THE POPE AT WAR

THE POPE
AT WAR

THE SECRET HISTORY
OF PIUS XII,
MUSSOLINI, AND HITLER

DAVID I.
KERTZER

RANDOM HOUSE

NEW YORK

Published in the United States by Random House,
an imprint and division of
Penguin Random House LLC, New York.

RANDOM HOUSE and the HOUSE colophon are
registered trademarks of Penguin Random House LLC.

LIBRARY OF CONGRESS CATALOGING-IN-PUBLICATION DATA

Names: Kertzer, David I., author.
Title: The pope at war : the secret history of Pius XII, Mussolini, and Hitler /
David I. Kertzer.
Other titles: Secret history of Pius XII, Mussolini, and Hitler
Description: First edition. | New York : Random House, [2022] |
Includes bibliographical references and index.
Identifiers: LCCN 2022000861 (print) | LCCN 2022000862 (ebook) |
ISBN 9780812989946 (hardcover) | ISBN 9780812989953 (ebook)
Subjects: LCSH: World War, 1939–1945—Diplomatic history. | Pius XII, Pope, 1876–1958. |
Catholic Church—Foreign relations. | Catholic Church—Relations—Judaism. | Judaism—
Relations—Catholic Church. | Pius XII, Pope, 1876–1958—Relations with Jews. |
Holocaust, Jewish (1939–1945) | World War, 1939–1945—Vatican City. | World War,
1939–1945—Religious aspects—Catholic Church. | National socialism and religion.
Classification: LCC D749 .K47 2022 (print) | LCC D749 (ebook) |
DDC 940.53/2545634—dc23/eng/20220127
LC record available at https://lccn.loc.gov/2022000861
LC ebook record available at https://lccn.loc.gov/2022000862

Printed in the United States of America on acid-free paper

randomhousebooks.com

Maps by Laura Maestro

1st Printing

FIRST EDITION

*Title-page images: (top) Pius XII giving benediction to crowd following his coronation,
Saint Peter's Square, March 1939. Popperfoto/via Getty Images;
(bottom) Hitler and Mussolini, Rome, May 1938. Fototeca Gilardi.*

Book design by Barbara M. Bachman

To the memories of my father,

Morris Kertzer,

and my father-in-law,

Jacob Dana,

chaplain and physician respectively

in the U.S. Army overseas

in the Second World War,

and to their great-granddaughter,

little Sol

CONTENTS

———

PART ONE

WAR CLOUDS

——

PART TWO

ON THE PATH TO AXIS VICTORY

———

PART THREE

CHANGING FORTUNES

———

PART FOUR

THE SKY TURNED BLACK

———

Illustrated map by Laura Hartman Maestro ©2021

Map of
Central
ROME
1939

0 100 200 300 400 500 600 700 800 900 1 Km.

Villa
Borghese

Viale del Muro Torto

Pincio

Galoppatoio

Viale del Muro Torto

Villa
Medici

Corso   d'Italia

To Villa
Torlonia
approx. 1km
Via Nomentana

Castro
Pretorio

Veneto

Via Vittorio

Ministero
delle
Finanze

Museo
Nazionale

Via del Tritone

(Montecitorio)
House of
Deputies

Ministero
della
Guerra

Stazione
Termini

Palazzo
Chigi

Piazza Colonna

Quirinal
Palace

Via del Quirinale

Via Nazionale

Ministero dell'
Interno

Via Cavour

ROMA TERMINI

Pantheon

Palazzo
Venezia
Piazza
Venezia

Via

Santa
Maria
Maggiore

Church of
Jesus

Victor
Emmanuel II
Monument

Via dell'Impero

Via Cavour

Via Giovanni Lanza

Synagogue

Foro Romano

Colosseo

Terme
di
Traiano

P.
Dante

Monte
Palatino

Via di S. Gregorio

Via
Claudia

Via S. Giovanni in Laterano

Via Labicana

Piazza
San Giovanni
in Laterano

Circo Massimo

Villa
Celi-
montana

Castel Gandolfo
(Pope's Summer
Residence)
approx. 24 Km

San Giovanni
in Laterano

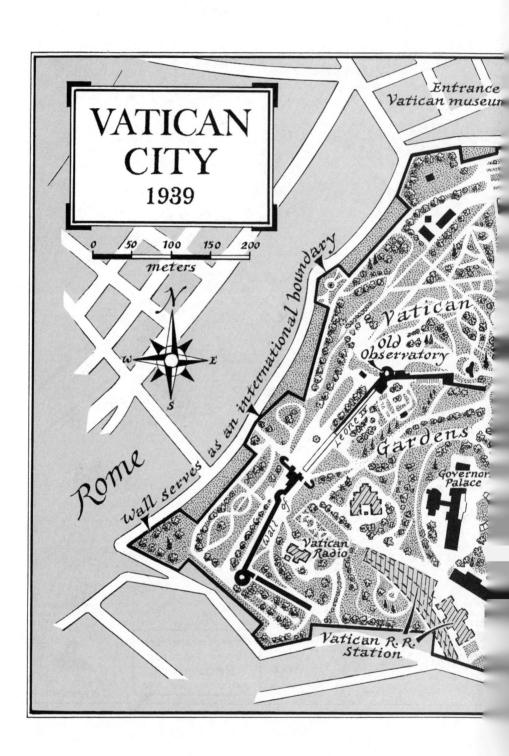

VATICAN
CITY
1939

0   50   100   150   200
meters

N
W   E
S

Entrance
Vatican museum

Wall serves as an international boundary

Rome

Vatican
Old
Observatory

Leone IV

Gardens

Wall of

Vatican
Radio

Governor
Palace

Vatican R. R.
Station

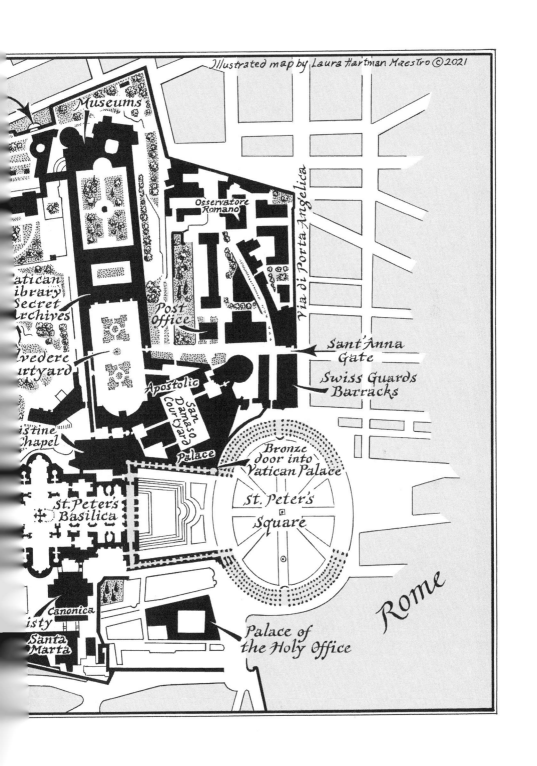

Illustrated map by Laura Hartman Maestro ©2021

Museums

Osservatore Romano

Via di Porta Angelica

Vatican Library Secret Archives

Post Office

Belvedere Courtyard

Apostolic Palace

San Damaso Courtyard

Sant'Anna Gate

Swiss Guards Barracks

Sistine Chapel

Bronze door into Vatican Palace

St. Peter's Basilica

St. Peter's Square

Canonica

Sacristy

Santa Marta

Palace of the Holy Office

Rome

LIST OF
ILLUSTRATIONS

———

CAST OF
CHARACTERS

––––––

THE POPE AND THE CHURCH

––––––

PIUS XII (EUGENIO PACELLI) (1876–1958): Son and grandson of lay luminaries of the Vatican, the frail but highly intelligent Pacelli never served as a parish priest or diocesan bishop but, following ordination, immediately joined the Vatican Secretariat of State. In Germany as nuncio from 1917 to 1929, he acquired a deep knowledge of that country before being appointed cardinal secretary of state by **Pius XI** in 1930. Ever cautious, and never comfortable with multiparty governments, on becoming pope in 1939 he attempted to repair frayed Vatican relations with **Mussolini** and **Hitler**.

BORGONGINI DUCA, FRANCESCO (1884–1954): A priest who had lived his entire life in Rome, Borgongini was appointed the Vatican's first nuncio to Italy following the signing of the Lateran Accords in 1929. He would remain at that post throughout the war and beyond. Although ignorant of the larger world and devoid of intellectual curiosity, Borgongini was one of Pius XII's key emissaries to the Fascist regime, which he constantly lobbied on behalf of the pope. Along with Father **Tacchi Venturi**, he repeatedly urged the Fascist authorities to spare baptized Jews from the draconian racial laws.

MAGLIONE, LUIGI (1877–1944): Through his intelligence and drive, Maglione, a Neapolitan from a poor family, made his way up through Rome's elite church training ground for the Vatican diplomatic service, serving as nuncio in Switzerland and then, from the mid-1920s to the mid-1930s, nuncio to France. Made a cardinal in 1935, he was one of the main contenders at the conclave that elected Pacelli pope. Although **Pius XII** named Maglione as his secretary of state, the two men never developed a warm relationship. Approachable, but careful about what he said, he was popular among the foreign ambassadors to the Vatican who met with him every Friday. Pius XII's discomfort with having anyone in the role of secretary of state became clear when, following Maglione's death, he decided not to name a successor.

MONTINI, GIOVANNI BATTISTA (1897–1978): From a prominent northern Italian Catholic family, his father having served as a member of parliament for the Catholic Popular Party before Mussolini disbanded it, Montini was appointed substitute for ordinary affairs, one of the two deputy positions in the Vatican Secretariat of State in 1937 under Cardinal Pacelli. He remained in that position following Pacelli's elevation to the papacy. Smart and refined in manner but with little worldly experience, he was a favorite of **Pius XII** and would himself one day become pope, taking the name Paul VI.

ORSENIGO, CESARE (1873–1946): A priest in Milan with no international experience and little knowledge of the larger world, Orsenigo was appointed nuncio to the Netherlands and then to Hungary in the 1920s before being named to replace **Eugenio Pacelli** as nuncio to Germany in 1930. A man of limited intelligence and enamored of **Hitler**, he would try to impress the Nazi officials with his sympathy for their cause, while wishing they treated the church better.

PACELLI, EUGENIO (see Pius XII)

PIUS XI (ACHILLE RATTI) (1857–1939): The then-archbishop of Milan was elected pope in 1922, the same year that the Fascist March on Rome led the king to appoint **Mussolini** prime minister. Remarking that God works in strange ways, Pius XI found in Mussolini a man who could help restore many of the privileges the church had lost in Italy the previous century. But by the last year of his life Pius XI began to regret all he had done to help the Duce solidify power in Italy, antagonized above all by Mussolini's embrace of Hitler, a man he despised as an enemy of the church and a proponent of a pagan ideology.

TACCHI VENTURI, PIETRO, S.J. (1861–1956): A prominent Roman Jesuit and from 1918 to 1940 rector of Rome's major Jesuit church, Tacchi Venturi became **Pius XI**'s unofficial conduit with **Mussolini** shortly after Mussolini came to power, meeting with the dictator regularly to convey Pius XI's requests. Although the Jesuit met with Mussolini less often during the war years, **Pius XII** would often take advantage of the huge network of contacts Tacchi Venturi had made with the leaders of the Fascist regime to convey papal requests. Among these were repeated attempts to have baptized Jews spared from the country's antisemitic campaign.

TARDINI, DOMENICO (1888–1961): From a modest Roman family, Tardini served in the Vatican Secretariat of State much of his life. Named substitute for ordinary affairs in 1935 and then secretary for extraordinary ecclesiastical affairs in 1937, he would share, with **Giovanni Montini,** the two major positions under the secretary of state over the following years. Sharp-tongued and quick-witted, he would regularly be called upon by the pope to prepare briefing papers to lay out his options during the war. Tardini trusted neither the Germans nor the Allies.

MUSSOLINI AND
THE FASCIST REGIME

MUSSOLINI, BENITO (1883–1945): Formerly a radical socialist, Mussolini was nothing if not an opportunist and realized that gaining Vatican backing would prove a great boon to his ambitions. Offering a range of benefits to the church, culminating in the Lateran Accords of 1929, which created Vatican City and ended the separation of church and state in Italy, he came to be hailed by the Vatican as the Man of Providence. But his increasing embrace of Nazi Germany in the late 1930s antagonized Pius XI. He would boast to Hitler that he knew how to keep the pope in line, and **Pius XII** relied on the Italian dictator to help convince the Führer to make peace with the church. As his own troubles mounted during the Second World War, Mussolini placed constant pressure on Pius XII to do nothing to undercut the Axis cause.

ALFIERI, DINO (1886–1966): Elected to parliament on the Fascist ticket in 1924, Alfieri rose through government ranks. In November 1939 Mussolini appointed Alfieri, then in charge of the government propaganda ministry, to replace **Bonifacio Pignatti** as Italy's ambassador to the Holy See. A few months later Mussolini would decide he needed an ambassador more kindly disposed to the Nazis to go to Berlin, and so he appointed Alfieri to the German embassy. At his last meeting with Alfieri before he left for Germany, the pope entrusted Alfieri with a message for Hitler, but then thought better of it.

ATTOLICO, BERNARDO (1880–1942): A southerner and career diplomat, Attolico married into the black aristocracy, the Roman elites whose families were closely linked to the popes. Following stints as Italian ambassador to Brazil and the Soviet Union, he was named ambassador to Germany in 1935. No friend of the Nazis, he tried to dissuade Mussolini from joining the Axis war. Switching positions with **Alfieri** in 1940, he served as the Duce's loyal ambassador to the Vatican until his death in early 1942. Typical of many men in Italy's foreign service, Attolico served the Fascist regime loyally and, following Italy's entry into the war, worked tirelessly to prevent any Vatican criticism of the Axis cause.

BUFFARINI, GUIDO (1895–1945): Perhaps the most intelligent member of Mussolini's government, the short, fat, ruddy-cheeked Buffarini was also among its most corrupt members. Among other side endeavors, he ran a booming business in falsifying parish records to make Catholics of Jews and so spare them the effects of the racial laws it was his responsibility to oversee. As in practice Mussolini's minister of internal affairs (a post technically held by the Duce himself), Buffarini greeted Cardinal Pacelli's election to the papacy by remarking, "He is just the Pope that is needed." Following Mussolini's initial fall, Buffarini served as minister of internal affairs in the Nazi-puppet Italian Social Republic.

CIANO, GALEAZZO (1903–44): His father was an early Fascist government minister, whose recently conferred aristocratic title of Count was then passed on to him. Galeazzo rose rapidly to the heights of the Fascist state thanks as well to his 1930 marriage to Mussolini's daughter, Edda. Appointed foreign minister in 1936 at the age of thirty-three, he remained his father-in-law's heir apparent for the next several years. Eager to stay on the pope's good side, he regularly offered professions of his deep Catholic faith to the pope's emissaries and cast himself as the pope's ally in trying to prevent Mussolini from joining the war. After briefly serving as the Duce's ambassador to the Vatican in 1943, he would end up facing a Fascist firing squad.

FARINACCI, ROBERTO (1892–1945): One of the original Fascists, boss of the northern city of Cremona, member of the Grand Council of Fascism from 1922, Farinacci styled himself as the most Fascist of Fascists and the one most devoted to Hitler. Mussolini would frequently use Farinacci and his anticlerical newspaper, *Il Regime Fascista,* as his stick to keep the pope in line. No one better incarnated what the pope considered the bad wing of the Fascist Party.

GUARIGLIA, RAFFAELE (1889–1970): Cardinal **Maglione** was delighted to learn of Mussolini's appointment of Guariglia, formerly ambassador to France, as Italy's ambassador to the Holy See following **Attolico**'s death in early 1942. He regarded Guariglia, a fellow Neapolitan, as a friend. Recognizing later in 1942 that the Axis was likely to lose the war, Guariglia hoped to find an escape for himself and for Italy. Sent to serve as Italy's ambassador to Turkey in early 1943, he returned following Mussolini's overthrow in July to serve briefly as Italy's foreign minister, meeting secretly many evenings with Cardinal Maglione as the Italian government faced a terrible dilemma.

MUSSOLINI, EDDA (1910–95): Mussolini's favorite child, and the one most like him, Edda was headstrong and independent. Initially enthusiastic about Hitler and having Italy join in the Axis war, she would turn against her father following the arrest of her husband, **Galeazzo Ciano**, and his subsequent execution.

MUSSOLINI, RACHELE (1890–1979): Semiliterate, the child of a poor peasant family, never comfortable around the opulence and pretensions of the Italian elite, her son-in-law included, Mussolini's wife was, according to her daughter, "the true dictator in the family." Although she despised her husband's young lover, she remained his staunch defender.

PETACCI, CLARA (1912–45): Clara was just a schoolgirl, the daughter of a Vatican physician, when she began sending **Mussolini** letters pledging her devotion. Beginning their affair in earnest in 1936, two years after her marriage, Clara developed an obsession for "Ben," as she called him. It was an obsession reciprocated by Mussolini, who often phoned her a dozen times a day and awaited her daily visits to the special room reserved for her at Palazzo Venezia. Over time, Clara began to offer her own political advice, reinforcing some of Mussolini's worst instincts.

PIGNATTI, BONIFACIO (1877–1957): Formerly Italian ambassador to Argentina and France, Pignatti was appointed Italian ambassador to the Holy See in 1935. Typical of many career diplomats, he made the transition from serving a parliamentary democracy to serving a dictatorship without any sign of difficulty and, until his retirement in 1940, would do all he could to ensure the pope's cooperation with the Fascist regime.

HITLER AND
THE THIRD REICH

HITLER, ADOLF (1889–1945): Since **Mussolini**'s ascension to power in 1922, Hitler had held the Italian dictator up as a role model. That affection would last through the war as the Führer's troops repeatedly saved the Italian army from catastrophe and then, following Mussolini's overthrow, rescued the Duce from his mountaintop prison and set him up as puppet leader of a new Fascist regime in the north. While Hitler, a Catholic by birth, had no affection for either the church or the Catholic clergy, he saw an opportunity with the election of **Pius XII** to ease the tensions that had marked the Third Reich's relations with **Pius XI**.

HESSEN, PHILIPP VON (1896–1980): Son of one of Germany's most prominent aristocratic families, his grandfather a German emperor, his great-grandmother Queen Victoria of Great Britain, Prince von Hessen married Princess **Mafalda**, King **Victor Emmanuel**'s daughter, in 1925, and then five years later joined the Nazi Party's storm troopers. Shortly after Hitler's ascension to power in 1933, he was named head of his province. One of the people closest to Hitler, von Hessen became the Führer's personal envoy to Mussolini. Shortly after Pius XII became pope, Hitler, seeking a possible opening, turned to von Hessen to conduct a series of secret meetings with the pontiff in the Vatican, meetings that have only now come to light.

RIBBENTROP, JOACHIM VON (1893–1946): Formerly a wine salesman, and a fanatic Nazi, Ribbentrop was named Germany's foreign minister in 1938. He would serve in that post until the war's end. "I have rarely seen a man I disliked more," said the American undersecretary of state after meeting him in 1940. Constantly promoting the virtue of war, and ever boasting of the inevitability of German victory, he had no affection for the church but nonetheless paid a dramatic visit to the pope only a few months after German troops launched the war.

WEIZSÄCKER, ERNST VON (1882–1951): Judged "a typical example of the German official of the old school of the nineteenth century" by the American undersecretary of state, Weizsäcker, product of an aristocratic German family, was appointed state secretary for international affairs, number two to **Ribbentrop** in the Third Reich's Foreign Ministry, in 1938. There he served Hitler efficiently through the first years of the war before being sent in the spring of 1943 to be Germany's ambassador to the Holy See. Liked by the pope, who, especially during the nine months of German military occupation of Rome, counted on him to help protect the Vatican, he would be viewed at the Vatican as an exemplar of the good side of the Nazi regime. Tried for war crimes at Nuremburg following the end of the war, Weizsäcker would be found guilty despite the Vatican's pleas on his behalf.

ITALY'S ROYAL FAMILY

VICTOR EMMANUEL III (1869–1947): Named for his grandfather, founder of the Kingdom of Italy, the Savoyard king suffered from a lifelong inferiority complex due to his short stature. Sharing with **Mussolini** a deep-rooted misanthropy, he was intelligent and well informed but weak-willed and pedantic. Long a willing enabler of the Duce, he would be slow to act when, as the war began to go against the Axis, he fended off increasingly insistent pleas that he replace the Duce as government head and extract Italy from the war.

MAFALDA OF SAVOY (1902–44): Second daughter of King **Victor Emmanuel III**, Mafalda married the German prince **Philipp von Hessen** in 1925 and subsequently shuttled between Italy and Germany, where her husband was becoming a prominent Nazi and confidant of Hitler. It would not end well for her.

MARIA JOSÉ OF BELGIUM (1906–2001): Daughter and sister of kings of Belgium, she married the Italian king's only son, Umberto, in 1930.

A strong-minded woman not comfortable with the constraints imposed on her by her position and by her gender, she developed an independent circle of friends among prominent Italian intellectuals, including, increasingly, those displeased with the Fascist regime. She would be among the first influential Italians to seek the Vatican's help in removing Mussolini from power and extricating Italy from the war, although in this she would have little success.

FOREWORD

I N MARCH 1939, AS THE WORLD HURTLED TOWARD A CATASTROPHIC war, the cardinals of the Roman Catholic Church gathered to elect a new supreme pontiff. The man they chose would become one of the most controversial popes in church history. Pushed for sainthood by some, vilified by others, Pope Pius XII has been the focus of bitter debates about his dealings with the Nazi and Fascist regimes and his actions during the Second World War. Critics accuse him of a weakness for dictatorships and a distaste for Jews, highlighting his decision to remain silent as six million Jews were murdered in the Holocaust. Mussolini and Hitler, they say, found him all too easy to intimidate and ever apt to embrace expediency over principle. Pius XII's defenders paint a very different picture, a portrait of great virtue. He was, in their view, a man of rare courage, a man who, threatened with kidnapping if not assassination, heroically stood up to the Nazis and their Italian Fascist allies. Far from showing indifference to the fate of Europe's Jews, in this account, he worked tirelessly and effectively to save them.

Previous research on World War II has shed light on some of these questions and offered a more nuanced view than either extreme, but a crucial piece of the puzzle has long been missing. The Vatican archives detailing the activities of the pope and the prelates around him during the war were sealed upon Pius XII's death in 1958. Since then, successive popes have faced intense pressure to open them. Finally, Pope Francis decided to order the archives for Pius XII's papacy open, and they were made accessible to researchers beginning in March 2020. Now a more complete story can be told of the controversial pope's actions during the war, and, perhaps as important, why and how, under great pressure, he made the fraught decisions he did.

The Pope at War offers readers the first full account of these events to take advantage of those recently opened archives. Its pages are full of previously unknown materials and new revelations. While researching this book, I read thousands of pages of these documents, those most closely bearing on the choices Pius XII made between 1939 and 1945. Many of these consist of internal memoranda prepared at the pope's request as he weighed how to respond to the ongoing Nazi attempt to exterminate Europe's Jews and to Mussolini's requests for greater Catholic support for the Axis war. Others consist of reports from the pope's nuncios and other church leaders in Nazi-occupied Europe detailing the atrocities they were witnessing and advising the pope on what action he should take.

As important as the Vatican archives are to the picture painted in these pages, relying on them alone would produce a one-sided and incomplete account. Piecing the full, dramatic story together requires exploiting the huge mass of relevant reports and correspondence found in other historical archives: in Italy, Germany, France, the United States, and Britain. Many of these documents, too, have become accessible only in the last few years, as the slow process of government document declassification has run its course. These include the reports that Mussolini's and Hitler's ambassadors to Pius XII regularly sent their governments, as well as similar reports from the British, French, and American envoys to the Vatican. When put together, these accounts from inside the Vatican provide virtually a day-by-day chronicle of the drama lived there from the war's beginning to its end. Offering an additional dimension, Benito Mussolini's many spies inside the Vatican regularly dispatched reports of the intrigue, backstabbing, and conflict within its walls during these years. I made use of similar informant reports in writing *The Pope and Mussolini,* my earlier book about Pius XII's predecessor, Pius XI, and the rise of Fascism in Europe in the years leading up to the war.

While Pius XII is at the center of the drama I examine here, *The Pope at War* offers a new account not only of the pope and the Vatican during the war but of how Italy experienced the war as well. Pius XII was Roman, the cardinals of the Curia were almost all Italian, and as bishop of Rome, the pope had special authority over Italy's church. How the pope balanced his public stance of neutrality while presiding over an Italian church hierarchy that offered enthusiastic support for the Axis war will become clear in these pages. How Italy's Catholic clergy urged all good Catholics to fight on Hitler's side, despite their uneasiness with the Nazi regime, is a story I tell here as well. Integral to all this is making sense of the strange relationship between the two men who, from Italians' perspective, stood out above all the rest: Mussolini and the pope. While the Italian dictator depended on the pope to ensure church support for the war, Pius XII would have his own reasons for wanting to remain in Mussolini's good graces.

For those fascinated by the drama and the tragedy of the Second World War, a handful of world leaders have stood out: Hitler, Mussolini, Churchill, Roosevelt, Stalin. The case can be made though that someone else should be considered. The pope had a status in war-torn Europe like no other man. Throughout the continent and beyond, many saw him as the only person whose position gave him unquestioned moral authority. To many he appeared as the last hope to stave off war and, once it had begun, to help bring it to an end. For Italians, he was the country's only authority independent of the Fascist regime, the lone man whose own charisma rivaled Mussolini's.

What follows is the story—sometimes shocking and often surprising—of a pope facing a world torn by war, fearing for the future of the church he led and under unrelenting pressure to denounce the evildoers. If the events recounted here offer a dramatic chapter in the history of the Roman Catholic Church, they are much more than that. They form an important and until now only partially understood chapter in the history of the Second World War itself. Perhaps, too, it is a story that offers lessons for our own world today.

PROLOGUE

———

THE TWISTED CROSS

ON MAY 2, 1938, THREE SPECIAL TRAINS, CARRYING HUNDREDS OF German diplomats, government officials, Nazi Party leaders, security agents, and journalists, left Berlin accompanying the Führer on his first—and what would turn out to be his last—visit to Rome. Luminaries of the Third Reich, including Joachim von Ribbentrop, Joseph Goebbels, Rudolf Hess, Heinrich Himmler, and Hans Frank, made the trip, leaving only Hermann Göring behind to keep the government going. Benito Mussolini, Italy's dictator, the man who invented Fascism two decades earlier, had insisted on the visit, eager to reciprocate for the huge, adulatory crowds that Hitler had turned out in Germany the previous fall in his honor.

The visit began awkwardly for the Führer. He assumed he would be accompanied through cheering crowds by the man he had long regarded as his role model, but on arrival in Rome, he found himself instead in an ornate, horse-pulled carriage sitting alongside Italy's small, introverted king. "Have they not heard of the invention of the motor car?" Hitler remarked later. The Führer's distaste for the weak-willed, white-mustachioed monarch was fully returned by King Victor Emmanuel III, who viewed the German leader as a drug-addled mental degenerate. But because it was the king and not Mussolini who was head of state, protocol demanded that the German chancellor be hosted at the Quirinal, the enormous royal palace constructed atop Rome's highest hill by Pope Gregory XIII in the sixteenth century.

Hitler found it a melancholy place, resembling nothing so much as an oversize antique shop. His hostess there, Italy's Queen Elena, towered over her husband by several inches. She bore a remarkable resemblance, observed the misogynist Führer, to one of the "horse guards."

Only at the end of the six-day visit was Hitler fully able to enjoy the sights, when he went to his favorite Italian city, Florence, having left the king and queen behind in Rome. Shortly after Mussolini's train arrived there, Hitler and his retinue pulled into track sixteen of Florence's train station, festooned with flowers, German and Italian flags, and large golden banners of the Fascist *fasces*. Amidst the stirring sound of the city band's rendition of "Deutschland über alles" and the Fascist hymn, "Giovinezza," came the roar of an Italian fighter squadron flying low overhead. The two smiling dictators sat side by side in the back seat of an open car as, surrounded by motorcycle police, they set off on their triumphal tour through the streets on their way to the Pitti Palace. A small army of architects, engineers, and artists had worked for months to decorate the city for the event. Tens of thousands of red and black swastika flags, interspersed with red-white-and-green Italian flags, hung from windows along the way. It was a beautiful spring day, and with a holiday declared throughout the Tuscan region, 350,000 people came to get a glimpse of the two great men, albeit with a clear preference for their own Duce. Thousands of Fascist militiamen and soldiers, lining the streets, held the crowds back. Hundreds of police, including a company brought in from Rome, along with fifteen hundred carabinieri from other districts, made their presence known as well. After a tour of the unparalleled art collection of the vast Renaissance palace—Mussolini, who had no patience for museums, had not joined Hitler for the viewing—the motorized procession resumed. The two men stopped at a shrine to a Tuscan martyr of the Fascist cause before going to a nearby hilltop so that Hitler could admire the city view.

Unknown to the guest of honor, a small contretemps preceded the gala dinner held that evening at Palazzo Medici Riccardi, the fifteenth-century rusticated graystone palace built by Cosimo de' Medici to house his family. According to a report prepared by the American consul in Florence, four female invitees were told at the last minute not to attend. The women's Jewish ancestry having belatedly been discovered, the local Fascist authorities deemed it best to avoid doing anything that might offend their German guests. In the end, as the consul's report explained, one final adjustment was made: "One lady made such a strong protest, proving she was not a Jew, that the request not to attend the dinner was withdrawn in her case."

Following the meal, the two dictators set out again, bound for the Teatro Comunale for a performance of Verdi's *Simon Boccanegra*. Afterward, late at night, they viewed a military display in their honor, with a light show featuring two huge sparkling inscriptions of "Führer" and "Duce." They then returned to the station where Hitler's train was waiting. As the two men stood on the platform saying their farewell, they struggled to contain their emotions. "Now," Mussolini told Hitler, "no force will ever be able to separate us." The Führer's eyes were wet with tears.[1]

WHILE THE DUCE AND the Führer were preening for the Italian crowds, the pope was fuming. Eighty years old, frail, and with less than a year to live, Pius XI, who in the early years of his papacy helped Mussolini solidify his dictatorship, had become alarmed with the Duce's ever-tightening embrace of the Nazi regime. In recent months the pope had become increasingly vocal in decrying the Nazis' attacks on the Catholic Church in Germany and their attempts to create a pagan religion of blood and soil with Hitler its new deity. When visiting Rome, heads of state typically came to see the pope, but Pius XI made clear he would grant the Führer an audience only if he promised to change course in dealing with the church. This the German dictator refused to do.

To signal his displeasure at Hitler's visit, Pius XI had left Rome, retreating to the papal palace at Castel Gandolfo in the nearby Alban Hills. He ordered the Vatican museums closed and directed that the lights illuminating the Vatican at night be extinguished. In addressing a group of newlyweds who came for a papal blessing while Hitler was in Rome, the pope strayed far from his usual bromides to lament the glorification of the swastika in Catholicism's capital. It was "the sign," he said, "of another cross that is not the Cross of Christ."[2]

For Mussolini, whose regime had long enjoyed a productive relationship with the Vatican, Pope Pius XI was becoming a problem. It was going to be difficult enough to win the support of Italians—no lovers of Germans with their talk of a superior Aryan race—for his alliance with Hitler without having the pope undermining him. But as long as Pius XI lived, Mussolini had little hope of relief. Indeed, many of the pontiff's subordinates in the Vatican were themselves unnerved by the pope's criticism of the Nazis, fearing it could jeopardize the church's privileged position in Fascist Italy. Among these prelates, none was more powerful than the Vatican secretary of state, Cardinal Eugenio Pacelli, second in authority only to the pope and a man widely viewed as Pius XI's likely successor whenever death came.

Pacelli himself had no love for Hitler or for the Nazis. Shortly after the Führer came to power in 1933, Pacelli had negotiated a concordat with him, seeking to protect the church's interests in Germany. The agreement was a great triumph for Hitler, whose ascent to power had been greeted with skepticism and alarm by other world leaders, and they were doing their best to isolate him. Now his new regime could boast of recognition by the pope himself. For the Vatican, though, the concordat proved a fleeting achievement at best. Hitler's failure to abide by its terms soon became clear as he methodically chipped away at the church's influence. Although embarrassed and unhappy with this outcome, Pacelli thought antagonizing the Führer would only make matters worse. He also viewed Germany as Europe's strongest bulwark against what he regarded as the church's greatest enemy, Communism. Rather than alienate Mussolini by condemning his alliance with Hitler, thought the cardinal, it would be more effective to keep him happy and take advantage of his close bond with Hitler to convince the Führer to make peace with the church.[3]

As the prelates around Pius XI worried where the pope's eagerness to speak his mind on the evils of Nazism might lead, Mussolini was growing ever more alarmed by reports coming from his ambassador to the Holy See and from his many spies inside the Vatican. The dictator learned late in 1938 that the pope was secretly working on an encyclical, a declaration aimed at Catholics worldwide, denouncing racism and antisemitism. Even more troubling were reports that Pius XI was planning to use his upcoming speech to all of Italy's bishops to denounce the Duce's embrace of Nazi Germany.

For the Duce, Pius XI could not die soon enough.

PART ONE

—

WAR CLOUDS

DEATH OF A POPE

E UGENIO PACELLI SAT IN A CHAIR BESIDE THE SIMPLE BRASS BED, watching as the once-robust pope, his face shrunken, labored to breathe beneath his oxygen mask. It was late at night, and although Cardinal Pacelli, the Vatican secretary of state, was accustomed to sleeping little, he decided to return to his rooms, two floors below in the vast Apostolic Palace, to get some rest. Awakened at four A.M. with news that the pope's condition had worsened, he rushed back to the pope's austere bedroom. Sweat poured down the pope's pallid face as he gasped for air. The cardinal got down on his knees and asked the dying pope for his blessing.[1]

It was early morning, February 10, 1939. For Pacelli, whom the pope had elevated to the cardinalate and appointed to the church's most influential position after that of the pontiff himself, it was a scene of great sadness. But there was much to be done, for the pope had also appointed Pacelli to be chamberlain, and it was now his job to ensure that all proceeded as it should until the cardinals could elect a successor.[2]

Pacelli's relations with the pope had been close but not particularly warm. Their personalities could scarcely have been more different and perhaps this was one reason Pius XI had valued him so highly. The tempestuous pope, prone to say what he thought and often seemingly impervious to the opinions of others, depended on the highly disciplined, diplomatic Pacelli to calm the waters he roiled.

The Vatican secretary of state had found himself caught in the middle. Not only did Mussolini's and Hitler's ambassadors complain to him about Pius XI and seek his help, but so did many high-ranking churchmen, worried that the pontiff was becoming reckless in his old age. True to his position and his vows, the cardinal would not fail to carry out the instructions the pope gave him. But he found ways to take the sting out of the pope's more acerbic remarks about the Italian and German regimes.[3]

Pacelli was a skilled diplomat and, despite a certain natural shyness, took great satisfaction in traveling the globe in a way no secretary of state before him had ever done. During his travels, he enjoyed meeting not only with the church's ecclesiastical elite but with the politically powerful in secular governments. In the fall of 1936, he became the first Vatican secretary of state to visit the United States, spending two months touring the country, picking up honorary degrees at several Catholic universities, and after thousands of miles crisscrossing the country by air, meeting with the American president.

The following year the cardinal was the guest of honor at the dedication of a new basilica in France, taking a side trip to meet with France's president and prime minister. A couple of weeks after Hitler visited Rome in May 1938, Pacelli left Italy again, this time going to Budapest, where he was the featured speaker at a Eucharistic Congress. His message everywhere was the same: The world was in crisis. It had turned its back on the cross of Christ. Only by returning to the bosom of the church would it be saved.[4]

While Pius XI was apt to bang his fist on his table and raise his voice in dressing down those foreign envoys whose countries' actions had displeased him, Pacelli sought to win foreign diplomats over by stressing what they had in common. Insofar as he felt the need to register complaints, he did so in a way that suggested he was speaking more in sorrow than in anger.

RELATIONS BETWEEN PIUS XI and the Führer had begun promisingly enough when Hitler came to power in 1933. Indeed, the pope initially harbored some hopes for him, impressed by the strength of his anti-Communist views. Pacelli, who had spent twelve years as papal nuncio, or ambassador, in Germany and knew the country well, remarked at the time that while Hitler was clearly a remarkably talented agitator, it remained to be seen whether he was "a man of government."

For his part, Germany's new leader was eager for the church to end its support of Germany's Catholic Center Party, the largest non-Marxist party standing in the way of his dictatorship. He made a series of conciliatory gestures, pledging to protect religious education and to guarantee a privileged place for the church in German society. It was amid these assurances that Germany's bishops fell in line with the new government head, and the Center Party was allowed to die. Their understanding was codified with the signing, in Pacelli's Vatican office only months after Hitler came to power, of a new concordat between Germany and the Holy See. The deal was a huge boost for Hitler's credibility not only domestically but also internationally, as the papal nuncio in Berlin himself pointed out a few years later in talking with Germany's secretary of state: "It does not seem possible to me that Signor Hitler has forgotten that, barely seven months after his arrival in power, when diffidence and hostility surrounded him both internally and externally, the Holy See extended its hand to him, contributing with its great spiritual authority to increasing faith in him and strengthening his prestige." Characteristically, Mussolini took credit for the agreement, having, he said, given Hitler his successful "recipe" for how to ingratiate himself to the Vatican.[5]

Hitler had long viewed the Duce★ as his role model. At a Munich rally held only days after Mussolini became Italy's prime minister in 1922, Hitler, then still one of many extremist claimants for attention in the German political firmament, was introduced as "Germany's Mussolini." "It marked," observed Hitler's British biographer, Ian Kershaw, "the symbolic moment when Hitler's followers invented the Führer cult." Over the next years, as Hitler plotted his rise to power, he kept a bust of Mussolini in his office. "Men like Mussolini are only

★ Pronounced DOO-chay.

born once every thousand years," he remarked after meeting the Duce for the first time in 1934. At the pope's urging, Mussolini took advantage of that meeting in Venice to offer Hitler his advice: it was best to keep the church happy.[6]

Following his meeting with Hitler, Mussolini wrote to Pius XI, reporting what he had told the Führer. He decided it best not to mention, he confided to his ambassador to the Holy See, "all the idiotic things that Hitler said about Jesus Christ being of the Jewish race, etc." What was important was that by the end of their conversation, Hitler made clear he did not want a religious war. It would be the first of many times the pope and Cardinal Pacelli would call on the Duce to speak with Hitler on their behalf.[7]

Pius XI's hopes for the German dictator did not last long. The Nazis soon began replacing Catholic parochial schools with state schools, abolishing Catholic youth groups, and limiting church activities to the purely sacramental. "The pope," a Vatican police informant in late 1934 reported, "has a strong personal antipathy toward Hitler. If it were not for Pacelli who is trying to bring more balance to the situation, the Secretariat of State would be even less tolerant of him."[8]

Pacelli too would lose patience with Hitler when, in 1935, he launched show trials of large numbers of Roman Catholic clergy, charged with a variety of sexual and financial crimes. The German bishops urged the pope to act, suggesting he issue an encyclical to protest Hitler's failure to abide by the terms of the concordat. Although Cardinal Pacelli, worried about antagonizing the Führer, advised against such a public protest, Pius XI went ahead. On March 21, 1937, Palm Sunday, bishops and priests throughout the Reich read the encyclical, *Mit brennender Sorge* ("With deep anxiety"), to their congregations, a shocking development in a country where any criticism of the Nazi regime risked violent reprisal. Predictably, Hitler was furious not only because of the pope's attack but by his ability to have the text secretly distributed and then read in churches throughout the Reich.

Hitler's occupation of Austria in March 1938 and its subsequent annexation into the Third Reich had been an embarrassment for Mussolini, for he had considered Austria as something of an Italian protectorate, a buffer between Italy and the powerful German state. Making matters worse, the Führer had informed him of the invasion only a few hours in advance. The next day Hitler triumphally entered Vienna to the ringing of the city's church bells, a celebratory touch ordered by the city's archbishop.

With millions more Catholics now under Hitler's rule, the pope and his secretary of state looked all the more urgently to Mussolini for help. Five days after Hitler's entry into Vienna, Cardinal Pacelli wrote Mussolini, thanking him "for Your moderating action with Signor Hitler, Chancellor of the German Reich, and for Your intervention against the continuation of the policy of religious persecution in Germany."[9]

HITLER'S REGARD FOR MUSSOLINI, already considerable, had grown further when, shortly after the Führer's spring 1938 visit to Italy, the Duce announced his new "racial" policy. Mussolini soon rolled out the first of Italy's anti-Jewish racial laws, closely resembling those Hitler had put into effect in Germany three years earlier. "After Italy's new policy regarding the Jewish problem," Hitler remarked, "the spirit of the Axis is complete."[10]

On January 30, 1939, the sixth anniversary of his ascension to power, the Führer gave a major address to the German Reichstag. He spoke for eighty minutes to the packed auditorium in his loud, strident voice, sprinkling in a series of ironic side comments. His themes were familiar ones, hailing the triumphs of the previous year in expanding the Reich by seizing Czechoslovakia's Sudetenland and all of Austria, and boasting of the German people's fervent support for the Nazi regime. He denounced foreign attempts to interfere with the Reich's treatment of Jews. Kristallnacht, the Nazis' horrifying pogrom, had savaged the country's Jews only two months earlier. Hitler then turned his attention to the question of the churches.

Italy's ambassador to Berlin, present for the occasion, reported that at this point Hitler adopted something of a defensive tone. "While clearly condemning the 'political' clergy," the ambassador wrote, "he reaffirmed the National Socialist government's wish to leave the Churches in peace" and highlighted the large financial subsidy the Reich gave them each year. But Hitler could not resist taking a jab at the Catholic Church, expressing "words regarding the pederasty and the sexual aberrations of some members of the Clergy."

In turning to foreign policy in the final portion of his speech, Hitler stressed the friendship that bound Fascist Italy and Nazi Germany, hailing all the Duce had accomplished. He followed this, wrote the ambassador, with a "clear, precise, unequivocal affirmation, that, in case of a war waged against Italy, the aggressor would find itself facing Germany as well." This, he reported, "triggered a great, enthusiastic demonstration by the Deputies and the public." Italy's ambassador, although not himself fond of Hitler, offered a comforting view back to Rome:

> The speech, of great range, seemed well constructed and well framed. It was, in substance, quite moderate, especially in relation to the man and to his previous speeches. Other than for the Jewish question, which he showed the clear intention of liquidating once and for all, Hitler was not excessive in anything. As regards the Church, one can say he was anticlerical but not antireligious. . . . Other than in connection with a defense of Italy, the Führer never spoke of war. On the contrary, he spoke a number of times of peace.[11]

Six weeks later Hitler's troops invaded Czechoslovakia and seized Prague, sending shock waves through much of the world. In the few weeks separating the Führer's speech from that invasion, a new pope would be crowned.

MUSSOLINI HAD BECOME PRIME minister in 1922, the same year Pius XI had become pope. At the time, the pontiff had good reason to be skeptical about Italy's brash new thirty-nine-year-old government head. Mussolini had previously been a prominent radical Socialist and anticleric, and it was only shortly before becoming prime minister that he had proclaimed his support for the church. Relations would improve dramatically, and over the next years, Pius XI would make a fateful agreement with the dictator, codified in the 1929 Lateran Accords. In exchange for Catholic support for his regime, Mussolini agreed to end separation of church and state in Italy, establish Vatican City as a sovereign state ruled by the pope, and grant the church political powers it had not enjoyed for many decades.[12]

Not that the pope had any illusions about Mussolini's own religious beliefs. The founder of Italian Fascism had never been known to attend a regular Sunday Mass, much less to take communion or observe other church rites. Although this seemed not to have unduly bothered the pope, he had, in recent years, become disturbed by Mussolini's ever-growing hubris. Increasingly, it seemed, the Duce regarded himself as a kind of deity, the church there to serve his interests. Most worrisome of all for the pope was Mussolini's embrace of Hitler, a man Pius XI viewed as the high prophet of blood-and-soil paganism.

The pope and the Duce were on a collision course. Although, as the German ambassador reported to Berlin in July 1937, Cardinal Pacelli had done all he could to rein Pius XI in, he "has not succeeded in persuading the aging, headstrong, and irascible Pope to exercise greater caution and restraint in his speeches." A year later, when Mussolini unveiled his new "racial" policy, the pope went off text in an audience to ask why Mussolini thought he needed to ape the Nazis, a remark that infuriated Italy's thin-skinned dictator.[13]

In December 1938 the Duce's ambassador to the Vatican reported that the recent friction with the Fascist regime had left the pope depressed and angry. In speaking of Mussolini with the prelates closest to him, he would frequently let this anger show. "The pope," recalled the ambassador, "threatened to do something before dying that Italy would remember for a long time." Perhaps, he speculated, the pope might issue "an encyclical against Fascism or even a condemnation of Fascism."[14]

Early in January 1939 the ambassador received confirmation that the pope was indeed about to issue an encyclical denouncing racism. The ambassador had confronted both Cardinal Pacelli and his deputy to ask if there was any truth to the report. They denied it, but the ambassador remained unconvinced. "Without further inquiries," he reported, "I definitely could not exclude the fact that a document denouncing the totalitarian States is being prepared."[15]

WHILE PIUS XI WAS SICK and depressed, Mussolini was feeling quite well. Returning on January 5 from a two-week vacation, Italy's dictator was still wearing his skiing outfit when he met the American ambassador, William Phillips, that afternoon in his cavernous office at the fifteenth-century Palazzo Venezia. The room, named the World Map Hall for the huge mosaic map that had once covered a wall, was sixty feet long and fifty feet wide, its frescoed ceiling forty feet high, its marble floor an intricately inlaid series of geometrical shapes and images.

Throughout their meeting, Mussolini's thirty-five-year-old son-in-law and foreign minister, Galeazzo Ciano, stood mutely at his side, giving Phillips the impression "of a thoroughly well-disciplined footman."[16] The son of an early Fascist government minister, he had married Mussolini's favorite child, his headstrong daughter Edda, in 1930.

At first, it was hard to take Ciano seriously. He was widely viewed as the spoiled son of Fascist aristocracy, the protected husband of the Duce's daughter. When Phillips first met Ciano, shortly after he became foreign minister, he had been unimpressed. Ciano's English was fluent and he was certainly affable, the ambassador reported to President Roosevelt at the time, but he was plump, fuzzy faced, and looked "astonishingly boyish," with well-oiled hair "slicked back in typical Italian fashion." Worse, he seemed more interested in chasing women at his golf club than in conducting serious business.[17]

Meeting Mussolini in the first days of the new year, the American ambassador found the dictator in a good mood but saw trouble ahead. Phillips had brought a letter from President Roosevelt to the Duce proposing that, in light of the persecution of Jews in Germany and elsewhere in Europe, a state be established for them in East Africa.

Roosevelt suggested setting aside the Plateau region straddling the southern border of Italy's Ethiopian colony and the north of the British colony of Kenya. The Duce surprised Phillips by interrupting him to express his strong distaste for Jews, saying they lacked any loyalty to the countries in which they lived and were the purveyors of financial fraud. Moreover, they were utterly incapable of assimilating with any other "race." There was no room for Jews in Europe, Mussolini told the American, and eventually they would all have to go, but he dismissed the idea of allowing Jews to settle in Ethiopia. He suggested that either Russia or North America, both having large sparsely settled areas, might better accommodate them.[18]

Down the hall in the Zodiac Room—its name deriving from the astronomical design painted on its sky-blue ceiling—the dictator's curly-haired, twenty-six-year-old lover, Clara Petacci, waited almost every afternoon for his visits and their lovemaking. Although he had had many lovers, and quite a few children by them, Clara was different. Not only was she much younger, but he had become obsessed with her, an obsession more than matched by hers for him.

Although she had not finished high school and had little experience of the world outside her corner of Italy, Clara, the daughter of a Vatican physician, had impressive drive. Through remarkable persistence, she had brought herself to the Duce's attention and then won him over. Undaunted by the fact she had been married two years earlier in a ceremony performed by one of the church's most illustrious cardinals, followed by a blessing given personally by the pope, Clara began her affair with Mussolini in 1936. By the following year, she would see or talk to him by phone virtually every day, and the diary she kept over the next several years would record practically every word he spoke to her, noting as well with her underlined code word *sì* (yes) each time they had sex. Her youthful pursuits—drawing, designing clothes, playing the violin, composing poetry—all came to take second place to her devotion to her lover, who was four months older than her father.

At home in the Villa Torlonia, Mussolini lived under the watchful eye of his wife, Rachele, the strong-willed ruler of his household, who kept chickens and pigs in their backyard. The daughter of a poor peasant family in Mussolini's hometown, she had met her future husband when she was only seven years old. The next year, following the death of her father, Rachele's mother took her out of school and sent her to work as a maid. Giving birth to Edda, the first of their five children, in 1910 when she was twenty years old, Rachele held fast to the anticlerical convictions of her youth and only reluctantly agreed to have her union with Benito consecrated by a church wedding fifteen years later. Spurning beauty salons and makeup, possessing only two modest coats, insisting on washing the dishes after their meals, and refusing to attend state functions, she nonetheless, in her elder daughter's words, was "the true dictator in the family." Although Mussolini diligently returned home every night, outside it he led a completely different love life.[19]

IN THE WAKE OF his 1936 conquest of Ethiopia and his declaration that after two millennia Rome once again had an empire, Mussolini was increasingly apt to see himself as infallible. He now dreamed of greater conquests. "March on to the ocean," he told the Fascist Grand Council at their early February 1939 meeting. Italy had to "escape from its Mediterranean prison." Too vain to be seen wearing reading glasses, Mussolini, like Hitler and for the same reason, had his text prepared on a special typewriter that printed letters three times their normal size. Perhaps sensing the feeling of alarm his remarks provoked among several of his fellow Fascist bigwigs, he added that he was not then planning any immediate military action.[20]

Mussolini had never felt comfortable around priests, and while he had earlier recognized the advantage of acquiring Vatican support in overwhelmingly Catholic Italy, he bitterly complained of the pope's recent barbs. It was not going to be easy to convince Italians to embrace Nazi Germany. The history of Italian diffidence toward Germans was a long one, not helped by the recent Great War the two nations had fought. Nor could most Italians feel comfortable with the Nazi ideology of Aryan supremacy. He could ill afford to have the church oppose his plans.

The barrage of criticism of Germany that appeared in the pages of the Vatican's daily newspaper in the first weeks of 1939 infuriated Mussolini. A typical *Osservatore Romano* article told of the recent closing of 180 Catholic schools in one region of the country. It went on to list other parts of the Reich that were now bereft of any Catholic schools, including all of Austria. An even more hard-hitting article appeared on the paper's front page in early February, giving a litany of Nazi measures aimed at undermining the church's influence. "They want to prevent and bleed away Catholic life," the Vatican paper charged, "and even more they want to destroy the Catholic Church . . . and even eradicate Christianity itself in order to introduce a faith that has absolutely nothing to do with the . . . Christian faith." Although the Vatican tried to keep up the fiction that *L'Osservatore Romano* was not the official newspaper of the Vatican, few took this seriously. In fact, it was closely overseen by the Vatican Secretariat of State and by the pope himself.[21]

On January 22 Bonifacio Pignatti, Mussolini's ambassador to the Vatican, went to the Apostolic Palace to complain. In his subsequent report, Pignatti expressed concern that the Vatican's attacks on Germany might weaken Italians' enthusiasm for their own Fascist regime. The problem lay with the pope alone, he said, for "no prelate, no matter how high up he is, dares oppose the Pontiff." "As I have repeatedly written," Pignatti advised, "only a new pontificate will be able to adopt a different, more conciliatory direction on the racial question." The prelates around the pope were themselves increasingly worried where his outbursts might lead. "The Holy Father is always very irritable," Monsignor Tardini, Pacelli's deputy in the Vatican Secretariat of State, wrote in a note at the time. "He once again repeated to me that Mussolini is a *farceur* [buffoon]. 'With me he has been rude and duplicitous.' And he adds, 'I say this to many people so that he too knows it.'" Tardini was at wit's end: "And unfortunately it's true. The pope does say it to many people. Ciano tells the nuncio that the pope . . . talks too much."[22]

Unlike many of the rumors that swirled around the Vatican, the whisperings that Pius XI was secretly preparing an encyclical denounc-

ing Nazi racism and antisemitism were grounded in fact. In the wake
of Hitler's visit to Rome the previous spring, the pope had decided
that just such an official papal pronouncement was needed. But he
worried that Cardinal Pacelli and the other high-ranking prelates of
the Vatican would try to talk him out of it. As a result, he turned to an
outsider, an American Jesuit, John LaFarge, to draft the encyclical. La-
Farge, known for his work opposing racism in the United States, had
sent the resulting text to the head of his order in September 1938, expecting him to deliver it to the pope within a few days. Instead, the
Jesuit superior general, Wlodimir Ledóchowski, a strident antisemite,
did all he could to sabotage it. The draft encyclical landed on Pius XI's
desk only in mid-January, with a cover note from the Jesuit leader urging him to abandon the project.[23]

The pope was planning another blow against Italy's embrace of
Nazi Germany as well. He had invited Italy's more than three hundred
bishops to Rome to celebrate the tenth anniversary of the Lateran Accords on February 11, 1939. There, at St. Peter's Basilica, he planned to
give them what he thought might well be his final message. When Pius
XI threatened to say something that would long be remembered, this
is what he had in mind, and it was this that had made Mussolini so nervous.

The pope prayed for God to allow him to live long enough to give
his message to the bishops, and to the world, but he had grown so weak
that by February 6 he was confined to bed. Other than his doctors,
only Cardinal Pacelli was allowed to visit him. Under the strain of the
pope's worsening health and increasing irritability, Pacelli himself appeared beaten down. The cardinal urged the ailing pope to delay the
upcoming anniversary ceremonies, but Pius XI refused. Concerned
that his voice might be too weak to be heard in St. Peter's immense
basilica, he ordered the Vatican printing office to make copies of his
remarks for all the bishops.[24]

"THE POPE IS DEAD," Galeazzo Ciano, Mussolini's son-in-law and
foreign minister, recorded in his diary on February 10. "The news

leaves the Duce completely indifferent." Indeed, on hearing of the pope's death, Mussolini made no effort to repress a big grin. "At long last he's gone!" he told his son Bruno. "That stubborn old man is dead." The death could not have come at a more opportune moment for the Duce, for it was the day before the pope was scheduled to give the address that Mussolini had feared. Indeed, some would later suspect the Duce of having found a way to hasten the pope to his tomb.[25]

While the Duce privately gloated, the official Fascist government reaction could not have been more respectful, for the image of the deeply Catholic Fascist state had to be maintained. The Grand Fascist Council's meeting scheduled for that day adjourned in a sign of respect and issued a statement that the Vatican's own newspaper highlighted in its front-page coverage of the papal death:

> The Grand Council of Fascism sends a reverent tribute to the memory of the Pontiff Pius XI who desired the Conciliation between the Church and the Italian state, a great event that, following sixty years of fruitless attempts, resolved the Roman Question with the Lateran Accords and, through the Concordat, established collaboration between the State and the Church to safeguard the Fascist and Catholic unity of the Italian people.[26]

The Fascist press devoted countless reverential articles to the deceased pope. *Il Regime Fascista,* the most anticlerical of all the major Fascist papers, was in this respect typical, filling page after page with praise for him. Its front-page story concluded: "While outside Italy the joint forces of Bolshevism, Judaism and the masonry, enemies of religion, of Jesus, and of Italian strength and world Peace, were working to provoke a war, Italy's Catholic and Fascist people testify to their sorrow for the death of the great Pope of Conciliation and of Peace."[27]

Ciano, as foreign minister, instructed Italy's ambassadors abroad to lower their flags to half-mast. Ciano himself went that evening to the Sistine Chapel, where Cardinal Pacelli awaited him. As they stood together at the foot of the towering catafalque on which the pope's body lay, Pacelli took advantage of the occasion to speak with Mussolini's son-in-law about church-state relations, a conversation that led Ciano to believe that with Pius XI dead, the Fascist-church alliance would soon be improving. The two men then got on their knees, side by side, their shoulders practically touching, facing the pope's body, as a crowd of prelates and aristocrats looked on. A photographer for the Vatican newspaper captured the image, as Mussolini's pudgy son-in-law, in his embroidered ministerial tunic, his short dark hair slicked back, pressed his hands together in front of his face in prayerful homage. Beside him, the gaunt, bespectacled, balding sixty-two-year-old Pacelli, in his clerical gown and long flowing red cape, did the same.[28]

Galeazzo Ciano and Cardinal Eugenio Pacelli in prayer at the body of Pope Pius XI in the Sistine Chapel, February 10, 1939

That weekend, instead of gathering to hear the pope denounce racism and Italy's embrace of Nazi Germany, Italy's cardinals and bishops came to Rome to mourn him. Mussolini initially balked at taking part in the funeral rites, but his son-in-law argued that his absence might prejudice their cause at the upcoming conclave. The Vatican would expect him to offer some gesture of respect. "The Duce," Ciano observed, "is always bitter about the Church." In the end, Mussolini agreed to attend one of the funeral ceremonies scheduled for the following week.[29]

Two days after the pope's death, Mussolini, still worried about the speech the pope had been planning to give to the bishops, directed his Vatican ambassador to find out whether any copies of it remained. The next morning the ambassador went to see Cardinal Pacelli, who confirmed that hundreds of copies of the speech had been printed. Distributing the dead pope's final message, remarked the ambassador, would not be a good idea. Pacelli agreed and ordered the Vatican printing office to destroy all copies. The vice director of that office assured the cardinal that he would personally see to their destruction, so that, as he put it, "not a comma" of the speech Pius XI had labored on in his dying days would remain.[30]

THE CONCLAVE

A WEEK AFTER THE POPE'S DEATH, MUSSOLINI'S AND HITLER'S ambassadors to the Holy See met to plan a common strategy. Bonifacio Pignatti, Italy's sixty-one-year-old ambassador, was an experienced diplomat and a man the Vatican viewed as a good, practicing Catholic. He would do all he could to ensure the new pope was someone congenial to the Fascist regime.[1] His German counterpart, Diego von Bergen, had been committed to improving relations between the Vatican and the Third Reich ever since Hitler came to power. Bergen had already spoken with Cardinal Pacelli, who wanted to let Hitler know that he hoped harmonious relations might now be restored between Germany and the Holy See. Should the conclave choose Pacelli, said Bergen, he would undoubtedly do everything he could to reach an agreement with Germany and would very likely succeed.[2]

As the day for the conclave neared, the two embassies continued to lobby the cardinals for Pacelli's election. The Italian ambassador sent his number two to meet with Fritz Menshausen, the number two at the German embassy. Menshausen "repeatedly insisted on the candidacy of Pacelli as Pope," reported the Italian ambassador. "That would represent the best solution for Germany and would perhaps allow reaching a detente in the relations between the Holy See and the Reich." Italy's ambassador thought the German cardinals were likely to support Pacelli's election. If the French, too, decided to vote for him, the other foreign cardinals were likely to add their support as well. What remained less clear was what the Italian cardinals—who formed a majority of the Sacred College of Cardinals—would do: "They fault the Cardinal Chamberlain [Pacelli] for his weakness of character, for being too prone to bend to pressure." Italy's ambassador added that in his opinion "these are quite well-founded concerns."[3]

Cardinal Pacelli presides over the Camera Apostolica, February 1939

The following day, forty-eight hours before the start of the conclave, the two ambassadors met again to compare notes. Bergen described his meetings with the German cardinals, who had assured him they would adopt a "conciliatory" attitude. One of them had met three times with Pacelli, who had expressed both his desire to bring about peace between the Vatican and the German Reich and his own interest in becoming pope. "It now seems clear to me," Pignatti reported, that "the obstacle to his election will come from the Italian cardinals, among whom he does not enjoy much sympathy."[4]

In the days before the conclave, Cardinal Pacelli had also met with the French cardinal Alfred Baudrillart. After a moment of hesitation, Pacelli spoke openly of his chances. "At the end of the day," wrote Baudrillart in his diary, "he will be a conciliator." The only holdout among France's papal electors was the youngest, fifty-four-year-old Eugène Tisserant, the Curia's lone outspokenly anti-Fascist cardinal, and the only non-Italian cardinal in the church's central administration. Pacelli certainly had his merits, the burly, bushy-bearded cardinal told the French ambassador, for he was a man of considerable culture and diplomatic ability, but he was too weak, too easily intimidated. Tisserant, whom France's ambassador characterized as "a bit like the *enfant terrible* of the group of our cardinals, wearying them with his quips and abrupt expression of his strong opinions," seemed to have "a personal antipathy toward the former secretary of state."[5]

IN THE PAST, CONCLAVES were held within days of a pope's death, and as a result the non-Italian cardinals often arrived too late to cast their votes. This time, to accommodate them, over two and a half weeks transpired between Pius XI's death and the convening of the conclave on March 1. Not all were pleased with the delay, unhappy with the spectacle of endless politicking, not least in a series of semi-secret meetings between foreign diplomats and their compatriot cardinals. "They ought to close in the cardinals just as soon as they arrive and make them recite the rosary from morning to night," quipped the papal nuncio in Lisbon.[6]

The opening ceremonies began with a morning Mass in the Apostolic Palace's Pauline Chapel. There, surrounded by its massive frescoed walls, graced by two of Michelangelo's masterpieces, the secretary of Latin letters, a man normally in charge of preparing the pope's Latin language correspondence, read a seemingly endless sermon in a glacial monotone. In the afternoon, the cardinals marched, each accompanied by a Roman aristocratic escort, to the Sistine Chapel. There, along either side of the famed frescoed sanctuary, small canopied tables had been set up for the sixty-two electors, with Boston's Cardinal William O'Connell rushing in at the last minute. Atop each table sat an inkwell, pen, blank ballots, a stick of red wax, matches, and a candlestick.[7]

The voting began the next morning. A two-thirds majority was required to elect a pope, and on the first ballot Cardinal Pacelli received thirty-two votes, followed by the archbishop of Florence, Elia Dalla Costa, with nine, and Luigi Maglione, former nuncio to France, with seven. Pacelli had won the support of a large majority of the non-Italians but only a minority of his compatriots. The French ambassador had speculated that if Pacelli did not get the needed two-thirds vote on one of the first two ballots, his candidacy would recede, and another cardinal would be elected. As the votes on the second ballot were opened and read aloud, Pacelli's name was pronounced forty times. He was still two votes short. Despite the ambassador's prediction, Pacelli was now too close to be denied. That same afternoon, on the third vote, at five P.M., forty-eight cardinals dipped their pens into their inkwells and scrawled Pacelli's name.

Following tradition, the cardinal deacon then approached Pacelli and asked if he would agree to serve. His acceptance, observed Cardinal Baudrillart, "was serious, dignified, and pious, but by a man who could not pretend to decline that which, though trembling, he has wanted for such a long time." Outside in the piazza, the growing crowd watched as white smoke emerged from the chimney of the Apostolic Palace, triggering excited shouts of *Il Papa è fatto!* (The Pope has been made!) A half hour later the cardinal deacon, surrounded by black-robed attendants, strode onto the loggia perched above the great front door of the basilica looking out on the vast piazza. In a strong voice, amplified by a loudspeaker system, he pronounced the traditional words *Habemus Papam!* The cardinals, he told the crowd in Latin, had elected Eugenio Pacelli, who had chosen the name Pius XII. Out then stepped the tall, thin, now white-robed figure, preceded by a prelate bearing a large cross, as other cardinals and Swiss Guards crowded around him. Tens of thousands of the faithful, packed into St. Peter's Square, dropped to a knee, as the new pontiff raised his arm to offer his blessing.[8]

AT THE TIME OF the new pope's election, the subordinate role he had played to Pius XI and his conciliatory style had led many to view him as weak. A couple of years earlier the Spanish ambassador to the Vatican remarked that "Pacelli presents no real counterweight to Pius XI, because he is completely devoid of will and character. He hasn't even got a particularly good mind." The chargé d'affaires at the British embassy, while characterizing the cardinal as "a good man, a pious man, not devoid of intelligence," added that he was "essentially there to obey." Similar thoughts were expressed by the elderly French cardinal Baudrillart, who confided in a 1938 diary entry that "despite all of his eminent qualities, Pacelli does not seem to have either a very strong intelligence or a very strong will."[9]

Having served as secretary of state for the past nine years, Pacelli had indeed become closely identified with his papal predecessor. But the two men were very different in both background and personality. Pius XI came from a modest northern Italian family, his father a textile factory manager. Pacelli came from the so-called black aristocracy, the Roman elites closely identified with the popes since the times they ruled the Papal States as pope-kings. His paternal grandfather had fled with Pius IX in 1848 when a revolution in Rome drove the pope into exile, and then, on their return, helped found the Vatican daily newspaper, *L'Osservatore Romano*. Pacelli's father, the dean of the Vatican's lawyers, had served as a conservative Catholic member of Rome's city council for two decades.

Born in Rome in 1876, Eugenio was a frail, bespectacled child who enjoyed playing his violin more than playing with other children. Following his seminary education in Rome, helped not only by his own considerable talents but by his family connections, he gained a position at the Vatican Secretariat of State. There he rose quickly through the ranks, becoming undersecretary of state in 1911. In 1917 Pope Benedict XV presided over Pacelli's consecration as bishop in the Sistine Chapel. A few days later, moving from his parental home for the first time, the newly minted forty-one-year-old bishop boarded a train bound for Munich to take up his new appointment as nuncio to Bavaria.

It was in Munich that a woman would enter his life, albeit not in a romantic way, as the twenty-three-year-old German nun, Pascalina Lehnert, the seventh of twelve children of a Bavarian mail carrier, came to manage his household. From that time to the later years when Pacelli brought her back to Rome to manage his Vatican household, her presence would generate constant rumors. As she established her rule over the household, seemingly ever present in her black nun's habit, some would find her a "troublesome" woman, but for Pacelli she would prove indispensable. Initially charged with seeing that the cleaning, cooking, and laundry all got done, she would become the one regular female presence in Pacelli's life, ensuring that all was just as he liked it, privately offering her advice and eager to shield him from any unpleasantness. This fiercely protective attitude—mixed with deep adoration for the man she would later campaign to declare a saint—was appreciated by her benefactor, but came to be resented by many, not least because of their chagrin at finding a woman exercising such influence at the heart of the Vatican.[10]

While in Munich, Pacelli had witnessed the early National Socialist movement and its charismatic leader, Adolf Hitler, who had his headquarters there. Pacelli was nearby when, in 1923, Hitler, inspired by the success the previous year of Mussolini's March on Rome, launched his Beer Hall revolt. It was an attempt to overthrow the Bavarian regional government as a first step in a half-baked plan to topple the national government. While the revolt was a fiasco, the episode only increased Hitler's visibility and popularity, not least in giving him time in prison to draft *Mein Kampf*. In 1925, the same year that manifesto was published, Pacelli left Munich for Berlin to take up the position of nuncio to the German government.

Throughout the dozen years he spent in Germany, Pacelli felt most at ease with the conservative Catholic upper classes. He regularly attracted attention, a distinctive tall, thin figure in his black clerical robe and red bishop's cape. "His face is ascetic," wrote a German journalist who observed him in 1927, "the features of his face hollowed out like an ancient gem, the shadow of a smile appearing only rarely." Striking too were his dark eyes, magnified by his glasses. He projected a calm dignity, and gifted in languages and having spent so many years in the country, he spoke German flawlessly.[11]

In his comfortable residence in Berlin, Pacelli often hosted receptions attended by members of the German elite. Among his guests were Germany's president Paul von Hindenburg, along with members of the German cabinet. As a popular dinner guest himself, Pacelli was appreciated for his ability to talk knowledgeably on a dizzying array of topics, from history and world affairs to theology, and for his ability to switch smoothly from one language to another with his delightful repartee. Although he was far from athletic and not one to readily take time off from work, Pacelli did enjoy the few days he was able to go horseback riding in the nearby Eberswalde woods, returning to a childhood pastime. Seeing how much pleasure this brought him, yet how infrequently he was willing to leave the nunciature for his equestrian expeditions, a thoughtful benefactor gave him an electric horse that imitated a galloping stallion. Although he mounted it regularly in Berlin and later had it brought to Rome, it got little use there. As Sister Pascalina noted in her memoir, "He used it about ten times at most as Secretary of State and Pope, not because he did not like it but simply because he did not have the time."[12]

Pacelli returned to Rome in late 1929, when Pius XI awarded him a red cardinal's hat and then appointed him Vatican secretary of state. Sister Pascalina followed him, and Pacelli asked her to furnish his new apartment in the Apostolic Palace just the way he had liked things in Berlin. She had his bookcases and favorite books sent, along with the desk that the German bishops had given him as a present, complete with a silver plaque on which they had their names inscribed.[13]

For the next nine years, Pope Pius XI and Pacelli would make an odd pair, the blunt-spoken, barrel-chested, temperamental pontiff, and the almost unhealthily slender, calm, quiet, highly controlled Pacelli, the consummate diplomat. Pacelli differed from the pope as well in carefully writing out the full text of his speeches, not trusting himself, as the pope did, to speak extemporaneously from notes. But he had a prodigious memory and often gave these speeches without having the text before him, the words, as he put it, scrolling down the page in his mind's eye as he spoke.[14]

———

IN REPORTING THE NEWS of Pope Pius XII's election, Pignatti, Mussolini's ambassador to the Vatican, explained that it "was facilitated by the fact that before entering into conclave Cardinal Pacelli had made clear that, while he had been the faithful executor of the orders given him personally by Pius XI, he had his own views that did not entirely correspond with the direction taken by the former pontiff, especially in recent years."[15] Ciano, Italy's foreign minister, recorded his own pleasure at the news of Pacelli's election in his diary. He recalled his conversation with the cardinal as they prepared to kneel in prayer before the pope's body: "He was very conciliatory, and it seems also that in the meantime he has improved relations with Germany. In fact, Pignatti said only yesterday that he is the Cardinal preferred by the Germans." The next day Mussolini expressed his own satisfaction with the news and remarked, with his customary hubris, that he planned to offer the new pope advice on "how he can usefully govern the Church."[16]

The Fascist press was effusive. *Corriere della Sera*, the country's top newspaper, dedicated its first three pages to the election, the front page featuring an article declaring that "Fascist Italy looks on the new pope with confidence and sympathy." The following day Roberto Farinacci, one of the most prominent members of the Fascist Grand Council and its biggest booster of Italy's alliance with Nazi Germany, offered an effusive editorial in his newspaper, *Il Regime Fascista*.[17]

FOLLOWING HIS FIRST APPEARANCE as pope on the loggia overlooking St. Peter's Square, the newly named Pius XII returned, exhilarated but exhausted, to his Vatican apartment. There Sister Pascalina, along with the other two German nuns who helped her run his household, awaited him. On seeing them now at the end of that historic day, the man famous for his ability to control his emotions finally let his guard down, if only a bit. Seeing the excited sisters sob with joy as they dropped to their knees to kiss the newly placed Fisherman's ring on the

Il Regime Fascista, March 3, 1939

finger of his right hand, he could not hide the tears that clouded his bespectacled eyes. Self-conscious, he glanced down at his new white robe. "Look how they've dressed me up," he quipped to the woman who had stood by him for so many years. But disciplined as he was, the pope let his guard down only for a moment. He had urgent matters to address and an important message to deliver.[18]

APPEALING TO THE FÜHRER

O N MARCH 4, 1939, TWO DAYS AFTER HIS ELECTION, PIUS XII ASKED the German ambassador to see him the next morning. Hitler had sent the new pope a congratulatory telegram, and it was all the encouragement he needed to turn to the most pressing item on his agenda. Italy's Catholic press seized on the Führer's message as well, hailing it as a clear sign that Hitler wanted to work with the new pope to improve relations.[1]

Pius XII began his conversation with the sixty-six-year-old Diego von Bergen, his first with a foreign diplomat as pope, by asking him to thank the Führer for his good wishes. Eager to dispel any impression he might be prejudiced against Germany's form of government, the pope quoted from the speech he had given the previous year at the Eucharistic Congress in Budapest: "It is not the business of the Church to take sides in purely temporal affairs and in the accommodations between the different systems and methods which may arise for overcoming the urgent problems of the present."[2]

The next day Pius XII wrote Hitler directly, expressing his hope that as pope he could restore harmonious relations between church and state in the German Reich. At the same time, he instructed the Vatican newspaper, *L'Osservatore Romano,* to end all criticism of the German government. A new era, it seemed, was about to dawn in the relations between the Vatican and the Third Reich.[3]

TO WIN THE SUPPORT of the French cardinals for his candidacy, Pacelli had promised to appoint Cardinal Luigi Maglione, the former papal nuncio to Paris, to be his secretary of state. Sixty-two years old, balding, but with an impressive fringe of white hair, Maglione was short and stocky, his face kindly, its most distinctive feature the deep dimple in the middle of his chin. He would be popular with the foreign diplomats at the Vatican, a warm man known for his sense of humor and his distinctive chuckle. Born to a modest family in a small town outside Naples, he had been left fatherless when he was a child. Despite this background, he was admitted to the Academy of Ecclesiastical Nobles, the Roman training ground for the Vatican diplomatic corps. He spent the early 1920s as nuncio to Switzerland before being

Cardinal Luigi Maglione

named nuncio to France in 1926, remaining there for a decade before returning to Rome.

"Cardinal Maglione," read a confidential profile prepared by the

Italian embassy to the Holy See, "is a man of spotless ecclesiastical life and vast culture. He has a mind open to understanding the necessities of the times and is a man of great tact in his relations with others and especially in diplomatic functions. A calm and reflexive character, he brings together with his other qualities an uncommon level of prudence in government and in practical affairs." Ciano described the new Vatican secretary of state as "a southerner full of talent and spirit," who "has a hard time notwithstanding his clerical education restraining the impulses of his exuberant personality." Both Ciano and Bergen, the German ambassador, saw in him a man with whom they could work.[4]

BEFORE DAWN ON SUNDAY, March 12, 1939, fifty thousand people began streaming into St. Peter's Basilica. Italian troops and police flooded the piazza and neighboring streets, where an even larger crowd of the faithful and the curious gathered. Later that morning a procession of royalty, government heads, foreign ministers representing thirty-six countries, cardinals, bishops, heads of religious congregations, and other church dignitaries began its slow march into the sanctuary. Among them was Galeazzo Ciano, representing the Italian government. President Roosevelt had sent Joseph Kennedy, one of America's most prominent Catholics and father of a future American president, to represent the United States.

At last, the pope appeared, carried into St. Peter's atop the papal *sedia gestatoria,* his traveling throne, to the sound of silver trumpets. He was swathed in layers of finely embroidered white vestments, wearing a tall white miter atop his head. In the atrium the procession stopped briefly so that the basilica's deacon could pay homage, kissing the pope's foot. As the lumbering procession, with its huge retinue of medievally garbed papal attendants, entered the main nave, the immense crowd inside erupted in applause. The pope, his face thin and pallid, slowly waved a white-gloved hand in repeated blessing.

Following the ceremonies, the guests began to emerge from the basilica. The broad steps of St. Peter's soon filled with dignitaries, whose places had been reserved to give them the best view of the main coronation ceremony, still to come. A long line of robed, white-mitered bishops exited the church, along with various Vatican armed corps, holding their papal banners aloft. In the piazza the papal forces exchanged salutes with the Italian military units that had been waiting outside. After the Vatican's Palatine Guard band finished playing the papal hymn, the band of the carabinieri, the national police under Italian military command, struck up the Royal March, followed by "Giovinezza," the stirring Fascist anthem.

By then all eyes were focused on the ornately adorned loggia, atop the central entrance of the basilica, where a golden papal throne, covered in red velvet, sat empty beneath a canopy made of the same material. The pope's Noble Guards were the first to appear, planting the church banner. The new pope then emerged to the sound of trumpets and the roar of the crowd below. Standing at the balustrade, he raised his hand in blessing, then turned to ascend his throne for the culmination of the ceremony. Removing the miter from the pope's head, the cardinal deacon replaced it with the heavy, three-tiered, bejeweled papal tiara. Pius XII then rose and lifted his right arm as he recited the "Urbi et Orbi" invocation, blessing Rome and all the world.[5]

It was after two P.M. when the pope was finally able to return to his apartment. As would become his practice, he ate alone in his private dining room. According to Sister Pascalina, the little canaries he kept in a cage by his side when he ate sang a particularly beautiful song on that propitious day. Ever attuned to the birds' moods, the pope interrupted his meal to open the little door and let them out. They flew onto the table and the empty chairs, keeping him company until he finished his meal. Then, one by one, he induced them to perch on his finger as he returned them to their cage and closed the little door.[6]

PIUS XII APPRECIATED PRECISION and lived by routine. He rose each morning at six-fifteen A.M., often after having gone to bed only at one A.M. or later, and even then, an insomniac, he did not sleep well. While dressing, he liked to turn on the radio to a foreign station, eager to keep

Pius XII coronation, March 12, 1939

up his English and French. His bedroom, on the top floor of the Apostolic Palace, had two windows overlooking St. Peter's Square. It was furnished plainly, with a simple brass bed, rug, small mirror, a mahogany desk, and a painting of the Virgin Mary. Enamored of devices of modern technology, he was fond of the electric shaver given him during his travels in the United States, sometimes using it while a canary perched on his free hand. At seven he went to his private chapel and knelt before the altar to pray. After putting on his vestments, he said Mass, surrounded by the nuns and priests of his household, and then went to his private dining room for coffee and a sweet roll. Although he ate alone at his table, his secretaries sat near him and handed him the latest dispatches. Following breakfast, he stepped into the elevator to descend the two floors to his office. There he read the most pressing correspondence, before the monsignor who served as his majordomo came in to hand him the list of the day's audiences. Typically, his appointments began with the secretary of state or one of his two deputies, who came in carrying a briefcase bursting with diplomatic papers. The cardinals who headed the various congregations at the heart of the Curia, the central government of the Holy See, then followed.

Those laypeople who were granted the privilege of private audiences were required to dress formally, women wearing black dresses and covering their heads with long black veils. For larger audiences, the pope often chose Clementine Hall, its towering walls covered in Renaissance frescoes and friezes, its ceiling decorated with Giovanni Alberti's *Apotheosis of St. Clement,* its floor patterned marble. When a trumpet blast announced the pope's arrival, all knelt. The pope passed, extending his hand so that visitors might kiss his ring. He then took his place on a modest throne raised on a short platform. After offering his remarks, he blessed his visitors' rosaries before moving on to the next group.

Following these audiences, the pope ate his modest lunch, often rice soup, along with fish or eggs, and vegetables and fruit. At lunch, too, his secretary sat nearby, reading cablegrams and important reports, or taking the pope's dictation while a radio broadcast the news. A couple of small saucers sat on the table, where his uncaged birds pecked at the food laid out for them. Gretchen, a white canary, the pope's favorite, sometimes seemed to tease him, or so Sister Pascalina thought, as the bird sat atop his head and pulled with her beak at the thin strands of dark hair that crossed his bald head.

After lunch, the pope rested briefly before his afternoon stroll. As secretary of state, he had been in the habit of taking long walks in the Villa Borghese, across the Tiber. Giving them up was one of the sacrifices he would have to make as pope. Now each afternoon a black sedan awaited him outside the Apostolic Palace for the two-minute drive to the Vatican Gardens. There the pope walked briskly, circling the gardens six times over the course of an hour, trailed at a respectful distance by one of the Noble Guards. He then stepped into the waiting car for the short drive back.

After returning to the chapel to recite the breviary, the pope met in the late afternoon with his two secretaries, both German Jesuits, or with others having urgent business. Unlike his predecessor, who refused to use a telephone, Pius XII did not hesitate to use his, and while sitting at his large walnut desk, decorated with a white statue of Jesus and a crucifix, he often pecked away on his American-made typewriter. Before dinner, he would summon one of the two deputy secretaries of state, giving them instructions and handing them the documents he had signed, having carefully lifted the white sleeve of his cassock before dipping his pen in the black inkwell. At eight P.M. the pope took his frugal supper alone, scanning news reports as he ate and listened to the radio. He drank wine with his meal rarely, a little glass of Bordeaux on the doctor's orders when ill. After returning to his private chapel for evening prayers, he worked late into the night in his private suite, drafting in his careful, elegant script the speeches he planned to give in coming days.[7]

ALTHOUGH THE BEGINNING OF the Second World War is typically dated to September 1, 1939, when the German army moved into Poland, it could just as well be said to have begun two days after Pius XII's coronation, when, on March 14, German forces entered Czechoslovakia, occupying Prague a day later. Less than half a year earlier, at a conference in Munich where Mussolini cast himself as the principal broker, it seemed that peace had been saved for Europe. In exchange for Hitler's pledge of no further aggression, Britain and France agreed to the German seizure of the Sudetenland, the largely German-speaking region of western Czechoslovakia. Now, with Germany's march through the rest of that country, it was clear Hitler's word meant nothing.[8]

All this was happening while the new pope was making overtures to the Führer in an effort to relax pressures on the church in Germany. The German assault on Czechoslovakia would be Pius XII's first test and in many ways presaged what was to come. Hitler's ambassador to the Vatican alerted Berlin to the pressure the pope was facing to protest the invasion. Thankfully, he wrote, "the Pope has declined these requests very firmly. He has given those around him to understand that he sees no reason to interfere in historic processes in which, from the political point of view, the Church is not interested."[9]

From the first days of his papacy, Pius XII decided it was best to tread a careful path. He was committed to maintaining the church's mutually beneficial collaboration with Italy's Fascist government and was eager to reach an understanding with Nazi Germany. But at the same time he had to avoid antagonizing the Catholic faithful elsewhere, especially in the United States, on whose financial support the Vatican depended.[10] Above all, his aim was to safeguard the church and thereby protect its God-given mission of saving souls.

At the heart of the pope's strategy was a decision to allow wide latitude to each country's church hierarchy in supporting its nation's rulers and policies, including making war. In this way, the church could enjoy good relations with governments anywhere in the world, regardless of their political nature, as long as they in turn supported the church's institutional interests. But as events would soon show, this approach had its drawbacks, putting the pope in an awkward position as he tried to cast himself as a moral leader and not simply the head of a huge international organization. His approach was particularly uncomfortable in dealing with Italy, for there it was the pope himself who was not only supreme pontiff of all the world's faithful but head of the nation's episcopate.

As war erupted in the months following his election, the pontiff carefully crafted his remarks to allow both sides to see them as supporting their cause. This was on display in his first speech, a widely reported address given in the Sistine Chapel the day after his election. Casting himself as an apostle of peace in a world threatened by war, he hailed peace as a "sublime Heavenly gift that is the desire of all good souls" and the "fruit of charity and justice." The coupling of his calls for peace with the caveat that true peace was one accompanied by justice would become a constant feature of his speeches in the coming months and years. It was a view heavily identified with Hitler and Mussolini, who had long complained that the Versailles Treaty ending the Great War could never be a true peace, for, they argued, it was unjust.

In reporting the pope's remarks, Italy's newspapers, from the hyper-Fascist *Il Regime Fascista* to the mainstream *Corriere della Sera,* assured readers that the new pontiff's idea of "peace with justice" reflected the same one the Duce had expressed from the balcony of Palazzo Venezia, "a concept that constitutes the essence of the policy of Fascist, Catholic Italy and that is the opposite of the peace of intimidation of the plutocratic Powers."[11]

ON MARCH 18, THREE DAYS after the German invasion of Czechoslovakia, a limousine carrying Italy's foreign minister entered the side gate of Vatican City and drove into the San Damaso Courtyard. As Galeazzo Ciano emerged from his car, the Vatican's Palatine honor guard greeted him, prompting him to raise his arm in Fascist salute. The pope's *maestro di camera* and a gaggle of Swiss Guards then accompanied Ciano up the stairway to Pius XII's private library, where the two men spent a half hour in conversation. They had last met on the day of Pius XI's death, when they had knelt side by side in prayer before the pontiff's corpse.

Romans had disparagingly dubbed Ciano "il Ducellino," the little Duce, and it did seem that Ciano was often trying to imitate his father-in-law. He was prone to posing with hands on hips, thrusting out his jaw, and speaking in staccato bursts. But the pose was rendered faintly ridiculous by his soft, boyish looks, his high-pitched nasal voice, and his peculiar flat-footed walk.

Despite these sporadic efforts to imitate Mussolini, Ciano could hardly have been more different, showing all the signs of his elite bourgeois upbringing and his inexperience with thuggery. The French ambassador to Italy saw the young foreign minister as the incarnation of moderate Fascism, a man who detested the violent, anticlerical "ultras" of the movement famous for the beatings they administered with their cudgels and the delight they took in humiliating their enemies by pouring castor oil down their throats. For Ciano, Fascism's great merit was in bringing the country's major power centers, the industrialists, the church, the military, and the monarchy into one harmonious whole. It was the brand of Fascism with which the pope, too, would feel most comfortable.[12]

On meeting Ciano that day at the Apostolic Palace, the pope had a matter he was eager to raise. Italian Catholic Action, the church's vast capillary organization of the laity, had long been a bone of contention between his predecessor and Mussolini. Divided into separate organizations of boys and girls, university students, and men and women, it had chapters in parishes throughout the country, each under control of the local clergy. "You have only to follow the advice and the instructions that come from above," Pius XI had once explained to a group of Catholic Action leaders. No church organization had been dearer to him, for he saw it as providing the lay ground troops for re-Christianizing Italian society. The Duce, having outlawed all popular organizations outside Fascist control, was never comfortable with these groups and suspicious that they hid opponents of the regime. He had focused much of his anger on Catholic Action's Vatican coordinator, Cardinal Giuseppe Pizzardo, but had never been able to convince Pius XI to sack him. Now, eager to overcome the tensions of his predecessor's last months, the new pontiff told Ciano he would remove Pizzardo from his post and issue strict instructions to ensure that Catholic Action limit itself to the purely religious realm. Ciano could not have had better news to bring back to his father-in-law.[13]

MUSSOLINI'S SUMMONS CAME AS a surprise to Father Pietro Tacchi Venturi. Under Pius XI, the seventy-seven-year-old Jesuit had served as the pope's personal emissary to the Duce, shuttling back and forth between the two men over a hundred times, carrying the pope's requests to the dictator. With his wide network of contacts among key government ministers and police officials, he had been an invaluable resource for the pope. An editorial of the time in a Fascist daily, mixing grudging praise with sarcasm, marveled at Tacchi Venturi's ubiquity: "He is a phenomenon, a super-phenomenon. For him the day has sixty hours. He is involved in everything. . . . Now you see him in the waiting room of a government minister, now he is going up the stairs of the military offices, now concentrating at his desk writing letters of recommendation left and right. . . . His fame in Italy now exceeds all limits."[14] But after the tensions arose between the Duce and Pius XI in the last months of his papal reign, Mussolini's enthusiasm for seeing the Jesuit had diminished, and their regular meetings had stopped.

Mussolini now summoned Tacchi Venturi, hoping to renew the Jesuit's role as intermediary with the pontiff.[15] First on the Duce's list of requests for the new pope was help in dealing with Spain. While Franco was wrapping up his successful war to overthrow Spain's leftist government, it was crucial, said Mussolini, that Spain's Catholic clergy offer him their strong backing. Next on the Duce's list was Croatia, which he feared Hitler might have in his sights. It was important, he told the Jesuit, for the pope to have Croatia's Catholic clergy make clear that their sympathies lay with Italy, not with Germany. Third on his list was Latin America, where Mussolini said the United States was trying to weaken the "Latin Catholic mentality" by "Protestant penetration." It would be important for Latin America's clergy to combat American influence and urge their governments to have closer ties with Fascist Italy.

Finally, Mussolini wanted to let the pope know how much he appreciated his decision to reorganize Italian Catholic Action. Once this was accomplished, he said, harmony between the Vatican and the regime could be fully restored.

Having outlined what he wanted from Pius XII, Mussolini asked whether there was anything the new pope might want from him. Indeed, replied Tacchi Venturi, there was. The Jesuit then showed the Duce a document whose text the pontiff had approved in their meeting several days earlier.[16] The pope was unhappy that the antisemitic racial laws that had been promulgated over the previous months were being used against those the church regarded as Catholics, not as Jews. He wanted "to see that all the descendants of mixed marriages, baptized in infancy, and brought up as Christians, be recognized as Aryans." The Jesuit explained to the Duce that such converts had, through their baptism, "become children of the Church no less than any others of Aryan descent."

The pope's emissary then reviewed the ways the pope proposed amending the racial laws. As the Duce read the list, he commented on each of the pope's points. Perhaps something could be done about the prohibition on baptized Jews employing Christians for domestic help, he suggested, and perhaps something might be done about allowing baptized Jews who had been engaged to marry Catholics before the laws had gone into effect to go through with the marriage. As for the rest of the pope's proposals, said Mussolini as he folded the pages and put them in a file on his desk, he would refer them to the commission he had established to oversee the racial laws.

The meeting, thought Tacchi Venturi, had gone rather well. It seemed, he reported, that the "period of diffidence characterized by constant jabs and pin pricks that made the last months of the glorious papacy of Pius XI of holy memory so bitter was about to end."[17]

Eager to begin his relations with the Italian dictator on a positive note, the pope acted quickly. He immediately responded to Mussolini's most pressing request, sending a personal telegram to General Franco to confer his blessing on him and to voice his gratitude to God for "Catholic Spain's victory." Franco replied by expressing his pleasure at the pope's words in praise of what he termed "the complete victory accomplished by our arms in the heroic crusade against the enemies of Religion, of the Fatherland, and of Christian civilization." Both messages drew extensive coverage in the Catholic press. Two weeks later the pope followed up by going on Vatican Radio to personally deliver a message to the Spanish people hailing Franco's victory and praising the Spanish dictator's "very noble Christian sentiment." Arrangements were also made to hold a special mass of thanksgiving for Franco's victory at Rome's historic Jesuit church, the Church of the Most Holy Name of Jesus, with the new Vatican secretary of state, Cardinal Maglione, prominently in attendance.[18]

THE FASCIST REGIME'S CAMPAIGN against Italy's Jews, initiated the previous year, was never far from the pope's mind. Indeed, if he were ever tempted to forget it, Father Tacchi Venturi would bring it up again. It had been Mussolini's announcement of his "racial" campaign in July 1938 that had caused the sharp escalation in tension between the

Duce and Pius XI. In the months that followed, Italy's government instituted a series of harsh anti-Jewish measures. Non-Italian Jews were ordered to leave the country. All Jewish children were barred from the nation's schools, and all Jewish schoolteachers and university professors were dismissed. Jews were thrown out of the country's military and civil service, barred from working in banks or insurance companies, forbidden from owning large businesses or farms, and forbidden from employing Christian household help.

To sell the anti-Jewish campaign to Italians, for whom it smelled suspiciously like an effort by the Duce to ingratiate himself with Hitler, the regime was counting heavily on the striking similarity between the new laws and the measures the popes had for centuries imposed on Jews in the Papal States.[19] Indeed, the Fascists boasted they were being softer on the Jews than the popes had been. After all, they were not herding Jews into ghettoes; nor were they imitating the earlier popes in requiring Jews to wear special marks on their clothes.

In the early months of Pius XII's papacy, laws barring Jewish professionals—doctors, lawyers, and others—from having Christian clients or patients were further tightened. Italy's tiny but flourishing Jewish population, not much more than forty thousand strong, and heavily located in a handful of large cities of the center and north of the country, was being reduced to penury. Perhaps worse, the government's propaganda branding Jews the scourge of Christians and enemies of the state was leading to their social isolation. Many Christians now stopped greeting their Jewish friends and neighbors.

Pius XII did nothing to disavow, much less express regret for, the church's long-standing demonization of Jews. The April 1939 lead story in the Jesuit journal *La Civiltà Cattolica,* whose pages had to be approved prior to publication by the Vatican secretary of state, offers some insight into views prevailing in the Vatican at the time. As Easter approached, the article explained, it was important to remember that "the Jews who mask their hatred for Jesus . . . are not simply actors in a drama limited to the obscurity of earlier times. They live again and reappear on the scene in all the persecutions aimed from time to time against the Church, faithful imitators of all the emissaries of the anti-

Church and of the most disparate synagogues of Satan." The article went on to brand Jews avaricious, lust-filled traitors and cowards.[20]

Given the church's view of Jews who were baptized as Christians, and the Fascist state's use of Catholic documentation in determining who was an "Aryan," many Jews saw baptism as their best hope for avoiding ruin.[21] Some of these were Jews who were married to Catholics. Such was the case of Emilio Foà, an executive in Turin. In the summer of 1938, following the announcement of the regime's new racial policy, and fearing, with good reason, the draconian anti-Jewish laws to come, he decided to seek baptism. "My dearest," he wrote Lina, his Catholic wife, "the papers bring you the news of what is happening. No one knows what will happen tomorrow as far as religion is concerned. For that reason, I have decided on conversion. I have the duty to defend your future and that of our children." As in many such cases, though, Foà's last-minute conversion did not save him from being dismissed from his job and left penniless. In May 1939, less than a year after Emilio's baptism, his eighteen-year-old son, Giorgio, found him lying in a pool of blood in his study, a gun in his hand and a bullet in his head. He had left a note for Lina: "My dear wife, I leave you. In that way I save my family. It would have been a life of poverty. With the insurance policies . . . you will have a sufficient income. . . . Do not condemn me. Love one another and remember me."[22]

THE PEACEMAKER

"THE ITALIAN PEOPLE ARE READY TO PUT ON THEIR BACK-packs," the Duce declared in a late March 1939 speech, "because like all young peoples, they do not fear combat and are certain of victory." Despite the war clouds gathering in Europe, few took him seriously. The American ambassador, for one, thought it all hot air. "No one here believes that he is prepared to strike in a military sense in order to achieve his goal," he reported to Roosevelt, "for it is a well-known fact that Italy is not prepared for war." Moreover, he added, "the Italian people are strongly against being drawn into any war."[1]

The ambassador's illusions would be short-lived. Eager to show that his Fascist regime belonged in the same league as his Nazi partner and to lay his own claims to the Balkans before Hitler could plant his flag there, Mussolini ordered Italian troops to cross the Adriatic and seize poverty-stricken Albania. On Good Friday, April 7, 387 Italian warplanes and 170 ships converged on the defenseless country. Twenty-two thousand Italian soldiers landed at its four ports.

Within days an Italian puppet government was in place. On April 16, in a tragicomic ceremony at Rome's royal palace, Victor Emmanuel III added King of Albania to his titles. Deeply self-conscious about his height—he was barely over five feet tall—the king found himself facing a group of hardy Albanians summoned to offer a veneer of legitimacy to the farce. Ciano described the scene as Victor Emmanuel rose to accept the crown: "The King responds with an uncertain, trembling voice. He is decidedly not an orator who impresses an audience, and these Albanians, a hard, mountain, warrior people, look on, while intimidated, with amazement at that little man seated on a huge golden chair."[2]

**King Victor Emmanuel III and Queen Elena at the
ceremony for the acceptance of the title of King of Albania,
Quirinal Palace, Rome, April 16, 1939**

The Catholic press joined the chorus heralding the invasion. "All the principal centers of Albania occupied by the magnificent Italian troops" and "Albania liberated from a shameful slavery" read the headlines of Milan's Catholic daily. Rome's Catholic newspaper published the text of a telegram that an Italian bishop had sent praising the Duce for the invasion. But signs of public enthusiasm in Italy were few. While the American ambassador condemned the unprovoked aggression, he clung to the line he had been feeding Roosevelt. He remained convinced, he told the president, that Italy was not planning any major war. But he sounded a note of caution: "We all admit that Mussolini is playing an exceedingly dangerous game."[3]

WHILE THE POPE HAD shown no particular interest in Italy's invasion of Albania, he was worried about the growing tensions between Italy and France. Mussolini had been demanding that the French cede some of their North African colonies to Italy. In April, Secretary of State Maglione repeatedly summoned the Italian ambassador to share the pope's concerns and urge the two sides to resolve their differences amicably.[4]

From the time he ascended to the papacy, Pius XII had dreamed of playing the role of peacemaker. It was an ambition his World War I predecessor, Benedict XV, had nourished as well, and his failure weighed heavily on the memory of his papacy. With Europe's peace threatened by two sources of tension, between Germany and Poland and between Italy and France, Pius XII decided to propose an international peace conference. First, though, he thought it best to consult Mussolini and so sent Father Tacchi Venturi to float the idea.

Would it not be good, the Jesuit asked the Duce at their May 1 meeting, for the pontiff to send a message to the five powers—France, Germany, England, Italy, and Poland—calling on them to resolve their differences peacefully at such a conference? The pope, he added, would not want to do anything that would displease him and would only go ahead if the Duce would support the initiative. Mussolini said he would give the matter some thought and asked him to return the next day.

The following evening the Duce told Tacchi Venturi he was willing to take part in such a peace conference but advised the pope to sound out the other governments before making his initiative public. Pleased by Mussolini's response, the pope quickly cabled messages to his nuncios in Paris, Berlin, and Warsaw and his delegate in London.[5]

Responding to the resulting request for a meeting from Monsignor Cesare Orsenigo, the papal nuncio in Germany, Hitler summoned him to his sumptuous mountain estate outside Salzburg. The nuncio had barely explained the reason for his visit when Hitler, who, Orsenigo reported, "had listened very deferentially, immediately expressed, as the first thing that came to his mind, his feeling of thanks toward His

Holiness for his attention and his interest, asking me to let the Holy Father know of these sentiments."

When the nuncio finished explaining the pope's proposal, the German dictator replied that before responding, he would need to discuss it with his Italian partner. Then Hitler, "almost in a tone of a simple friendly conversation, added, 'However I don't see any danger of a war. I don't see it in the case of Italy and France, because Mussolini's requests . . . Tunisia, the Suez Canal, and Djibouti, which I find to be reasonable and fully support, are not such as to lead to a war, but only to negotiations.'" Nor, the Führer added, did he see any reason why Germany's dispute with Poland should lead to war.

Following their hour-long conversation, Hitler invited the nuncio to join him in a nearby room for tea. With their official business behind them, Hitler rhapsodized about his visit to Italy the previous year. Italy's art, said the Führer, was of incomparable beauty. The country was fortunate as well, he added, in having the Duce and Fascism. Without Mussolini, Communists would have reduced all of Italy's artistic treasures to rubble, as, Hitler said, they had recently done in Spain. Indeed, Mussolini deserved praise from all of Europe, for had he not led the way, the continent would by now be one big Bolshevik empire. Finally, the German dictator returned his attention to the Vatican, expressing his pleasure that the pope spoke German so well. He only regretted, he told the nuncio as the tea was coming to an end, that in his recent visit, he had been unable to visit St. Peter's Basilica.

"There was once a wise man," replied the nuncio, "who said it was a very good thing not to see everything one wanted to see, so that even in old age there would still be things to which one could look forward."[6]

Word of the pope's proposed peace conference had in the meantime triggered frenetic exchanges between London and Paris. The British, inclined to take up the pope's initiative, suggested holding two separate sets of negotiations, one involving Germany and Poland, and the other France and Italy, but the French were wary. All the evidence, argued the French government ministers, suggested that the pope had coordinated his initiative with Italy's Fascist government to push Mussolini's territorial demands. The Italians, they feared, would take advantage of their privileged relations with the Vatican in any such negotiations.[7]

While these conversations were under way, Joachim von Ribbentrop, the forty-six-year-old German foreign minister, boarded a train to Milan to meet with his Italian counterpart. There Ciano informed him that, notwithstanding what Mussolini had told the nuncio a few days earlier, the Duce had no intention of having his dispute with France brought to any papally sponsored conference. The two foreign ministers agreed they would thank the pope for his efforts but ask him to abandon the effort.[8]

Germany's official reply to the pope came a few days later, when State Secretary Ernst von Weizsäcker delivered Hitler's decision to the nuncio. The prospects for success, the German diplomat told him, did not seem sufficient to justify the sort of conference the pope had in mind. Orsenigo's reaction to this news offers an inkling of the kind of emissary the pope kept in Berlin throughout the war. "The Nuncio," Weizsäcker recalled, "scarcely spoke of the matter itself again, and merely said, with reference to a remark of mine, that he, too, was not quite clear as to what urgent and menacing reports the Vatican could have received to cause a *démarche* to be made."[9]

PIUS XII'S EAGERNESS TO play a visible role in world affairs was making Mussolini uneasy. Insofar as the Vatican played any political role, from the Duce's perspective, it should be confined to efforts aimed at supporting his regime. Nor was the Duce eager to see the pope's stature grow, believing Italy had room for only one heroic figure. Better for the pope to remain in his chapel and pray.

The Duce's unhappiness with the pope's *protagonismo* grew further in mid-May, when Pius XII made known his plans to go in formal procession to the Basilica of St. John in Lateran, on the opposite side of the city from the Vatican. It was an ancient ritual whereby a new pope, as bishop of Rome, took possession of his diocese. The massive ancient basilica traced its origins to the fourth century and had been home to many of the early pontiffs. The origins of the papacy itself and its

Pius XII in his *sedia gestatoria,* May 1, 1939

claim to authority over the church worldwide were rooted in the pope's role as bishop of Rome, and the bishop's seat was at the Lateran.

For the Duce, the less the pope traveled outside the walls of Vatican City, the better. Especially infuriating for the temperamental dictator were any public spectacles in Rome where the pope could equal—or worse, surpass—the crowds of devotees and popular enthusiasm he himself attracted. When the pope's predecessor had made the same trip to the Lateran basilica, he had done so in a closed car, traveling at considerable speed, and once there, he had remained inside the church. Pius XII had something very different in mind, and nothing Mussolini's ambassador said to dissuade him would have any effect.

When the day of the procession came, a long line of cars left the Vatican, accompanied by armed Swiss Guards. The pope sat in the back seat of a slow-moving open car, as the crowds lining the streets cheered. Once at the basilica, the pope, seated in his *sedia gestatoria,* was carried around the vast piazza, circumnavigating the massive Egyptian obelisk at its center. An impressive procession of papal prelates marched with him, accompanied by colorfully uniformed Noble Guards, their ceremonial sabers unsheathed, and a gaggle of Palatine Guards, armed with rifles and bayonets.

"I can predict," Italy's ambassador observed in reporting the spectacle, "that Pius XII will seize any favorable occasion to go out from Vatican City. As much as he is an ascetic, he does not shy away from the pomp that, in his mind, befits the Roman Pontiff. Moreover, being profoundly Roman, the Pope is, without any doubt, seeking popularity, especially among his fellow Italian citizens. If we allow it, we will all too often see Pius XII in the streets of Rome, and probably in other cities of the Kingdom."[10]

THE ITALIAN AMBASSADOR'S GERMAN counterpart, Diego von Bergen, eager to ease tensions between the Vatican and Berlin, continued to send Berlin reports on the pope's pro-German views. The first months of the new papacy had indeed seen a dramatic easing of those tensions. On April 20, the pope had instructed his Hitler-friendly nuncio in Berlin to personally bring the Führer the pope's birthday wishes. On that day, too, the bells of Germany's Catholic churches pealed in celebration as priests and their parishioners prayed for God to bless the Führer.[11]

"Pope Pius XII," Bergen wrote in mid-May, "has the desire to go down in history as a 'Great Pope' . . . as a messenger and accomplisher of peace on the basis of justice, as a bringer of peace to the world." No goal was more important to him, asserted the ambassador, than overcoming the church's differences with Italy and Germany. While the Vatican's relations with Italy's Fascist government had deteriorated in the last months of Pius XI's papacy, that crisis had mercifully passed, reported Bergen, "thanks to the greatest accommodation shown by both sides." While the pope's views of Germany were more complicated than those toward Italy, he explained, Pius XII had "stated quite openly . . . that he 'loved Germany' and hoped for nothing more fervently than for an early peace with us." To reach that goal, the new pope "would be prepared for far-reaching concessions, provided that the vital interests of the Church and principles of dogma were not endangered."[12]

Relations between the Vatican and Italy's Fascist regime had indeed dramatically improved under the new pontiff. In late May Giuseppe Bottai, Italy's minister of education and one of the key members of the Fascist Grand Council, met with the pope. In his recent Easter Sunday radio address, Bottai had stressed the religious value of the government's newly unveiled national school policy. Highlighting all the measures the Fascist regime had taken to provide Catholic instruction in the public schools, Bottai announced that they were being enshrined in the nation's new school charter. Italy, he declared, viewed "Christian teaching in the manner of Catholic tradition as the foundation and high point of public education." He promised, too, that, in cooperation with the Vatican, he would expand Catholic religious instruction in the nation's secondary schools.[13]

In meeting Pius XII, the Fascist leader marveled at the contrast with his predecessor, whom he had also visited. Although the new pope received him in the same room, it looked very different. In Pius XI's time there had been, Bottai noted in his diary, a "picturesque disorder of furniture, decorations, trinkets, papers, newspapers, books." Now everything was in meticulous order. The new pope had also moved his desk. Pius XI had positioned his between the room's two windows, so that sunlight washed across the pope's shoulders. The new pope had moved the desk to be along the wall to the right as his visitors entered. In the place of the old clutter, it was now cleared of all but a few essential items. "One has the immediate impression," observed the Fascist minister, "that the man who sits there knows his 'job' well. . . . Pius XII immediately gives the visitor the sensation of a mystic, but a mystic who works, who weighs his words carefully, who knows what he wants and how and where and when he wants it."[14]

Observers of the new pope saw an unusual combination of an ascetic man intensely interested in the news of the world, someone who labored well past midnight each night, but who, in the privacy of his bedroom, delighted in having a canary perched on his shoulder, a man who, although nervous of crowds, seemed never to tire of offering them painstakingly prepared speeches on almost every conceivable subject, a man who would never miss his hour-long walk through the Vatican Gardens but rarely looked up from his papers to take in the nature around him, a man whose natural aloofness struck many as coldness, yet who could also be charming. By temperament mild and shy, Pius XII at the same time basked in the majesty of his office, eager to cast himself as God's messenger of peace on earth.[15]

Rome now had two men who towered over all the rest, and to whom Italians looked in worshipful adoration. Despite all the fears of war, doubts about the German alliance, and questions about what seemed to some the inexplicable campaign against the nation's Jews, Mussolini's popularity appeared undiminished. Ambassador Phillips reported to Roosevelt in late May that the Duce continued to rouse the crowds, his staccato speech laced as always with pithy phrases, military metaphors, and references to faith and sacrifice. There was no hope, Phillips advised Roosevelt, that Italians would turn against him.[16]

NOTWITHSTANDING HITLER'S ASSURANCES, PIUS XII was becoming increasingly worried that the German demand that Poland return Danzig might trigger a war. A city of 400,000 inhabitants, it was composed overwhelmingly of ethnic Germans. As part of the punitive conditions of the Treaty of Versailles at the conclusion of the First World War, the German region of West Prussia, on the eastern border of Germany, had been given to the newly reconstructed state of Poland. It cut the German region of East Prussia off from the rest of the country. The port city of Danzig, on the Baltic coast in West Prussia, was given special status, under the protection of the League of Nations, but with special ties to Poland. The loss of Danzig and West Prussia had led to a wave of nationalist resentment in Germany, and now following the Reich's absorption of Austria and the Sudetenland, it looked like Germany was preparing to take the region back.

On May 22, 1939, Ciano and Ribbentrop met in Berlin, where in a well-photographed ceremony they signed the Pact of Steel, Italy's formal alliance with Germany. This prompted the pope to write directly to the Duce. It was his fervent wish, Pius XII told him, that he "use his great influence on Chancellor Hitler and the German government to ensure that the Danzig question be dealt with in a calm way."[17]

Following the signing of the Pact of Steel, Berlin, May 22, 1939:
Bernardo Attolico, Hermann Göring, Adolf Hitler,
Galeazzo Ciano, Joachim von Ribbentrop

At the same time, the Duce sent Hitler a considerably less pacifistic message: "War between the plutocratic and therefore self-seeking conservative nations and the densely populated and poor nations is inevitable."[18]

The pope would learn of Mussolini's gloomy prediction soon enough, having dispatched his Jesuit envoy once again to urge the Duce to do all he could to prevent the outbreak of war. Tacchi Venturi met Italy's dictator at Palazzo Venezia two weeks after the signing of the Pact of Steel and sent his report back the following day: Mussolini had listened to the pope's plea "with glacial coldness without saying a word." Discomfited by the dictator's demeanor, the Jesuit asked him, "But then Your Excellency believes war to be inevitable?"

"Most certainly," replied the Duce.[19]

"PLEASE DO NOT TALK TO ME ABOUT JEWS"

WHEN THE BRITISH GOVERNMENT SENT THE THEN FIFTY-
one-year-old Francis D'Arcy Osborne, a career diplomat, to be
its envoy to the Vatican in 1937, it did not expect much of him. A Protestant, representing a country lacking formal diplomatic relations with
the Vatican, Osborne's situation did not seem particularly propitious.
But the dapper diplomat would become something of a fixture in
Rome and, following his ten years representing Britain at the Holy
See, would never leave the Eternal City for more than a few weeks at a
time. Indeed, he remains there still, his body buried in the city's Protestant Cemetery.

Osborne came from an aristocratic family and would later inherit
the title of Duke of Leeds. Unmarried, tall and slim, with a receding
hairline, he tended to a formality typical of his class, a "grand *gentil-
homme*," as the French ambassador would put it, a bit stiff but charming and sociable. Although he had little money, he had extravagant
tastes, was fond of elegant clothes, well-aged wine, and whiskey, as
well as fine furniture and silver. When meeting with the pope or Cardinal Maglione, he spoke in French, in which all were fluent. With
Maglione's two deputies, he spoke Italian. A High Church Anglican,
he was enamored of the Vatican's architectural marvels and ornate rites
and of the glories of Rome itself.

Osborne reflected the British aristocracy in another way as well, in
his tolerance for Italian Fascism and disdain for Communism and Jews,

as his early reports from Rome to London reveal. "The methods of the Comintern,★" he observed in 1937, "are devised to a large extent by the brilliant imaginativeness, mental agility and disintegrative predilections of the Jew, combined with the semi-asiatic fanaticism of the Russian. The first works on the intellectuals, the second on the mob of under-dogs." The next year, in a report to the British foreign secretary, he remarked that Lenin had relied largely on "the mental agility, the cynical adaptability and the amoral ingenuity of the Jew."[1]

On an early July day in 1939, as the crisis over Danzig was heating up, Osborne left his pleasant residence, with its view overlooking the vast Villa Borghese Park, and made his way to the Apostolic Palace at the Vatican. He came with a warning from his government: If the Italians thought the British would stand idly by while the Germans seized Danzig, they were deluding themselves. It would mean war. When Osborne left, Cardinal Maglione summoned the Italian ambassador, asking him to pass the British message on not only to Mussolini, but to the Germans as well.[2]

Neither potential victim of Axis aggression was happy about the pope's efforts to get involved in negotiating a resolution of their disputes. In late June the American ambassador in Warsaw reported on the dismay felt in the upper echelons of the Polish Catholic Church at what they saw as the pope's pro-German attitude and what they feared was his willingness to sacrifice Poland in order to protect the Catholic Church in Germany. At the same time, during a visit back to Paris, François Charles-Roux, the French ambassador to the Vatican, complained to the nuncio there about the contrast he saw between the new pope's attitude toward the Axis powers and that of his predecessor. Since Pius XII's election, observed the ambassador, the Vatican's loud complaints about the treatment of the church in Germany had abruptly come to an end.

In addition to informing the pope what the French ambassador had said, the nuncio had further disturbing news. For some time now, he wrote, "one observes a certain change in attitude toward the Holy See

★ The Third Communist International.

in French public opinion, not, unfortunately, excluding some Catholic circles. One had already heard complaints that the Holy Father did not speak out on the occasion of the bombardment of Albania, which took place on Good Friday." The unhappiness, he reported, had grown as French newspaper accounts of the pope's abortive peace initiative portrayed it as designed to favor the totalitarian states.[3]

When the French ambassador returned to Rome, the pope summoned him. Charles-Roux had barely sat down when the pope surprised him by saying, "So I hear that you are not happy with me!"

The ambassador found himself at a loss for words.

"Yes, yes, I know it well," insisted the pontiff.

Charles-Roux decided to be frank. People in France, he said, had the impression the pope was reacting against his predecessor's approach.

Not at all, said the pope. True, his methods were a bit different, but the French needed to understand that, following Germany's annexation of Austria and parts of Czechoslovakia, forty million Catholics now lived within the Reich. He had to be careful not to do anything that could make their situation worse. "If there was a chance to ease their difficulties," asked Pius XII, "does the Pope not have the duty of seizing it?"

Admittedly, the pope acknowledged, the results of his efforts had thus far been disappointing. The religious situation in Germany hadn't changed, although there were some bright spots, as the treatment of the church in the German press had improved. None of this was to say he had any faith in Hitler. That faith had long been undermined by the Führer's failure to observe the terms of the concordat that the pope himself, then the Vatican secretary of state, had negotiated shortly after Hitler came to power.[4]

It would be folly, replied the French ambassador, for the pope to offer Hitler any further concessions.

To this, the pope offered no objection but instead shifted the subject. Should war erupt, he observed, Germany had a great deal of military might.

So do the French and British, the ambassador replied.

As for Italy, said the pope in concluding the audience, it was his impression that the Italian people did not approve of the government's pro-German policies, although they had little influence.[5]

If the French ambassador was frustrated by what he saw as the pope's apparent tilting to the totalitarian states, he, along with his government, would only become more worried when, in mid-July, the pope decided to revoke his predecessor's condemnation of France's Action Française. Thirteen years earlier the Vatican had placed the newspaper of the antisemitic, monarchist Catholic movement on the Index of Prohibited Books, the publications that no good Catholic should read. In reporting Pius XII's decision to Ciano, the Italian ambassador linked it to what he referred to as the new pope's "strong sympathy, I would say almost a weakness, for the nobility." The new papacy, he concluded, "is progressively taking on its own distinctive complexion, one that has nothing to do with that of the preceding one."[6]

WITH THE ELECTION OF Pope Pacelli, one matter Mussolini would no longer have to worry about was the likelihood of papal protest against the Duce's campaign against Italy's Jews, who had been driven out of the nation's schools and universities, and out of their jobs. No such criticism of the racial laws would ever escape the pope's lips or pen, not in 1939, nor over the following years in which they were in force.

While the pope offered no public sign of displeasure with the anti-Jewish campaign, he continued to lobby on behalf of Catholics who had formerly been Jews or were the children of Jews. "These unfortunates, as Catholics," the pope's Jesuit envoy argued, "are children of the Church, with the same rights and duties as any other Catholic." Should the church not come to their aid, it could "spark the doubt in their souls of being abandoned by the Church: which might make them come to curse the day of their conversion, or worse, to commit apostacy in the hope, albeit illusory, of being effectively helped by the Israelites."[7]

Mussolini's top official overseeing the campaign against the Jews was forty-four-year-old Guido Buffarini Guidi, undersecretary of internal affairs. Mussolini kept for himself the position of minister. With the country's prefects and police reporting to Buffarini, he had enormous power. Portly, ruddy-cheeked, crafty, and ruthless, he was regarded by the German embassy to the Vatican as Italy's most talented Fascist. Mussolini is reported to have said, "Buffarini is such a liar that one does not dare believe even the least percent of what he says," yet he relied on him for handling the everyday machinery of government.[8]

Buffarini made the most of his position, running a side business offering fake certificates of Catholic identity to selected Jews for a handsome price, complete with a cottage industry in producing forged parish baptismal records. For a price, too, officials would discover that the children born to Catholic women married to Jewish men were actually the product of their mother's adulterous affair with a Catholic lover. Such children could enjoy their new status as pure Aryans, that is, pure Catholics.[9]

In late August, the papal nuncio to Italy, Monsignor Borgongini,

Guido Buffarini with Heinrich Himmler,
Palazzo Venezia, Rome, May 4, 1938

was dispatched to bring Buffarini the pope's latest complaint about the government's treatment of baptized Jews. As the nuncio entered the undersecretary's office, he was momentarily taken aback by the sign he saw on the wall: "Please do not talk to me about Jews." Indeed, when the nuncio began to raise the subject, Buffarini interrupted him: "But this isn't the moment because, as you know, as part of its recent effort to promote war, the international Synagogue has stood against Italy."

"It is just because we are on the brink of war," replied the nuncio, "that I can assure you that many baptized Jews, who have been excluded from the army, would like to fight for Italy. So I suggest you change the date of October 1, 1938 [after which baptism would not exempt Jews from the racial laws], for example, to December 31, 1939." The new date would give "the Jew the possibility of redeeming himself by receiving baptism, and then be a soldier in defense of his country. In that way, seeing as he would be risking his life, you will no longer be able to suspect that these people are simply getting baptized for selfish reasons."

The deputy minister gave no ground but promised that if war were to break out, he might reconsider the proposal.[10]

CIANO WAS RELAXING ON the beach at Ostia, near Rome, on a warm August afternoon, when an aide arrived with a message. The German foreign minister wanted to meet him the next day in Austria. Ciano rushed back to Rome to alert his father-in-law and prepare for the trip.

On arriving in Salzburg, Ciano was driven the twenty-six kilometers to Ribbentrop's lavish lakeside summer residence, Schloss Fuschl, a fifteenth-century castle built originally by the prince-archbishop of Salzburg. Dressed in his smart military uniform, Ciano was discomfited to find Germany's foreign minister wearing casual civilian clothes. His discomfort only grew when Ribbentrop, who greeted him rather icily, told him that he had asked him to come so that he could inform him that Hitler had decided on the "merciless destruction of Poland." The German foreign minister brushed off Ciano's protests that this would trigger a larger conflagration. Neither Britain nor France, he said, would in the end risk war.

If Ribbentrop had a new home in the Salzburg area, he was following the example of many of Hitler's ministers, for during the warmer months if they wanted to see the Führer, this was where they needed to be. Hitler had earlier acquired his mountain retreat nearby, in Obersalzberg, on the German side of the old border with Austria. Over the previous years the original building had been dramatically expanded, the massive complex amid the mountains dubbed the Berghof, a palace fitted for the demanding dictator. The day following his uncomfortable meeting with the German foreign minister, Ciano went there to see Hitler.

The Führer spoke with Ciano while standing in front of a large wall map of Europe. As a great nation, he said, Germany could not continue to abide Poland's provocations without losing prestige. But, he insisted, the fighting would be limited. While one day it would be necessary to fight the western democracies, that day remained in the future.

Ciano said he hoped the Führer was right but felt less sure the war could be contained and worried that Italy was not ready to throw itself into a Europe-wide conflagration. In the wake of the recent Ethiopian war and then Italy's support of Franco's revolt in Spain, his country's stores of raw materials were completely exhausted. He then listed Italy's other vulnerabilities should war erupt: its industries were clustered in the north, making them easy targets for air strikes; its African colonies were only lightly defended; and a million Italians were working in France. Ciano even pleaded that Mussolini had put great stock in hosting a world's fair in Rome in 1942 to celebrate the twentieth anniversary of his regime, and ambitious construction for the event was already under way.

None of this impressed Hitler. If he turned out to be wrong, said the Führer, and the Polish invasion triggered a larger war, so be it. It was just as well that it be fought while the Duce and he were still young.[11]

CHAPTER

6

———

THE NAZI PRINCE

———

I N AUGUST 1939, AS HE WAS FINALIZING PLANS FOR INVADING
Poland, Hitler was also engaged in negotiations with Pius XII so secret that not even the German ambassador to the Holy See knew about
them. The existence of these talks, initiated shortly after Pacelli became pope, have only now come to light with the opening of the Pius
XII archives at the Vatican. Both Hitler and the pope thought it in
their interest that no one be aware of them, and it was a secret the
Vatican was eager to maintain long after Pius XII's death. In publishing
from 1965 to 1981 their massive twelve-volume compilation of the
Holy See's documents on the Second World War, which to date has
constituted the official record of Vatican activity during the war, the
four Jesuit editors systematically expunged all reference to those secret
meetings.[1]

The key player in the negotiations was thirty-six-year-old Prince
Philipp von Hessen. Von Hessen proved of special value to the Führer
because he was the son-in-law of Italy's King Victor Emmanuel, having married the king's daughter, Princess Mafalda, in 1925. It was all
part of a pattern of aristocratic marriage, Philipp's younger brother
having married Princess Sophia of Greece, whose own brother Philip
was the future Duke of Edinburgh. Indeed, there were few German
aristocrats with a more illustrious pedigree than Philipp, whose grandfather was the German emperor Frederick III and whose great-
grandmother was Britain's Queen Victoria. Philipp was a man of

medium height, with blond, rapidly balding hair. He kept what hair remained short and combed straight back. His full-page photo in the 1941 almanac of German aristocrats shows him in profile, wearing his dark Nazi uniform, the large swastika patch on his left arm impossible to miss.

The Nazi prince had experience keeping secrets. While courting Mafalda in the early 1920s, he had made sure his clandestine amorous relationship with the English poet Siegfried Sassoon never came to light; nor would his other homosexual liaisons ever become public.[2]

Within five years of their marriage, Mafalda's husband had joined the SA, the Nazi Party's storm troopers, and wore its brown-shirted uniform. What Mafalda thought of her husband's embrace of Hitler remains unclear. Some historians argue she was repulsed by the Nazis, but whether she was or not, she remained loyal to her husband while raising their four children. In the end, she would pay the price as the Führer lashed out at her and her husband following the Italian king's turn against the Duce in 1943. Princess Mafalda would die a gruesome death a year later in the Buchenwald concentration camp, buried beneath a plain marker reading simply *Eine unbekannte Frau,* an unknown woman. She was forty-one years old.[3]

But this was still years in the future. When Hitler came to power in 1933, he rewarded von Hessen by appointing him governor of his home province of Hesse-Nassau in Prussia. Although in the first years of his marriage he had lived largely in Italy, von Hessen would now spend most of his time in Germany. Along with other highly visible and deeply conservative aristocrats, he proved valuable to the dictator in lending legitimacy to the Nazi regime, enveloping the Third Reich in the cloak of German tradition. As one of Hitler's most prominent German biographers put it, between 1938 and 1942, next to Albert Speer, Philipp was "Hitler's closest friend in terms of a foremost unpolitical relationship." Few had as easy access to the Führer as the prince, who served not only as Hitler's private conduit to the Italian government and to Italy's royal family but as his adviser on the acquisition of Italian art.[4]

To maintain their secrecy, the talks between von Hessen and the

**Prince Philipp von Hessen and Princess Mafalda,
June 8, 1933, Hesse-Nassau, Germany**

pope had to be arranged through unofficial channels. The roundabout route, which would be used repeatedly over the next two years, involved a rather shadowy friend of Mafalda's brother, Prince Umberto, Italy's future king. Raffaele Travaglini, a man with valuable Vatican connections, had a secret police file dating back to 1931 that painted him as a schemer and self-promoter. Born in 1900, Travaglini had fought in the First World War and joined the Fascist Party in 1922. After some experience as a journalist, he was appointed in 1927 as Italy's vice consul in Jerusalem thanks, as he later put it, to his ability "to utilize my modest relations in the Vatican and my modest competence in ecclesiastical matters." By 1931, back in Italy, he had acquired a position in the bureaucracy of the Fascist afterwork program and began attracting the attention of Mussolini's police chief as a suspected spy for the Vatican. "Travaglini," reported a police informant in 1933, "is someone who has traveled a lot and has easy access to and is very well known in Vatican circles. . . . It is likely that Travaglini is engaged in a double game (if he is indeed one of our agents) with us and with the Vatican."[5]

Travaglini was not only an avid Fascist but deeply enmeshed in a church social network that reached into the Vatican. On March 9, 1939, only a week after the pope's election, he wrote to Cardinal Lorenzo Lauri, a member of the Curia in Rome and a former nuncio to Peru and Poland. Lauri's closeness to the new pope was reflected in Pius XII's appointment of him later in the year to be chamberlain, in charge of the Vatican in the event of the pope's death. As he would in all his subsequent correspondence with the cardinal, Travaglini wrote on the stationery of the Order of Malta, the knightly Catholic religious organization. Beginning in June, the stationery identified him as the Order of Malta's special representative to Germany.

In the first of his many letters, now found in the archive of the Vatican Secretariat of State, Travaglini informed the cardinal he had recently returned from a trip to Germany in a successful effort to protect the Order of Malta's assets in the Reich. For this result, he said, much thanks was due to leading Nazi officials. While he was in Germany, he recalled, "Many notables of the Reich and the Party assailed me with questions about the new Holy Father." He told them how fortunate the Third Reich was to have Pacelli as pope.[6]

Within weeks of Pacelli's election to the papacy, Hitler summoned von Hessen to his office. Given the new pope's evident eagerness to turn the page on the Vatican's rocky relations with the National Socialist regime, Hitler, after discussing the matter with Hermann Göring, decided to explore the possibility of a deal. For this, he thought von Hessen, whom he had already been using as his unofficial go-between with Mussolini, best suited to act as his emissary. Von Hessen was told to see if he could arrange a secret meeting with the pope to begin the discussions.

On a Sunday in mid-April, barely a month after Pacelli had become pope, Prince von Hessen summoned Travaglini to the Italian royal residence in Rome. There he explained that Hitler had asked him to initiate negotiations with the new pontiff outside normal diplomatic channels. He was turning to Travaglini because he knew of his high-level contacts in the Vatican. Travaglini, excited, immediately wrote Cardinal Lauri, telling him what Hitler had requested and asking for the cardinal's help in arranging a meeting between von Hessen and the pope.[7]

The pope agreed and met Hitler's envoy for the first time on May 11. To help ensure secrecy, the pope took the highly unusual step of holding the meeting in Cardinal Maglione's apartment. The two men spoke in German, although von Hessen, who had spent years living in Italy, could also speak Italian, and the Vatican archives contain a German-language account of their conversation.[8]

After welcoming von Hessen, the pope took out a copy of the letter he had sent Hitler shortly after his election as pope two months earlier. He read it aloud to the prince, then read Hitler's reply.

"I have been very considerate, and the Reich Chancellor's reply was very kind," said the pope on finishing his reading. "But the situation has since deteriorated." By way of example, he cited the closing of Catholic schools and seminaries, the publication of books attacking the church and the papacy, and the slashing of state funds benefiting the church in Austria. He told the prince he was eager to reach an agreement with the Reich and was ready to compromise insofar as his conscience allowed, "but for that to happen, there must before anything else be a truce. . . . I am certain that if peace between church and state is restored, everyone will be pleased. The German people are united in their love for the Fatherland. Once we have peace, the Catholics will be loyal, more than anyone else."

Von Hessen explained that the National Socialists were divided into pro-church and anti-church factions that were "bitterly opposed to each other." If the church would agree to confine itself to church matters and stay out of politics, the pro-church faction could prevail.

The church, replied the pope, had no interest in involving itself in partisan politics. "Look at Italy. Here too there is an authoritarian government. And yet the Church can take care of the religious education of the young. . . . No one here is anti-German. We love Germany. We are pleased if Germany is great and powerful. And we do not oppose any particular form of government, if only the Catholics can live in accordance with their religion."

Von Hessen asked if the pope was willing to put the church's commitment to stay out of politics in writing.

The problem, replied Pius XII, evading the question, was to be clear what was meant by "politics." Religious education of the young, for example, should not be considered political.

Von Hessen then brought up what had been another sore point in the Vatican's relations with the Reich, the much-publicized "morality" trials of German priests. Hundreds of priests had been charged with sexual crimes, including the abuse of children. "Such errors happen everywhere," observed the pope. "Some remain secret, others are exploited. Whenever we are told of such cases, we intervene immediately. And severely. If there is mutual goodwill, we can set such matters straight. . . . As I said, especially within the Church they should not occur and are deplorable, and when they happen the Church acts immediately."

That the Secretariat of State a year earlier, then under Cardinal Pacelli's direction, had taken immediate action in dealing with such cases is now clear from the Vatican archives. A folder there, labeled "Vienna: Order to burn all archival material concerning cases of immorality of monks and priests," describes the decision, in the face of an ongoing police investigation, to order the destruction of all church files documenting cases of Catholic clergy sexual abuse in Austria.[9] To date, historians have largely dismissed the police investigations of clerical sexual abuse of minors during the National Socialist regime as evidence of the regime's anti-Catholicism. It is indeed likely that the prosecution of the clergy was motivated by attempts to place pressure on the church. However, there were reasons that the church was so vulnerable to this variety of blackmail. The fact that the Vatican has never made its own records dealing with cases of clerical sexual abuse available to scholars has contributed to the failure by historians to pursue how such cases were handled. It was only many years later that, under pressure, the German church hierarchy authorized an investigation of clerical sexual abuse, and it focused exclusively on the decades following the war. That investigation found thousands of such cases, most involving the abuse of boys under age thirteen. The story of the earlier decades remains unknown and largely unexamined.[10]

Throughout their meeting, von Hessen expressed his nervousness that word of it might leak out. "No one knows we're having this conversation," the pope assured him. "Even my closest associates don't know about it."[11]

Following their encounter, von Hessen returned to Berlin to tell Hitler what the pope had said. Three weeks later, having returned to Rome, employing what would become their standard practice, von Hessen called Travaglini to the royal palace and recounted what Hitler had told him. Travaglini in turn relayed this in a letter to Cardinal Lauri, which the cardinal then sent on to the pope.

"The Fuehrer," the message began, "was very satisfied with the secret discussion that the Prince had with His Holiness on the evening of May 11, 1939. . . . Following that meeting various conversations took place in Berlin with the Führer and with Goering and Ribbentrop." As a result:

a)   The pope's meeting with von Hessen had changed Ribbentrop's attitude toward reaching an agreement between the Reich and the Vatican, which he had previously opposed but now supported.

b)   As of May 25, the German press was ordered to end its attacks on the Catholic religion and Catholic priests in Germany and on the contrary, to speak well of them if good occasions should arise to do so.

c)   Hitler called on various regional officials to send reports on the religious situation in their regions, in order to be in a position to negotiate with the Vatican regarding its concerns.

d)   The decision was made to send Prince Philipp to Rome

with a message of homage and good wishes for the Holy
Father, accompanied by some concrete proposals, to initiate official contacts via the respective diplomatic channels
for the hoped-for accord.

Von Hessen's message went on to stress the importance Hitler
placed on having the negotiations remain secret and on ensuring that
no sign of them appear in any of the official diplomatic channels linking the Holy See and Germany. Should the negotiations become public, they would raise expectations of a deal that might in the end prove
impossible. For Hitler, reaching out to the pope in this private way
could be seen as a sign of weakness, and unless an agreement could be
had with the pope, there was no benefit to letting word of his initiative
get out.[12]

Through the summer of 1939, as Hitler prepared his invasion of
Poland, he continued to use the same channel to hold out hope to Pius
XII of reaching an agreement that might usher in an era of harmonious
relations between the Vatican and the Third Reich. In early July, the
pope received a new report via Cardinal Lauri. Prince Philipp, briefly
in Italy for a royal wedding, had summoned Travaglini to the royal
palace to pass on the Führer's latest message. At a meeting with Hitler
a few days earlier, von Hessen had asked him whether the proposals for
the pope were ready. The prince reported that while the Führer was
"now predisposed to conciliation," he "asked to be excused if, given
the current extremely delicate international situation, he hadn't been
able up to now to adequately study the current complex problems of
the Catholic Church in the Reich in order to be able to bring the Holy
Father, with devout and respectful sentiments of great esteem and
sympathy, concrete proposals." But, von Hessen hastened to add, he
was convinced that the much-desired religious peace could be achieved,
and he hoped soon to return again to Rome to meet with the pope.[13]

Von Hessen's next secret meeting with Pius XII took place the following month, less than a week before the Führer's invasion of Poland.
It was preceded on August 21 by a long, encouraging report that Travaglini sent the pope, again via Cardinal Lauri. Typical in including a

large dollop of self-promotion, Travaglini informed the pontiff that he had himself returned recently from Germany, where he had lobbied the Nazi higher-ups on behalf of the Vatican, telling them that "Pope Pacelli is their Pope." Von Hessen, he reported, wanted Pius XII to know that not only had Hitler ordered the press to stop its criticisms of the church but also that, in order to create the necessary atmosphere for reaching an accord with the Vatican, he was subtly distancing the Reich from Alfred Rosenberg, Nazism's foremost anti-church theoretician. "Now the problem," wrote Travaglini, "is in the exclusive hands of the Führer and von Ribbentrop."[14]

"A half hour ago," reported Travaglini three days later, in a letter to Cardinal Lauri, "His Royal Highness Philipp von Hessen arrived from Germany with some extremely urgent messages from the Führer for the Holy Father. I believe we have now arrived at the official start of the Negotiations. The Prince has to leave again by air tomorrow evening or at the latest on Saturday after having seen the Holy Father." Travaglini then asked for instructions on how to arrange for this new meeting. He noted that the prince would be using the same alias he had employed in his earlier visit: Marquis Turri. In forwarding Travaglini's letter to the pope, the cardinal emphasized in a cover note that von Hessen had come to Rome "by order of the Führer to once again negotiate the noted affairs secretly and personally with Your Holiness."[15]

A detailed account of von Hessen's next encounter with the pope, which took place at Castel Gandolfo, comes in the form of a German-language record found in the newly opened Vatican Secretariat of State archives. Labeled "Secret Audience of His Royal Highness Prince Philipp von Hessen, Saturday, 26 August 1939, Evening, 6 pm," it describes the dramatic meeting that took place less than a week before Hitler sent German troops into Poland, setting off the Second World War.

The German prince began, as was by now becoming familiar, by telling the pope that Hitler wanted to assure him of his "most fervent desire" to restore peace with the church. The Führer, said von Hessen, did not believe that any "big issues" divided them. Seemingly oblivious to the apparent contradiction, the prince then said that Hitler thought the "biggest issues" needing to be resolved, if an agreement was to be reached, were two: the "racial question," and what the Führer saw as the clergy's meddling in Germany's domestic politics. Hitler thought that the first of these obstacles to an agreement, the "racial question," could be "avoided," presumably by continuing the new pope's policy of remaining silent about the issue. What was needed if an agreement was to be concluded, then, was reaching an understanding on the proper role of Germany's Catholic clergy.

In responding, the pope first expressed his gratitude to the Führer for his warm greeting. He, too, he said, would like to see the church reach an honorable agreement that would ensure religious peace in the Reich. As for Hitler's concerns about political activity by the German clergy, there should be no grounds for worry, as the church had no reason to engage in partisan politics.

The Führer, replied the prince, was convinced that their talks could well lead to a new, revised concordat with Germany, one that included Austria, now part of the Reich, as well.

"We will promote the achievement of an honorable religious peace with utmost vigor," said the pope.

Such a peace, the prince assured the pontiff, "really is the Führer's deep wish. He hopes to see your Holiness when he comes back to Rome for official purposes." The Führer had hoped by now to have provided the pope with a series of points to move the negotiations along. Unfortunately, "the Russian affair came up," distracting Hitler from the matter. Von Hessen did not need to explain his reference, for the German-Russian nonaggression pact, signed three days earlier in Moscow, had already been reported in the press. But the negotiations with the pope, insisted the German prince, remained of the utmost interest to the Führer. That was why Hitler had ordered him to make this trip to Rome, wanting to move the discussions ahead. At the same time, they all realized that everything had to be done in secret if they were to prevent "hostile interference" by those eager to prevent any agreement between Pius XII and the Führer.

It was certainly true, said the pope, that there were those who would not like to see the conclusion of such a peace, but Hitler needed have no concerns about maintaining secrecy on the Vatican's side. "The *secretum,*"★ said the pontiff, "is sacred to us."

As the meeting neared its end, von Hessen, although himself a Protestant, asked for the pope's approval of his plan to dedicate a small Madonna in the pope's honor "in remembrance of this day." It was an appropriate offering, as Pius XII had a long-held devotion to the Virgin Mary. Expressing his appreciation for the German prince's gesture, the pope agreed.[16]

Pius XII would next meet with Hitler's emissary two months later. By then, the world would be much changed, a terrible new war begun.

★ Secret. The pope apparently used the Latin term here.

SAVING FACE

"WE ARE PASSING THROUGH A VERY MYSTERIOUS MOMENT here," Ambassador William Phillips wrote President Roosevelt on August 18, 1939, "and underlying the deadness of mid-August in Rome there is a feeling of general alarm." Ever since Ciano's return from Salzburg, Phillips had been trying unsuccessfully to see him to discover why Hitler had summoned him there so urgently. "The Pope," added Phillips, "is said to be seriously alarmed."[1]

Mussolini continued to affect a boastful, if not megalomaniacal, swagger. But doubts from his generals about the military's preparedness, and reports of Italians' lack of enthusiasm for a war, were giving him some pause. His mood swings were becoming ever more frequent. Irritated by a London newspaper's claim that Italy's military wasn't ready to fight a war, he vented his fury with his son-in-law. He had been considering remaining neutral, he told Ciano, but now he was inclined to go to war at Germany's side. "Otherwise," remarked the Duce, "we would be dishonored for a century."[2]

The next day Mussolini was relaxing—that is, insofar as he was capable of relaxing—in his Palazzo Venezia hideaway with his lover, Clara Petacci. Adjacent to the room was a small bathroom where, after sex, Mussolini liked to freshen up, splashing his face with his favorite cologne. Still in the early years of their affair, Clara, then twenty-seven years old, was thrilled by her proximity to the man she and many other Italian schoolgirls had grown up idolizing as the heroic incarnation of virility. As she waited for him each afternoon in the Zodiac Room, she whiled away her time stitching new gowns, scribbling in her burgeoning diary, or simply lying on the sofa, daydreaming.[3]

This day, like many, offered Clara something of a political education, as Mussolini pontificated on the world situation, an endless stream combining acute analysis with the rankest vitriol. England, Mussolini told Clara that day, should never have given its guarantees to Poland without first reaching an agreement with Russia. "Now Russia is going to screw them!" Without Russia's support, explained the Duce, the English would soon realize they had put themselves in an impossible situation. "They'll begin to say: 'It's not worth dying for Danzig . . . for something that has nothing to do with us.' . . . Ah! The Germans are lucky. They always find themselves facing morons or cowards."[4]

The following day Mussolini's ambassador to Germany, Bernardo Attolico, appeared at Palazzo Venezia, having arrived by train from Berlin bearing urgent news. A career foreign service officer and former ambassador to the Soviet Union, Attolico looked as soft as the Duce was hard. Tall, overweight, and balding, with protruding ears, his sparse gray hair combed back, the ambassador wore round, thick-lensed glasses.

"Duce!" said the breathless Attolico, "in Berlin they've decided to wage war, now, within a few days!"

The Duce ran his tongue over his lips and thought the matter over a moment before saying matter-of-factly, "In that case . . . Italy's road is clearly marked: we must honor the alliance."

Attolico, shocked, stood mute. Mussolini broke the silence: "There is nothing else to do! I told the rally in Maifeld★ that Fascist Italy spoke with a single voice and a single will. I told Germany in front of a million Germans gathered there that with friends one goes all the way."[5]

ON AUGUST 22 THE world's press carried the surprising news that Germany was entering a nonaggression pact with its archenemy, the

---

★ The May field was created for the 1936 Olympics in Berlin. Mussolini appeared with Hitler there in the fall of 1937.

Soviet Union. A German attack on Poland now appeared imminent. The day after Joachim von Ribbentrop and his Russian counterpart, Vyacheslav Molotov, signed the agreement, both the French and the Polish ambassadors rushed to the Vatican with the same request: Should Germany invade Poland, a Catholic country, it was crucial that the pope publicly condemn it.[6]

The next day Italy's ambassador arrived at the Apostolic Palace, where, with Cardinal Maglione awkwardly still away on his summer vacation, he met with his deputy, Monsignor Domenico Tardini.

While the ambassador would rather have met with the cardinal himself, he realized that as far as access to the pope was concerned, he lost little by seeing either Monsignor Tardini or the cardinal's other deputy, Monsignor Giovanni Montini. Indeed, it was clear to all in the Vatican that the pope felt closer to the two deputies than to the secretary of state himself.

The pope never would develop a warm, personal bond with Maglione and never felt entirely comfortable with him. Practically the same age as Pius XII, nuncio to France while Pacelli had been nuncio to Germany, and Pacelli's rival at the recent conclave, Cardinal Maglione had a hard time playing the subservient role that the pope found most congenial in those who worked for him. But it was just such devoted service that the pope found in Maglione's two principal deputies, who had loyally served in their present positions under him when he himself had been secretary of state.[7]

The two deputies were very different. Forty-one-year-old Giovanni Battista Montini, the pope's favorite, came from a prominent Catholic family from the northern city of Brescia. The product of elite Catholic seminaries and colleges, Montini was appointed substitute* of the Vatican Secretariat of State in 1937.

Almost a decade older than Montini, Domenico Tardini was at the same time named secretary of the Curia's Congregation of Extraordinary Ecclesiastical Affairs, responsible for relations with the govern-

---

* Substitute is the title given to the head of one of the two major departments into which the Vatican Secretariat of State was divided.

ments of the world. The son of a Roman family of limited means, he was as rough around the edges as Montini was genteel. "Monsignor Tardini is a short, stocky man, rather common, and of modest origins," observed the French ambassador, "with a very lively spirit, of mediocre culture, impulsive." Although Tardini said only what he wanted to say, he was inclined to be more frank than others in the Secretariat of State. For this refreshing trait, as well as for his wry wit, he was popular among the foreign envoys at the Vatican.[8]

The French ambassador captured Giovanni Montini well, with a play on words: "He is a little bit the Pope's *enfant de choeur*—*ou de coeur* [altar boy—or child of his heart]." He was, in some ways, much like the pope: from an elite Catholic family, intellectual, innately rather shy and soft-spoken, cautious in his speech: "emotional, indecisive, unsure of his judgments, he is at the same time very likeable, very sincere, very frank and yet elusive." The ambassador concluded the sketch by noting that people in the know thought Montini was likely to become a pope himself one day. Indeed, over two decades later Montini would be elected to the papacy, taking the name of Paul VI.[9]

Meeting now with Mussolini's ambassador, Tardini said the pope would welcome any suggestion the Italian government had for preventing the outbreak of war. The ambassador replied, as he had in the past, that the only thing the pope could do to be helpful was to urge Poland to cede Danzig to the Germans.

Tardini immediately informed the pope of the Italian request. The following day, at their early morning meeting in Castel Gandolfo, the pontiff handed him the text of a telegram to send in code to the nuncio in Warsaw. Its message was clear: "If Poland were to give some satisfaction on the question of Danzig, it might open a path to détente." This was not the pope's first effort to convince the Polish leaders to be more flexible. Earlier in the month he had instructed his nuncio in Warsaw to urge compromise on the Polish government. Now, on receiving this latest telegram, the nuncio met again with Poland's foreign minister, this time specifically urging Poland to cede Danzig to the Germans. The Polish minister refused the request out of hand.[10]

Monsignor Domenico Tardini, Cardinal Luigi Maglione,
Monsignor Giovanni Montini, and (seated) Kazimierz Papée,
Polish ambassador to the Holy See, March 16, 1939

DESPITE ALL HIS BLUSTER, the Duce did not share the Führer's rosy prognosis for how quickly Poland could be conquered, and he was even less convinced of an easy victory over Britain and France should those two powers follow through on their threats to come to Poland's aid. Nor, despite his repeated proclamations of Fascist Italy's might, was he without doubts about the country's ability to wage a European war. At his twice-weekly meetings with the king, the constitutionally mandated commander of Italy's military, Victor Emmanuel made no secret of his belief in the poor state of the country's forces, the woeful quality of its generals, his worry that Italy could be exposed to a French attack across the Alps, and, not least, his belief that Italians were not psychologically prepared for a war. Nor did the monarch have any love for the Germans, much less Hitler, whom he detested.[11]

On the afternoon of August 25, Hans Georg von Mackensen, the German ambassador to Italy, hand-delivered a letter from Hitler to Mussolini belatedly informing him of the signing of Germany's non-aggression pact with Moscow. Sitting at his desk in Palazzo Venezia, Mussolini, who prided himself on his knowledge of German, read the Führer's text carefully. His reaction was rather muted. He was reconciled to the idea that a European-wide conflict was about to erupt, but, he said, he would have preferred Hitler to delay the war another year or two so Italy could be better prepared.[12]

While he assured Mackensen that Italy would honor its pledge and stand by Germany in war, the Duce was already looking for a way out. The next day he sent Hitler a message. The chiefs of staff of the Italian military, he told the Führer, had identified all the materials they would need Germany to supply to enable them to take part in a war that might last as long as a year. An extensive list followed, beginning with six million tons of coal, two million tons of steel, and seven million tons of petroleum. It was a request Mussolini knew the Germans could not satisfy. He ended his message on a rather discordant note: "If you think that there is still any possibility whatsoever of a solution in the political field, I am ready—as on other occasions—to give you my full support and to take such initiative as you may consider useful for the aim in view."

Hitler replied the same day. Presiding over a military high command that had a poor opinion of the abilities of its Italian partners, Hitler had always been the main booster of the Italian alliance. He still retained a strong affection for the Duce, recalling the early days in Munich when Mussolini served as his role model and inspiration. He would now do what he could to help him save face. Regretfully, Hitler informed his Italian partner, Germany could not furnish all the materials requested. "In these circumstances, Duce, I understand your position, and would ask you to try to achieve the pinning down of Anglo-French forces by active propaganda and suitable military demonstrations such as you have already proposed to me."[13]

Hitler's message served its purpose, for it allowed Mussolini to claim that if he was not sending Italian troops to fight alongside his

German allies, it was only because Hitler had not asked for them. But there was no getting around the fact that this came as a great humiliation for the Duce—the first of what would be many for him in the war—after all the years he had boasted of turning soft, mandolin-playing Italians into hardened Fascist warriors.

THE NEXT DAY, A Sunday, a large crowd gathered in Piazza Venezia, clamoring for the Duce to appear outside his window. They had come to express not their enthusiasm for war, but their faith that their leader would somehow help avert it. After stepping onto the tiny balcony outside his office window and raising his arm in salute, Mussolini went directly to Clara in the Zodiac Room.

"Sweetheart, did you see? They needed to see me and then I warmed their hearts with my smile, as I made a sign as if to say that things are getting better. These people don't want war. . . . People are writing me from all over the world calling on me to act as mediator." Then, as was often the case, Clara turned the subject from the political to the personal, her jealousy over Mussolini's other lovers. Especially weighing on Clara was Margherita Sarfatti, Mussolini's most serious affair, although it had ended over a decade earlier. For the Duce, Clara's mention of Sarfatti brought to mind the last time his wife had lectured him about his relations with other women. It had been ten years earlier, he told Clara, when Rachele caught him on the phone with Margherita. Now, though, his wife showed no interest in his affairs or, for that matter, in him. "No," he assured Clara, "I don't love her. She is the mother of my children. . . . We are always very distant, very: we are too different." Clara felt reassured for the moment, but her doubts, her insecurity would soon return.[14]

The pope was meanwhile growing increasingly uneasy. As German troops massed on the Polish border, the French ambassador returned to the Vatican to plead for a papal declaration in support of Poland. "His Holiness," wrote Monsignor Tardini, in recalling Pius XII's response to the request, "says that this would be too much. One cannot forget that there are forty million Catholics in the Reich. Just think what they would be exposed to if the Holy See were to do something like this!" The pope, however, deciding some action was needed, sent Father Tacchi Venturi, his Jesuit envoy, to meet with Mussolini and urge him to do all he could to preserve Europe's peace and, in any event, keep Italy out of the war.[15]

That Mussolini was eager to see the pope's messenger was evident from the speed with which he agreed to the meeting. Tacchi Venturi sent his request to meet at twelve-thirty P.M. and an hour later was told to come to Palazzo Venezia that same afternoon at five. There the Jesuit found Mussolini in a rather good mood and eager to get his own message to the pope. Germany today, the Duce observed, was much stronger than it had been in 1914, and even back then it had taken all the world's forces several years to defeat it. But, said the Duce, there was still hope. Here he took out a piece of paper on which he had written a message. It was advice he wanted the pope to send to Poland's president.

The text was brief: "Poland does not oppose the return of Danzig to the Reich and calls for direct talks with Germany on concessions allowing Polish traffic through the Danzig port; on the corridor; on reciprocal matters concerning minorities."[16]

Although Mussolini could often be abrupt, and meetings with him short, he seemed in no rush to see his old Jesuit partner leave. It would be criminal, said the Duce, for a world war to erupt simply over the question of Danzig. But should it happen, he added, anticipating the Jesuit's next plea on the pope's behalf, he would not rush to throw Italy into it.

Tacchi Venturi hurried to get the dictator's note to the pope. On learning what Mussolini had asked of him, Pius XII had telegrams prepared for his nuncios in Warsaw and Berlin. The telegram to Berlin, signed by Cardinal Maglione, went out quickly:

Some diplomat has suggested the following solution for the Danzig question: "The Polish corridor and the adjacent territory could become an independent state like Monaco, Liechtenstein, etc., guaranteed or administered by neutral Powers, which would assure complete freedom for all nationalities and for commerce." As the situation now seems extremely serious, I communicate the above to Your Excellency on the august order of the Holy Father, so that you make such use of it as you believe possible and opportune.[17]

Maglione's deputies found the task of drafting the message to Poland more difficult. Indeed, the ever-cautious Monsignor Tardini questioned whether it was wise for the pope to send any such message at all. Aside from the likelihood that the pope's secret efforts would come to light, he saw three other reasons why it would be best to abandon the idea. First, "it would seem as if the Holy See was playing into Hitler's hands. He would bite off another big mouthful with Danzig and then next spring would begin all over again." Second, "the Holy See would have seemed to accomplish another Munich," which Tardini described as consisting of "Hitler screamed, threatened and obtained what he wanted." Third, advised the monsignor, "the Holy See would seem a bit too tied to Mussolini. It would seem easy enough, in fact, to know that the person who made the suggestion . . . was him. That all worries me because these are exactly the accusations that are now being made against the Holy See." Spurning Tardini's advice, the pope decided to send the telegram anyway, directing his nuncio in Warsaw to meet with the Polish president.[18]

Although the pope threw himself into this last-minute effort to broker a peaceful settlement of the German-Polish dispute, he had little confidence he would succeed. "Poland is going to be crushed within a few days," he told a visiting French prelate. "And France isn't able to do anything for Poland, absolutely nothing. Do you know what strength Germany has? It is overwhelming."[19]

But the pope made one last effort. On August 31, only hours before the war would erupt, he had Maglione summon the ambassadors of all five countries at the center of the crisis—Britain, France, Poland, Germany, and Italy—to the Vatican. Each, separately, was handed a copy of the pope's plea to avoid war.[20]

———

MUSSOLINI WAS HIMSELF IN a state of great nervous tension, but it was a nervousness mixed with excitement. The previous day he had taken time, as he often did, to call Clara several times before her arrival at their room in Palazzo Venezia. When she appeared late that afternoon, he gave her a humor magazine to read, telling her he had to wait for an important phone call before he could be free for their lovemaking. But his impatience got the better of him. He roughly pulled her dress over her head, and as Clara recorded that day in her diary, they made "savage love." She added, "I cry for joy."

Mussolini soon got the call he was waiting for, as Ciano briefed him on the latest German-Polish developments. When Mussolini returned to Clara, he told her the news: war was about to break out. "The poor Poles, poor Poles, what a disaster they're making!" said the Duce. "How can they fool themselves into believing in help from the French or the English?"[21]

WAR BEGINS

T HE GUNS OF THE GERMAN BATTLESHIP BEGAN FIRING ON THE Polish military garrison at Danzig's port before dawn on September 1, 1939. At the same time, sixty-two German army divisions supported by thirteen hundred warplanes crossed the border into Poland, one major group attacking from Prussia in the north and one from Slovakia in the south. By six A.M. the first bombs began falling on Warsaw. German Stuka dive-bombers swooped down to wipe out scattered concentrations of Polish troops, while the Luftwaffe tried to destroy as much of the Polish air force as possible before it could leave the ground. The air attack targeted towns and villages as well, causing the terror-stricken residents to clog the roads and so block the flow of Polish reinforcements to the front. Monsignor Rarkowski, the field bishop of the German army, sent an urgent message to the Catholic soldiers of the Wehrmacht that day: "In this grave hour, when our German people face a test of their resolve under fire and have come forward to fight for their natural and God-given rights, I address myself to you soldiers. . . . Each of you knows what is at stake for our people . . . and each man sees before him, as he goes into action, the shining example of a true fighter, our Führer and Supreme Commander, the first and bravest soldier of the Greater German Reich."[1]

Over the first three days of the war, the German forces would carry out seventy-two mass executions, both of captured Polish soldiers and of men, women, and children shot in anger at popular resistance to the German occupation. In one incident on September 8, a shot fired from a high school hit a German army officer; the Germans responded by executing fifty students in reprisal, despite the fact that the boy who fired the shot had given himself up. That same day, after a German company commander was killed in fighting south of Warsaw, enraged Germans led three hundred Polish prisoners of war to a ditch and machine-gunned them, leaving their bodies strewn aside the road.[2]

In their desperation, Poland's leaders sent urgent appeals to the French and British governments to come to their aid, but the Germans continued their brutal march unbothered by any significant foreign interference. Over the next few weeks, they carried out more than six hundred massacres, some in retaliation for the death of a German officer, in one case in response to the death of two German horses caught in a crossfire. Within those first few weeks, too, the roundup of Poland's Jews began, a roundup that ultimately led to the death of three million of them.[3]

IT WAS THE MOMENT Pius XII had been dreading. Not only was he horrified by the devastation of Poland and its largely Catholic population, but he knew that pressure for him to condemn the Nazi invasion would become almost unbearable. Mussolini himself had reason to believe the pope might speak out. "It is not improbable," a secret police report informed the Duce, "that the Pontiff who, as is well known, has the existence of Poland close to his heart, will intervene publicly with a statement."[4]

Mussolini need not have worried. On the day after the assault began, the French ambassador asked Cardinal Maglione if the pope would make his voice heard. No, replied the cardinal. It was not the pope's style. He preferred "letting the facts speak for themselves." The French ambassador was quickly followed by Poland's own ambassador, there to make the same request. All he could get from the cardinal was the promise that the pope would have Poland in his prayers.[5]

———

GERMANY'S ATTACK LEFT THE Duce in an uncomfortable position. He was not ready to throw Italy into the war, but he dreaded being seen as too cowardly to join his ally in battle. On the day of the invasion, he had phoned his ambassador in Berlin. He needed Hitler to send him a message saying he had no need at the moment for the Duce's help. The Führer quickly obliged.[6]

At three P.M. that day, Italy's government ministers nervously gathered at Palazzo Venezia to learn what the Duce had decided. Mussolini arrived wearing his all-white summer military uniform. He looked, thought his justice minister, Dino Grandi, as though he had aged ten years, "his face pale, crossed by deep wrinkles that reflected the internal drama that had tormented him for two weeks and that he did not succeed in hiding behind the mask of his glacial calm." Mussolini told them he had made Italy's position clear to the Führer: the country would not be ready for war until the end of 1942. "While Mussolini spoke," Grandi recalled, "his eyes and his face visibly betrayed an internal storm. Hitler's telegram and Italy's abstention from the war meant for him if not the first, certainly the greatest defeat of his life. . . . Contradictory feelings buffeted through him all at the same time: jealousy, anger, delusion, humiliation."

The new watchword, said Mussolini, was "nonbelligerency." "Neutrality" was not a term the Duce could ever abide.

Following the meeting, Mussolini waited nervously to see the effect his announcement would have. His aides suggested he summon an adulatory crowd to the piazza outside Palazzo Venezia for a triumphal address, but he dismissed the idea. The prospect of Fascists cheering a decision not to take military action was repugnant to him.[7]

Fears that Germany's invasion of Poland would trigger a wider conflict soon proved well founded. On September 3, Britain declared war on Germany. That afternoon France did as well. But as the German army advanced rapidly through Polish territory, it remained unclear how either nation would be able to do anything to stop it.

For the Duce, the speed with which Germany's massive offensive

was churning through Poland proved intoxicating. Entering the dictator's office on September 5, Giuseppe Bottai, minister of education,
found him standing at a table looking down at a large a map of Europe.
"The French," he said, as he looked up to greet his visitor, "don't know
either where or how to wage this war, which, by the way, they don't in
any case want to do." He looked down again at Europe. "Within a
month," he predicted, "the Polish game will be over."[8]

IT DID NOT TAKE long following the war's outbreak for Mussolini to
deliver his first warning to the pope. On September 3, barely forty-
eight hours after German troops crossed into Poland, Italian police
came to arrest Guido Gonella, one of the Vatican daily newspaper's
most prominent writers. Along with Giuseppe Dalla Torre, the director of *L'Osservatore Romano*, Gonella had long been seen by Fascist officials as an irritant, an anti-Fascist voice protected by the Vatican.

Gonella oversaw the column of the Vatican paper that reported
world events. His arrest was prompted by an article he had published
the previous day, "First Reflections on the Grave Conflict." Mussolini's
ambassador to the Vatican, angered by what he viewed as the paper's
unflattering view of the German invasion, suggested that Mussolini
put pressure on the pope by arranging to have Gonella denounced in
the pages of *Il Regime Fascista*.[9] Mussolini had regularly used the newspaper for this purpose, and its director, Roberto Farinacci, was always
happy to oblige. It was the old strategy of the carrot and the stick, with
Farinacci delighting in his role as the cudgel.[10]

Unfortunately for Gonella, the Duce thought a firmer measure was
required. The day after the offending article appeared, he personally
ordered the Vatican journalist's arrest.[11] Gonella was locked into Rome's
venerable Regina Coeli prison, its ironic name—Queen of Heaven—
deriving from its seventeenth-century origins as a Catholic convent.
The news quickly reached the pope, and despite the lateness of the
hour—after ten P.M.—Cardinal Maglione phoned the Italian ambassador to demand an explanation. The next day Ambassador Pignatti

came to see the cardinal and told him that as an Italian citizen, Gonella had no right to publish an article harmful to the national interest.

The cardinal threatened to have the pope publicly protest the arrest, but this failed to move the ambassador. Maglione decided to take a more conciliatory approach. Given the delicate moment, he said, a public quarrel would be damaging for both sides. He promised that the Vatican paper would publish no such critical articles of the German invasion in the future.[12]

Pignatti soon noted the improved atmosphere, reporting that one could now read the pages of the Vatican newspaper without fear of any unpleasant surprises. Indeed, the men of the Secretariat of State themselves seemed properly chastened. Mussolini personally ordered Gonella's release.[13]

WHILE THE ITALIAN DICTATOR was pressuring the pope to remain silent about the German invasion of Poland, the Polish ambassador kept trying to convince him to speak out. Reports from his country were indeed alarming. As the German forces moved through western Poland, destined to be absorbed into the Reich, hundreds of priests, thought to be inspiring Polish nationalism and Polish resistance, were being arrested. German priests were being brought in to replace them. In the end, more than half the priests in western Poland would end up in concentration camps, where many would die, while many seminaries, church schools, monasteries, and convents were shuttered. Church charitable institutions were closed, and outdoor shrines, crosses, and other church ritual sites dismantled.[14]

The day after the invasion of his country, the Polish ambassador met with the pope, proposing that he allow the Polish press to print a statement that the pope had blessed Poland. Although Cardinal Maglione and Monsignor Tardini found this unobjectionable, Pius XII demurred, initially proposing he instead release a statement of his own saying that as the pope loved all peoples, he also loved the Polish people. In the end, nothing came of this. Ten days later, the Polish ambassador asked the pope to meet with a group of Poles living in Rome. "At a time of extreme agony," said the ambassador, "they would like to gather around their common Father." The pope refused. "One does not see," reads a Secretariat of State note on the request, "how an Audience can be granted that would not then take on a political value of great resonance."[15]

The French ambassador to the Vatican continued his own attempts to convince the pope to break his silence, visiting Pius XII twice in the first week following the invasion. Explaining his decision to say nothing, the pope cited his desire not to do anything that might worsen the church's situation in Germany. It was a rationale that the prelates of the Secretariat of State would often repeat as well. "All in the end told me," Ambassador Charles-Roux reported, "that there were now around forty million Catholics in the Reich and that the Holy See could not expose them to reprisals. In short, I spoke in terms of morality, rights, honor, justice; and they responded to me in terms of method, practicality, tradition, and statistics."[16]

Sixteen days after the German invasion, Soviet troops crossed Poland's eastern border, and the country began to be carved up from both sides. Still the pope remained silent. Cardinal Tisserant, the Curia's lone non-Italian and its only outspoken anti-Fascist, sent his own impassioned plea: "Soviet troops entered Polish territory yesterday. The soldiers of Adolf the Apostate and those of the atheist State are uniting to destroy Catholic Poland. Will the Holy See not protest?"[17]

Oddly, despite the international crisis, Cardinal Maglione had returned to his summer vacation home near Naples, leaving his two deputies to fend off pleas for a papal protest. The French ambassador had heard that Maglione had decided to leave the field clear for his two deputies, thinking they had more influence with the pope. While Charles-Roux had doubts this was true, he noted that "there is not great mutual sympathy between Pius XII and Cardinal Maglione." The French diplomat thought Monsignor Montini, the man closest to the pope, would have liked him to utter some words of protest, but "the Holy Father, in his isolation at Castel Gandolfo, remains silent."[18]

At the end of September, the arrival in Rome of Poland's cardinal primate, August Hlond, led to new hopes the pope might finally speak out. Meeting with the pope at his summer palace, the cardinal and the Poles he brought with him were disappointed. Pius XII, noted Britain's envoy to the Vatican, offered them "no word of reprobation of either the German or the Russian invasion of Poland."[19]

If many were surprised by the pope's silence, Hitler was not. A week into the Polish campaign, the German ambassador to the Vatican had sent Berlin a telegram: "Pope's refusal to take sides against Germany would be entirely in harmony with assurances he has repeatedly conveyed to me through trusted agent in recent weeks."[20]

THE PRINCE
RETURNS

LTHOUGH MUSSOLINI WAS IMPRESSED BY THE GERMANS' RAPID
advance through Poland, he was well aware of his countrymen's
lack of enthusiasm for their German ally. Rachele, his wife, who had
recently been on a train filled with soldiers, had heard the same thing
from enlisted men: "For the Duce we would certainly go off to kill,
but for Hitler . . . not even if God Almighty sent us."[1]

Italy's dictator found himself in a difficult balancing act, eager to
cast himself as the one man who could bring about peace in Europe
without tarnishing the aggressive image of Fascism he had spent the
past two decades crafting. "In a situation full of unknowns like the current one," he told Fascist Party leaders in Bologna in a mid-September
speech, their task was clear: "Prepare militarily to be ready for any
eventuality, support all efforts for peace, be vigilant and work in silence." Two weeks later he struck a more aggressive pose in meeting
with Fascist Party leaders from Genoa: "We are prisoners of the Mediterranean. It is a large prison, but a prison just the same. . . . You must
prepare the Italian people for the eventuality of war."[2]

In the early years of his regime, one of Mussolini's favorite boasts
was that he had saved Italy from the Communists. Now some found it
surprising that he seemed unbothered that Hitler had partnered with
Stalin in dividing up Poland. Shortly after the Red Army crossed the
Polish border in mid-September 1939, Mussolini explained the situation to Clara. "The Russians are Slavs, just like the Poles: great enthu-

siasm but no preparation." The contrast with the Germans, he told her, was stark: "a German soldier has his own culture, he reads, he understands everything. . . . Of every ten Russian soldiers, at least eight or nine don't know how to read or write: they're illiterate." Hitler's alliance with the Russians, he predicted, would not last long: "You will see I am a prophet: I would put my hand over the fire to swear that Germany and Russia will attack each other like two beasts."[3]

DESPITE CARDINAL MAGLIONE'S PROMISES that *L'Osservatore Romano* would not publish anything the Duce might deem offensive, the newspaper remained a point of friction between the Vatican and the Fascist regime.[4] A mid-September article on the war provoked yet another protest from the Italian ambassador, who thought the piece had an anti-German tone. Confronted with the new complaint, Maglione briefly lost his patience. The government, he told Pignatti, could hardly expect them to transform the Vatican paper into another organ of Italian propaganda.[5]

The Italian ambassador decided the matter was important enough to raise directly with the pope. The key to the continuing problems caused by the Vatican newspaper, Pignatti told the pontiff at his late September audience at Castel Gandolfo, was its director, Giuseppe Dalla Torre.[6] Ever since the new pope had so speedily heeded Mussolini's request and dismissed the cardinal coordinating Italian Catholic Action, it seemed likely that Dalla Torre, long a point of friction with the regime, would be next on the papal chopping block. Mussolini viewed him as a dangerous anti-Fascist, and of Dalla Torre's anti-Nazi sentiments there was no doubt. But although the pope had, over Dalla Torre's protests, forbidden him from publishing any more articles critical of Germany, he was reluctant to remove him from his post.[7]

When Pignatti broached the subject of the Vatican newspaper, the pope responded by recalling the recent imprisonment of Guido Gonella, the writer for the paper. "The Holy Father," reported the ambassador, "spoke to me of the Gonella affair with great calm, without making the least complaint, not even for the removal of his Fascist membership." What bothered the pope, according to Pignatti, was the injustice of Gonella suffering for something that was really not his fault, but Dalla Torre's.[8]

The focus of the ambassador's new complaint was an article in the Vatican newspaper that cast President Roosevelt in a good light. Hearing Pignatti describe the offending piece, the pope lashed out with uncharacteristic vehemence at Dalla Torre. He had repeatedly warned him, he said, yet he kept pushing the boundaries he had clearly been instructed not to cross.

Pignatti offered the pope a simple solution: "Send him away."

Pius XII would make no promises. The paper's director was intelligent and able, he said, but undisciplined. If Dalla Torre were left on his own, "he would strike out at half the world with his sarcasms." In an effort to show his goodwill, the pope promised to turn down Dalla Torre's request to buy new printing machines to meet the increased demand for the Vatican newspaper, and he led the ambassador to believe he would order a reduction in the number of copies printed. The next day the pope confirmed that he had put measures in place to ensure that *L'Osservatore Romano* would give the government no grounds for further complaint.[9]

ANGER AT PIUS XII'S silence continued to build, both in Poland and among its allies. By mid-October, Hitler had annexed a large swath of western Poland to the German Reich while the rest of the country was divided by a ragged border separating the German and Soviet zones of occupation. The Polish ambassador to the Holy See had repeatedly urged the pope to speak out, but to no avail. Britain's envoy to the Vatican complained that the pope "has carried caution and impartiality to a point approaching pusillanimity and condonation." While Osborne rejected his French colleague's belief that the pope had come under German influence, he acknowledged that "the Pope's silence seems hard to explain and defend."[10]

Pius XII defended himself by arguing that as pope it was his role to attend to spiritual, not political matters.[11] But the line separating the two was less than clear, as would be evident in the pope's first encyclical, a message addressed to all the world's archbishops and bishops. The Italian press treated the encyclical not only as a statement of the pope's theology but as the program of his papacy. Dated October 20, 1939, and issued from Castel Gandolfo, *Summi Pontificatus* bore the subtitle "On the Unity of Human Society." Composed of 117 numbered paragraphs, it attributed the evils of the world to the spurning of Christ's teachings. The pontiff urged "the Soldiers of Christ," as he termed loyal Catholics, to combat "the ever-increasing host of Christ's enemies."

Preaching the value of "universal brotherhood," and the "unity of mankind," the pope castigated those nations that would separate church from state. While citing the church's teaching of "obedience and respect for earthly authority which derives from God its whole origin," he condemned any attempt by the state "to attribute to itself that absolute autonomy which belongs exclusively to the Supreme Maker. It puts itself in the place of the Almighty and elevates the State or group into the last end of life, the supreme criterion of the moral and juridical order."[12]

In reporting the encyclical to Ciano, Ambassador Pignatti highlighted the "beautiful words" the pope had devoted to Italy and to the Lateran Accords: "There can be no doubt of the political importance of the papal speech given the fact that the 'Conciliation' is not only accepted but exalted by Pius XII." In its coverage of the encyclical, *Il Popolo d'Italia,* the newspaper that Mussolini himself had founded and that had launched his Fascist career over two decades earlier, likewise highlighted the pope's praise for the Italian regime.

The government office overseeing the foreign press in Italy prepared a critique of foreign coverage. What naturally made the greatest impression among the correspondents for the democratic countries, it reported, were the pope's remarks condemning those who would place allegiance to the state over allegiance to God. "They however make clear that the Holy Father intended to identify in his condemnation only Germany and Russia, it being implicit, when he spoke of the good relations existing with Italy, that he intended to exclude Italy

Official portrait of Pius XII at his desk, ca. 1940

from it." But the Vatican's own paper, in an apparent attempt to calm any ruffled German feathers, highlighted the positive German press reaction to the encyclical. It offered lengthy quotes from the positive review in *Deutsche Allgemeine Zeitung*. The pope's words, said the German newspaper, were in harmony with the aims of the National Socialist government. Even Farinacci's *Il Regime Fascista* offered a respectful summary of the encyclical.[13]

WITH HIS CONQUEST OF Poland now complete, Hitler let the pope know he was ready to resume their secret negotiations through Prince von Hessen.[14] The next meeting took place on October 24, 1939. Again, we find in the newly opened Vatican Secretariat of State archives a quasi-transcript of their German-language conversation. The record makes clear that, even after the invasion of Poland and the start of the larger war, the pope was eager to reach an understanding with Hitler. At the same time, the pope wanted the Führer to know that any agreement depended on a change of those German policies that had harmed the church. The record offers a precious and long-sought-after insight into the pope's thinking at the time.

As von Hessen sat down, the pope asked how Hitler was doing.

"He is doing very well, the considerable tensions notwithstanding," replied the prince. Unfortunately, the Poles had brought disaster on themselves, their stubborn refusal to recognize their defeat having had tragic consequences. The Polish Military Command's decision to continue the pointless resistance, said von Hessen, had needlessly sacrificed many lives.

But, replied the pope, even the Germans had to recognize the bravery of the Polish soldiers.

All in all, said von Hessen, passing over the pope's remark, the Führer was very pleased with the military and political progress he had made in Poland.

How, asked the pope, were the German people faring?

"They are doing well. Food ration cards have been introduced. But the people are optimistic."

The pope acknowledged that there did now seem to be calm on the military side.

Indeed, replied the prince. Perhaps he was being overly optimistic, he said, but he saw signs that peace might now be returning to Europe. He added that he had recently shared these views with Ciano, Mussolini's son-in-law.

As Ciano's thirty-three-year-old sister, Maria, had died only two days earlier, the mention of his name led the pope to express his sympathy for the family and ask the prince for details about Maria's illness and the last days of her life.

As it happened, said von Hessen, he had seen Ciano the day before his sister's death and had used the occasion to discuss how to go about bringing peace between the Third Reich and the Vatican. Ciano had been enthusiastic, believing that an end to the tensions would be beneficial not only for the German government but for Italy's as well. Here von Hessen added that following his previous meeting with the pope, he had returned to Germany and discussed with the Führer what the pope had told him about the importance of coming to an understanding. "He was in complete agreement," said the prince, but he was then regrettably distracted with the many other urgent issues he had to address. Still, the prince assured the pope, "the intention remains."

They had finally gotten around to the issue the pope was most eager to discuss. Unfortunately, said Pius XII, the news from Germany was not such as to encourage a rapprochement with the church. Even those who preferred an authoritarian regime were concerned about the way religious institutions were being treated.

At this point the pope decided to bring up an argument he thought might appeal to Hitler. Germany's enemies were making ample use of the Reich's poor treatment of the churches. All this, added the pope, alluding to the pressures on him to speak out against Hitler's anti-church measures, was making his own position and that of the Vatican difficult. The Germans' systematic attack on the church had to stop. If Hitler were to give a signal and the situation were to improve, it would pave the way for productive negotiations. "I understand other tasks require the Führer's energy right now," said the pope. "But such a signal, such a 'Stop!' is possible and most important. That is because, and there is no doubt about it, the persecutions go on. Deliberately and systematically."

Perhaps, suggested the prince, it might be best to begin by holding preliminary negotiations in Berlin, where the Führer spent most of the time. There the papal nuncio could preside over the talks. "So many countries have joined the Reich," added von Hessen, that clearly a new concordat with the Vatican was needed.

Did he have in mind forming a committee to organize such talks? asked the pope.

No, he had been given no such instructions. He was simply thinking out loud. On the German side, the prince suggested, the talks would need to involve the Foreign Ministry along with the Reich minister for church affairs. "If His Holiness would agree in principle, then—"

The pope interrupted. What was important for any such talks to be fruitful was the creation of a propitious atmosphere by means of a signal from the Führer.

"I will gladly advocate this."

"I have always desired peace between Church and State and continue to do so," said Pius XII.

Von Hessen repeated a point he had made at their earlier meeting: While he was among the many in the National Socialist Party who favored coming to an understanding with the church, another faction of the party, an anti-Christian faction, opposed it. But it was the Führer alone, he added, who made all important decisions.[15]

Realizing that this might raise in the pope's mind the question of Hitler's responsibility for Germany's recent nonaggression pact with the Soviet Union, von Hessen launched into a preemptive defense. Hitler had made that agreement, he explained, out of political necessity, designed "to cover our back." It certainly would lead to no inroads of Communism in Germany. Russia had agreed not to engage in propaganda activity in Germany, as the Germans had in Russia.

So, said the pope, no propaganda on either side. . . .

Naturally, said von Hessen, Germany's police were very strict. Under no circumstances would the Führer be willing to countenance the revival of Communism in any part of the Reich.

"It would be a blessing for everyone," said the pope, if the "moral conflicts" now faced by Germans loyal to the church were eliminated. The Reich's Catholics would then no longer feel any conflict in their dual loyalties to church and state.

As Pius XII rose to bring their meeting to an end, he told the prince how much he appreciated his visit and asked that he bring Hitler his warm greetings.[16]

―――

A PAPAL CURSE

―――

OVER THE COURSE OF THE FALL OF 1939, ITALIANS' FEARS OF being dragged into an unwanted war began to ebb. The press devoted little attention to the Rome-Berlin Axis, and even a visit to Rome by Heinrich Himmler attracted little notice. "While the Government is not ready to declare its neutrality and the officially inspired press still maintains its pro-German tendencies in order not to incur German hostility," wrote the American ambassador, offering Roosevelt advice he would soon regret, "I believe that Italy will avoid at all cost any trouble with the Allies."[1]

Mussolini himself was unsure of the best path forward. Hitler, he remarked to Clara, should have listened to what he had told him: "Don't fool yourself that this time England and France won't intervene: it's crazy to think so." The Führer was delusional, a fanatic, a visionary, Mussolini said. He refused to listen. "In short, Hitler has made a mistake, he has committed serious errors. Now he has to either arrive in Paris or go into exile!" Conquering France, said the Duce, wouldn't be easy, predicting that at least a million Germans would die. But this wouldn't be an entirely bad thing, he added, for having an overbearing Germany weakened was not without its advantages for Italy.[2]

Further signs that the Duce might be slowly drawing back from his embrace of Hitler came at the end of October, when he fired the Fascist Party head along with a number of government ministers known for their enthusiasm for the Nazi alliance. These were the same men most identified with the anti-church, antimonarchical wing of the Fascist Party, "eaters of priests and Jews" in the words of Dino Grandi, minister of justice and one of the most prominent anti-Nazi Fascists. Vatican secretary of state Cardinal Maglione expressed satisfaction at the ministerial changes, judging them a victory for Ciano and the government's pro-church forces.[3]

PIUS XII'S REFUSAL TO condemn the Nazis was becoming more uncomfortable for him as reports mounted of the horrors they were inflicting in the lands they had seized. In late November, he learned that all Vatican efforts to send relief supplies to German-occupied Poland were being rebuffed. Meanwhile, the Germans' brutal campaign against Poland's Catholic clergy, along with its nobility and intelligentsia, continued in an effort to throttle any Polish patriotic resistance. In the large slice of western Poland that the Germans had annexed in early October, many priests had been deported or imprisoned. A later Vatican report described the situation: "The churches, which are only permitted to open for two hours, once per week, remain closed because of the lack of officiants. No sacraments, no preaching, no religious instruction. Absolute destruction of the once flourishing Catholic press. . . . No seminaries. No convents."[4]

A mid-November *Osservatore Romano* article recounted without editorial comment how the Jews of Poland were being separated from the rest of the population and made to wear a "yellow cloth triangle" stitched to their clothes to distinguish them from what the Vatican paper termed the "Aryan" population. Later in the month a second article described the Nazis' creation of a "reserve" in Poland into which all Jews from the German-occupied countries were being sent, under the authority of Hans Frank, the German minister in charge of the occupied territories. Earlier that month, on learning that Hitler had escaped unharmed from an assassination attempt, the pope had sent the German dictator his congratulations.[5]

Pius XII now worried what would happen if the war were to last into the spring and the Germans mounted their threatened campaign against France. Meeting with the French ambassador, the pope pressed him on the solidity of the Maginot Line, the string of large fortresses, blockhouses, and bunkers that the French had built along their border with Germany over the previous decade to prevent invasion. It was, the ambassador assured him, "impenetrable."[6]

If the pope had any worries at the time about Mussolini's intentions, they would not have been apparent to Italians. On December 7, in a colorful and widely reported ceremony at the Apostolic Palace, Dino Alfieri presented his credentials as the new Italian ambassador to the Holy See, replacing Pignatti, who had reached retirement age. Met at the Vatican by a phalanx of Palatine Guards who offered their honors, Alfieri responded by raising his arm in Fascist salute. He was then led through the halls of the Apostolic Palace as Swiss Guards and other pontifical gendarmes added their ceremonial tributes. The pope, seated upon his throne, awaited him in the Throne Room, surrounded by his ornately dressed noble court. "It was the glory of Your Venerated Predecessor," said the new ambassador in his remarks to the pope, "to bring about new relations between church and state in Fascist Italy." The pope ended his own remarks by invoking God's blessing on Italy's royal family and on Mussolini. The Vatican newspaper coverage included a warm profile of Alfieri, one of the major figures of the Fascist regime and a man with no previous diplomatic experience. Lest anyone miss the message, the arch-Fascist Farinacci dedicated a front-page editorial to the event in his *Il Regime Fascista:* "The Pope's words do not admit of any doubt. He blessed Italy which is Fascist, and our Duce." The pope also, Farinacci wrote, blessed the new ambassador, who, he pointed out, had been minister of popular culture when a year earlier the government "put the same racist laws into effect that various [church] councils had instituted over the centuries."[7]

The following day, in another event attracting major newspaper coverage, Pius XII traveled across the Tiber to Santa Maria Maggiore to give his annual "Urbi et Orbi" Christmas blessing addressed to the city of Rome and to the whole world. One of Rome's four major basilicas, tracing its origins to the fifth century, the massive Santa Maria

Dino Alfieri with Rudolf Hess and Joseph Goebbels, Germany, July 19, 1939

Maggiore boasts rich mosaics dating from that early period and a cor-
nucopia of artistic splendors added over the following centuries. Riding to the basilica from the Vatican in a black sedan with the convertible
top covering the back seat folded down, the pope kept his right hand
raised as he nodded repeatedly to acknowledge the enthusiastic crowd
greeting him along the way. Men waved their hats, while awestruck
nuns, recognizable in their white headcoverings, ran alongside his
slow-moving car. As the car pulled up to the basilica, an Italian military unit saluted the pontiff while a band played the papal hymn. After
blessing the soldiers, the pope entered the basilica, where he quickly
changed from his simple white robe into an elaborate white embroidered one and replaced the broad-brimmed black clerical hat he had
worn in the car with his impressively tall white miter. Emerging from
the church borne aloft in his *sedia gestatoria,* with attendants on either
side holding a white ostrich plume over his head, he waved again at the
huge crowd. Italian troops, standing at attention along the basilica
stairs, presented arms as a military band again struck up the papal

hymn, which they followed with the Fascist anthem "Giovinezza." It was in many ways a typical mix of papal and Fascist symbolism that Italians had by now come to take for granted.[8]

AS 1939 WAS DRAWING to a close, Italians learned of plans for an even more dramatic display of papal friendship with the government. The pope and the king would mark the holiday season with an unprecedented exchange of visits. The highly publicized events began with the royal family's intricately choreographed visit to the pope on December 21. A dozen black limousines set out from the king's Quirinal Palace for the procession across the city to the Vatican. Troops lined the streets as Romans crowded behind them, cheering as the royal family passed through. The French ambassador described the scene at the Vatican as the royal couple stepped out of their car: his tunic covered with a jumble of ribbons and medallions, "the puny, stunted king, in his general's uniform," emerged and stood next to the large "Queen Helen, imposing, in white dress and mantilla." Joining them was Mussolini's son-in-law, Galeazzo Ciano, wearing his embroidered ministerial jacket.

At the pope's private meeting with the royal couple in the Small Throne Room of the Apostolic Palace, he complained about Germany's treatment of the church, a message that found a welcome audience in the viscerally anti-German king. Following their brief conversation, the pope invited the rest of the king's large retinue to enter. Ciano led the way.[9]

"There is no doubt," the French ambassador reported the next day, "that King Victor Emmanuel III's visit yesterday to the new pope furnished new proof of the desire for détente and collaboration between the two powers that share Rome." With the fast-moving developments in Europe, the veteran French ambassador offered a new theory of what Fascist Italy hoped to achieve by further strengthening its ties with the Vatican. Less than a month earlier, the Soviet army had invaded Finland and speculation was rife as to what its next victim would be. With the Germans now in league with the Soviets, "Fascist Italy

intends to create a united bloc with the Catholic Church." Casting itself as the defender of the Faith, the Fascist government "hopes to be
able to count on the Holy See's collaboration when the right moment
comes to propose a compromise peace to the belligerents in the name
of Christianity and in the higher interests of European civilization."[10]

If the king's visit to the Vatican provoked public excitement, the
pope's decision to reciprocate produced an even greater impression.
The last time a pope had set foot in the Quirinal Palace, it had been his
own property, for the Quirinal had long been home to the popes.
When the troops of the present king's grandfather and namesake, Victor Emmanuel II, had deposed Pius IX as ruler of the papal states and
occupied the papal palace in 1870, the pope had excommunicated him.
Indeed, it was believed that on that day the pope had put a curse on the
Italian monarch's presence in the Quirinal. In any case, the vast edifice
was anything but cozy, its 110,000 square meters making it one of the
largest palaces in the world. The royal family, in fact, lived elsewhere,
using the Quirinal for ceremonial occasions.[11]

In Milan, Cardinal Schuster, archbishop of Italy's most important
archdiocese, characterized by some as a "convinced fascist," was overjoyed by news of the visit. Vicariously sharing in the historic event, the
cardinal arranged his own ceremonial exchange of visits with the head
of Milan's provincial Fascist Party branch. The local Catholic newspaper featured a photo of Cardinal Schuster arriving at Fascist headquarters, surrounded by black-shirted men giving him a Fascist salute. He
proceeded through a Fascist honor guard to meet the *federale,* the provincial Fascist Party head, with whom, the paper recounted, he had a
"long and cordial conversation."[12]

The papal cortege that made its way to the royal palace in Rome on
that gray December day included an impressive number of cardinals
and other church dignitaries, traveling between two lines of Italian
troops along a route decorated with a mix of Italian flags and papal
banners. Pius XII, as had now become his practice, traveled in the lone
uncovered limousine so that the crowd could see him and, undaunted
by the rain, raised his arm in benediction. Met by an Italian battalion in
the huge piazza outside the Quirinal Palace, the pope and his retinue

were escorted to the ceremonial stairway, at the top of which the king waited to greet him. Colorfully uniformed royal guards, chosen for their height, stood on either side of the monarch, making the king seem all the smaller.[13]

Victor Emmanuel and the pontiff made an odd pair, but despite their obvious differences, they were similar in certain ways, both high strung and neither one wholly comfortable around other people. Following family tradition, the king was more anticlerical than religious, while in the Vatican, resentment for the royal conquest of the papal states and occupation of Rome seven decades earlier still simmered, albeit at a low boil. But as Pius XII explained to the French ambassador the next day, he was eager to do his part to shore up the king's popularity. In the king, thought the pope, he had an ally in ensuring that Italy stayed out of the war.[14]

MAN OF STEEL

A S 1940 BEGAN, THE TENSION THAT HAD MARRED FASCIST-papal relations in the last days of Pius XI was a distant memory. A stream of police informant reports told Mussolini of the popular enthusiasm generated by Pius XII's exchange of visits with the king, and of the widespread belief that the combined efforts of the Duce and the pope would keep Italy out of a war that no one wanted.[1]

At the same time, the pope continued his efforts to improve relations with Hitler's regime. In his New Year's audience with the German mission to the Vatican, the pope denied he had any objection to the totalitarian states. Indeed, he pointed out, the Vatican's harmonious relations with the Italian regime proved the opposite. Fritz Menshausen, the German embassy's number-two man, complained to the pope that the western democracies were casting the pope's speeches as critical of the totalitarian regimes. Surely, replied the pope, the same thing happened on the other side, with the press in the totalitarian countries citing his words to show he opposed the democracies. "The Pope further explained," Menshausen reported to Berlin, "that his speeches were of a general nature as a matter of course and he deliberately composed them in a way that they could not be interpreted by Germany as directed against it."[2]

On the morning of February 10, Pius XII marked the first anniversary of his predecessor's death with a brief ceremony in St. Peter's. The following day the anniversary of the 1929 Lateran Accords provided the occasion for the Fascist regime to show its solidarity with the Vatican. Italian flags hung from all public buildings, and special lights illuminated their facades at night to mark the day that Mussolini put an end to the decades-long conflict between church and state. Italy's new ambassador to the Vatican, Dino Alfieri, hosted a reception at the embassy, standing under a large portrait of Pius XII. Seventeen cardinals attended, including Secretary of State Maglione and his two deputies, Montini and Tardini. Present too were all the foreign diplomats accredited to the Holy See, together with a bevy of government officials, Fascist Party leaders, and a flock of Rome's aristocracy. Each scarlet-robed cardinal made a separate ceremonial entrance, accompanied by four footmen carrying large lighted candles.[3]

At the dinner, Cardinal Maglione pressed Italy's foreign minister for news of Hitler's intentions. Again, Ciano cast himself as the peacemaker, telling the cardinal that in signing the military pact with Germany the previous spring, he had made clear that Danzig should not constitute a reason to go to war. While it was true that Mussolini had a more favorable view of Germany than his own, said Ciano, his father-in-law recognized that it was in Italy's interest to stay out of the conflict.[4]

A few days later the pope met with one of the men whose views of the military situation he most valued. Enrico Caviglia, seventy-seven-year-old hero of the Great War, held the title of Marshal of Italy, the highest rank of the Italian military. He was a member of the Senate as well. Caviglia had never been enamored of Mussolini and opposed involving Italy in a war at Germany's side.

Given his rank, the marshal received a full-scale ceremonial welcome when he arrived at the Apostolic Palace for his noon audience with the pope. Swiss Guards, Palatine Guards, Noble Guards, and assorted footmen in red damask uniforms all stood at attention, lining the frescoed hallways as he passed through. Arriving at the ornate Small Throne Room, Caviglia was met by the pope's *maestro di camera,* who then led him to the adjoining door of the pope's study. The pope, seated at his table, greeted him warmly.

Caviglia was struck by how emaciated the pope looked, his spectacles standing out on his face. "A sweet voice, affable, simpatico," observed the general, contrasting Pius XII with his predecessor, who had been more likely to lecture his visitors than to listen to them.

The two men spoke of the difficulty of forging a lasting peace deal. "It is not possible," said the pope, "to trust a man who goes back on the word he has given," referring, without naming him, to Germany's leader.

At his recent meeting with Mussolini, said the marshal, he had urged him to keep Italy out of the war, appealing to the Duce's vanity by telling him that in doing so he would come to be looked upon as a truly great man.

"God bless you," replied the pope, urging the marshal to keep repeating that message. "Not all men are advising Mussolini in this sense."[5]

AMONG THOSE MOST WORRIED about where the European war was heading was the American president, who was facing reelection in the fall. In late February, Roosevelt sent his undersecretary of state, Sumner Welles, to Europe to sound out leaders on both sides of the conflict. In Rome, his first appointment was with Italy's foreign minister. The American entered the meeting with low expectations, having heard that the Duce's son-in-law radiated a sense of self-importance. Welles was pleasantly surprised. "His manner was cordial and quite unaffected, and he could not have been simpler nor more frank in the expression of his views." It no doubt helped that Ciano spoke English. It also helped that, in Welles's words, "he spoke with no effort at concealment of his hearty dislike of Ribbentrop."

It was only at the end of their meeting, when photographers were called in, that Welles saw the Ciano he had been expecting: "That was the only time I saw the 'chest out, chin up' Ciano of which I had heard. Until the cameras began clicking, he could not have been more human, more simple, nor more seemingly frank in everything he said."[6]

Welles's impression of the Duce, whom he met later that day at Palazzo Venezia, was very different.

Ciano accompanied Welles along with Ambassador Phillips to Mussolini's office. There Welles was struck, as all were, by the grandeur of the cavernous room, but also by how sparsely furnished it was. The Duce greeted Welles at the door and walked him the length of the largely empty space to his desk on the other side. Ciano, Welles, and Phillips sat in the three chairs arranged in front of the desk.

The American visitor was shocked by Mussolini's appearance. He looked, he thought, fifteen years older than his fifty-eight years: "He moved with elephantine motion. Every step appeared an effort. He is very heavy for his height, and his face in repose falls into rolls of flesh. His close-clipped hair is snow white. During our long and rapid interchange of views, he kept his eyes shut a considerable part of the time, opening them with his dynamic and oft-described wide-open stare only when he desired particularly to underline some remark." Phillips had thought the conversation would take place in French, which both Welles and Mussolini spoke, but the Duce said he preferred speaking in Italian and had Ciano translate. Asked by Welles if he still rode a horse every morning, the Duce said he did, proudly adding he had recently taken up tennis and was now, he boasted, regularly beating the pro who played with him. Welles presumably regarded both claims as implausible.[7]

WHILE THE AMERICAN UNDERSECRETARY of state was meeting with the Duce, Pius XII was preparing to receive another American, a man who would play an important role in the years to come. Two months earlier, President Roosevelt had notified the pope of his intention to send his own personal representative to the pontiff. At the time, the United States had no diplomatic relations with the Holy See—Protestants in Congress adamantly opposed the idea—and thus no ambassador. Roosevelt appointed the envoy in the hope that Pius XII might play a role in bringing peace to Europe and, in any case, as a way of solidifying his support among America's large Catholic population in the lead-up to the fall 1940 presidential elections.

Myron Taylor, the man Roosevelt chose for the role, had until re-

Mussolini at his desk, Palazzo Venezia, February 1, 1940

cently been president of U.S. Steel, the largest producer of steel and one of the largest corporations in the country. A sixty-six-year-old Episcopalian—appointing a Catholic to the position would have been politically impossible—Taylor owned a villa outside Florence where he often vacationed. With combed-back gray hair he had an unmistakably distinguished appearance, comfortable in his dark three-piece suit or in the white bow tie and tails he wore to papal audiences. He had, as well, an additional qualification that recommended him for the post. He was a man of great wealth, and Roosevelt did not want to have to ask Congress to fund a mission that was bound to provoke much unhappiness among the country's Protestants.[8]

Taylor arrived in Rome on February 20, 1940, and moved into a large suite in the luxurious Excelsior Hotel on the fashionable Via Veneto. At his first meeting with Taylor a week later, the pope, speaking in English, offered his view of the European crisis. The German people had not wanted war, he said, but intimidated by the Gestapo, they were powerless. The German generals likewise were not eager for war, but they too were not prepared to voice their opposition. As for Italy, said the pontiff, Ciano was opposed to the war, as were most Italians, but the Duce, it seemed, was wavering.[9]

Although unhappy about Mussolini's embrace of Hitler, Myron Taylor, like most of the American business elite, had previously been an admirer of the Duce. He had, they thought, crushed the socialists, ended labor unrest, and brought a sense of order to a country viewed in the United States as poorly governed and chaotic. The day after his first meeting with the pope, Taylor had dinner with Mussolini's justice minister. There, the Fascist minister recalled, Roosevelt's envoy "declared with great emotion that the Duce is the arbiter of the situation in Europe and that his intervention can be decisive. During the meeting, Signor Taylor expressed himself in very deferential and admiring terms toward the Duce. He recalled with evident pleasure having been received by Him four times."[10]

FOLLOWING HIS THIRD SECRET meeting with the pope the previous October, Prince von Hessen had returned to Germany and briefed Hitler. Thinking the time had come for discussions to move to the next level, the Führer decided to send Foreign Minister Ribbentrop to meet with the pontiff. He said the pope could choose the format for that meeting. If it were to be an official one, Hitler would have his ambassador to the Holy See make the formal request. Should the pope prefer the meeting to remain secret, they could continue to use the von Hessen-Travaglini-Cardinal Lauri channel to arrange it.

At the end of December, Hitler sent von Hessen back to Rome to discuss these arrangements with the pope. Since his last meeting with the pontiff, von Hessen had also had a number of conversations with the Duce and his son-in-law. Following the Führer's instructions, he had asked for their support in helping establish amicable relations between the Reich and the Holy See. Both Mussolini and Ciano had readily offered to do whatever they could.

Von Hessen's message to the pope, sent through Travaglini on the first day of 1940, informed him of these conversations and concluded with what appeared to be a promising sign. Hitler and Ribbentrop "would be pleased to know immediately, through the usual channel, which problems most urgently concerned His Holiness, so that they could be resolved before the above-cited visit [by Ribbentrop] . . . and that with the goal of creating in these days an atmosphere of trust and hope." The prince asked the pope to meet with him to discuss next steps, saying he would soon have to return to Germany.[11]

Following their now familiar path, Travaglini, the Order of Malta go-between, took his written account of what von Hessen had told him to Cardinal Lauri. The cardinal then sent it on to the pope on January 2, 1940, with a cover letter urging the pontiff to quickly let him know how to respond to the prince. A separate typed note on a plain sheet of paper, found together with the cardinal's letter in the recently opened Vatican's secretary of state archive, shows how quickly the pope agreed to the meeting and gives a flavor of its cloak and dagger nature: "January 3, 1940 (12:15 P.M.). The Most Eminent Cardinal Lauri informs that 'the noted person' returned this morning in Rome and appropriately advised, will come this evening at the agreed-upon time."[12]

In preparing for the meeting, Pius XII hastily assembled a document listing five requests for the Führer. He gave it to von Hessen when the prince, using his alias, appeared that evening at the Apostolic Palace.

The pope prefaced his five points by expressing his pleasure in seeing that "some of the propagandistic publications against the Church or Church organizations [in Germany] have been withdrawn." However, other signs were less encouraging, for reports of anticlerical and anti-Christian propaganda in Germany kept coming in. "We continue to perceive that there are those in the Party—especially in those circles that regard themselves as the foremost representatives of today's Germany such as in the SS, the SA, the Labor Front, the Hitler Youth, the Federation of German Girls—who seek to separate Catholics spiritually and, if possible, visibly from their Church. For example, one cannot advance in the SS without having discarded one's membership in the Church." To "detoxify the public atmosphere before any talks begin," suggested the pope, it would be important for the German government to take certain measures. He then listed the five steps he urged Hitler to take:

1. Ending the attacks against Christianity and the Church in Party and State publications, and the withdrawal of particularly offensive past publications. Some of the worst publications against the Church have indeed been withdrawn from the market, but far from all. . . .
2. Cessation of anti-Christian and anti-Church propaganda targeted at youth, in the school and beyond. . . .
3. Restoration of religious education in schools in accordance with the principles of the Catholic Church and led by Church-approved teachers, in most cases Catholic clergy.
4. Restoration of the Church's freedom to defend itself publicly against public attacks against Church doctrine and Church organizations. . . .
5. Cessation of further sequestrations of Church property, in anticipation of the mutual examination of past measures.[13]

The morning after meeting with the pope, von Hessen, using a prearranged code, briefed Ribbentrop by phone on what Pius XII had told him. The Nazi foreign minister asked for further clarification, and so the prince summoned Travaglini to pass on the German foreign minister's question: Did the pope regard his five points as an "absolute condition" for holding their meeting? That same day Cardinal Lauri transmitted Ribbentrop's query to the pontiff, adding that, should the pope desire it, von Hessen was willing to return the following evening for further discussion.[14]

The pope did not think it necessary to meet again with von Hessen so soon and instead sent him a note, in German, responding to Ribbentrop's question. "His Holiness," the reply explained, had offered

the five points "to give the Reich Foreign Minister some indication of
what the Church considers to be beneficial for the creation of a propitious atmosphere for visits and negotiations. In doing so, the Holy Father merely sought to make sure, as far as he can, that the prospects of
success of the prospective, strictly confidential visit by the Reich Foreign Minister are as great as possible." Three days later, on January 8,
Cardinal Lauri telephoned with the news that "the noted person was
pleased with the response received and wanted to be sure the Holy
Father was immediately informed of this."[15]

On his return to Germany in early January, von Hessen briefed
Hitler and gave him the five-point German-language memo Pius XII
had prepared. Sent back to Rome early the next month to continue
the negotiations, von Hessen summoned Travaglini to the royal residence with a new message for the pontiff. After Hitler had read the
pope's memo, he had discussed next steps with Ribbentrop and agreed
in principle with the terms the pope had set out. He had decided that it
would be best if the upcoming meeting of his foreign minister with the
pope be an official one and so not remain secret. It should be billed as a
discussion of the points of tension between the Reich and the Vatican.

Curiously, in advising Pius XII on the planned meeting with Ribbentrop, von Hessen conveyed Hitler's wish that the pope flatter his
foreign minister as much as possible: "During the meeting that von
Ribbentrop will have with the Holy Father—perhaps a decisive one
for the relations between the Church and the Reich—the Führer
would like the Holy Father to employ many, many sweet words in regards to his Minister of Foreign Affairs, as he is very susceptible to such
expressions, and as von Ribbentrop is the executor of future oversight
in this area." Hitler, said the German prince, "is expecting much from
this audience."[16]

While the pope was eager for the meeting with the Nazi foreign
minister, Hitler's decision that the encounter should receive wide publicity made him nervous. Given the delicate dance he was engaged in
with the Poles and others who were calling on him to denounce the
Reich, being seen in collegial conversation with Ribbentrop could

have unpleasant consequences. On February 8 the pope had a new German-language note prepared for von Hessen:

> · The news we have received up to the beginning of the current month on the Church's situation in Germany does not indicate the beginning of a détente in line with the five mentioned points.
>
> Under these circumstances His Holiness believes that it remains more beneficial to make the first encounter between him and the Reich Foreign Minister a confidential one, to permit an open discussion without interference about the necessary . . . points for the agreement.
>
> His Holiness hopes that such an encounter will yield clarity and, potentially, agreement on those issues that should feature most prominently in the upcoming settlement.[17]

On February 18, 1940, the Nazi prince returned to Rome, where Travaglini gave him the pope's message. Travaglini's account of his conversation with von Hessen, which Pius XII received via Cardinal Lauri, featured the prince's latest enticements for the pope. The Führer and Ribbentrop were "cautiously and discreetly applying the five points of [the pope's] Note." They planned to complete that task and potentially do even more to please the pope following Ribbentrop's visit. To make all this possible, the Nazi leaders had agreed that, while the foreign minister's visit could be considered "private," it was important that it be accompanied by all the ceremony appropriate for an event of such importance. Von Hessen's message for the pope ended on an optimistic note: "After the visit and the Holy Father's open, frank discussion with von Ribbentrop, a new era of pacification of Catholicism in Germany may dawn."[18]

None of the secret correspondence involving Cardinal Lauri, Travaglini, and von Hessen appears in the twelve-volume compendium of documents dealing with the Second World War prepared by the Vatican. The thousands of pages of documents found there, published between 1965 and 1981, make only oblique reference to them.[19]

———

ON FRIDAY, MARCH 8, Prince von Hessen sent word to Pius XII that Ribbentrop hoped to meet the pope three days later. Only after getting a phone call from von Hessen later in the day, communicating the pope's approval, did the German foreign minister board the train for Rome.[20]

It was a tense weekend for the pope, as the notes Monsignor Tardini, the deputy secretary of state for international affairs, jotted down that Saturday make clear. Those notes have become accessible to researchers eighty years later:

> Monday, the 11th, von Ribbentrop will come to see the Holy Father. The audience has been prepared secretly for some time. Through Prince von Hessen and Travaglini. The Holy Father gave him five points which are desired by the Holy See (all prepared by him personally and until now unknown to the [Vatican secretary of state] office). The German government declared that they could constitute a basis for an agreement.

Tardini added that it was only the previous day that Ambassador Bergen, ignorant of the secret talks between von Hessen and the pope, had finally been told what was going on and had come to see Cardinal Maglione with the formal request for the audience.[21]

The pope's negotiations with Hitler over the first year of his papacy remained unknown outside a small circle, but his encounter with the Führer's foreign minister, coming after months of preparation, was now about to become known to the world.

A PROBLEMATIC
VISITOR

O N MONDAY MORNING, MARCH 11, 1940, FOUR BLACK VATI-
can limousines pulled up in front of the palazzo housing the German embassy to the Holy See. Two colorfully clad Vatican attendants,
each with a sword strapped to his side, emerged from one of the cars to
greet the pope's guest, Hitler's foreign minister. Forty-six-year-old
Joachim von Ribbentrop, the "boundlessly vain, arrogant and pomp-
ous former champagne salesman," had become one of the Führer's
closest confidants, although looked on with contempt by most of the
top Nazi leadership.[1] After Ribbentrop and his entourage boarded the
limousines, they set off for the Apostolic Palace, entering Vatican City
through the Porta Sant'Anna in the imposing protective wall that
stretched to the right from St. Peter's Square. There Harlequin-striped
Swiss Guards saluted them before the cars made their way into the San
Damaso Courtyard, surrounded by the tall walls of the fifteenth-
century Apostolic Palace.

Awaiting the German delegation at the foot of the grand ceremonial stairway that led into the Apostolic Palace was Carlo Pacelli, the
thirty-six-year-old prematurely balding, mustachioed son of the
pope's brother. Having taken over his father's law firm, specializing in
canon law, Carlo was one of the handful of laymen in whom the pope
had complete confidence. The pope regularly called on him to represent his interests with the outside world. Now, dressed in a dark
double-breasted diplomatic uniform with golden epaulets and a silver

cross hanging from his neck, he greeted Ribbentrop, who wore a formal, if somewhat less impressive, dark uniform. Escorted by a phalanx of Swiss Guards, the men then formed a procession as they climbed the stairway. On their arrival at richly frescoed Clementine Hall, a double line of Swiss Guards paid tribute to Ribbentrop, who was then led by a prelate to the antechamber of the papal apartments where the pope's master of ceremonies and several high-ranking prelates greeted him.

Ribbentrop entered Pius XII's private library, with its large carved desk, set near one wall, with a white statue of the Madonna, her arms outstretched, standing along the adjoining wall. The foreign minister, who declined to kneel as was the custom in approaching Pius XII, began the conversation by conveying Hitler's greetings. In response, the pope spoke of his many years in Germany, which he said had perhaps been the happiest of his life.

Ribbentrop said he hoped they could speak frankly. Hitler believed that settling their differences "was quite possible" but depended on first ensuring "that the Catholic clergy in Germany abandon any kind of political activity," that is, not offer any criticism—explicit or implicit—of government policies. Of course, wartime was not the moment for entering into any new formal agreements, said the German, but "in the opinion of the Führer, what mattered for the time being was to maintain the existing truce [between church and state] and, if possible, to expand it." Hitler, said Ribbentrop, was doing his part in bringing this improvement about. He had quashed no less than seven thousand indictments of Catholic clergymen, charged with a variety of financial and sexual crimes, and was continuing the National Socialist government's policy of giving a large annual financial subsidy to the Catholic Church. Indeed, the pope had much to be thankful to Hitler for, suggested Ribbentrop, for if the church still existed in Europe, it was only thanks to National Socialism, which had eliminated the Bolshevist threat.[2]

Here the German and Vatican accounts of the conversation begin to differ. According to the German version, "The Pope showed complete understanding toward the Foreign Minister's statements and admitted without qualifications that the concrete facts were as mentioned. True, he attempted to turn the conversation toward certain special problems and complaints of the Curia, but he did not insist on going on."

The pope's account of the conversation was prepared by Monsignor Tardini, based on what the pope told him shortly after Ribbentrop departed. We also now have further insight into the conversation thanks to a lengthy German-language memo prepared in advance of the meeting as a guide to what Pius XII intended to say. The memo, which only recently came to light with the opening of the Vatican archives, offered a reminder of the five points the pope had sent to Hitler via the prince in January and outlined the steps the pope had asked the Führer to take to improve the atmosphere for negotiations. It included as well other important issues the pope hoped to bring up.

The list was long: "There have been cases of offices of high Church officials, including bishops, being searched . . . by the Gestapo." Such actions violated the provisions of the concordat the pope had negotiated with the German government shortly after Hitler had come to power. It had to stop. Claims that the German clergy were working against the National Socialist government were groundless. "The storm against Church and priests notwithstanding, the clerics always knew how to restrain themselves and adhere to the law. This suggests an extraordinary amount of loyalty to the state on their part." Then there was the sensitive issue of Poland. The pope's concern focused on the negative impact the German conquest was having on the freedom of the church and the welfare of its clergy:

> Give Us the opportunity to look for the truth in Poland. If this truth is positive for Germany, We are willing to clear up any misunderstandings. . . . The Holy See has the gravest concerns over the current situation of the Church in Poland, especially because of the extreme restrictions imposed on the bishops and priests; the restrictions on Church activities, even on Sundays, that prevent priests and the faithful from executing the most necessary religious acts; and the closing of many religious institutes and Catholic private schools.[3]

Following the meeting, the pope remarked that Ribbentrop had struck him as a rather vigorous young man, but one who railed like a fanatic when he spoke. Ribbentrop had told the pope he had once been a wine merchant with little interest in politics. He believed in God, he said, and had been born a Protestant but belonged to no church. In response to Ribbentrop's complaint that the pope's predecessor had used strong words against Germany, Pius XII pointed out that by contrast in his own first encyclical, released the previous October, he had taken care not to offend the Germans, and in his subsequent Christmas address, his mention of the suffering of a "little people" had referred not to Poland, as some had claimed, but rather to Finland, which the Russians had recently overrun.

Ribbentrop tried to impress the pope with the Germans' certainty of winning the war before the year's end, a claim he kept repeating. "I had never seen a man of ice until I had met with von Ribbentrop," Giuseppe Bastianini, Mussolini's undersecretary for foreign affairs, had observed, and now the pope was seeing the famously warmongering Nazi in action. Every German, said Ribbentrop, stood with Hitler.[4]

Eager to turn the subject back to the situation of the church in Germany, the pope, diplomatic as ever, told the foreign minister that while he did not doubt Hitler's good intentions toward the church, the facts showed that a war was being waged against it. Here he cited various examples, highlighting the widespread closing of Catholic schools. When Ribbentrop then returned to his argument that the Third Reich was giving the church a great deal, emphasizing the large financial subsidy it provided the church each year, the pontiff replied that much was also being taken away from it, including its educational institutions and its properties.

The audience lasted a little over an hour. The pope, surprisingly, said that it had been quite friendly. Apparently the German foreign minister had the same impression. "In the antechamber," observed Monsignor Tardini, "they say that von Ribbentrop entered the Holy Father's chamber a little worried and nervous. He left with a satisfied air."[5]

Ribbentrop also met twice that day with his Vatican counterpart,

Secretary of State Maglione, an hour-long meeting at the Apostolic Palace and then a shorter one when the cardinal returned the visit by going to the German embassy. Maglione memorialized his conversations in notes later in the day. Ribbentrop had recalled that he had seen Pacelli, the future pope, when he was nuncio in Berlin in the 1920s and knew how much people admired him. When he had first heard the news of Pacelli's election to the papacy, he had remarked, "Now, there's a true Pope!"

Ribbentrop told Cardinal Maglione how pleased he was that Pius XII was eager to reach a "solid, long-lasting understanding with Hitler," as the Führer wished for the same thing. He then repeated much of what he had told the pope, about Germany now being in the midst of a great war that would decide the nation's future, and how every German stood with the Führer, certain of victory. The problem, said Ribbentrop, was that the Catholic Church, and the Protestants, too, had inappropriately strayed into the political sphere.

The cardinal interrupted him. "Can you now say," he asked the Nazi leader, "that the clerics, bishops, priests, members of the orders are mixing themselves in political party matters? . . . If it were true, you would only need to give us their names." The fact is, argued the cardinal, they were not. Having listened impatiently to Ribbentrop's long monologue, he now offered his own litany of complaints: the closing of almost all Catholic schools in Germany and Austria, the suppression of religious classes in many elementary schools, the removal of crucifixes from classrooms, and replacing the teaching of the Christian catechism with the Nazi *Weltanschauung*. "Who can believe," asked the cardinal, "that all this has been done because the Catholics are mixing in politics?"

Unintimidated by Ribbentrop, the cardinal continued his attack: the National Socialist government had closed many seminaries, big and small, had suppressed religious houses, abbeys, and Catholic charities, and jailed many priests.

"I have no knowledge of that," replied the German foreign minister.

Incredulous, the cardinal suggested that Ribbentrop read the reports the Vatican had been regularly sending the German embassy. Ribbentrop countered by handing him a German publication describing the many atrocities that Poles had allegedly inflicted on Germans and asking him to give it to the pope. Maglione seized on the subject to complain about Germans' treatment of the Catholic Church in Poland.

In concluding his account of their conversations, the cardinal noted that the German foreign minister had twice told him he had long abandoned any religion. "He believes and says naively that he can be objective in evaluating religious matters just because he has no religious ideas himself!" The conversation had been civil enough, thought the cardinal, but "I have the impression that one can expect very little to come from the Foreign Minister's visit to the Vatican."[6]

Indeed, the newly opened Vatican archives reveal that the Nazi leader was himself none too pleased with the cardinal secretary of state. Later recounting his Vatican meetings to Jozef Tiso, the priest who led the pro-Nazi Slovakian state, Ribbentrop offered his impressions: "On the orders of my Führer I went to the Vatican to clarify various things with the Holy Father, and I found him to be cordial, conciliatory, educated and well informed. He made an extraordinary, I would say almost mesmerizing impression on me. By contrast, I found in the Cardinal Secretary of State an enemy of German National Socialism."[7]

ALTHOUGH THE PRIMARY REASON for the Nazi foreign minister's trip to Rome was to see the pope, his meetings with Mussolini and Ciano while in Italy's capital were important as well. Indeed, if a date were to be given for Mussolini's ultimate slide toward war, it might be during this visit. On Ribbentrop's arrival at Rome's train station, Ciano had met him rather icily, unhappy that the Germans had notified him of his planned visit only a couple of days earlier. Ribbentrop's previous encounter with his Italian counterpart had been their uncomfortable meeting in Salzburg the previous August when he told Ciano of Hitler's decision to invade Poland.[8]

Meeting with Mussolini at Palazzo Venezia, Ribbentrop handed him a letter from Hitler. Mussolini's decision not to enter the war up to that point, wrote the Führer, was certainly understandable. Indeed, perhaps it had been for the best. "But, Duce, I believe that of one thing there can be no doubt: the outcome of the war will also decide Italy's own future." Playing on Mussolini's vanity, his lust for the limelight, his resentment over Italy's secondary status in world affairs, and his envy at Germany's military successes, Hitler had struck the right chord. The letter ended with a stirring call: "Sooner or later destiny will force us to struggle together. That means that You too will not be able to keep yourself out of the conflict. . . . It means all the more that your place will be at my side, just as I will be at yours."⁹

Hitler's letter to the Duce was linked to the message that Ribbentrop had come to deliver. The Führer had decided to launch an attack on France and Britain, certain of being able to defeat the French army by some time in the summer and chase the English forces from the continent before the fall. The Führer had studied the military situation carefully, Ribbentrop told the Duce, and he knew the battle would not be as easy as the conquest of Poland had been. But he was convinced that both France and England would be not only defeated but annihilated. Ribbentrop acknowledged that at Salzburg he had downplayed the likelihood France and Britain would back up their pledge to come to Poland's aid, but, he said, it was all working out for the best. A final showdown with the western democracies was inevitable. There was not a soldier in Germany, said the foreign minister, who did not believe that victory would come before the end of the year.

When the Duce responded by observing that the morale of French troops did indeed seem low, given all the Communist propaganda there, Ribbentrop smiled. A number of those French Communist papers, he boasted, were being printed in Germany.¹⁰

Mussolini took advantage of the meeting to ask how Ribbentrop's audience with Pius XII had gone. The pope, replied the German, agreed with the Führer that it was possible for the two sides to come to an understanding. The Duce, eager as always to offer the Nazi leadership his own advice on the church, remarked that it was best to avoid antagonizing a pope. It could, he said, be "quite troublesome."¹¹

Waiting at Berlin's train station along with other dignitaries to meet

Ribbentrop on his return late the next evening was Monsignor Cesare Orsenigo, the papal nuncio. He proudly reported back to Rome that the foreign minister, on descending from the train, had made a point of greeting him first. After then greeting the others, Ribbentrop made his way back to Orsenigo to tell him how pleased he was with his meeting with the pope. "In general," reported Orsenigo, "both among the diplomats and the men of government, even those least enthusiastic about the regime, a sense of relief prevails. Many also told me of their satisfaction, interpreting Signor von Ribbentrop's step as, if not the beginning of a new orientation for the religious policy in Germany, at least

**Nuncio Cesare Orsenigo with Adolf Hitler at
Reich Chancellery, Berlin, 1936**

as a clear distancing from all those revolutionary elements who would have liked to eliminate any trace of Christianity."[12]

SOON AFTER RIBBENTROP LEFT Rome, Sumner Welles, the American undersecretary of state, returned to the Italian capital. Since his previous visit earlier in the month, he had traveled to London, Paris, and Berlin, where he had met with Hitler. "Hitler is taller than I had judged from his photographs," Welles observed. "He has, in real life, none of the somewhat effeminate appearance of which he has been accused. . . . He was dignified both in speech and movement, and there was not the slightest impression of the comic effect from moustache and hair which one sees in his caricatures." But Welles found the Führer uninterested in discussing the kind of peace the American had in mind, one involving the withdrawal of German forces from the lands it had conquered. "I did not want this war," Hitler told him. "It has been forced upon me against my will." His aim, said the dictator, was simply to attain "a just peace."[13]

In his second visit to Rome, the American diplomat again shuttled between the Italian leadership and the pope and his secretary of state, with all eager to hear what he had discovered in his travels.[14] In going to see Pius XII on March 18, he brought Myron Taylor, Roosevelt's personal envoy to the pope, with him. Welles spoke to the pope in French, but Taylor was limited to English, and while the pope could read English easily and spoke it fairly well, he was not always able to follow what Taylor said.[15] One thing became clear to both Americans: Pius XII had excellent sources on Europe's unfolding drama. Indeed, it was the pope who explained to them the course the war was about to take. The Germans were planning an offensive on the western front, he said, but it would not begin for at least another month.

Taylor asked the pope if he thought the Italians would revolt if Mussolini led the country into war on Germany's side. The pope looked startled by the question and remained silent a long time before responding. Speaking slowly in English, he said that it was true Italian public opinion opposed the war, but he very much doubted there would be any revolt against Mussolini should he decide to join it.

"The Pope was exceedingly cordial," the undersecretary of state observed in concluding his report to Washington. "He impressed me as having a very well-informed and analytic intelligence, but as lacking the force of character which I had previously attributed to him. I found

Cardinal Maglione far more direct and unevasive in his discussion of present conditions."

The American diplomat's contrast between the pope and Maglione found an echo in observations the French ambassador to the Vatican would record later that year. The Frenchman sensed a certain rivalry between Pius XII and his secretary of state. The two men had never enjoyed good personal chemistry. The French ambassador thought Maglione more intelligent than the pope, more decisive, and a better judge of people. "Because he is endowed with great perspicacity, people call him crafty." But the cardinal also had a very human quality that, the ambassador observed, could be appealed to, but only on condition that one never pressed him too hard, for that would immediately put him on the defensive. The ambassador thought part of the reason Maglione was hesitant to speak his mind was that he did not think his own position was entirely solid. He sensed he was not a "persona grata" to the Pope, "nor to the fascist milieu that has influence at the Vatican."[16]

THE DAY BEFORE UNDERSECRETARY Welles's March 18, 1940, audience with the pope, Mussolini and his son-in-law, Ciano, accompanied by an assortment of top Fascist officials, had boarded a special train in Rome. They were bound for Mussolini's first meeting with Hitler since the historic September 1938 Munich encounter in which Britain and France had agreed to Hitler's demand to seize the Sudetenland in exchange for a promise of peace. It was late at night when they arrived at the German-speaking town of Bressanone, ceded to Italy only two decades earlier from what was left of the Austrian empire. In the wake of the incorporation of Austria into the Reich, it was now the last Italian town before the German border. The next morning, in the midst of a snowstorm, their train pulled into the small station at the Brenner Pass, at an altitude of 4,500 feet, in the shadow of the Alps. A half hour later Hitler's train approached the station, which was decorated with both Italian tricolor and red-and-black swastika flags.

Mussolini, waiting with Ciano under the protection of a small shelter by the side of the track, was wearing the uniform of commander
general of the Fascist militia. As Hitler descended from the train, an
Italian military guard offered its honors while the Führer greeted the

**Adolf Hitler and Benito Mussolini at train station, Brenner Pass,
March 18, 1940 (Galeazzo Ciano looking on with chin thrust out)**

Duce. After Ribbentrop stepped out of the train, he and Hitler greeted
Ciano as well. Fighting off the snow, the military band played the two
nations' anthems as the men climbed into the dark wood-paneled salon
compartment of the Duce's train for their meeting. Hitler sat at one
end of the long table there, Mussolini and Ciano across from each
other on either side of him.[17]

It did not take long before the Führer launched into one of his familiar messianic monologues. Recalling the meeting later, Hitler observed he had found Mussolini "visibly embarrassed, like a pupil who
hadn't done his homework." It did not help that Hitler knew only
German and Mussolini was too proud of his own linguistic ability to

allow a translator. Between his own difficulties with the language and the sonorous quality of the Führer's endless harangue, the Duce missed much of what the German dictator said, but his main message was clear enough. The decisive battle was about to begin. Soon Paris would fall, and London would as well unless it wisely agreed to peace terms. Italy was bound to Germany by a solemn pact. "If Germany were to lose—"

Here Mussolini interrupted him. "Then Italy has lost too!"

The Führer continued: "If Italy is content with a second-rate position in the Mediterranean, then she need do nothing more."

Increasingly under Hitler's spell, and ever more impressed with Germany's military might, Mussolini told the Führer he needed only a little more time to make final military preparations, and then Italy would march proudly at Germany's side. Hitler promised that once France was conquered and England forced to sue for peace, Italy would become master of the Mediterranean.

After two and a half hours, following a quick lunch, the men left the Duce's compartment and walked the short distance back to Hitler's awaiting train. The snow had stopped. Back inside his own compartment, the Führer spent a few minutes chatting amiably with Mussolini through his pulled-down window before, as the train pulled out, the two dictators raised their right arms in final salute.[18]

THE U.S. UNDERSECRETARY OF state had delayed his departure from Rome, hoping to learn from Ciano about the Brenner Pass encounter. Preferring not to call public attention to his meeting with the American, Ciano arranged to see Welles at his golf club on the southeastern outskirts of the city. Ciano often spent afternoons at the club, which had been founded earlier in the century by British expats. It boasted scenic views of the Appian Way, the ancient Roman road connecting Rome to the southern tip of Italy's heel. Ciano told the American undersecretary that Hitler had done practically all the talking at their meeting, telling them that the western offensive would come soon but was not imminent. It was Hitler's intention, said Ciano, to send his warplanes to bomb British ports and cities, including London.

In Welles's final report on his mission, he wrote that Mussolini's decision to throw Italy into the war would depend on whether Germany won rapid victories in its drive westward. Opposing the decision would be virtually all those who counted in Italy, beginning with Ciano, who, wrote the undersecretary, is "violently against it," as was the king. "The entire Church is openly against it," he added, and "so are the financial and commercial interests, and every ordinary man and woman." But if Germany seemed to be heading to certain victory, little could prevent Mussolini from joining. As for the pope, "I fear [he] is discouraged and, in a sense, confused."[19]

Two weeks after Mussolini's meeting with Hitler, the Duce sent a top secret memo to the king, Ciano, and the heads of the military. If the war continues, he told them, "believing that Italy can remain out of it to its end is absurd and impossible. Italy is not off in a corner of Europe like Spain. . . . Italy is in the middle of the belligerents." Two days later he sounded a similar note in a meeting of his cabinet. To remain neutral "would reduce Italy from being a great Power for a century and from being a true Fascist Regime for eternity." It was time for Rome to regain its Mediterranean empire.[20]

The Duce's impatience only increased when, on April 9, he received a letter from Hitler announcing his plans to send German troops into Norway that same day. Thanking Mussolini for all he had done so far, Hitler concluded the letter, "I am deeply moved, Duce, by the belief that Providence has chosen us two for the same mission." Late the following night Mussolini received another message from Hitler: German troops had completely occupied Denmark and seized Oslo.[21]

"I hate this Italian rabble!" Mussolini told Clara the next day. While the Germans were fighting bravely, Italians cared only for their peace and quiet. "I've had the chance to measure the temperature of this people for eight months now," said the Duce, referring to the time since the war erupted. "They're cowards, weak, full of fear." Warming to this, one of his favorite themes, he added, "Ah, you know, certainly it's all useless: one doesn't undo three centuries of slavery in eighteen years of regime!" He had done his best to turn Italians into a courageous, martial force but had accomplished little. "We'll have the enemy on our doorstep, and they will still just keep babbling."

"Yes, my dear," concluded the Duce, "I am upset, upset and disgusted."[22]

His mood had not been helped by his meeting with the king that morning. Mussolini needed the king's support to fulfill his promise to Hitler, for the king was the ultimate commander of the military, and the army had a long tradition of allegiance to the Savoyard monarchy. But Victor Emmanuel, always a cynic, and no lover of the Germans, had shown no eagerness to send Italy's troops into battle.

"It's humiliating," remarked the Duce later that day, "to stand with your hands in your pockets while others are writing history."[23]

PART TWO

—

ON THE PATH TO AXIS VICTORY

AN INOPPORTUNE TIME

USSOLINI'S SON-IN-LAW WAS LEAVING THE GERMAN EMBASSY'S dinner party after midnight when Hans Georg von Mackensen, Hitler's ambassador to Rome, took him aside at the door. It's likely, Mackensen said, that he would have to disturb him early in the morning. At home, Ciano found it difficult to sleep. At four A.M. his phone rang. Mackensen said he would be at his door in forty-five minutes. When the German arrived, he informed Ciano that Hitler wanted him to deliver a message to Mussolini at five A.M. exactly. Asked why all this could not have been done the previous day at a more reasonable hour, Mackensen fumbled through an excuse about a diplomatic courier who had been delayed. The two men then made their way through Rome's deserted streets to Villa Torlonia, the dictator's residence. It was May 10, 1940.

"Duce," Hitler's message began, "when you receive this letter, I shall already have crossed the Rubicon." He had ordered German troops to launch their attack on Belgium and the Netherlands at 5:35 A.M. After carefully reading the letter and the enclosures, all in German, Mussolini looked up and said he fully approved of the decision. He cabled Hitler to thank him for his message. "I feel that time is pressing for Italy too," he told the Führer. "As for the Italian armed forces, the navy is ready, and by the end of May two army groups in the east and west as well as the air force and the antiaircraft formations will be ready."

The Duce's eagerness to join his forces with Hitler's would only grow over the next days as German troops advanced with startling speed through the Netherlands, Belgium, and Luxembourg and on toward Paris. His daughter Edda, unlike her husband, shared his enthusiasm. If the country was to uphold its honor, Mussolini's headstrong daughter told her father, Italian intervention in the war could not come soon enough.[1]

ALARMED BY SIGNS THAT Mussolini was preparing to plunge Italy into war, Pius XII had written him a letter two weeks earlier. "Beloved Son," it began. "We know . . . the noble efforts you have made from the beginning to avoid and then to localize the war." The pope went on to express his hope that "thanks to your initiatives, to your steadfastness, and to Your Italian soul, Europe is saved from greater ruin and more numerous sorrows; and in particular that Our and Your beloved country is spared such a great calamity." At the same time, the pope reaffirmed instructions to the Vatican newspaper to avoid publishing anything that might offend the Duce.[2]

Mussolini's reply to the pope was anything but comforting: "Your recognition, Most Blessed Father, of the fact that I have tried every avenue to avoid a European conflagration has given me legitimate satisfaction." While he had kept Italy out of the war so far, he told the pontiff, he could not guarantee he could continue to do so. Then with a large dose of hubris, he cited the pope's own words as justification: "The history of the Church, as You have taught me, Blessed Father, has never accepted the formula of peace for peace's sake, for peace 'at any cost,' for 'peace without justice.'" "It is a consolation to me," he added in a final burst of insincerity, "that, in either eventuality, God will want to protect the fate of a population of believers like the Italian people."[3]

The pope had coordinated his letter to the Italian dictator with the American president, who sent a similar appeal. Roosevelt cabled his plea to his ambassador in Rome with instructions to deliver it personally to the Duce. On May 1 Mussolini received Ambassador Phillips at his office in the Ministry of Internal Affairs. Although the Duce was initially alone, Ciano joined them midway through the half-hour meeting. Conscious of the limits of Mussolini's English, the ambassador read Roosevelt's message slowly to him. Mussolini voiced his Italian translation of each sentence as Phillips proceeded. When Phillips finished, he handed the text to Mussolini, who then read it again.

Having finished his reading, Mussolini asked Phillips why the Americans would want to get involved in the war. In his cable, the president had called himself a realist. He too was a realist, said the dictator. For better or worse, the reality was that Germany had conquered Poland and Czechoslovakia, and the new map of Europe would have to reflect those facts. As for Italy, said the Duce, it was no longer the agricultural country it had long been, but a heavily industrialized one dependent on international trade. It could not remain a "prisoner within the Mediterranean" forever. It needed an outlet to the Atlantic. Italy, he told Roosevelt, had never interfered in American affairs. It had a right to expect the Americans to stay out of Europe's.[4]

THE POPE LEARNED OF Germany's offensive from his nuncio in Brussels, who cabled the news that day that the Belgian capital was under air attack. Urged by the French and British governments to condemn the invasion, the pope felt he had to do something. Sitting at his small American typewriter late on the evening of May 10, he drafted telegrams in French to be sent to the sovereigns of each of the three countries under attack. He worked for several hours, correcting the typed pages by hand and crafting an individualized message to each.

"For the second time," the pope wrote King Leopold, "the Belgian people, against their will and their rights, see their land exposed to the cruelties of war." "Profoundly moved," he wanted to send the king and the entire Belgian nation assurance of his paternal affection, along with his prayers that Belgium soon regain its freedom and independence. To Queen Wilhelmina of the Netherlands, he wrote, "Learning with deep emotion that Your Majesty's efforts for peace were unable to prevent your noble people from becoming, against their desire and their right, the scene of a war, We beg God, supreme arbiter of the destiny of nations, to hasten through his all-powerful help the reestablishment of justice and freedom." He sent Grand Duchess Charlotte of Luxembourg a similar message.

The pope had the text of the three telegrams published, albeit only in their original French, on the front page of *L'Osservatore Romano*. When the issue hit the Italian newsstands, angry local Fascist Party officials and their minions seized copies, roughed up the vendors, and made a great show of burning piles of the newspaper in the streets.[5]

"If we continue with our neutrality, as many would like," remarked the Duce on learning of the pope's messages to the European sovereigns, "we too will one day get a fine telegram of outrage from the pope to wave in front of the occupying German troops!" Mussolini, Ciano noted in his diary that night, "often repeats that the papacy is a cancer that eats away at our national life, and that he intends—if necessary—to liquidate this problem once and for all." As was often the case, it fell to Ciano to calm him down.[6]

While the pope's three telegrams angered the Duce, they did not satisfy the Nazis' victims or their allies. On the morning of the German invasion, the French ambassador urgently requested an audience with the pontiff. The entire world, he told the pope, was waiting for him to pronounce his "solemn condemnation" of the "odious attack of which two Catholic nations are victim." British foreign secretary Lord Halifax sent a similar plea, hoping that a papal denunciation of the Nazis would make it more difficult for Mussolini to join the war.[7]

Three days later François Charles-Roux, the French ambassador, returned to the Vatican to press for a stronger papal response. "All the Catholics in France, England, Belgium, Holland and Luxembourg are waiting for the Holy Father to condemn the crime the Germans committed with their invasion of three neutral countries." The pope's own prestige, he argued, was at stake.[8] The pope, aware that he had already angered Mussolini with his three telegrams, would do no more.

The Wehrmacht's advance went more swiftly than anyone could have imagined. Within four days, the Dutch resistance was largely crushed, and the Belgians were in retreat. The massive German tank assault on France had begun. Worried that the Italians would soon join the attack, the French saw the pope as their last hope. "Nearly every member of the French Government and many French Senators have appealed to me today," the American ambassador in Paris informed the U.S. secretary of state on May 14, "to ask you to make a final effort to keep Italy from entering the war as Germany's ally." The French officials had made clear, said the ambassador, "that the most powerful weapon to employ against Mussolini would be a statement by the Pope . . . denouncing the barbarities which Germany has inflicted on the Netherlands, Belgium and Luxemburg, combined with a papal edict excommunicating Hitler."[9]

In their desperation, France's leaders made the same plea more directly as well. Returning to the Apostolic Palace, Charles-Roux read the cardinal secretary of state a long telegram from Paris calling on the pope to pronounce "an explicit and formal condemnation of the German aggression." He had no luck. The pope would do no more. It had already become clear to the pope that it was a war that Germany was likely to win.[10]

ONLY A COUPLE OF weeks earlier Dino Alfieri had been sitting at his desk in the Italian embassy to the Holy See when he received an urgent summons from the Duce. Arriving at Palazzo Venezia, he was immediately ushered into Mussolini's office, where the Duce and Ciano greeted him with a Roman salute. To Alfieri's surprise, Mussolini told him to pack his bags. He was to leave immediately for Berlin to become Italy's new ambassador to Germany. "I hope you're satisfied," said the Duce. "Today Berlin is the most important post in the world."

On his way out the door, still trying to absorb the news, Alfieri turned to Ciano and said, "But I don't speak any German."

"Neither does Attolico," replied Ciano.[11]

Mussolini knew the move would please the Germans, who had long suspected Bernardo Attolico, the current ambassador, of undermining their efforts to bring Italy into the war. In Alfieri they would have someone much more well-disposed to the Third Reich.[12]

Soon thereafter Alfieri went to the Apostolic Palace for his final papal audience as Italian ambassador to the Vatican. After an initial exchange of pleasantries, his tone grew serious. The telegrams sent to the three sovereigns, he told the pope, had greatly upset the Duce. He reminded the pontiff that he had often warned him against having the church get involved in politics, and indeed, with Italy now likely soon to join its Axis partner in war, the consequences for the church of doing so could be grave.

"The Pope," Alfieri reported, "listened to my words with emotion and surprise, evidently not expecting my ceremonial visit of departure to have such serious contents." Pius XII replied that he had heard no complaints about his telegrams from Germany, and so he did not see why the Italian government should be concerned. All he had done, he insisted, was to express well-known church principles. Speaking with growing emotion, "the Pope," Alfieri recalled, "added that his well established and sincere attachment to Italy—an attachment that had not failed to lead to unhappiness with him in certain foreign quarters—could not prevent him from the essential exercise of his mission."

"I am profoundly and firmly convinced," said the pope, "that I have done my precise duty, taking care not to offend anyone, avoiding any particular references, indeed, studiously taking care to say the least possible. I certainly did not want to do something displeasing to Italy, which up to now is absolutely not involved, much less to the Duce."

Warming to his theme, the pope added, "They can even come to take me to a deportation camp, I have absolutely nothing to regret, if not perhaps having been too discreet and too reserved in the face of what happened and what followed in Poland. . . . We must each answer for our actions to God."

Telling Alfieri he was eager to maintain good relations with Italy's government, the pope asked if having the Vatican newspaper publish Queen Wilhelmina's response to his telegram would cause any problem. "As I expressed the view that it would be best if such a publication not happen," Alfieri reported, "the Pope personally got up from his work table and telephoned a secretary, telling him to suspend its publication."[13]

Before the ambassador left, the pontiff told him he was considering asking him to deliver a message to Hitler and Ribbentrop when he got to Berlin. He wanted to let the Nazi leaders know he was still hoping to reach an understanding with them. Religious pacification in Germany was possible, he believed, as long as the Reich protected the legitimate rights of the church.

Alfieri had barely left the Vatican when the pope began to have second thoughts about the mission he had just given him. Bombarded by pleas to denounce the Nazi leadership, perhaps now, three days after the massive German invasion of the western countries, was not the time to renew such an approach. After discussing the matter that evening with Monsignor Montini, the pope sent word to Alfieri not to raise the matter. Should a better moment come, he would let him know.[14]

The next night Alfieri boarded a train for Berlin.[15] There he gave the German Foreign Ministry a full briefing on his last encounter with the pope, telling them of the pope's insistence that in drafting his telegrams to the three European sovereigns, "he had intentionally avoided using both the words 'Germany' and 'invasion'" and "had promised to give instructions once more that [*L'Osservatore Romano*] should not take sides with England and France." Alfieri advised the Germans that it was "in the interests of both Germany and Italy to be on good terms with the Vatican," albeit adding the caveat, "at least for the duration of the war." In one of Alfieri's first official acts in Berlin, following an exchange of Roman salutes, he presented Hermann Göring, whom months later Hitler would name Marshal of the Empire, the Italian king's Collar of the Most Holy Annunciation, the same honor that he had, on Victor Emmanuel's behalf, bestowed on Cardinal Maglione less than half a year earlier.[16]

AS THE GERMAN TANKS rolled relentlessly toward the French capital, the American ambassador in Paris, William Bullitt, brought an urgent request to the papal nuncio there. The last thing the French needed now was for Italy to join the war and attack France from the south.

The only way Mussolini could be prevented from entering the war, thought the ambassador, was for the pope to threaten to excommunicate Mussolini should he do so.[17]

Maglione's response to the American request offers a glimpse at how successful Mussolini had been in intimidating the pope. The Holy Father, the cardinal told the nuncio, had done all he could. "Unfortunately, one doesn't see what is still possible to do, all the more so given the continued opposition to the distribution of *L'Osservatore Romano* and the fact of the innumerable, regrettable incidents in that regard."[18]

Pius XII was feeling pressure to prevent Italy's entrance into the war from within Italy as well. A letter to the pope from Naples in mid-May told of the violent seizure of the Vatican newspaper by Fascists there. "Italy, which is an eminently Catholic people," the man wrote, "should not sacrifice some millions of human lives for nothing or for the caprice of one man alone. . . . In Your power, Holiness, the Italian people seek protection from You, they do not want war nor civil war."[19]

Another letter at the same time, its author identifying himself as "A civilized and Christian Italian," sounded a similar note: "The Holy Father's power could help our Italian people . . . not only to avoid war by threatening the King with excommunication but seeking to help them to liberate themselves from this cynical scoundrel who plunders us and leaves us in poverty, while he and his Pretorians accumulate thousands." A man he knew who was reading the Vatican daily, he told the pope, had it torn from his hands and shredded into pieces that were made into balls he was forced to eat, washed down by castor oil. "We call on the Holy Father to help us. Have the King set the Army against these assassins and the people, the whole Nation will be with You. . . . Help us not only with prayers, but with facts."[20]

Women, too, addressed their pleas to the pope, including one signed anonymously, if presumptuously, "The Catholic women of Italy":

> Holy Father, In every tormented and broken heart of Your
> faithful, Catholic people lives today one fervent hope, that Your

Holiness prevent this monstrous, cowardly war that the frater-
nal friend of the criminal Teutonic vandal is preparing. . . . In
past ages, the Holy Pontiffs excommunicated monarchs and po-
tentates many times solely for having rebelled against the sacred
laws of the church. Today . . . then, excommunicate these mon-
sters or it will be too late.[21]

As far as we can tell from the Vatican archives, Pius XII never seriously considered excommunicating either Hitler or Mussolini, who
were both nominally Catholic. But the Nazi leadership showed some
concern he might. On May 22 Hermann Göring asked the Italian ambassador whether he thought it possible that the pope would excommunicate the Duce if he entered the war on Germany's side. Alfieri
replied he thought it highly unlikely. But he admitted, if the pope
were to do so, "it would have a dangerous influence on popular opinion."[22]

The prospect that Italy would soon enter the war was producing
another kind of concern as well, worries for the safety of the pope
himself and whisperings that the pontiff might be planning to leave
Italy altogether. On the eighteenth, D'Arcy Osborne, the British emissary, received a surprising message from the London Foreign Office.
Should Italy join the war, the French Foreign Ministry had advised
them, the pope might move the Vatican Secretariat of State to a neutral
country such as Switzerland, where foreign ambassadors to the Holy
See would be expected to relocate, while the pope himself would remain in the Vatican. The British Foreign Office had also learned that
President Roosevelt was considering offering the pope asylum in the
United States. In response, members of the Foreign Office were toying
with the idea of offering Pius XII refuge in Malta. Speculation about a
possible papal relocation was rife in Rome as well, with one police informant reporting the rumor that if Italy joined the war, the pope
planned to move to Lisbon.[23]

A few days after Germany launched its westward attack, Cardinal
August Hlond, primate of the Polish church, asked the pope for permission to address a message to the Polish people via Vatican Radio.

The cardinal explained that he had designed his message "to sustain the faith of the nation, a faith put to harsh test by both the religious persecution and by the very sad living conditions." A week after receiving the request, the pope sent his response to the cardinal. "Taking into consideration the extremely delicate current circumstances, His Holiness does not believe that this is the opportune moment to deliver allocutions, even with the noble intent of lifting up the faith and the depressed spirits of a disturbed nation." Having faced Fascist ire for sending his telegrams to the three European sovereigns, the pope was not inclined to do anything that might further provoke the Duce's displeasure.[24]

AN HONORABLE
DEATH

T IS IMPOSSIBLE TO UNDERSTAND THE POPE'S ACTIONS WITHOUT recognizing he had good reason to think the church's future would likely lie in a Europe under the thumb of Hitler and his Italian partner. Many were convinced the war would be over in a matter of months, with the continent in the hands of the Axis powers and Britain suing for peace.[1]

While most Italians had opposed joining the war, news of Germany's surprisingly rapid advance, reported enthusiastically by the Fascist and Catholic press, was beginning to win some converts. A police informant in Genoa was among the first to report signs of the changing attitude: "public opinion is undergoing a major evolution, due to the impressive German victories. It is brought about by the fact that everyone is convinced that the war will only last a few months, and that victory will come easily, thanks to the defeats being suffered by the French and British." The Ministry of Popular Culture reported that Italians were "stunned and amazed" by the resounding German victories and the rapid collapse of Allied resistance. German military might was frightening yet intoxicating. "Some are delighted; others, on the other hand (and there are more of them than the first kind) are upset, disoriented and alarmed."[2]

Although popular opinion was mixed, Mussolini's enthusiasm for joining the war was growing. By May 12, 1940, only two days after the invasion had begun, the German army, having marched through Belgium, was crossing into France at Sedan. Luftwaffe bombers were routing French troops, while German fighter planes were repelling the Allied air forces. Winston Churchill, having become British prime minister on May 10, asked Parliament three days later for a vote of confidence for his wartime cabinet. "I have nothing to offer but blood, toil, tears, and sweat," he famously told them. Prospects were not looking good for the British. On May 20 German troops reached the English Channel on the northeastern coast of France at Abbeville and encircled the Allied armies. In a report Hitler sent the Duce on May 25, he boasted that his forces were encountering no serious opposition as they moved through France. The British, in full flight from the continent, were hurriedly boarding ships from the beaches of Dunkirk.[3]

The breathtaking speed and ease of the German advance had also made a great impression on the Duce's son-in-law, who was beginning to rethink his opposition to joining the war. Ciano's May 28 meeting with Monsignor Borgongini, the papal nuncio to the Italian government, was notable for the absence of his previous mantra that he was doing everything he could to keep Italy out of the fighting. That same day Ciano was even more frank with his friend, the fifty-eight-year-old industrialist Alberto Pirelli. Pirelli, who headed the eponymous rubber-producing company founded by his father, had often conferred with Mussolini over the preceding two decades. Having extensive contacts throughout Europe and the Americas, he was among the Italian business elite with the deepest knowledge of the world. No better exemplar could be found of the industrialists whose support—sometimes grudging, sometimes enthusiastic—had helped prop up the Fascist regime.[4]

Should they join their ally and declare war on France, said Ciano, they stood to gain not only Corsica but also Nice, on the coast near the Italian border. They could also acquire the entire northwest African coast including French Morocco and, with it, access to the Atlantic. Hitler, he told the industrialist, had agreed to let Italy replace England in Egypt and had assured the Italians he had no aspirations for Germany to gain a Mediterranean port. Nor did the formerly war-shy Ciano limit himself to this already long list of targets for Italian conquest. "We will take Crete and Corfu," he told Pirelli, "and we ought to control all of Greece."[5]

AS THE DAY OF Mussolini's fateful declaration of war drew near, Bernardo Attolico, who until days earlier had been ambassador to Germany, presented his credentials at the Vatican as Italy's new ambassador to the Holy See. People who met Attolico thought he had something of a professorial air, a serious man with thick glasses and a somewhat stooped posture. The move to Rome was one Attolico was happy to make. A conscientious career diplomat of considerable intelligence, he had never felt comfortable among the Nazis, and he was not in the best of health. The previous year, following the signing of the Pact of Steel, he had confided to a friend, "I am sick, I don't have long to live, I've wanted to leave this horrible atmosphere. But I can't." Hitler himself had now helped grant Attolico's wish, having let Mussolini know that Italy's unfriendly ambassador was no longer welcome in Berlin.

The Vatican appointment had an added benefit for Attolico, for while he came from a middle-class southern Italian family, his wife, Eleonora, was a product of the Roman elites closely identified with the popes. She had strong family ties with the upper reaches of the church.[6]

Attolico's new task, as he saw it, was to ensure harmonious relations between the Italian government and the Vatican. Unlike his predecessor, Dino Alfieri, a hard-line Fascist and strong supporter of the German alliance, Attolico was more typical of the conservative Italian elite who supported a Catholic Fascist state but had no love for Hitler or the Nazis. Aware of the recent tensions sparked by Fascist assaults on the vendors and readers of the Vatican newspaper, he urged the Duce to bring them to an end and avoid any other actions that might offend the pope. Next to these two points in the text of Attolico's report, Mussolini himself wrote, in his colored pencil: "Yes, M." It was just as well not to go too far.[7]

Pius XII himself was eager to do what he could to avoid further conflict over the Vatican newspaper. In exchange for a promise by the new Italian ambassador to allow *L'Osservatore Romano* to be distributed

**Ambassador Bernardo Attolico and Eleonora Pietromarchi Attolico
with Adolf Hitler, Berlin, December 10, 1937**

and read freely, the pope directed it not to publish any more pieces that were, as Attolico put it, "in apparent contrast with the supreme interests of the country."[8] Italy's new ambassador promised the pope that he would do all he could to eliminate any points of friction between the Vatican and the government and expressed hope that through the open exchange of information, he and the pontiff could be successful. The pope assured him that these were exactly his own thoughts.[9]

"THE DECISION HAS BEEN made. The die is cast." So Ciano recorded Mussolini's decision on May 30 to enter the war at Hitler's side. "The Italian people," the Duce wrote in a letter to the Führer that day, "are impatient to be at the side of the German people in the struggle against the common foe." Italy would be ready to enter the war in six days, said Mussolini. William Phillips, the American ambassador, sent a blistering letter to President Roosevelt: "We are dealing with an Italian peasant who has . . . not the imagination to see beyond the overwhelming power of German armaments."[10]

Mussolini had decided to throw Italy into the war without convening either the Grand Council of Fascism or his own cabinet ministers. Only after making his decision did he summon the heads of the military to inform them. None voiced opposition, perhaps intimidated by the experience Marshal Pietro Badoglio, supreme commander of the military, had had when he voiced his objections a few days earlier. Badoglio argued that, given their limited number of planes and tanks, entering the war would amount to national suicide. "You, Signor Marshal," replied Mussolini, who was rapidly losing faith in his military head, "haven't the calm necessary for an accurate evaluation of the situation. I tell you that by September all will be over, and I need only a few thousand dead to be able to sit at the peace table as a belligerent."[11]

A SHORT WAR

TENS OF THOUSANDS OF ROMANS STREAMED INTO PIAZZA VENEZIA on the afternoon of June 10, 1940, waiting for Mussolini to appear at his office balcony. In the central piazzas of towns and villages throughout the country, loudspeakers attached to radios were set up to broadcast the Duce's speech to crowds mixing enthusiastic Blackshirts with others herded in by earnest Fascist officials.

Earlier that afternoon Ciano had summoned the French and British ambassadors to read them the king's proclamation.

"I imagine you know what I have to say," remarked an ill-at-ease Ciano, dressed for the occasion in his air force commander uniform, when André François-Poncet, France's ambassador to Italy, arrived.

"One need not be very intelligent to understand," replied the ambassador. "Your uniform is eloquent enough."

After Ciano read the king's war declaration, the Frenchman, unable to hold his temper in check, lashed out: "You have waited until we were face down in the ground to then stab us in the back. In your place I would be very proud!"

Ciano's cheeks reddened. "My dear Poncet," he responded, "all this won't last long." Surely, they would soon meet again in more pleasant circumstances.

"On the condition," replied the ambassador, "that you haven't been killed!"[1]

The Duce was filled with nervous excitement that day, worried that if he failed to act quickly, the war would be over before he fired a shot. His only doubt was whether the British would agree to make peace once France was conquered; if they did not, the Axis would have to attack the British Isles as well. He spent the morning at home working on his speech, which he wanted to memorize, but paused three times to phone Clara, telling her to be at Palazzo Venezia by midafternoon. Groups of youths in their black Fascist uniforms, carrying banners and signs, were already streaming into the piazza when she arrived. She found Mussolini in a state of great agitation. "The time for poetry is over!" he said by way of greeting.

At six P.M. Italy's dictator stepped out onto his small balcony. Wearing a dark militia uniform and cap, he stood with his hands perched over the thick black belt on his hips, his chin jutting out, his chest puffed up. Chants of *doo-chay, doo-chay* greeted him. The immense crowd flowed well beyond the capacious piazza down the broad Via dell'Impero, which led on a straight line to the nearby Colosseum. When the crowd quieted, he delivered his speech, his gaze fixed in the indeterminate distance. He spoke in his characteristic pugnacious, staccato bursts, pausing for the oceanic shouts of enthusiasm that greeted each pithy phrase:

> Combatants on land, on sea, and in the air! Black shirts of the revolution and of the legions! Men and women of Italy, of the empire and of the Kingdom of Albania! Listen!
>
> An hour marked by destiny strikes in the sky of our fatherland. The hour of irrevocable decisions. The declaration of war has already been delivered to the ambassadors of Great Britain and France. We enter the battle against the plutocratic and reactionary democracies of the West. . . .
>
> This gigantic struggle is . . . the struggle of the poor, numerous people against the exploiters who ferociously hold onto the monopoly of all the world's riches and all its gold. It is the struggle of the fertile, young peoples against the sterile people who are facing their decline. . . .
>
> The watchword is one alone, categorical and incumbent on

all. . . . Victory! And we will win in order to finally give a long period of peace with justice to Italy, to Europe, to the world.

People of Italy! Run to take up arms, and show your tenacity, your courage, your valor![2]

The roaring crowd called him back to the balcony time and again. Finally, his nervous energy spent, Mussolini returned to greet Clara. He now showed his tender side, and Clara's gray-green eyes clouded with tears. Life would never be the same, he told her, but he would always love her, he would never leave her. When, later that evening, it was time for her to go, he held their parting kiss for what, she wrote in her diary, seemed a long time. That night he would phone her at home three more times to hear her voice and reassure her of his devotion.[3]

In London, Prime Minister Churchill was awakened from a nap to be told the news. "People who go to Italy to look at ruins," he snapped, "won't have to go as far as Naples and Pompeii in future." In Paris, there would be little time to react, as the members of the government were hastily fleeing from the capital as the German army approached.[4]

In Washington, the news of Mussolini's declaration of war was not unexpected, but it came as a blow to President Roosevelt, whose pleas to the Duce had been dramatically rebuffed.[5] Much less bothered by the new development was the pope's nuncio to Germany. Indeed, if Monsignor Orsenigo was unhappy about Italy's entrance into the war at Hitler's side, it was not apparent to the German undersecretary of state, with whom he happened to be meeting at the time. "In the conversation," the German official recalled, the nuncio "gave very cordial expression to his pleasure at the German victories. It seemed as if he could not wait for Italy to enter the War and he remarked jokingly that he hoped the Germans would march into Paris by way of Versailles."[6]

Mussolini had expected Rome's church bells to ring to offer a festive conclusion to his speech, but they remained silent. Alerted in advance of the government's plans, the pope insisted he could never countenance sounding Rome's bells to celebrate a declaration of war. If the Fascists wanted to have them ring, they would be able to do so only by force. In the end, no one made such an attempt. This was not a time to antagonize the pope.[7]

For his part, the pontiff was not inclined to risk antagonizing either the Duce or Hitler. A week earlier he had given a highly publicized address at St. Peter's to mark St. Eugenius I's Day, his namesake holiday. The speech was vintage Pius XII: written with great care, memorized, and delivered in a monotonous tone devoid of any hint of spontaneity. As Europe was being ravaged by the rapidly advancing German army, and as hundreds of thousands of British troops were being evacuated at Dunkirk, the pope sought above all to avoid saying anything that could be deemed offensive by either side.[8]

Italian press coverage of the pope's remarks that day emphasized his use of the same phrase Mussolini had continually repeated: "peace with justice." Indeed, the Duce used the words again in his declaration of war. It was a peace that Mussolini contrasted with the peace that had prevailed in Europe since the end of the Great War, a peace that in the Fascist view was unjust, a product of the much-vilified Versailles Treaty.[9]

AS CHARLES-ROUX, FRANCE'S AMBASSADOR to the Holy See, was called back to France to help deal with the crisis there, a new French ambassador came to Rome. On June 9 he met the pope for the first time amid circumstances that could hardly have been worse for his country. Fifty-one-year-old Vladimir d'Ormesson came from an illustrious French family, his first name deriving from the fact that his father, a prominent diplomat, had been serving in the French embassy in Russia when he was born. Badly wounded in the Great War, he had become one of France's most prominent Catholic journalists, and although in the past he had occasionally been tapped for brief diplomatic missions, he was not a diplomat by profession. The Italian government viewed him with suspicion, aware of his critical writings about Mussolini. His hatred of Nazi Germany could hardly have been greater, for his son, in the French army, had been killed by the Germans only weeks before. He was "a man of exceptional ability, courage, and charm," thought the British envoy to the Vatican. The new French ambassador's detailed reports over the next months would offer clear-eyed insight into the murky world of papal politics.[10]

After an initial ceremony in the papal Throne Room, d'Ormesson followed the pope into his study for a private conversation. "Given the tragic circumstances in which our country finds itself," the ambassador would later remark, "one would have thought the Holy Father would have avoided taking advantage of this occasion to give us a 'moral' lesson." Rather than castigate the Germans for their invasion of his country, the pope, while expressing sympathy for the trials that the church's "elder son" was undergoing, told d'Ormesson that France's problems were self-inflicted. It was the result of its de-Christianization, the country's strict policy of separation of church and state.

The pope could also not refrain from voicing his amazement at the rapid disintegration of the Maginot Line, which the French had characterized as an impregnable barrier to German attack. "Where," Pius XII asked him, "was the France of Verdun," which had held off the German army for years in the Great War? While the pope expressed sympathy for France, observed d'Ormesson, "the Holy Father is a little too easily resigned to playing only a passive role in the drama that is ravaging Christianity." The pope, he thought, was not a man of action. His head was too high in the heavens.[11]

IT DID NOT TAKE long after Mussolini's proclamation of war for him to apply new pressure on the pope. Two days after his announcement, British warplanes bombed both Turin and Savona, a fact reported in the French media but not in Italy. The new Italian ambassador rushed to the Apostolic Palace to urge that the Vatican paper not print news of the attack or any other stories on the war not found in official Italian press releases.[12]

Following the ambassador's visit, the pope turned to his most trusted adviser, Monsignor Montini, the future Pope Paul VI, to help frame his options. In his hastily scribbled memo, Montini outlined the possibilities. The Vatican daily could publish official war communiqués from both sides of the conflict, but this would mean having the paper banned in Italy and antagonizing Mussolini. It could confine itself to publishing only Axis war communiqués, but that would damage the Vatican's prestige abroad. Publication of the paper could simply be suspended, but that, judged the monsignor, would be "catastrophic today and extremely dangerous for the future." This left only one realistic option, having the paper focus entirely on church business and religious life.[13]

The matter was urgent for the pope, as that day's edition of the Vatican paper was about to go to press, and following recent practice, it contained without comment not only the Italian and German war bulletins but those from France and elsewhere as well. Although he could often be indecisive, on this day the pope acted quickly. He ordered the immediate suspension of the day's printing.[14]

But as it happened, copies of that evening's edition of the paper had already been printed. Perhaps, Cardinal Maglione told the Italian ambassador in explaining what the pope had decided, they could allow this one last issue to appear uncensored. This Attolico would not tolerate. The pope ordered all copies pulped, and word was sent to the country's newsstands that due to "broken machinery," *L'Osservatore Romano* would not be appearing that day. "The question," Attolico concluded in his report to Ciano, "has therefore been definitively resolved."[15]

FOLLOWING MUSSOLINI'S DECLARATION OF war, the headline in Italy's leading Catholic daily, *L'Avvenire d'Italia,* screamed "VICTORY!" followed by a front-page editorial by the paper's director, which began "Today the duty is but one: TO SERVE. Wherever. However." The next day the paper featured the message that Bologna's archbishop had directed all clergy of his archdiocese to read from the pulpit: "The one who has high government authority has taken the decision and our Italy has entered into war. To the Sovereign's Majesty and to Those who share with Him the supreme responsibility of na-

L'Avvenire d'Italia, June 11, 1940

tional life we all owe, following the law of our Faith, the most complete, fullest obedience."[16]

The directors of Italy's Catholic papers—who would not print any
editorial they thought displeasing to the pope—filled their pages with
heroic portraits of the Duce and enthusiastic calls by Italian clergy for
Catholics to answer the nation's summons to war. At the same time,
the Vatican newspaper remained quiet. "It is certain," remarked the

new French ambassador, "that the Holy See's newspaper is going to reduce itself little by little to the proportions of a 'Parish Bulletin.'"[17]

With his government in flight and German troops advancing rapidly on Paris, d'Ormesson tried to persuade the pope to speak out, but without success. "It is infinitely probable," the ambassador observed, "that the Holy Father will say nothing for the moment and will only take advantage of the first occasion he has to speak publicly to emit some pious and expertly balanced moans."

D'Ormesson did find one ally in the Vatican, the physically imposing, bushy-bearded Cardinal Tisserant. The lone non-Italian cardinal in Rome, who dined with the ambassador's family each week, was secretary of the Curia's Congregation for the Oriental Churches. He "seems to me," the ambassador confided to his diary, "the elephant in the china shop." The cardinal's propensity to say what he thought came as a breath of fresh air in a Vatican full of secrets, where obfuscation was a way of life. Indeed, he would soon acquire the nickname Cardinal De Gaulle, in reference to the French resistance leader. D'Ormesson worried that the Fascist authorities would find a way to throttle the outspoken cardinal, and Tisserant's bulging political police files offer testimony to the often hapless efforts made to tail him whenever he left Vatican City, as he often did. But the pope himself had little sympathy for the French cardinal, never forgiving him for his all-too-well-known opposition to his election.[18]

Shortly after Mussolini's declaration of war, Cardinal Tisserant lashed out at the pope's inaction in a letter to the archbishop of Paris. Several months earlier, he recalled, he had unsuccessfully pressed the pope to issue an encyclical on the individual's duty to obey his conscience, the hallmark, he argued, of Christianity. "I fear that history will have much to reproach the Holy See for in having adopted a policy of convenience for itself and not much more. . . . It is sad in the extreme, above all when one has lived under Pius XI."[19]

The day after Tisserant wrote his letter, Roberto Farinacci, former secretary of the Fascist Party, editor of that most Fascist of Italy's newspapers, *Il Regime Fascista,* and strident critic of the Vatican, sent

Cardinal Eugène Tisserant

the Duce a warning about the French cardinal. He enclosed a typed, unsigned letter that he identified as written by the head of the Vatican police, whom he described as "our most faithful comrade." The passage dealing with the cardinal was written all in capital letters: "It is necessary for Italy to keep an eye on all movements into and out of the Vatican. IT IS NECESSARY TO PUT THE MOVEMENTS AND THE CONTACTS OF CARDINAL TISSERANT UNDER STRICT SURVEILLANCE." The Vatican police head's letter—if it was indeed written by the head of one of the Vatican police forces—concluded with the Fascist cry: "ALALA."[20]

Arturo Bocchini, Italy's skilled national chief of police, who reported each morning to Mussolini, had no need to wait for Farinacci's message before putting the Vatican under surveillance, and he did not particularly appreciate the gratuitous advice. Nor was the surveillance a secret to the French and British diplomats who were in the process of settling into their modest quarters in Vatican City. Mussolini's spies, it seemed, were everywhere.[21]

THE ITALIAN CLERGY AND the country's Catholic institutions, which all came under the pope's authority as bishop of Rome, continued to proclaim their strong support for Italy's entrance into the war at Hitler's side. Attracting special attention in both the Catholic and the Fascist press was the patriotic message by Bishop Evasio Colli, national director of Italian Catholic Action: "In this grave, solemn hour in which the Fatherland calls upon all its children, the members of Italian Catholic Action respond to this appeal with that sense of profound duty and generosity that is the fruit of their Christian education." Leaders of the various subgroups of Catholic Action added their own calls urging members to support the war. Typical was the letter of the national president of Catholic Men: "Italy has entered the war. The Head of the Government has proclaimed it to all of Italy. . . . We, Men of Catholic Action, leap to our feet and shout our *'Presente!'*"[22]

Mussolini's Vatican embassy kept track not only of these national church appeals but also of the many messages of support for the war that the nation's archbishops and bishops were sending their flocks.[23] Meanwhile the Catholic and Fascist press was giving special prominence to the call to arms by one of Italy's most esteemed churchmen, Father Agostino Gemelli, founder and head of the Catholic University of Milan. "We must all prepare for the victory," Gemelli urged. "May God hear our prayers, may the Holy Virgin protect us, and may she be the star that guides our Fatherland to victory."[24]

SURVEILLANCE

———

MUSSOLINI WAS EAGER TO GET ITALIAN TROOPS INTO FRANCE before Germany's conquest would deprive him of any claim to French territory. But despite the Duce's years of bellicose bluster, the Italian military had no clear plan for an invasion, nor did its generals believe they were ready to launch one. The attack that finally did come, sending Italy's antiquated tanks through Alpine passes, to the west of Turin, that were little more than mule tracks, would prove less than overwhelming.

On June 14, 1940, four days after the Duce's declaration of war, the German army entered Paris. Still no significant movement of Italian troops across the border had occurred. A new French government, led by the aged Great War hero Marshal Philippe Pétain, was quickly formed and immediately asked for an armistice. Pétain sent his plea to Germany through Madrid, and the one to Italy through the Vatican. Informed of the French request for an armistice by his nuncio in France, the pope immediately passed it on to Mussolini.[1]

On June 17 Pétain publicly broadcast his call, *il faut cesser le combat* (the fighting must stop). Furious, Mussolini called on the Italian army to launch its assault. With the French military overwhelmed by the Germans farther north, he imagined it would have few troops free to resist the attack.

Following a series of confusing and contradictory orders by Mussolini and his generals, the Italian offensive was finally launched the morning of June 21, begun by air force bombardment of the French fortifications arranged along France's mountainous southeastern border with Italy, known as the Little Maginot Line. The advancing Italian troops, three hundred thousand strong, largely ignorant of the location of French gun emplacements, were soon overwhelmed by enemy fire and ambushed by French soldiers hiding along the mountain mule tracks. Italian air force support was less than effective, partly due to the heavy fog and their outdated maps and partly due to lack of adequate pilot training. Indeed, some of the Italian planes ended up bombing their own troops. Much to the Italians' dismay, the French stood and fought, and after only four days, the brief Franco-Italian war ended with Italy's General Pietro Badoglio signing an armistice agreement outside Rome with the French general Charles Huntziger. In the end, the fighting at the French border had cost the Italians 642 dead, 2,631 wounded, and 616 missing, with another 2,151 soldiers suffering from frostbite. The Italian military had succeeded in occupying only a tiny sliver of southeastern France. The contrast with the German military's rapid advance across the Netherlands, Belgium, and France was painfully obvious to all.

FRENCH AMBASSADOR D'ORMESSON, MEETING with the pope while Italy's troops were still fighting, found him open to the idea of helping to broker a peace deal between France and the Axis powers. But as often happened, the pope soon had second thoughts. The next day he informed the French ambassador he did not think it wise for him to get involved. The only chance France had of receiving relatively favorable terms, given its crushing military defeat, thought the pope, was for Mussolini to exercise a moderating influence on Hitler.[2]

Pius XII's faith—or perhaps better put, his hope—in Mussolini's moderating influence on the Führer had never been more misplaced. The Duce was in fact meeting with the German dictator in Munich at the time. Things had begun well enough for Mussolini there, a massive rally welcoming him on his arrival at the train station, but his mood soon soured. In their initial one-on-one meeting, Hitler lectured him for two hours on his plans for France. It would be advantageous, the Führer insisted, to ensure that the country had a functioning government of its own, for otherwise they risked having the French set one up in exile in London. In any case, he added, it would save the German military a great deal of manpower if it did not have to bother with the day-to-day administration of the country. For all this to happen, they would need to handle the French carefully. It would not do, as Mussolini proposed, to insist on an armistice that would give the Italians Corsica as well as the French colonies of Djibouti and Tunis. Such a demand, said Hitler, would make it politically impossible for Pétain to collaborate. In the end, all that Mussolini would get for his belated military efforts was the modest strip of French land at the Italian border that his troops had occupied. It contained fewer than 30,000 inhabitants; the only town captured was the small tourist city of Menton, on the French Riviera at the Italian border.[3]

ON THE NIGHT OF June 12, barely forty-eight hours after Mussolini's declaration of war, the first group of thirty-six RAF bombers hit Turin, the center of Italy's heavy industry, followed over the next few days by British bombardments of cities throughout the country. Milan, La Spezia, Livorno, Cagliari, Trapani, and Palermo were all bombed. Although damage was limited and victims few, the British succeeded in delivering a loud message.[4]

The attacks underscored what would become a constant preoccupation of the pope, preventing the Allies from bombing Rome. Within twenty-four hours of Mussolini's declaration of war, the pope had his secretary of state summon the French and British emissaries to make this request. The French were no longer in a position to bomb anyone. The British, who were, assured the pope they would never bomb Vatican City, but for the rest of Rome, they would make no commitment.[5]

With Italy's entry into the war, what friction still existed between the Vatican and the Fascist regime largely evaporated. "The Pontiff," reported Mussolini's ambassador to the Holy See, "has personally desired to suppress any center of possible anti-Italian and defeatist propaganda that might take root in the Vatican." At his weekly general audience on June 19, Pius XII reminded his countrymen of "the duty they have to pray too for their Fatherland which, fertilized by the sweat and perhaps too by the blood of their ancestors, asks its children to be generous in serving her."[6]

The speed of the Germans' drive through France had made a deep impression on the pope and the cardinals of the Curia. Fear of where Germany's seemingly unstoppable march would lead Europe and anxieties about the church's future further reinforced the pope's inclination not to expose himself to Fascist or Nazi retribution. Cardinal Maglione, for one, thought the war might soon be over, with France defeated and Britain likely to reach a deal with Germany to protect its empire. "He always finds the means to excuse Italy," observed the French ambassador after his latest conversation with the Vatican's secretary of state. Referring to the dramatic change that readers saw in the Vatican newspaper following Italy's entry into the war, he added, "This silence is equivalent to submission. The Holy See is aware of this and is not proud of it."[7]

Britain's envoy, too, was struck by the change that had come over the Vatican. From the moment Italy entered the war, Osborne observed, "the moral prestige of the Papacy began to decline. . . . Axis methods of blackmail were used to good effect." The pope was giving in to Mussolini's and Hitler's none-too-subtle pressures. By contrast, he recalled, Pius XI had "fearlessly pronounced the moral verdict of Christian civilization" against Nazi worship of the state. His successor carefully tailored his words "to the exigencies of an anxious neutrality." Osborne attributed the change in part to a difference of personality. "The Pope," he wrote, "sensitive and impressionable by temperament and naturally inclined to caution and compromise, bowed to what he conceived to be both duty and necessity." But the British diplomat saw another motive behind the pope's decision to remain silent, the desire to play a role in brokering an eventual peace. "He does not realize," reflected Osborne, "that the abnegation of moral leadership in the interests of a strict neutrality is likely to hinder rather than to advance that ambition."[8]

Pius XII indeed still hoped to play the role of peacemaker. In the wake of France's defeat and the routing of British forces from the continent, Hitler was signaling a willingness to make a deal: in exchange for Britain's acquiescence to Germany's control of the continent, he would spare it from attack and allow it to keep its far-flung empire. In late June, the pope decided that such a peace deal might be possible. He sent a letter to the Italian and German ambassadors to the Holy See, as well as to his nuncios in Rome and Berlin and the apostolic delegate in London, asking them to sound out the governments in Berlin, London, and Rome to see if they would consider a peace conference. He did not want to make a formal proposal unless he could be sure it would be accepted by all three governments.

On the morning of June 28, Cardinal Maglione presented the pope's idea to Diego von Bergen, Germany's long-serving ambassador to the Vatican. Bergen sounded encouraging. The Führer, he told the cardinal, had always said he was open to negotiations. He promised to cable Berlin immediately. The Italian ambassador likewise promised to refer the proposal to his superiors without delay. It seemed that the two Axis powers might well support the papal plan.

Archbishop Godfrey, the papal delegate in London, met a far less friendly reception. Foreign Secretary Lord Halifax brusquely dismissed the pope's idea of a peace conference and told Godfrey to leave Pius XII in no doubt of Britain's "determination not to acquiesce in Hitler's programme for making himself master of Europe." Godfrey himself was sufficiently alarmed by the foreign secretary's reaction that he urged the pope not to make his appeal public. Such a step, he advised "might easily be badly interpreted as if the Holy See was associating itself with the invitation to surrender, calling on Great Britain to sue for peace terms." Pius XII's tentative peace initiative would remain stillborn.[9]

While German troops now controlled a vast stretch of Europe, from France, Belgium, and the Netherlands through Austria, Czechoslovakia, and Poland, Italian forces had at this point only poverty-stricken Albania and a skinny stretch of sparsely populated French Alpine borderland to show for their war efforts. At the same time as the Italians were struggling to conquer that meager territory, the Red Army had occupied all three Baltic states, soon to be incorporated as Soviet republics. Eager to have more to show for his efforts, Mussolini looked to North Africa and told his military command to plan for an invasion of Egypt from Italy's Libyan colony. Hitler offered heavy bombers in support of an Italian assault on the British position there.[10]

At the Vatican, virtually everyone expected Hitler to launch his invasion of Britain in July, and it seemed likely he would succeed in adding Britain to his conquests.[11] Meanwhile Italy's Catholic clergy and church institutions continued to do what they could to encourage popular support for the war. The pope, as primate of the church in Italy, could have put a stop to it, but he had no intention of doing so. Italian Catholic Action, the church's vast, capillary organization of the faithful, was certainly doing its part. Not only had its leaders issued widely publicized calls for getting behind the war effort, but as the Italian embassy to the Vatican reported, "all the weekly publications of Catholic Action have . . . offered a ringing endorsement in their editorials. The Catholic daily newspapers have been second to none in voicing the highest notes of patriotism in this situation." Likewise, the new issue of the *Rivista del Clero Italiano,* the journal devoted to Italy's priests, carried a stirring call by Father Gemelli. "The time of war," Milan's Catholic University head said, "is not the time for discussion or for dissent, but for harmony, obedience, action."[12]

As usual, Italy's Catholic newspapers looked to the Vatican-supervised Jesuit biweekly, *La Civiltà Cattolica,* for papal guidance. An early July article on Italy's decision to join the war immediately prompted front-page stories in the major Catholic dailies. Italian forces, the Jesuit author explained, were locked "in a giant struggle aimed at giving the world a new order." He recalled that the pope, in his recent saint's day speech, had highlighted a quote from Saint Augustine: "We do not seek peace in order to be at war, but we go to war that we may have peace."[13]

The police chief of Borgo, the Roman district bordering the Vatican, responsible for surveillance of Vatican City, offered what he presented as further evidence of papal blessing for the war. In the most recent beatification ceremony held in St. Peter's, he reported, the pope had instructed that members of the Italian armed forces be admitted without the need for the ticket that was normally required. The pope took this action, said the police chief, "due to an express desire . . . to see himself surrounded by many soldiers in order to be able, through them, to bless the entire Italian Army."[14]

Ambassador Attolico was likewise pleased by the pope's supportive attitude. "In private conversations," he wrote Ciano in early July, "the Pope has expressed his favorable impression of Germany's conduct in the war," saying that "the German army was acting well, without excesses, trying to avoid destruction, respecting, as far as possible, civilian populations." The ambassador was also pleased to point out that, along with the Vatican's embrace of the Fascist slogan of peace with justice, the other much vaunted Fascist war goal, fighting to create a "new order," seemed to be finding increasing favor there.[15]

REPEATEDLY VISITING CARDINAL MAGLIONE and his two deputies, France's ambassador tried to impress on them "how much the Sovereign Pontiff's silence and reserve, at such times, pained the French," and he warned of the "dire consequences" that might result. Monsignor Montini offered a glimmer of hope in meeting with d'Ormesson on the last day of June, hinting that the pope was considering saying something soon. "Believe me," added Montini, "the Holy Father is perfectly aware of the situation. I can even say that it is, for him, an acute concern." For d'Ormesson, what that meant was not entirely clear. Perhaps the pope had in mind addressing a letter to the French cardinals or to the archbishop of Paris. "What is likely, however," the ambassador feared, "is that this document will be written in the rather convoluted and overly flowery style in which Pius XII delights. What is certain . . . is that each of his phrases will be carefully weighed not to provoke any negative reaction on the part of Germany or Italy. Extreme prudence is now more than ever the order of the day at the Holy See."[16]

The Frenchman saw in Attolico, the bland, courteous Italian ambassador to the Holy See, a dangerous tool of the Fascist regime, "all the more dangerous because he is himself Catholic and related, through his wife, to the Vatican milieu. He is a skillful, shrewd, cunning, wily man. His wife and he have entered into the good graces of the Secretariat of State." Attolico knew the right button to push: the Vatican should stick to its religious mission. He was an effective complement to Bergen, his German colleague, both men conservatives of the old school. Attolico was no fervent Fascist and Bergen no zealous Nazi, but it was just this that made them so useful to the two regimes in preventing the pope from doing anything that might be harmful to the Axis cause.[17]

D'Ormesson's flickering hopes that the pope would speak out would soon be extinguished. In his public audiences, the pope stuck to the familiar bromides, avoiding any attempt to cast blame. His July 10 address was typical, developed on the theme that Christianity teaches that one should not hate one's enemy at a time of war or fall prey to feelings of revenge. As an example of the proper Christian attitude, he pointed to the virtue of caring for the wounded on the battlefield regardless of which side they were on.[18]

As for the Vatican paper, it paid remarkably little attention to the war. "To read it," observed the French ambassador in July, "one would think that the missions to Paraguay or the concordat with Portugal were currently Christianity's sole objects of concern." The Fascist government's campaign of intimidation, thought the French ambassador, had succeeded. The pope's three telegrams to the sovereigns of the invaded countries and their publication in the Vatican paper had been met by violence against the paper's vendors and readers. The pope, explained d'Ormesson, being "extremely sensitive," was shocked at the time to learn that shouts of "Down with the Pope" had been heard on the streets of Rome. Indeed, the pontiff frequently remarked on the unsettling impression it had made on him.[19]

IN EARLY JULY 1940, Mussolini sent his son-in-law to Berlin to plan the war's next moves with Hitler and Ribbentrop. He wanted to impress on the Führer his eagerness to have Italian forces participate in what he expected to be the impending invasion of the British Isles. He also wanted to ensure that the moves Marshal Pétain, the head of France's new collaborationist government, was making to cooperate with the Axis powers would not end up "defrauding" Italy of the French booty that, as he saw it, was Italy's due.

Hitler, in a buoyant mood, took Ciano for a tour of the sites of Germany's recent triumphs: the Maginot Line, which had been so easily breached; Dunkirk, from which the British troops had fled in chaotic retreat across the Channel; and Bruges, in northwestern Belgium. The tour ended in Salzburg, Austria, where they were met by a huge popular demonstration of support.[20]

The following week Pius XII, meeting with the French ambassador, told him how impressed he was with Marshal Pétain. Having been worried in the past that Communists might take over France, the pope welcomed the appearance of a strong leader who could expunge that danger for good. It had indeed been Communist subversion, thought the pope, that had led to France's humiliating defeat. He told the ambassador of a report he had heard that, as the German army approached, a large number of French troops deserted while singing the Communist "Internationale." Perhaps the pope even believed the implausible story. "What a difference from the war of 1914," remarked the pontiff.[21]

Ambassador d'Ormesson asked Pius XII what he thought the Italians would demand of France. "Nice, Corsica, Tunisia," replied the pontiff. Distraught, the Frenchman told him how much the French were counting on him to protect them. "The Pope listened to me attentively," the ambassador later recalled, "approving my words, but nothing in his attitude or in his words left any hope that he was resolved to take a vigorous position in any near future. Pius XII has been crushed by recent events. . . . I fear that his personal character is not equal to the dramatic situation found in Europe today." What seemed to worry the pope most in the negotiations then under way was that the Germans would try to take the Congo, home of a well-developed network of Roman Catholic missions, away from Catholic Belgium.[22]

The pope's nervousness about the Congo reflected the Vatican's continuing discomfort with the German government, seen as weakening church influence in the lands it conquered. The sharp-tongued Monsignor Tardini dubbed Hitler the "Motorized Attila." Even among those Italians who were more positively inclined to the war, the Nazis were not particularly popular. A police informant reported that the image of King Victor Emmanuel in a newsreel at a Rome movie theater provoked enthusiastic applause. The subsequent projection of an image of the Duce prompted a similar reaction. "But Hitler's appearance," the informant recalled, "passed amid the most absolute indifference." In an effort to do his patriotic duty, the informant said he had tried to encourage the audience by enthusiastically clapping, but "it

Rome's Catholic newspaper, *L'Avvenire*, July 21, 1940: "A Great Speech by Hitler"

was followed by barely a dozen people who immediately got tired of applauding."[23]

Although not standing up and applauding for Mussolini, the Vatican authorities were doing all they could to remain in his good graces.[24] Attolico continued his stream of encouraging reports on the Vatican's cooperation. On July 24 he sent a clipping from its newspaper featuring Father Gemelli's new call to support the Axis war. "I want to immediately bring to your attention," wrote Attolico, "how the attitude of *L'Osservatore Romano* not only no longer gives rise to concerns but has assumed, and I've been assured that it will always assume in the future, an attitude of greater understanding." Father Gemelli's well-publicized support for the war, he said, was priceless.[25]

Attolico, career diplomat, devout Catholic, unsympathetic to the Nazis, and never a true-believing Fascist, continued to be one of Mussolini's most valuable assets. Showing increasing initiative, in late June he had written to Arturo Bocchini, Italy's talented police chief. The Italian ambassador, who used the informal "tu" form in his note, had a request to make:

"Dear Bocchini, I know that an opportune surveillance is exercised by the Borgo police commissioner over Vatican City. Given the particular moment, do you think it possible to allow the Commissioner of Borgo to give me contemporaneously those reports that he may judge of interest to the Embassy?"

"Dear Attolico," replied Bocchini, "I can assure you I have given instructions to the Commissioner of Borgo to act in accordance with your request."[26]

THE POPE, EAGER TO avoid antagonizing Mussolini, was keeping a close eye on the pages of the Vatican newspaper. In mid-August, a rather minor infraction gave rise to a sharp papal rebuke to the paper's director, delivered via Monsignor Montini. "It is not without pain this evening that I must echo what the Holy Father said about publication of the article on the third page reviewing the book by Seppelt and Loeffler, which lacked prior approval. . . . You were told, only this past

June . . . not to publish anything regarding Germany or books by German authors without first getting approval from this office, such being the delicacy of that situation and all the interest that it attracts." Thus chastised, Giuseppe Dalla Torre immediately sent a notice to the paper's editorial staff warning them not to publish anything regarding Germany without his approval, not even a book review.[27]

By all reports, the pope had become depressed, despairing at the devastation Europe was suffering, but despairing too at his own plight. To criticize Mussolini would be to end the mutually beneficial relations the Vatican had long enjoyed with the Fascist regime. To criticize Hitler and the Nazis would be to risk further actions aimed against the church in the largely Catholic lands that the Germans had recently conquered and to turn the millions of German Catholics loyal to the Nazi government against him. To add to his hesitancy, he thought it only prudent to plan for protecting the interests of the church in a future Europe dominated by the Axis powers. His nervousness was heightened when, in mid-August, Germany began its massive air attacks on Britain. By the end of the month, over a thousand German sorties each day were dropping bombs on the island in preparation for a landing on British soil, a landing that seemed imminent. The end of the war, it appeared, might well be near.[28]

To understand the pope's actions, it is also important to realize he shared a view largely prevailing in the Curia, one that distinguished between good Fascists and bad Fascists. The good ones—men like Attolico—were loyal, conservative Catholics who sought a close, mutually respectful collaboration between the church and the regime. The bad Fascists, men like Farinacci, frequently from socialist backgrounds, were anticlerics, regarded as left-wing Fascists by the Vatican. Although they often posed as defenders of the church, they were interested only in using the clergy, the pope included, as their lapdogs.

Monsignor Tardini explained all this to the French ambassador in late August. The Fascist Party, as he put it, was torn between two tendencies. One consisted of the bellicose, antireligious fanatics who were strong supporters of the Third Reich and adversaries of the Holy See. The other was composed of more moderate people who dreaded German hegemony, had advocated Italian neutrality, and were sympathetic to the church and the Vatican. With Italy's entry into the war, it was clear it was the first group that had won Mussolini over.

In lamenting this situation with d'Ormesson, the tart-tongued Tardini may have said more than was prudent. "You see," he told the French ambassador, "all the courtesy, the moderation, the benevolence, the goodwill, all that has no chance of success in dealing with the Fascist leaders. On the contrary! All that does is excite them. . . . Pope Pius XI sometimes spoke to them without mincing words, harshly. . . . And, well, they respected him and they feared him." The monsignor did not need to draw the obvious conclusion. "It is clear," observed d'Ormesson, "that Pius XII's policy, which has consisted up to now of dealing carefully with the Fascist government and giving in to certain of its demands . . . does not seem, in Monsignor Tardini's eyes, to have had happy results."[29]

While anguish was the dominant mood behind the walls of Vatican City, and with it fears of what a Nazi-dominated Axis victory would bring, Italy's Catholic laity had little idea the church was anything other than fully supportive of the Axis war. Bishops and other influential prelates continued to urge the faithful to rally to the nation's armed cause.

The daily Catholic press joined in the chorus. As the summer of 1940 was coming to a close, Milan's Catholic daily published a big front-page editorial, "The New European Order," echoing the Fascist watchword. It incorporated many of the regime's main propaganda points: "There has been much talk in recent times of a new European order, which will come about the day in which, with their definitive victory, the two Powers of the Rome-Berlin Axis prevail over the Anglo-Saxon plutocracy and will finally be in a position to reestablish a peace based on justice." Axis victory, the Catholic paper predicted, would bring about the collapse of "the territorial political system based on the Peace Treaty that emerged from the world war of 1914–18 and on the League of Nations, ruled over by the two hegemonic Powers and by the Jewish-masonic international cliques."[30]

THE FECKLESS
ALLY

I
N THE THREE MONTHS SINCE ITALY'S DECLARATION OF WAR, THE
pope had said little publicly about it, but on September 4, 1940, he
gave voice to the modus vivendi he had reached with Mussolini's Fascist regime. Speaking at the Vatican to two thousand Catholic Action
leaders and assembled church dignitaries, the pontiff stressed the duty
all citizens had to their country. He quoted Romans 13:1: "Let every
person be subject to the governing authorities. For there is no authority except from God, and those that exist have been instituted by God."
He urged members of Catholic Action to "offer loyal and conscientious obedience to the civil Authorities and their legitimate prescrip-
tions." They should show that they were "not only the most fervent
Christians, but also perfect citizens, not exempt from the high duties
of national and social life together, lovers of the fatherland, and ready
as well even to give their life for it every time that the legitimate good
of the Country calls for this supreme sacrifice."

Warm applause greeted the pope's remarks.[1]

Mussolini had reason to be pleased not only by the pope's speech
but by the police reports describing the vocal support other churchmen were giving to the war effort. "The clergy in general," read one
such report, "and the parish priests in particular have offered praise-
worthy proof of patriotism ever since the declaration of war. In all the
correspondence they are sending members of the military they are,

yes, expressing the wish for world peace, but also for the victory of Italian arms."[2]

Some idea of the pope's thinking at the time comes from his remarks to the French ambassador. The London blitz had recently begun, with hundreds killed in the initial air attacks. The daily bombardment would continue to drive Londoners into shelters every night for many months to come. The blitz followed weeks of heavy German bombing of British military bases, airfields, and industrial plants. Commenting on the German assault, the pontiff expressed his admiration for the Britons' courage, especially praising the example the king and queen offered by refusing to leave the capital. Even if the Germans did succeed in occupying the country, thought the pope, the British would likely continue their struggle. Perhaps they would make Canada their center of operations. There they could closely coordinate their efforts with the United States.

The pope then turned to a familiar theme, lamenting Germany's continuing campaign of "de-Christianization," especially in Catholic Austria. On the other hand, the pope told the French ambassador, Italy was a completely different story. Mussolini's government had given the church a position of honor and made Catholic religious instruction obligatory in the nation's schools. Finally, the pope turned to what he saw as the greatest threat the church faced, expressing his alarm at the advance of Russian troops in Europe. A month earlier the Soviet Union had annexed Estonia, Latvia, and Lithuania, having earlier in the summer occupied portions of Romania. "One gets the impression," reported d'Ormesson, "that for him, communism is 'public enemy Number 1.'"[3]

WHILE VATICAN RELATIONS WITH the Italian government continued to be good, Roberto Farinacci's attacks on church figures in his front-page editorials in his newspaper, *Il Regime Fascista,* continued to anger Pius XII. If he wanted to upset the pope, he could do no better than the new target he chose late in the summer of 1940, Francis Spellman, whom the pope had appointed archbishop of New York the previous year. "He is a great friend of the Pope's to which his unexpected promotion was undoubtedly due," the British envoy to the Vatican observed. Indeed, Spellman was by far the member of the American church hierarchy whom Pius XII knew best. Not only had he served for years, beginning in the 1920s, in the Vatican Secretariat of State, but during Eugenio Pacelli's grand tour of the United States in 1936, he served as the then cardinal's companion and guide.[4]

In 1932 Pius XI had forced Spellman on William O'Connell, the strong-minded archbishop of Boston, to serve as his auxiliary bishop. To show his displeasure, O'Connell had refused to see his new number two for a month after his arrival. Seven years later, now in his new post in New York, the politically savvy Spellman won the confidence of the American president. Roosevelt came to see the talented and ambitious new archbishop as a valuable resource in garnering the support of America's large Catholic electorate. In a typical message, in March 1940, Spellman sent Roosevelt a handwritten letter telling him of his St. Patrick's Day speech "thanking you in the name of 21,000,000 Catholics for your logical and courageous action in sending Mr. Taylor to the Holy Father. . . . I took advantage of the occasion of a very important function with bishops in attendance from all over the US, 65 of them . . . to explain our gratitude to you." Along with his note he sent the president a series of press clippings covering his speech.[5]

In the wake of Farinacci's two editorials attacking him for his support of Roosevelt and charging him with being a stooge of America's Jews, Spellman registered his displeasure with Italy's consul general in New York. The archbishop's complaint was later relayed to Mussolini's son-in-law. The consul reported that Spellman had long been a friend of Italy and found it outrageous he should be attacked in the Fascist press.[6]

In late September the Duce received further news of the problems that the *Regime Fascista* attacks were creating for him in the United States. A group of prominent Italian American public officeholders and judges, presenting themselves as representing more than a million Catholics in New York City "of Italian race," sent a telegram to Rome. They called on the Duce "to stop Minister Farinacci in his campaign

Monsignor Francis Spellman, Archbishop of New York

against the Holy Father that wounds our Catholic sentiments and, provoking general resentment in America, increases antipathy toward
Italy."[7]

The pope himself soon made his unhappiness known. At a September 22 audience, Bernardo Attolico found Pius XII in an unusually
combative mood. Italy's ambassador had come with a request to make.
Mussolini wanted the pope to raise the archdiocese of Bari, facing the
Adriatic atop Italy's heel, to the status of a cardinal's seat. As the ambassador explained, the Duce wanted the port city to become the "ring
linking west to east, the instrument of Italian expansion in the Mediterranean and beyond." The pope seemed in no mood to discuss the
question. He would study the proposal, he said impatiently, but he had

something else on his mind, an article that had appeared the previous day in a Roman newspaper.

"I had barely received assurance that all polemics in *Regime Fascista* against my person and against the Holy See would be stopped," said the pope, "when the polemics are reopened by the *Popolo di Roma*. This pains me. I deceived myself and harbored the illusion for all the past year that relations between Church and State in Italy could be perfect. This was my dream, the dream that has inspired all my speeches and all my actions."

By way of example of the support he had lent the regime since the war began, the pope cited his speech earlier in the month to members of Italian Catholic Action. There, he told Mussolini's ambassador,

> in a perfectly national setting, I reminded the faithful that it is their duty to sacrifice for the Fatherland, even, if necessary, with their life. I have neglected nothing on my part, and I would be disposed to do even more. I reduced *L'Osservatore Romano* to a publication that now no one reads. In return, they feel free to insult me publicly without—even if they suspend the campaign for a few days—giving me any public satisfaction. They abuse me because I do not respond. But one day I might indeed speak and then I would speak without any worry for the human consequences.

While saying all this, the pope sat with one hand resting on a large folder filled with the offensive newspaper clippings.

Taken aback by the pope's uncharacteristically aggressive tone, Attolico tried to turn the pontiff's attention to happier matters. Mussolini, he told him, hoped to have Italy replace Britain as the protector of the Holy Land and so was working to provoke an Arab revolt there.

The pope was in no mood to be distracted. As Attolico tried to engage him in a conversation about how the Italian government could cooperate with the Vatican in managing Palestine's Holy Places, the pope interrupted. "Yes, this too would be possible, but only in an atmosphere of harmony and reciprocal understanding, which is now lacking."

The pontiff returned to his lament about how he had deceived himself by dreaming of complete harmony with Mussolini's regime. "The Pope said all this," Attolico later recalled, "in a tone of bitterness, no longer that of resignation as before but as that of a person who is now ready for the worst." It was crucial, Attolico advised his government, for Italy's press to avoid any more criticism of the Vatican and find an occasion in the near future to heap praise on Pius XII.[8]

Told of the pope's unhappiness, Mussolini instructed his ambassador to return immediately to calm the Holy Father. He was to let the pope know that he was committed to respecting both the letter and the spirit of the concordat, including its provision making insults to the pontiff a criminal offense. He would also give new instructions to have the press attacks stopped. But along with these carrots came the stick: the pope was to be told of a disturbing report Mussolini had received. Several local Catholic Action groups were involved in unacceptable political activity. It went without saying that government action might be needed.

Meeting with the ambassador only five days after their previous encounter, the pope reacted to the Duce's complaint with what, for the highly controlled pontiff, was practically an explosion of anger. If there were any such incidents of inappropriate behavior by Catholic Action groups, said the pope, he was unaware of them. Again, he cited his recent allocution to the leaders of Catholic Action, calling on their members to be ready to sacrifice their lives for their country. "And here," reported the ambassador, the pope's "eyes were almost sparkling, thanks to the intimate pleasure produced by recalling the 'burst of enthusiasm' that these words evinced in the crowd."

All that might be true, countered Attolico, who was in fact sympathetic with the pontiff's views, but he insisted there might still be isolated Catholic Action groups harboring "nostalgic adversaries of the totalitarian regimes." If so, replied the pope, "give me the specific cases. Give me the concrete facts, and I won't hesitate for a single moment to remedy them."

"I would like the relations between us, beyond simply being those of reciprocal understanding, to be based on trust," said the pope, now in a more conciliatory mood. "One should not always believe the information that one receives. If there is something that, in the opinion of the Italian government, needs to be corrected, tell me clearly, openly. I will always be very pleased, and our relations can only gain from it."

Expressing his pleasure at the Duce's restatement of his commitment to the concordat, a key component of the 1929 Lateran Accords, the pope recalled that it was his older brother, Francesco, who had negotiated them. As he spoke of his brother, who had died several years earlier, the pope's voice softened. Francesco, said the pope, had praised the Duce's "precious contribution" in crafting the historic accords and had said what a great and intelligent man he was. His brother had regarded Mussolini not only "with the greatest esteem, but also the deepest admiration." Warming to his subject, the pope added that no one should forget all the Duce had done for the church, giving civil effect to religious marriages, introducing religious instruction in the public schools, and so many other things. The pope, Attolico was relieved to report, had clearly calmed down.[9]

ITALY'S CATHOLIC PRESS CONTINUED to offer strong support for the war. In early October a *Civiltà Cattolica* article declared that the rebirth of an Italian empire would strengthen the Roman Catholic Church's influence in the world. "The article," the Italian ambassador reported to Ciano, "took its inspiration directly from the Duce's words." Indeed, it quoted Mussolini by name, expressing support for the rationale he had given for the war, achieving a "Europe of justice for all," and followed the Duce in blaming the war on the evil wrought by the Versailles Treaty. "I would be grateful," Attolico told Mussolini's son-in-law in conclusion, "if these articles . . . were made known to the Duce."[10]

Italy's Catholic daily newspapers meanwhile continued to do their part in promoting the idea that the Axis cause was the church's own.

The country's most prominent Catholic daily, *L'Avvenire d'Italia,* owned by Catholic Action and jointly supported by the ecclesiastical hierarchy of four regions of the northeast of the country, published a stream of praise of the regime and its war aims. Raimondo Manzini, the paper's director—whom years later Pope John XXIII would appoint director of *L'Osservatore Romano*—penned a front-page editorial praising the latest group of volunteers going off to fight and chronicled all the important changes brought about in Italy by two decades of Fascism, replacing a liberal society with one respectful of authority.[11]

IN MID-SEPTEMBER 1940 MUSSOLINI'S troops based in Italy's Libyan colony crossed into Egypt and quickly captured the small Mediterranean town of Sidi Barrani, about a hundred kilometers east of the Libyan border, the first step in the effort to wrest the Suez Canal from the British. The approaching confrontation seemed a mismatch, with a quarter-million Italian troops based in Libya arrayed against perhaps 36,000 British troops stationed in Egypt. Emboldened, the Duce decided to open a second front, turning his sights to Greece.[12]

While Hitler had supported Mussolini's decision to march on Egypt, he was not pleased by this new development. The Führer's own long-term plan was to defeat the Soviet Union after he dispatched Britain. Stirring up war in the Balkan Peninsula now would, he feared, be an invitation to have the Soviet Union move troops in that direction. Making the invasion even less palatable to Hitler, the head of Greece's government, Ioannis Metaxas, was a pro-Nazi dictator who had studied in Germany. The Führer decided to travel to Italy to try to dissuade his Italian comrade.[13]

Hitler's nine-car train arrived at Florence's train station at midmorning on October 28. Mussolini waited at the platform, a military band behind him. When the train stopped, the Duce, in an ebullient mood, waved his arms as if conducting the band as it played its musical tribute. The Führer leaned out of his window and forced himself to

Mussolini and Hitler in Florence, October 28, 1940

smile as he watched Mussolini walk along the red carpet that had been laid out for the welcome. "Führer," said the Duce, "we are on the march. My troops victoriously entered Greece at six this morning."

Hitler, who realized he had come too late, remained silent.

"Don't worry," said Mussolini, "in two weeks, it will all be over."[14]

THE GREEK FIASCO

TALY'S INVASION OF GREECE RAPIDLY TURNED INTO A FIASCO. AT Greece's mountainous border with Albania, torrential rains transformed the dirt roads into mud traps, and bad weather prevented both air support and the landing of supply ships. For four days Italian soldiers slogged onward, crossing swollen streams and rivers as fallen trees and drowned sheep swept by. Much to the soldiers' surprise, Greek artillery soon began shelling their positions. After briefly capturing a handful of Greek villages near the border, the Italians were surrounded by Greek troops assisted by hostile locals. The weather became even worse, as rain turned to snow, and temperatures plunged. Weapons and feet froze, and at night the shivering soldiers huddled together beneath piles of blankets in the holes they had dug. On November 14 a full-scale Greek counteroffensive began. Within days the Italians' modest gains were wiped out, as they hurried in embarrassing retreat back into Albanian territory. To make matters worse, British bombers flying from the aircraft carrier HMS *Illustrious* succeeded in sinking a not insignificant part of the Italian naval fleet, anchored across the Adriatic at the Italian port of Taranto.[1]

Hitler was not pleased. "The situation which has now arisen," the Führer wrote the Duce, "has very grave psychological and military repercussions." The Italian attack had given the British an excuse to establish air bases in Greece, which now threatened the Romanian oil fields on which the Germans depended. It also threatened to draw the Russians into the Balkans. In his reply, the Duce assured Hitler that he was readying new divisions "to annihilate Greece," adding, in a note that would have brought little comfort to his countrymen south of Rome, that he was unconcerned about British bombings of southern Italian cities, as they contained no industrial plants of any importance.[2]

For Hitler's war effort, Italy's unfolding catastrophe in Greece would soon appear as only a temporary setback, but for Mussolini it marked a major turning point. Until then, it seemed to many Italians that he had gone from victory to victory, bringing the country ever greater respect in the world. He had conquered Ethiopia and declared the birth of a new empire. He had sent Italians to Spain and helped win Franco's victory. He had invaded Albania and, in a matter of days, and with little bloodshed, added King of Albania to Victor Emmanuel's titles. Few Italians had questioned their military's ability to prevail over Greece, regarded as a small, third-rate power. Now, for the first time, confidence in the Duce began to waver. When, over the next few weeks, the British began a successful counterattack on Italy's troops in Egypt, the shock of defeat gave way to national embarrassment and disorientation, then to despair.[3]

The Greek disaster would be a turning point for another reason as well. It marked the beginning of the end of Mussolini's conceit that he was fighting a "parallel war" alongside his German ally, with the Italians expanding their empire in the Mediterranean while the Germans took the lead farther north. The Italian military, never taken very seriously by the German military command, would have to be repeatedly rescued by the Germans, and both the Allies and the Germans would come to view Italy as the soft underbelly of the Axis.[4]

UNSURPRISINGLY, MARSHAL PÉTAIN, LEADER of the French collaborationist government, wanted to have an emissary to the pope he could trust, and the outspokenly anti-Fascist d'Ormesson was certainly not such a man. In his final report, in late October 1940, the outgoing ambassador, a perceptive observer, recorded his impressions of the pope and of the mood prevailing in the Vatican five months after Mussolini's declaration of war.

When Pius XII was elected, d'Ormesson recalled, many had thought he would simply continue his predecessor's policies. After all, he had not only been Pius XI's secretary of state, he had chosen the pope's name as his own. But these predictions had proven false. "In reality," wrote the ambassador, "Pius XI and Pius XII were very different men. In the place of a robust mountaineer from Milan came a more passive Roman bourgeois." Pius XII "is good, fine, sensitive, it is even said oversensitive. But in my opinion, he lacks personality, or more exactly he lacks strong character." Pacelli had spent his entire adult life as a Vatican diplomat and had never held a pastoral position. This had left him, thought the ambassador, with habits of reserve, of prudence, of finding "balance" that led him to avoid offering any harsh words of criticism. Coupled with his taste for what d'Ormesson dubbed a "beau style" of florid speech, this robbed his words of any clarity.

"The Pope seems to me above all to be a conservative of a monarchical stamp," observed d'Ormesson, "enemy of all demagogueries, whether they be communist or National Socialist (but of the communists above all). . . . He openly collaborates with fascism and, although sometimes treated roughly by Mr. Farinacci, and, above all, treated with great indifference by Mr. Mussolini, he seizes every opportunity to show his loyalty to the Fascist government. He had not a single word, nor gesture, even an indirect one, to criticize Italy for its entry into the war." Pius XI, thought the Frenchman, would have publicly condemned the Axis aggression, but the horrific violence simply served to drive Pius XII back into his shell. All this played into Mussolini's strength, for if ever there was a master of exploiting the weaknesses of others, it was the Duce, and Mussolini had become an expert in manipulating the pope to get what he wanted.

The pope's refusal to take a public stand had continually frustrated the French diplomat. His speeches, since the war began, had been devoid of specific references to what was happening in the world. "Each time I approached the Pope and spoke to him of the future condition of Europe, I was always struck by the lack of clarity of his responses. . . . Obviously, he did not want to compromise himself, much less to commit himself." It was crucial, the ambassador believed, to understand that the Vatican made a "total distinction between Germany and Italy, the latter power continuing to benefit from a very favorable prejudice." He explained, "Despite fascism . . . despite Monsieur Mussolini's own flippant attitude toward the Holy See (and this attitude is total), the Holy See remains and will always remain infinitely favorably disposed to Italy. . . . They are certainly conscious of its faults, and even of its villainy, but they are always ready to find excuses for it." By contrast, the prelates offered no such excuses for the German regime. Not a trace of "Nazi-philia" was to be found in the Vatican.

Only one development could alter this picture, thought the ambassador. Should Germany renounce its pact with the Soviet Union and turn against it, all might change. Italian Catholics would rally enthusiastically to the anti-Bolshevik cause, and the war would become "a sort of crusade." "Bolshevism being the principal enemy for the Church, Germany, in crushing it, would quickly regain sympathy and prestige at the Vatican. . . . In such a scenario, the Axis would appear as the 'secular arm' of the Church." But for the moment, the prevailing attitude toward Germany in the Vatican, reported d'Ormesson, was fear: fear of German power and of the fate of the church in a Europe under the thumb of a triumphant Germany.[5]

The pope received d'Ormesson for a final audience on October 29, 1940. Mussolini had met with Hitler in Florence the previous day, the same day he had launched his invasion of Greece. For Hitler, it had been the last stop on a train trip that had stops for talks with Marshal Pétain in France and with Spain's new dictator, Francisco Franco. Hitler had been disappointed by all three of the meetings. Pétain, he thought, was old and weak, and Franco evasive about joining the Axis. Mussolini had stubbornly gone ahead with his attempt to take Greece despite the Führer's misgivings.[6]

The French envoy was eager to get the pope's reaction to the Italian invasion of Greece, but he found that "as was the case every time that

Italy's behavior came into question," the pope was reluctant to say anything. "One gets the strong sense," reported the ambassador, "that the Pope has such a fear that a phrase, a word of his might be repeated and escape the walls of Vatican City, that he prefers to remain silent, and merely nod and look up, raising his eyes to the sky."

The next day Pius XII hosted an audience attended by two hundred Italian soldiers, along with the priests who served as their chaplains. Blessing them and their "precious Fatherland," he praised them for serving their country with "such faith, loyalty, and courage." Attolico happily reported all this to Ciano, noting that the pope had made his remarks soon after learning the news of Italy's invasion of Greece.[7]

REMAINING SILENT WAS NOT without its risks for the pope. In early November Cardinal Maglione received a long memo from Kazimierz Papée, the Polish ambassador to the Holy See, still hoping the pope would speak out against the horrors that the Nazis were visiting on his country. The Germans, Papée told him, were using the fact that Pius XII had received Hitler's foreign minister, Ribbentrop, in March, months after the invasion of Poland, to claim the pope approved of Germany's action. After all the outrages the Nazis had committed against the Catholic clergy and church institutions in Poland, people were asking why he had still said nothing. Many Poles wondered why Vatican Radio, while occasionally speaking of Soviet misdeeds in Poland, had remained silent about the German occupation of the country, and *L'Osservatore Romano* made no mention at all of the German assault on Poland.[8]

The ambassador's plea had little effect. On November 10, in an event the Italian ambassador reported on at length to Ciano and Mussolini, the pope hosted five thousand youth members of Italian Catholic Action. At the special mass held in St. Peter's Basilica following the pope's remarks, Monsignor Colli, bishop of Parma and national leader of Catholic Action, addressed the crowd. Quoting liberally from the pope, the bishop urged them to support the war. "The youths of Italian Catholic Action," Colli told them, "do not forget—something which the Holy Father continues to urge on them—that 'we have here too a Fatherland that is dear to us, to which we owe a cult of faithful love.'" All good Italians, the bishop told them, quoting the pope, were obliged to "serve it as 'perfect citizens . . . ready even to give our lives every time that the legitimate good of the country requires this supreme sacrifice.'"⁹

The church continued to signal its support for Italy's Fascist regime in many ways. The unexpected death of Mussolini's longtime police chief, Arturo Bocchini, a man who every morning brought him the latest informant reports to review, produced the latest signs of the close ties between church and state. Rome's Catholic daily, *L'Avvenire,* offered the good news that Bocchini had still been conscious and filled "with a feeling of great piety" when his parish priest gave him the last rites. Monsignor Borgongini, the papal nuncio, had been present at his deathbed, bringing the main architect of Italy's police state the comfort of the pope's blessing. Archbishop Bartolomasi, head of the military chaplaincy and outspoken shill for the Fascist regime, presided over Bocchini's funeral mass at one of Rome's historic churches.¹⁰

CRITICIZED FOR HIS SEEMING invisibility amid the drama engulfing Europe, the pope decided he needed to do something to appear in the public eye. He planned a special mass honoring the victims of war to be broadcast from St. Peter's. Virtually all of the twenty-four cardinals resident in Rome were present for the ceremony held on Sunday, November 24, 1940, and a large crowd filled the pews. Following a long disquisition on Christ's teachings, sprinkled liberally with references to verses from the New Testament, the pope turned to the crux of his message. It was crucial, he said, that an order be restored among the world's peoples "that is more equitable and universal, based on that justice which calms the passions." It was an order, he explained, "that tends to attribute to all peoples, in tranquility, in freedom and in security, the part that is due each of them in this world."¹¹

While the pope had understandably lamented the suffering caused by war, observed the Italian ambassador in reporting the speech, he "knew how to find the right equilibrium." Indeed, there were parts of the speech, Attolico suggested, that the Axis could use to show the pontiff's support for their cause, including his statement that a more equal division of the earth's riches was needed. Pius XII had also again praised the soldiers for heroically fulfilling their duties, even to the point of sacrificing their lives for their Fatherland. In its coverage of the event, Mussolini's own newspaper highlighted much the same points. Farinacci's paper likewise gave glowing coverage to the speech, quoting the same lines.[12]

Disappointed but not surprised, Britain's envoy attributed the pope's words to the fact that he was "anxious and cautious by temperament," and "desirous of avoiding any charge of political partisanship so as to be in a position to exercise his influence when the moment comes for initiating peace negotiations." Pius XII, he noted, remained "firmly convinced of German victory."[13]

A NEW WORLD ORDER

F OR ITALY'S JEWS, THE HUMILIATIONS WERE ENDLESS. ONE SUMMER
day—to cite a typical story—parents of a young family from
Rome's old ghetto decided to escape the sweltering city and give their
children a treat. They went to a beach resort at nearby Ostia that they
had often frequented in the past. When they arrived, the proprietor,
who had in earlier years welcomed them warmly with a smile, now
had an unmistakably severe look on his face. "What do you want?" he
asked brusquely. The Jewish father had barely begun to respond with a
"Buongiorno" when the proprietor cut him short. "Don't you read the
papers?" he shouted. "Beginning this past year, people of the Jewish
race are not allowed in this establishment. You can't come here again!
Go away!" Rather than subject his family to further embarrassment as
other beachgoers looked silently on, he took the hands of his crest-
fallen children and returned to the city.

With their children ejected from the country's public schools in
1938, Jews in Rome and in other Italian cities having sizable Jewish
populations created new private Jewish schools. There was no lack of
potential instructors, as the country's Jewish schoolteachers and university professors had all been fired. Now cast out of many of the jobs
that had supported them—the ban on selling used clothing hit the Jews
of more humble station in Rome particularly hard—many struggled
daily to afford food. A typical account tells of a nine-year-old boy
from Rome's old Jewish ghetto selling individual cigarette-rolling pa-

pers outside bars to help support his family. To prevent Catholics with Jewish-sounding names from being unfairly targeted, the government allowed them to have them changed.[1]

For over two years, Italians had been subjected to a barrage of newspaper and magazine stories warning them that Jews were their enemies, that on the one side were the true Italians, Aryan avatars of Fascism and Catholicism, and on the other stood the evil Jews. Indeed, the distinction between Aryan and non-Aryan in Italy was based for the most part on whether a person was Christian or Jewish.

In introducing his "racial" campaign two years earlier, Mussolini had worried about the possibility of church opposition. In the first months of the campaign, which had coincided with the last months of Pius XI's papacy, the pope's rebukes had enraged him. Pius XI's opposition to the anti-Jewish "racial" laws threatened not only to weaken public support for the antisemitic campaign but also to diminish public enthusiasm for the dictator himself. Now, as the end of 1940 neared, the last thing Mussolini needed was for his increasingly harsh campaign against Italy's Jews to do anything to undermine Italians' support for his regime. Fortunately for the Duce, since Pius XII's election, he had little grounds for complaint.

The Vatican newspaper reported the ever more oppressive racial laws without comment. "Yesterday," noted a March 1940 article, "the deadline passed for canceling from the rolls those professionals considered to belong to the Jewish race who practice the professions of doctor, surgeon, pharmacist, obstetrician, lawyer, public prosecutor, public defender, shopkeeper, accountant, engineer, architect, chemist, agronomist, surveyor, agricultural consultant and industrial consultant. No delays have been granted."[2]

In the late 1930s many Jews escaping persecution farther north in Europe—from Germany, Austria, and Czechoslovakia—had fled to Italy. Five days after Italy's entry into the war, the government ordered all foreign Jews arrested and moved to "appropriate concentration camps currently being constructed." Soon thousands of Jews who had sought refuge in Italy would be confined in such camps. In all approximately two hundred camps were established, scattered throughout the country, some housing not only Jews but others deemed "enemy aliens" or ethnic undesirables.[3]

Since the beginning of the racial campaign in 1938, many of Italy's Jews had tried to escape persecution by getting baptized, but while church doctrine made no distinction between Jews who had converted before the racial laws went into effect and those who had been baptized after, Fascist measures did so, provoking a litany of church complaint. Typical was a letter that the cardinal responsible for the Sacred Apostolic Penitentiary★ sent Monsignor Montini in August. It told of a young Jewish woman who had been baptized and who now sought to marry a Catholic. The cardinal called on Montini to help win state recognition of the marriage. The reply sent to the cardinal was simple: "there is, unfortunately, nothing to be done. . . . Ever since the racial law began to be promulgated, the Holy See tried, but in vain, to have the civil effects of mixed marriages recognized whenever both newlyweds were of Catholic religion. The Government responded with a flat refusal."[4]

Despite official church dogma that there was nothing "racial" separating Jews from Catholics, attitudes that smacked of racism had long been found in the Vatican, so that Jews who were baptized remained racially marked. The prelates of the Vatican readily picked up the distinction that identified Christians as Aryans and Jews as non-Aryans. We can see some of these attitudes reflected at the time in the pope's handling of a gift of $125,000 given him by the American United Jewish Appeal to use in relief work to aid war refugees fleeing religious persecution. The pope used a good part of the American Jewish fund to support Catholics who had been Jewish before being baptized, but he also used it to aid an "Aryan" Austrian Catholic couple as well. When the concern was raised in the Secretariat of State that the funds might have been intended to be used only for "non-Aryans," Monsignor Tardini looked further into the matter.

In his subsequent report, Tardini quoted from the auxiliary bishop

★ The Apostolic Penitentiary is a tribunal of the Holy See, responsible for providing "absolution in the name of the pontiff on grave matters presented at court for the pope's opinion." Noonan 1986, p. 84.

of Chicago's transmittal letter of the gift. The bishop, wrote Tardini, had specified that the funds were to be used to aid the victims of persecution "without regard to race or religion." And so, advised the monsignor, "these funds can certainly be used to aid some Aryans." He added, "if up to now those who were Jews by race but Catholic by religion have been preferred, there is no need to continue on this path." Tellingly, while the above note is found in the Holy See's authoritative volumes of Vatican documents dealing with aid to war victims, the published version omits an uncomfortable phrase by one of the prelates closest to the pope, and a man who would become Pope John XXIII's secretary of state. Next to "Jews by race but Catholic by religion," Tardini had commented parenthetically that such "Catholics" had, "by the nature of their action more honored . . . their race than their Catholicism." In the place of the phrase in the Vatican publication is a square bracket containing three dots and a footnote: "Personal notes omitted."5

In November Italy's minister of popular culture, in charge of the government's antisemitic propaganda campaign, asked Attolico to update him on the Vatican's position on the racial laws. The ambassador offered a comforting reply: "As for racism, it is true that certain of the theories that have been advanced are condemned (at least implicitly) by the Church, but they are only those theories that contrast with [church] dogma. A racism that is limited to the biological sphere is not condemned." As for the racial laws themselves, observed the ambassador, "The Church cannot approve of any 'persecution' against the Jews, but it is not opposed to prudent measures, aimed at rendering the Jews harmless in relation to the society in which they live. Indeed, that is what the Church itself did by instituting the 'ghettoes' and with other measures."6

All this was welcome news for the propaganda minister, for one of the government's favorite arguments in promoting public support for the racial laws was identifying them with the restrictions the popes had long thought necessary to impose on Jews when they had the power to do so as rulers of the Papal States. The popes had confined the Jews to

ghettoes, forbidden them from practicing professions or owning property, and sought to isolate them from the Christians around them.
Farinacci repeatedly published articles recounting this history, liberally quoting from past popes and past church councils, as did the rest of
the Italian press.

Meanwhile in France, the Pétain regime was beginning to enact anti-
Jewish measures of its own. An October 1940 law duplicated many of the
measures Mussolini had earlier put in place in Italy, excluding Jews from
teaching in the public schools, ejecting them from the civil service, judi-
ciary, military, and journalism. In response, the French Catholic press
offered similar support. In a late November article titled "Are the Jews
cursed by God?" the venerable *La Croix* took up the theme widely found
in Italian Catholic publications: while the church opposed "an overly
sectarian anti-Semitism," it had long recognized the need to act to protect Christian Europe from Jews' pernicious influence.[7]

WHILE THE VATICAN WAS causing Mussolini no problems, the news
from the battlefront was. Winter having descended in the mountains
of Greece, frostbite was proving as damaging as bullets to the poorly
outfitted Italian soldiers. The news from North Africa was no better.
The Italian troops whose capture of the coastal towns of Egypt had
earlier so excited the Duce were now being pushed back over the Libyan border, and by early January 1941, 130,000 Italian troops would
surrender to a smaller British force.[8]

The reverses were producing a wave of public unhappiness with the
war, prompted by the contrast between the rhetoric of Fascist invinci-
bility featured in the nation's press and the stories being told by soldiers
returning from the front. As would become his habit, Mussolini blamed
the military command and dismissed Marshal Pietro Badoglio, head of
the Italian military and hero of the Ethiopian war. The ever-tighter
rationing of basic foodstuffs and coal did nothing to help the public
mood, which America's military attaché in Rome captured well in a
mid-December 1940 report:

Faced with the prospect of a long war with the outcome in doubt the morale of the Italian people is exceedingly low. The successes of the Greek Army in Albania have profoundly shocked the whole country. The Greek Army was unheard of by the people at large, whereas the Italian Army over a period of 15 years had been played up as one of the world's great military machines. Therefore, the events in Albania have left them bewildered and uncomprehending.[9]

In hopes that Italians might rise up against the Duce, British prime minister Churchill took to the radio to broadcast a Christmas Eve appeal. One man, he said, was responsible for taking the country to war against Britain and leading the country to ruin. "It is all one man—one man, who, against the crown and royal family of Italy, against the Pope and all the authority of the Vatican and of the Roman Catholic Church, against the wishes of the Italian people who had no lust for this war; one man has arrayed the trustees and inheritors of ancient Rome upon the side of the ferocious pagan barbarians."[10]

Whether many Italians were brave enough, or motivated enough, to risk arrest for listening to an enemy radio broadcast, we do not know. It was another Christmas Eve speech that dominated the Italian press, as amid the drama of the war, all awaited Pius XII's annual Christmas address to the Sacred College of Cardinals. If Italians were looking for some concrete guidance from the pope, however, they were disappointed. As had by now become his practice, he went on at length at a level of abstraction and abstruse ecclesiastical language that flew over the heads of all but the most erudite church intellectuals. In the words of a Fascist police informant, "The Pope could have said more by saying less. . . . The great prolixity of Pius XII's speeches comes at the expense of their substance."[11]

After speaking at length in this fashion, the pontiff finally did turn his attention to the war. Here he developed two themes. He first devoted considerable verbiage to self-congratulation, as would become a standard feature of his wartime oratory, recalling all he had done to try to prevent the war from breaking out and then all the humanitarian relief efforts the Vatican was making to relieve the suffering caused by the war. The title he gave to the next section of his speech—"The premises of a just and lasting peace"—borrowed the phrase Mussolini was fond of using, and the pope followed this with a section bearing a phrase likewise claimed by Mussolini as his own: "aspirations for a new order." When the pope reached his conclusion, he at last used language that was uncharacteristically plain: "Among contrasting systems [of government] . . . the Church cannot be called upon to make itself a partisan of one course rather than another."[12]

Attolico immediately sent Ciano news of the speech, praising the pope's words, highlighting his "affirmation of the necessity of a new world order," underlining these last words, and suggesting which of the pope's phrases they might best be able to exploit in press coverage of his address.[13]

ONCE THE CHRISTMAS RITES were concluded, the pope began to receive the ambassadors to the Holy See for their annual New Year's audiences. It was the first time for France's new ambassador, Léon Bérard, recently sent by Marshal Pétain to replace d'Ormesson. Sixty-four years old, a lawyer and an academic, a devout Catholic, a conservative, and a former French education minister, Bérard was as reserved and cautious a man as his predecessor was outgoing and outspoken. Representing a government that was collaborating with the Germans, he would never be comfortable being confined to the same Vatican City hostel that housed the ambassadors of the enemies of the Axis.[14]

Their first encounter, earlier in the month, consisted in good part of the pope offering his praise for Marshal Pétain, pleased by all the ways his government was bringing back privileges the church had lost decades earlier in France. Bérard had himself been pleased that the pope proved so understanding of the new government's need to have "relations of collaboration" with the Germans, as the pope shared his oft-repeated observation that the Germans had many good qualities. That said, the pope made clear that he was very concerned by what he saw as the Nazis' antireligious doctrine and their anti-church measures.[15]

At his own New Year's audience with Pius XII on the same day, Italy's ambassador took the opportunity to thank the pontiff for his recent Christmas address. It had, Attolico said, made an excellent impression, citing especially the pope's condemnation of "ignorant and depressing pessimism." The ambassador expressed the hope that the pope's words would make Italians realize that at a time of war it was the church's role to strengthen public morale. "I found the Pontiff," Attolico observed, "agreeing perfectly with this concept."[16]

Indeed, the war did seem to be going well for the Axis powers, despite Italy's own military failures. On the last day of 1940, Monsignor Borgongini, the nuncio to the Italian government, offered the pope's New Year's greetings to the king. Victor Emmanuel told the nuncio he didn't think the British could hold out much longer, for amid the relentless bombing, London was suffering "immense disasters." While some were worried that America might enter the war, there was little reason to be concerned. The Americans seemed unlikely to want to do so, and even if they did, the king assured him, with German U-boats patrolling the Atlantic, they would never succeed in landing troops on the continent.[17]

HITLER TO
THE RESCUE

B Y THE TIME 1941 DAWNED, ITALY'S MILITARY HAD BECOME THE laughingstock of Europe. "Even before the war," read an early January German analysis, "it was the firm conviction of the German General Staff that not too much could be expected from the Italian Army." Hitler's generals had had higher hopes for Italy's air force and navy, but they too would disappoint. The air force had hardly been heard from, and as for Mussolini's much-vaunted navy, after only half a year of war, it "has relinquished naval supremacy completely to the English, both in the Mediterranean and in the Red Sea—actually without a fight." Anthony Eden, the UK's foreign secretary, referring to the recent surrender by Italian troops in North Africa, quipped, "Never had so much been surrendered by so many to so few." Back in Italy, the last of the large colored plaster maps set up in town squares throughout the country, with movable pegs to show the forward position of Italian troops, were being discreetly removed.[1]

Following the string of Italian military reverses abroad, and the sporadic British bombardments of the country's cities, public opinion was souring on the war. While there were still relatively few victims of the bombings, Italians found the lack of air defenses astonishing after years of regime boasts of invulnerability.[2] Mussolini's ambassador to the Holy See brought Cardinal Maglione, the pope's secretary of state, a list of parish bulletins seized by the police on the grounds they were undermining public morale. Maglione replied he had recently discussed the problem with Pius XII, and as the ambassador later reported, "the Pontiff himself had recognized the necessity of an intervention."[3]

After a new appeal by the bishop heading Italian Catholic Action for support of Italy's military efforts, the director of Italy's most important Catholic daily, *L'Avvenire d'Italia,* devoted a huge front-page editorial to hailing the pontiff's presumed approval for the Axis war: "People are asking today for a better division of land and wealth. Pius XII has said many times that this ideal is legitimate." Archbishop Bartolomasi, head of the military chaplains, added his voice to assure Italians of the pope's blessing for the Axis cause. He sent the chaplains a circular, featured in the Catholic press as well, praising the value of their work "in these days of a war that must, at any cost, be won. It must be won . . . for a better division of the wealth . . . for a better understanding and realization of the Gospels' ethical-social principles." All this, proclaimed the archbishop, reflected "the intention of the Holy Father's august Christmas speech to the College of Cardinals."[4]

IN THE WAKE OF Italy's continuing reverses in Greece and North Africa, Galeazzo Ciano was in a bad mood, as Monsignor Borgongini, the papal nuncio, discovered when he went to see him. The nuncio had come to ask for the foreign minister's help. Due to wartime rationing, the Vatican was encountering difficulties getting its own food supplies, as even basic items like bread, olive oil, and pasta were becoming scarce. He suggested that Ciano might have a word about the matter with his father-in-law.

"That would not be in your interest," Ciano replied, "because he has recently been talking to me, in a tone I have never heard before, in a rather violent way against the Vatican." Ciano explained that he was doing his best to calm his father-in-law down. "I do it happily for you as a fascist, as an Italian, and as a Catholic, and I would like to have the Holy Father know it. However, at moments like this it becomes difficult to do even for me." What had prompted the Duce's ire, said Ciano, was a recent police informant report claiming that a clique revolving around the director of *L'Osservatore Romano* was secretly conspiring against the regime. It would be well to be careful, Ciano warned. "I wouldn't want the Duce to take some disagreeable action. You know his style when he intervenes."[5]

Ciano's mood was not helped by the fact that his father-in-law, in an effort to tamp down public grumbling about the war, had decided to send the government's ministers to the front as ordinary military officers. Ciano himself was only partially spared, ordered to go south to the air force headquarters in Bari. A police informant from inside Vatican City offered a glimpse of the souring public mood: "Catholic circles are becoming increasingly impressed by the continually growing cost of living and the difficulty of finding many basic foodstuffs. Naturally all this leads to a pronounced unhappiness and sharp criticisms against the Government's policies."[6]

With signs that public support for the war was weakening, Father Gemelli, rector of the Catholic University of Milan, published a proposal to build up support for the war effort in the national magazine devoted to the nation's clergy. He called on every parish in the country to hold a special Mass on Sunday, February 2, 1941, to pray for Axis victory. Accepting the sacrifices imposed by the war, and praying regularly, declared Gemelli, "make us await with faithful certainty the hour of God and brings closer the dawn of victory." The country's Catholic newspapers offered enthusiastic support for the initiative, as did Italy's cardinals. The resulting ceremonies, held in churches and cathedrals throughout the nation, were deemed a great success, as parishioners crowded into the pews behind the black-shirted local luminaries of the Fascist Party who filled the front rows.[7]

Yet the war, or at least the Italian part of it, continued to go badly. In early February British ships entered the waters outside Genoa uncontested and, with their planes circling overhead to identify targets, subjected the port city to sustained naval bombardment. Genoa's historic cathedral came close to being destroyed when an errant projectile pierced its muraled wall and skidded to a stop unexploded along the marble floor. Another shell hit one of the city's hospitals, killing seventeen inside. Although half of the projectiles fell harmlessly into the ocean, twenty-nine of the fifty-five ships anchored there were damaged or sunk. In all, well over a hundred *genovesi* were killed, and many more injured. The propaganda ministry told the nation's newspapers to omit any details of the destruction. They were encouraged instead to feature stories about President Roosevelt's alleged Jewish ancestry.[8]

Although news of the bombardment of Genoa was kept out of the Italian press, it circulated through the country, further depressing public morale. Mussolini uncharacteristically acknowledged the setbacks in a speech later in the month, but he offered hope that the country's fortunes were about to improve, no doubt based on the messages he was getting from Hitler that help was on the way. Indeed, in mid-February the German general Erwin Rommel, the "Desert Fox," arrived in North Africa and launched an offensive against the British. There is "a growing conviction," Ambassador Phillips wrote President Roosevelt, "that the war will be over by September next with a complete German victory."

Recognizing that Italy's fate depended on its obtaining help from Germany, public opinion toward the German troops who were increasingly streaming into the country was also changing. The Germans were helping shore up Italy's defenses and stopping in the country on their way to North Africa. It seemed, reported the American ambassador, "that the Italians, rather than resenting their presence, are beginning to be grateful to them for helping them out of a bad situation." Pius XII, too, was hosting more German military men, who were eager to boast of having had an audience with the pope. "On February 12," read one police informant report from Vatican City, "the Holy Father received a group of German officers and soldiers in private audience. He met with them for a while speaking with them in German. This audience, like the other one a few days ago, has made a great impression in the Vatican, and is being commented on favorably as one of the many signs of a German-Vatican rapprochement."[9]

But in his audience with Pius XII in early March, the French chargé d'affaires found the pope more depressed than ever about what the future would bring. The combination of German air supremacy and its lethal submarine blockade was proving, or so it seemed, fatal to the

British cause. The likelihood that the United States could or would intervene in time to save Britain seemed small. With spring approaching, a German landing on British soil appeared imminent.[10]

While the pope despaired, Italy's churchmen continued to do their part to bolster their countrymen's support for the war. In late February, in one of countless such events taking place through the country, Rome's Catholic Action University chapter sponsored a Mass on behalf of its members who had been called up for military service. In his sermon, the officiating priest prayed that "the God of Armies smile on and bring very soon the most radiant victory of Italian arms, which will bring peace and justice to Europe and to the world."[11]

Each spring Italy's ambassador to the Vatican closely monitored the Easter messages the country's bishops sent their flocks.[12] Of all those sent by the bishops of Italy's 284 dioceses that year, reported Attolico, only two were deemed problematic. And of the Easter messages sent by the pastors of the country's twenty-seven thousand parishes, only about ten were judged objectionable.[13] At the same time, the ambassador called attention to the recent patriotic initiative by Bologna's archbishop, Cardinal Giovanni Nasalli Rocca. The cardinal had proposed holding regular masses in all the churches of his archdiocese "for our glorious dead who sacrificed their lives for us and for our well-being." Catholics, in this time of war, explained the archbishop, should see themselves as soldiers "in the Christian militia." He had concluded by invoking the pope's call for a "new order."[14]

The nation's largest circulation newspaper, *Corriere della Sera,* featured the Easter message of another, albeit less prominent, bishop, whose calls to rally to the Fascist cause could hardly have been more strident: "The Man sent by God who now guides the Fatherland's destiny was the first one to understand the need for extending a friendly hand to Germany in order to see so many injustices righted." What was so regrettable, the bishop lamented, was that so many Christian nations had allowed themselves to hold out a hand "to the descendants of those Jews who had crucified Jesus." In "the new European world," he vowed, there would be no place for Jews.[15]

———

MUSSOLINI HAD INITIALLY DISMISSED his generals' worries about the country's limited war supplies by telling them the fighting would be over in a matter of months. Now, with the likelihood it would drag on for some time, reports of shortages kept streaming in. With bronze among those resources in short supply, he turned his eye to the country's seemingly limitless number of church bells. Conscious of the delicacy of the request, the government devised a plan to proceed incrementally, where possible finding churches with multiple bells, so that some might be taken while leaving at least one in each to ring. In any case, the bells of the nation's cathedrals were to be spared. Prefects were instructed to meet with the local bishop or archbishop in each province to coordinate a census of the bells and prioritize their removal. Authorities were then to report on the weight and composition of each of them, and to list those that the bishops proposed to exclude, along with their rationale for leaving them in place. Lists were to be sent to Rome by the end of March 1941.

In early February, after discussing the matter with Cardinal Maglione, the Italian ambassador drafted what he described as "the basis for a possible agreement between state and ecclesiastical authorities regarding the contemplated requisition of the church bells for use in the war."[16] Maglione had told him that if it proved necessary to take the bells for this purpose—which of course he hoped it would not—it was important that in each case an agreement be reached with the local bishop to determine which bells were to be selected. It would be best, the cardinal suggested, to begin by reaching agreements with the archdioceses presided over by a cardinal, for once that was done, it would be easier to convince the bishops who came under their authority to go along. Maglione drew the line at Rome. No church bell could be taken from the city whose bishop was the pope himself. The cardinal had one last request: no public notice should be made of the Vatican's collaboration in crafting the measures. Over the following two years, government agents removed more than 13,600 bells from Italy's churches, to be melted down to make weaponry. Many had been crafted by artisans centuries earlier.[17]

AFTER A SERIES OF Italian defeats at the hands of the British in North Africa, the Axis war there was now turning around thanks to the arrival in February 1941 of Germans troops led by General Rommel. Over the next months, Germany's Desert Fox would drive the British from the positions they had gained in Libya and capture two top British generals in the process. But the situation in Italy's prized East African colonies was very different. In declaring war on Britain the previous June, Mussolini seems to have given little thought to the implications for Italian East Africa, as Italy's colonies of Eritrea, Ethiopia, and Somaliland were collectively known. In fact, it was completely cut off by enemy forces, its 3,900 kilometers of coast immediately blockaded by superior British naval forces, and its 4,800 kilometers of land border all exposed to attack from British colonies having open supply lines.

In the six weeks from the beginning of the British East African offensive in mid-January to late February, commonwealth troops occupied over six hundred thousand square kilometers of Italian East African territory. The Somali capital of Mogadishu fell to British Commonwealth forces on February 25, Eritrea's capital, Asmara, on April 1. A month later Haile Selassie, the emperor of Ethiopia, having been chased from his capital by Italian troops five years earlier, made his triumphant return to Addis Ababa. Italy had begun the fighting with a great numerical advantage, with over 90,000 Italian troops augmented by close to 200,000 indigenous troops, arrayed against approximately 20,000 British troops, mainly coming from the British dominions, India among them. By the end of the fighting, over 15,000 Italians had been killed and many more taken prisoner.[18]

Mussolini would get much better news from the Balkans, as German troops poured in to rescue the embattled Italian forces. With Luftwaffe support, the German army needed only eleven days to conquer Yugoslavia. The country was quickly divided between Rome and Berlin, along with an independent Croatia. Two months later Croatia, under the rule of Ante Pavelić, champion of Croatian Catholic Fascism, would formally join the Axis. Germany's Twelfth Army then crossed the border into Greece, occupying Thessaloniki on April 9. Two and a half weeks later German motorcycle troops entered Athens. Although fifty thousand of the British Commonwealth soldiers who had tried to shore up Greece's defense succeeded in escaping, several thousand others were captured. The ease with which the Germans conquered Greece, after the hapless performance of the Italian military there, made a mockery of Mussolini's earlier boasts of Fascist military might.[19]

While elsewhere this turn of events was making the Duce an object of ridicule, the same was not true in Italy, thanks in good part to strict government censorship. The American ambassador, writing in mid-April to President Roosevelt, explained, "Since the collapse of Yugoslavia, the Italians have begun to feel greater confidence and of course are not permitted to be aware how little their own forces have done in this connection." He added that there was a "great deal of 'wishful thinking' in government circles," where people were now convinced that the war would be won by the end of the summer. Romans who, thanks to the presence of the pope, thought they had little reason to fear British bombings themselves, were doing the best they could to forget an unpopular war. Early each evening they filled the city's bars, theaters, cinemas, and brothels before hurrying home in time for the nightly blackout at eight-thirty P.M.

Although censorship meant that Italians had a distorted picture of the war, returning soldiers brought word of the weakness of their own army and the overwhelming strength of the Germans. But if people were unhappy with the war, they had to be cautious about expressing it openly. "The police are everywhere," reported the American military attaché in Rome, "especially the plain-clothes-men, who are, as always, the backbone of the local espionage service. Every hotel, restaurant, apartment house, etc. has its police agents. Many telephone lines are tapped and people are naturally afraid to speak freely." Although Italians feared what the overweening Germans might visit on their country, everyone, reported the American adviser, expected Germany to win the war. The only impact Italians thought American entry would have would be to prolong the misery before that inevitable victory came. At the same time, America's ambassador in Rome offered his own assessment to President Roosevelt: "Paradoxically enough, Mussolini's failure in the war has temporarily strengthened his hand; most people feel that Fascism and the Duce are finished but they feel that if they fell they would be replaced by a Nazi régime."[20]

Indeed, the Fascist system of censorship and surveillance was ramping up. In mid-April the military intelligence service informed Mussolini that all telephone calls coming from Vatican City were being monitored. Bowing to government pressure, the Vatican was itself collaborating in the surveillance, having its own gendarmes spy on the movements of diplomats from enemy countries living in Vatican City.[21] Responding to government protests about Vatican Radio running news stories in some of its foreign broadcasts reflecting unfavorably on the German military, the pope quietly allowed the papal police to spy on the movements of the Jesuits involved in the broadcasts. "As a result of a campaign of menace and intimidation," Osborne, the British envoy, wrote, "the Secretariat of State issued orders that the Vatican Radio should not mention Germany at all." Osborne complained to Pius XII, handing him a note arguing that "a policy of appeasement with Hitler led nowhere." The pope denied having made any agreement with the Axis powers to muzzle Vatican radio, but Osborne did not believe him.[22]

Britain's envoy might have been even more skeptical had he known that Hitler had a secret channel to Pius XII through Prince Philipp von Hessen, for the pope's meetings with the Führer's envoy had not ended with Ribbentrop's visit a year earlier. Again, these meetings have come to light only with the recent opening of the Vatican archives, but even from these newly available documents, we do not learn why Hitler kept sending the prince to meet secretly with the pope, other than perhaps to string him along and help keep him silent. One of these encounters was arranged, by the usual channel, in late March 1941, and took place in early April. The prince, Cardinal Lauri explained to the

pope in passing on the request for the meeting, would as usual be accompanied to the pope's antechamber by his Italian Order of Malta
shadowy go-between, Raffaele Travaglini.[23]

BELIEF IN THE LIKELIHOOD of Axis victory was widespread in the
halls of the Vatican. In late April Harold Tittmann, Roosevelt's envoy
to the Holy See, ran into Monsignor Bernardini, papal nuncio to Switzerland, who was visiting the Vatican. Even if the United States did
enter the war, said the nuncio, Germany could not be defeated. It
would be better to arrange a compromise peace. Tittmann asked how
he, as a churchman, could favor a compromise that would mean a
"Hitler-controlled" Europe. Bernardini replied that the Vatican had no
reason to be alarmed, for he was "certain that within a few years the
Nazi prejudice against Catholics was destined to die out."[24]

Even those who had been critical of tying Italy's fate to the Nazis
were now trying to get on the Germans' good side. Emblematic was
the artfully worded letter, marked "personal," that Bernardo Attolico,
Italy's ambassador to the Vatican, sent Hitler's ambassador in Rome in
early May. Attolico, who kept to himself his belief that Hitler was a
warmongering madman, wrote, "I listened to the Führer's speech on
the radio yesterday not once but twice. It is the most elevated, most
noble one that he has ever given and such as to leave all who hear it an
absolutely unforgettable and everlasting impression. Permit me to express, as a simple citizen, the most fervent and heartfelt congratulations."[25]

Amid the growing certainty of German victory, the pope was unsettled by a troubling rumor. Ribbentrop was said to have told Ciano
that once the war ended, the Axis powers should evict the pope from
Rome. The new Europe, the German foreign minister was alleged to
have said, would have no place for the papacy. Cardinal Maglione immediately summoned the Italian ambassador. Although Attolico dismissed the report as preposterous, he promised to speak to Ciano about
it. Ciano then sent his own heated denial.

Still nervous, the pope took the unusual step of making a direct inquiry of the Duce. Knowing of a monk who, as chaplain with the Italian troops in Albania, had spent time with the Duce there, the pope called on him to tell Mussolini how astonished he was to have heard such a report. Mussolini, who was sitting at his desk as the monk recounted the rumor, stood and pounded on it with his fist. "I am astonished too," he said. The account, he insisted, was a complete fabrication, undoubtedly planted by Italy's enemies.[26]

While Pius XII carefully avoided any condemnation of Hitler or the Nazis, there was one evil he had no trouble denouncing. His late May 1941 speech to the members of the Girls' Catholic Action organization warned of what he portrayed as the dangerous enemy they faced. As was his custom, he arrived at the event carried in his *sedia gestatoria,* the four thousand girls standing excitedly before him, all dressed in white. The event, the organization's annual "crusade for purity," was seen as sufficiently notable that it merited a special report from the local police commissioner, who described Pius XII's "important speech" there.

Comparing the battle to be fought today with the "glorious" Crusades of old, the pope told the girls it was crucial for them to help government authorities "combat the dangers of immorality in the areas of women's fashion, sport, hygiene, social relations, and entertainment." Rome's Catholic newspaper explained that the pope had in mind the scandal of women's and girls' immodest dress, their participation in sports wearing outfits that left parts of their bodies exposed, and their yielding to the temptation of inappropriate dancing, theater, books, and magazines. Pius XII would continue to warn of these dangers throughout the war years.[27]

The pope's own knowledge of girls and women was limited, for aside from the nuns who ran his household, he lived in a world of men. There was only one woman in whom he felt free to confide, his longtime household manager, Sister Pascalina. "What is so amazing," a police informant reported at the time, "is the full command assumed by the German nun who, since the time he was a cardinal, acts as the Pope's private secretary. . . . The thing logically leads to much gossip for malicious tongues say all kinds of things about it, and apart from these calumnies, there remains the evident fact of the command exercised by the secretary, who does and undoes what she likes at her pleasure." The informant went on to give as an example the current work being done on a Vatican City renovation project of interest to the pope, noting, "She herself oversees the work on the building making various visits in the evening, when there are no workers there. . . . Every order by the above-mentioned nun is as if given by the Pope and is obeyed to the letter."[28]

THANKS TO THE ARRIVAL of German troops in the Balkans and North Africa, the war was now going better for Mussolini. But he seemed oddly removed from its day-to-day oversight, spending an inordinate amount of time with Clara Petacci. Mussolini's affair, Ambassador Phillips had told Roosevelt back in January, was prompting increasing criticism in Rome. In a reference to her distinctive hairstyle, Phillips had dubbed Clara "Madame Pompadour," and he offered the president the salacious, if erroneous, detail that Mussolini had taken both Clara and her younger sister as his lovers. So consumed was the Duce with his mistress, claimed Phillips, that "for weeks, the army did not see him."[29]

Troubling, too, were signs that competing groups were forming around Mussolini's uneducated but highly opinionated and strong-willed wife, Rachele, whom their children regarded as the true boss of their household, and the scheming Petacci family members around Clara. "For some months now," Ciano noted in his diary in mid-May, "Donna Rachele has been agitated, cold, and involving herself in policeman-like manner in things that don't concern her." As an example, he cited a report—albeit one that seems hard to believe—that she was going around in disguise, dressed as an impoverished Roman, to see what people on the streets were saying. Ciano was far from an impartial witness to his mother-in-law's behavior, for the two had never gotten along. For Rachele, who came from the same modest anarcho-socialist background in Romagna as her husband, Ciano represented all that had gone wrong with Fascism, as it attracted the soft, well-heeled men of the economic elite who found it a useful way to defend their privilege.[30]

For Ciano, the problem with Clara was not that she was Mussolini's lover but that their affair was becoming such a scandal. In 1939, with an extravagance hard to miss in the case of the family of a Vatican physician, Clara's family moved into a sprawling, luxurious villa on Monte Mario, in the periphery of the city overlooking the Vatican. While full public attention to the Duce's weakness for Clara and her parasitical family was still a couple of years away, police informant reports were already filled with accounts of popular anger at the Petacci family's flaunting of the riches it was assumed Mussolini must have been showering on them. The needy dictator often visited his lover's home, welcomed by Clara's mother, herself the undisputed ruler of her household. A devout churchgoer, she had long made peace with her daughter's doubly adulterous affair and was now enjoying its fruits, as were Clara's brother, Marcello—a man more devoted to questionable business schemes than to his own medical career—and her glamorous younger sister, whose dreams of a career as a film star Mussolini would help fulfill. Marcello, the inspector general of Italy's police told the finance minister, "is doing more harm to the Duce than fifteen lost battalions." Key to funneling government support to the family was Mussolini's undersecretary, Buffarini, who somehow succeeded in casting himself simultaneously as an ally to both of the warring parties: Mussolini's wife and his lover.[31]

Mussolini himself now seemed rarely in a good mood. In a typical choleric outburst, after reading a speech given by Roosevelt, he raged against the American president: "In all of history, there has never been a people led by a paralytic. There have been bald kings, fat kings, handsome yet stupid kings, but never a king who in order to go to the bathroom . . . had to be assisted by other men."[32]

Roosevelt, in turn, had a dim view of the Duce but had little faith that the Italians would turn against him. The American ambassador in Rome had been reporting on the combination of low public morale and Italians' growing conviction that the Germans would win the war. But, thought Phillips, Mussolini remained popular, and he advised the

Clara Petacci

president against following Winston Churchill's tack of denouncing the Duce to the Italians. A better approach, he thought, was to try to separate the Italians from the Germans by distinguishing between the two rather than casting them together in his denunciations of the Axis. It was a suggestion Roosevelt rejected out of hand. "At the present time there appears to be little possibility that the Italian people are willing to do more than passively accept the ignominious position which their alliance with Germany has forced upon them." He added that "there would be little support in this country for a declaration of this sort."[33]

THE CRUSADE

O N JUNE 22, 1941, IN AN ACTION DUBBED OPERATION BARBAROSSA, Hitler attacked the Soviet Union with three-quarters of the German army, 160 army divisions, along with twenty-five hundred warplanes. Before long, 3.5 million German soldiers, joined by 700,000 German-allied troops, including the Italians, would face a Red Army numbering 5.5 million men. Within six months, as the Wehrmacht drove toward Moscow, the Red Army would suffer 4 million casualties, including 3 million starving in German POW camps. Although Hitler had been planning the attack for months, he informed Mussolini only a few hours before it began, with the German chargé d'affaires delivering the Führer's letter to Ciano at his home at three A.M. Despite the hour, Ciano picked up the phone to tell Mussolini the news.[1]

Encouraged by the ease of his march through western Europe the previous spring, and by the difficulty the Red Army had had, in the winter of 1941, overcoming Finland's tenacious resistance to its invasion, Hitler thought the eastern campaign would take no more than a few months. Nor were the Allies confident that the Russians could hold out long, believing their army was grievously weakened by Stalin's purges of its officer ranks over the preceding years.

At the Vatican, news of the German attack on the Communist state was greeted with great relief, for the prelates had long worried about the prospect of a triumphant Russia sharing in an Axis victory. For the pope, the news cast the war in a very different light, as the Nazis took aim at what he viewed as Christianity's greatest foe. Mussolini's ambassador to the Vatican was pleased as well. He believed Hitler's move would undermine the Allies' efforts to present themselves as fighting on behalf of Christianity, battling both the Nazis and the Communists.[2]

First reports from the battlefield lent credence to the hopes and fears of a lightning German victory. No one was more euphoric than Mussolini and his son-in-law. Ciano noted in his diary that seventeen hundred Russian planes were reportedly destroyed in the first night of war. General Ugo Cavallero, the new head of the Italian military, advised the Duce that the poorly trained and equipped Soviet soldiers would quickly abandon the fight. The chargé d'affaires of the German embassy in Rome offered Ciano a similar view. The German military command, he reported, was predicting they would soon have five million Russian prisoners. Although Hitler had not asked for Italian help, Mussolini insisted on sending troops: "In a war of this nature," the Duce wrote him, "Italy cannot remain on the sideline." The campaign would culminate in "a dazzling victory . . . the prologue to the total victory over the Anglo-Saxon world."[3]

Church enthusiasm was immediately clear to Italy's faithful from Catholic press coverage. L'Avvenire d'Italia published an editorial alongside the front-page news of Italy's declaration of war against the USSR. "The Cross," predicted the paper's director, "will once again appear atop the Kremlin's cupola." The editor of Rome's Catholic newspaper added his own blessings a few days later, on the departure of the first Italian military units for the Soviet front. They were on their way to do battle, he wrote, "against the murderers of Catholic Spain, the 'Godless,' the irreducible enemies of Christian civilization. . . . In these days, our prayers rise up all the more fervently to God, that the Axis affirm this God-given historical task."[4]

The declaration of war against the Soviet Union likewise triggered an outpouring of renewed support for the Italian war effort by Italy's church hierarchy, encouraged by the Vatican.[5] Cardinal Adeodato Piazza, patriarch of Venice, offered stirring patriotic remarks at San Marco Basilica to the troops leaving for the Russian front, concluding with the wish that they soon return to San Marco "to sing the Te Deum of Victory." The archbishop of Catania, at the other end of Italy, pronounced much the same hope. The reports on the clergy that prefects from each province sent monthly to Rome similarly painted a gratifying picture for the Duce. "The clergy and Catholics in general," wrote the prefect of Salerno, "learned with enthusiasm of Germany's actions against Russia" and were now describing the struggle as a "holy war . . . the crusade against the Godless. . . . All these manifestations of a national character by the high Italian clergy draw their inspiration directly from the Pontiff who has, personally as well, not failed in recent times to eloquently express his sympathy and his faith in Italy and in Rome's mission."[6]

The imagery of the Axis cause as a Christian crusade was becoming common not only in the Catholic press but in the Fascist press as well. In July Mussolini's newspaper featured a pastoral letter of the archbishop of Gorizia, in northeastern Italy. All good Catholics, he said, should be willing to shed the last drop of their blood for the victory of Christianity against the darkest barbarism. "It is like the time when the venerable hierarchs of the Church saluted and blessed the voluntary militias leaving for the Orient to liberate the Sepulcher of Christ."[7]

While Mussolini was no doubt pleased by the clergy's support, he wanted the Vatican to do more. A week into the Russian campaign, Ciano sent a message to his ambassador at the Vatican: "There is no doubt that for the purposes of propaganda in American Catholic circles, and especially for the isolationist Irish [Americans], nothing would make a greater impression at this moment than a clear and unequivocal condemnation of bolshevism by the Holy See." Mussolini's greatest fear was that the United States would enter the war. Anything the pope could do to prevent or even delay it would be exceedingly valuable.[8]

By midsummer, Ambassador Attolico and his chargé d'affaires, the veteran diplomat and fellow conservative Catholic Francesco Babuscio Rizzo, were regularly meeting with Cardinal Maglione and his deputies, pleading with them to get Pius XII to issue a strong denunciation of Communism. But the pope was far from eager to take an action that, given the timing, would be widely viewed as publicly throwing his support to the Axis powers. It was one thing for the Italian church, albeit under the pope's authority, to cast its lot with the Axis cause, but quite another for the pope to do so personally. Cardinal Maglione told Babuscio that since Vatican opposition to Communism was well known, there was no need to repeat it now. He invoked another argument, one the Vatican would repeat many times. If the Italian government really wanted the pope to speak out against the Soviets for their persecution of religion, the pontiff could hardly fail to mention the Nazis' ill treatment of the Catholic Church as well. According to the reports they were getting, said the cardinal with a bit of exaggeration, the first thing the German troops did when they occupied new territory was to throw all the nuns, monks, and priests onto the street.[9]

THERE WAS GOOD REASON to believe the Soviet army would soon collapse and in doing so bring the war to an end. The Germans were rapidly marching along a vast front, stretching from the Baltic Sea in the north, where they had occupied Estonia, Latvia, and Lithuania, through Minsk in Belarus, and down past Odessa on the Black Sea. Meanwhile Britain, suffering from unremitting bombing and increasing isolation, seemed to have little choice but to sue for peace.

In late July, D'Arcy Osborne, Britain's Vatican envoy, warned London that Hitler might try to enlist the pope in a peace offensive in the fall. The British envoy believed the pope's "natural caution" would incline him against involving himself in an initiative that was likely to fail, but there was some reason for worry: "Great pressure and even blackmail from the Axis may be expected and the Pope is obsessed with the ambition to play a part in the restoration of peace."[10]

As primate of the Italian church, the pope was trying to keep the Duce happy by doing nothing to discourage Italy's most prominent churchmen from giving their vocal support to the Axis war. To Mussolini's dismay, however, the pope remained unwilling to compromise himself with the British or, especially, with the Americans. In the days following the German invasion of the Soviet Union, the closest he came to praising the Axis cause was in his late June speech marking the celebration of Rome's two patron saints, Peter and Paul. The German press trumpeted his words on that occasion—his reference to the "great courage shown in defending the bases of Christian civilization and confident hope in their triumph"—as a clear endorsement of their war.[11]

With reports of the Germans' ill treatment of the church continuing to come in, the pope decided at the same time to find a safe way to make church displeasure at the German government known. In mid-August Cardinal Maglione sent the papal delegate in Washington new instructions: while no American bishop should publicly express support for either side of the war, "it is, however, desirable that some of them . . . find a way to let their faithful know the painful conditions in which religious life operates in Germany and in the occupied countries. In doing so, they must act as if on their own initiative and not in the name of the Holy See." Papal deniability was crucial. Any bishop calling attention to the issue must "not suppose, much less bring attention to the fact, that the news given comes from the Holy See."[12]

In fact, tensions over the war were mounting within an American church hierarchy that was riven by factions and personal rivalries. Not long after Maglione sent his instructions to Washington, the American prelate closest to Pius XII, Archbishop Spellman of New York, wrote to tell the pope how uncomfortable the situation had become. Bishop Joseph Hurley had triggered the latest embarrassing public display in a speech that branded Nazism as worse than Communism and called on Catholics to support the president's plan to send aid to Russia. "Catholic papers openly attacked Bishop Hurley and in an unprecedented incident in American history," wrote Spellman. "Archbishop [of Dubuque, Francis] Beckman attacked Bishop Hurley in a radio address. In short, things are in a turmoil here."[13]

IN LATE AUGUST 1941, after a three-day journey aboard his special train, Mussolini reached Görlitz, at what is today the border between Germany and Poland. In addition to his own generals, his large retinue included Hans von Mackensen, the German ambassador to Italy, whose cigars stank up much of the train, and Lieutenant Colonel Eugen Dollman, head of the German SS in Italy.[14] Hitler came to the station to meet the Duce and then accompanied him to his newly constructed "Wolf's Lair," a few kilometers to the east, the huge palatial complex Hitler had built to be his headquarters for Operation Barbarossa. Thousands of workers had cleared the forest nearby to construct the Führer's vast underground complex, surrounding it with minefields and barbed wire. Nothing remotely like it existed in Italy.

Ever eager to impress Hitler and convinced that victory was near, Mussolini told him it was his great wish to have the Italian armed forces play a larger role in the war against the USSR. The Führer, confident of victory himself and with his generals seeing little value in the Italian army, tried unsuccessfully to dissuade him, citing Italy's great distance from the Russian front and the logistical difficulties they would face.[15]

Back at the Vatican, the first news was coming in of resistance the German troops were encountering in their eastern drive and even instances of counterattack from the much-disparaged Red Army. While the pope and the men of the Curia feared an all-powerful, triumphant Nazi Germany, the alternative, unlikely as it then seemed, of Russian success against the Wehrmacht raised the possibility of a victory conference at which Europe's future could lie in Stalin's hands, a prospect they dreaded. But there was a third possible outcome, one that offered a glimmer of hope. What God, in his mysterious ways, might intend was a brutal war between Russia and Germany that would bring about the end of Communism but leave Nazism grievously weakened. In such a scenario, the pope might well come to play a crucial role in negotiating a peace settlement. Indeed, he might one day be hailed as Europe's savior.[16]

AS ROOSEVELT WAS RAMPING up his efforts to send aid to Britain, while fending off his countrymen's pleas to keep the United States out of another European war, he decided to send his envoy back to see the pope. "Duce!" read an anonymous note to Mussolini. "Myron Taylor is coming back to Rome. He is a Jew and hides himself behind the Vatican. Be on guard!"[17]

Roosevelt gave Taylor a dual mission. In the face of widespread American Catholic opposition to his support of Britain, and to his efforts to prepare the country for the possibility of war, he thought publicly renewing his bonds with the pope would be politically valuable. Taylor's new trip to Rome also came shortly after Roosevelt had met the British prime minister in Newfoundland, where they drafted the eight points of what came to be known as the Atlantic Charter. It was a statement of their goals for a postwar world, including the disarmament of aggressor nations and the right of all people to self-determination. The president hoped to convince Pius XII to signal his support for the charter.

Taylor was well on his way to developing a strong bond with the pope. The imposing American business tycoon could display a softer side, as he listened respectfully to the pope and delighted in the Vatican's ornate rituals. Although a Protestant, Taylor never failed to genuflect to the pope and ask for his blessing at the end of every audience. The pontiff appreciated Taylor's can-do attitude, backed by America's vast resources, and Taylor's personal friendship with the president offered the pope a key resource. Osborne noted an additional trait the two men shared, a "militant Christian idealism."[18]

On September 9, 1941, Taylor met with Pius XII. He brought a letter from Roosevelt expressing the hope that the pope might publicly support the aims he and Churchill had set forth. The pontiff, ever cautious, said he would give the matter some thought. Taylor then met with Cardinal Maglione, urging the importance of papal support for the Atlantic Charter's eight points. Only two people on earth, said Taylor, were in a position to speak out credibly for "the triumph of justice": the pope and the president of the United States.

What exactly Pius XII promised the American when they next met would be a matter of disagreement. In Taylor's account, the pope said that, given his desire to maintain a "role of independence," he could not "make such a statement immediately without a suitable occasion to inspire it. He agreed, however, to do so at a reasonably early date."[19]

No sign of such an agreement can be found in the Vatican records. Indeed, aware of Mussolini's nervousness about his meeting with the American envoy, the pope had his secretary of state brief the Italian ambassador on it immediately. The cardinal made no mention of Roosevelt's proposal. The purpose of Taylor's visit, Maglione told Mussolini's ambassador, was simply to show America's Catholics that he remained in contact with the pope and to convey the American president's views on the war.[20]

As was often the case in such matters, the pope depended on Monsignor Tardini, Cardinal Maglione's clear-eyed and plainspoken deputy, to prepare notes to help guide his response to the American president's request. They offer precious insight into the views of the pope and his closest advisers.

"To defeat Nazism," wrote Tardini, "the United States is supporting Russia," in effect supporting Communism, that is, "militant atheism . . . battle against religion, ruthless war above all against all of Catholicism!" While Roosevelt was eager to get American Catholic support, "the leaders of the Catholic Church [in America] are instead persuaded that Nazism and communism are two extremely dangerous enemies of the Church. Both need to be destroyed. Whichever one of the two were to survive, it would be the ruin of humanity." How, asked Tardini, could they say the American church leaders were wrong?[21] The following day he added additional notes: "Roosevelt's letter made a painful impression on me. It is an attempted (although unsuccessful) apology for communism. . . . In an exhausted Europe and with Germany annihilated, it would become the absolute ruler over continental Europe."

In the end, the pope decided it best to say as little as possible, offering the American president generic good wishes while avoiding any statements that could pin him down.[22]

WHILE TAYLOR WAS STILL in Rome, the Italian ambassador came to see the pope to find out what the American had come for, and to renew his attempts to persuade the pope to issue a public denunciation of

Communism. It was a frustrating meeting for the ambassador, as the pope clearly had Germany, not Russia, on his mind.

"If I were to talk about bolshevism—and I would be very ready to do so," the pope added—"should I then say nothing about Nazism?" The situation in Germany was dramatically worsening. Even if, as he had been told, the Führer had ordered the suspension of the persecutions aimed at the church, "that doesn't mean that Christ has been readmitted to the schools . . . or that the numerous convents and religious institutions that had been closed will be reopened . . . or that they will suppress the prayer that German children are made to recite in which, parodying the Pater Noster, they thank Hitler for their daily bread."

After going on in this vein for a half hour, the pope told Attolico he was glad he had come because there was a matter he wanted to ask about. He had long been hearing it said that some in Germany were aiming "to do without the Vatican" in the new European order that the victorious Axis armies would usher in. "Now," said Pius XII, "they are telling me that, even in Hitler's meeting with Mussolini, the Führer is reported to have said it was necessary to 'do away with' the Vatican. Is that true?"

Attolico assured the pontiff that such reports were totally false. Hearing this, the pope, Attolico reported, "was pleased, and I would say almost relieved, showing how much the belief, I would almost say the nightmare, of new and more serious persecutions weighed on his soul." Thus reassured, the pope recalled the many pleasant years he had spent in Germany. "Oh, if Germany had only left me in peace," he told Mussolini's ambassador, "my attitude in this war, especially at this moment, would have been very different."[23]

IN FRANCE, THE PÉTAIN government had begun introducing its own draconian antisemitic laws shortly after taking power the previous year. Initially worried that these might prompt a protest from the Vatican, the collaborationist officials were reassured by Léon Bérard, the French ambassador to the Holy See. "There was nothing," he told them, "that can give rise to criticism from the Holy See's point of view." In a subsequent letter, he explained that although the church condemned racism, it had long recognized that a "Jewish problem" existed, and indeed from the time of the Middle Ages, the popes themselves had acted to keep Jews from a variety of occupations. He added that the church's only objection to the anti-Jewish campaign was the treatment of baptized Jews as Jews rather than as Catholics. This the church could never accept.[24]

Although he would voice no objection to the antisemitic state campaigns under way in Italy, France, or elsewhere, Pius XII could never feel comfortable about the reports that were beginning to come in describing the Germans' systematic murder of Europe's Jews. His discomfort comes through clearly in notes that Monsignor Angelo Roncalli made in his journal following an audience with the pope in October 1941. "He asked me," wrote the future Pope John XXIII, then visiting Rome from his post as papal envoy to Turkey, "if his silence regarding the Nazis' actions is not a mistake."[25]

Germany's campaign of extermination of Europe's Jews was indeed accelerating as its troops moved eastward. Since the invasion of the Soviet Union began in June, special German mobile killing units—*Einsatzgruppen*—had begun murdering Jews with the help of local antisemites. On June 27 an *Einsatzgruppe* unit together with local Ukrainians killed two thousand Jews in Lutsk. That same day a German motorized unit burned hundreds of Jews alive in a synagogue in Bialystok, Poland. Early the next month, at least six thousand Jews were shot to death and dumped into a trench in a Lithuanian forest, assisted by locals. All across the vast territory through which the German army was moving, Jews were being shot en masse, their bodies shoved into ditches they were forced to dig.[26]

In October 1941 the pope received one of the first unmistakably credible accounts of this massacre of Europe's Jews. The nuncio in Bratislava passed on a report from the bishop in charge of Slovakia's military chaplains. The previous November Slovakia, along with Hungary and Romania, had joined the Axis. While other war prisoners were being sent back to their homes, the bishop reported, "the Jews are simply being shot . . . systematically murdered, without distinction of sex or age." The day the bishop sent his report, the pope was busy offering his blessings to an audience of eighty German soldiers, something he would continue to do over the next many months. That day, too, the pope had an appointment sitting for a sculptor commissioned to create his bust. The artist found his subject skittish and ill-tempered, as the pope directed agitated bursts of German to the nuns who ran his household. The nuns told the sculptor it was a miracle he had agreed to all the two-hour sittings. Normally, he was too high strung to stay in one place so long.[27]

In November 1941 Pius XII would learn in much greater detail

Pius XII poses for sculptor, 1941

about the unfolding mass murder of Europe's Jews when Father Pirro Scavizzi, an Italian military chaplain, gave him a bloodcurdling account on his return from the eastern front. While aboard an Italian military hospital train as it passed through Ukraine in late October, the Roman priest had jotted down his observations: "the Jews here are very numerous and hated by everyone." As soon as the German army arrived, "a massacre of the Jews took place in the most atrociously exemplary and terrifying way. Several hundred of them were enclosed, piled like animals, into old train cars, and beaten down in every way, and then, after several days of this martyrdom, they were murdered." The Germans were dynamiting synagogues, and "a day does not pass without other murders of Jews taking place." A few days later he wrote: "massacre of hundreds of Jews, forced first to dig a ditch, then machine-gunned and thrown inside."

Father Scavizzi met with the pope on his return from that trip in November, when he described at length what he had witnessed. The pope listened with great interest, growing increasingly distraught as the priest recounted the horrors the Germans were inflicting on Jews, Catholic Poles, and others on the eastern front. "I saw him cry like a child and pray like a saint," the Roman priest later recalled. Along with his oral report to the pope, Scavizzi delivered an impassioned letter from a Polish priest. Describing the terrifying events unfolding in Poland, the priest said that the Poles could not understand what they termed the Vatican's "crime of silence." He begged the pope to make his voice heard.[28]

A NEW PRINCE

W ITH JAPAN'S ATTACK ON PEARL HARBOR ON DECEMBER 7, 1941, the war entered a new phase. The following day Ambassador Phillips ordered all sensitive papers at the American embassy in Rome burned. Harold Tittmann, Myron Taylor's assistant in Rome, came to Vatican City to ask if the apartment was ready that the Vatican Secretariat of State had reserved for him in case Italy declared war on the United States. On December 11 Ambassador Phillips received a summons from Mussolini's son-in-law. When he arrived at the foreign minister's office, Ciano rose from his desk and, with all the formality he could muster, stiffly told him: "I have sent for you to tell you in the name of my King and in that of the Italian Government that as of today Italy considers itself at war with the United States." Hitler declared war on the United States that same day.

None of this was greeted with much enthusiasm by the Italian public. The obligatory crowd outside Mussolini's window was quickly assembled, mixing enthusiastic Fascists with dragooned government employees and students. The Duce emerged onto his balcony, attempting his usual swagger but looking rather pale. His speech would be brief:

Men and women of Italy . . . hear this!
This is another day of solemn decisions in the history of Italy. . . .

The powers of the Pact of Steel, Fascist Italy and National-Socialist Germany, ever more closely united, stand beside heroic Japan against the United States of America. . . .

Neither the Axis nor Japan wanted the expansion of this conflict. One man, a single man, an authentic and democratic despot, through an infinite series of provocations, deceiving with supreme fraud the very populations of his own country, has wanted the war and has prepared it day by day with diabolical pertinacity. . . .

Italian men and women, standing once again, show yourselves worthy of this great hour.

We shall be victorious![1]

Cheers from the crowd came as they always had at the appropriate times, following mentions of Nazi Germany and Japan, and following the Duce's concluding and now ritualistic vow of inevitable victory, but they were markedly less enthusiastic than those that had greeted Mussolini's similar performances in the past. As the dictator went back inside Palazzo Venezia, the crowd quickly melted away, returning home to their rationed suppers.[2]

For Mussolini, the pope's support would now be even more important. Within days of America's entry into the war, the king conferred the title of prince on all the descendants of the pontiff's beloved older brother, Francesco, who had died several years earlier. It was Francesco Pacelli who had negotiated the Lateran Accords on Pius XI's behalf with Mussolini. The benefits for the regime from conferral of the honor could be seen immediately: the Vatican newspaper reported that the government's ennobling of the pope's kin "constitutes new proof of the faithfulness to these historical events and to the happy consequences that have flowed from it in line with the great Christian traditions of the Italian nation."[3]

Britain's emissary to the Vatican, D'Arcy Osborne, observed that the ennoblement might have been understandable but for two facts: it was done so many years after the event that it claimed to be honoring, years too after the honoree had died, and in the meantime, Pacelli's brother had become pope. The most plausible explanation for the granting of the honor, wrote Osborne, was "to affirm the '*italianità*' of the Vatican, and thereby to indicate to the Italian people that, in the present world struggle, the Papacy must necessarily be on the side of the Axis Powers." Unfortunately, thought the envoy, Italians were likely to draw exactly that conclusion. "The Pope, I was told, was somewhat embarrassed, as the transaction now savoured faintly of nepotism."[4]

CHRISTMAS 1941 WOULD AGAIN see Pius XII broadcasting a holiday message to the world. Typical of his speeches, it was so long and of such rarefied language that it would fly over the heads of most Italians. Once again the pope fashioned it in a way that would allow both sides to read into it an offering of support.[5]

In its coverage of the speech, the national bulletin of Italian Catholic Action highlighted what it took to be the pope's main message: "What is the cause of so many evils? Men have rebelled against true Christianity." One should not oppress minorities; one should not try to monopolize the earth's resources; there is no place for persecution of religion or of the church. The French ambassador explained to Vichy that the pope was calling for governments to do exactly what Pétain's was doing, restoring "the values of Christian civilization and the rules of religious morality by maintaining good relations with the Church." The ambassador pointed out that while the pope, in bemoaning persecution of religion and the church, had not named any guilty parties, he surely must have had both Stalin and National Socialism in mind.[6]

While Mussolini's newspaper relegated its story to the second page, it offered a respectful account, offering its own paraphrases. Farinacci offered effusive praise for the speech in a lengthy front-page editorial, ably offering selective quotes from the pontiff's words to turn it into a brief in favor of the Axis war. The German ambassador to Switzerland shared with the nuncio there his view that the pope's speech was "very beautiful" because "every word is measured and it contains ample material for all the belligerents to reflect upon."[7]

In sending an English translation of the radio address to London, Osborne tried to put as positive a spin on it as he could, calling attention to the pope's generic denunciation of religious persecution. Members of the British Foreign Office were less deferential. As one noted, the pope's praise of those governments having amicable relations with the church must be seen as "a compliment to Mussolini." That, he added, seemed "scarcely necessary, even though the title of Prince had just been conferred upon the Pope's nephews in strangely tardy recognition of his late brother's assistance in negotiating the Lateran Treaty." At the same time, the German Foreign Ministry newsletter hailed the pope's speech as offering support for the theories at the heart of National Socialism and Fascism. It explained as well that the pope, in his reference to "oppressed minorities," undoubtedly had in mind the prewar German minority in Poland.[8]

At his New Year's audience, the British envoy found the pope unhappy about America's recent entry into the war and the war's resulting expansion. Contributing to the pope's glum mood was Churchill's speech, three days earlier, to a joint session of Congress in Washington. The prime minister had predicted that the war would last into 1943, when the tide would finally turn. The British Foreign Office sent Osborne's report on the audience to King George VI with a scribbled note: "Mr. Osborne twice stresses the Pope's depression. This is likely to increase owing to pricks of conscience caused by his timid policy." In his end-of-year report for 1941, Osborne linked the pope's insistence on remaining impartial in the war to his belief it would enable him to play a key role in brokering a peace. In the meantime, the pope immersed himself "in multifarious charitable activities and in indulgence of his weakness for oratory." The path the pope had chosen, concluded the British envoy, came "at the expense of the moral prestige of the Papacy bequeathed to him by Pius XI."[9]

WHILE MUSSOLINI HAD JETTISONED many of the beliefs he had once held as a young radical socialist, he never lost his visceral distaste for the Catholic clergy and Catholic doctrine. While these feelings erupted in periodic bursts of venom in the privacy of his encounters with Clara and his conversations with his son-in-law, he had long recognized the wisdom of exhibiting a different attitude in public, and his more caustic views on the church had rarely reached Pius XII's ears.

This was now beginning to change. In speaking to the Fascist Party directorate in early January 1942, the Duce asked how it was that while America's Catholic bishops had issued a declaration supporting their president, the Italian episcopate had made no similar joint declaration of support for him. "There are traitors in the Vatican," someone shouted. "Down with the priests!"[10]

When, a few days later, the pope's nuncio went to meet with Guido Buffarini, Mussolini's undersecretary, he got to hear an echo of the Duce's complaints. "It was easy for me," Monsignor Borgongini recalled, "to rebuff the accusations and emphasize the words of praise that the Holy Father had pronounced for Italy, along with the patriotic work of the Bishops and the Italian clergy in these moments." He told Buffarini that the pope could hardly fail to criticize the Germans' treatment of the church, yet despite all the provocation, Pius XII had always done so "with extreme delicacy."[11]

In fact, Mussolini would have little grounds for complaint in the months ahead. In mid-January his own newspaper featured an address by the bishop of Trieste to the priests of his diocese, warning that Communism was Christianity's dangerous enemy and had to be defeated.[12] A week later, at a high-profile church ceremony, Cardinal Carlo Salotti, one of the Curia's most prominent members, invoked the Madonna's "protection of our soldiers who are fighting for a more just society and for certain victory."[13]

As February began, the Vatican-supervised Jesuit journal added its own support for the Axis cause, publishing an article titled "Vital Space," echoing the concept that both Nazis and Fascists were using to justify the war. The pope, it told its readers, had insisted that all people had a right to their fair share of the earth's resources. That right, it quoted the pope as saying, "applies equally to the State. . . . Thus the State . . . has the right to possess the amount of goods necessary for the fulfilment of its essential functions, or, in modern terms, it has the right to such vital space as is indispensable for the preservation of its social life and for the material and moral welfare of its citizens."[14]

In an effort to retain good relations with the moody dictator, Pius XII decided to send him a private message. The opportunity came in mid-January 1942 when the pope agreed to an audience with Pietro Fedele, Mussolini's former minister of education and a longtime member of the Senate. The pope asked Fedele to tell the Duce how much he appreciated the recent conferral of nobility on his family, adding that he regarded Mussolini with *"great admiration and profound devotion."* In reporting the pope's remarks in a letter to Mussolini, Fedele underlined these last words, further emphasizing the phrase by noting "I repeat His words verbatim." He added that the pope expressed his "joy that the Italian Bishops, at least in great part, are acting in full harmony with the political Authorities and with the Hierarchs of the [Fascist] Party."[15]

While church relations with Italy's Fascist regime remained for the most part friendly, the pope's suspicions of Germany's intentions were only increasing. In the latest incident, the number two in Germany's embassy to Italy was reported to have remarked, "Oh, the Vatican! That's a museum that within a few years we'll have people visit with a ten lire admission ticket."[16]

The pope sent a military chaplain to speak to the Duce about these latest rumors. Father Giacomo Salza met with the Italian dictator on February 4 and told him of the pope's alarm.

"Dear Father," replied the Duce, "there is no incompatibility between the Vatican and Fascism. . . . I am in Rome, and as long as I am here no one is going to touch the Vatican. The Vatican is almost two thousand years old. It will have at least another two thousand. Of this I am certain."[17]

ON FEBRUARY 9, 1942, Mussolini's ambassador to the Vatican, Bernardo Attolico, who had long suffered from heart and liver ills, passed away. Father Tacchi Venturi presided over his funeral Mass at the Jesuits' central church in Rome, with Cardinal Maglione attending as well. Galeazzo Ciano led the large government delegation.[18]

Mussolini's choice to replace Attolico, fifty-three-year-old Raffaele Guariglia, a career diplomat, was greeted warmly at the Vatican. Not only was Guariglia regarded as a good, observant Catholic, but he and Cardinal Maglione, both proud Neapolitans, were old friends.[19]

In the new ambassador's first papal audience in late February, Pius XII gave voice to his fears, beginning with his continuing nervousness over rumors that people from "beyond the Alps," as he delicately put it, were threatening to turn the Vatican into a museum. Such stories were ridiculous, said Guariglia, as ridiculous as a threat would be to turn all of Italy into a museum. Somewhat reassured, the pope returned once again to the theme he seemed never to tire of repeating whenever the subject of Germany came up: his great affection for the German people and his failure to understand why the German leaders—or at least some of them—had turned against the church. "He concluded," wrote Guariglia in his report of this initial papal audience, by "expressing, by contrast, full faith in the political wisdom of the Duce."[20]

A month later—following meetings the new ambassador had with the pope, with Cardinal Maglione, his deputies, and numerous cardi-

Raffaele Guariglia and wife, Francesca Maria Palli, with Cardinal Maglione, following presentation of his credentials as new ambassador to the Holy See, February 24, 1942

nals and bishops—Guariglia reported to Ciano what he had learned. "The central preoccupation that dominates everyone around the Vatican," he wrote, "concerns Germany's anti-Catholic policies, and the ideas that are spreading in some German circles in favor of a new, one might say 'theo-Nazi,' religion." The church's leaders "say it is not true that the Vatican, as some have accused it, has particular theoretical or practical sympathies for the democratic organization of states, since, as far as Italy is concerned, it must recognize the fact that only Fascism has brought the Catholic Church the great benefits that had been denied it by the preceding regimes." The problem, rather, came when, instead of drawing strength from the Catholic Church, as the Fascist regime did in Italy, the totalitarian state sought to put its own national religion in its place.

In all his conversations at the Vatican, Guariglia heard the same fear, that following its inevitable victory, Germany might try to get Italy to adopt a religious policy like its own. The best protection for the church, the prelates were convinced, was for the Holy See to keep its close ties to Mussolini and the Fascist government.

For this reason, the new Italian ambassador advised that "all segments of the Vatican—and not only the Pontiff and the directors of the Holy See's policies—place their full, sincere trust in the proper policies of Fascism and in the wisdom of the Duce, that is, the Author of Conciliation." The occasional brush-up over *L'Osservatore Romano,* and the periodic outbursts in the columns of *Il Regime Fascista,* "are not in reality facts of such a nature as to in any way erode the realistic understanding of a broad commonality of interests which, without any doubt, especially at the current political moment, exists between the Italian Fascist state and the Church of Rome."[21]

THE POPE CONTINUED TO receive detailed reports of Hitler's campaign to exterminate Europe's Jews. They came not only from Jewish and press sources, but from churchmen in whom he would have complete faith. On January 9, 1942, the Roman military chaplain, Father Scavizzi, returned from another trip to the eastern front and met with the pope, giving him a hair-raising account of what he had seen.[22] "It is clear," the priest reported,

> that it is the government of occupation's intention to elimi-
> nate as many Jews as possible, killing them using the various
> systems of which the most frequently employed and the best
> known is that of machine-gunning them in mass. They trans-
> port groups of hundreds and even thousands of Jews from their
> communities. There they make them dig a big ditch, then they
> machine-gun them and throw the cadavers in the ditch. The
> number of killings of Jews is now approaching about a million.[23]

"A young German officer," the Roman priest recounted, "boasted of having learned how to kill both a mother and her child with a single shot." Moments later the soldier proudly took out a photo of his own wife and children to show the priest. Tears clouded the soldier's eyes as he spoke of his deep love for them.

Pius XII told the priest he occasionally thought of excommunicat-ing those who would commit such atrocities, but had decided against it, believing it would not stop the slaughter and might even spur greater anger against Jews. Following their conversation, Scavizzi sent the pope a written report on what he had witnessed. For Hitler's sol-diers in Germany, Poland, and Ukraine, he wrote, "The watchword is: 'exterminate [the Jews] without pity.' The mass murders are multiply-ing everywhere."

More gruesome details followed. At the end of March, the priest sent additional documentation to the Vatican Secretariat of State, ask-ing that L'Osservatore Romano publish it. The pope judged that inop-portune. It was best not to alienate either Mussolini or the Führer.[24]

In March, too, the pontiff heard again from his nuncio in Bratislava, who told of "the imminent mass deportation of all of the Slovakian Jews in Galicia and the Lublin region regardless of age, sex, religion." The "atrocious plan," the nuncio reported, was the work of Josef Tiso, a Catholic priest who since 1939 had been president of the Slovak Re-public, a client state of Nazi Germany. He had ordered the deportation of the nation's Jews to the death camps on his own initiative, needing no prompting from the Nazis. When the nuncio had gone to protest, Tiso "dared to say (he who makes such a show of his Catholicism) that he does not see in it anything inhumane or anti-Christian." The nuncio himself had no doubt as to the Jews' fate. "Deportation of 80,000 people to Poland at the mercy of the Germans," he wrote, "is equivalent to condemn the large part to certain death."[25]

In Italy the pope's interest in the "Jewish question" continued to focus not on the ongoing persecution of the country's Jews but on the application of the racial laws to those he considered Catholics, that is baptized Jews and the baptized children of "mixed" marriages.* Cardinal Maglione repeatedly sent Father Tacchi Venturi to complain to Mussolini's undersecretary about the unfairness of applying laws aimed at Jews to those the church considered Catholics.

In meeting with the pope's Jesuit emissary in late March, Buffarini, the undersecretary of internal affairs, had initially seemed to agree to an amendment to the racial laws declaring "Aryan the whole family in which one of the two spouses is of Aryan race." However, in the end he had backed away from any commitment. "Because of this rigid application [of the racial laws]," lamented the Jesuit emissary, "many Catholics and their offspring were and continue to be treated as if they were pure Jews!"[26]

---

* Most often in Vatican documentation, "mixed" marriages refers to marriages of two Catholics, one of whom is a convert from Judaism.

BEST TO SAY NOTHING

THE FIRST DARK-SUITED MEN, LUGGING THEIR BULKY FILMING equipment, appeared one spring day in Vatican City. Soon, it seemed, they were everywhere, setting up their tripods and lights in the frescoed halls of the Apostolic Palace, in St. Peter's Basilica, in San Damaso Courtyard, and along the walkways of the Vatican Gardens. The sight of the camera-toting laymen hurrying through these sacred spaces seemed odd, but it was the ascetic pope himself who had agreed to this unprecedented incursion of the outside world of cinema into the timeless precincts of the Holy See.

As the resulting film would explain in its opening capital-lettered panels, a twelfth-century Irish bishop had predicted that Peter's two hundred and sixty-second successor to the pontifical throne would come be known as Pastor Angelicus. In late 1941, to promote this image of a pontifical champion of peace amid war, Pius XII had authorized the making of this ambitious, hagiographic feature-length film. Titled *Pastor Angelicus,* it would be shot in the Vatican and star the pope.[1]

The Vatican newspaper had announced the film project in December: "The spectator preparing to watch the vast documentary on Pius XII must approach it with that attention and reverence, that Faith and veneration, which must animate the soul of every Catholic on beholding the representative of God on earth. And, in fact, from his face, from the austere and sublime acts of the Vicar of Christ, torrents of light and goodness flow." The Vatican paper predicted that for those having the good fortune to be admitted to the Holy Father's presence by viewing the film, "the emotional impact will be immediate."[2]

Now, in the spring of 1942, the camera crews were busy following the pope in his daily schedule, as he sat on his throne for audiences, walked through the Vatican Gardens, conferred with his clerical atten- dants, lifted his white-robed arms to bless a crowd, and offered his hand to be kissed by a grateful black-veiled woman on her knees. The filming coincided with an ambitious Vatican effort to burnish the saintly image of the pope, using the twenty-fifth anniversary of his elevation to the episcopate—that is, his rise to the status of a bishop—to create a series of major public events. In March, on the anniversary of his papal coronation, the Vatican had issued a special medallion to mark the day. It showed the distinctive profile of the pope on one side and a haloed image of Jesus on the other. The following month, plans for his episcopal anniversary featured construction of a church in his honor dedicated to his namesake, the obscure seventh-century pope Saint Eu- genio I. The Italian dictator was among the many who contributed to the fund.[3]

WHILE THE CAMERAMEN WERE busy setting up the scenes for their film, their subject was receiving ever more alarming accounts of the Germans' campaign to exterminate Europe's Jews. In May the pope got yet another bloodcurdling report from Italian army chaplain Fa- ther Scavizzi on his return from his latest trip to the eastern front. "The massacre of the Jews in Ukraine," he reported, "is now complete. They want to likewise finish off with their system of mass killings in Poland and Germany."[4]

Monsignor Orsenigo, the longtime papal nuncio in Berlin, well aware of the Jews' fate, did not seem overly concerned. He told the secretary of Italy's embassy in Berlin he had tried to intervene various times "to soften the action against the Jews, at least the Christian Jews," but had not had any success. The embassy secretary reported this con- versation to Ciano, observing that "the nuncio did not fail to point out to the Jews how the excessive racial sense that characterizes them has come to be used against them." The nuncio's warm regard for Hitler had earlier been noted by Italy's ambassador to Berlin. "Orsenigo," he observed, "is viewed favorably and respected by the Führer himself."[5]

The nuncio was also doing his best to minimize fears that the Nazis were trying to create a new religion of their own, insisting the rumors were overblown. He told an Italian diplomat in Berlin that while unfortunately some Nazis would be happy to see this happen, there were many "reasonable people in the bosom of National Socialism with whom one could talk." With 40 or 45 million Catholics in the newly expanded Reich, he added, it would be suicidal for Hitler to turn against the church.[6]

In Italy, Mussolini had recently ordered Jews to form domestic labor brigades, saying it was scandalous that Jewish men were left undisturbed at home while good Catholic Italians were risking their lives on the battlefield. (The racial laws had banned Jews from serving in the country's military.) Photographs of bare-chested Roman Jews doing hard physical labor along the banks of the Tiber soon appeared in the country's newspapers. Upset by the images, Cardinal Maglione sent Father Tacchi Venturi to speak with the authorities about the new policy. Antonio Le Pera, head of the Department of Race and Demography, assured him that contrary to newspaper reports, members of the "noble professions, like doctors, lawyers, accountants," would not be made to do the humiliating physical labor. Rather it would be limited to Jews of a humbler station. The Jesuit then went to speak with Le Pera's boss, undersecretary of internal affairs Guido Buffarini. After expressing his unhappiness at seeing Rome's Jews humiliated in this way, Tacchi Venturi told the undersecretary that "should they decide at any cost to put the requirement into practice, it would at least be important to order a perfect separation in the forced labor between the Jews who had become Christians and those who remained as Jews."[7]

The Fascist press meanwhile continued to publish articles justifying the anti-Jewish measures as simply carrying out the same policy that the Catholic Church itself had long championed. A July article in Mussolini's *Popolo d'Italia* gave prominent coverage to a recent speech by Farinacci in Milan, in which he read aloud what he identified as "maxims" from the Talmud. "Italy and Germany," the paper reported "were able to be inspired by an ancient anti-Jewish tradition . . . nourished by the Catholic Church itself, through the words of its popes and the decisions of its Councils." The accompanying photo showed Farinacci speaking to a packed hall decorated with both Nazi and Japanese flags. A week later, in his own newspaper, *Il Regime Fascista,* Farinacci repeated what had become his constant refrain: "We, Fascist Catholics, are anti-Jewish because we have learned to combat these enemies of Christian civilization from the Doctors and Saints of the Church."[8]

Roberto Farinacci

Italy's Catholic press meanwhile reported the recent roundup in Paris—by French police—of twenty thousand Jews destined for concentration camps and death in Poland. A few days later an assembly of French cardinals and archbishops met to discuss the situation, but the minority calling for a public protest was overruled. Instead, the archbishop of Paris wrote Marshal Pétain a private letter expressing their concern.[9]

WITH THE SUCCESS OF the new Axis offensive in North Africa and regular reports of the sinking of Allied merchant ships by German U-boats in the Atlantic, the summer of '42 brought Mussolini a raft of good news. Following months of widespread pessimism, his spies were reporting an improvement in public morale. If the Germans now took Egypt, President Roosevelt observed at the time, the Nazis and their Japanese allies would control a vast stretch of land and sea extending from the Atlantic to the Pacific.[10]

Along with reports of the Germans' military advances in North Africa came new accounts of their mass murder of civilians in central and eastern Europe. D'Arcy Osborne, Britain's envoy to the Vatican, renewed his pleas for the pope to speak out, but as he reported to London on July 12, his efforts were proving futile. There was no point in having the pope protest the atrocities, said Cardinal Maglione, as the Germans would simply deny that the charges were true. But Osborne sensed the cardinal was himself uncomfortable with the pope's silence: "He has to defend the policy of the Pope, whether he approves of it or not." On the text of Osborne's report, a London Foreign Office official added a handwritten note: "Papal timidity becomes ever more blatantly despicable."[11]

If Cardinal Maglione was becoming embarrassed, his deputy, Monsignor Tardini, was growing ever more irritated, but not with the pope. The constant parade of diplomats complaining about Pius XII's failure to denounce the Nazi crimes was beginning to wear on him. The Polish ambassador came again to see Tardini, asking, in the monsignor's words, "for the umpteenth time that the Holy See say a word publicly in favor of the Poles and against the terrible persecution they are being subjected to." The next day Osborne came "to say more or less the same thing." To both, Tardini replied the same way: the Holy See found it most effective to act privately, discreetly. To speak out publicly risked compromising that valuable work.[12]

Tardini's irritation was no doubt heightened when Osborne handed him a letter he said a "friend" at the Foreign Office had written him but that reflected the Foreign Office's views. It was a rather curious subterfuge, avoiding representing the letter as an official message from the Foreign Office. "Ever since the entry of Italy into the war," it argued:

> the Pope has more and more assimilated himself to the status of a sovereign of a small neutral State in the geographical neighbourhood of Axis Powers, and, for worldly rather than spiritual reasons, has allowed himself, like others, to be bullied. In short, we feel that His Holiness is not putting up a very good fight to retain his moral and spiritual leadership, when he should realise that in Hitler's new world there will be no room for the Catholic religion and that if the Papacy remains silent, the free nations may find that they have little power to arrest the anticlericalism which may follow the war.

A handwritten note made on the text the following day reads "Seen by the Holy Father."[13]

A week later, Osborne took the unusual step of writing directly to the pope. Again, he used the tack of presenting his harshest language in the form of a text written by someone else. Marking his letter "personal and confidential," he told the pope he wanted to pass on an extract from a letter he had received "from a great friend of mine in England," whom he described as "a devout Catholic, the mother of six children."

> I think that the Vatican is very poorly thought of indeed in this country at the moment, and not only by Protestants! . . . What no one understands is why His Holiness goes on talking about what people ought to do, instead of giving some kind of lead in condemning what they are actually doing. Why does He not speak out, with names attached, about the really appalling fate of Poles, Jews, Czechs, etc. under the Germans?

There is no indication the pope responded to Osborne's letter, but a penciled note written in the margin, perhaps by Tardini, consigned it to a now rapidly growing pile, labeling it simply, "Pressures for the Holy Father to speak out against German barbarism."[14]

The evening before he sent his letter, Osborne was walking in the Vatican Gardens, as he did most evenings, when he encountered a strange sight. The band of the Palatine Guard was marching around and around a little path on the top of the hill that overlooked the back of St. Peter's Basilica. Puzzled, it dawned on him that this was part of the shooting of the pope's *Pastor Angelicus* movie. "I find this very regrettable," Osborne wrote in his diary, "and much too reminiscent of Hollywood publicity." With the pope feeling under such great pressure to speak out, "I fear his holiness sublimates his frustration in overdoing the Pastor Angelicus. . . . Only why then does he not denounce the German atrocities against the populations of the occupied countries?"[15]

TALL, SLENDER, ATTRACTIVE, HER photographs gracing countless Italian magazines, the thirty-six-year-old Princess Maria José could not fail to attract attention when she appeared by herself in the Apostolic Palace, leaving her driver to wait outside. She had come to make an urgent, secret request. Perhaps it was appropriate that in those halls entirely dominated by men, it was she, wife of Umberto, the king's son and heir, who would first come to ask for the pope's support in ridding Italy of Mussolini and extracting the country from the war.

It was especially ironic that Maria José would play this role, as it was her sister-in-law, Mafalda, who was married to the Nazi prince Philipp von Hessen, Hitler's secret emissary to the pope. Maria José's husband, Umberto, the prince of Piedmont, had followed the long tradition of intermarriage of Europe's royalty in marrying her, daughter of the former king of Belgium and sister of its current king, now a hostage of the Germans. A patron of the arts and especially archaeology, she had a strong interest in politics too, something neither the pope nor the king appreciated in a woman. The princess had also developed a thick

Princess Maria José and Prince Umberto, heir to the Italian throne, 1939

network of contacts among intellectuals unsympathetic to Mussolini
and to his alliance with Hitler, and she had close ties as well to several
of the Italian military command. "She hates the Germans with all her
soul," Ciano had noted after one of her visits in late 1939.[16]

A few months after Hitler's forces occupied Belgium in 1940, Maria
José had gone to Germany on her brother's behalf to plead with the
German dictator for better treatment of her native country.[17] In her
account of that meeting, the Führer took her hand and said, "You
know that you are the perfect model of an Aryan Princess? Your eyes
are the color of the German sky." But he was not so smitten as to ac-
cede to her request. She returned to Italy ever more repelled by the

Nazi regime and more eager to see Italy remove itself from the war. For those of the upper classes and upper regions of the military in Italy who viewed the monarchy as their only hope for deposing Mussolini and were unhappy that the king and his son Umberto were unwilling to countenance any such talk, she had become the center of a loose network. Resented by her father-in-law for inappropriately mixing herself in political affairs, she was the first to admit how little influence she had over him. She likely kept her husband informed of her activities, but he would do nothing to challenge his father.

The princess's visit to the Vatican was prompted by news that Myron Taylor, President Roosevelt's envoy to the pope, would soon return to Rome. She wanted to get a message to the pope and decided to do so by meeting Monsignor Montini, known to be the man closest to him. She told Montini she had come on her own initiative, eager to have Pius XII tell the American envoy that Italians wanted to get out of the war and were willing to support a new leader for that purpose. She warned that in negotiating Italy's exit, the Americans should not deal with those in the Duce's inner circle. There were other men, men with links to the military, who could take over. She named various people she thought the Allies could deal with, and who, with the church's support, could win Italians' confidence. The alternative, said the princess, was not only continued war and suffering but the likelihood it would lead one day to what she called an "anarchical revolution." It would be in the interest both of the royal family and of the church to prevent any such popular uprising and its unpredictable consequences.

It isn't clear if Prince Umberto knew in advance of his wife's trip to the Vatican, although his father certainly did not. Subsequently informed of her attempt to enlist the pope's help, Victor Emmanuel, who came from a long line of anticlerics, replied in Piedmontese dialect, "I don't want priests underfoot." He need not have worried. Pius XII, although not happy about Italy's continuing involvement in the war, showed no inclination to act on the princess's suggestion that he help bring about Mussolini's fall. But Montini did keep in touch with her, and over the next months, they arranged a series of secret meet-

ings, something he is unlikely to have done without the pope's blessing. Those meetings were held not at the Vatican, where it would be
difficult to keep them from the eyes of informants, but at private resi-
dences in Rome. In the princess's telling, she arrived at such rendezvous incognito in an unmarked car, wearing large sunglasses with a
kerchief covering her hair. Montini's accounts of these meetings, if
they exist, have yet to be found.[18]

THE POPE WOULD ENJOY no respite from the continued pressures to
speak out against the mounting scale of German atrocities. Shortly
after the princess's visit, Monsignor Montini tried to deflect the British
envoy's complaints by referring him to a recently published article in a
Swiss newspaper, titled "Vatican Policy in the Second War." The monsignor's clear implication, reported the British envoy, was that it represented an accurate statement of the course charted by the pope. Its
theme was, as Osborne reported,

> insistence on the political and moral neutrality of the Vatican
> in the interests of "the preservation of the freedom of the
> Church and her hierarchy, of her members and their profession
> of faith." Thus it is stated that the exercise of the right to take a
> moral stand will be subordinated to political exigencies. . . . We
> have here the admission that the moral leadership of the Papacy
> is conditioned by considerations of opportunism and expedi-
> ence. This means, for instance, that the Pope does not condemn
> Nazi religious persecution because, if he did so, the lot of the
> Catholics concerned might be worsened. . . . (This is a favourite
> argument at the Vatican.)

Osborne, who over the next years would wax hot and cold on the
pope, concluded his report with a sharp rebuke: "But a moral leadership the exercise of which is governed by practical expediency must
lose its validity, and this is what has happened. . . . I have often pointed
out here, and shall continue to do so, that the Pope's policy of silence

and neutrality at all costs is destroying the moral authority of the Vatican."[19]

The pope meanwhile continued to receive new reports of the mass murder of Europe's Jews, including one from a particularly reliable source, the archbishop of the Ukrainian Greek Catholic Church, who wrote the pope directly in late August 1942 describing the German occupiers' "diabolical" depredations in Ukraine:

> The Jews are the first victims of it. The number of Jews killed in our little area has certainly exceeded two hundred thousand. As the army advances eastward, the number of victims grows. At Kiev, in just a few days, as many as a hundred thirty thousand men, women and children were executed. All the small towns of Ukraine have seen similar massacres. . . . As time has passed, they have begun to kill the Jews in the streets, in view of the entire population and without any shame.[20]

Reports were also coming to the Vatican from Italy's own concentration camps, into which foreign Jews had been herded since the imposition of the country's racial laws four years earlier. On September 10 a Franciscan friar reported to the Vatican on his recent visit to the concentration camp at Ferramonti, in Calabria. Fourteen hundred foreign Jews were confined there, scattered among scores of barracks. They had created a certain degree of self-governance, regulating religious life and setting up a school for the children. Now news of the recent mass deportation of German Jews living in France to Polish death camps was creating panic. The visiting priest had unsuccessfully tried to calm the Jews at Ferramonti, telling them there was no immediate danger they would meet the same fate. But, he thought, their fears were understandable. They knew that deportation meant an unspeakable death.[21]

At that time, too, the pope received another firsthand account of the fate of Poland's Jews when a prominent Italian Catholic, Giovanni Malvezzi, came to see Monsignor Montini. As part of his duties as vice director of the Italian government's giant holding company, which controlled a good part of Italy's economy, Malvezzi had recently traveled to Poland. "The massacres of Jews," the future pope noted after the meeting, "have reached horrifying proportions and horrifying forms. Incredible slaughters are carried out every day."[22]

Two months earlier the Brazilian ambassador to the Holy See, frustrated by Pius XII's refusal to condemn the Nazi crimes, proposed a coordinated effort by like-minded colleagues to put pressure on him. After the foreign diplomats received authorization from their governments, their pleas began to pour in.[23] On September 12, 1942, the Belgian and Polish ambassadors came to the Apostolic Palace to bring their joint appeal. Meeting with Monsignor Tardini, they told him that the representatives of the other German-occupied nations—the Netherlands, Norway, Czechoslovakia, and Yugoslavia—had all subscribed to their message as well.[24]

Two days later it was Osborne's turn. He sent the British plea in the form of a letter to Cardinal Maglione: "I have been instructed by my Government to urge that His Holiness the Pope should carefully consider the expediency of a public and specific denunciation of Nazi treatment of the populations of the countries in German occupation." After dismissing the pope's generic words denouncing the crimes of war as of little use, Osborne warned, "A policy of silence in regard to such offences against the conscience of the world must necessarily involve a renunciation of moral leadership and a consequent atrophy of the influence and authority of the Vatican." That same day the American envoy, Harold Tittmann, sent a similar appeal on behalf of the American government.[25]

"Even Peru!" wrote the disconsolate Tardini as the last of these pleas came in at the end of the month. A separate handwritten note in the bulging Secretariat of State file observed, "Almost no one is lacking from the chorus."[26]

ON SEPTEMBER 19 ROOSEVELT'S envoy, Myron Taylor, met with Pius XII. It was his first visit since the United States entered the war nine months earlier, and the audience lasted almost two hours. Taylor thought the pope appeared to be in good health, albeit thinner, "heightening his ascetic appearance." He devoted this first audience to impressing on the pontiff his country's confidence that it would win the war, pointing out that America had an abundance of material resources, while its enemies' resources were steadily dwindling. He argued as well that if the Axis were to triumph, it "would destroy all semblance of Christian Europe." But he took care to distinguish between American attitudes toward Germany and Italy. In the United States, popular anger focused almost entirely on Germany and Japan. One seldom heard any harsh words aimed at Italy. If Italy were now to renounce its alliance with Hitler, it might yet escape the fate that would one day befall the defeated Axis powers.

Roosevelt had another message for Pius XII as well, which Taylor handed him in the form of a ten-page document. As the memo put it, there was reason to believe "our Axis enemies will attempt, through devious channels, to urge the Holy See to endorse in the near future proposals of peace without victory. In the present position of the belligerents, we can readily understand how strong a pressure the Axis powers may bring to bear upon the Vatican." With German troops occupying much of Europe, such a peace conference would only end up ratifying Hitler's conquests. Roosevelt wanted to be sure the pope resisted those pressures.[27]

Three days later, Taylor met again with the pope, this time handing him a report documenting German atrocities. "It is widely believed," Taylor told him, "that Your word of condemnation would hearten all others who are working to save these thousands from suffering and death."[28] He coupled this appeal with a long memo, addressed to Cardinal Maglione, containing reports of the ongoing slaughter of Poland's Jews. It painted a horrifying picture:

Liquidation of the Warsaw Ghetto is taking place. Without any distinction all Jews, irrespective of age or sex, are being removed from the Ghetto in groups and shot. Their corpses are utilized for making fats and their bones for the manufacture of fertilizer. . . . Jews deported from Germany, Belgium, Holland,

**Myron Taylor returning from European trip,
New York, October 1942**

France, and Slovakia are sent to be butchered. . . . Inasmuch as butcherings of this kind would attract great attention in the west, they must first of all deport them to the East, where less opportunity is afforded to outsiders of knowing what is going on. During the last few weeks a large part of the Jewish population deported to Lithuania and Lublin has already been executed. . . . Arrangements are made for new deportations as soon as space is made by executions. Caravans of such deportees being transported in cattle cars are often seen.

Taylor's memo concluded, "I should much appreciate it if Your Eminence could inform me whether the Vatican has any information that would tend to confirm the reports contained in this memorandum. If so, I should like to know whether the Holy Father has any suggestions as to any practical manner in which the forces of civilized public opinion could be utilized in order to prevent a continuation of these barbarities."[29]

Although a note in the recently opened secretariat files shows that the pope read this memo immediately, he was slow to respond. A handwritten note on the memo, dated September 30, responded to the question of whether the Vatican had any reports confirming that the Nazis were engaged in slaughtering Jews. It read "There are those of Signor Malvezzi," referring to the Italian business leader's recent account of his trip to Poland. The pope had received many other such reports, including the recent one the Ukrainian archbishop had sent him, as well as the many detailed reports he had been getting from Don Scavizzi's trips to the eastern front.

Taylor would leave Rome before receiving any response to his request.[30] A few days after his departure, Harold Tittmann, his assistant, now resident in Vatican City, went to the Apostolic Palace to follow up. A note in the secretariat files explains that the American envoy came "to pray that a response be given, even at any hour, to the memo left by His Excellency Myron Taylor on the killings of the Jews."[31]

The following day, October 2, 1942, Monsignor Dell'Acqua, the member of the Secretariat of State staff whom the pope viewed as his expert on questions regarding Jews, offered his advice on how to respond.[32] Over the next years, Dell'Acqua's antisemitic comments would mark many of the documents dealing with requests to the pope to speak out on behalf of persecuted Jews. His future in the church would be a bright one. In 1953 he would replace Monsignor Montini as substitute of the Secretariat of State office, and then in 1967 Montini himself, as pope, would appoint Dell'Acqua cardinal vicar of Rome.

It was best, Dell'Acqua suggested, to delay saying anything in response to the American request: "There is no doubt that the news contained in Ambassador Taylor's letter is very serious. . . . It is necessary, however, to be certain that it corresponds to the truth, because exaggeration comes easily also for the Jews." True, he noted, the pope had in the last months received very similar accounts of the mass murder of Jews from the Ukrainian archbishop and from Malvezzi. Here the pope's adviser added parenthetically, apparently referring to the Ukrainian archbishop, "the Orientals too are not in fact an exemplar of sincerity." "But," advised the monsignor, "even given that the news is true, it will be wise to proceed with great caution in confirming it to Signor Tittmann because I seem to also perceive a political (if not purely political) aim in the American Government's move, which would perhaps not fail to give publicity to the Holy See's eventual confirmation." In short, the Allies might cite the Vatican in support of their charge that the Nazis were systematically slaughtering Europe's Jews. That, argued Dell'Acqua, "could have unpleasant consequences not only for the Holy See, but for the Jews themselves who find themselves in German hands. . . . One could ask the opinion of the nuncio in Berlin, but whatever will that poor man be able to say with certainty!"[33]

The following day the Polish ambassador would provide the pope with further news of the ongoing mass murder of Jews in his homeland: "The Germans' massacres of the Jews in Poland are of public notoriety." He went on to give details of the deportation of tens of thousands of Jews to their deaths in concentration camps, concluding, "In the course of the next months, one expects that all of the Jewish population of the Warsaw ghetto, consisting of 300,000 Jews, will be sent there, and that the homes of that part of the city will be given to 'Aryans.'"[34]

Coincidentally, while the pope was mulling over how to respond to the American president, Father Scavizzi, following his most recent return from visiting Italy's troops on the eastern front, sent in yet another report of atrocities. "The elimination of the Jews, with mass killings, is almost total, without regard to children, not even those who are nursing. . . . It is said that over two million Jews have been killed."[35]

On October 10 Cardinal Maglione finally handed the pope's re-

sponse to Tittmann. The statement, unsigned, acknowledged that reports of "severe measures taken against non-Aryans" had also reached
the Holy See from other sources, "but that up to the present time it has
not been possible to verify the accuracy thereof." The pope had accepted Monsignor Dell'Acqua's advice. Best to offer the Allies no confirmation of the reports of the Nazis' mass murder of Europe's Jews
and risk having the Vatican invoked in confirming the Allies' charge. In
fact, best not even to use the word "Jews" at all.[36]

PART THREE

—

CHANGING FORTUNES

ESCAPING BLAME

L ATE ON THE NIGHT OF OCTOBER 22, 1942, WAVE AFTER WAVE of British bombers swooped below the 2,500-foot cloud cover over Genoa and released hundreds of bombs and incendiary devices. Two searchlights pierced the skies as the city's antiaircraft guns, positioned on the nearby hills, fired haplessly at their elusive targets. The attack would usher in a new phase in the Allied air war, a campaign of "area bombing" aimed at terrorizing and demoralizing the Italians. The port, the city center, residential areas, hospitals, and churches were all hit. Two days later it was Milan's turn, the first time British bombers attacked in broad daylight, leaving 132 people dead. By war's end, Genoa, Milan, and Turin would each have suffered over fifty Allied bombing raids.[1]

Along with this unwelcome new development came one even more consequential for the Axis cause. On the night of October 23, Allied forces under British general Bernard Montgomery began their offensive in Egypt at the central Egyptian Mediterranean town of El Alamein. Montgomery commanded 190,000 men, equipped with over a thousand tanks. He faced German war hero Erwin Rommel, who had 116,000 German and Italian troops under him, along with 540 tanks. Montgomery's assault began with a massive artillery barrage on the Axis troops, followed by a harrowing tank attack through the minefields Rommel had planted. Within ten days the Allies had sent the

Axis troops into flight, although not before half of Rommel's men were killed, wounded, or taken prisoner.

To make matters worse for the Axis, on November 8, the first American GIs, under General Dwight Eisenhower, began flooding into the French colonies of Morocco and Algeria. Together with their allies, they defeated German and Italian forces there in short order. Until then France's position had remained ambiguous, with the loyalty of the French military in the North African colonies not entirely clear. The fact that the French troops, who came under the authority of Marshal Pétain and his Vichy collaborationist government, failed to contest the Allied assault led the Germans to send their own troops into the southeastern portion of France. Until then, that large swath of France had been left under French military control.

For Germany and Italy, the new developments in North Africa were a disaster. The Allies were not only in the process of removing hundreds of thousands of Axis troops from battle and destroying a good deal of Axis war matériel; they were also creating a major staging ground for an assault on Axis-controlled Europe from the south. Italy lay tantalizingly close to the Allies' new airfields and ports.[2]

EVER SINCE THE GERMAN army had moved so rapidly through western Europe two years earlier, Axis victory had seemed inevitable to many in Italy and in the Vatican. Germany's troops had seized much of Europe, penetrated deep into the Soviet Union, and routed British forces in North Africa, while Japan had conquered an enormous swath of territory in Asia and Oceania. Now a very different future was beginning to emerge.

Mussolini needed someone to blame for the country's mounting disasters. "The bombings of Genoa and Turin are entirely the Vatican's fault," he told a surprised Raffaele Guariglia, his ambassador to the Holy See. Myron Taylor, said the Duce, had sensed a defeatist attitude during his recent visit to the Vatican and assumed it reflected a more widespread lack of Italian enthusiasm for the war. "So he went to London and suggested they intensify the terrorist bombings in Italy, certain that the Allies would bring about our country's collapse that way."

Guariglia tried to convince Mussolini he was mistaken. Vatican prelates would never do anything to undermine war morale, he said, for they lived in fear of doing anything that might provoke Fascist hotheads to strike out against the Holy See.

"It's true," replied Mussolini, "for it would be very easy to send a few hundred people to attack the Vatican."[3]

At the same time, the Italian ambassador decided to speak with his German counterpart about what he saw as the greatest threat to the pope's willingness to be cooperative. Pius XII was under great pressure to denounce German measures undermining the church, Guariglia told Ambassador Bergen. The pope had recently commissioned a report examining the situation of the church in German-occupied territories, and it painted an alarming picture. In Austria, all the seminaries were closed, and children were being sent to schools where any discussion of religion was forbidden. In Czechoslovakia, a number of priests had been sent to the Dachau concentration camp. At the camp at Mauthausen, according to the report received by the pope, "there are about 42,000 people, between Jews, priests, and those condemned for political reasons. It is a place of suffering and of the cruelest and most inhumane treatments, including the use of asphyxiating gas."[4]

Despite all the alarming news of this sort coming in to the pope, Guariglia told Bergen, "the Pope has restrained himself as a courtesy to Germany, which is beneficial to Italy too." But if the Germans continued to act against the church, the pope's policy of silence could become untenable.

The German ambassador heartily agreed and now had a new note to strike in his pleas to Berlin. He wrote to Berlin on October 12, 1942:

Ambassador Guariglia recently expressed his grave concerns about the progressive deterioration of German-Vatican relations and cautiously asked if Germany could not be somewhat more accommodating towards the Curia, for instance with respect to

the confiscation of monasteries and Church property. . . . As in
every conversation, he raised the issue of the unbearable Anglo-
Saxon propaganda, which portrays England and the United
States as pillars of religious freedom against the Axis powers. He
also fears that this propaganda could lead to pushing Argentina
and Chile into the enemy camp.

Bergen concluded with this advice to the German Foreign Ministry: "I
suggest you reflect on potential repercussions for our allies. Open conflict with the Pope would have a drastic negative effect on public opinion in Italy, which generally is not very good vis-à-vis Germany, and
it would promote the machinations of those who seek to separate Italy
from Germany."[5]

AS THE NIGHTLY BOMBINGS of the northern Italian cities continued,
Giuseppe Bottai, Mussolini's minister of education, went to warn him
about the souring public mood. Don't worry so much, replied the
Duce. Following the invasion of Ethiopia seven years earlier, he reminded Bottai, the war at times had seemed to be going badly, and
people's enthusiasm had flagged, but once the war began to go well
again, they were more enthusiastic than ever.[6]

Yet things were only getting worse. On the night of November
20, 250 Allied planes dropped bombs and incendiary devices on Turin,
flattening entire neighborhoods and causing 117 deaths. A witness described the scene: "a cloud of fire, made all the brighter by the dark-
ness, has descended on Turin." Eight days later a new wave of RAF
bombers appeared, dropping huge bombs and phosphorous incendiary
devices on the city.[7] Turin's archbishop sent the pope a barrage of telegrams and letters chronicling the damage. In early December, as the
bombings continued, he wrote: "Churches hospitals ruined, Seminary
and Cathedral intact. Household and myself safe." D'Arcy Osborne,
Churchill's envoy at the Vatican, reported to London on the pope's
reaction:

There can . . . be no doubt that the recent heavy bombardments of North Italian cities have greatly upset the Pope and his
entourage. Owing to the fact that His Holiness never made any
specific condemnation of the deliberate slaughter of thousands
of civilians in German bombardments, such as those of Warsaw,
Rotterdam, Belgrade, London, Coventry and other British cities, he is precluded by the most elementary logic from condemning our recent raids on Milan, Genoa and Turin.[8]

Nor were matters going better for Italian and German troops on
the Russian front. On the snowy, foggy morning of November 19,
1942, over a million Soviet soldiers launched an attack on the German
army besieging Stalingrad. Soon the three hundred thousand Axis soldiers found themselves encircled. Over the next three months, the Red
Army would tighten its vise, as Axis rations ran out, a typhus epidemic
raged, and the wounded and sick were left outside to freeze to death.
The frozen bodies of German, Italian, Hungarian, and Romanian soldiers soon dotted the frosted wasteland amid the rubble of the city and
its hinterland.[9]

In the privacy of her time alone with Mussolini, Clara witnessed
her lover's nervousness about the war's new turn. "I'm disappointed
and tired," he told her on the last day of November. "Everything is
very different from what I was expecting and what I had hoped. . . .
Nothing interests me any longer, not even you." Clara would always
meet these episodes of self-pity and venom by doing her best to buck
up his spirits, knowing that any passing cruel words he aimed at her
would soon be replaced by renewed professions of his love. His mood
could indeed change quickly. Only a few days later Mussolini was euphoric, back from a trip to Milan where he reveled in the enthusiastic
reception he had received from the crowd that came to hear him speak
there. "He is already in a divine mood," Clara recalled happily.[10]

Despite the bombings of Italy's cities and the recent stall of the
Axis advance in Russia, Italy's king, too, remained convinced the war
would soon be won. "The Allies do not find themselves in a terribly

comfortable position and I believe that they will not be able to win," he told the papal nuncio, who met with him in late November. The king had advice for the pope as well: "In His exalted mission the Holy Father must maintain the strictest neutrality. However, I believe that in His heart he cannot wish for the victory of the Jews, the Bolsheviks, and the Lutherans."[11]

THE INTENSIFYING ALLIED AIR assault on Italy's cities prompted new fears that Rome might soon be targeted. In early December 1942 the pope learned of a Radio London broadcast threatening to extend the Allied bombing campaign to the Eternal City. He decided to contact not the British prime minister but the American president. He had good reason to believe Roosevelt would be more open to his plea, because Catholics were more politically important to the American president than they were to the British prime minister, and because it was London, not Washington, that had suffered from devastating Axis bombings.

The pope made use of both official and unofficial channels. Monsignor Amleto Cicognani, the papal delegate in Washington, alerted Archbishop Spellman, who immediately telephoned the president. Such was the New York archbishop's clout that Roosevelt scheduled a meeting with him three days later. At the same time, Cicognani informed the American assistant secretary of state of the pope's threat to protest publicly if Rome were bombed. That route proved less effective, as the American official responded by asking whether Pius XII had ever protested when London was bombed.[12]

At the Apostolic Palace, Cardinal Maglione summoned Mussolini's ambassador. Whenever they asked the British to spare Rome from attack, he told him, they always received the same response: not only had the pope made no protest when Italians took part in bombing London, but Rome was the headquarters of both Italian and German military command centers. It was crucial, the cardinal told Guariglia, for the Duce to move all military activities out of the city.[13]

Mussolini soon sent back word signaling his agreement. The king, eager to avoid having British bombs fall on his palace, agreed as well.[14]

Frenetic negotiations followed, with the American envoy, Harold Tittmann, and his British colleague, D'Arcy Osborne, meeting almost daily with Maglione as the cardinal tried to broker a deal. Osborne, however, never had much confidence that Mussolini would abandon his capital. He also found the pope's intense interest in protecting the Axis capital from harm unseemly. Instead of thinking only of protecting Rome from attack, Osborne noted in his diary, the pope would be better advised to consider his duty in the face of "the unprecedented crime against humanity of Hitler's campaign of extermination of the Jews," in which, he pointed out, "Italy was an accomplice as the partner and ally of Germany."[15]

ITALIAN MEDIA MEANWHILE CONTINUED to feature the clergy's patriotic appeals in support of the war. In December, Italy's state radio broadcast a special Mass praying for Axis victory. A few days later similar masses were held in churches throughout the country. Celebrating a "Day of Faith," they brought Fascist officials and military officers together with the faithful. Mussolini's paper offered enthusiastic coverage of the event, giving special attention to the ceremony held at Bologna's central church, San Petronio. The head of the Fascist Party for the province was present, along with the *podestà,* the prefect, and local military commanders. "After the Mass," the paper reported, "Cardinal Nasalli Rocca, archbishop of Bologna, pronounced a most noble speech, exalting the heroism of our soldiers, who are fighting and dying for Italy, cradle of Christianity, beacon of civilization to the whole world." In December, too, the pope, as he had in previous years, personally authorized the holding of a special Mass of mourning on the anniversary of the death of Arnaldo Mussolini, who had succeeded his brother as director of *Il Popolo d'Italia.*[16]

The main source of church complaint about Italy's government at the time, according to the monthly reports of the nation's prefects, stemmed not from any unhappiness with the war but from the regime's failure to sufficiently police the nation's entertainment. What particularly attracted the outrage of the church's moral arbiters was the country's popular variety shows, to which large numbers were streaming as a diversion from the rigors of wartime life. A lengthy late 1942 report of the national Catholic Action secretariat for morality recounted that its members had recently monitored 229 such shows. It called on the government to suppress them all. The secretariat complained that the actors were getting laughs by portraying husbands cuckolded by their wives, while female dancers wore costumes so minimal that they sometimes revealed their navels. Homosexuals, rather than being denounced for their depravity, were being portrayed in a comic light, "and dances, without exception, have one purpose only: that of provoking sexual orgasm in the spectators."[17]

Luigi Lavitrano, one of the three cardinals charged by the pope with overseeing Italian Catholic Action, found the matter sufficiently serious that he wrote a long letter directly to Mussolini. Speaking on behalf of the entire Italian episcopate, he called on the Duce to address "a serious problem of a moral nature that deeply worries pastors of souls and educators of youth," namely variety shows, which had been spreading into movie theaters throughout the country and threatened to become the nation's most popular form of entertainment. "The moral consequences," wrote the cardinal, "are extremely pernicious."[18]

PAPAL PREMIERE

W ITH THE ALLIES FIRMLY ENSCONCED IN NORTH AFRICA, FEARS they might now be planning a cross-Mediterranean attack on Italy led to a flow of thousands of German troops down the peninsula to bolster Italian defenses.[1] One effect of the increasing German military presence was the ever-larger number of German soldiers eager to attend a papal audience and receive a papal blessing. The frequent audiences granted to the German soldiers were pleasing to the pope, who remained not only fond of Germans from the many years he had spent in that country but also proud of his ability to speak with them in their own language. Neither Hitler nor his colleagues were amused. A December 8 complaint from the Nazi Party Chancellery to the German Foreign Ministry called for better enforcement of the requirement that any such visits by members of the army be approved in advance by the German embassy in Rome.[2]

At the same time, the increased German military presence in the country was prompting new nervousness in the Vatican. "One hears talk," Cardinal Maglione observed, "of invasion or bombardment of the Vatican by the Germans, of seizure of the archives, of expulsion of the diplomats from the countries that are the enemies of the Axis, etc." Maglione was also concerned by the old rumor that had so unnerved the pope about German plans to turn the Vatican into a museum.[3]

The pope was feeling pressure from the British as well. On December 18, 1942, Osborne, the British envoy, briefed Monsignor Tardini, head of the Vatican Secretariat of State office dealing with foreign relations, on the systematic murder of Jews in German-occupied lands. Before leaving, he handed him a written report to give the pope. A few extracts offer some flavor of what the pope was to read:

> December 8th: Polish Government in London informs Mr. Eden and Mr. Maisky that the Nazis have up to date massacred more than a million Jews in Poland. Meanwhile 180,000 Jews have been deported from Roumania and deportation is similarly proceeding from France, Holland, Norway (where heartrending scenes are today reported on the rounding-up of the Jewish victims), Croatia and Slovakia. The deportees are sent to Poland, which appears to have been selected as the extermination centre for European Jewry. [British Archbishop] Cardinal Hinsley denounces the policy of extermination.

> . . . Dec 10th: Polish Government address a Circular Note to all other Governments regarding the German massacres of the Jews. One out of three million Jews in Poland have already been murdered. Speaking in London the Archbishop of York declares that "we are witnessing the deliberate massacre of a nation."

> . . . Dec 13th: New evidence is coming in of the unspeakable cruelty involved in Hitler's war of annihilation against the Jews of Europe, to which he referred in his last speech. . . . Entire communities in Poland were massacred to a man and there were several thousand deaths a day. After Hitler had sent Himmler to Poland to make the arrangements for wholesale extermination, a number of special execution camps were organized.

> . . . Dec 16th . . . Up to date about 500,000 Jews have been transported from Occupied Europe or countries under German influence to Poland for liquidation.[4] They include 50,000 from France, 70,000 from Alsace and Lorraine, 250,000 from Rouma-

nia, 57,000 from Slovakia and 50,000 from Luxembourg. These are distinct from the million Polish Jews already slaughtered.

"I had a rather distressing conversation with Mgr Tardini this evening about the attitude of the Holy See to the Jewish persecution," Osborne began in reporting the reception he got when he presented the memo for the pope. "He was, I think, uncomfortable and on the defensive." Would the pope not finally denounce the Nazi campaign? asked Osborne. Tardini offered the reply he had given many times before. The pope could not speak out against the outrages being committed against Jews, or those against Catholic Poles, without seeming to take sides in the war. Moreover, argued Tardini, giving another oft-repeated, albeit disingenuous, defense for the pope's silence, they had not been able to verify the atrocity stories.[5]

The pressure wasn't coming only from the British. Poland remained a particularly sensitive subject for the pope, as its overwhelmingly Roman Catholic population looked to him to condemn their oppressors. Three days after Tardini met with Osborne, the Polish ambassador, representing a government that since the German occupation of his country had operated from exile in London, came with much the same request. He brought a memo informing the pope that the Germans were in the process of murdering the entire Jewish population of Poland, with those killed to date exceeding one million. The ambassador asked the pope to "strongly and clearly condemn these as well as other German crimes, whose scale exceeds anything known in history."[6]

Raffaele Guariglia, Italy's ambassador to the Vatican, happened to be in Cardinal Maglione's office at the time, delivering a very different message. The Duce wanted the pope in his upcoming Christmas broadcast to avoid any "incitements to peace that could have a debilitating effect on the Italian people." The pope's response the next day was vague. He would take the Duce's suggestion into consideration and deal with it as best he could, given what his papal mission required of him.[7]

Three days later Osborne made a brief note in his diary: "Having been reliably assured that the Pope was going to speak out this Christmas, I am now equally reliably assured that he is not. The Vatican will be the only State which has not condemned the persecution of the Jews."[8]

AMID ALL THE POPE'S worries that Christmas season, there was one bright spot. *Pastor Angelicus,* the film on which he had lavished so much time over the past year, was finally having its premiere. It was a historic event, the first time a pope was protagonist in a film designed to present himself to the world. The product of the Catholic Film Center, it benefited from the work of twenty-five cameramen who had followed the pope around the Vatican for several months. The goal was to show the film in every Italian city and in many other countries as well. More than two hundred showings would take place in German-occupied Paris alone.

Osborne noted that the Vatican was now employing modern techniques to craft the pope's public image. "His Holiness," he observed, "is not altogether free from the human vanity of the artist. Flattery on this score of his eloquence does not come amiss and is not neglected by his entourage, while any suggestion that the baroque architecture of his discourse might prejudice the force or the clarity of his teaching is ill-received." If the British diplomat found the film project in the midst of the war in poor taste, the Duce was even less pleased. Although the Fascist government had supported the making of the film, he resented it, jealous of any display of papal charisma that risked eclipsing his own.[9]

Mussolini's unhappiness with the new cinematic paean to the pope was no doubt magnified by his own miseries. He had long been plagued by periodic attacks of crippling stomach pains, caused, it seemed, by stress-triggered ulcers. For years he had kept to a spartan diet, avoiding meat, alcohol, and coffee. The previous July, when his pains had flared up following a lengthy visit to Italian troops in Libya, doctors initially thought he had picked up a stomach amoeba. By November the pains had become much worse, and as Christmas approached, he was spending many days in bed. He had fought a lifelong campaign against a family tendency toward fat, but now he had lost a quarter of his body weight and looked gaunt and older. Clara's father, a Vatican physician, visited Mussolini regularly to give him injections of vitamin supplements, while the Duce took antispasm pills and administered his own sodium bromide injections.

In speaking with Clara several times each day by phone, Mussolini sought her commiseration as he lamented that his life was a failure. "It is not the ulcers, Clara, that's killing me," he told her. "It's seeing twenty years of work and sweat destroyed and useless." He gave vent as well to his jealousy of the pope's popularity in Rome, complaining, as usual without any trace of self-consciousness of his hypocrisy, about the ongoing Allied bombing of Italy's cities. "All the cities should be respected in Christ's name . . . this is what the Pope should have been asking for . . . not defending only Rome because he is there."[10]

The morning following Rome's gala premiere of *Pastor Angelicus,* Mussolini awoke with a sharp pain in his stomach and reached again for his pills and his syringe. Clara soon arrived and gave him a soothing massage. Depressed, he told her he did not think he could go on; it was time to quit. Clara had only a limited formal education and little direct knowledge of the larger world. In their first years together, she was more likely to simply add her support to whatever opinion her "Ben," as she called him, expressed. Now she felt bolder in offering her own views, albeit those of a staunch, Mussolini-worshipping Fascist. Hoping to buck up Ben's spirits, she urged him not to "yield to the English and the priests." Then, as they often did when they wanted to relax, they put a record of classical music on the phonograph, beginning with their favorite, Beethoven's Seventh Symphony. While they listened, Mussolini, lying on the floor beside her, began to cry. The symphony often had that effect on him. What particularly irked him, he said, was having to depend on the pope to get the British to spare Rome from bombardment. Again, the thirty-year-old Clara tried to shake him out of his self-pity. He should not let himself be defeated by the "Anglo-priestly" forces, she said. Doing so would leave Rome in the hands of the Vatican and its "priestly power."[11]

———

THE POPE WOULD HAVE been surprised to learn that among those tuning in to his Christmas radio broadcast on December 24 was the Duce himself. Unsurprisingly, Mussolini was unimpressed. Turning to Ciano, who was listening with him, he said, "God's Vicar, that is, the representative on earth of the governor of the Universe, should never speak. He should stay up in the clouds. This is a speech filled with commonplaces that might as easily have been given by the parish priest of Predappio."★ [12]

As was his custom, the pope had words that both sides of the war could interpret as supporting their cause. Mussolini's newspaper offered a respectful summary of the speech, highlighting the pope's condemnation of "Marxist socialism" and his defense of private property. A paragraph in bold then followed: "the Pope said that this war represents the unravelling of a social order that, behind the false face or mask of conventional formulas, hides its fatal weakness and its unbridled instinct for profits and for power." [13]

On the twenty-fourth page of the pope's text were words that defenders of Pius XII would later cite in trying to cast the speech as a ringing papal denunciation of the ongoing massacre of Europe's Jews. [14] Although the pope nowhere mentioned either Nazis or Jews, he lamented in that well-buried passage the "hundreds of thousands of people who, through no fault of their own and solely because of their nation or their race, have been condemned to death or progressive extinction." In his end-of-year report, Osborne recalled that the pope seemed "pained and surprised" that these words had not satisfied those who had been calling on him to speak out. "While the address strikes me as being the most effective of the Pope's recent pronouncements," Osborne told London, "it suffers from the usual defect of exorbitant length and from the fact that . . . his teachings are weakened by the oratorical flux in which they are invariably enveloped."

Father Vincent McCormick, American Jesuit and former rector of

---

★ Mussolini's small hometown in Romagna.

Rome's Gregorian University, living a stone's throw from the Vatican, expressed his own disappointment in the pope's speech. As usual, he wrote, it was "much too heavy," its message "obscurely expressed." Tittmann, meeting with the pope shortly after his speech, likewise found him miffed that his words were thought insufficient. As Tittmann reported to Washington, Pius XII "stated that he 'feared' that there was foundation for the atrocity reports of the Allies but led me to believe that he felt that there had been some exaggeration for purpose of propaganda."[15]

Two days after Christmas the Polish ambassador, Kazimierz Papée, came for his New Year's audience with the pope. Once again the ambassador began with accounts of the Germans' horrendous persecution of both Jews and Catholics in Poland. In response, the pope reiterated his argument that any papal protest risked bringing new misfortune and added that he had already spoken out quite clearly in his Christmas broadcast. Expecting to get some positive acknowledgment of this from the Polish diplomat, he was unhappy that the ambassador met his claim with silence. "I am deeply convinced," Papée reported following the audience, "that he spoke sincerely. The pope is now convinced that he clearly and strongly, albeit generically, condemned German crimes in occupied countries." The ambassador added, "There lies the source of difficulties. . . . Pius XII . . . due to his sensitive and delicate nature, the character of his studies and a certain one-sidedness of his career—exclusively diplomatic and far from [real] life—cannot speak a different language and passes by the realities of our time, not realizing how little an average Catholic can understand and remember from his enunciations, isolated from facts, complex and carefully polished."[16]

Diego von Bergen, the German ambassador, had his end-of-year audience with the pope the same day. It would turn out to be his last. Ever since Hitler came to power, Bergen had sought to smooth relations between the pope and the German Reich, and to convince Ribbentrop and Hitler it was in their interest to have better relations with the pontiff. In his report of the papal audience to Berlin, Bergen wrote that Pius XII had made clear his recognition of "the historic significance of the heroic German struggle in the East; the danger of Bolshevism to which the British and the Americans wanted to expose Europe." If the pope offered any harsh words in private to the German ambassador about the atrocities the Germans were committing, the ambassador would not want to upset the already precarious relations between the Vatican and his government by passing them on to Berlin.[17]

The year ended, then, with Mussolini ailing, the pope feeling unfairly attacked for his silence, Vatican public relations efforts busily crafting a heroic image of the pontiff, and Italians' misery growing. Food shortages, a staccato of reports of military reverses, and air raids on cities throughout the country that threatened only to get worse all fed the increasingly depressed public mood. The ranks of avid Fascists were rapidly dwindling, and while public anger had long focused on the men around the Duce, something new was becoming ever more apparent. The myth of the omniscient leader that had powered popular enthusiasm for the regime for so many years was finally beginning to crumble.[18]

CHAPTER

2 6

———

DISASTER
FORETOLD

———

THE WAR COULD SCARCELY BE GOING WORSE FOR MUSSOLINI as 1943 began. "A very heavy day," wrote Ciano in his diary in mid-January. "The retreat continues in Russia and it seems that in some areas it is becoming a rout. In Libya, the infantry divisions are abandoning Tripoli, headed west, while the rearguard is trying to slow Montgomery's prudent but inexorable advance. I speak on the phone with Mussolini, who seems depressed." Three days later Ciano added, "The Duce judges today's German military bulletin the worst since the beginning of the war. And in fact, it is. In retreat at Stalingrad, in retreat on the front almost everywhere, the fall of Tripoli near."[1]

While Mussolini was depressed, he had little to worry about as far as the Vatican went. At the beginning of the year, Francesco Borgongini sent in a review of his work as papal nuncio to the Italian government over the previous three years. While noting that not once in that time had Mussolini received him, following the Duce's decision to meet with no ambassador other than Germany's, his report reads like a paean to the Fascist leadership. The nuncio boasted that he had "entered into a practically intimate" relationship with Ciano, who was especially helpful in dealing with the ongoing problem of the anti-clerical Farinacci and his newspaper, *Il Regime Fascista*. Giuseppe Bottai, the minister of education, reported the nuncio, was "always kind," as was Guido Buffarini, undersecretary of internal affairs, whom he often met with in dealing with the racial laws. "Minister [of Justice Dino]

Grandi was always very kind and openly professed that he was a believer." Grandi, he added, had been particularly helpful in squelching any attempt to legalize divorce. Borgongini also had words of praise for the minister of finance who "has shown himself always well-disposed in the various measures allowing the Church to be exempted from various fiscal burdens."

The nuncio's report went on to chronicle many of the other areas of ongoing church-state collaboration: "In these three years there has been a noticeable relaxation in all conflicts with Catholic Action and a better attitude toward the Clergy." The government had also shown its regard for the pope by acceding to his pleas to prevent Protestants from proselytizing in Italy. Indeed, the outbreak of the war had "favored the battle against Protestantism, because all the funding sources for the sects come from countries that are at war with Italy." Even the church's battle for morality had seen many successes thanks to government action, albeit this was an area in which Ciano and other Fascist leaders seemed less enthusiastic. Nonetheless, bowing to the church's desires, Buffarini, along with the minister of popular culture and the police chief, had all cooperated in shutting down variety shows and seizing books and magazines the church found objectionable.[2]

EARLY IN JANUARY, IN keeping with long Vatican tradition, Pius XII held the annual papal New Year's reception for the Roman aristocracy. Speaking on behalf of the nobility, Prince Marc'Antonio Colonna, who bore the title Prince-Assistant to the Pontifical Throne, offered words of homage to the pontiff. The pope then gave a long speech, published by Italy's leading Catholic newspaper under the title "The Mission of the Ruling Classes."[3]

The day following the ceremony, Prince Colonna hosted a private lunch at his home, arranged at Ciano's request. Italy's foreign minister had something to communicate to the pope outside official channels, and so the prince invited Monsignor Montini to join them. After lunching with the prince and princess, Ciano and Montini were given a room to themselves. There they spoke privately for an hour.

The Duce's son-in-law began by praising the pope's recent Christmas radio address, which, "even if dense with doctrine and in erudite form," was in keeping with "the dignity of the person who pronounced it." Ciano also told the monsignor how pleased he was by the pope's recently released film, *Pastor Angelicus*.

Ciano then turned to the subject of the war. He began by saying he had opposed Germany's decision to launch the war in 1939 and claimed he had opposed Italy's entry as well. He then came to the topic he was most eager to communicate to the pope. While the war would not end soon, when the time came, he hoped the Vatican might help broker an acceptable peace deal. He ended the unusual meeting by telling the monsignor of his deep faith in God, recounting how much he liked to visit his private sanctuary in Tuscany to pray in solitude.[4]

Ciano's latest bid to win the pope's favor and begin to plan for Italy's exit from the war had come amid more bad news for the Axis. In the face of the Allied offensive in North Africa, German and Italian troops were abandoning the last pockets of Axis-occupied North Africa. The situation would only get worse for Italy over the next days as Allied planes flying out of North Africa began bombing the ferry facilities that linked Sicily to the mainland. Most disastrously of all for the Axis powers, on February 2, the Germans' Sixth Army, with a quarter-million of its soldiers trapped at Stalingrad, surrendered to the Russians.[5]

In late January the Polish ambassador returned to the Apostolic Palace, having received new instructions from his government in exile in London stressing how important it would be for the pope to speak out. "In Poland," the ambassador told the pope, "new events have taken place: their horrific character cannot be compared to anything known to history." He then read a personal plea from the Polish president.

As he listened, Pius XII smiled nervously. "First of all," said the pope when the ambassador finished, "I wonder if Monsieur le President has read my Christmas message. I am surprised, I am even hurt. Yes, I am, it pains me. Not a word of thanks, of recognition, I mean of recognition"—here the pontiff, not sure if the French word captured his thoughts, added the German term *Anerkennung*. "And yet I said everything. I was clear and distinct." At this point the pope began to quote passages from his Christmas radio address from memory, pausing at his condemnation of the persecution of national minorities and races.

The ambassador responded that the Polish bishops had not found his words adequate, as he had nowhere mentioned the Nazis nor what, specifically, they were doing. The pope interrupted him: It was easy for the bishops living in exile to speak impudently, but those still in Poland would have to pay the price. The Germans were only waiting for a pretext for further persecution.

The Germans, replied the ambassador, had no need for pretexts. The Polish people had no patience for such excuses.[6]

Nor was it only the Germans who were engaged in a war of conquest and committing atrocities against civilian populations. Although few Italians would ever admit it, the Italians were as well. This was noted a couple of weeks later by the American Jesuit in Rome, Vincent McCormick, in his diary:

> Holy See seems to manifest very keen interest in sufferings of civilian population when this population is Italian. They are fully aware of what cruel sufferings have been inflicted on civil population in Slovenia, Croatia and Greece, and this by Italians—burning of whole towns, murder of innocent hostages in revenge, and no letter of sympathy has been published as sent to Bishops of those parts. I am finding it more and more difficult, really impossible to defend the neutrality of the present-day Vatican. Catholicity is very much compromised.[7]

NEWS OF THE AXIS debacle at Stalingrad, the defeat of Axis forces in North Africa, and the Allied bombing raids on Sicily, together with the worsening food shortages, with meat, dairy products, bread, pasta, and much else in short supply, was fast eroding popular support for the Fascist regime. Concluding that bold action was needed to deflect blame and regroup, Mussolini decided to dismiss nine of his twelve government ministers, as well as Guido Buffarini, who, as his own undersecretary, had in effect served as the powerful minister of internal affairs.

On the afternoon of February 5, the Duce summoned his son-in-law to his office. When Ciano arrived, Mussolini, ill at ease, surprised him by asking, "What would you like to do now?" The question would have seemed odd had it not been immediately followed by the dictator's explanation that he had decided to change the entire government. Ciano was shocked, and Mussolini, embarrassed, and perhaps afraid of the reaction his mercurial daughter Edda would have to the sacking of her husband, quickly tried to turn the conversation to the question of what new post his son-in-law might like. Perhaps, the Duce suggested, he might want to be put in charge of Albania.[8]

Ciano had no interest in going to Albania. Instead, he surprised his father-in-law by naming the post he did want: ambassador to the Holy See. Eager to bring the awkward encounter to an end, Mussolini signaled his approval. Early the next morning Ciano, fearing his father-in-law might have second thoughts about the appointment, informed the Vatican of the decision.[9]

Ciano's overnight transformation from Mussolini's number two, responsible for foreign affairs in the midst of a world war, to ambassador to a postage-stamp-size state, triggered frenetic speculation in Rome's diplomatic community. The German ambassador sent a telegram to Berlin arguing that Ciano had long been preparing the way for this "retreat" by his repeated efforts to win the pope's sympathy. A British intelligence report suggested Mussolini might have designed the move "to pave the way for Italy's withdrawal from the war and eventually to open negotiations for peace with the aid of the Vatican." In his diary, the industrialist Alberto Pirelli speculated that Ciano was probably happy with the move, thinking it put him in a good position to detach Italy from Germany. Harold Tittmann offered a similar view to the American secretary of state: "Because of his reported pro-Ally proclivities," Ciano "would be fitted to work through the Vatican on the United Nations representatives [i.e., the British and American envoys] in the Vatican City in favor of a compromise peace holding up to them the Russian danger."[10]

The pope himself had mixed feelings about the news. As a lightning rod for Italians' unhappiness with the war, Ciano was arguably the most unpopular man in the country. Making matters worse, his well-known playboy antics and widely rumored affairs were an embarrassment. Nor was the pope happy that Mussolini kept changing ambassadors. Ciano would be Italy's fifth since he had become pope less than four years earlier. But the pope would see a positive side to the appointment as well. It would be hard to imagine an ambassador with easier access to the Duce, or one better placed to argue the pope's cause.[11]

Among those pleased by the demotion was Clara, Mussolini's lover, who saw Ciano, along with his wife, Edda, as enemies, conspiring to turn the Duce against her. But news that Buffarini too would lose his position infuriated her, for Clara viewed him as her most effective defender among the men surrounding the Duce. In the first of what would turn into a long series of letters to Mussolini casting Buffarini as his most loyal and able government servant, she urged him to create the new position of minister of the police for him. Later in the year, under dramatically different circumstances, her letters would become lengthy daily missives.

In increasingly offering "Ben" her political advice, Clara had something of a role model in Margherita Sarfatti, the Venetian Jewish woman who, during the time Mussolini came to power, had not only been his lover but had acted as an important political adviser as well. Indeed, Clara herself would later make oblique reference to the role her predecessor had played. "Ben," she wrote, "I don't know exactly how much you value what I tell you. . . . You are prejudiced, having had a sad experience with a woman, the ridiculous Jewess Sarfatti. But the difference is substantial, not only due to Race, to blood—a clear distinction to which I hold dear—but because her advice was not motivated by love, but by her own personal interests . . . out of an inordinate pride in wanting to be the *Presidentessa*. The Jewess, that is, who exploits the Great One for her own advantage."[12]

THE CHANGE IN MUSSOLINI'S cabinet came only a few days before the anniversary of the Lateran Accords, an annual occasion for the Fascist and Catholic press to lavish praise on the Duce and highlight the regime's strong ties with the church. Mussolini's own newspaper featured a front-page article noting that, as each year on that date, Italian flags were hung festively both from public buildings and from private homes. "Italy, Fascist and Catholic," the article concluded, "has, with the Conciliation, given new strength to its religious conscience, and, in the new climate created by the Revolution of the Blackshirts, rediscovered the road of its precise historical mission: defense of immortal Rome's spiritual values and civilization."[13]

The pope, until recently worried about the church's fate in a Europe dominated by Hitler, was now increasingly worried about the impact of a German defeat.[14] Fears of the catastrophe that would befall Europe and the church should the Russians destroy the Axis army were being stoked by Italy's own propaganda efforts, reflected daily in both the Fascist and the Catholic press. A February 21 editorial by Father Mario Busti, director of Milan's Catholic daily, went so far as to quote approvingly Nazi propaganda czar Joseph Goebbels, long viewed in the Vatican as one of the Reich's leading anticlerics. The priest hailed Goebbels for warning of the need "to eliminate the danger that is coming from the east, to Germany first and then to all of Europe . . . by the Bolshevik wave." Quoting the Nazi leader again, Busti added, "only the German army and its allies possess the force to save Europe from this immense danger."[15]

As the likelihood of Axis victory receded, speculation increased that Mussolini or other Fascist leaders would look for a way out of the war and in doing so would need to rely on the pope to broker a deal. In mid-February Harold Tittmann, from his apartment in Vatican City, informed Washington that the pope might be interested in supporting such an initiative. Perhaps, thought Tittmann, Ciano, as Mussolini's new ambassador to the Holy See, "would be in a position to attempt through the Vatican to open negotiations with the Allies with a view to having Italy withdraw from the war through a separate peace." The American envoy believed the interests of the Vatican and the Italian government were now converging, both eager to save Italy from destruction. Fearing that the fall of the Fascist regime might trigger a popular uprising, the Vatican would not want to risk any dramatic change in Italy's government.[16]

What the Allied diplomats in the Vatican found wholly lacking, despite the turn in the war, was any indication that Italians would rebel against their government. The Allies had designed their bombing campaign with the aim of provoking just such a popular uprising. But as British foreign secretary Anthony Eden wrote in a confidential memo, the lack of any sign of popular revolt was no reason to halt the air attacks. On the contrary, he thought they should be intensified. Rather than pursue a separate peace with the Italians, he advised, "we should aim at provoking such disorder in Italy as would necessitate a German occupation. We suggest that the best means of achieving this aim is to intensify all forms of military operations against Italy, particularly aerial bombardment." Forcing the Germans to send soldiers desperately needed elsewhere in Europe into Italy could, thought the British foreign secretary, only aid the Allied cause.[17]

HOPES THAT PIUS XII might help Italy break with Hitler and exit the war were not confined to whispered conversations among the foreign envoys at the Vatican. On February 22 General Ettore Bastico, who until the recent routing of the Italian army in North Africa had served as governor of Libya, came to see Pius XII. He hoped to enlist the pope's aid for just this purpose, telling him it was the only way for the country to avoid ruin. Bastico would leave disappointed. "I tried to interest the Holy Father in the real situation in which Italy finds itself in this war," he recalled, "but the Pope kept himself so far above it all, eager to avoid engaging the question, and leaving me without letting me know his august opinion."[18]

With fears of an Allied invasion growing, other worried members of Italy's elite were now making their way to the Vatican, hoping to

find a lifeline. Notable among them was the rubber czar Alberto Pirelli. Long a pillar of the Fascist regime, he, like others of his class, was
now among those desperate to find a way to avoid the popular uprising
that he feared would follow military defeat. He met with Cardinal
Maglione to test the waters.

Maglione asked the industrialist whether he thought Italy could
negotiate a peace deal separately from Germany.

No, Pirelli replied. Not only would it be too humiliating for the
nation to abandon its German partner that way, but if they attempted
to do so, the Germans would make them "pay dearly" for their betrayal. Their only hope was to try to negotiate a peace that included
Germany as well.

"Who," asked the cardinal, "could take the initiative?"

"My people are looking to the Vatican, albeit understanding the
difficulties."

Maglione could not see how the Vatican could succeed in such a
mission. The Allies had made clear they would not negotiate with either Mussolini or Hitler. While Italy had a king who, at least in theory,
could replace the Duce, Germany had no king and so no obvious way
to remove the Führer. "Besides," the cardinal told the industrialist,
"Germany has truly sown hatred in all of Europe. . . . As for the atrocities committed against the Jews in Poland and everywhere else, the
proofs we have are terrifying!"

If Maglione had any encouraging news for Pirelli, it was his concluding thought. Italy might yet be spared. It seemed unlikely to him
that the Allies would land their troops on Italian soil. More likely they
would open their new front on the northern coast of France instead.[19]

WITH THE SOURING OF the public mood, Mussolini was now all the
more eager to avoid any criticism of the war by the Catholic clergy. As
Easter approached, the prefects in each province, aided by local party
officials and eager local Fascists, pored over the bishops' annual Lenten
messages. Authorities seized copies of the bishop of Verona's Easter
message, deemed guilty of calling the war a punishment inflicted by

God for Italians' obscenities and their profanation of the Holy Name. But for the most part the government would be pleased with the church, as both the Fascist and the Catholic press continued to trumpet messages by bishops stressing the importance of Axis victory.[20]

American warplanes were now joining the British as they stepped up their bombing raids. Each day as evening approached, in cities from Naples to Milan, long lines of people on foot, on bicycle, and on donkey-pulled carts headed out to the countryside seeking to escape the death that rained down from the nighttime sky. People looked back at the sky over the city, reddened by flickering flames rising from factories and fuel depots. Turin, center of Italy's heavy industry, suffered over twenty massive bombardments. Much of the city lay in ruins, whole working-class residential areas destroyed, electricity, gas, and water lines repeatedly cut. In Naples, open-bed trucks with cadavers piled high headed to makeshift cemeteries where the bodies were dumped into common graves. A single cross stood atop each, bearing the hastily scrawled names of all those entombed below.[21]

Francis D'Arcy Osborne, Britain's envoy to the Vatican, during visit to London, April 14, 1943

In early April the pope, having heard that Osborne, the British envoy, was about to go to London for consultations with the Foreign Office, asked to meet with him. He had a request to make. Would Osborne convey to his government the pope's wish that the Allies not invade Italy? Such an invasion, said the pope, would not be in the interest of future good relations between the two countries. Knowing the rude welcome such a request would meet in the British capital, which had suffered months of murderous Axis bombardment, Osborne apparently judged it best not to mention the papal plea on his subsequent visit to London.[22]

A THORNY
PROBLEM

I N MID-MARCH 1943 ANGELO RONCALLI, THEN PAPAL DELEGATE
in Istanbul, sent a coded telegram to the Vatican; fifteen years later
Roncalli would succeed the current pope and take the name of John
XXIII. Once the text came back from the Vatican decrypting office, it
presented the pope with a particularly delicate dilemma. The twenty
thousand Jews still remaining in Slovakia, reported Roncalli, "run the
risk of deportation to Poland at the end of the month. They beg the
Holy Father to intervene with that government . . . so that one thousand Jewish children can emigrate to Palestine, with English authorization . . . and be permitted to transit through Turkey." The Jews were
turning to the pope in hopes that he would use his influence with the
head of the Slovakian government, the Roman Catholic priest Jozef
Tiso.[1]

The problem for the pope was that, following the policy his predecessors had adopted ever since the Zionist movement began, he opposed the creation of a Jewish state in Palestine and was not eager to see
more Jews living there. As we now know from the recently opened
Vatican archives, Roncalli's request was turned over for evaluation to
Monsignor Giuseppe Di Meglio, on the staff of the Secretariat of State.
Di Meglio's lengthy report, "Palestine and the Jews?" would eventually be sent to the pope.[2]

Reviewing the history of the Zionist movement, Di Meglio observed that until recently Jews had not been eager to go to Palestine. He explained why he thought this was so:

> Now it is known that most Jews are mainly dedicated to industry and, for the most part, commerce. This commerce remains quite profitable for them when they find themselves living among Christians. If, on the contrary, *all* and *only* the Jews come together, one has an enormous gathering in of . . . swindlers, while lacking those to be swindled. Therefore, most Jews had no desire to migrate to Palestine.[3]

Di Meglio added that in the past a further obstacle to the success of the Zionist plan had been the Holy See's steadfast opposition. He saw no reason for the Vatican to change its policy, for "to give Palestine now to the Jews in dominion and absolute predominance would mean offending the religious sentiment of all Catholics and all those who . . . call themselves Christians."

If in the past Europe's Jews showed no great desire to go to Palestine, now, amid the threat of annihilation, wrote Di Meglio, they were eager to do so, with backing from England. The request for Vatican assistance in helping Jews escape to Palestine put the Holy See in an awkward position. "The Holy See, for its part . . . cannot easily in the present stage of the war raise questions and voice protests. . . . The Holy See is being beseeched to help this emigration only in order to save thousands of people (especially children) from certain death."

Cardinal Maglione brought the monsignor's report to the pope, who decided to use it to have his staff draft a response to Monsignor Roncalli's message. Monsignor Tardini's resulting brief advised that the Holy See should "continue to follow the same line of conduct, endeavoring, that is, as in the past, to prevent the creation of the feared Jewish supremacy in Palestine." At the same time, the Vatican should tread carefully, for given the persecution Europe's Jews were facing, "it would make a bad impression if the Holy See now appeared to refuse . . . an act of humanity."[4]

In early May, the pope sent a telegram containing his decision to Monsignor Roncalli in Istanbul: The Holy See "has repeatedly intervened with the Slovakian Government in favor of non-Aryans with special regard to youths. It is still interesting itself in trying to get all transfer of Jewish residents in Slovakia suspended." The response made no mention of Palestine.[5]

Roncalli renewed his plea later in May, asking to help fifteen hundred Jewish children from Slovakia obtain transit permission from the Hungarian government to escape to Palestine. This time Roncalli's note was given to the Secretariat of State's expert on Jews, Monsignor Dell'Acqua. He advised that they first try to find out from the priest-president of Slovakia whether the "transfer of Jews" was being suspended, "because it seems more opportune for the Holy See to insist that the Slovakian Jews remain in Slovakia and not be transferred to Palestine." If Tiso were to inform them that the deportations had in fact been suspended, concluded Dell'Acqua, "a telegram could be sent with this news to Roncalli," adding "he should not give too much support to the emigration of the Jews to Palestine."[6]

PIUS XII WAS WELL aware of the fate that awaited the Jews being deported to the Nazi death camps, but he continued to resist pressures to intervene publicly, arguing that his words would hold little sway with the Germans and any papal criticism risked provoking a backlash against the church in German-occupied Europe.[7] Among the many pleas he received at the time was a lengthy telegram from Generoso Pope, the influential publisher of America's most prominent Italian-American newspaper, *Il Progresso Italo-Americano*:

> In the name of Christianity and human decency I humbly implore you to once again lift your sacred universal voice against intensified unchristian persecution being perpetrated by Nazi regime against Jewish people. Americans of all faiths and racial origin are filled with horror and shocked by brutalities against millions of Jews. Savage Nazi national cult is cruel travesty on

Christian conscience and human spirit. . . . I pray and hope that intercession by Holy See ever a seat of racial spiritual tolerance and justice will arouse world conscience and help halt Nazis' orgy of savagery.

Following what had by now become standard practice, a brief response was drafted calling on the apostolic delegate in Washington to "confidentially" assure the American publisher that the Holy See was doing all it could. A note at the bottom of the suggested reply from the plainspoken Monsignor Tardini, who drafted the telegram, explained: "I thought to add 'confidentially' because, as [Generoso] Pope is the proprietor of the daily newspaper 'Il Progresso Italo-Americano,' he would easily publish the Holy See's response. On the one hand this would be a good thing, but on the other. . . ." Here, the ellipsis at the end tells the story. Beneath this Maglione added a handwritten note: "*sta bene,*" that's good.[8]

Monsignor Cicognani, the pope's delegate in Washington, was himself besieged with pleas to get the pope to speak out publicly against the ongoing extermination of Europe's Jews. His correspondence with the Vatican soon took on a defensive tone, as he realized that his transmission of a continuing stream of complaints about the pope's silence was not appreciated. A telegram he sent Cardinal Maglione in late March makes this clear. After receiving the cardinal's latest three messages, he explained,

> I ought not dare present new appeals, but three Rabbis representing various of their associations, in the face of alarming news coming especially from London of the systematic, rapid extermination that is said to have been recently decreed by Hitler and inexorably begun, especially in Poland, came to me today tearfully begging for the Holy Father to make a public appeal and prayer to stop the massacre and the deportation.

Cicognani ended his telegram with a further apologetic note: "I had to promise them this transmission."[9]

If Pius XII could argue that his influence over the German government was limited, he could not say the same for his influence in Italy.
In April, Jewish organizations informed him of the German request
for the deportation of the Jews from Italian-controlled areas of France
and the Dalmatian coast. The pope decided to act, instructing his Jesuit
envoy to raise the matter with Italy's new undersecretary of foreign
affairs, Giuseppe Bastianini.[10]

Bastianini assured the pope's envoy that Italy would not hand the
Jews over to the Germans. Mussolini's maxim, he said, was "with the
Jews, separation, not persecution." The Jews in the Italian-occupied
territories would be confined to Italian concentration camps. He explained, "We don't want to be executioners. . . . The Church too always called for separation from the synagogue."[11]

IN EARLY APRIL 1943, Hitler again summoned Mussolini to discuss
the war. Having missed his previous appointment with the Führer because of his ills, Mussolini, although still sick, reluctantly boarded a
special train. Sharp stomach pains forced him to order it stopped periodically along the way so that, with an aide supporting him on either
side, he could make his way down the steps and take deep breaths of
fresh air. On the Duce's arrival at Salzburg, Hitler, shocked by his ally's
sickly appearance, begged him to allow German doctors to examine
him, but Mussolini refused.

Although weak and ill, Mussolini did muster the strength to urge
the Führer to make peace with Russia and so free the Luftwaffe to defend Italy from Allied assault. Hitler remained unmoved.

Once back in Rome, the Duce remained bedridden with excruciating stomach pain for another month. "In his yellowed face," observed
a visitor, "one sees the mark of his suffering." Italy's dictator would do
his best to keep up his pugnacious front, but the note of defensiveness
that now crept into his voice was hard to miss. "They say that I'm finished, out of it, done for," he said. "Well, they'll see!"[12]

AN AWKWARD
REQUEST

L EAVING HIS SICKBED ON MAY 5, 1943, MUSSOLINI MADE WHAT
would be his final address from the balcony of Piazza Venezia. His
appearance came following a meeting of the Fascist chiefs. There the
newly appointed head of the party, Carlo Scorza, offered his own
blend of Fascism and Catholicism: "The Fascist people," he told the
black-shirted bigwigs, "will win the war and the peace, because they
possess the three elements that guarantee eternity: their belief in the
Catholic religion, their recognition of the House of Savoy as the symbol of continuity and glory, their obedience to and faith in the genius
of the Duce." In short, Fascism's holy trinity: the church, the monarchy, and the Duce. Stepping onto the small balcony outside his window, Mussolini echoed Scorza's words. "I, like you," he told the hastily
assembled crowd, "am certain that the bloody sacrifices of these difficult times will be compensated by victory, if it is true, and this is true,
that God is just and Italy immortal."[1]

With Italians ever wearier of a war that most had not wanted, Italy's press continued to invoke the words of church leaders to boost
morale. The May 9 issue of Rome's Catholic daily was typical in featuring the patriarch of Venice's recent blessing of the troops. "All
Italy," said the patriarch, "is proud of you. It knows with what vehemence you stand as a barrier to the enemy's great power, it knows that,
from a sense of duty, you do not shrink from making supreme sacrifices." That barrier was in fact rapidly crumbling.[2]

WHILE THE DUCE'S STAR was falling, the pope's was rising, and Vatican efforts to cast Pius XII as heroic prince of peace were growing ever more intense. The pope's name day, June 2, the feast of Saint Eugene, offered the latest opportunity. Following words of homage by the nineteen cardinals present in Rome, the pope gave a speech, broadcast by radio, that would be widely—albeit selectively—quoted in Italy's press. The banner headline in *L'Osservatore Romano* proclaimed "The Supreme Pastor's Incessant Activity to Soothe the Sufferings of War and His Appeal for the Return of True Peace in the World." Reprising a theme he had briefly introduced in his radio broadcast the previous Christmas, the pope expressed his desire to respond to those who had asked for words of comfort, "troubled as they are," as the pope put it, "by reason of their nationality and their descent." He went on to express his affection for those "minor Nations" that, due to their geographical position, were exposed to problems as a result of the struggles between the Great Powers and had suffered terrible horrors. This he followed with an expression of sympathy for all the pain suffered by the Polish people. The pontiff concluded his remarks with the wish that peace soon descend on earth.[3]

Once again both sides were able to point to signs of support in the pope's words. The British envoy, emphasizing the pope's expression of sympathy for those who were persecuted due to their ancestry and for the Polish people, referred to his address as "the most outspoken speech to be made by him since the outbreak of the war."[4] *Il Regime Fascista,* the newspaper of the arch-Fascist Roberto Farinacci, offered its own lengthy, respectful paraphrase of the speech, while Ciano prepared a long analysis for Mussolini's benefit. The pope, said Ciano, felt he had to say something "to dispel the impression of the political passivity of the Holy See that has been spreading through Catholic circles." The pope had been very careful in dealing with the two "particularly delicate points" he felt compelled to address. By pairing his expression of concern for the peoples of the occupied countries with his lamentations about the cruelties of the air war, it was "almost an effort to equally divide the blame and the responsibilities of the two groups of belligerents and thereby to emphasize the universality and impartiality of the Holy See." Clearly, by his reference to the occupied peoples, the pontiff had been referring to those occupied by the Axis, but it was significant that even there the only place he singled out was Poland. "Evidently, he wanted to choose a country that, after the [recent] revelations of the massacre of Katyn [where in 1940 the Soviets had executed thousands of Polish military officers and intelligentsia], no one could say whether they suffered more from the hardship of the German occupation or from the wickedness of the USSR." On the other hand, claimed Ciano, the pope's call for a return to the principles of basic humanity in the way the war was being waged was an implicit rebuke of the Americans and the British for their brutal air war.[5]

THE POPE'S SPEECH HAD come in the wake of the collapse of the Axis army on the Russian front. Italy's own expeditionary army in Russia had been smashed, and those not captured or killed desperately retreated through the terrible cold and deep snow. One survivor recalled seeing the sides of the road "dotted with these grotesque, immobile figures, human statuary marbleized with snow and ice." In all, over 87,000 Italians soldiers there were dead or missing, and thousands more wounded and frostbitten. The remnants of the army that returned to Italy that spring spread horrifying details of what had happened.

To add to the Italians' miseries, food shortages were worsening, British and American air attacks on their cities were intensifying, and an Allied landing on Italian soil seemed near.[6] In early May British bombers flew over Rome, dropping flares and leaflets that threatened Italians with destruction if they did not renounce the Axis alliance. It was the first time Allied planes had appeared in the skies over Rome since the war began.[7] The pope felt he had to do something. He was, after all, not only supreme pastor of all the faithful but also head of the Italian church.

On May 10 Monsignor Tardini prepared notes on the challenges they faced. Mussolini cared for nothing other than holding on to power, while amid the destruction and privation the germs of Communism were spreading. Tardini put his next point delicately, although he underlined it for emphasis: "In the face of this sad spectacle one might ask if an intervention by the Holy See is not advisable."

In setting out the pope's options, Tardini acknowledged there were arguments for the pope to continue to say nothing other than periodically lament the war's miseries. But given the Vatican's location, its close historical ties to Italy, and the fact that the Italian people looked to the pope for help in this hour of need, he suggested, "it would be useful to be able in the future to demonstrate that the Holy See had seen things as they were and had done what was possible on behalf of Italy." Here the monsignor added parenthetically, "One should not forget that all the anticlerics and many antifascists are accusing the Holy See of having supported fascism!" Any papal action would need to meet certain criteria. First, it would have to remain secret. Publicity might come later, "when one can and should demonstrate all the good work done by the Holy See." In any case, "It would be necessary to studiously avoid all that could be interpreted as an 'invitation' to make a separate peace, or as a proposal of mediation."

The monsignor proposed two possible forms this expression of papal concern could take: a letter the pope could write directly to Mussolini, or an informal verbal message transmitted via Cardinal Maglione to Ciano, then from him to the Duce. Given that many people were now looking to the king to bring an end to Mussolini's reign, thought Tardini, it would not be a good idea for the pope to send a similar communication to the monarch, for "it is necessary to avoid having the Holy Father appear, in one way or another, as a supporter of that plan."[8]

The next day the pope reviewed Tardini's memo with its attached proposed text for a papal message to the Italian dictator. While acknowledging that some sign of papal initiative was called for, he balked at sending the Duce a formal letter, favoring the more modest step of a verbal communication via Ciano. On May 12 Ciano came to the cardinal's office, where Maglione read him the pope's message before handing him the page to read himself.

The message could hardly have been shorter, consisting of four sentences. As father of all the faithful, and concerned as he always was to spare civilians the scourge of war, said Pius XII, he was saddened by all the suffering the conflict was causing "to His beloved Children of Italy." But he was even more worried about the future, which threatened to bring even greater sorrows and ruin. Given this situation, as bishop of Rome and primate of Italy, he wished "once more to declare to the Honorable Mussolini that He, as always, is ready to do whatever is possible to come to the aid of the people who are suffering."[9]

Given the dramatic circumstances, a weaker message would be hard to imagine. Even Ciano said it seemed rather vague. Looking over the sheet Cardinal Maglione had handed him, Ciano read it again, taking notes, for the pope did not want Mussolini to have anything in writing. Ciano said he would bring the pope's message to the Duce immediately, but he was not optimistic that his father-in-law would be pleased to receive it, with its implicit suggestion that something should be done to extract Italy from the war. While Ciano acknowledged that peace talks were indeed urgently needed, he said Mussolini opposed them, and in any case the Allies would never negotiate with him. Nor, Ciano added, was the king showing any signs of taking matters in hand.[10]

The pope would not have to wait long for the Duce's response, as that same afternoon Mussolini dictated it to Ciano, who no doubt crafted some of the more respectful wording himself: "The Duce thanks the Holy Father . . . for the interest he has demonstrated for the sufferings that have been inflicted on the Italian people." It was indeed likely, Mussolini told the pope, that the Allies would continue their attacks and so bring more ruin and more sorrow. But still eager to cast himself as the peacemaker, he added, "The Duce himself is suffering personally from this situation, given that between August and September 1939 he made every possible effort to avoid the conflict." The dictator then got to the nub of his wholly predictable response: "The Duce thanks the Pope for his good intentions but given the current state of things there are no alternatives and therefore Italy will continue to fight."[11]

The next day Ciano brought his father-in-law's reply to the Vatican and read it aloud to Cardinal Maglione. He told the cardinal that Mussolini regarded the pope's message as yet another attempt by the pope to burnish his own image at Mussolini's expense.[12]

WHILE THE DUCE WAS fending off the pope's carefully couched plea, the last Axis forces in North Africa were surrendering in Tunisia, and the Allies were taking prisoner another 120,000 Italians and 130,000 Germans. Meanwhile, in an effort to keep the Italians guessing about where they might land, Allied planes were dropping bombs on both coasts of Sicily as well as on Sardinia.[13]

With the Allied invasion nearing, those in the upper echelons of Italian society were frantically seeking a way to save themselves. For Italy's military leadership, there could be only one point of reference, the king, to whom they traditionally pledged their allegiance and for whom they served. It was the king who retained the right to choose the head of government, a fact reflected in the requirement—never abandoned in the years of the dictatorship—that Victor Emmanuel sign all legislative acts before they could go into effect.

The pope was aware that secret meetings were being held at the Quirinal, the royal palace across the Tiber from the Vatican. Giuseppe Dalla Torre, the *Osservatore Romano* director, who had good contacts with the conservatives now scheming to save the salvageable, was keeping the pope up to date.[14]

The notoriously reclusive king, long under Mussolini's spell, and fearful that the fall of Fascism might mean the end of the monarchy, was growing more nervous with each new approach. In early May his cousin, the count of Turin, a military commander in the First World War, urged him to act. The king refused. "There were still fifty thousand people there applauding the Duce in Piazza Venezia the other day," he replied. "I don't want to provoke a civil war."[15] To his military aide-de-camp, Victor Emmanuel confided his fear that "at any moment the English and the King of England are going to turn to me directly to negotiate a separate peace. It would put me in a very embarrassing position. If this were to happen, I would act openly, I would speak with the Duce so that we could agree on the line to follow."[16]

THREE MONTHS EARLIER PRESIDENT Roosevelt had asked the pope an awkward series of questions. What form did he think a new Italian government should take? Who should be entrusted to lead it? Should the Italian monarchy be retained or ended?[17]

The pope had delayed responding but now decided he could put it off no longer. Cardinal Maglione and Monsignor Tardini prepared three drafts before the pope, making final edits, agreed on the text. The most sensitive point was identifying potential leaders of a new government. Initially, Tardini omitted any names, deeming it too risky to list them. The pope called for a new draft. Because the Americans had asked for names, the pope thought they needed to provide some, but he cautioned that they not be put in writing. Rather, the names were to be conveyed orally and cast not as people whom the pope himself was proposing, but rather, as the pope phrased it, "putting everything in the mouths of informants and public opinion."

Following these instructions, a new draft included the names of those the pope favored, albeit couched in a way that offered some distance: "large sectors of public opinion hold that, at least for an initial transitional period, those suited to lead the government, among others, are Vittorio Emanuele Orlando, Marshal Enrico Caviglia, and Luigi Federzoni." The elderly Orlando had been Italy's prime minister during the First World War, Caviglia was a similarly aged military hero of that war, and Federzoni a prominent, pro-church member of the Fascist Grand Council.[18]

Bringing this latest draft to the pope, Cardinal Maglione voiced his own uneasiness with the pope's request that names be included in responding to the American president. There was always the danger the message might fall into the wrong hands. Nor was it only Mussolini they were worried about. Many men were eager to succeed the Duce, and were any of them to see they were not included on the pope's list, the result could prove damaging. In the end, the pope agreed. The brief cable to Cicognani in Washington, in cipher, would go out with the names deleted. The pope focused on one issue only: his belief in the importance of retaining the monarchy. As for the matter of who might head a future government, the reply was curt. This matter, under the Italian constitution, was for the king to decide.[19]

While the pope's reply to Roosevelt's request was brief and sent through his apostolic delegate in Washington, he at the same time wrote directly to the president on a matter he thought more pressing. The intensified Allied bombardment of Italy's cities, along with the realization that invasion might be near, led him to fear Rome might soon be the target of Allied air assault. He began his letter, as had become his custom in speaking of the war, by praising his own ceaseless efforts on behalf of peace: "And when the awful powers of destruction broke loose and swept over a large part of Europe, though Our Apostolic Office places Us above and beyond all participation in armed conflicts, We did not fail to do what We could to keep out of the war nations not yet involved and to mitigate as far as possible for millions of innocent men, women and children, defenseless against the circumstances in which they have to live, the sorrows and sufferings that would inevitably follow." He asked Roosevelt to spare Italians from further tribulations and to protect "their many treasured shrines of Religion and Art—previous heritage not of one people but of all human and Christian civilization."[20]

ON MAY 29 WINSTON CHURCHILL and his foreign secretary, Anthony Eden, joined General Dwight Eisenhower and the Allied military command at their headquarters in Algiers to plan the invasion of Italy. Landing would take place on the shores of Sicily in an operation code-named "Husky." The date of the invasion was not yet set, but it would come soon.[21]

At the same time, Myron Taylor, President Roosevelt's emissary, paid a visit on the apostolic delegate in Washington, Monsignor Cicognani, with a message for the pope. Although Taylor said he was only speaking personally, Cicognani was convinced Roosevelt had sent him. Taylor said Italians faced a fateful choice. Should they not quickly depose Mussolini and renounce their alliance with Germany, the future would bring horrible ruin, death, and poverty, and in the end, they would suffer the fate of all conquered peoples.[22]

News of this conversation prompted anguished discussion between Cardinal Maglione and the pope. Clearly, if Pius XII wanted to play a role in bringing about Italy's renunciation of its alliance with Hitler, he would need to encourage King Victor Emmanuel to remove Mussolini from power, for only the king had the legal authority to do so. In sketching what such an attempt might look like, Monsignor Tardini even drew up a lengthy text that the pope might send the king. It tried to finesse the matter by putting some distance between the pope and the American request, phrasing it as passing on Taylor's message "solely as a matter of information."

Tardini was himself conflicted. If the pope decided to say nothing to the king, he thought, "it would seem that the Holy See wanted, at any cost, to save Mussolini." But for the pope to do anything that suggested Mussolini be deposed ran risks of its own.[23]

Despite the urgency of the American appeal, the pope decided to buy some time. He asked his delegate in Washington to find out from Taylor whether his message had the approval of the American government.[24]

On the same day as the pope sent this question to Washington, Monsignor Tardini prepared a new memo, this one outlining all the reasons why it would be unwise for the Vatican to do anything to help bring about Mussolini's fall. The Allies wanted Italy to renounce its alliance with the Nazis, eliminate Fascism, and under the guise of offering Italy its protection, use the country as a convenient base for attacking Germany. The Allies' threats of what they would do should Italy not comply—destroy Italy's cities, massacre its population, ruin its economy—were outrageous. "Does this not seem," asked Tardini, "a Nazi program?" And then, he thought, there was another consideration. The Germans had spies everywhere and undoubtedly had a plan ready to occupy Italy if the country made any move to replace Mussolini and disengage from the Axis. Indeed, he was convinced the Germans had "a great wish of striking against the Holy See." It would be unwise for the Vatican to do anything to anger them.[25]

THE FIRST ITALIAN TERRITORY to fall to the Allies was the small island of Pantelleria, midway between Sicily and Tunisia. After three days of intensive air bombardment, the military garrison surrendered, its ten thousand soldiers taken prisoner. On June 11, following the surrender, Roosevelt broadcast a radio appeal urging Italians to depose Mussolini and cast off their German ally. Later that day Myron Taylor again visited the papal delegate in Washington, bringing a final ultimatum from Roosevelt. If Italy and its king would heed his call, the United States stood ready to aid the beleaguered country and support a new government. This was their last chance. The Allies were determined to bring down Fascism and National Socialism. They would bomb any target that would hasten that goal, whether military or nonmilitary. Not even Rome would be spared.[26]

Pius XII could put off contacting the king no longer. On June 17 he sent his nuncio to meet with the monarch, using the pretext of giving the king a series of medallions commemorating the pope's twenty-fifth episcopal anniversary. The nuncio, Francesco Borgongini, perhaps the king's match as a pedant, spent the first several minutes of their forty-minute meeting explaining the history of each item to him. The monarch reciprocated by offering his compliments to Pius XII, saying how much he admired the pope's ability to craft his speeches in a way that ensured they would offend no one.

Roosevelt's radio address of a few days earlier gave the nuncio the opening the pope had sought to raise the delicate subject. The American president had said the United States was not ill disposed toward Italy and it would be in Italy's interest to withdraw from the war. If

Italy did so, Roosevelt had promised the country would have America's support. If it did not, the consequences would be terrible. In summarizing Roosevelt's radio message for the king, the nuncio made no direct mention of Mussolini or the desirability of replacing him.

As the king failed to take the bait the first time and went off on a tangent, the nuncio tried another tack. He told the king the Holy See had learned that the president really did mean what he had said regarding the support the country would get if it withdrew from the war. Here the king showed a flicker of interest, but then again changed the subject, asking how the church was structured in the United States.

Once more the nuncio tried to move the conversation in the right direction: "The monarchy is well regarded and loved by the Italian people and the government depends on Your Majesty."

The king, a coward but not a fool, could see what Borgongini was getting at. A wry smile appeared on his face. "I am not like the Pope."

The king said the Allies would find it difficult to land troops in Sicily. It would take more men and more large ships than they had. More likely, he speculated, they would aim for Sardinia. Or they might well not be planning to invade Italian territory at all, but rather would head for Greece. In any case, the king assured the nuncio, no landing on Italian soil was imminent, as the military had been keeping a vigilant eye and saw no signs of it.[27]

Mussolini's need for church backing for his faltering efforts to retain popular support had never been greater. The same day as the nuncio met with the king, the national head of the Fascist Party convened a meeting of thirty military chaplains, ten attached to the army, ten to the Young Fascist paramilitary groups, and ten to the Fascist militia. Present with them was the national head of the military chaplains, Archbishop Bartolomasi. The party secretary proposed holding a series of party-organized popular assemblies in cities throughout the country aimed at "inciting resistance" to the approaching Allied armies. Each event, scheduled for the first and third weeks of July, would consist of speeches by Fascist Party dignitaries, wounded veterans, and a local chaplain. The archbishop offered his strong support for the initiative and promised the Catholic clergy's "loyal collaboration."[28]

———

WHILE THE POPE HAD long been nervous about what a Europe under Nazi control would mean for the church, he also worried about what a resounding Allied victory might mean. A memo that Monsignor Tardini prepared for the British embassy offers a valuable glimpse into the thinking in the Vatican now that the war had turned so decidedly in the Allies' favor. Christian Europe and Christianity faced two dangers: Nazism and Communism, both materialist, antireligious, totalitarian, tyrannical, cruel, and militaristic. In response to Vatican worries that an Allied victory would result in Communist domination in Europe and so produce no better result than a Nazi victory, the Allied diplomats had argued that the two situations were very different. While an Axis victory would mean control of Europe by the Nazis alone, there were three major powers behind the Allies, and in a postwar world the British and Americans would counterbalance Russia's influence.

Tardini deemed this argument weak. There was in fact good reason to fear that an Allied victory would result in a Europe dominated by Russia and with it "the destruction of European civilization and Christian culture." He predicted that once the fighting in Europe was over, the Americans and British would need to focus on the war in the Pacific. While they were busy dealing with Japan, Russia's massive army would complete its occupation of much of Europe. Nor would their advance depend on military conquest alone, for Russia's unexpected victories against the German army had greatly impressed the working classes of Europe. In the aftermath of the war, the western Europeans, living in hunger and misery, would be easy prey for the Communists, while the Slavs, thought Tardini, had a natural affinity for the Russians and for Communism. The Communist conquest would be made easier by the fact that even after Japan was defeated, a totalitarian regime like Russia could continue to mobilize for war, while the democracies, subject to the popular will, would be eager to reduce their armies and enjoy the fruits of peace.

The monsignor concluded that the ideal outcome of the war would be elimination of both dangers, Nazism and Communism. Should

Communism survive—much as if Nazism were to survive—the result would be catastrophic.[29]

PIUS XII KNEW THAT neither the Italians nor the Germans had abided by the agreement to remove their military from Rome. But Roosevelt's threat that, if Italy continued to fight on the Axis side, he would not spare the city led the pope to renew his earlier admonition. If the Allies bombed Rome, he would loudly protest. In a message for the president, he warned: "Those effecting such a bombardment will be held responsible by Catholics the world over and by the judgment of history."[30]

Roosevelt and Churchill had given considerable attention to the question of whether Rome should be bombed, viewing the issue almost entirely in terms of Catholic sensitivities. But they had very different views. Foremost on the president's mind was the domestic political fallout he would face from American Catholics. For the British prime minister, it was outrageous that the pope should shield Mussolini's capital from attack after he had said nothing to protest the savage Axis bombing of London. In the end, as the Allied invasion of Italy neared, General Eisenhower in Algiers received new instructions, approved by both Roosevelt and Churchill, authorizing the daylight bombing of Rome's railway yards, a major transit point for Axis troops and supplies. Prior to launching any such attack, all pilots were to be thoroughly briefed on Rome's geography, with instructions to steer clear of Vatican City.[31]

Reluctant to alienate the pope, Roosevelt had not abandoned his hope of finding a way to declare Rome an "open city"—that is, one free of military activity and so not subject to attack.[32] His efforts met strong opposition not only from the American military command but from his own secretary of state, Cordell Hull. In late June, Hull explained his reasons in a long letter to the president: Given Rome's strategic position in the peninsula, the city remained a major rail hub linking north and south. Indeed, despite the Vatican's earlier assurances that the Italian and German military headquarters were being removed from Rome, they had good evidence that they had not, "and in fact there is every evidence that Mussolini continues to use Rome as the capital of Fascist Italy."[33]

WHILE IT MUST BY then have been clear to the pope that Mussolini's days were numbered, he remained careful not to antagonize the Duce or the Fascist government. But the disastrous turn in the war was leading an increasing number of the country's priests to express their unhappiness with the continued fighting. The result was a stream of prefect and police informant reports flowing into Rome complaining that parish priests were depressing public morale.

In mid-June, Ciano's second-in-command at the Vatican embassy argued that these cases of "defeatist" priests should not be given much importance. What was significant, he advised the Italian Foreign Ministry, were the strong words of support for the war that continued to come from some of the country's most influential bishops and cardinals. He cited the recent blessing the patriarch of Venice had given Italy's troops, praising them for battling "the enemy's oppressive power" and for "spreading Roman and Christian civilization in the world." He also quoted the recent remarks of Cardinal Carlo Salotti, a member of the Curia, hailing Italian soldiers' willingness to sacrifice their lives on behalf of their country, "proud in their Christian faith."[34]

As the Red Army was marching westward, and underground Communist Party organizers were helping foment strikes in factories of the north of Italy, the pope was becoming increasingly worried that a Communist wave might soon wash over the country. In mid-June, he addressed twenty-five thousand Italian workers gathered in Vatican City's Belvedere Courtyard. Cautioning them against the "lying promises" of the advocates of revolution, he warned that the Communists would reduce them all to slavery.

In reporting the speech to London, the British envoy wrote, "I am inclined to attribute the vehemence of the Pope's warnings against social revolution to the fear lest reaction from Fascism in Italy may take a Communist form." Osborne's chargé d'affaires followed up with a further critique. The pope "denounced 'social revolution' so severely and painted its consequences in such dark colours that the Fascist and Nazi press were able, by dint of judicious omissions, to represent the speech as having been little more than an attack on Communism." The Nazis made ample propaganda use of the speech. Italy's chargé d'affaires in Berlin reported that it was distributed "practically in its full text," presented "as the most explicit denunciation of communism that the Pope has ever uttered."[35]

Despite the turn the war had taken, the ongoing exchange of favors between Vatican prelates and the leading Fascist government officials continued. It would be an exchange for which many of the leading figures of the Fascist regime would later receive ample repayment from the Vatican. Throughout the war, Cardinal Maglione and those around him had used their government ties to protect their own relatives from the dangers posed by the war, especially to prevent their young kin from being sent off to the killing fields. The latest example, in May 1943, was emblematic. Maglione penned a letter to Francesco Babuscio, then chief of staff of the Foreign Ministry, addressing him as "dear friend." He asked that the orders to have the nephew of the papal nuncio in Belgium sent off to the front be countermanded and that he instead be assigned to the Rome office of the Foreign Ministry.

Babuscio replied two days later: "Permit me to tell you right away that it gave me immense pleasure to once again see your handwriting." He also wrote to the general under whose command the nuncio's nephew served. "It is in our great interest," Babuscio explained, "to maintain relations of confident sympathy with Cardinal Maglione." As expected, the general complied with the request.[36]

FROM ITS BASE IN ALGIERS, Eisenhower's Operation Husky now neared its final planning stages. Despite all the people involved in the effort, the secret of where and when the Allies would strike remained well kept. A massive invasion was coming soon.[37]

THE GOOD NAZI

O N JULY 5, 1943, THREE BLACK VATICAN LIMOUSINES DISPLAYING both white papal banners and red-and-black swastika flags pulled up at the German embassy to the Holy See, located in the majestic, columned, eighteenth-century Villa Bonaparte. The estate had been the Roman residence of Napoleon's sister Paolina over a century earlier. The Vatican attendants had come to accompany the new German ambassador, Ernst von Weizsäcker, and his entourage as they traveled the short distance to the Apostolic Palace for his presentation of credentials to the pope. Weizsäcker would later have the distinction of being the only wartime diplomat at the Vatican to be convicted at Nuremburg for crimes against humanity.[1]

As a young man, Weizsäcker had served in the German military during the Great War before entering the diplomatic service. Following stints as ambassador to Norway and then, in the early years of Hitler's reign, to Switzerland, he returned to the Foreign Ministry in Berlin. In 1938, when Hitler chose Ribbentrop to be his new foreign minister, Ribbentrop selected Weizsäcker to be state secretary, the top job under him.

Sumner Welles, the American undersecretary of state, had met Weizsäcker in Berlin during the same 1940 European trip that had brought him to the Vatican. He found him "a typical example of the German official of the old school of the nineteenth century." Like many who served in Hitler's government, Weizsäcker would later claim never to have really been a Nazi and to have been appalled by its excesses. But it was men like him who ensured the smooth functioning of the Third Reich. For the first four years of the war, he had run the Foreign Ministry and, as one historian put it, "supplied Nazi diplomacy with a civilized façade." He had been pleased by the early conquests that had expanded the Reich, and his office had played an instrumental role in deporting Jews from the occupied countries of Europe to their deaths in Nazi extermination camps. He would later claim he had no idea what awaited them there.[2]

Although the pope had had an ally in Diego von Bergen, Germany's long-serving ambassador to the Vatican, he would see some advantages in the new appointment. Bergen had little influence with Hitler and, ailing in recent months, had rarely been seen by anyone at the Vatican. By contrast, there was no better connected or more professional German diplomat than Weizsäcker, who, self-confident, well spoken, and projecting sincerity, immediately began to inspire trust and sympathy in the pope and in the men of the Secretariat of State.[3]

Indeed, from the Vatican's perspective, Weizsäcker epitomized the good Nazi. He was, as the pope's nuncio in Berlin put it, among those "men of Government who are not fanatics for National Socialism." The new ambassador, a Protestant, would ingratiate himself to the men of the Vatican by asking their help to enroll in a course on Catholic religious culture.[4]

After presenting his credentials, Weizsäcker accompanied the pope to his study. There the pope sat at his desk, while the ambassador dragged a chair from a corner of the room to be closer to him. As he always did on such occasions, the pope began by fondly recalling the many years he had spent in Germany. When the conversation turned to the war, the ambassador stressed Germany's central role in combating Communism. Pius XII then spoke of his own unpleasant experiences as nuncio in Munich in 1919, when Communists briefly took over the city. Weizsäcker reported to Berlin that in commenting on the war, the pontiff "condemned the mindless slogan of our enemies about an 'unconditional surrender.'"

Hitler's new ambassador felt he could build a good relationship with the pope. He found him easy to talk to, was delighted at the pope's excellent German, and could even occasionally get the pope to laugh. He later wrote, "I should enjoy my job more if the pope was a bit less ascetic and of a less frail disposition. . . . He is first a very faithful Catholic priest, and second a practical man." Doing his best to meet all the cardinals of the Curia in his first weeks in Rome, Weizsäcker was pleased by what he found. "What they were hoping for above all," he reported to Berlin, "was an agreement between England and Germany to unite against the Russians. Great is their disappointment that the British show no willingness to pursue this goal."[5]

The day before Weizsäcker made his ceremonial entrance to the Apostolic Palace, a different kind of ceremony was held in the cathedral of Frascati, on the outskirts of Rome. The local priest had summoned the faithful to take part in a procession "to implore the Madonna for 'peace with justice' and victory over the forces opposed to Christianity and to our country." He praised the efforts of the archbishop of Milan, who had recently convinced hundreds of thousands of the faithful to sign a pledge that they deposited at the feet of the Madonna at the city's famed Duomo. If the Madonna agreed to bring Italy victory in the war, they would all say the rosary daily, stop going to see movies that promoted immodest fashions, and devote their families to the Sacred Heart of Mary. Frascati's priest circulated his own version of the petition and urged his parishioners to sign.[6]

THE ALLIED LANDING IN Sicily was now only days away, but the king still dithered. The latest of the military command to urge him to act was General Vittorio Ambrosio, the nation's military head, who called on the monarch to replace the Duce with a military dictatorship that could negotiate a separate peace with the Allies. But the king insisted that such dramatic action was premature, indeed dangerous, arguing that after two decades of Fascist rule, one could not simply bring the regime to an end overnight.[7]

As Operation Husky—the landing in Sicily—was about to launch, Roosevelt and Churchill decided to jointly address a message to the

Italian people. There was one note, though, that the American president insisted on writing himself. "I am sending the following message to the Pope," the president wrote Churchill on July 9, "and feel that this should come from me instead of from both of us because of the large percentage of Catholics here, and because the Pope and I have a rather personal relationship, especially during the last few months."

Roosevelt's note to Pius XII began: "By the time this message reaches Your Holiness a landing in force by American and British troops will have taken place on Italian soil. Our soldiers have come to rid Italy of Fascism and all its unhappy symbols, and to drive out the Nazi oppressors who are infesting her soil." He assured the pontiff that the Allies would do everything possible to avoid damaging churches and religious institutions.

Informed of Roosevelt's planned message, the British foreign secretary Anthony Eden and Britain's ambassador to the United States Lord Halifax wrote both the president and General Eisenhower in Algiers to voice their disapproval. "We doubt whether message would help towards reconciling the Pope to an Allied invasion. The Pope must know anyway we intend to respect the neutral status of the Vatican, freedom of religion, and as far as possible ecclesiastical buildings and institutions; and to assure him that we intend to do so will not influence his attitude towards invasion." Undaunted, Roosevelt sent his message anyway.[8]

On the night of July 9, the Allied armada, consisting of 2,590 ships, left the shores of North Africa, headed for Sicily's southeastern coast. Defending the island were a quarter million ill-equipped and dispirited Italian soldiers and thirty thousand German troops. A forty-mile-an-hour gale produced boatloads of seasick GIs and wreaked havoc on the Allies' plan to land gliders behind the Axis lines. Thousands of paratroopers were blown off course but still succeeded in cutting Axis communications. In the early morning of July 10, the first shipborne troops landed on the still dark beaches, the British Eighth Army under General Bernard Montgomery and the Seventh U.S. Army under General George Patton. Over the next three days, 3,000 ships would deliver over 150,000 ground troops, supported by more than 4,000 aircraft. By evening of that first day, the British had walked into the southeastern Sicilian city of Syracuse virtually unopposed.[9]

The pope received Roosevelt's letter that same evening. His mood was not helped by the fact that Allied radio had broadcast its content before he read it. Monsignor Tardini dismissed the letter as nothing but a public relations effort by the American president, its intended audience not the pope but the 24 million Catholics in the United States.

Once again, the pope had Monsignor Tardini prepare a memo to help him decide how to respond to the president. As Tardini noted, Roosevelt's letter cast the Allied battle as a crusade, and he seemed to want to portray the pope as his partner. But while he had offered assurances that he would respect Vatican City, the president had said nothing about Rome. "He proclaims that he will as far as possible spare the churches," but only "after having destroyed so many extremely precious churches in Sicily and elsewhere!" Tardini suggested that the pope reply by reaffirming the Holy See's neutrality, repeating his entreaties for the Allies to protect civilians and church buildings and reminding the president of Rome's sacred character. The pontiff should "proclaim one more time that the pope's teachings and activities are inspired by and aim at true peace, at a pax Christi." Here the monsignor added, "Very different I believe from the one that in reality if not in his words Roosevelt is pursuing!"

The tart-tongued Tardini added an additional complaint: "This so-called Liberator of Italy (unfortunately the Liberators sow nothing but ruins!) pretends almost to be the pope's friend."[10]

When Mussolini learned of Roosevelt's letter to the pope, he had his son-in-law register his unhappiness with Cardinal Maglione and insisted that the government had a right to know how the pope would respond. Ciano reported that the cardinal looked "visibly upset" by the president's letter and had "excluded most emphatically that the Church had done anything to even indirectly encourage such a message." Saying the Holy See itself could not take sides in international conflicts, the cardinal reminded Ciano of all the statements Italy's cardinals and bishops had issued in support of the country at war and all the support provided by Italy's Catholic press. "From the conversation," concluded

Ciano, "I got the clear impression that Roosevelt's message was the first bomb to fall on the Vatican. The Holy See is in fact aware of the embarrassing position in which Roosevelt has tried to put the pope." Despite the urging of Tittmann, the American envoy, to have the president's letter published in the Vatican newspaper, the pope judged it best not to further anger the Duce.[11]

Two days later Pius XII sent his response to Roosevelt via a short telegram to his delegate in Washington. While he was thankful for the assurances the president had given regarding religious life and the safety of Vatican City, he said he was disappointed that the president had given no such assurances for Rome. He reiterated his plea that the city be spared.[12]

AS THE ALLIED ARMIES closed in, among those in the Fascist government eager to avoid disaster was the undersecretary of foreign affairs, Giuseppe Bastianini. With Mussolini retaining for himself the position of foreign minister following his cabinet purge of a few months earlier, Bastianini functioned in effect in that role. The day after the Allies landed in Sicily, he sought help from Cardinal Maglione, whom he had known for almost two decades. The previous twenty-four hours had been among the most dramatic in Italy's history. When Bastianini sat down in the secretary of state's large, richly furnished red-damask-upholstered study, its windows offering a spectacular view of Rome, the cardinal reached out and placed a hand on his.

Bastianini had come to ask for the cardinal's help in opening negotiations with the British. He wanted to send an envoy to make contact with the British government, but someone who could be dismissed as having no official government role if the matter came to light. Toward this end, he thought it best if the envoy were to carry a Vatican City passport and pose en route as a member of the Vatican's administrative staff. Exactly what kind of deal with the Allies Bastianini had in mind remains unclear. In meeting earlier with Alberto Pirelli to discuss the matter, he had said there needed to be a government of national unity, in which the industrialist himself might serve as foreign minister, but he left vague whether Mussolini would remain head of it. The plan was to sound out the British on the possibility that Italy could lead a group of Axis countries—Romania and Hungary among them—in withdrawing from the war.[13]

Who might this unofficial envoy be? asked the cardinal, nervous about handing out Vatican identity documents for such a purpose. Bastianini suggested Giovanni Fummi, a Roman banker who had once represented American financial groups in Europe.

Seeing the cardinal's reluctance, Bastianini stressed the danger the Vatican would face if a defeated Italy were at the mercy, as he put it, of "a coalition of communist forces in league with the anti-papists and Protestants." The cardinal raised his eyes and pointed with his hand to the ivory crucifix on his desk. "Yes, we are in God's hands."

In the end, Maglione agreed to furnish the envoy with the documents and assured him he would inform the pope of the plan, although he added that he doubted it could succeed. The British and Americans had repeatedly made known their opposition to negotiating with Italy's Fascist government. If that objection were raised, replied the undersecretary, Fummi would have a ready reply. The alternative to such a negotiation would be a "Russified" Italy and the end of Christian civilization in Europe.

Two days later Fummi appeared at the Vatican, where his papers were waiting for him. As the cardinal had predicted, his mission would go nowhere.[14]

OVER THE PAST MONTHS, Mussolini had been receiving a series of police reports detailing popular anger at the corruption surrounding his lover's family. Clara's brother, Marcello, was constantly getting into trouble with his shady business schemes, taking advantage of his government connections. His most recent escapade involved using contacts in Spain to organize an international trade in contraband gold. Clara's father's column in the local newspaper and her younger sister Miriam's acting career—she had gotten her first starring role in the Italian film *The Ways of the Heart* the previous year—were both thought to be the product of the Duce's influence. Meanwhile, the source of the family's income for their lavish spending was generating much unwelcome speculation. Edda constantly complained to her father about the affair. Indeed, she had gone so far as to persuade a friendly member of the government to compile a dossier documenting the illicit dealings of Clara's brother, which she brought to her father. "The woman will be liquidated, and all these swindles will be over," Mussolini assured his favorite child. There followed a series of half-hearted attempts by the Duce to end his affair with Clara.

Early in May Mussolini ordered the police official stationed at the back entrance of Palazzo Venezia not to allow Clara to come in. Shocked when the policeman barred her way, she protested loudly but failed to convince the officer to admit her. Back home, she took to her weapon of choice, her pen, and wrote her lover a scathing letter: "You have tried to free yourself from me in the most brutal and definitive manner, creating a scandal. . . . You have treated me like a thief and a prostitute." She would die, she said, "crushed by the pain forever." Clara's ever-protective mother wrote her own letter to the Duce. She told him not to believe the calumnies that Ciano, Edda, and others had directed at Claretta, as she called her, for her daughter's love for him knew no bounds. "Claretta's life lies in your hands."[15]

Mussolini had put Clara under police surveillance, not least because of his suspicion she was cheating on him. But in the murky world of the secret police, the surveillance came not only at Mussolini's direction but also on the order of others who found it profitable to gain more information on the Duce's second family.

Shortly after noon on July 15, 1943, offering some pretext for his visit, a general of the intelligence services arrived at the Petaccis' garish family home on Monte Mario. A crystal facade covered the entire ground floor of the enormous house, making the structure appear, observed the general, "like a large box sitting on a bar of ice." His report offers a glimpse of what life was like at the Petacci mansion, built with funds widely believed to have been funneled from the country's coffers by one of Mussolini's enablers. After a family servant succeeded, with difficulty, in pushing open the massive crystal sliding door, the general was ushered into the vast living room, graced with twenty plush chairs, a grand piano, and a harp. "On one wall," he observed, was "an incredibly ugly picture of an ugly girl." All the floors in the house were marble. Told that Clara would receive him in her bedroom, he was able to offer a detailed description of its opulence, not failing to mention the fact that the attached bathroom was entirely constructed in black marble. On the bedroom wall was a large color photo of Mussolini, alongside a cabinet filled with a great quantity of medicines. Clara confided in him, he reported archly, that she suffered "from many imaginary illnesses."[16]

Mussolini's tempestuous relations with his lover came at a dramatic time for him. Italians were suffering, making do with rationed pasta, bread, and other foodstuffs. There was widespread discontent as people found themselves caught between the Anglo-American forces on the march and a distrustful but powerful German ally. Police reports told the Duce of efforts being made to convince the king to depose him. Two months earlier Clara herself, his staunchest defender, had warned him of the threat posed by Marshal Badoglio and the other generals: "Your general staff is a nest of filthy snakes." She accused Edda and her husband of betraying him in league with Victor Emmanuel, or the "dwarf king," as she called him.

On July 18, following the third time Clara was refused entry to Palazzo Venezia, she renewed her warnings: "If you fall like a Myth, like God, the only thing left for me to do will be to kill myself." Her desperation stemmed not only from her exclusion but from her well-founded suspicion that her Ben was seeing other women. "You have the power of life or death over me," she wrote in her typically melodramatic style. "The sentence must be worthy of our love." Two days later she wrote again. "I would like to kill Ambrosio, Badoglio . . . Cavallero, the whole Military Command and all the ministers who are betraying you myself. . . . Save yourself . . . react, take supreme decisions, kill if necessary."[17]

DEPOSING
THE DUCE

A S ITALIAN SOLDIERS IN SICILY WERE FLEEING FROM BATTLE, jettisoning their uniforms along the way, and Allied troops were beginning their rapid march across the island, a delegation of Mussolini's longtime Fascist colleagues—Bottai, Bastianini, and Farinacci among them—took the unprecedented step of going together to Palazzo Venezia to press on him the precariousness of their situation and call for a meeting of the Fascist Grand Council. They found the Duce looking better than he had in a long time, but, as they regaled him with accounts of the disaster that was then unfolding, he listened in silence. "All right," he responded, "I'll convoke the Grand Council. In the enemy camp they'll say that it's being held to discuss surrender. But I'll convene it." He dismissed them without further comment. It would be the first time the council had met in over three years.[1]

Operation Husky had caught Hitler by surprise, for he had thought Sardinia the more likely Allied landing site. With only two German divisions in Sicily, and reports of Italian soldiers running from battle, the Führer was informed that the island's defenses could not long hold. Alarmed, he asked Mussolini to confer with him immediately, even offering to meet in Italy. Their encounter north of Venice at Feltre, not far from the Austrian border, would be the last time Hitler set foot on Italian soil. On July 19 both men flew into the Treviso airport and then traveled another hour by car to the villa that had been reserved for their rendezvous.

Mussolini's conceit that these were meetings of equals, longtime comrades, continued to be pushed by the Italian propaganda mill, but for the Duce they had become scenes of humiliation, as he sat through his erstwhile acolyte's lengthy harangues. This time was no different, as Hitler, looking pallid, spoke uninterruptedly for two hours, like a man possessed. He proposed that the poorly functioning Italian military come under German command. Mussolini, only sporadically able to follow what he was saying, sat on the edge of a chair too wide and too deep for him, his hands folded patiently over his crossed knees. The Italian military entourage that the Duce had brought with him, men whose German language skills were rudimentary at best, understood even less. At times, Mussolini seemed close to dozing off, but as Hitler's shrill tirade turned to Italy, he came back to life. Every so often he nervously passed his right hand over his mouth while his left hand briefly rubbed the pain radiating from his belly.[2]

The news that reached the Duce in the middle of the summit could not have helped his ability to pay attention. As the two dictators were in their cars headed for Feltre, American and British warplanes flying from Tunis and Malta had appeared over Rome and begun dropping bombs, in a daylight attack aimed at the city's railyards and airport. Rome had been warned. At midnight the previous day, British planes had appeared over Rome, triggering antiaircraft fire from the ground while red flares and tracer bullets lit up the sky. As the Allied diplomats housed at the Vatican guesthouse ran outside to see the spectacle, they could hear the nuns in the nearby chapel raise their voices in prayer. What rained down on the city that night, though, was not bombs but leaflets warning that Rome would be bombed the next day and urging residents to remain far from the railyards and airfields.[3]

Seven hundred Romans would be killed in the Allied assault, sixteen hundred injured, and the homes of many more left in ruins. The first bombs fell at eleven A.M., the last bomber leaving Rome's cloudless skies four hours later. Over five hundred Allied planes took part in the attack. They encountered little, wholly ineffective antiaircraft fire. A handful of Italian fighter planes initially flew up to meet them but quickly turned around rather than face obliteration. According to

Eisenhower's report the next day, 769 tons of bombs were dropped, yet "no damage is visible to historic or religious buildings except that preliminary interpretation of photographs indicate that the roof of church on edge of bombing area damaged, but strong possibility this resulted from blast rather than bomb strike."[4]

While Roosevelt had long worried about the public relations disaster bombing Rome might cause, and the propaganda coup for the Axis powers that the pope's threatened denunciation could bring, his British counterpart had few compunctions. When told that the bombing of Rome had begun, Churchill was delighted. "Good. And have we hit the Pope?" he quipped. "Have we made a hole in his tiara?" According to Pirelli, the Duce's first comment on the bombing after his return to the city the next day was bittersweet: "And so ends the myth of papal Rome."[5]

AT THE SOUND OF the first bombs exploding across the Tiber, Pius XII went to his window, where he could see the swarm of planes against the clear blue sky and smoke rising from below. Later in the day, eager to show himself to his wounded flock, he ordered a Vatican car to be readied. Three hours after the last plane flew away, the pope made his way through the rubble-strewn streets to view the scenes of destruction.

What most drew the pontiff's attention were reports that one of Rome's major basilicas had been destroyed. San Lorenzo Fuori le Mura, one of the seven destinations for Catholic pilgrims in Rome, lay not far from the railyards and, along with many of the buildings nearby, was heavily damaged. As the pope's slow-moving car drew near the devastated basilica, people recognized the white-robed pontiff and began to follow along. By the time the car stopped and the pope opened the door, a growing throng of traumatized Romans surrounded him, hailing the man of peace. Unable to enter the church, whose facade had been largely destroyed and its roof caved in, the pontiff sank to his knees and recited a prayer for the dead. Rising to his feet and turning to the crowd, he called on them to pray "so that the Lord turns this pain into a blessing for you and for all of Italy." As he raised his arms in benediction, hundreds of Romans dropped to their knees.[6]

On Mussolini's return to the city, the German ambassador went to see him to express his solidarity. "You see, Mackensen," the Duce responded, "I believe that the ruins of the Basilica of San Lorenzo will prove to be fatal to our enemies. It may be that from this very event their defeat has begun, and that from now on the wheel of fortune will turn in the opposite direction." Unhappy to learn of the popular adulation that had greeted the pope on the city's streets, Mussolini had initially ordered the newspapers not to publicize the pope's visit to the scene of destruction. But the dictator's resolve quickly crumbled, as he realized the propaganda value of featuring the pope's anguished appearance amid the rubble of the sacred Catholic site.[7]

The day after the attack, Mussolini's own paper led the way, with a large front-page photo of the damaged basilica, its banner headline reading "The Pope Kneels on the Ruins of the Destroyed Basilica of San Lorenzo." No mention was made of the train station, railyards, or military airfield that were hit, for according to the paper, the Allies' aim was destruction of Rome's churches and homes. A subtitle referred to the "profanation" of the Verano cemetery, also hit by the bombs: "The impiety of the gangsters of the air . . . did not even spare the dead." Another story told in loving detail of the pope's arrival at the devastated basilica: "The Pope saw all of this, and his heart wept, while from his trembling lips a prayer poured out." Afterward the pope let those close to him kiss his hand. As he drove away, the article concluded, in an embellishment that few but the most credulous Romans could have believed, "Those present erupted in a single enthusiastic shout: *Viva l'Italia!*"

Alongside the news article, Mussolini's paper carried an editorial: "With Judaic impudence, Roosevelt had promised, in one of his special 'messages' to the Pontiff, that in the course of the increased air actions against Italian cities the churches would be spared." It detailed the great religious significance of the basilica that the Allies had destroyed, recalling that it was the resting place of many of Pius XII's papal predecessors. "The Pontiff did not let much time pass after the last wave of the assassins to leave his distant residence to visit the place that had been hit. The Christian and Roman greatness of this gesture will cause the meretricious man responsible and his clique of Jews . . . to sink into the slime of shame that will remain indelible for centuries."[8]

FOLLOWING THROUGH ON HIS oft-repeated threat to protest the bombing of Rome, the pope directed his secretary of state to send a letter to all the principal nuncios and apostolic delegates of the Allied and neutral countries informing them of the bombing and of the pope's "bitterness" at the devastation it had wrought in "the city that is the center of Catholicism." The message concluded with the pope's request that Catholics make their displeasure known: "The Holy Father would like to hope that this Episcopate, clergy, and Catholic people show that they share in such great unhappiness."[9]

The pope's own public protest came in the form of a letter addressed to the cardinal vicar of Rome and published not only in the Vatican's *L'Osservatore Romano* but in Italy's Fascist newspapers as well. After reminding the cardinal he had long lamented the carnage and ruin that war inflicted on innocent populations and on religious and cultural monuments, he then turned to his repeated efforts to spare Rome from bombardment: "But, alas, this so reasonable hope of Ours has been deceived. What we so greatly deprecated has now happened."

Pius XII had felt it his duty to speak out should Rome be attacked, and indeed he had told the Allies so often he would do so that he could hardly remain silent now, but his words read as uttered more in sorrow than in anger. Osborne, the British envoy, deemed the pope's response "singularly mild." Likewise, Myron Taylor reported to Roosevelt that the pope had intentionally used moderate language so that it might not be used against the Allies by the Nazis or Fascists.[10]

Despite the pope's caution, the Fascist press did its best to cast his letter as a ringing condemnation of the Allies' barbarism and anti-Catholicism. "The Bombing of Rome: The Pontiff's Condemnation Brands the Aggressors with Eternal Infamy," read Farinacci's headline.

The article recounted how the "Anglo-Saxons" in London and Washington were all the more pleased with the bombing "because it struck, simultaneously, the capital of both Italy and of Catholicism."[11]

The Jesuit Father McCormick, among the few prominent anti-Fascist clerics in Rome, was unimpressed by the pope's letter. He noted in his diary that it made no mention of the targets of the Allied bombing. "But why did not the Vat[ican] let the world know more clearly, honestly, that the chief offenders are those who have delivered Rome over to the enemy by using it as a military centre! . . . There seems to be no courage for saying anything that might offend and show up Ger[mans] and It[alians] in a bad light."[12]

THE KING COULD NOT wait much longer. On Thursday, July 22, news came that Palermo had fallen to the Allies. What resistance the American and British troops were meeting was coming largely from the German troops on the island, and embarrassing stories of Allied soldiers being greeted enthusiastically by Italian civilians were doing nothing to encourage the king to tie his fate to the Duce's any longer. Men who had been central to the operations of the Fascist regime were now desperately looking for a way to distance themselves from it and begin the process that, over the next years, would rewrite their personal histories.

Among them was forty-eight-year-old Dino Grandi, one of the early Fascist bosses and president of the lower house of parliament. On the day Palermo fell, he met with Giuseppe Bottai, until recently minister of education. The two looked over a draft resolution Grandi had prepared for the meeting of the Fascist Grand Council planned for that Saturday. In light of the unfolding military disaster, the resolution called for returning authority over the military to the king, a constitutional role that Mussolini had taken from him earlier in the war. While the resolution called for restoring the authority of other institutions of government, it did not go so far as to ask directly for Mussolini's removal.[13]

The country's economic elite, too, were now rapidly deserting the

Duce. Emblematic was Alberto Pirelli, who on July 23 met with Duke Pietro d'Acquarone, the king's right-hand man, to see what the king was planning. Clearly, the industrialist now realized, Mussolini had to go, but the question was how he could be removed without creating dangerous unrest in the country. Although d'Acquarone would not say what the king had decided to do, Pirelli got the clear sense that Victor Emmanuel was finally about to act. It would be important, advised the industrialist, that the new prime minister, most likely a general, announce that Italy was continuing the war on Germany's side. If Italy was to negotiate with the Allies, it should do so on behalf of its Axis partners as well. That way, if the Allies were to present reasonable peace conditions and the Germans rejected them, Italy could announce its withdrawal from the war without being open to accusations of betrayal.

In sharing these suggestions with d'Acquarone, Pirelli said the Vatican would be their best bet for brokering any negotiations with the Allies. Both men agreed it would be wise to notify the Vatican only a few minutes before the king acted, lest news of the plan to depose Mussolini leak out prematurely.[14]

THE FASCIST LEADERS WHO arrived at Palazzo Venezia for the five P.M. meeting of the Grand Council that Saturday, July 24, had ample reason to be nervous. More than one wondered whether, when they next exited the building, they would be arrested, if not summarily shot. None had ever dared to challenge the Duce in this way. In the hours before the meeting, Ciano and Bottai had both worked with Grandi on his draft resolution and lobbied other members of the council for their support.

At five-fifteen P.M., dressed in his black Fascist militia uniform, the Duce entered and took his usual place at the head of the long U-shaped table. He began by launching into a history of the war. True, he admitted, Italians were now unhappy with it, but all wars were unpopular. He went on to outline his plan for a new line of defense against the Allied assault.

After Mussolini finished, Dino Grandi stood up to make his motion, but first he did the unthinkable, delivering a long, impassioned denunciation of the Duce. He accused him of turning the early comradely ideal of Fascism into a personal dictatorship and of failing to convene the Grand Council or to seek its advice before making the decision to go to war. Having for seventeen years retained for himself the ministries of all three branches of the armed forces, charged Grandi, Mussolini had failed to prepare the country for the war, and the disastrous consequences were there for all to see. Throughout Grandi's speech, Mussolini remained silently in his seat. His face betrayed no emotion.

He remained silent as well when his son-in-law then got up to speak. Ciano turned to his favorite argument: Germany had constantly deceived its Italian ally. It had plotted its attack on Poland without consulting them, and the Germans had decided on all their subsequent invasions—Norway, Denmark, Belgium, France, Russia—without any consultation. Far from being guilty of betrayal in wanting to separate their fate from Germany's, they were the ones who had been betrayed.

The debate would last many hours, the session adjourning only at two-thirty A.M. In the end, nineteen of the twenty-seven members voted in favor of Grandi's motion calling for the return of the position of military commander-in-chief to the king and, more ambiguously, the return of constitutional powers to the crown, the Fascist Grand Council, the government, and parliament. What exactly the nineteen Fascist leaders who voted for the motion thought would result from this vote remains, even today, unclear. That they still hoped to save themselves from the coming reckoning seems to be the only thread that tied them together.[15]

At seven A.M. Alberto De Stefani, one of the Grand Council members who had voted for Grandi's motion, appeared unannounced at the quarters of a high Vatican official he knew. He said he had urgent news to convey to the pope.* His next stop would be the royal palace to inform the king, but it was the pope whom he wanted to notify first.

---

* De Stefani, formerly one of the Catholic Center Party's pro-Fascist members, had served as minister of finance during Mussolini's first years in power. It was Monsignor Costantini, secretary of the Vatican congregation of Propaganda Fide, whom he came to see.

Summoned by phone, Monsignor Montini quickly joined them. On his arrival, De Stefani explained that the Grand Council had just approved a resolution that could mean the end of the dictatorship. Yet Mussolini still seemed confident the king would never countenance any effort to relieve him of his position.

Although saying that what the king would do remained unclear, De Stefani wanted to let the pope know what he thought needed to be done. In this, he said he was confident he spoke for the majority of the Grand Council. Two sets of negotiations had to begin immediately, one with Germany and the other, brokered by the Vatican, with the Allies. They would need to convince Germany it was in its own interest to allow Italy to withdraw from the war. The rationale they would give the Germans was that by no longer having to defend Italy, the Germans could redirect desperately needed troops to their eastern and western fronts. In Italy's negotiations with the Allies, it was clear that the country would be required to disarm, but the key, said De Stefani, was to have the Allies grant the country neutral status and forswear military occupation.[16]

WORD OF THE GRAND Council vote served to hasten the decision the king had already taken to replace Mussolini as head of government with Italy's former military leader, General Pietro Badoglio. At the time, Badoglio was best known for leading the Italian army in its conquest of Ethiopia, for which he had been awarded the title Duke of Addis Ababa. A longtime member of the Fascist Party, he had led Italy's military at the start of the war and overseen its invasion of France, but then, blamed for the debacle in Greece, he had been replaced in late 1940. A proud man, he would not forgive the Duce for that humiliation.[17]

At three forty-five A.M., shortly after the Grand Council meeting ended, Mussolini phoned Clara. She warned him not to trust the king. Still nursing the wounds from her recent exclusion from Palazzo Venezia, she added, "Remember who loves you and who never tires of giving herself to you." On his return home, Mussolini's wife would give him much the same advice, albeit without a profession of love.[18]

Mussolini arranged to see the king later in the day, hoping somehow to explain away the Grand Council vote. Clara wrote him a long tear-soaked letter. Again, she mixed her injured love for him with her unsolicited political advice: "You don't want to see me, to let me embrace you again after so much drama, to let me tell you that I love you all the more now that you have been betrayed. . . . It is all as my blood had told me: you have been betrayed, by your son-in-law first of all. Ben, you push away my love and my words, you keep humiliating me, but it doesn't matter." She begged him, belatedly, not to go see the king. "What must I do to get you to listen to me! Does history not teach you anything!! Listen to me. . . . Believe me it is the king who has wanted this. It is the king who betrays you with the whole Military Command, and he made use of those vile, timid, fatuous reptiles. Ben, arrest them! Ben, kill them and then let the king know you have brought justice to those who betrayed the Fatherland at war."[19]

The fainthearted king had initially thought he could simply inform Mussolini of his decision to appoint a new head of government and then let him go free. Only at the last minute did the generals convince him that the Duce would have to be arrested and removed from Rome. At his awkward half-hour conversation with Mussolini that afternoon, the king made no mention of the fact he had ordered his arrest. Only when the deposed dictator walked back toward his car in the courtyard did an awaiting carabiniere captain approach him.

"Duce, in the name of His Majesty the king we ask you to follow us to protect you from any possible violence by the crowd."

"But there's no need!" responded Mussolini.

"Duce, I have an order to carry out."[20]

The radio announcement of Mussolini's "resignation" and the king's appointment of General Badoglio as head of a new military government came shortly before ten P.M. on July 25. The Vatican newspaper announced the news the following day with a small headline buried beneath its "International News" rubric. There it also published Badoglio's address to the Italian people. For the many who hoped the change in government would mean Italy's swift exit from the war, Badoglio's words were disappointing: "The war continues. Italy, hit hard, its provinces invaded, its cities destroyed, keeps its word, jealous custodian of its age-old traditions." No public demonstrations of any kind would be tolerated.

Two days later *L'Osservatore Romano* added more detail, attributing the change in government to the Grand Council vote and the king's subsequent action, and adding a note on Germany's positive reaction to Badoglio's statement that the war would continue. It also listed the

General Pietro Badoglio

new members of the government, beginning with the new foreign minister, Raffaele Guariglia, who, until his replacement a few months earlier by Ciano, had been the Fascist government's ambassador to the Vatican. In a further sign of the repackaging of men who days earlier had been stalwarts of the Fascist regime, Gaetano Azzariti, the man who headed the special Fascist court overseeing the racial laws, was named Italy's new minister of justice. He would later become chief justice of the country's highest court.[21]

Corriere della Sera, which for years had been filled not only with paeans to the Duce but with the vilest antisemitic attacks, greeted news of his overthrow with big photos of the king and Badoglio, along with an article titled "Milan Exults." Fascists who had proudly worn their black shirts now found places to hide them. One man, slow to see the way the winds had shifted, was forced off a tram, his black shirt torn from his chest and set afire. Elsewhere, images of the Duce and Fascist symbols were ripped from walls and shredded. Monsignor Costantini went out walking toward the Vatican on the day following the announcement of the change in government. "Everywhere there is lively gaiety, everywhere joyful voices," he wrote in his diary, "everywhere the fluttering of the tricolor." What the Monsignor did not mention is that shouts of "Death to Father Tacchi Venturi" could also be heard on Rome's streets. It would be a warning to the pope. The time had come for the Vatican to begin rewriting its own history as well.[22]

The pope, though, had a more immediate problem on his mind. Although the new government had publicly announced its intention to remain at Hitler's side, behind the scenes it would clearly be looking for a way to extract Italy from the war. As the Vatican had good relations with the Allies, and the pope's eagerness to play the role of peacemaker was well known, the new government seemed likely to call on the Vatican to act as intermediary to arrange Italy's exit from the war.

Following the king's dismissal of the Duce, the pope had Monsignor Tardini prepare a memo on the urgent question he expected soon to face. Tardini drafted it even before the Italian public learned what had happened and gave it to Cardinal Maglione that same evening. Now come to light with the recent opening of the Vatican archives, his handwritten brief offers a clear view of how the pope's closest advisers saw the dramatic choices he faced.

Tardini's advice was clear: the Holy See should refuse any request by the new government to serve as intermediary in its efforts to leave the Axis. The Allies had made clear they would accept only Italy's unconditional surrender, and the pope could do nothing to change that. If the Vatican got involved in arranging such a painful exit from the war, it might well "greatly damage the prestige of the Holy See in the eyes of the Italian people who would have earlier placed many hopes in the papal intervention and would then remain bitterly disappointed." The fact that the Allies would subsequently proceed to occupy Italy "will humiliate the Italians and diminish the Holy See's prestige in their eyes." Nor were the reasons for the pope to refuse to help the Italians make peace with the Allies limited only to potential damage to the pope's reputation in Italy: "The Germans might blame the Holy See for their defeat." True, many Germans would be happy to liberate themselves from Hitler, "but it is also true that the Allies will treat Germany in such a harsh and inhumane way that all Germans, even the good ones, will remain embittered and indignant. This bitterness and indignation of theirs might well be directed, in part, against the Holy See, should it have acted to facilitate Italy's peace with the resulting abandonment of Germany."

After recalling the bitterness produced in Germany by the Treaty of Versailles, at the end of the previous war, Tardini came to his recommendation:

> Because the humiliations and the punishments inflicted on the Germans this time will be even worse than those that followed Versailles; because the Allies, blinded, unfortunately!, by hatred, will commit countless arbitrary and unjust actions against the Germans without any sense of proper measure; because (even if unjustly) a hostile attitude of the Germans to the Holy See would make the future conditions of Catholicism very difficult in Germany (where the Church needs to make up for the losses already suffered), it would seem opportune for the Holy See now to avoid any gesture that might in any way lend itself to being used one day to accuse it of having taken part (if only minimally) in Germany's defeat.

The next morning Cardinal Maglione discussed Tardini's memo with the pope. Pius XII felt torn. Tardini had certainly captured his own worries, the pope mused aloud, but after all the times he had hailed the value of peace, how could he refuse a request from Italy's new leaders if they asked for his help?[23]

That evening, buffeted by a potent mixture of elation, apprehension, and disorientation, large numbers of Romans made their way to St. Peter's Square, hoping the pope would come out to bless them and so share in their joy and their hopes. The pope must have been tempted to come onto his balcony to bathe in their acclaim, but he was a cautious man. It would be more prudent not to take part in what could be construed as a celebration of the end of the Fascist dictatorship. Despite the calls from below, Pius XII remained inside, his window closed.[24]

MUSICAL CHAIRS

THE DUCE'S ARREST WAS CAUSE FOR CELEBRATION IN WASHINGTON and London. Writing to Churchill, Roosevelt insisted they demand an unconditional surrender from the Italians. "It seems highly probable," replied Churchill, "that the fall of Mussolini will involve the overthrow of the Fascist Regime and that the new government of the King and Badoglio will seek to negotiate a separate arrangement with the allies for an armistice."

But the nature of Italy's new government remained unclear. As an American intelligence report put it, "There is no indication that the forces which supported the Mussolini regime—namely, the monarchy, the armed forces, the Vatican, the Catholic Church in Italy, and the industrial and agricultural backbone of the Fascist party—have relinquished their power or their principles in accepting Mussolini's resignation." The newly announced slate of government ministers was filled with men from its Fascist predecessor.[1]

Italy's new prime minister, the seventy-two-year-old Pietro Badoglio, had himself been far from a minor player in the two decades of Fascist rule. As head of the military chiefs of staff from the time Mussolini proclaimed the dictatorship in 1925, he had overseen the fascistization of the armed forces. As governor of the North African colonies of Tripolitania and Cyrenaica in 1930, he had employed brutal measures to put down the Libyan resistance, herding the native population into camps where sixty thousand died. In 1940 he oversaw Italy's invasion of France and was forced out of his position only as a result of the humiliating defeat in Greece.[2]

Churchill thought the Allies should not be overly particular about who was in Italy's new government. What mattered was that whoever they were, they be in a position "to deliver the goods." There was also the question of what should be done if Mussolini and "his partners in crime," as Roosevelt called them, were captured. Churchill reviewed the options: "One may prefer prompt execution without trial except for identification purposes. Others may prefer that they be kept in confinement until the end of the war in Europe and their fate decided together with that of other war criminals. Personally I am fairly indifferent on this matter." What was of concern was that prominent Fascists would seek refuge in neutral countries. Roosevelt and Churchill sent a joint telegram to the states they were most worried about, including the Vatican, warning them against assisting such individuals "in any effort to escape their just deserts." Britain's envoy gave the message to Cardinal Maglione. At the bottom of his official request was a one-word handwritten note by Monsignor Tardini: "Wait . . ."[3]

From Algiers, Eisenhower urged rapid diplomatic action while there was still an authority in Italy with the ability to surrender: "If the King of Italy remains for more than a very short time as head of a country still at war with the Allies, full odium in our 2 countries now concentrated on Duce will be transferred to the King. Situation might therefore arise where it will be impossible to arrange an honorable capitulation with the King and we may be left without any other responsible authority." Eisenhower proposed broadcasting a message to the Italian people, commending them on ridding themselves of Mussolini, "the tool of Hitler," and calling on them to cease all activities in support of the Germans. Roosevelt and Churchill tweaked Eisenhower's text before authorizing its broadcast. On July 28 Roosevelt wrote Churchill: "It now appears possible that by skillful handling of the situation we may be able to get Italy out of the war without the sacrifice of large numbers of our soldiers and sailors." In retrospect, the president's forecast appears tragically naïve.[4]

Unlike the Americans, who had joined the war late, the British had a significant number of prisoners of war in Italy, and their fate was much on Churchill's mind. Forty-two thousand British soldiers and another 26,000 from elsewhere in the British Commonwealth were imprisoned in seventy different locations scattered through the Italian Peninsula, from reconverted orphanages to newly built prison camps. "Discarding etiquette," he wrote Roosevelt on July 29, "I have sent a direct message to the King of Italy through Switzerland emphasizing our vehement and savage interest in this matter." When Churchill had earlier raised the issue with Roosevelt, the president volunteered to use his good relations with the pope to help. "I am most grateful for your promise to put the screw on through the Pope or any other convenient channel," Churchill responded. But he added a warning, "If the King and Badoglio allow our prisoners and keymen to be carried off by the Huns without doing their utmost to stop it, by which I mean using physical force, the feeling here would be such that no negotiations with that Government would stand a chance in public opinion."[5]

While joy and optimism greeted news of Mussolini's overthrow in the Allied capitals, the reaction in Berlin was very different. The Führer's outrage was further stoked by his fear that Mussolini had been executed. He immediately summoned Goebbels and others of his inner circle to prepare a response, placing no faith in Badoglio's public declaration that Italy would continue to fight on the Axis side. Indeed, Hitler suspected that Badoglio had moved against Mussolini only after reaching a secret agreement with the Allies. The Führer's first thought was to direct a German parachute division based in France to occupy Rome, seize Badoglio, the king, and the whole royal family, and take them to Germany. Hitler suspected, wrongly, that the Vatican had played a key role in the king's decision to replace Mussolini, and he railed against the pope and the Holy See. Goebbels, his propaganda chief, helped persuade him that taking any action against the pope or the Vatican would be unwise, for it would undercut their claim to be defending Christian Europe from the Jews and the Communist hordes. He described the discussion in his July 27 diary entry: "The Fuehrer at first intended, when arresting the responsible men in Rome, to seize the Vatican also, but Ribbentrop and I opposed the plan most emphatically. I don't believe it necessary to break into the Vatican, and, on the other hand, I would regard such a measure as exceptionally unfortunate because of the effect our measures would have on the whole of world opinion."[6]

The fate of Mussolini and his family was on the pope's mind as well. Two days after the dictator's arrest, Cardinal Maglione made a note of these concerns. He knew Mussolini was in a nearby military base, although he did not know that he would soon be spirited off to a more remote location. Perhaps the military authorities would allow the Holy See to send Archbishop Bartolomasi, head of the military chaplaincy—and, until then an avid cheerleader for Mussolini and Fascism—to visit the fallen leader to comfort him. The cardinal, shortly after learning of Mussolini's arrest, had also sent a message urging the police chief to give precise instructions "for the security of the poor woman Rachele Mussolini." Maglione followed this up later in the month by sending a detailed list of Mussolini's extended family members—twenty-six in all—and their whereabouts to the Italian embassy with a recommendation that no harm come to them.[7]

Early on the morning of July 30, Dino Grandi, the main author of the Grand Council resolution, came to see the pope.[8] He later recalled: "Pope Pius XII greeted me with paternal benevolence. He asked that I sit near him and tell him in minute detail about the events in which I took part on the eve of July 25, my last conversation with the Duce, the preparations for and the night of the Grand Council, my contacts with the king and with the ministers of the Royal House." In Grandi's subsequent account, which must be viewed with some skepticism, he also told the pope that Badoglio's hopes for Italy to withdraw from the war were illusory and that Italy should prepare to defend itself against a German invasion. While he and the pope were talking, they heard an ear-shattering air raid siren. At first, according to Grandi's account, the pope did not move, but after a moment he got down on his knees and, with his palms pressed together in front of him, began reciting the Lord's Prayer. Grandi knelt down next to him, joining the pontiff in reciting the familiar words.[9]

There was a kind of musical chairs quality to the hasty formation of the new government, as evident in the fate of Mussolini's undersecretary for foreign affairs. On July 31, the king summoned Giuseppe Bastianini, who arrived early the next morning at the king's study in the Quirinal Palace. Victor Emmanuel wore his military uniform. Bastianini, in tails, sat before him, his cylindrical black top hat perched on his lap. The king first thanked Bastianini for all the work he had done under difficult conditions over the past few months as, in effect, Mussolini's last foreign minister. He then said he was appointing him ambassador to Turkey. The position was vacant in the wake of the appointment of Raffaele Guariglia, Mussolini's former ambassador to the Holy See, and for the past several months Italy's ambassador to Turkey, as the new foreign minister.[10]

Among Guariglia's first challenges on returning to Rome from Ankara was what to do about Mussolini's son-in-law, who remained the country's ambassador to the Holy See. Clearly, he could not stay in that position. But, Guariglia later recalled, "Taking any administrative action against him was repugnant to me given the personal relations I had had with him and the appreciation I had always had of his good qualities." Instead, he sent a Foreign Ministry assistant to ask for the resignation, and Ciano readily obliged. Placed under house arrest, Ciano remained in his home as he mulled over his options.[11]

Rather than replace Ciano as ambassador to the Vatican, Guariglia decided to leave the position vacant. Having held that post until Ciano took his place earlier in the year, and having a close relationship with Cardinal Maglione, Guariglia decided it best to manage relations with the Vatican by himself. He appointed his longtime colleague, forty-six-year-old Francesco Babuscio Rizzo, to the post of chargé d'affaires of Italy's embassy to the Holy See. Guariglia's ties to the Vatican secretary of state did not escape the notice of the German ambassador. "Foreign Minister Guariglia and Cardinal Secretary of State Maglione keep close contact," Weizsäcker advised Berlin. "Both come from the same region close to Naples. Guariglia is a devout Catholic. I do not think that there are any matters in Italian foreign policy that Maglione does not learn about."[12]

———

NOW THAT MUSSOLINI HAD fallen, the church faced the urgent task of denying it shared any responsibility for having promoted popular support for his regime. The dangers the churchmen faced were evident from Milan, where despite Badoglio's ban on popular demonstrations, workers hostile to his government were demonstrating in the streets. On the morning of July 26, a crowd sacked the Fascist Party headquarters in Milan, as similar crowds did elsewhere in Italy. That evening thousands marched in a spontaneous demonstration making their way through the streets of Milan to Piazza Duomo, facing the city's famed cathedral. Shouts were heard against Cardinal Schuster, Milan's archbishop, a longtime supporter of the Fascist regime. Smaller groups of demonstrators broke off to gather around orators who called for an end to Fascism and an end to the war. Over the following days, the government vigorously enforced the ban on demonstrations while censorship prevented newspapers from reporting the cases of popular violence against particularly reviled local figures of the Fascist regime. At the same time, strikes broke out in factories as workers called for better wages and better working conditions.

Nor was the turmoil limited to the center and north of the country. On July 28 in the southern city of Bari, police opened fire on two hundred demonstrators, mainly high school and university students and their teachers, as they marched by the Fascist headquarters and called for removal of the Fascist symbols decorating its exterior. Twenty of the marchers lay dead in the street. Similar bloody encounters of protesters with the government's armed forces occurred in central Italy as well. In all, it is estimated that in the days following the announcement of the new government, ninety-three demonstrators were killed, over five hundred injured, and more than two thousand arrested.[13]

Bishop Colli, who, as national director of Catholic Action, had repeatedly urged all good Catholics to support the Axis war, now issued new instructions to the membership. They were to obey the new government. In what would become the anthem of the Italian church in general, the bishop added: "Italian Catholic Action has nothing to repudiate in its past work."[14]

In the wake of Mussolini's fall, the pope worried about the possibility of a popular uprising and the threat it posed not only to the Vatican but to his own personal safety as well. On August 7 the commander of the Swiss Guard warned that Vatican security forces were woefully undermanned and underequipped to deal with the new threats. The "development of the uncertain events, full of surprises," he advised Cardinal Maglione, "requires a major improvement in the weapons at the Guard's disposal." Accompanying his plea was a memo prepared for the pope, who reviewed it on August 9. Should a regular army unit attack the papal residence, there was no hope of prevailing and, the papal officer suggested, only symbolic resistance could be mounted. Fortunately, however, such an assault seemed unlikely. "On the other hand, a defense promises success against the more likely attacks from revolutionary masses in case of possible political disorders." In such a case, it would only be a matter of holding off the anticlerical mob long enough for the forces of the regular army to come to their aid. But such assistance, the Swiss Guard commander advised, might "only arrive after the rabble had amassed around the Gates and Entrances of the Vatican and had eventually climbed the Vatican's walls and forced open one or another entrance."

The commander thought it crucial that his forces be equipped with automatic weapons, including machine guns, weapons they did not have. "The revolutionary crowd, especially after a war, will certainly have armament superior to that of the Vatican, that is automatic arms, cannons, tanks, etc." The use of heavy weapons by Vatican forces outside the walls of Vatican City to prevent the mob from entering would be politically impossible, advised the commander. Therefore it was crucial they be able to stop the rioters once they had breached the Vatican perimeter. He recommended that a request be made to the Italian government for twenty-four machine guns, as well as "a certain number of defensive hand grenades." With those arms, they would be able "to guarantee the safety of the Holy Pontiff and all those in the Sacred

Apostolic Palaces." To this he added another note: the Swiss Guards would need to replace their decorative antique helmets with modern ones made of steel and procure sandbags sufficient to protect the papal troops in case of attack.

The pope considered the recommendations but judged some of them a step too far. Among those the pope approved was setting up a direct phone line to the Italian police and finding better ways to protect the entrances to Vatican City and the Apostolic Palace. He also asked that means be examined to disperse any crowds that might gather at a Vatican City gate, suggesting, adding a question mark indicating his hesitancy, "Water hoses? Use of smoke?" The pope put off the question of procuring heavy arms, saying he would discuss the matter with Cardinal Canali, responsible for overseeing Vatican City. The Swiss Guards would never get the heavy weapons their commander had urged on the pope.[15]

ITALY'S NEW PRIME MINISTER faced an impossible dilemma. To continue to fight the Allies would be to ensure national ruin, but to announce that the country was abandoning its Axis partner risked disaster as well. Hundreds of thousands of Italian troops were stationed alongside the Germans in the Balkans and elsewhere. The day Italy announced an armistice, the Germans would likely seize them all, if they did not simply shoot them as turncoats. The tens of thousands of German soldiers in Italy itself were undoubtedly a more potent military force than the demoralized Italian troops. Nor was there any doubt that should the new prime minister announce a separate peace with the Allies, Germany would flood thousands more men into the peninsula.

In late July, Badoglio was still mulling over how best to make contact with the Allies without letting the Germans know. He also feared that Hitler might try to restore Mussolini to power. To gain time, he instructed the head of Italy's military mission in Berlin, General Luigi Efisio Marras, to meet with the Führer. The general's task was not an easy one, for Hitler was furious with the Italians, and Marras was charged with offering assurances he knew were being made in bad faith.

Thanking the Führer for meeting so speedily, the general did his best to convince him that the change in Italy's government had nothing to do with Italy's commitment to the Axis cause. As Badoglio had publicly proclaimed, the war at Germany's side would continue.

Hitler listened for a while without interrupting. Then when the general paused, he launched into a lengthy lecture. What Italians lacked, said Hitler, was courage. German cities were being bombed too, yet Germans stood strong. "The day will come," the Führer predicted, "when we will be able to take our revenge." He reminded the general of Mussolini's favorite adage, "Better to live one day as a lion than a hundred years as a sheep." If Italy were to lose the war, he warned, it would also lose not only its hard-won African colonies but Sicily and Sardinia as well.

What most concerned the Führer, it seemed, was the fate of his former comrade in arms, and the general repeatedly tried to assure him that the Duce was alive and well. "All things considered," Marras concluded in his report to Badoglio, "the Führer exhibited a calm, a composure and even a cordiality greater than could have been expected given the situation."[16]

The meeting might have been cordial, but Badoglio was getting alarming news from Italy's northern border. German troops were pouring into the country both at the Brenner Pass in the northeast and across the French border on the northwest. The Germans brushed off the feeble challenges they met from Italian border officials who had no orders to use force to stop them, nor could they. In the northeastern city of Bolzano, German units quickly occupied power stations, bridges, and other strategic points. The same pattern would soon be repeated elsewhere.[17]

Badoglio still clung to the belief, or at least the hope, that Italy could find a path out of the war that did not appear to be a betrayal of its Axis partner. He sent a message to the Führer suggesting that together they find a way to bring the war to a "dignified" end. Told of the message, Hitler erupted, "This is the greatest insolence the world has ever seen! But what is this man thinking? That I believe him?"[18]

Worried that violent conflict with Germany might be about to

erupt, Cardinal Maglione convoked a joint meeting with the ambassadors of Portugal, Spain, Argentina, and Hungary, all countries having
good relations with the Third Reich. As Italy might soon break off
relations with Germany, he told them, Germany might send its troops
to occupy key points in Italy, including Rome and perhaps even Vatican City. The cardinal then put the matter diplomatically. He himself
had faith that Italy and Germany would find a way to come to an agreement. He also had faith that even if relations between Italy and Germany were broken, Germany, which had recently protested so loudly
against the Allied bombing of Rome, would respect the city and its
sacred character, as well as Vatican City, which remained neutral in the
war. Given all this, asked the cardinal, might it not be opportune for
the ambassadors to speak with their German colleague at the Vatican
and express their faith in Germany's good intentions toward the Holy
See? After briefly discussing the question among themselves, the ambassadors promised that they would raise the matter with their German counterparts at the first opportunity.[19]

The ambassadors were as good as their word, for the next day
Weizsäcker sent a message to Berlin reporting on their visits. The Vatican, they had told him, was worried, for it had received reports that
Germany was planning military action in the next few days aimed at
toppling the Badoglio government. "When they spoke to me about
this," Weizsäcker informed Berlin, "I said all of this was pure fantasy."
He added, "I could not ascertain whether they believed my denial."[20]

Italy's new government, while still publicly reaffirming its commitment to the Axis, was eager to keep the Allies from resuming their
bombing of Rome. The government had changed, but its belief that
the Vatican offered its best hope to protect the nation's capital had not.
On the last day of July, Italy's new foreign minister asked Cardinal
Maglione for the Vatican's help in getting the Allies to declare Rome
an "open city" and to find out what they would require to do so.

In discussing the matter with the cardinal and most likely with the
pope as well, Monsignor Tardini expressed doubts about getting the
Vatican involved in such sensitive discussions. It seemed that Italy's
new government was simply stalling for time, since the Allies' demands

regarding demilitarization were well known, and past assurances notwithstanding, the city was still buzzing with military activity. Unwilling to forgo another chance to act as protector of the Eternal City, Pius
XII brushed aside Tardini's reservations. Maglione wrote to the apostolic delegates in both Washington and London to pass on the government's query.[21]

On receiving Maglione's note, the papal delegate in Washington
contacted Sumner Welles, the U.S. undersecretary of state. The Vatican request, coming on August 2, arrived at an awkward moment, as
Eisenhower had scheduled his second bombing mission over Rome for
two days later, and Roosevelt was on a fishing trip on a Canadian island
in Lake Huron. The American war department sent a radio message to
Eisenhower in Algiers: "Italian government via Vatican requested US
to prescribe conditions for declaring Rome open city. Pending further
instructions it would appear desirable to refrain from air activities
against the city of Rome proper."

Eisenhower replied the next day, after receiving an additional message reporting on a subsequent exchange between the British prime
minister and the American president. It was now only a day before the
planned attack. "The meaning of the President's reply to the Prime
Minister . . . quoted in your message is not entirely clear to us," wrote
the American general. "We assume, however, that it means he does not
wish to interfere with the attack on the marshalling yards at Rome
planned for tomorrow August 4th of which you have already been informed but that further raids on Rome should not be made pending
the outcome of Vatican efforts." Eisenhower followed this up with a
message to General George Marshall, army chief of staff, reiterating his
plan to attack Rome's railyards the next day but adding: "I do not intend to overdo operations against Rome as I fully realize all the implications and repercussions which are bound to result, but the presence
of our planes over the city, dropping leaflets and, when appropriate,
bombs undoubtedly has a marked effect."[22]

The U.S. War Department had prepared a list of twenty-five conditions that would have to be met to declare Rome an open city. From
his fishing retreat, Roosevelt cabled Churchill, "I think we would be in

a difficult position if we were to turn down the plea to make Rome an open city. I have just received from Washington the proposed conditions and given my approval in principle but I think we must be very sure of the inspection if the terms are accepted by Italy."

The British prime minister remained unsympathetic. "The time for negotiating about Rome being an open city has passed," replied Churchill. It would only "encourage Italy to attempt further negotiations for the neutralization of Italy itself."

Roosevelt replied immediately. Given the imminence of Eisenhower's planned air raid over Rome, it would be unwise to try to halt it now. "However," he added, "pending the outcome of Vatican efforts, I am of the opinion that further raids should not be continued."[23]

The frenetic transatlantic exchange of messages was followed by something of an anticlimax. Due to bad weather, Eisenhower called off the bombing mission at the last minute. Given the need to give priority to air support for the Sicilian operation, he reported, no new attack on Rome's railyards could be contemplated immediately.[24]

Within hours of learning that the day's bombing mission was canceled, Churchill sent Roosevelt word of the latest discussion of his War Cabinet. The effect on British public opinion of sparing Rome from attack "would be most unfortunate. . . . It would be taken as a proof that we were going to make a patched-up peace with the King and Badoglio and had abandoned the principle of unconditional surrender." The world would see the decision as a ringing success for the new Italian government. "No doubt their greatest hope is to have Italy recognized as a neutral area, and Rome would seem to be a first instalment." There was another reason as well for Churchill's insistence that the Allies reject the Italian request, for they hoped to have Rome in their hands soon, and it would then be of great help to be able to use the city as a staging area for their own military efforts farther north. Should they proclaim Rome an "open city," that would be impossible.[25]

Roosevelt was getting much the same message from his own joint chiefs. "It is inadvisable," they warned him on August 5, "from a purely military viewpoint, to decide the question of the recognizing of Rome as an open city at the present time. By such recognition we would deny ourselves the use of communications through Rome which would be vital to operations to the north." But they recognized why the president was reluctant to reject the pope's plea. "For political reasons," they acknowledged, "it would appear that the necessity of a direct denial of this request should be avoided." Their advice: delay responding to the pope as long as possible. "It is our view that the communication facilities, plants, and airfields in Rome and its immediate vicinity are important military targets and should be attacked."[26]

BETRAYAL

F EARING, FOR GOOD REASON, THAT HITLER WOULD TRY TO LIBERATE
his fallen Italian comrade, Badoglio initially sent Mussolini to the
tiny island of Ponza, in the Tyrrhenian Sea between Rome and Naples.
He did not remain there long, for Badoglio, worried that the Germans
might be close to locating him, had him board a navy ship that sailed
northward to Maddalena, a small island off the northern coast of Sardinia.

Shortly after Mussolini arrived at the semiabandoned villa that
would be his home on the grounds of the small naval base there, he was
handed a small package. Within a day of learning of Mussolini's arrest,
the Führer had ordered the SS to find the deposed dictator and free
him, but he had not yet succeeded in locating him. He did succeed,
though, in having the Italian government deliver this gift. Mussolini
had turned sixty on July 29. Unwrapping the package, he found a book
inside, sent by the man who, as a young rabble-rouser, had looked up
to the Italian leader as a role model. It was the first volume of a luxury
edition of the complete works of German philosopher Friedrich
Nietzsche. The Führer had scrawled his own dedication: "Adolf Hitler, to his dear Benito Mussolini."[1]

IN ROME, DUKE PIETRO D'ACQUARONE, minister of the royal household, sent an urgent summons to industrialist Alberto Pirelli. On the

tire magnate's arrival on August 3, 1943, the duke accompanied him to the office of Italy's new foreign minister, Raffaele Guariglia. The situation, Guariglia told the two men, was bleak. If Italy were to ask the Allies for an armistice, Hitler would order the thousands of German soldiers already in the area to move on Rome, seize control of the government, and most likely arrest the king. The Germans might conceivably force the pope out as well, as Napoleon had done a century and a half earlier to Pius VII. Guariglia predicted that additional German troops would then pour into the country and take over much of the rest of the peninsula, aiming to keep the Allied armies far from German soil. In light of these dangers, the new government's most pressing task was to calm the Germans' fears. The industrialist agreed: they must do nothing to appear to be betraying their German allies.[2]

Relations between an Italian foreign minister and a Vatican secretary of state had never been closer. On leaving his office late at night, Guariglia would often go to the Apostolic Palace to brief Cardinal Maglione on the latest developments. Given the potentially momentous events about to unfold, Maglione decided to convene a meeting of fourteen cardinals resident in Rome to brief them on what he had learned. Thirteen of the fourteen were Italian.

The Holy See, Maglione told them, had played no role in the king's recent dismissal of Mussolini, yet it now faced the consequences of that action. German troops were progressively occupying Italian cities near the Austrian border, and motorized German divisions were nearing Rome. The new Italian government feared an imminent German seizure of the nation's capital, and there was no guarantee the Germans would not invade the Vatican as well. Among the rumors he had heard was one claiming that the Germans planned to relocate the pope to Munich.

The cardinal told his colleagues it was crucial that the Holy See do nothing that the Germans could view as helping Italy reach a separate peace with the Allies. Italy had no choice but to continue the war on Germany's side. But this would lead the Allies to resume their deadly bombardments. The result, he feared, would be not only more devastation and suffering but chaos that would offer fertile field for the spread of Communism.[3]

Amid all the tension, Ernst von Weizsäcker, the German ambassador, remained committed to promoting smooth relations between the Vatican and the Third Reich. To this end, he reported to Berlin that the Vatican was not entirely happy with Italy's new government. He cited Vatican displeasure with the government's loosening of the previous regime's strict censorship of speech and the press. Rome was now flooded with leaflets denouncing the Vatican for its past support of Fascist rule. "Currents hostile to the Church are spreading in Rome to such an extent," observed Weizsäcker, "that the Vatican is secretly assuming a defensive position. . . . What is certain is that the Church is anxious, and its arch enemy continues to be Communism."[4]

WITH ALL THE UNCERTAINTIES in the aftermath of Mussolini's fall, Pius XII had thought it best to remain publicly silent, but on August 7 he decided to take a public initiative. He called on Italians to take advantage of the approaching Feast of the Assumption of the Blessed Virgin to pray for peace. Referring to the sorrow that the Mother of God felt at "the sight of the slaughter of so many of her sons," the pope, in a text published in the Vatican newspaper, expressed the hope that "Christian peace" might soon be brought about, "by means of which alone the conquering and conquered peoples, reunited not through force but through justice and equity, may be enabled to enjoy a long tranquility and prosperity."

In his diary entry that day, Father Vincent McCormick, the former head of the Gregorian University, expressed his disappointment in the pope's first words since the ending of the Fascist regime:

> I take it to be a document published to defend Vatican before Italy against the charge of doing nothing for peace. For Vat[ican] seems to be victim of terror now lest Rome or Italy be taken over by Germans or anti-clerical Italians. But what an unfortunate document! At a time when Sicilians are jubilant over their liberation, and hundreds of millions of people from Norway to the Medit[erranean] are breathing a sigh of hopeful

relief, seeing at last after four years of subjection to tyranny and slavery the light of freedom begin to spread along the horizon, the H[oly] F[ather] speaks to tell us that the heavens, far from clearing, are becoming blacker than ever, Christianity is threatened. Is that His true feeling about a German defeat, or is it that His horizon is bounded by the Alps and the Sicilian straits. The robbed and starving in Greece, in France, in Belgium, Holland, Austria, in concentration camps—religious, priests, seminarians, the enslaved workers—does their liberation mean nothing to Vat[ican]? Sad, sad.[5]

As the pope was lamenting the suffering on both sides of the war, Italy's new head of government, Pietro Badoglio, found himself engaged in a dangerous double game of his own. On August 6, while continuing to reassure Hitler that Italy remained a loyal partner, he dispatched two emissaries, one to the Allied headquarters in Tangiers and the other to meet with Allied diplomats in Lisbon, to explore the possibility of negotiations. In Tangiers, his emissary explained to the British consul general that initiating negotiations through the Vatican had become "impracticable," and so this more direct, if informal and secret, approach was being made. Fearful of the Germans, Badoglio could not appear to be authorizing any such talks. Indeed, he was soon scheduled to meet with Hitler, where he would renew his public call for Italy to continue to fight at Germany's side. But, his emissary explained, these were not his true sentiments nor those of his government. They were, unfortunately, necessary to gain time.[6]

IN HIS FOUR YEARS as pope, Pius XII had never spoken out against Italy's anti-Jewish racial laws. He had, though, frequently complained to the Fascist government that the laws were being unfairly applied to families who were, in the church's eyes, Catholic. Jews who had been baptized should be exempt from the racial laws, the pope believed, as should baptized children of "mixed marriages." The fall of Fascism now offered the prospect of bringing about the changes to the racial laws the pope had long sought. The newly opened Vatican archives reveal that Badoglio himself was sympathetic to a change in the racial laws. Within a few days of being appointed prime minister, Badoglio had sent word to the pope that he would like to abrogate them, "especially those regarding marriage," but could not do so immediately due to his fear of what the Germans would think.[7]

In the five years since those laws had gone into effect, Father Tacchi Venturi, the pope's unofficial Jesuit emissary to Mussolini, had repeatedly complained to the government on his behalf about the ways they were being applied. Now the Jesuit was eager to act. Seeking papal approval, he wrote Cardinal Maglione urging that they take advantage of the changed government to remedy "the painful condition in which, due to their ancestry, not a few Catholics of so-called mixed families find themselves." He reported that he had already sounded out members of the Ministry of Internal Affairs and found them sympathetic to such a papal request.

He then outlined the changes needed. The revised laws should grant "full Aryan status to all mixed families." This would ensure that those children of mixed marriages who had been baptized after the inception of the laws "are no longer, as they are at present, declared members of the Jewish race, and, while being Christian, are treated as Jews." He ended his letter, "I await your instructions."[8]

Four days later Pius XII told Monsignor Tardini how to respond: "One can write to P.T.V. [Padre Tacchi Venturi] in the sense he has desired." Cardinal Maglione added his own note to the Jesuit's proposal: "Affirmative. Do it on behalf of the Holy See." On the eighteenth, Maglione sent the papal envoy a letter authorizing his approach to the new government, reiterating that the changes were to be made to ensure that the racial laws were applied only to those whom the church regarded as Jews.[9]

Later in the month, the Jesuit reported back to Maglione on his efforts. "In dealing with the matter with His Excellency the Minister of Internal Affairs, I necessarily limited myself to the three points [regarding mixed marriages and converted Jews] specified in Your Eminence's letter of August 8 . . . taking good care not to call for the total abrogation of a law which, according to the principles and traditions of the Catholic Church, while having some provisions that should be abrogated, certainly contain others that merit being confirmed."[10]

AFTER A BRIEF PAUSE following Mussolini's overthrow, Allied air attacks on Italy resumed in the second week of August, heavily damaging Turin and Genoa and engulfing Milan's famed La Scala opera house in flames. Rome fell victim as well. Late on the morning of August 13, Allied planes appeared over its skies, again targeting the city's railyards and raining destruction and death on nearby residential neighborhoods. Knowing that the planes would steer clear of Vatican City, many Romans crowded into St. Peter's Square as soon as they saw them approach. A Swiss journalist described the scene:

> People huddled like chickens under the colonnade. Long files of cars parked all over the place; cabs with steaming horses obviously driven here at a great speed; and people still pouring in from every direction, in cars, on bicycles and on foot. . . . In the basilica a crowd. But even here people shiver and tremble, hearing the dull thud of the bombs. They also run from one corner to another, always thinking that not theirs but the opposite one is the safer.
>
> But best of all was the sight of an Italian soldier, obviously on duty . . . timidly hiding himself in a corner of the porch. I grinned at him and he grinned back, as if saying, "Yes, I know I ought not be here, but you see, here I am safe!"

In early afternoon, the pope once again got into his car and headed for the scene of destruction. Stopping briefly in front of the Basilica of St. John in Lateran, he raised his arms in blessing as the distraught Romans gathered around him.[11]

The next day Badoglio's government announced it was unilaterally declaring Rome an "open city." On hearing the news, which linked the city's self-declared immunity from further bombing to its status

Pius XII at scene of Allied bombardment of Rome, August 13, 1943

as the world center of Catholicism, several thousand Romans rushed to the Vatican. Gathered below the pope's window, they shouted "Long live the pope! Peace! Peace!" The pontiff stepped onto his balcony three times to bless them. A witness from Italy's Foreign Ministry offered his own ironic observation in his diary that day: "The Roman crowd, jubilant once more, goes to the Vatican and shouts 'vivas' to the pope with the same fervor with which yesterday they shouted to Badoglio and the day before that to Mussolini."[12]

Uncertain how Roosevelt would react to Italy's "open city" announcement, and with a further air assault on Rome planned for the next day, the combined chiefs sent Eisenhower a curt message: "Pending clarification and further instructions it is desired that you make no further attacks on Rome." Eisenhower was not pleased but, having no choice, canceled the strikes planned for the fifteenth. "All our information indicates," he wrote, that "attacks on Rome have had most profound effect on Italian morale. We believe here that we shall miss another golden opportunity if these operations are restricted before a bilateral declaration is made. It will certainly be some time before Government Agencies, War Factories and German Troops will be clear of the city."

Eisenhower would not have to wait long, receiving new instructions within hours: "Standstill order issued by Combined Chiefs of Staff in their message of 14 August regarding bombing of Rome is revoked. . . . You are free to carry on these operations to the extent that you consider necessary or advisable subject to previous limitations regarding safety of Vatican."[13]

ONE MORNING IN LATE AUGUST, the much-dreaded sound of the air raid siren again pierced the air. People streamed into the baroque Church of the Holy Name of Jesus in the center of Rome, the same church where Father Tacchi Venturi had lived for many years. False alarms had been common, and all hoped this would prove to be another, but in the absence of bomb shelters, the massive church seemed to offer the best hope for safety. Seeing a group of women huddled together, some weeping, a priest went to offer words of comfort.

"There are fourteen million Catholics in the U.S.A.," said the Jesuit, "and they will immediately kick Roosevelt out if he dares to bomb Rome again especially now when it is an open city."

"It is not," objected one of the women, her voice raised. "I serve a General who is with Badoglio and he says the city is full of Germans."

The Swiss journalist who witnessed this scene added a note of her own: "As a matter of fact everybody knows that Rome is packed full of German troops. Yesterday, crossing Piazza Navona, I noticed that all the adjacent streets were full of armored cars. There were at least a hundred of them."[14]

AS AUGUST WORE ON, the police forces of the new government were rounding up and jailing more of the former Fascist elite. Some had succeeded in fleeing to Germany, Ciano among them. It was a move he would soon come to regret. Mussolini himself had been moved from one island imprisonment to another and would soon be brought back to the mainland to a remote mountaintop. Mussolini's wife, Rachele, was left alone, but his lover, Clara, along with the rest of her family, was arrested. Indeed, for Badoglio's government, the Petacci family came to symbolize the corruption of the Fascist government, and word of the reversal of the Petacci family's fortunes produced widespread glee. From her jail cell, Clara wrote to Mussolini, assuring him that she, her mother, and her sister prayed day and night to the Madonna of Pompeii for his liberation. "I have faith," she told him, "I have faith." "The Führer will save you, I feel it!" she wrote later in August. "It is not only I who need you, but the world, History." In Rome, a group of Ursuline nuns moved into the newly vacated Petacci mansion, setting up an orphanage. It housed fifty children quite comfortably.[15]

For the precarious Italian government, the drama could hardly have been greater. The Allies were demanding unconditional surrender and threatening further bombardment and invasion of the mainland. Badoglio's public proclamations of loyalty to the Axis cause were antagonizing the Allies yet doing little to reassure Germany. At the end of the month, Foreign Minister Guariglia drafted a memo for Badoglio setting out the unappetizing choices they faced:

The Germans viewed Italy as a crucial shield for keeping the Allies far from the Reich. This left the government with only two alternatives. It could continue along its current path and drag its feet on the war while making whatever concessions were necessary to Germany to keep it at bay. Alternatively, it could break off relations with Germany. For this second path to have any chance of success, there would need to be sufficient Italian military force to hold off the Germans long enough to reach a military and diplomatic agreement with the Allies. It would also require having the Allies immediately begin furnishing all the basic goods that Italy had been importing from Germany.

Guariglia was pessimistic. Should the government renounce its alliance with the Reich, German troops would immediately occupy Rome. Italian soldiers in the Balkans would be herded into German prison camps, and the disorganized Italian troops in Italy would likely meet the same fate. The hundreds of thousands of Italians who were working in Germany would be imprisoned. The basic materials and foodstuffs Italians needed to survive would be cut off. Italy, or at least a large part of it, would be occupied by the Germans, a situation that would be made worse by the Germans' thirst for revenge for Italy's betrayal.

Perhaps, thought Guariglia, the Allies would soon succeed in crossing over from Sicily onto the Italian mainland, but if so, their advance up the peninsula would be slow. Meanwhile Rome would be devastated, and Italy would be carved in two, oppressed by a dual enemy occupation. "The truth is we do not have the force necessary to undertake a policy that can allow the country to enter into a conflict with Germany." Nor did Guariglia have any faith in the British. He told Badoglio it was a dangerous illusion to think Britain was positively disposed toward them. Indeed, Britain would rather treat Italy as a defeated enemy than a belated ally and had been careful not to promise that if it renounced Fascism, it could retain any of its hard-won African colonies.

The Americans and British, whom Guariglia referred to as "our enemies," thought not of Italy's interests but only of their own. They would land wherever it most suited their goals, and, Guariglia concluded, "it might be more convenient for them to have the Italians and Germans massacre each other, weakening Italy's defense, before they intervene."[16]

WHILE THE POPE HAD been careful to do nothing that might turn the Germans against the Vatican, Italy's situation had become so desperate, he now decided—against the advice of Cardinal Maglione—to risk sending a secret emissary to the United States. The pope entrusted Enrico Galeazzi, the Vatican's chief engineer, with the task. Galeazzi had accompanied the then Cardinal Pacelli on his lengthy tour of the United States in 1936 and had close ties to New York's Archbishop Spellman. Responsible for much of the day-to-day administration and facilities of Vatican City—Tittmann described him as "the uncrowned governor of the Vatican State"—and long enjoying a close personal bond with the pontiff, he seemed a good choice.[17]

Galeazzi was to give Roosevelt a two-part message from the pope. Part one explained that while both the Italian government and its people sought peace, they were unable to put this wish into practice due to the German military forces in the country. Not only were the Italians not in a position to force the Germans out, but they would be helpless should the Germans decide to take control of Rome. And here the pope expressed his greatest fear: "In such an eventuality, it is predicted that Vatican City, which houses the diplomatic representatives of the Allied countries, would not be spared and the very august person of the Holy Father might also be in danger."

Secondly, the pope warned that Communism was fast spreading in Italy, especially among the working class. Contributing to the Communist appeal were "the very serious damage and massacres produced by the recent terrorist bombings of the Italian cities, which have caused great resentment among the people, who had earlier been well disposed toward the Allies and especially toward the Americans, pushing them increasingly toward . . . communism." The pope warned that since the fall of Fascism there was clear evidence of well-organized Communist attempts at subversion. "That said," the papal message concluded, "it is easy to predict how difficult, not to say impossible, it would become for the Holy See and the government of the universal Church should Italy fall in the hands of communism."[18]

With this secret mission under way, the pope decided a public appearance was also in order. What perhaps the pope did not realize was that the announcement of his planned address would trigger sky-high expectations among Romans. When they learned he would broadcast a special radio message to the world on September 1, the fourth anniversary of the war, rumors exploded. Perhaps, people thought, he would be announcing his success in arranging an end to the bombing of Rome or, indeed, even an end to the war in Italy.

Sitting on his throne, dressed in his white robe, a white skullcap atop his head, the pope spoke into the microphone in his nasal voice. Thousands crowded into St. Peter's Basilica and Square, where loudspeakers broadcast the pope's words. His delivery, never one of his strong points, came in staccato bursts of three or four words at a time, the pontiff carefully emphasizing each phrase. Elsewhere in Rome, crowds gathered in cafés whose radios blared at their highest volume.

Those who were hoping to hear good news were disappointed. The French ambassador told of a "certain delusion" caused by the pope's remarks, which while expressing heartfelt wishes for a "just and lasting peace," offered nothing more specific. "As in his preceding messages, the Holy Father energetically affirmed his impartiality with respect to all of the belligerents, his equal solicitude of all peoples." Osborne, the British envoy, reporting on the speech to London, wrote that while a number of his diplomatic colleagues thought the pope's main motive in speaking was to appeal to the Allies for better treatment of Italy, "I rather think he felt it was time for him to make the front page and re-pledge himself as champion of peace."

Although many Romans felt let down, Pius XII still, as they saw it, remained their best bet for extracting them from impending disaster. Italy's hapless government certainly inspired little confidence. When, following the broadcast, the pope stepped out from his apartment to the window and raised his arm, a sea of hands in the huge crowd below shot up, waving their hats and their white handkerchiefs to salute God's vicar on earth.[19]

THE NEWLY FORMED GOVERNMENT'S secret talks with the Allies began in Lisbon in mid-August. At the end of the month, they moved to a newly established Allied military base in southeastern Sicily. Robert Murphy for the Americans and Harold Macmillan for the British flew there from Algiers to finalize the negotiations with Prime Minister Badoglio's emissaries, Generals Giuseppe Castellanos and Giacomo Zanussi. Roosevelt and Churchill had set out the terms of the armistice and were impatient for the Italian government to sign on. But since the meetings in Lisbon, the Italian attitude had become more cautious. As German troops continued to pour into Italy from the north, Badoglio, his fears fanned by his foreign minister, was growing increasingly nervous. They would not sign the agreement, the Italian generals now insisted, unless the Allies could guarantee that they would land troops north of Rome at the same time as the armistice was announced. Murphy reported to Roosevelt: "They asserted that if we only land south of Rome the Germans will take the city and everything north of it. In their minds the slaughter, pillage and destruction would be too awful to contemplate."

If the Italians were trying to put pressure on the Allies, they were playing with a weak hand. Should they fail to sign the surrender terms now, Murphy and Macmillan warned them, three things would happen:

> The King and the present Italian Government would be all through as far as the Allies are concerned.
>
> We would be obliged to incite disorder and anarchy throughout Italy. . . .
>
> We would obviously be obliged to bomb relentlessly and on a large scale until all the major Italian cities, including Rome, would be reduced to ashes and piles of rubble.[20]

That evening, the two Italian generals flew back to Rome to inform Badoglio of the ultimatum.

"It is clear," Eisenhower wrote to the War Department in Washington, "that the Italian Government will not pluck up courage to sign and announce an armistice unless they are assured of Allied troops being landed in the Rome area and to give them some guarantee of protection against the Germans." In light of this, "We believe that the employment of an Airborne Division for this purpose . . . would be a good gamble, because the success of AVALANCHE [the landing planned on the mainland near Salerno south of Naples] may very likely turn upon obtaining a degree of Italian help that will materially delay movement of German forces." Eisenhower concluded, "Consequently, under my instructions to support any Italian units that would actually fight the Germans, I have determined to employ an Airborne Division in the Rome area if we can be sufficiently assured of the good faith of the Italians."[21]

The next day, September 2, 1943, Roosevelt and Churchill sent a joint response to Eisenhower: "We highly approve your decision to go on with AVALANCHE and to land an airborne Division near Rome on the conditions indicated."[22]

On September 3 Eisenhower flew to Sicily to be present for the ceremony in which Castellanos, acting on behalf of Badoglio, would sign the surrender agreement. It was to be made public a few days later, when the Allies would land a major force near Salerno and airlift troops to Rome. The plan depended on having the Italians safeguard Rome's airfields to allow the U.S. 82nd Airborne Division to land and help prevent the Germans from occupying the city. Roosevelt and Churchill planned to issue a joint announcement of Italy's surrender on September 8. Badoglio was told to make it public at the same time.[23]

But all threatened to come undone at the last moment. The day before the armistice was to be announced, Badoglio abruptly tried to put it off, saying he could no longer guarantee control of the airfields outside Rome that the Allied airborne troops would need to land. Early on the day when the armistice was supposed to be made public, he sent Eisenhower an unwelcome message: "Owing to changes in the situation which has broken down and the existence of German forces in the Rome area it is no longer possible to accept immediate armistice since this proves that the capital would be occupied and the government taken over forcibly by the Germans."

The Allies would now be unable to airlift troops to Rome, but they had already launched Operation Avalanche and urgently needed the armistice to be announced before the troops landed on the Italian mainland. In sending Badoglio's message on to Washington, Eisenhower made clear his own view of what should be done: "we would like to have . . . your thought on whether or not we should proceed with the armistice announcement for the tactical and deception value it might have. Certainly the Italian government itself deserves no consideration."[24]

Washington's response came quickly: "It is the view of the President and the Prime Minister that the agreement having been signed you should make such public announcement regarding it as would facilitate your military operations. No consideration need be given to the embarrassment it might cause the Italian Government." Eisenhower sent Badoglio a final ultimatum: "I intend to broadcast the acceptance of the Armistice at the hour originally planned. . . . If you or any part of your armed forces fail to cooperate as previously agreed, I will publish to the world full records of this affair. Today is X day, and I expect you to do your part."[25]

Dragging his feet, Badoglio made his announcement only late in the evening, after Italy's capitulation had already been broadcast on the radio. People took to the streets. Some among the young were singing, dancing, and waving Italian flags, but many of their elders experienced more mixed emotions, pained at their nation's humiliating defeat and fearful of what was to come. A few thousand Romans streamed into St. Peter's Square, where they shouted out their hopes for peace and beckoned the pope to come to his window. But the pope would not grant their wish. Knowing how vulnerable Rome now was to German occupation, the pope was not eager to be seen celebrating Italy's betrayal of its Axis ally. When, despite their repeated calls, he failed to appear at his window, the disappointed crowd slowly drifted away.[26]

PART FOUR

—

THE SKY TURNED BLACK

CHAPTER
3 3

FAKE NEWS

I N THE HOURS AFTER THE ANNOUNCEMENT OF THE ARMISTICE, Italy's seventy-four-year-old king anxiously followed news of the approach of German troops. Fearing that the Quirinal Palace might not be secure, he spent the night sleeping on a couch in the palazzo housing Italy's War Ministry. Word came late at night that German forces had begun advancing on Rome, occupying the old port city of Civitavecchia to the northwest and the naval fortress town of Gaeta to the south. Only one road leaving Rome, Via Tiburtina, remained clear, but it would not stay that way very long. It was still dark at five A.M. on September 9, 1943, when a caravan of five cars formed in the courtyard of the palazzo. The king and queen got into the first car, a gray-green Fiat 2800, Prime Minister Badoglio and the king's adviser Duke d'Acquarone into the second, and Prince Umberto into the third. A phalanx of carabinieri on motorcycles led the way. Over the next two hours, many of Italy's top generals and admirals followed their example, as did a bevy of valets and household servants of the royal family who brought hastily prepared baggage. All made their way east across the Apennines, headed for the Adriatic port city of Pescara.

Among those missing from the royal caravan was the king's daughter Mafalda, who was in Bulgaria at the time to be with Giovanna, her younger sister, for the funeral of Giovanna's husband, King Boris. Mafalda would never see her father again, for shortly after her return to Rome later in the month, the Gestapo seized her and flew her to Ber-

lin. From there she would be sent to the concentration camp at Buchenwald, where she would die a gruesome death.[1]

Princess Mafalda

On the royal party's arrival at Pescara's airport, Victor Emmanuel
had expected to find a plane waiting to take him south to safety. He
never did board a plane there, although whether it was because of fear
of German aerial interception or refusal of the Italian airmen to participate in such a humiliating spectacle remains unclear. The royal
party decided instead to summon a naval warship for the evacuation.
As they waited for its arrival, news of the king's attempted escape
began to circulate through Pescara, triggering fears of popular protest.
At the last moment, the warship *Bayonet* was redirected to Ortona, a
small port town to the south. There the king, queen, prime minister,

and fifty-six other members of the royal party boarded the small war vessel, which set off immediately to Brindisi, on Italy's heel. In their haste to escape, neither Badoglio nor the king nor the military chiefs of staff had given instructions for the army or the government ministers whom they left behind. Raffaele Guariglia, the foreign minister, had spent the night preparing dispatches for Italy's diplomats abroad informing them of the armistice; no one had told him the king and prime minister were leaving.[2]

Later that morning, on learning of the flight of the king and his prime minister, two of Guariglia's assistants rushed to the Vatican to let the pope know. Guariglia himself took refuge in the Spanish embassy to the Holy See, where he would remain for the next nine months. Later that day an Italian military officer representing what was left of the military command came to see Monsignor Montini, the man closest to the pope, seeking Pius XII's help. Might the pope prevail on the Allies to hasten the arrival of their troops in Rome? The pope left the request unanswered. With Rome about to be occupied by the Germans, this was no time to antagonize them.[3]

"Ever since Mussolini's exit," Goebbels wrote in his diary that day, "we have anticipated and expected this development. . . . We can now set in motion what the Führer really wanted to do immediately after Mussolini's fall." Within hours of the armistice announcement, German soldiers occupied the cities of northern Italy without encountering any notable resistance. Meanwhile the Allies were focused on Operation Avalanche, landing their troops near Salerno, south of Naples.[4]

Among the first to appear at the Vatican that morning was Ernst von Weizsäcker, the German ambassador. Eager to let the pope know that the German troops headed for Rome would respect Vatican neutrality, he met with Monsignor Montini. He coupled this news with a discordant note: Persistent rumors that the pope had played a part in deposing Mussolini were not helping matters. Indeed, a Roman newspaper article claimed that the pope had had a long phone conversation with Roosevelt shortly before the Duce was removed.

The story was pure invention, said Montini, who arranged to have the next day's *Osservatore Romano* publish a front-page denial. Weizsäcker then cabled Berlin: "based on declarations by authorized Vatican bodies, the phone talks between Pope and Roosevelt are revealed to be pure fantasy."[5]

The next evening Ambassador Weizsäcker phoned the Vatican to offer reassurances from the general in charge of German military forces in Rome: they would respect Vatican City and those institutions that depended on it. Goebbels's diary entry of the next day confirms that the order came from Hitler himself: "The Vatican has inquired of our Ambassador whether its rights would be safeguarded in the event of our occupying Rome. The Führer sent an affirmative reply."[6]

THE BRITISH ARMY CROSSED the Messina Strait from Sicily onto the Italian mainland on September 3, occupying Reggio Calabria at the toe of the peninsula. Six days later Allied troops landed at Taranto, at the base of Italy's heel. From there, the Allies soon reached Brindisi. It was in this protective pocket of the extreme south of the peninsula that Victor Emmanuel and Prime Minister Badoglio would establish their makeshift royal government.

By the time the king reached safety in Brindisi, messages from Roosevelt, Churchill, and Eisenhower would be waiting for him: with Hitler's army invading the peninsula, it was his job to rally the nation to fight back. Badoglio duly put out a weak call for Italy's military to resist.[7]

"Our army," the socialist leader Pietro Nenni recorded in his diary at the time, "melted like fog in the sunshine. . . . The spectacle of an army in ruin, without leaders, without arms, without discipline, with really only one wish: not to fight anymore against anyone, for any reason. . . . Everywhere the same story: arms abandoned, camps and barracks abandoned . . . in the face of an order from an exiguous number of Germans." In the end, few Italian troops in Italy or abroad heeded the call to resist. The Germans disarmed over a million of them, killed about ten thousand officers and soldiers, and in most areas with few shots being fired, took six hundred thousand Italian soldiers for forced labor in Germany.[8]

On the night of September 10, the Germans issued an ultimatum to the scattered Italian forces offering resistance in Rome. They should surrender by midnight and allow the city to come under German control. The Vatican, promised the Germans, would be left alone. The following morning the radio announced that an accord had been reached between the Italian and German forces, and the fighting would end. An Italian general, Giorgio Calvi di Bèrgolo, married to the king's oldest child, would assume responsibility for working with the Germans in overseeing the city.

Monsignor Costantini described the scene as he walked through Rome's streets that day:

> The city is peaceful; the stores are closed; all work has been suspended. Groups of people gather on the sidewalk with an air of astonishment and a kind of contained anxiety. There is not one smiling face. A kind of nightmare weighs on everybody's soul. . . .
>
> [A]t Piazza Venezia, I saw a column of a great many German armored vehicles with machine guns levelled and with an arrogant attitude shown by the soldiers. . . . The vehicles were going in every direction. One got the impression that they were joyriding . . . an ostentatious show of force, a type of triumphal celebration in the streets of the Eternal City.

A few days later the monsignor added, "We are at war. I have confidence, however, that the Holy See and Rome will be respected."[9]

On the fourteenth of September 1943, half a dozen German troops stationed themselves at St. Peter's Square. The Vatican offered to put up a small wooden shed just outside Vatican territory to shelter them from the weather, and the offer was accepted. As the French ambassador to the Holy See put it in his report the next month, "Worried above all about surviving the storm, the Vatican is seeking to avoid any possible cause of friction with the Germans. It is being aided in this by the German ambassador [Weizsäcker], who seems to be showing good-will."[10]

HITLER ACTED QUICKLY TO free Mussolini from his latest place of imprisonment, atop the Gran Sasso mountain, in the Apennines north-east of Rome. On September 12 German soldiers in gliders landed at the remote site, while German troops seized the funicular that gave access to the base. The two hundred well-armed carabinieri guarding Mussolini surrendered without a shot being fired by either side. Italy's fallen Duce was then flown to Germany, where he joined the other Fascist leaders who had found refuge there.

After some disagreement with his military brass, Hitler decided it would be in the Reich's interest to install a new Italian government under Mussolini. As a result, on the evening of the eighteenth, German radio broadcast a speech by the Duce. He was once again, he proclaimed, assuming the direction of Fascism in Italy.

The Germans had released Clara, her sister, and her parents from their jail cells in Novara, in northwestern Italy, the previous day. From there she had traveled northeast to her brother's house in Merano, near the Austrian border. On arrival, she first kissed the image of the Madonna of Pompeii to whom she had prayed for this moment, then pressed her lips to a photo of Mussolini. In her diary, she recalled her thrill at hearing his voice on the radio: "You speak, you speak to the people still . . . but to me it seems you speak also to me. Your soul passes into mine in drops and I feel you within me as before. I am transfused as always! Your unique words, your touching phrases, your way of speech, so human, simple, precise, poetic." A week later Mussolini's Italian Social Republic was officially announced at the first meeting of the new puppet government. The optics were less than optimal, as the gathering was held at the German embassy in Rome, and Mussolini himself was absent.[11]

Eager to cooperate with the Germans in order to protect Vatican City, Pius XII found a willing partner in Hitler's ambassador. On September 16 Weizsäcker, carrying an envelope stuffed with cash, met with Monsignor Montini at the Vatican. He said the money was to compensate the Vatican for damage done to one of the basilicas a week earlier during the brief combat in the city. When Monsignor Montini balked at taking it, Weizsäcker told him to consider the cash "for the poor" and insisted on leaving it.

Weizsäcker said that General Reiner Stahel, the German military commander now in charge of Rome, was eager to show his goodwill to the Vatican and so had asked to come to the Apostolic Palace to meet Cardinal Maglione. The ambassador explained he had thought it best to dissuade him. Weizsäcker worried it could lead to unwanted rumors.[12]

Word that General Stahel was not being received at the Vatican triggered suspicion among some in Berlin that the pope had refused to see him. Asked by Ribbentrop if this was true, Weizsäcker responded he too had heard the rumor, along with the opposite rumor that Field Marshal Albert Kesselring, Germany's commander of the entire Mediterranean theater, had already met with the pope. "Both stories are false," wrote the ambassador. "In truth, the Field Marshal has made no attempt to be received by the Pope, neither he himself nor his envoy."[13]

There was one irritating matter the ambassador did raise with Cardinal Maglione. After German troops seized Rome, the British had been spreading "a series of false news reports: the Germans had disregarded the neutrality of the Vatican; had entered the Vatican City; the Pope had surrendered and was a hostage in German hands; the Vatican [radio] broadcast was surveilled by Germans; and so on." The ambassador informed Berlin that he had asked for official Vatican denial of the reports, and he was pleased to report that both *L'Osservatore Romano* and Vatican Radio had issued a "public correction."[14]

When "enemy propaganda," as Weizsäcker characterized it, continued to push the claim that German troops were mistreating the Vatican and looting Rome's churches, he asked the Vatican to reaffirm its denials. The Vatican newspaper soon published a new, more extensive refutation, and the ambassador proposed that the German government issue the following statement:

Since German troops have entered Rome, enemy propaganda, with fabrications of all kinds, has sought to portray the city of Rome and its people, but especially the Vatican, as a victim of German tyranny. The German military and German policy are to be disparaged to the Catholics of the world.

These attempts are futile. It is a matter of course that Germany fully respects the sovereignty and integrity of the Vatican state and that the German troops present in Rome act accordingly.

Weizsäcker followed this up with a detailed report to Berlin on all the ways the German authorities were cooperating with the Vatican to ensure its continued smooth operation. "For these reasons I have recently had constant contact with the Cardinal Secretary of State. Of course, Maglione fervently insisted on the rights of the Curia. But our talks have proceeded in mutual agreement. The Curia has repeatedly expressed its respect for the German actions." Germany's ambassador concluded by trumpeting how beneficial the statement he had put out had been in countering enemy propaganda, noting that it was published in *L'Avvenire,* which, "as is well known, is a Catholic paper close to the Vatican."[15]

Weizsäcker was also eager to impress Ribbentrop and Hitler with the pope's helpful attitude. "By chance," he wrote Ribbentrop the following day, "I was able to have a glimpse at three documents that are indicative of the Pope's political position. All three documents were written after July 25." He went on to describe them:

The first document includes an intervention by the Curia with the Badoglio government on behalf of old Fascists.

In the second, the Curia, on the Pope's orders, pleads for the Duce and his family, listing about twenty members of the family by name. The names of Count Ciano and Edda Ciano are not among them, though.

The third document is of particular interest. It included Cardinal Secretary of State Maglione's analysis of imminent global threats. . . . Maglione says that Europe's fate depends on Germany's successful resistance on the Russian front. The German army is the only possible bulwark against Bolshevism. If it crumbles, that would be the end of European culture.[16]

In Berlin, the papal nuncio to Hitler's government, Monsignor Orsenigo, went to see the German state secretary and had a congenial conversation at his Foreign Ministry office. The German told the nuncio that it was only through their speedy military intervention that the Germans had prevented a Communist uprising in Milan and Turin. He recorded Orsenigo's reaction: "The Nuncio then said that, in his view, only Germany and the Vatican could face the Bolshevik threat, Germany on a material and the Vatican on a spiritual level." The nuncio, he added, "would be pleased if we gave the Vatican the opportunity for common action against Bolshevism."[17]

ITALY NOW HAD TWO governments, the royal government headed by Badoglio, isolated in its Allied-protected enclave in the extreme south of the peninsula, and Mussolini's republican government, the Italian Social Republic, based around Salò, a small town on the banks of Lake Garda in northeastern Italy, not far from the Austrian border. Their competing claims of legitimacy posed an immediate problem for the Holy See and an even more pressing problem for the men of the previous Italian administration, who were being called upon to support Mussolini's new Fascist regime.[18]

Neither of the competing governments offered a very appealing sight. Harold Macmillan, the British diplomat, and Robert Murphy, his American counterpart, who had negotiated the armistice for the Allies, offered Roosevelt their view of the king's rule in late September: "The Government, from the military and civil point of view, is little more than a name. Its importance is that it has unchallenged claim to legality." The aged king was "physically infirm, nervous, shaky, but courteous, with a certain modesty and simplicity of character which is attractive. He takes an objective, even humorously disinterested view of mankind and their follies." He was not, however, "capable of initiating any policy, except under extreme pressure." His interests were "his family, his dynasty, and his country, in that order." As for the men of his government, the Allied diplomats wrote, they "inspire sympathy rather than confidence. They are old and unimaginative. . . . The Marshal [Badoglio] has courage and a high sense of duty. The rest are men of ordinary parts. . . . They hate the Germans, but they fear them equally. All their divisions, in Italy and the Balkans, are 'surrounded' by a smaller number of German troops. . . . There is an atmosphere of well-bred defeatism."[19]

THE CLAIM THAT HITLER was planning to kidnap the pope, later often cited by defenders of Pius XII in explaining his actions, was an invention of Allied propaganda. It had gained sufficient traction by early October 1943 that the Nazi press office thought it necessary to issue a long denial, broadcast on Mussolini's newly installed radio station. "For a few weeks now," it began, "the Vatican and the Pope have been the hobbyhorse of English-Jewish-American propaganda, which is capable of the most shameless and absurd fantasies as we know from long and daily experience." Radio stations from America to Great Britain and the Soviet Union, the Nazi press release complained, were claiming that "Hitler's SS had taken over the personal custody of the Pope, who thereby became a prisoner of Germany. . . . Notwithstanding the denials published by 'L'Osservatore Romano' and broadcast by Vatican Radio, these propagandists in the service of Jewry continue their work and fantasize about the imprisonment of the Pope and pretend to be deeply aggrieved and indignant because of this egregious injustice towards the representative of God on Earth."[20]

Undaunted by the German denials, Allied propaganda put out ever more elaborate tales of a Nazi plot to kidnap the pope. On October 9 the British Political Warfare Executive arranged for a bogus "German" radio broadcast reporting that all preparations were now complete for the removal of the pope to the German Reich. Two days later it added a further embellishment: the Lichtenstein castle in Württemberg was now ready to receive not only the pope but the cardinals of the Curia as well.[21]

HAVING RECEIVED THE LATEST Vatican plea to recognize Rome as an open city, Weizsäcker went to discuss the matter with Cardinal Maglione. Perhaps, said Weizsäcker with a smile, the Vatican could take care of the problem simply by persuading the Allied troops to turn back, "just like Pope Leo the Great did with Attila." The cardinal laughed but quickly turned serious. He was hoping all three governments might reach an agreement to prevent a destructive "battle for Rome." Not being a military man, he said, he could not say exactly how this would work in practice. Perhaps one "party" might leave Rome before the other "party" reached the city.[22]

The pope and the cardinal feared not only the physical consequences that a pitched battle over Rome might cause, but the possibility of a Communist insurgency amid the destruction. In mid-October, Maglione told Weizsäcker that the lack of a robust Italian police force in the city worried him. A week earlier the Germans had seized the carabinieri barracks in Rome, forced over two thousand carabinieri housed there onto a train, and sent them off to the Third Reich. The limited number of police remaining in the city, said the cardinal, would be unable to quell a Communist insurrection.

Maglione sent a parallel plea on the pope's behalf to the American president via Monsignor Cicognani, the apostolic delegate in Washington: "Should the Germans be forced to evacuate Rome, there are serious worries for the period in which the city, before the arrival of the Allied troops, would remain practically on its own." The cardinal argued that "the few remaining police forces would not be in a position to stop many riotous elements, especially the communists." In his cover letter, passing on Maglione's plea to Roosevelt, Cicognani added further explanation: "From reliable sources it has been learned that the Communists are plentifully supplied with arms and might embark upon a program which would result in wholesale robbery and the complete sacking of the city. Such an eventuality . . . would hardly exclude the possibility of an attack upon Vatican City itself."[23]

While the pope was sharing his fears of Communist insurrection with the American, British, and German envoys, the Nazi SS was exploring how it might be able to exploit the Communist threat even after the Allies captured Rome, as now seemed inevitable. British intelligence intercepted an October 12 telegram that the German Foreign Ministry Intelligence Service sent to Rome. It offers a tantalizing glimpse into the contacts the Nazis had—or at least thought they had—with the Italian Communist Party leadership:

> Please investigate most carefully the possibility of organizing Communist coup after the Anglo-American occupation of Rome. The object, among other things, would be to exert pressure on the Vatican. Please examine the possibility and, if favourable, make preparations. Prinzing, who has contacts with the Communist Party leadership, is to be incorporated. The affair is to be handled as a special assignment and a state secret matter.

Albert Prinzing, professor of Italian studies at the University of Berlin, member of the National Socialist Party since 1934 and of the SS since 1935, was responsible for intelligence on Italy at the German Foreign Ministry. What contact he might have subsequently made with the Italian Communist Party leadership, if any, remains unknown.[24]

As the fateful date of October 16, 1943, approached, Pius XII had another meeting with Ambassador Weizsäcker. Both were eager to ensure smooth relations between the Vatican and the German military forces occupying Rome. The pope began the audience by thanking the ambassador for all he had done thus far. When Weizsäcker brought up "the aspersion against our troops in Rome spread by our enemies," the pope commiserated with him, and the two men discussed how the pope might best help combat the stories.

Hitler's ambassador would next appear in the Apostolic Palace a week later, but that meeting would take place under dramatically different circumstances.[25]

THE POPE'S JEWS

O N SEPTEMBER 24, 1943, BARELY TWO WEEKS AFTER GERMAN TROOPS seized Rome, Heinrich Himmler's Reich Security office in Berlin cabled orders to Herbert Kappler, head of the SS in the city: "All Jews, without regard to nationality, age, sex, or condition must be transferred to Germany and liquidated there."[1]

In January 1942, at the Wannsee Conference, top Nazi officials had met to coordinate plans for the "Final Solution of the Jewish Question." Six months later the SS began gassing operations at its Treblinka killing center in Poland. Over the following sixteen months, nearly a million Jews along with an unknown number of non-Jewish Poles, Roma, and others were put to death there and at other such sites. In December 1942 the Allies issued a declaration stating that the Germans were engaged in the mass murder of Europe's Jews and warned that those responsible for this "bestial policy of cold-blooded extermination" would "not escape retribution."[2]

Now that they controlled much of Italy, the Germans could add the murder of all of Italy's Jews to their plans. Approximately forty thousand Jews were then living on the peninsula. The Germans began almost immediately, improvising a bit at first. Within a week of the announcement of the armistice, members of the "Adolf Hitler" Panzer Division seized fifty-four Jews in towns around Lake Maggiore in the north, shooting some and drowning others. They had apparently taken the initiative on their own. A few days later as many as four hundred

Jews, in good part refugees escaping the Nazis in southern France, were rounded up in the Cuneo area in the northwest. Most were put to death at Auschwitz.[3]

Within a day of the German troops' entrance into Rome, the city's chief rabbi went into hiding with his family. Israel Zolli had until a few years earlier lived in Trieste and had close ties with his rabbinical colleagues in central Europe. He urged the lay leaders of Rome's Jewish community to close the synagogue, destroy the list of members, distribute all its accumulated emergency financial aid to the poor, and encourage all of Rome's Jews to hide as well. But Zolli was not on good terms with the community leadership, and with his German accent and a personality judged cold, he was not popular among the city's Jews. The community's lay leaders rejected his advice, worried that it would trigger panic.[4]

Jews had been living in Rome for over two thousand years. Four centuries earlier, when Pope Paul IV first mandated that they be confined to a walled ghetto, locked in at night, twenty-five hundred Jews had lived in Rome. In good part impoverished, they were subject to draconian laws mandated by the popes to keep them in their humble state and to limit all contact with their Christian neighbors. They were further humiliated by the requirement that they regularly attend conversionary sermons at a nearby Catholic church. They lived in fear as well that church authorities would seize their children. Church practice demanded that Jewish children who were baptized, even without the knowledge or consent of their parents, could not be raised by Jews and so were to be taken from their families. Under the thumb of the popes, and at their mercy, the Jews in Rome came to be known as the Pope's Jews. The situation came to an end only with the conquest of Rome by Italian military forces in 1870, and with it the end of the Papal States.[5]

Many of the twelve thousand Jews who now lived in the province of Rome were poor, especially those living in the city's old ghetto, on the banks of the Tiber, not far from Palazzo Venezia and the Pantheon. In the wake of the German occupation, those with more means, scattered through the city, hurriedly packed up their Jewish books, magazines, and newspapers, stored away their Chanukah menorahs, and pried the mezuzahs from their doorposts. On September 29, 1943, German troops sacked the archives of the Jewish community and smashed down the door of Rabbi Zolli's home, having brought an expert to go through his collection of rare Jewish books to determine which were worth carting off to Germany.

In late September as well, Kappler, for reasons that remain unclear still today, summoned the two lay leaders of Rome's Jewish community and demanded that the city's Jews provide him with fifty kilograms of gold within forty-eight hours. He warned that if they did not, he would select two hundred Roman Jews by lot and have them deported. Worried they might not come up with sufficient gold in time, a delegation of Jews went to the Vatican to ask the pope's help. Although the pope, it was reported, agreed to offer whatever might be lacking, in the end his help was not needed. Two days later the two Jewish leaders, accompanied by the head of the Office of Racial Affairs of Rome's police department and by two Italian policemen, delivered a pile of the requisite weight of gold jewelry to Rome's SS headquarters.[6]

On October 11 Kappler received another telegram from Berlin, this one ordering "the immediate and complete elimination of Jewry in Italy." Other members of the German command in Italy were told of the order at the same time, including General Stahel and Germany's new ambassador to Italy, Rudolf Rahn, who had replaced Mackensen. Additional members of the SS were sent to Rome to help put the plan into action.

SATURDAY, OCTOBER 16, WAS both the Sabbath and the third day of the Jewish holiday of Sukkot. It was still dark on that cold, wet morning when a hundred SS officers marched double file into Rome's old ghetto to get the *Judenoperation* under way. Another 265 fanned out to other parts of the city carrying clipboards with lists of the Jews who lived there. When the Jews of the ghetto first peered out their windows that morning, drawn by the commotion, many assumed the Germans had come to search for the men who had been evading the recently declared conscription for forced labor. Indeed, having feared such an event, most of the younger Jewish men had already gone into hiding. It still did not occur to those who saw the Germans approach that they had come to seize all Jews, women as well as men, babies as well as the elderly. Checking the address of each building against their lists, the SS men methodically banged on each door, smashing down those where no one answered. Shocked by the order for them all to come out, the Jews tried to draw some hope from the Germans' written instructions—the SS men themselves spoke no Italian—to lock the door behind them and keep their keys. Surely, many thought, or at least hoped, they would soon be coming home.

As the morning progressed, the dramatic roundup was attracting the attention of passersby, who stood mutely watching the horrific scene as uniformed SS marched hastily dressed families in ragged single file through the wet streets amid pleas, sighs, tears, and shouts. Anguished mothers carried infants in their arms while gripping the small hands of those old enough to walk. A sick, deaf eighty-five-year-old woman was marched by, along with a paralyzed man who had to be carried aloft in his wheelchair. A woman holding her baby opened her blouse to nurse in the hopes of convincing the German officer to let them go, but he merely responded by poking her with the muzzle of his rifle, telling her to move along with the others. The men of the SS led the Jews in the old ghetto to an excavated area below street level near the ancient Roman Theater of Marcellus, where three or four tarpaulin-covered trucks shuttled back and forth, taking batches of distraught Jews to their destination, a military college complex across the Tiber, near the Vatican.

Some succeeded in escaping, warned by the shouts from neighboring apartments, while others simply froze in fear. Rosa Anticoli fled her home with her four little children before the SS arrived, desperate to reach a nearby tram stop. Slowed down by her young daughter, sick with diphtheria, she had not gotten quite far enough when a suspicious SS officer, spotting her, shouted, *Jude! Jude!* Rosa fell to her knees and pleaded for mercy. Prodding her with the butt of his rifle, he marched her and her four children to an awaiting truck.

Outside the ghetto, when a group of SS came to seize a Jewish family from a middle-class apartment building on Via Flaminia, a neighboring woman, looking on, berated the SS officer. He had a ready defense: Germany's ambassador, he told her, had recently met with the pope and told him of the plans to round up the city's Jews. "If you have to deport the Jews," the SS officer quoted the pope as saying, "it is well to do it quickly." Needless to say, no such conversation with the pope had taken place, but the fact that the pope had never spoken out either against Italy's own racial laws or against the Nazis' systematic murder of the Jews allowed such stories to be spread among the SS and the German troops.[7]

In all, the Germans wrested 1,259 people from their homes, many from the old ghetto, but many too from apartments scattered throughout the city. All were trucked to the military college compound just outside the old walls of the Vatican. On their arrival there, the 363 men were separated from their families and sent to a different part of the compound. Two hundred seven children and 689 women were imprisoned there, the oldest ninety years old. The trauma caused one woman to go into labor, resulting in an additional imprisoned Jew the next day.[8]

PIUS XII LEARNED OF the roundup early that morning. Among those to inform him was the young Princess Enza Pignatelli, who, alerted by a friend to the unfolding tragedy, rushed to speak with the only man the Romans thought to be in a position to stop it. Somehow she succeeded in reaching the pope's private chapel, "pushing aside with her elbows those who wanted to stop her."[9]

The pope could have no doubt about the fate that awaited the Jews. Making matters worse, the seizure of Rome's Jews and their detention a stone's throw from the Vatican, where they awaited deportation to their deaths, put his policy of not criticizing the Nazis' ongoing extermination of Europe's Jews to an excruciating test. For centuries, the popes had, as bishops of Rome, cast themselves as protectors of the city's Jews, even as they had forced them into a ghetto. Only two months earlier the pontiff had for the second time raced to the site of an Allied bombing to publicly express his solidarity with the victims. How could he remain silent now?[10]

The pontiff phoned Cardinal Maglione and asked him to summon the German ambassador immediately. Meeting Weizsäcker that afternoon, the cardinal, invoking the ambassador's sense of Christian charity and humanity, asked if he might intervene: "Excellency, you who have a tender, good heart, see if you can't save so many innocents. It is painful for the Holy Father, painful beyond all measure that in Rome itself, under the eyes of the Common Father so many people are made to suffer simply because they belong to a particular race."

Weizsäcker reflected for a moment, then asked, "What would the Holy See do if things were to continue?"

"The Holy See," said Maglione, "would not want to be constrained to say a word of disapproval."

"It has been more than four years," responded the ambassador, "that I have been following and admiring the Holy See's attitude. It has succeeded in steering the ship amidst rocks of every kind and every size without any collisions, and even if it had more faith in the Allies, it has known how to maintain a perfect balance. I ask myself whether, right at the time that the boat is about to reach port: is it a good idea to put everything in danger? I think of the consequences that a step by the Holy See would provoke. . . . The instructions received come from the highest source."

After a pause to let the cardinal reflect on his unmistakable reference to Hitler as responsible for the order to round up Rome's Jews, Weizsäcker asked, "Does Your Eminence leave me free not to report this official conversation?"

"I observed," Maglione recalled in his notes of the encounter, "that I had asked him to intervene by appealing to his sense of humanity. I left it to his judgment whether or not to mention our conversation, which had been so friendly."

Maglione went on to assure the German ambassador that, as Weizsäcker himself had noted, the Holy See had always been careful not to give the Germans the impression of having done "even the least thing against Germany during a terrible war."

"Meanwhile," concluded the cardinal, "I repeat: Your Excellency told me that he would do something for the poor Jews. I thank you for it. As for the rest, I leave it to your judgement. If you think it more opportune not to mention our conversation, so be it."[11]

In fact, Weizsäcker never promised to do anything on behalf of Rome's Jews and never did. What he did do was inform Berlin the next day that the Curia was "particularly shocked that the action took place, so to speak, under the pope's windows," and that groups hostile to the Germans were trying to exploit the roundup "to force the Vatican out of its reserve." He added that people were beginning to contrast the silence of the current pope to "his much more fiery predecessor Pius XI."[12]

At the military college, the Jews were forced to sleep on the floor. The incessant weeping of women and children, along with the pangs of hunger and the stench from the lack of lavatories, made sleep impossible in any case. All wondered what would become of them, although most imagined some kind of work camp would be their destination. Few could imagine the fate that awaited them.

As the thousand terrified Jews huddled a few hundred meters from the Vatican, pleas kept coming to the pope to do something. On the day after the roundup, Pius XII received an urgent letter from a group of Roman Jews who had eluded capture, begging him to intervene. That day, too, he received a letter that an elderly Jewish woman "in precarious condition of health" had somehow smuggled out of the military college where she was among the imprisoned. She pleaded for his "authoritative intervention." At the same time, a number of other Roman Jews reached the Vatican Secretariat of State office to plead for papal help on behalf of their family members who had been seized.[13]

That morning Monsignor Montini had obtained German permission to send a member of his staff to the place of the Jews' imprisonment. The Jews, the emissary learned, had been given nothing to eat or drink since their capture. Doctors who treated those who had been beaten were on their way out the door as he arrived. He learned something else of interest from speaking to those milling around outside the military college entrance. "It seems, according to some who were outside and knew people interned there, that they also included people who had already been baptized, confirmed, and celebrated a Church wedding."[14]

In fact, among those rounded up were quite a few Christians, that is, baptized Jews, as well as Jews married to Christians. Within hours of the arrests, pleas were coming into the Vatican to take action to have them freed. At seven A.M. on October 16, an employee of the Vatican Library learned of the plight of his relatives who were among the first taken in the raid. He rushed to the Vatican, where he found a cardinal he knew who advised him to speak with Monsignor Dell'Acqua in the Secretariat of State. This he did, but at the same time, taking advantage of his acquaintance with Monsignor Montini, he sent him an urgent letter: "I turn to Your Excellency with the most fervent prayer to use Your authority with the German Embassy so that Catholic people, and fervent Catholics like my aunt and my cousins are saved. . . . It is an intervention that cannot come quickly enough, if (God forbid!) it is not already too late."[15]

At the same time Monsignor Montini learned of another such case and hastily wrote to Cardinal Maglione: "This morning the lawyer Foligno was 'taken' . . . Catholic by birth with his Aryan wife and children." A note three days later reported the good news: "Mr. Foligno . . . comes to the Secretariat . . . to give thanks for what has been done for him: he was liberated after only a few hours." The day after the roundup, the Roman office of the Order of Malta advised the Vatican Secretariat of State of another such case. Although the man in question had a Jewish father, the letter explained, he had been baptized at birth. He had been seized in the German raid. Three days later the office of the Order of Malta followed up with a letter reporting that the Germans' error had been rectified: "fortunately for him, before embarking for an unknown destination . . . he was let go." In fact, the Vatican Secretariat had hastily drawn up a list of those among the imprisoned whom the church deemed Catholic and had given it to the German ambassador.[16]

Early on Sunday, the Germans began carefully reviewing their captives' identity documents to determine which Christians had erroneously fallen into their net. Over the next hours they would release not only former Jews who had been baptized but also those Jews married to Christians. This was Rome, not Poland or Russia, and the Germans did not want to unduly provoke the Vatican.[17]

Beginning at dawn on Monday, October 18, the 1,007 remaining Jews were loaded into trucks, which then rumbled through Rome's streets to the Tiburtina train station. Among them were 105 children under age five. At the station, the trucks pulled up alongside a long train that waited on a dead-end track. Ordered to get out, the Jews were forced into eighteen windowless cattle cars. Hours later the train pulled out of the station. As it made its way north, witnesses reported hearing plaintive cries emanating from its forlorn human freight.

Monsignor Montini met with Pius XII to ask how he should reply to a letter that relatives of the captured Jews had sent the previous day, pleading for the pope to intervene. "Let them know," instructed the pope, "that one is doing everything that one can." Lutz Klinkhammer, the foremost historian of Germany's military occupation of Italy, summed up the pope's reaction to the roundup of Rome's Jews: "It is more than clear that all their efforts were aimed above all at saving the baptized or the 'half-Jews' born from mixed marriages."[18]

The day after the trainload of Jews pulled out of the Roman train station, a member of the Vatican Secretariat of State office handed Ambassador Weizsäcker the latest Vatican list of those among the seized who should have been considered Catholics. "Among the various cases of 'non Aryans' not previously made known to the German embassy," a note in the newly opened Vatican archives explains, "there are the two attached: they involve 'non-Aryans' who have been baptized, but not freed as others have been in their condition."[19]

It was still dark when the train arrived at Auschwitz on the morning of October 23, exactly a week since the Roman roundup had begun. As the disoriented, exhausted, freezing, famished, filthy Jewish captives stepped out of the train, they were met by the camp's medical director, the infamous Josef Mengele. As husbands and wives, fathers and their children rushed to find one another, they were immediately stopped, ordered not to move. Mengele directed the children and those men and women he deemed too old or too sick for physical labor to move to his right. The others were directed to his left. The elderly, the children, the sick, and the fragile were then loaded onto trucks and taken directly to the gas chamber. The youngest, born at Rome's military college the previous Sunday, was not yet a week old. Slave laborers would later remove the victims' gold teeth. The rest of the Jews, 149 men and 47 women, were sent to a labor camp where most would die from exhaustion or disease. Of the more than one thousand Jews who had been put on the train in Rome, only sixteen would emerge alive.[20]

On the day the Jews were being forced onto the train in Rome, Osborne, the British envoy, had a long audience with Pius XII. Appearing "well and in good spirits," the pope shared two concerns. First, Rome's food shortages might worsen should the Germans retreat from the city and the Allies not immediately arrive. This concern brought up the second one, that unrest might explode in the city during such an interval. Osborne asked the pope whether the Germans were treating the Vatican well. The pope replied that "he had no grounds for complaint against General von Stahel and the German police who had hitherto respected neutrality."[21]

The next day the American envoy Harold Tittmann visited the pope and offered a similar account. The pope took the opportunity to tell Tittmann "that so far the Germans had respected the Vatican City and the Holy See's property in Rome and that the German General Officer Commanding in Rome seemed well-disposed toward the Vatican." Apparently, the pope made no mention of what had happened to Rome's Jews in his meetings with the two envoys, or if he did, it was regarded as too inconsequential for them to put in their reports.[22]

Those Jews who had escaped the roundup were now on the run. The day after the train departed, in one of what would be many such scenes, a nun went to respond to a knock on her convent's door. There she found a Jewish couple, the woman holding a baby in her arms. "Take him," said the man, "and if you like, baptize him. If you don't take him, I will kill him and kill myself." Monsignor Costantini, who recorded the episode in his diary that day, added, "The child remained with the nuns. And the two forlorn Jews vanished, looking to escape from the Gestapo."[23]

Pleas from Rome's Jews kept coming to the pope. On the twenty-seventh, a Roman rabbi, David Panzieri, wrote directly to Pius XII, begging him to convince the Germans to return the victims of the October 16 roundup to their families, unaware that most had already been gassed and incinerated. But in the days following the roundup, the Vatican's main focus was to alert the German authorities to the fact that, despite the earlier efforts to identify them and have them freed, some with bona-fide Catholic credentials had been among those forced onto the train.

On October 20, an accountant working in the administrative offices of the Vatican sent Monsignor Montini a plea on behalf of a family he knew: "Last Saturday, October 16, at 5 A.M., the following men, of Jewish origin, but converted to Catholicism and baptized, as seen from the attached certificates from the Most Excellent Vicariat of Rome, were taken by German armed forces from their home, together with their mother." He listed the two men, Aldo Veneziani and his brother Dario, along with the dates of their baptism (1940 and 1941). The two men, wrote the accountant, were eager to bring the certificates proving their baptism to the attention of the German authorities in the hope that they would then set them free. He asked as well whether the Vatican secretariat would be "willing to interest itself in the pitiful case" of the men's elderly mother, "although not Catholic, in consideration of her venerable age and her precarious state of health."

Three days later, having received word of two other baptized members of the Veneziani family who had been taken on October 16, the Vatican secretariat sent a note to the German embassy. "Particular interest in the liberation of the below noted persons, arrested because of their descent, has been requested." The Vatican note listed five Veneziani family members, identifying all but the elderly mother as "baptized." It concluded, "The documents proving the Baptism of the above-mentioned persons are conserved at the Secretariat of State of His Holiness."[24]

On October 29, Maglione's office sent Weizsäcker another such appeal: "The most excellent German ambassador to the Holy See is asked for his benevolent interest in the release of Count Victor Cantoni and his mother, who were deported by the German troops from Rome, where they live, to an unknown destination. Count Cantoni, Catholic, was baptized thirty years ago as a child, and his mother was baptized in 1927." A week later, writing on behalf of all those who had been arrested that day, although still avoiding the use of the word "Jews" in referring to them, Maglione sent a letter to the German ambassador. He asked if it was possible for him to satisfy the "many relatives or friends of the non-Aryans, recently arrested in Rome, who would like to have news of their loved one and eventually to have some material help."[25]

At the same time, Weizsäcker sent Berlin the welcome news that the pope had decided to say nothing about the roundup of Rome's Jews:

> Although he has been beseeched by various parties to do so, the Pope has refrained from making any ostentatious remarks on the deportation of the Jews from Rome. Even though he must expect to be criticized for this for a long time by our enemies, and Protestant circles in Anglo-Saxon countries will exploit this for propaganda purposes, on this issue too he has done everything possible not to strain relations with the German government and the German authorities in Rome.

Weizsäcker noted that the Vatican's newspaper had published only one oblique reference to the roundup. Written "in the paper's characteristically long-winded and unclear style," the ambassador reported, it stated that "the Pope grants his paternal care to all people, regardless of nationality, religion, and race. The diverse and ceaseless activities of Pius XII, it says, have even intensified as a result of the suffering of so many unfortunate people." The German government, concluded Weizsäcker, should find nothing to object to in the Vatican statement, a German translation of which he enclosed, "especially since its wording will be understood by very few people as a specific reference to the Jewish question."[26]

The pope's silence as the Jews of Rome were being sent to their deaths was so striking that it even led to a complaint by the German priest who served as chaplain to the SS stationed in Rome. Speaking with the Italian priest who served as chaplain to the Roman police force, he said that some among the German military in Rome were unhappy about the deportation of Rome's Jews. They were struck, he said, by the "indifference" shown by church authorities. Scrawled on the report to Montini containing the chaplain's complaint is the comment, "H[oly] S[ee] had done what it could."[27]

In the absence of any news of what had happened to the Jews once their train had left Rome, anguished relatives kept bombarding the pope with pleas. Perhaps none attracted his attention more than the one from a Roman Jewish family with personal ties to his own family. Four days after the roundup, Pius XII received word that among those seized was the niece of one of his former classmates from the Ginnasio Visconti, the Roman secondary school he had attended. In a letter his old classmate recounted what had happened: "One of my most beloved young nieces, Nella Pontecorvo, married name Mieli, guilty only of being born Jewish, was taken last Saturday from her own home in Via Padova 43 together with her tender young children, Marina age six and Claudia age four. . . . We know nothing more of them except, it seems, that after forty-eight hours they were forced to leave Rome for a destination unknown." He added a note recalling that his niece's grandfather "was tied by profound esteem and intimate friendship" with the pope's own father.

Following the pope's direction, the Vatican Secretariat of State contacted the cardinal vicar of Rome to verify that Nella and her two children had been baptized and so should have been exempted from the SS roundup. On December 13, Monsignor Montini, the future Pope Paul VI, wrote on the family's behalf to Ambassador Weizsäcker to ask if he could arrange "to have news of the children and their mother, and obtain, possibly, their liberation." Montini explained: "They are non-Aryan Catholics and the documents of their Baptism are available at the Secretariat of State of His Holiness." Unfortunately for Nella and little Marina and Claudia, evidence of their baptism arrived much too late. The children had been sent directly to the gas chamber on their arrival at Auschwitz. Their mother, after having her little children taken from her, was perhaps sent to the slave labor camp. She had recently celebrated her forty-first birthday. It would be her last.[28]

BASELESS
RUMORS

ON THE CLOUDLESS EVENING OF NOVEMBER 5, 1943, FOUR BOMBS
fell on Vatican City. One exploded in the gardens near the Vatican
radio station, two others near administrative buildings. The fourth
crashed through the roof of the Vatican's mosaic factory. Remarkably,
no one was badly hurt, although Monsignor Tardini, responsible for
international relations at the Vatican Secretariat of State, narrowly escaped injury. He had been heading for his study in the governor's palace when one of the bombs blew in its windows and collapsed the
ceiling. Finally, quipped the sharp-tongued prelate, they had succeeded
in creating an "open city."

Although the damage could have been much worse, it was considerable. Blast marks could be seen up to the fourth floor on the exterior
of many buildings. The mosaics laboratory was strewn with wreckage,
a water main broke, and one of the buildings housing foreign diplomats had narrowly missed a direct hit. Although St. Peter's Basilica
largely escaped damage, some of its windows shattered.[1]

The search for the guilty party began quickly, as did the Axis use of
the episode for propaganda purposes. The Vatican sent evenhanded
notes to the American and British envoys and to the German ambassador detailing the damage and asking for an investigation to determine who was responsible. British foreign secretary Anthony Eden
sent a telegram to Allied headquarters in Algiers: "Enemy propaganda
is making great play with the alleged bombing of Vatican City by Al-

lied aircraft at 2100 hours on November 5th. If as we assume there is no truth in this story we suggest that A.F.H.Q. should issue an immediate denial that any Allied aircraft were over the Rome area on this date." At the same time, the American War Department cabled Eisenhower in Algiers recommending he issue a prompt denial as well.[2]

The day after the bombing, the Fascist media was filled with expressions of outrage. "A criminal air raid attack was made yesterday at about 9 P.M. against Vatican City," announced a Rome radio broadcast. "The holy city . . . which is being protected by Reich troops from any possibility of violation, was hit by four heavy bombs which caused considerable damage. It is very probable that the attack was directed against St. Peter's Basilica." A banner headline in Rome's major newspaper screamed "Criminal Anglo-Saxon Attack on Vatican City." The headline in Farinacci's *Il Regime Fascista,* back in business after having been briefly shuttered following the Duce's overthrow, proclaimed, "Another Evil Act of the 'Gangster' of the Air: Vatican City Bombed: The Premeditated Barbarous Incursion."[3]

Eisenhower quickly issued a denial: "Crews adhered to their definite instructions and did not bomb the Vatican City."[4] The following day, November 8, a statement prepared at a meeting of the British War Cabinet read "Enquiries showed that the bombing of the Vatican City during the previous week could not have been done by Allied aircraft."[5]

The following day the British prime minister would receive an unwelcome message in the form of a cable from the chief British diplomat in Algiers, Harold Macmillan. "We think that we probably did bomb the Vatican," he wrote. "It was a very small affair anyway of possibly one machine that had lost its way." The British government quickly buried Macmillan's report. The next day the U.S. State Department put out its own press release responding to the Vatican request for an investigation: "A reply has now been received from General Eisenhower which establishes beyond any doubt that the attacking plane was not an Allied aircraft."[6]

Cardinal Maglione came to know of the Allies' suppressed account of what had happened thanks to a letter sent eight days after the incident by Monsignor Carroll, the only American working in the Vatican Secretariat of State. Carroll happened to be in Algiers. "In a conversation with the American Chief of Staff during the past week, I was informed very confidentially that they feel that the bombing of the Vatican is probably attributable to an American pilot who lost his way." In fact, explained the American prelate, "another American pilot reported seeing an Allied plane dropping its load on the Vatican." The American general had expressed his regret and pledged that strict measures would be taken to ensure it would never happen again.[7]

AT THE END OF OCTOBER, Clara Petacci finally got to see her lover again. Having been freed by the Germans from her brief imprisonment, she had been sending Mussolini a stream of long handwritten letters, a curious stew mixing attempts to buck up his spirits, protestations of her undying love, complaints about his failure to sufficiently appreciate her, unsolicited political advice, and warnings about his enemies. Over the next year and a half, she would write him over three hundred of these, and although he repeatedly urged her to destroy their correspondence, she not only kept all his letters but made copies of her own. Clara's visit that day to Mussolini's residence at Gargnano, on Lake Garda about ten miles up the lake from Salò, was made possible because the Duce's wife, Rachele, had yet to return from Germany. In the car on the way to see him, Clara clutched her rosary in her hands and prayed to her favorite saint, Rita. Entering a side entrance to Mussolini's villa, she described her first sight of him: "I see him advance slowly in the shadow. I feel dizzy. . . . I see him, I see him again. He takes hold of my hand, he holds me, we look at each other, we tremble violently." They spent the night together, a privilege they would not often get to repeat, for Rachele, Clara's archenemy, would soon be returning and would use all the arms at her disposal to keep Clara away.[8]

For his part, Mussolini felt as much prisoner as dictator, resenting the Germans' control and no longer confident of his ability to dictate to his own Fascist underlings. The ministries of his government were scattered across the Veneto region, while his villa served as both his office and his home. He had long reveled in the popular adulation that met him wherever he went and the oceanic crowds roused by his combative speeches. Now he felt alone, rarely venturing from his villa and not fully trusting the men who guarded him. He had not been back in Rome since he had been so abruptly removed by the king; nor would he ever return there. At the balcony of Palazzo Venezia where he had given so many memorable harangues, the only sign of his presence now was a picture of him, his arm raised in Roman salute, hung from the balustrade. Guarding the entrance of that building were no longer his own troops but a German tank and four armored German cars. Most humiliating of all, perhaps, were the widespread rumors in Rome that he was dead.[9]

THROUGHOUT THESE FIRST WEEKS of German occupation, relations between the Vatican and the Germans continued to go smoothly, much to the pope's relief.[10] On October 8, Weizsäcker had asked the pope to issue a statement denying the Allied tales of German mistreatment of the Vatican. The pope hesitated. If he were to issue his own statement, he said, all he could do would be to confirm that the Germans had thus far acted properly. He suggested that a statement by the German authorities would be more valuable, for it could not only speak to the past but offer guarantees for the future as well.[11]

In the end, the pope agreed to a joint declaration, signed by the German ambassador and Cardinal Maglione, published prominently in the October 30 issue of *L'Osservatore Romano* and then reprinted in *La Civiltà Cattolica:*

> In order to put an end to baseless rumors now in circulation, particularly abroad, concerning the attitude of the German troops towards Vatican City, His Excellency the German Ambassador to the Holy See, on the instructions of his government, has informed the Holy See that just as Germany has hitherto respected the institutions and activity of the Roman Curia as

well as the sovereign rights and integrity of the Vatican City
State, it is determined to respect them in the future as well. The
Holy See, recognizing that the German troops have respected
the Roman Curia and Vatican City, have gladly taken note of
the assurance given by the German Ambassador as regards the
future.[12]

In helping nurture good relations between the Vatican and the German military authorities in Rome, no one was more active than Father
Pancratius Pfeiffer, the German superior general of the Salvatorian religious order. Sympathetic to the Axis and a native speaker of German,
he eagerly offered to serve as the intermediary in Vatican dealings with
the occupying forces. The pope would have at least a half-dozen meetings with him during the nine months German troops remained in
Rome.[13]

Having quickly become a familiar figure to the German military
command in Rome, Father Pfeiffer was invited to an October 30 dinner held in honor of General Stahel on his departure from his post as
commander of German troops in Rome. Pfeiffer was given the seat
between Germany's ambassadors to Italy and to the Holy See. In his
notes on the event, Pfeiffer wrote, "Weizsäcker congratulated me for
making myself so useful in such difficult times. At this, Ambassador
Rahn observed that he too would always make himself available,
should he ever be able to be helpful. It would be sufficient to drop him
a line."

In his remarks that evening, General Stahel spoke of his pride in
having been chosen to be commander of Rome during such difficult
times. He expressed special satisfaction for all he had done to ensure
the well-being of Vatican City.[14]

EVER SINCE THE KING and Badoglio abandoned Rome, Italy's emissary to the Holy See had found himself in an awkward position. The
new republican Fascist regime was calling on all members of the Italian
government to swear their allegiance. Although Francesco Babuscio

had for many years loyally served the Duce, he had always viewed this as in harmony with his attachment to the Italian monarchy. Also weighing against swearing allegiance to the reconstituted Fascist government was his awareness that the Allies were likely to win the war. Caught between the two competing calls for his allegiance, he was not particularly eager to draw attention to himself.[15]

In mid-October, cut off from any communication with the royal government in exile, Babuscio asked Cardinal Maglione to help him establish contact with it. Loath to risk upsetting the Germans or provoking Mussolini's republican government, and unsure that a communication such as Babuscio proposed could be kept secret, Cardinal Maglione turned down the request.[16]

Nor was Pius XII eager to bring attention to the awkward situation he faced with his own nuncio to the Italian government, Francesco Borgongini. The pope made no attempt to have Borgongini contact the royal government in the south, and in these months of German occupation, the pope did not want to be seen having anything to do with that government. At the same time, he would not want to have his nuncio deal with Mussolini's republic, for that would be tantamount to offering it official recognition. It was best to have the nuncio do nothing.[17]

AS PART OF THE Allies' armistice terms, they had demanded that Italy's racial laws be scrapped. When, two months later, in November 1943, still no move had been made to nullify the laws, the Naples city administration, acting on its own, declared them no longer in effect. The Allies had entered Naples the previous month. Angered by the unilateral move, Prime Minister Badoglio complained to the Allied Control Commission in Brindisi.

Having learned that Naples had "decided to consider null and void all fascist antisemitic laws," the secretary-general of Badoglio's Foreign Ministry wrote, the ministry wanted the Anglo-American authorities to know that the royal government had the question of abolishing these laws "under consideration. . . . In the meantime, I would be grateful if, while informing the Anglo-American authorities in Italy of the foregoing, you could impress on them the value of not encouraging isolated actions in this field by provincial or city authorities."[18]

Replying three days later, the Allied authorities stressed the urgency of putting an end to the racial laws and reminded Badoglio that his government was obligated to do so by the armistice agreement. The Allied officials also took the opportunity to ask a series of questions: Were the anti-Jewish measures still in effect? Had the large number of Jews interned in Italian concentration camps been freed? Were Jews receiving the government's support in efforts to regain their property and the jobs that had been taken from them? Were Italian Jews now able to resume their normal lives and rebuild their communal institutions? What must have been clear to the Allied authorities was that none of the major figures in the royal government had shown the least interest in these questions.[19]

While the racial laws were still on the books in the Kingdom of the South, as the royal government came to be known, Jews living there, thanks to the presence of Allied troops, were at least safe. The same could not be said for the great majority of Italy's Jews, who found themselves in regions under the control of the Germans and their Italian collaborators.[20] In Rome and elsewhere in German-occupied Italy, Jews sought refuge where they could, and many found shelter in convents and monasteries. Such was the case of Enzo Finzi who, fleeing the October 16 roundup in Rome with his wife and family, sought refuge at the city's Monastery of the Carissimi, where there was someone they knew. Although it was already crowded with an assortment of political dissidents, Italian soldiers, carabinieri, and other men not wanting to serve the Nazi-Fascist cause, the monks took the Jewish family in.

While many Jews succeeded in finding safety in this way, others were less fortunate. Some, on presenting themselves at the door of a Catholic religious institution, were told that they would be admitted only if they agreed to convert. Others were simply turned away. Emma Fiorentino, a Roman Jew, to cite but one case, received a telephone warning on October 16 that the roundup had begun. Desperately searching for somewhere that would let her and her children in, she thought of a nearby convent which housed two nuns she knew. The nuns refused to admit them. Emma and her family then walked from convent to convent pleading for shelter, but they were turned away everywhere.[21] To cite another example, in the days that followed the October 16 raid, a parish priest wrote to the Vatican to plead for help for two Roman Jewish children, a girl aged nine and a boy fourteen. Their parents, he explained, wanted "to entrust them, respectively to male and female religious institutions," but as they desperately went from one to another of them, "some of them refused to accept them because they are Jews, claiming a prohibition by the order of higher authorities." The priest reported that they had yet to locate a Roman convent or monastery that would take them in.[22] Although as these and other examples suggest, there is no evidence the pope ever directed church institutions to take in Jews, and many did not, he was aware that among the large number of refugees concealed in Rome's religious buildings were many Jews.[23]

Guido Buffarini, the new republican Fascist government's minister of internal affairs, played a central role in the murderous new phase of Italy's anti-Jewish campaign. Following Mussolini's overthrow a few months earlier, Badoglio's government had jailed him. Within days of his imprisonment, the mother superior of Rome's Institute of the Most Holy Crucifix wrote directly to the pope to plead his cause: "Holiness, remembering the infinite number of benefits and favors received for so many years that His Excellency Buffarini lavished on the works of our Congregation," she wrote, she prayed that the pope would intervene to have him freed from prison and allowed to remain at home. Following the mother superior's plea, the papal nuncio spoke with the chief of police on Buffarini's behalf. The police chief assured him that while the prominent Fascist would need to remain in prison, he would be treated "with all possible consideration." He remained imprisoned until the Germans freed him in early September.[24]

On November 30, 1943, in his new role for the Italian Social Republic, Buffarini sent a telegram to the prefects of all the provinces under his control: "The following police order is being communicated

for immediate execution. . . . All Jews . . . of whatever nationality re-
siding in the national territory must be sent to special concentration
camps. All their possessions, including their real estate and other properties, must be subject to immediate seizure." In deference perhaps to
the repeated requests the pope's emissaries had made to him in his former role in overseeing Italy's racial laws, he added a note: "Jews born
of mixed marriages should be considered Aryans."[25]

Indeed, the Vatican's efforts to shield baptized Jews from such measures were still very much alive. Four days before Buffarini's order,
Cardinal Maglione wrote the German ambassador with his latest request. The bishop of Trieste had implored the Vatican to see that the
dire situation of the "non-Aryans" in his diocese was not aggravated by
the ever more stringent measures being adopted against them. "It
seems," Maglione informed Weizsäcker, "that the local German authorities have proceeded to the arrest and requisition of the property
of a number of Jews, without even making a distinction between the
baptized and those not baptized, or those married to Catholics."
Maglione asked the ambassador to intervene.[26]

The patriarch of Venice, Cardinal Adeodato Piazza, was likewise
moved to write to Rome to express his unhappiness that baptized Jews
were being treated as Jews and called on the Holy See to do all it could
to save them. He voiced another concern as well, which he registered
in meeting with the German consul in Venice. It was disturbing, he
said, to see Italian Fascist zealots invading the houses of poor, old, and
sick Jews and arresting them while leaving the wealthier Jews to move
freely around the city. "This injustice was disturbing him so much,"
wrote the consul, "that the only solution he could see would be for the
measures against the Jews to be carried out by German authorities, because then justice would at least be guaranteed for all. It is well known
that the Patriarch's chief wish is to have all Jews and half-Jews shut up
in a ghetto."[27]

News of Buffarini's order to arrest all of Italy's Jews, confiscate their
property, and send them to concentration camps prompted an unusual
comment on the front page of the Vatican newspaper. In its December
3 issue, *L'Osservatore Romano* asked what could have prompted the au-

thorities to feel the need to drastically modify the existing racial laws. If Jews were thought to be responsible for some new danger, surely merely adding additional police surveillance would have sufficed. The Vatican paper expressed special concern for "the painful recognition that the new measures strike some who are Catholics from birth, children of Catholic parents, along with individuals who have sincerely converted and been practicing from the time of their youth or for many years, in any case entered into the bosom of the Church and Christian life, participating in the divine grace and in the communion of the Saints, like all those who are baptized."[28]

The U.S. intelligence report for southern Europe that week commented on the Vatican's response to the newly announced roundup of Italy's Jews: "After several unofficial and fruitless appeals, the Vatican openly, but with characteristic mildness, takes issue with the neo-Fascist government over the latter's drastic antisemitic campaign being planned and executed with Nazi-like ferocity." The pastoral letters of the bishops of northern Italy "merely exhort their flocks to docility and patience 'during these most trying times.'" If Hitler had any concerns that the pope might speak out against the new anti-Jewish campaign in Italy, Weizsäcker would assure him he need not worry. "As for a protest by the pope for the arrest of the Jews," Weizsäcker reported to Berlin in mid-December, "it is not even being considered."[29]

Italy's Jews were now regularly being rooted out of their hiding places. Among the traces they would leave behind, as they were sent off to their deaths, were hastily penned letters that came fluttering out of the trains taking them north. One such note, written by twenty-three-year-old Abramo Segre to Lucia, his fiancée, emerged from a train passing through Brescia on December 7, 1943. In the train with Abramo were his mother and sister.

Dear Lucia,

I entrust my letter to the goodness of someone who will want to mail it. This is the second day that I find myself closed in a cattle car with my family and with two hundred other people on our way to the concentra-

*tion camp. I face the terrible prospect of eight days of travel to reach Cra-
cow in Poland.*

*I have the feeling unfortunately that, for me and my family, this
voyage is one without return, because if we don't succumb to the hunger
and the exhaustion to which we will be exposed we will not be able to resist the terrible cold, being scarcely dressed and shoed as we are. Our last
hope is in God who, unfortunately, up to now has not helped us, but to
whom nonetheless we continue to pray.*

*The sufferings of prison were a paradise compared to what we are
facing. . . . Here we don't even have a name, but only a number, like
animals.*

*The train goes not very fast but inexorably toward the border. I must
now end this brief letter that has little chance of reaching you.*

The letter never did reach Lucia. Abramo, his mother, and his sister
Rosa would all die at Auschwitz.[30]

As the roundup of Italy's Jews intensified, it was impossible for the
pope to ignore. In mid-December, the archbishop of Ferrara became
the latest to implore the Vatican's intervention in favor of the victims,
"especially those members of mixed families." A note in the Secretariat
of State files reveals the reply sent to the archbishop: "one can respond
saying that the Holy See, as it had done in the past, tries in the current
circumstances as well to aid the non-Aryans to the extent it can, particularly those in mixed families." It was unlikely that they would
achieve any result, "but, if nothing else, one will always be able to say
that the Holy See has done everything possible to help these unfortunates." The note added, "One might also ask Mons. Nuncio to say a
word or arrange to have a word said, confidentially, with Marshal Gra-
ziani★ or with Buffarini asking that mercy be used especially toward
the mixed families."[31]

The dramatic new order to arrest all of Italy's Jews, confiscate their
property, and send them to concentration camps made the pope's con-

★ General Rodolfo Graziani, minister of defense in Mussolini's Italian Social Republic.

tinuing silence ever more embarrassing. Believing some kind of Vatican action was called for, Father Tacchi Venturi decided to take the initiative and sent the pope a lengthy appeal. He did not go so far as to call for a public papal protest, but he urged that a Vatican brief be presented to the German ambassador calling on his government to end its homicidal campaign against Italy's Jews. In mid-December 1943 the Jesuit prepared a draft of the brief.

While the appeal was to be made on behalf of Italy's Jews, it did not stray from the church's longtime teachings: Jews should be kept separate from Christians and prevented from acquiring positions of social influence. However, it was not permissible to physically harm them. In pleading to have the deportations and murders stopped, Tacchi Venturi argued that Mussolini's racial laws, instituted five years earlier, had successfully kept the Jews in their proper place, and as a result there was no need for these new measures. Jews did not present the grounds for serious government concern in Italy that they did elsewhere. Nor had they engendered the same hostility from the "Aryan" population that they did in other countries. This was partly, he argued, because there were so few Jews in Italy and partly because so many of them had married Christians. The new laws confining Italy's Jews to concentration camps offended the "good sense of the Italian people," who believed that "the racial laws enacted by the Fascist Government against the Jews five years ago are sufficient to contain the tiny Jewish minority within the proper boundaries."

"For these reasons," wrote the pope's Jesuit envoy, "one trusts that the German Government will want to desist from the deportation of the Jews, whether those done *en masse,* as happened last October, or those done individually." He returned again to his earlier argument: "The above-mentioned racial laws of 1938, rigorously observed, already took care of the indisputable difficulties caused by Judaism when it comes to dominate or to enjoy much reputation in a nation. But as this is not the case in Italy at the moment, one does not understand why . . . there was a need to return to a question that Mussolini's government considered already taken care of."

Tacchi Venturi suggested the pope might conclude the message to the German government with a threat to speak out, proposing the following wording: "If the harsh measures are renewed against the small Jewish minority, which includes a notable number of members of the Catholic religion"—that is, Jews who had converted to Catholicism—"how will the Church remain silent and not express great sorrow for the fate of men and women not guilty of any crime . . . without failing in its divine mission, its compassion, and all of its maternal care?"[32]

On December 19, Cardinal Maglione sent Tacchi Venturi's text to Monsignor Angelo Dell'Acqua to get his opinion. Whether the Jesuit's plea to the pope had first been read by the pontiff and it was the pope himself who asked to have it sent to Dell'Acqua, or whether Maglione thought it best to have the opinion of the office's resident expert on Jewish questions before showing it to the pope remains unknown. Dell'Acqua would later become cardinal vicar of Rome, but at the time he was a forty-year-old staff member of the Secretariat of State. He had earned the pope's confidence in questions regarding Jews.

A month earlier, Dell'Acqua had been called upon to advise the pope on how to respond to a plea from the bishop of Trieste in the wake of the German occupation of that city and the beginning of its roundup of the city's sizable Jewish population, one of Italy's largest, numbering six thousand at the start of the war. "I do not share the thought of Monsignor bishop of Trieste that the current situation in Venezia Giulia [the region in which Trieste is located] favors such an official intervention by the Holy See in favor of the Jews. . . . An official intervention by the Holy See might confirm the Nazi leaders in the false idea, that is, that the Holy See is in agreement with international Jewry, which preaches the necessity of the destruction, or virtual distruction of the German people."[33]

Dell'Acqua sent back a lengthy critique of Father Tacchi Venturi's proposed plea on behalf of Italy's Jews two days after receiving it. He advised against the protest, not least because, in his view, the Jesuit's text was overly sympathetic to Jews: "The persecution of the Jews that the Holy See deplores is one thing, especially when it is conducted with certain methods, but quite another thing is to distrust the Jews' influence, because this can certainly be opportune." Indeed, the

Vatican-overseen Jesuit journal, *La Civiltà Cattolica,* had been repeatedly warning of the need for governments to introduce laws to restrict the rights of the Jews in order to protect Christian society from their depredations. How could the Vatican justify taking such a great interest in the Jews, asked Dell'Acqua, when it had not complained about the violence Germany had directed against "Aryan people who have professed the Catholic religion from birth"?

Dell'Acqua also argued that the Vatican should not, as the proposed statement did, deny there had long existed in Italy an "Aryan environment" that was hostile to the Jews. After all, he wrote, "in the history of Rome there is no lack of measures adopted by the Pontiffs to limit the Jews' influence." He also appealed to the pope's eagerness to do nothing to antagonize the Germans. "In the Note the mistreatment that the Germans are alleged to subject the Jews to is highlighted. It may even be true, but is it the case that one should say it so openly in a Note?"

Dell'Acqua listed twelve objections in all to Tacchi Venturi's draft before reaching his conclusion. It was inadvisable to send off such a note, even if it was only delivered orally to the German ambassador. It

General Graziani with Hitler and Mussolini, E. Prussia, July 20, 1944

would be better simply to have a more informal word with Weizsäcker, "recommending to him that the already serious situation of the Jews not be worsened." One might also ask someone to have "a little word with Marshal Graziani so that the Republican Government proceeds prudently." The monsignor ended his recommendations with a final suggestion, reflecting his irritation at the Jews' constant appeals for the pope's help. "It is also necessary to let the Jewish *Signori* know that they should speak a little less and act with great prudence."[34]

Weighing the memos for and against making such an appeal to the German ambassador, the pope, siding with Dell'Acqua, decided to stay the course. He might have been influenced in this decision by news he had recently received.[35] Mussolini had ordered that "mixed families" be exempted from the order to deport all Jews, and it seemed that other "modifications" of a similar kind were under study. There the matter rested. Over the next several months hundreds more Jews from Rome would be captured and sent north to their deaths, and thousands more from northern Italy. The pope judged it best to say nothing.[36]

TREASON

As 1944 dawned, Galeazzo Ciano, Mussolini's son-in-law, longtime foreign minister and, until recently, ambassador to the pope, sat in a cold prison cell in Verona, charged with treason.

When the king removed the dictator from power on July 25, 1943, Ciano had found himself in an impossible position. Fearing arrest by the new Italian government, several Fascist leaders had fled to Germany, Farinacci among them. But for those like Ciano whom the Germans were blaming for the Duce's fall, Germany seemed a risky destination. By the end of July, Ciano was under house arrest, the entrance to his home guarded by carabinieri. His wife, Edda, contacted the Vatican requesting refuge for the family, but given the delicate moment, the pope did not want to be seen shielding the person who was among the most reviled men in Italy.

Dino Alfieri, one of the Fascist leaders still free in Rome, had come to visit Ciano at his home confinement. Ciano embraced his old comrade and, speaking of his imprisoned father-in-law, burst into sobs: "He was a great man, a real genius." Then Edda came into the room. She looked, recalled Alfieri, "pallid, emaciated, her lips pale, her large, luminous eyes sunken and veiled with sadness. . . . For the first time she appeared to me a simple and poor woman." Although for years the couple had lived largely separate lives, in the months that followed Edda would become her husband's tenacious defender.[1]

Spain had been a more appealing destination for Mussolini's son-in-law, given the role he played in supporting Franco's successful revolt. The problem was how to get there. In August, desperate for a way out, he made what would prove to be a fatal mistake, using German contacts to arrange an escape for him and his family. Hitler, whose approval was necessary for the plan, had great affection for Edda but none for her husband. Initially he gave approval only for Edda and her children to come to Germany, apparently thinking she would be happy to free herself of the man who had betrayed her father. When told she insisted on having her husband with her, the Führer reluctantly agreed.

Their escape was dramatic. Early on the morning of August 27, Edda dressed her children in a double set of clothes. Leading them out of their home in the fashionable Parioli residential neighborhood in the north of the city, she told them, "Pretend we're going for a walk." At a nearby piazza, a black American car with two Germans inside pulled up. Edda and the children climbed in, and they sped off. At the same time, Ciano, wearing large, tinted glasses, stepped out of the door to his building and, before the carabinieri had a chance to react, jumped into a slowly moving car that came by with its back door open. There is some question as to whether the police on duty were bribed by the Germans to allow Ciano to get away. Ciano's biographer, Eugenio Di Rienzo, recently advanced an alternative theory, speculating that Italian authorities were complicit in Ciano's escape. He theorized that Italy's new leaders feared that if the Allies got their hands on him, he would provide detailed evidence of the connivance of the Vatican and the monarchy in the Fascist regime.[2]

The two cars carrying the Ciano family pulled into a Roman courtyard, where a closed Wehrmacht truck waited to take them to Rome's airport. There a Junkers 52 military plane with engines running awaited them, bound for Munich. Shortly after arriving in Germany, Ciano acquired a fake moustache and glasses along with a passport identifying him as an Argentinian of Italian origin. Edda's name, according to her new passport, was Margaret Smith, an Englishwoman born in Shanghai.

Mussolini arrived in Germany two weeks after his daughter. Hitler, meeting the Duce for the first time after his rescue, told him, "I don't doubt that you will agree with me in believing that one of the first acts of the new [Italian] government will have to be death sentences for the traitors of the Grand Council. I judge Count Ciano four times a traitor: traitor to his country, traitor to fascism, traitor to the alliance with Germany, traitor to his family."[3] It would be best, added the Führer, for the death sentence to be carried out in Italy. The prospect of executing his grandchildren's father sickened the Duce, but Hitler was unbending.

In Munich on October 19, 1943, ten men of the SS escorted Ciano onto a plane bound for Verona. Members of Mussolini's Italian Social Republic militia met him on his arrival. Informing Ciano he was under arrest, they drove him to a sixteenth-century monastery that had been converted into a prison. There cells had been prepared for each of the men who had voted against Mussolini at the July 24 Grand Council meeting. Subject to a humiliating body search, he was allowed to keep only the small icon of the Madonna he always carried with him and photographs of Edda and his children. He would spend the next weeks awaiting a trial that, he knew, could have only one result.[4]

Edda returned to Italy with her children to plead with her father. She threatened him as well, saying that if the sentence were carried out she would release Ciano's diary, filled with embarrassing revelations. Despairing at his own powerlessness and perhaps sensing that his own end could not be far off, Mussolini told her the matter was no longer in his control. The die-hard Fascists who now dominated the republican government viewed Ciano as a traitor and wanted his head. Were he to try to intervene on his son-in-law's behalf, he would appear unforgivably weak both in the eyes of his own Fascist entourage and in those of the Germans on whom he depended. Edda remained nearby, continuing her fight while friends arranged to smuggle her three children across the Swiss border. On the night of December 12, her middle child Raimonda's tenth birthday, the children made their escape, spending their first night in Switzerland in the residence of the bishop of Lugano.

After being allowed to visit her husband in his jail cell only once and fruitlessly repeating her threats to release his diary, Edda made

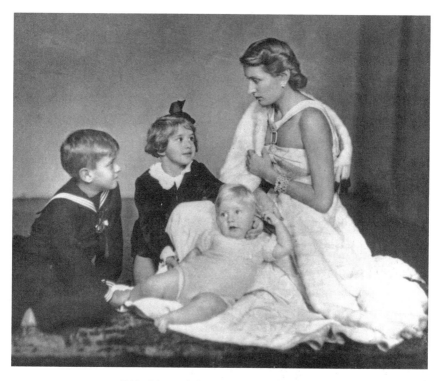

Edda Mussolini with her children, 1938

plans to join her children in Switzerland. The Germans were alarmed. On January 9, 1944, the SS in Verona received a telegram with new instructions: "Watch closely the daughter of Mr. Mayer [the German code name for Mussolini]. She can move and go where she wants, but she is not to put a foot in Switzerland. An eventual attempt by her to leave must be impeded even by force. The diaries of the son-in-law of Mr. Mayer are still to be found. Search for them." On that same night, despite the efforts of the SS to find her, Edda slipped across the Swiss border.[5]

On January 10, following a three-day trial conducted by a special court of the Italian Social Republic in a riverside fortress in Verona, Ciano was found guilty of treason. He had conspired, the court ruled, to remove Mussolini from power. Along with four other members of the Grand Council who had voted against Mussolini at that fateful Grand Council session, he was sentenced to death by firing squad.

Mussolini learned of the verdict at his residence on Lake Garda. He took the news calmly, at least on the surface, but showed signs of not having slept well over the previous nights. His stomach pains, which had earlier subsided, had now returned.

That evening the prison chaplain came to visit the condemned men, who asked to make Confession and take Communion. He remained there through the night as the men reminisced about their lives and their families. At six A.M., the eldest of the condemned men, Marshal Emilio De Bono, one of the four leaders of the Fascist March on Rome that had brought Mussolini to power in 1922, hearing the chiming of the bell from the nearby convent, stood up. They should all, he proposed, offer a final earthly salute to the Madonna, whom they would next see in Paradise. Led responsively by the priest, they recited the Angelus:

The Angel of the Lord declared unto Mary,

And she conceived of the Holy Spirit.

Hail Mary, full of grace. . . .[6]

Soon the men were placed in a police van and driven to a nearby fort. The seventy-seven-year-old Marshal De Bono, who had led the initial invasion of Ethiopia in 1935, stepped out of the police van first. Easily identifiable by his trademark white goatee, he wore a dark suit and black hat. He was followed by Ciano, who wore a gray overcoat against the cold. The men were marched into a nearby field where, blindfolded, they were made to sit backward on rickety wooden chairs, their hands tied behind their backs. The makeshift firing squad lined up in two rows. Five bullets struck Ciano in his back, but he did not die right away. Others also writhed on the ground, their chairs tipped over, and so the firing squad was ordered to aim another round into their bleeding bodies. Ciano still somehow managed to murmur, "Oh, help, help!" The squad's commander walked up to him, revolver in hand, and fired a bullet into his head. "It was like the slaughtering of pigs," recalled a German diplomat present at the execution.[7]

ON THE FIRST DAY of 1944 the pope learned that Mussolini's government wanted to replace Francesco Babuscio, responsible for Italy's em-

Execution of Galeazzo Ciano, Verona, January 11, 1944

bassy to the Holy See. For months, Babuscio had remained in his uncomfortably ambiguous position, for it was unclear which of Italy's two competing governments he represented. In December, when he succeeded in making his first secret contact with the royal government in the south, he had left the embassy building in Rome and taken up residence in Vatican City. The move did not go over well with the Fascist government, which informed him he was being recalled. To avoid a direct confrontation with the Vatican, he was told to go on "medical" leave.[8]

The pope, not wanting to force the issue of which Italian government Rome's embassy to the Vatican represented, had a Vatican Secretariat of State staff member, Monsignor Testa, speak with a foreign service officer still at his post in Rome. "I just met again with our friend the Monsignor [Testa]," the ministry official reported. "He informed me that the Holy Father wanted us to be told 'I pray that they not insist on taking a formal position.'"[9]

A few days later, the Fascist government sent the pope its response: "In conformity with the specific instructions given by the Head of the

Government, the Ministry of Foreign Affairs has always taken care after September 8 to avoid any attitude that might bring attention to the question of the relations between the Republican Government and the Vatican." It was Babuscio who had compromised this delicate balance by abandoning the embassy and moving into Vatican City.

Monsignor Testa suggested that Babuscio be asked to give up his position "for that well-being of the Holy See that he always says he wants to serve. He could . . . find a pretext to suspend his functions." If Babuscio presented the decision as his own, suggested the monsignor, "the Holy See would avoid the danger of a clamorous break with the Republican Government, as it would also avoid that of a [formal] recognition of that same Government." Babuscio, however, refused to step down. In the end, it was Mussolini's government that backed off, judging it best to leave the current ambiguous situation as it was. Babuscio would spend the next months in his new lodgings in Vatican City.[10]

IN THE WAKE OF Ciano's execution, Mussolini was feeling ever more miserable. Trying to save the father of his grandchildren would have made him look weak to his Fascist supporters and his German allies, but allowing his daughter's husband to be executed as a traitor was humiliating as well. Now Edda, his favorite child, the one most like him in so many ways, was refusing to speak to him and had, embarrassingly, fled to Switzerland.

Clara, for whom Edda had long been an enemy, did what she could to revive her lover's spirits. He needed, she told him, to act like a "real dictator" again.[11] She showered "Ben" with detailed political advice as well, regularly mixing in reproaches for his failure to fully appreciate her. Among the targets of her tirades, both Jews and "plutocrats" featured prominently. As two historians who studied her closely observed, "If she were not a woman, Clara would be the 'new man' imagined by fascism to regenerate Italians." Indeed, Clara kept urging Mussolini to act tougher, to whip Italians into proper Fascist shape, and to assert himself more forcefully with Hitler, who, she assured him, was his great supporter and friend.[12]

An indication of Mussolini's state of mind at the time, or at least his daughter's view of it, is found in a U.S. intelligence service memo from Switzerland written after Edda's arrival there. She is reported to have said that her father "is convinced that everything is over and that nothing more is to be done. He is a prisoner of the Germans and of the neo-Fascists, and the latter have no love for him. His authority is dead. He is without strength, sad, sick, and eaten by bitterness at finding himself abandoned even by his closest friends."[13]

Some confirmation of this view comes from a letter Mussolini wrote Clara on February 4: "I am a kind of *podestà* of a large town with highly limited powers. A State without arms is merely a parody. The Pope is infinitely better armed that I am. The Palatine Guard, according to the newspapers, while being the refuge of all the draft-dodging nobility, has its own arms and light artillery. I still have nothing. . . . Yes, I am the 'living corpse.' . . . I am a living, ridiculous corpse. Ridiculous above all."[14]

Later that month Mussolini again gave vent to the self-pity that would come through in many of his letters to Clara in these months of his puppet government. Ever since that fateful Grand Council meeting the previous July, he wrote, "I am dead. . . . My authority lies more in tatters by the day. My prestige too. I used to be someone. Even if they had hung me from the Tower of London, I would have been someone. Now I am nothing. . . . The only sector over which I rule is the mortuary police." In showering Clara with laments of this kind, the fallen dictator knew he would trigger new attempts to bolster his spirits, as she did that day in a typical effort to waken him from his stupor: "Lift off this gloom that envelops you, get back your energy and your vibrancy, your will. It is not events that ought to dominate you, but you the events."[15]

Such was the Duce's desperation that he enlisted a priest, Father Giusto Pancino, to send his daughter a message. Pancino had gotten to know Edda in the weeks she had spent as a nurse with the Italian troops in Albania, where he was then serving as a chaplain. Mussolini sought to win back her affection, worried that in the wake of her husband's execution she now despised him. To locate Edda and accomplish his mission, the priest would need to get help from the Vatican, and so the priest headed not north but south to Rome.[16]

Succeeding in arranging a meeting with Monsignor Tardini, Father Pancino had a dramatic story to tell. Mussolini wanted to convince Edda he was not responsible for her husband's death, that it was the Germans' fault. He said he had tried to have his son-in-law pardoned, but the Germans had delayed word of his decision until too late. While the Duce recalled these events, said Father Pancino, he had begun to cry. The priest also had something he wanted to bring Edda, the little Christian devotional volume, *The Imitation of Christ,* that her husband, the priest said, had always carried with him. Indeed, Ciano had had it with him at the time of his death. The priest asked Tardini for a letter of introduction to the nuncio in Bern, whose contacts would enable him to find Edda.

Tardini agreed to do what he could and gave Pancino an embossed card of the Vatican Secretariat of State with a simple, if purposely vague, message for the nuncio: "The priest Giusto Pancino is coming to Switzerland for a work of charity, which he will explain to you orally. Try to help him."

Tardini took advantage of the priest's visit to ask him to bring Mussolini a message on his way to Switzerland: He wanted Mussolini to know that the Holy See, too, had been concerned for Edda's welfare. They knew she had succeeded in entering Switzerland but did not know her exact address. He also wanted Mussolini to know that the Vatican had taken an interest in the welfare of his other family members in the weeks following his arrest the previous summer. But while apparently trying to win goodwill from Mussolini, Tardini could not resist adding a barb. Tell him, said the monsignor, that if he had only heeded Pius XI's warning, when the previous pope urged him not to tie Italy's fate to the Nazis, the country would not now find itself in such a sad situation. And while Mussolini might be able to convince his daughter he was not to blame for her husband's execution, Tardini added, no one else in Italy would believe it.[17]

Thanks to the help of Monsignor Tardini and Nuncio Bernardini in Switzerland, Father Pancino was able to complete his mission for the Duce. Mussolini's goal in sending him to Switzerland, Pancino told the nuncio, was to achieve a "rapprochement" with his daughter who, "following the death of her husband, nourishes a hatred for all of her family." In the end, the mission would bring the fallen Duce little satisfaction. Edda took advantage of the visit to give the priest a letter for her mother-in-law, asking her to arrange to have her son buried near his father's tomb and to ensure that fresh flowers be regularly placed there. The message she asked the priest to give her father was brief: "Tell him that I feel sorry for him and that he should leave the position he holds which is without either any authority or prestige."[18]

ON JANUARY 21, 1944, a new Allied assault began. Twenty-eight destroyers, 103 other warships, and 241 landing craft left Naples harbor headed north and arrived at Anzio beachhead, sixty kilometers south of Rome, shortly after midnight. Allied planes flew 1,200 sorties to protect the landing beaches as over 36,000 men and 3,000 vehicles made their way onto shore that first day. The Germans were initially caught off guard, the area lightly defended. Some say that if the Allies had been more aggressive, they could have quickly seized the Alban Hills to the north, cut off the German lines, and then rapidly driven the Germans from Rome. But the commander was cautious, finding it hard to believe the area was as poorly defended as it was. While the Allied troops dug in at the beachhead over the next two days, the Germans rushed in reinforcements, taking up positions in the hills overlooking Anzio and aiming their deadly artillery fire on the troops below. Seven thousand Allied bodies would soon fill a large cemetery adjacent to the beach, its vast sea of white crosses, sprinkled with stars of David, still attracting visitors today.[19]

Although the Anzio landing offered the Vatican hope that Rome might soon be liberated, it also brought with it a variety of fears. Most unwelcome was the Allies' plea that the Romans do all they could to weaken the German occupation army: "The hour has arrived for Rome and all Italians to fight in every possible way with all forces. . . . Sabotage the enemy. Block his roads of retreat. Destroy his communications. . . . Strike against him everywhere continuing the fight indefatigably." As the men of the Vatican kept assuring the German occupiers, they were urging the Italians to reject the Allies' entreaties, arguing that such resistance led only to more violence. Whether they were influenced by the church's advice or simply because of their own inclinations, only a modest number of brave Romans would be involved in the resistance that the Allies were recommending, and of the insurrection that the Allies hoped to trigger, there was no sign.[20]

The Allied advance raised another fear in the pope's mind. Four days after the landing at Anzio, he had Cardinal Maglione give Osborne an urgent message. The British envoy in turn sent it on the same day to London: "Cardinal Secretary of State sent for me today to say that the Pope hoped that no Allied coloured troops would be amongst the small number that might be garrisoned at Rome after the occupation. He hastened to add that the Holy See did not draw colour line but it was hoped that it would be found possible to meet this request." That the pope's appeal attracted high-level attention we know from the records of the Foreign Office: it reached Foreign Secretary Anthony Eden. He then sent a copy to Lord Halifax, the British ambassador in Washington, with the request to alert the Americans.[21]

The situation of Italy's Jews, already dire, was becoming worse, as increasing numbers were being rounded up, in no small part by Italian police and militias, and sent north to the Nazi death camps. In February the recently appointed head of Rome's police, Pietro Caruso, launched a new Jew-hunt that would ensnare several hundred victims. They could take little comfort from the fact that in January Badoglio's government in the south had finally gotten around to striking down the racial laws.[22]

It was a cold winter. Lacking coal, the marble-floored halls of the Vatican were frigid, and on rainy days life there was miserable. "We are dying of cold," complained the Brazilian ambassador. The pope thought it important that he should suffer along with the rest of Rome, and so he forbade the use of heaters. When he was out of his rooms, Sister Pascalina, observing that the pope's slender hands seemed practically frozen, would sometimes sneak in an electric stove, taking care to remove it before he returned. Outside the walls of the Vatican, food was critically short; the Fascist police scoured the streets searching for those suspected of conspiring against the regime; and German soldiers dragooned men to send north for forced labor. "To add to these immediate troubles," Osborne reported to London in early February, "hopes of early relief by Allied landing forces are weakening."[23]

As the front neared Rome, Allied planes began attacking German convoys in the Alban Hills to the south of the city. On February 1 one of the bombs landed on a convent adjacent to the papal villa at Castel Gandolfo, killing seventeen nuns. The next day bombs fell inside the papal estate itself, causing another fatality. It seemed a miracle that more were not killed, as thousands had taken refuge in and around the papal grounds, thinking themselves safe from Allied and German attack. That good fortune ran out on February 11, when a third Allied bombing hit the papal property, killing hundreds of refugees. Osborne had alerted London immediately after the first bombing and urged that the military avoid future such incidents. Ian Eaker, the British general in charge of the air assault, responded to the Foreign Office justifying the campaign. "This area," he wrote the day after the first attack, "is now in the midst of the battle area and contains essential road communications. I have discussed this matter with Alexander★ who feels that we cannot prejudice the success of the Rome operations by providing in the middle of the battle a sanctuary for the opposing Germans."[24]

ON THE NIGHT OF February 3, Republican Fascist policemen dressed in civilian clothes surrounded the Basilica of St. Paul Outside the

---

★ General Harold Alexander was commander of the British forces trying to force their way up the peninsula.

Walls, located near the Tiber River in the southern part of the city. Originally built in the fourth century as a shrine over the grave of Saint Paul, it was one of Rome's four major basilicas, exceeded in size only by St. Peter's. At eleven-thirty P.M., while most inside slept, an advance party climbed the wall at the back of the complex and dropped into the garden below. The Lateran Accords had granted the basilica extraterritorial status, and it was protected by members of the Palatine Guard. On seeing the first black-shirted figures clambering over the wall, a guardsman fired his rifle into the air and ran to alert his sergeant. When the sergeant confronted the intruders, they quickly disarmed him.

At the same time, the bell inside the front entrance of the basilica began to ring, and the porter came to the door. Without opening it, he asked who was there. A voice responded that they were two monks from Florence seeking shelter for the night. When, after a moment's hesitation, the porter unlatched the door, a crowd of pistol-wielding men burst in, one of them exclaiming, enigmatically, "We know everything!" Throwing another Palatine Guard to the ground and taking his rifle, the men, now a hundred strong, began banging on the doors where people slept. Striking some of the refugees in the stomach with the butts of their rifles, firing into the air to intimidate them further, and roughing up others with their fists, they herded their terrorized victims into two large rooms for interrogation, while hurling insults at the monks who tried to block their way. Squad members tore through the refugees' belongings, eagerly dividing up their booty, from watches and coats to sugar and coffee.

"You've disgraced your dignity as a priest," one of the policemen told the Benedictine abbot in charge of the basilica, "hiding Jews, draft dodgers and military officers, allowing subversive newspapers to circulate." When, many hours later, the intruders left, they led out scores of people who had been hiding there. Some were Jews, many others were men seeking to escape service in the Fascist army, and one, their prize catch, was an Italian air force general unsuccessfully disguised as a monk.

Present for the whole operation, although trying to remain at a comfortable distance from the scene, was Rome's chief of police, Pietro Caruso. The infamous Pietro Koch, the man who ran the show, was inside the basilica directing the action. Ardent Fascist and leader of a violent squad that specialized in intimidation, torture, and murder, Koch was known for the special delight he took in helping the Germans round up Italy's Jews.[25]

Learning early that morning of the assault on the basilica, the pope was outraged. The Vatican Secretariat of State staff worked all day on a protest note to give the German ambassador. At eight-thirty P.M. Father Pfeiffer, the Vatican's intermediary with the German military authorities, ever eager to smooth relations, telephoned the Secretariat of State office. The German military command denied having anything to do with the raid, he told them. Indeed, they were indignant at the very suggestion and speculated that the desecration of the basilica might well have been an act of sabotage aimed at discrediting them.[26]

The next morning Cardinal Maglione met with the pope to review the final draft of the letter of protest for the German ambassador. They also reviewed statements on the basilica assault to be published in *L'Osservatore Romano,* broadcast on Vatican radio, and sent to the members of the foreign diplomatic corps at the Vatican. Shortly after noon Ambassador Weizsäcker arrived. He insisted the Germans had known nothing about the assault on the basilica, saying it was all the work of the Italian republican police. He cautioned the cardinal against putting out any statement on what had happened. It might, he feared, leave the impression the Germans bore some responsibility for the attack.[27]

Maglione found himself on the defensive. If anyone were mistakenly to interpret the planned statement on the invasion of the basilica as casting aspersions on the Germans, he told the ambassador, "I would be ready to offer my apologies. . . . But I don't believe I have been unclear, and I am sure I have not allowed responsibility for what happened to be attributed to the Germans, even though I was earlier informed that a certain Koch, who accompanied Police Chief Caruso in the much deplored undertaking, had stated in the presence of both Caruso himself and Vatican functionaries that the German authorities were aware of it."

The cardinal then showed Weizsäcker the letter addressed to him that the pope had approved. It named Rome's police chief as leader of the expedition and made no mention of any German involvement. Nodding his approval, the ambassador nonetheless suggested it would be better if the cardinal did not insist that he take it. Now that he had read the letter, what was the point? It would only mean he would need to communicate it to Berlin, and this, he suggested, did not seem a good time to do anything that might upset the harmonious relations between the Vatican and the Reich.

Maglione agreed to bury the letter but asked that Weizsäcker note its request for the German authorities to reimburse the Vatican for the damage caused by the attack and to take steps to ensure that nothing like it happened again. Even admitting that Italians and not Germans were behind the assault, Germany, as the occupying power, was responsible for maintaining public order and ensuring that the Holy See's rights were respected.

Before Weizsäcker left, he made a request of his own. He wanted Maglione to tell the ambassadors from neutral countries that the Vatican thought the Germans had nothing to do with the raid. "I have no problem doing so," the cardinal replied, "if Your Excellency agrees that I can inform them of the assurances you have given me." Weizsäcker signaled his approval.[28]

A few days later, the cardinal received a report confirming his suspicions. It came from Giovanni Gangemi, a general in the Fascist militia. Characterized in the Vatican's notes as a practicing Catholic and the nephew of a prominent nun, Gangemi told of a conversation he had with Pietro Caruso on the day following the basilica assault. The general knew Rome's police chief well, for Caruso had served under his command until only a few months earlier. When the general told Caruso how unfortunate he thought the attack on the basilica had been, Caruso gave this response:

> They made me. Already when I had barely been named police chief I was called by [Eugen] Dollmann [head of the German SS in Rome,] who instructed me, "You will keep this

position of trust if you know how to be remorseless toward the Jews, Communists, and deserters!" And a few days ago I was called by Dollmann again, who forced me and planned the details for raiding San Paolo and, to be sure of me and my agents, placed one of the men of his confidence, Koch, at my side.[29]

Although the pope had every reason to find this report credible, he deemed it unwise to call attention to German responsibility for the assault on the basilica.[30]

THE INVASION OF THE basilica left Pius XII nervous about the continued concealment in church institutions of Jews, Italian military officers, and others fleeing the Nazi and Fascist authorities.[31] Rome's major newspaper, *Il Messaggero,* had reported that those seized in the St. Paul raid included, in addition to the air force general, four other Italian military officers, nine Jews, two police functionaries, and forty-eight young men fleeing conscription.[32] Of special concern to the pope was the presence of such refugees in Vatican City itself. Shortly after the incursion, the three cardinals composing the Pontifical Commission overseeing Vatican City summoned the three canons of St. Peter's Basilica. The priests were known to be sheltering refugees at the Canonica, their residence adjacent to the basilica. Cardinal Rossi, known for his strong Fascist sympathies, presided over the commission. He ordered them to eject the refugees.

A few days later the papal chaplain prepared a report addressed to Pius XII listing the people sheltered at the canons' residence. He began with those he was housing in his own rooms: "Signor A. and his family . . . who, while of Catholic religion do not have what is necessary to be considered Aryan [i.e., they were baptized Jews] and for that reason are actively being sought to be sent to Poland." He listed by name eight other priests living at the Canonica who were sheltering refugees, some of whom were there "because lacking in the Aryan requisites," as he put it, and many others for political reasons or because they were fleeing military service. Last on his list, he noted: "On the ground floor with the custodians and the sacristans, various people have been taken in, mostly Jews who had been baptized several years earlier." In summary, he concluded, the priests were sheltering "about fifty individuals in grave danger of being arrested and shot or deported. Those facing the least danger have already spontaneously left; those remaining prefer to face any danger in the Canonica in the shadow of the Father's house to whom they address the anguished invocation: *salva nos, perimus!*"[33]

In his brief account of these events, Monsignor Tardini noted that the cardinal's order to evict the refugees had produced considerable unhappiness among Vatican clergy, and on February 10, at the gathering of cardinals at St. Peter's marking the fifth anniversary of Pius XI's death, a number of cardinals urged Cardinal Rossi and his two colleagues of the Pontifical Commission to relent. Rossi initially refused, saying he was merely implementing an order from a "higher" authority, the pope. According to Tardini, the other cardinals then prevailed on Cardinal Maglione to speak with Pius XII and convince him to rescind the order, which he had given in a moment of nervousness about the basilica raid. This, in the end, he did.[34]

ON FEBRUARY 12, 1944, bombs again began to fall on Rome, with an initial series of Allied bombing raids lasting three days. Again the local officials—most notably General Domenico Chirieleison, Italian commissioner for the administration of Rome—looked to the Vatican to use its influence to stop them. The pope once more had Cardinal Maglione appeal to Washington and London for an end to their assault on the world center of Catholicism. Although the pleas made repeated reference to Rome as an "open city," the pope knew it was being used as a major transit point for German troops. The fact that London was itself suffering from heavy German bombing raids at the time did nothing to help the pope win British sympathy for his plea.[35]

It was farther south that Allied bombs would cause the greatest damage to the church, and with it offer the Germans and their Fascist partners a propaganda bonanza. The Allied efforts to move up the peninsula had bogged down at what became known as the Gustav line, in the rugged Apennines between Naples and Rome. Taking advantage of the high ground, the Germans had repeatedly foiled Allied assaults, at great loss of life. At the center of the Gustav line stood the sixth-century mountaintop monastery of Montecassino. On February 15, suspecting that the Germans were using the ancient monastery as a base of military operations, American bombers dropped over a thou-

Abbey of Montecassino after the Allied bombing, 1944

sand tons of bombs on it. Little but rubble remained. As it turned out, the only people in the complex were monks and refugees. It had never been used by the German army.[36]

Cardinal Maglione summoned Harold Tittmann, the American envoy, and gave vent to his anger. The Germans had maintained their word and honored the sacred status of the priceless abbey, said the cardinal, and the church had repeatedly assured the Allies it harbored no German troops. The bombing was "a piece of gross stupidity."

"German propaganda is naturally making full use of this windfall," an American intelligence report noted six days after the bombing. "A raging campaign has been let loose." Osborne, unsettled by the disastrous attack, likewise recounted the propaganda use the Germans were making of it. The goal of "the present German Catholic campaign," he told the British Foreign Office, was to cast the Allies as the enemies of the Catholic Church and the Germans as its defenders. "Its primary purpose is to put the screws on the Vatican by means of pressure by the clergy and the faithful in the hope of inducing the Pope to declare himself publicly against Anglo-Saxon powers. Thereby the Germans hope to swing the Catholic vote in the US against the President in forthcoming elections and also to work on public opinion in Catholic Spain and South America."[37]

The men of Mussolini's Italian Social Republic were also quick to use the Montecassino bombing to cast themselves as defenders of Roman Catholicism against Anglican England and its allegedly Jewish-run American ally. A small group of Fascist prelates in the north of the country had been recruited to the cause and launched a new journal, *Crociata Italica* (Italian Crusade), edited by a priest. The bombing fit neatly into their narrative.

But most Catholic clergy were keeping their distance from Mussolini's Blackshirts. Indeed, many would aid the resistance. It was now clear to almost everyone that the rump Fascist government was going to be on the losing side of the war, while the violence of its goons was generating widespread anger.[38]

No man was more influential in the church hierarchy in northern Italy than the archbishop of Milan, Cardinal Schuster, and as the drama unfolded, he would play a highly visible role. An American intelligence report of late February offered a snapshot: "In Milan the Neo-Fascists are making desperate attempts to win over the clergy or to frighten them into collaboration, but with practically no success. The Cardinal Archbishop of Milan, Schuster, who at one time flirted with Fascism, has become soured now on Neo-Fascism, and the Catholic clergy among whom Fascist influence has been strong have now completely veered around."[39]

To say Schuster had "flirted with Fascism" was putting the matter rather delicately. Schuster had long been central to the Fascist regime's efforts to identify itself with the church in northern Italy, and the fact that he refused to bless the new republican regime sparked charges of betrayal among its leaders. In a front-page "Open Letter to His Excellency Cardinal I. Schuster," Farinacci shed his own crocodile tears. Even before Schuster had been named archbishop of Milan in 1929, wrote Farinacci, he had found him "close to my spirit as an Italian and as a fascist Catholic," pleased by the cardinal's "words of admiration for our Duce and for the work that fascism was doing." For many years subsequently, recalled Farinacci, his hopes had been fully realized by "your fascist activity, your participation in the most important [Fascist] ceremonies, your flights to visit our colonies, the pleasure of finding you in our midst." What could have happened to cause the archbishop to turn his back on Fascism? How could he have been won over by Roosevelt, who had revealed himself to have the soul of a Jew and had "betrayed the Pontiff notwithstanding his solemn promises, betrayed the Catholics of the whole world? Today he is destroying the Churches, the seminaries, the convents, the religious institutions, he is massacring the clergy, he is killing thousands of women and children." And how could it be, Farinacci asked the archbishop in his open letter, that "you are only concerned about threatening anathemas against those priests of *Crociata Italica* who want to save the Fatherland and save the Church from the Judaic and communist hordes?"[40]

A GRATIFYING
SIGHT

O N THE FIRST DAY OF MARCH 1944, A SOLITARY PLANE FLEW OVER
the Vatican and dropped six small bombs. Three months earlier
four bombs had struck Vatican City. While none of the bombs hit inside this time, a number exploded just outside its walls. "Anglo-Saxon
Bombs on Vatican City," read Farinacci's front-page headline in *Il Regime Fascista*.[1]

While the Allies blamed the Italian Fascists for the raid, it had been
an Allied plane that dropped the bombs. The American and British
chiefs of staff received the unwelcome report from British Royal Air
Force headquarters later in the month. Visibility had been poor that
night, and it added, in an apparent attempt at exculpation, "Captain of
aircraft was P/O [pilot officer] McAneny who is of Roman Catholic
faith."

What to do? By the time this report was received in late March
1944, the Allies had spent weeks denying responsibility. A flurry of
communication between London and Washington resulted in something of a compromise. In the future, they should immediately admit
when such mistakes were made. "Nevertheless," advised the British
chiefs of staff, "it would be unwise to admit the particular mistake . . .
gratuitously so long after the event. To do so would . . . invite the
enemy to meet any future denials with the rather awkward taunt 'wait
a month or two and they will admit it.'" The Allies never did admit

that it was their bombs that had come close to crashing through the roofs of St. Peter's Basilica and the Apostolic Palace that day.[2]

Two days after those bombs fell, the Allies resumed their large-scale air assaults on Rome. On March 3 American warplanes flew low over the city and, facing little enemy fire, bombed their targets, among them an ammunition train, triggering a series of explosions that could be heard for another hour. The U.S. intelligence report on the operation boasted of its "perfect accuracy." It expressed unhappiness over the Vatican newspaper's account of the attack, which "overlooks the fact that the town is shamelessly used by the Germans as their main center of communications for all their military transport." Although the bombing might have been accurate from the American military's perspective, it resulted in hundreds of civilian deaths and many homes destroyed. The American analyst's conclusion seems, in retrospect, to have been overly rosy: "Roman press attempts to gain a propaganda victory from the attack were meeting with no success" for "the Romans remain as usual completely indifferent; their main concern is always to get food and to avoid conscription."[3]

EAGER TO CELEBRATE THE fifth anniversary of his papal coronation on March 12, 1944, Pius XII decided to invite the faithful to St. Peter's Square and address them from his balcony. Neither the Allies nor the local Fascist officials were pleased to learn of the event. The day before, Rome's police chief warned that subversives were planning to take advantage of the crowd to provoke an anti-Fascist, anti-German demonstration. At the same time, the British envoy D'Arcy Osborne rebuffed the pope's request that the Allies promise not to bomb Rome that day. He sent his reply to Maglione's office:

> You should inform the Cardinal Secretary of State that we very much regret not to be able to give any assurance that Allied planes will not fly over Rome during the afternoon of March 12. You should make clear to His Eminence that we cannot accept

any responsibility for what could happen if large crowds assemble in the middle of an active war zone and that if the Pope goes ahead with his intention, it will be at his own risk and on his own responsibility.[4]

The pope was not to be dissuaded. Romans flocked to St. Peter's, as rumors spread that he was planning to use the occasion to make an important announcement. Perhaps he had succeeded in convincing the Allies to stop the bombings of their city or had arranged to have additional supplies of food brought in, or perhaps he had even convinced the Germans to end their roundup of men for forced labor. For many, amid the devastating bombings by the Allies and the depredations of the Germans and Fascists, the pope seemed their only possible savior.

A crowd of tens of thousands filled the piazza facing St. Peter's, enclosed by Bernini's colonnade. Their eyes were fixed on the balcony over the basilica's central door. In front of it stood a line of Palatine Guards, and near them a large contingent of priests and seminarians. In one of the loggias overlooking the piazza sat members of the Vatican diplomatic corps along with various dignitaries of the papal court. As they waited for the pope to emerge, the crowd sang sacred songs, their voices mixing with the pealing of the city's church bells, which rang nonstop for five minutes.

At exactly three-thirty P.M., the white-robed pontiff and his entourage stepped onto St. Peter's central balcony. After pausing to allow the applause and cheers that greeted him to subside, the pope began his speech. His first sentence, characteristically convoluted, was 116 words long:

> In the desolation that has deprived you of domestic happiness, you, beloved sons and daughters, whom the present calamities have forced to scatter, without a home, perhaps separated from one and another of your own family, often ignorant and roaming, without news of them, to whom your blood and love bind you all the more, worried for their fate, just as they are worried for yours; you, however, to whom faith points

to a heavenly Father, who has promised those who love him to turn all to the good, even the most oppressive and bitter things (cfr. Romans 8:28); you have come today, attracted and propelled by filial impulse, to receive from the Vicar of Christ a word of blessing and of comfort.

The pope continued at some length in the same vein, lamenting the people's suffering while expressing faith that the Lord would one day restore their happiness. That the pope had nothing new to tell the Romans that afternoon, no new grounds for hope, was profoundly demoralizing. But as he completed his remarks, and the choir sang the hymn "Christus vincit" (Christ conquers), cries of *Viva il Papa!* rose from the crowd. Police fears of possible unrest at the papal event turned out to be not altogether unfounded. Following the speech, some scuffles broke out in St. Peter's Square, while many from the disappointed crowd headed for the bridge over the Tiber to cross to the other side of the city. As they went, some hurled insults at a passing German car, while other brave souls handed out anti-German leaflets. Policemen shot their guns into the air to disperse the crowd and arrested several suspects before they succeeded in clearing the street.[5]

The German ambassador offered a glowing account of the pope's speech to Berlin, writing that "the Pope publicly denounced the Allied raids on Rome with unusual harshness. The crowd in St. Peter's Square applauded most wildly." Weizsäcker was also pleased to convey what he termed the pope's "grateful recognition of the aid provided by the German Command for Rome's food supply."

Indeed, there were signs that the Romans' attitudes toward the Allies were souring, as Osborne reported to London. The continued bombing raids, he wrote, were "slowly but surely turning Italian opinion against us. . . . The destruction of civil life and property is altogether disproportionate to military results obtained." All this "is leading the Italians to think that German occupation is almost a lesser evil, generally detested as the Germans are, than Anglo-Saxon liberation. . . . The Germans are effectively exploiting the bombing damage, especially in Rome." Making matters worse, thought the British envoy, Communist propaganda was becoming ever more effective, with its argument that only Russia's "people's army" was strong enough to defeat the German military without at the same time wreaking destruction on civilian populations. Osborne warned that, with Allied forces still bogged down south of Rome, "I fear it will crystalise in anti-Anglo-Saxon feeling almost comparable to the existing anti-German sentiment, while sympathy for Russia will correspondingly increase, to the advantage of Italian Communist party."[6]

As the front drew ever nearer, the pace of Allied bombings picked up. In all, before the Allies reached Rome, twenty-five bombing runs would leave more than 4,000 dead and 10,000 wounded, with 2,500 buildings destroyed or badly damaged. Even for those Romans whose homes remained standing, conditions were rapidly worsening, with water, gas, and electricity knocked out for prolonged periods and food scarce.

Eager to show their regard for the Vatican, as well as to burnish their image as cultured patrons of the arts, the German authorities enlisted the Vatican's help in a hurried effort to save Italy's artistic masterpieces from destruction. It was Buffarini who had proposed to Mussolini the previous month that they should work in cooperation with the Germans to send important art works to safety inside Vatican City. Nor was it only Rome's wealth of historic art that was at risk. The city now housed much more, including priceless works of art moved from the Montecassino abbey before its destruction and from museums in Naples, Milan, and other cities that had long been under Allied bombardment. German military convoys moved truckloads of art to safety in Vatican City.[7]

The pope continued to do what he could to convince the Allies to stop bombing Rome, calling on the Vatican's representatives abroad to enlist the local episcopate and loyal Catholics in each country to raise their voices in protest. Responding to the latest of these requests, Ireland's prime minister, Eamon de Valera, no friend of the British, denounced the Allied attacks. The chargé d'affaires of the Irish embassy to the Holy See sent Maglione a copy of the prime minister's protest and asked if the pope would like to see it published. The Irish leader, he said, would do whatever the pope wanted. Tardini's notes record the pope's instructions: "Respond: Thank you. If they want to publish it, go ahead. . . . I think that, given the importance the Irish have in the United States, and given the attachment they have to De Valera, the Irish Government could give special publicity to its Note in the United States. That you can say, but do not put it in writing."[8]

Amid the anger in the Vatican for the Allies' stepped-up bombing of Rome, President Roosevelt's mid-March response to the latest protests did nothing to win him friends there. In the margin of the printed text of the president's remarks, next to his assurance that "We have tried scrupulously and often at considerable sacrifice to spare religious and cultural monuments and we shall continue to do so," Monsignor Tardini scribbled his own comment: "Declarations: in large part false, untrustworthy in themselves, dangerous for the future." Roosevelt "tends to deny any responsibility and to open the way for the continual bombardment of Rome, following a system that is by now well known. . . . 1) exaggerate the military importance of Rome for the Germans . . . 2) place priority on so-called military exigencies, and 3) place all blame on Hitler and on the Germans."[9]

IF THERE WAS ANY chance Romans might view the German occupation as preferable to the treatment they were receiving from the Allies, the events of March 23 would have quickly put that to rest. An SS battalion, composed of men recruited from Italy's German-speaking Bolzano region bordering Austria, was marching through a narrow Roman street when partisans detonated explosives planted in a garbage bin, killing thirty-three of them. The Germans, who had no success finding the partisans involved in the attack, vowed to execute ten Italians for every SS member who had died, and Hitler himself ordered the executions to take place within twenty-four hours. The Germans hurriedly assembled the victims, selected for the most part from those they had already imprisoned in Rome, including seventy-seven Jews. While most of the non-Jewish victims had been jailed for anti-Fascist activities, the Jews had been arrested for being Jewish and, unlike the others, arrested in family groups. The youngest, Michele Di Veroli, had celebrated his fifteenth birthday only the month before. He was selected along with his father. Another family group of six included the oldest victim, Mosè Di Consiglio, age seventy-four. Among those with Mosè was his seventeen-year-old grandson, Franco. The SS herded those chosen into trucks and drove them to man-made caves on the outskirts of Rome, known as the Fosse Ardeatine. There the unfortunate victims were led in groups of five into the caves, where the Germans shot each one in the back of the head. Belatedly, the Germans realized they had brought 335 to the killing ground rather than the requisite 330, but rather than return the additional five to Rome, they murdered them as well. When the Germans were finished, they planted explosives in the caves to bury the bodies and conceal the scene of the crime.[10]

The pope had been notified of the German reprisal plan no later than ten A.M. that morning and, it appears, managed to get a few people whom the church favored taken off the list of those to be executed, each to be replaced with someone lacking such Vatican connections. Neither the pope nor anyone else at the Vatican raised a voice in protest. On the contrary, that evening the Vatican newspaper published a denunciation of the partisans' assault on the SS troops, admonishing the Romans not to engage in acts of violence against the occupiers. It was a message the Vatican would continue to repeat as long as the Germans remained in Rome.[11]

Over the following weeks, the anguished families of those murdered at the caves, unsure of what had happened to them, turned to the Vatican for help. A month after the killings, the pope had his secretary of state send an appeal to the German ambassador. It began by assuring Weizsäcker that the Holy See realized he bore no responsibility for what had taken place, yet it asked him to help answer the pleas of those who feared for the fate of their loved ones. While the ambassador sent the Vatican request on to Berlin, he would never reveal what had happened. The truth of the mass executions at the Fosse Ardeatine would come out only after the Allies had driven the Germans from the city.[12]

WEIZSÄCKER CONTINUED TO SEND Berlin reassuring accounts of the pope's cooperation. He claimed that Pius XII, consumed with fear that a Communist tide might sweep through Europe, was sympathetic to their cause. As Weizsäcker put it in a message on March 29, 1944, "The pope is working six days a week for Germany, on the seventh he prays for the Allies."[13]

The pope had been denouncing the Allies' bombing of Rome, but he knew the Germans were using the city as a major transit point for military operations. Worse, they were now using train lines that ran alongside Vatican City. In early April this prompted Cardinal Maglione to send the German ambassador a note. In the last few days, he complained, thirty-nine train cars containing explosives had stopped along the tracks of St. Peter's train station. In addition, four train cars containing antiaircraft artillery, guarded by German soldiers, had stopped on the track that linked that station to one inside Vatican City.

In an unusually frank note, Monsignor Tardini confided his discomfort at the position in which the Vatican now found itself. Allied bombs had recently destroyed Rome's Ostiense train station and in doing so caused the explosion of a trainload of weapons, yet the pope complained only of the destruction of churches and homes and offered no acknowledgment that the Allies were targeting military facilities. "We give the 'news' on Vatican Radio," Tardini wrote, "but only of the killing of civilians, without saying anything of the military objective hit. With this, is Vatican Radio truly remaining 'impartial'?"[14]

Five hundred kilometers to the north, Mussolini found himself in a quandary of a more domestic kind. Clara, his ever-faithful lover, was now lodged with her family in an estate along Lake Garda, twenty kilometers down the waterfront from Mussolini's lakeside villa. Rachele, with the help of her son Vittorio, was doing all she could to prevent her husband from seeing his young lover. In this she was helped by the hard-line Fascists who now populated the puppet government, for they viewed the affair as an embarrassing bourgeois scandal. Clara, frustrated but unbowed, kept up her stream of passionate letters, mixing protestations at her poor treatment with attempts to improve Mussolini's spirits and regular dollops of unsolicited political advice. In mid-April she sent "Ben" an image of her holy protector, Saint Rita. "I kept it in jail," she wrote him, "which is why it is so ragged because of the continual, insistent, devoted prayers to it, for the tears that fell on it during those long, anguished nights. . . . Don't lose it, love. . . . Keep it always, keep it dear to you as I kept it dear to me, and trust in Her miraculous help, for She is truly the Saint of the impossible." At the same time, she wrote of the birthday they might have been celebrating that month, reflecting on her one, ill-fated pregnancy: "Mine—ours—would now be a little over two years old, now three perhaps this month, being born in April! What bad and evil fortune! This joy too was denied to me, your child, made by you and me."[15]

As Mussolini prepared for a meeting with Hitler, his first since the founding of the Italian Social Republic several months earlier, Clara sent him a packet of materials, coupling detailed political advice with a photo of herself. She urged him to assert his "absolute parity" with the Führer. Since the last meeting of the two dictators, the war had turned further against them, as the Red Army drove the Wehrmacht out of much of the Russian land it had earlier occupied and was now in the process of pushing the Germans out of Crimea to the south. The likelihood that the Allies would soon attempt a major landing in France was becoming ever greater.

The meeting took place on April 22, 1944, in the grand ballroom of the Baroque Klessheim Castle just outside Salzburg, near Hitler's Berghof retreat. Mussolini knew it well, familiar with its eighteenth-century decor, its high mirrors and grand staircases, having had earlier meetings with his German comrade there. Speaking from a text he had prepared in German, Mussolini began by complaining about the poor conditions the six hundred thousand Italian troops faced in the prison camps the Germans had placed them in following the Italian armistice. He then protested the demand that the Italians provide yet more workers for Germany, saying it was unreasonable. It was important, too, he said, that Italians not think that his government was under German control.

Hitler had little patience for the Duce's arguments. "But what was this Fascism if it just melted like the snow?" asked the Führer. He rejected Mussolini's requests but did his best to project optimism, predicting that the alliance between the western Allies and the Soviet Union would soon come undone. At the meeting's end, Hitler decided it wise to conclude with a more inspiring message. Fascist Italy was his closest ally, he told his Italian partner, the regime closest in ideology to his own. The two of them needed to stand together still, for he and the Duce were the two most reviled men in the world. Germany and Italy had to win the war. If they did not, both countries and both peoples would perish.

Following the meetings, the two men posed amiably for the cameras. "This is no time for recriminations," Mussolini told his son Vittorio the next morning in explaining what had happened. "It appears that the secret weapons are now ready to be deployed. They are supposed to turn the situation around in our favor. I sensed much tension between the Nazi leaders and the generals. When things go wrong, the whole world is the same."[16]

When the Duce returned to Italy from the meeting, having failed to accomplish the goals Clara had set out for him, she wrote again, bewailing the death she envisioned awaited them, "buried under the wreckage caused by drunken negroes, Jews, plutocrats." Meanwhile, her mother, upset by signs that Mussolini's wife was poisoning him against Clara, wrote the Duce a letter of her own, accusing Rachele of "having entered a state of insanity with murderous ideas based on a senile postmenstrual phobia." Clara's twenty-one-year-old sister added her own letters of a similarly denunciatory kind to the beleaguered dictator. Nor was the correspondence one-way. In the nineteen months of the Italian Social Republic, Mussolini would write over three hundred letters to Clara.[17]

AS THE SPRING OF 1944 wore on, life in Rome was becoming ever grimmer. The German and Fascist police continued to raid homes in search of *partigiani,* the armed underground resistance fighters engaged in sporadic attacks on German troops and Fascist forces. They looked as well for men to send off to forced labor, shooting at those who tried to flee. A booming black market charged exorbitant prices for basic goods, including potable water, which was in short supply. With electricity and gas intermittent and coal lacking, women and children trudged into the nearby countryside to gather bundles of wood. They could not use their bicycles, as they had been forbidden since an incident in December when a partisan tossed a bomb from one and pedaled away. In January the Germans imposed a five P.M. curfew as collective punishment for another partisan attack in the city.[18]

Waiting in endless lines to get their meager hundred-gram daily portion of bread, the women of Rome were desperate to find enough food to feed their starving children. The city's walls were covered with the same message, painted in large letters: *VOGLIAMO PANE! PANE! PANE!* "We want bread!"[19] Worst off were the estimated two to three hundred thousand recent arrivals from outlying areas under bombardment who had flooded into Rome. Having no access to ration cards, they had little access to food.[20] But the situation of the native Romans was little better. In April a series of spontaneous assaults on bread stores, bakeries, and trucks taking food to German troops led to explosive skirmishes with the Fascist and German armed forces. The Roman police files for April were full of accounts of desperate women and their children raiding bakeries and food depositories, sometimes with the connivance of the proprietors. "At 6:30 A.M.," read one April 25 report, "about fifty women and children in the Tiburtina Terzo neighborhood tried to attack the bakeries of the zone, and, although contained by the Police Forces, succeeded nonetheless in seizing . . . four hundred kilograms of bread." A similar police file of a few days later, reporting on the situation in the Porta Pia neighborhood, recounted: "in via Nomentana 433, some hundreds of persons coming from the neighborhoods of the [city's] periphery assaulted the bakery of Luigi Franzoni, making off with bread, flour, and pasta totaling in all about 800 kilograms. With the arrival of police agents three persons were arrested."[21]

The Vatican organized a relief service in Rome amid the crisis, trucking in desperately needed food supplies. "Sixteen small Vatican vans carrying provisions are circulating through Rome," one police report recounted. Each bore the emblem of Vatican City on its sides. The author of the report, an officer of the Fascist government's police force in Rome, added a suggestion: "Why, in agreement with the German authorities, don't we see that at least two hundred such vans provide food to the city, with 'Italian Social Republic' written on its sides, to contrast with those of 'Vatican City'?"[22]

These Vatican efforts to bring food to Rome by ship and truck quickly became a source of conflict with the Allies, who made little effort in their air attacks to spare the Vatican's convoys. Responding to a Vatican request that Allied bombers steer clear of them, a British Air Ministry memo on April 21 explained: "The British and US Governments consider that the responsibility for supplying the population of Rome with food rests with the so-called Fascist Republican Authorities or their German masters. . . . His Majesty's Government and the US Government . . . regret that they are unable to accept the general proposal."[23]

Informed of the decision, Osborne sent a heated message to London: "It is going to cause an extremely painful impression if I have to tell the Pope that His Majesty's Government appreciates his desire to save Roman population from starvation but unfortunately 'for military reasons' they cannot give their assent to methods proposed." Rome's population, Osborne reported, was on the verge of starvation and already dependent on the food the Vatican had succeeded in bringing in. "Unless supplies of flour can reach the city by sea, in Vatican ships or otherwise, famine seems inevitable. . . . [U]nless we can within immediate future either ourselves provide for essential supply of flour to Rome or enable Vatican to do so we shall be inviting a catastrophe by which the sole beneficiaries will be the Germans."[24]

Further pleas to the Allies to permit the Vatican food convoys led to a top secret military memo from the head of the Allied air command. Issuing orders to avoid bombing convoys of trucks with Vatican markings, he wrote, "would result inevitably in hampering the efficiency of our action against enemy communications and probably in unnecessary loss of life to aircrews endeavoring to identify Papal vehicles." The Allies were in the process of besieging Rome by land from the south, by sea from the west, and by air from the north and east. In running regular food convoys to Rome, he wrote, "the Vatican . . . is surely performing an unneutral act since, in effect, it is working to defeat one of the recognized instruments of siege warfare, the starvation of the populace." It was an accepted principle of war, he argued, that the occupying military power is responsible for feeding the local population. If the Germans proved unable to do so, "it is surely not for us to help them by action which has for us the doubly deleterious effect of solving their difficulties in Rome and hampering our military actions designed to wrest Rome from their hold."[25]

THE GERMANS WERE MEANWHILE continuing their roundup of Rome's Jews. Since the initial SS seizure of more than a thousand of them the previous October 16, many hundreds more were wrested from their hiding places over the next months of German occupation. Roman Jews who survived tell of living in constant fear of having their hiding places revealed by their neighbors. Indeed, most were discovered only as a result of Roman informants who received hefty payments for turning in each Jew.[26]

In other parts of German-occupied Italy, thousands more Jews were seized in these months and deported to Nazi death camps. None were more visible or more vulnerable than the spiritual leaders of Italy's Jewish communities. Of twenty-one chief rabbis in the country, nine were sent off to their deaths at Auschwitz. In these months, the primary concentration camp to which captured Jews were first shipped was Fossoli, in the town of Carpi, near Modena. In theory under an Italian camp commander, it was in practice run by an SS officer. From Fossoli, the Jews would be periodically placed on trains bound for the death camps in Poland.

Some of the captives never made it that far. Pacifico Di Castro had not been at home in Rome the previous October 16 when the SS seized his wife and seven children and sent them to their deaths at Auschwitz.

Discovered later at his hiding place, he was sent to Fossoli. There, falling ill, he failed to perform a work assignment. A prison guard murdered him on the spot. A similar fate met a deaf elderly Jewish man at Fossoli, shot in the back of the head for his failure to respond "present" when his name was read at roll call.

Many of Italy's Jews sent to Fossoli seemed unaware of the fate that would meet them at the end of their train trips farther north. Such was the case of Tranquillo Sabatelli, his wife Enrica, and two of their four children. In order to avoid detection after escaping from the October 16 roundup in Rome, the family split up. Tranquillo, in hiding with one of his sons, was discovered, and the two were sent to Fossoli. There they discovered that his wife and their other son had previously been found out and sent to the concentration camp. Only their two daughters still remained hidden. On May 16, 1944, Tranquillo succeeded in sending a letter from Fossoli to the elder of the two, shortly before he, his wife, and his two sons were sent off to Auschwitz:

> *Dear daughter,*
>
> *It's papa who writes you from Modena, because I was transferred here from Verona with Carlo and they brought us to the camp at Carpi where with surprise and sorrow I found Mamma and Mimmo. . . . Now we are all leaving in a convoy for unknown destination, who knows where, but I think far from Italy. We are going to find Uncle Angelino. [His brother, Angelo Sabatelo, was among those seized in Rome on October 16 and sent to Auschwitz, never to return.] I beg you, dear daughter, not to cry and to be strong, take good care of Mara [her young sister]. . . . We will return, I swear it to you, and I will always be close to mamma, as I am now. Be strong. . . . After the misfortune, the Lord God has at least wished to have the four of us united together.*[27]

In April, the plight of one of the country's more prominent Jews reached the pope. Mario Segrè was a world-renowned professor of Latin epigraphy. His mother and sister had been deported to Auschwitz and to their deaths in the October 16 roundup, but he, his wife, and one-year-old child had found refuge in Rome's Swedish Institute of

Classical Studies. Informed on by an Italian, they were arrested by two Italian policemen on April 5 and sent to Rome's Regina Coeli prison to await deportation.

The Brazilian embassy to the Holy See sent the Vatican Secretariat of State a letter informing them of the arrest. Monsignor Montini scribbled his own anguished note in its margin: "Professor Mario Segrè has already been transferred into the hands of the Germans! With his wife and boy!" Their only hope, thought the future pope, was to convince Weizsäcker to intervene, and he soon raised the matter with the German ambassador. We have no record of his reply, but it is easy to imagine that Weizsäcker took no responsibility for what his fellow Germans were doing as they sent thousands of Italy's Jews to their deaths. Professor Segrè, his wife, Noemi, and Marco, their toddler, were all sent to the Italian concentration camp at Fossoli, then on to Auschwitz where, on May 24, the day of their arrival, they were led in a line of their fellow Jews into the gas chamber.[28]

At the time, Vatican City itself was sheltering 160 refugees, many in the lodgings of the canons of St. Peter's, others elsewhere in that same building of the Canonica. Since the attempt made in February to have all the refugees evicted, which the pope was finally convinced to retract, the numbers had not grown dramatically. It seems that virtually all had found a way into Vatican City despite Vatican attempts to keep them out. Among them were various aristocrats, high-ranking Italian military officers, judges, and wealthy businessmen, all either wanted for their dissident activities or for escaping service in the Fascist military or government.

A June 2, 1944, Secretariat of State enumeration of the refugees in Vatican City counted among them "around forty . . . of the Jewish race, about fifteen of whom had been baptized." Indeed, some of the Jews had been baptized since their arrival. In theory, none of the refugees were supposed to be there. Some had entered in cars bearing diplomatic or Vatican City license plates, some had made their way from St. Peter's Basilica into the Canonica through the sacristy, the room that stores priestly vestments, and others, as a Secretariat of State report explained, employed "some little stratagem to elude the vigilance of the guards at the Vatican's entry gates." The only way any of them could be induced to leave, the report concluded, was by force, as all knew the fate that awaited them outside.[29]

THE ALLIED CONQUEST OF Rome was finally at hand. After having been pinned down for many months by German forces in the mountains south of Rome, and suffering tens of thousands of casualties, the Allied armies finally broke through in late May. On May 25 General Mark Clark, commander of the Fifth U.S. Army, riding in an open jeep, followed by two dozen war correspondents, rode up to the point in the Anzio-Terracina road where his troops had met up with the Allied troops that had been trapped at the Anzio beachhead. For the benefit of the cameras, the gum-chewing soldiers took off their helmets, grinned, and engaged in much backslapping. The time for the final assault on Rome was now at hand.[30]

With the pope's approval, Tardini summoned the German ambassador, informing him that the Vatican had sent new instructions to Rome's parish priests. They were to urge their parishioners to remain calm should German troops be leaving the city and Allied forces entering. They wanted to ensure there was no violence. At the same time, Tardini told the ambassador, it was crucial that the Germans do nothing that might provoke the populace. It was especially important for the Germans to exert their moderating influence on the Italian Fascists, "because they are the hardest and most violent."

Germany would continue to honor its commitment to protect Rome, replied Ambassador Weizsäcker, who met biweekly with General Kesselring, the German military commander in Italy. Tardini, relieved, replied that he personally was confident of the German government's "good intentions" and "likewise persuaded that Marshal Kesselring's tactics are aimed at saving Rome."[31]

The Germans' "good intentions" were less evident to the Romans as the first two days of June saw a frenetic effort by the German military to round up young men and women to send north for forced labor. A flood of anguished reports came to the Vatican reporting on German raids on Catholic shelters housing people whose homes had been destroyed. A June 1 note from a school attached to one such shelter reported that at one A.M. it had been surrounded by German soldiers, assisted by Italian police. Fortunately, "The boys all succeeded in fleeing thanks to the help of the Italian police. The girls, gathered in a large ground floor room, all escaped through a window." A priest from another such school reported that at two A.M. that same night it too had been surrounded by armed forces and five young women and four men were seized and placed on a truck. "I omit," wrote the priest, "describing the heart-rending scenes of the family members, especially of the mothers who saw their young daughters torn from them by force." In an effort to respond to these pleas for help, the Vatican Secretariat of State contacted Father Pancrazio Pfeiffer. The result is described in a note dated June 4: "Father Pancrazio communicates that the boys and girls that were taken by the Germans in these recent days are being sent to Germany to work. They will be well treated and well paid."[32]

After months of nervousness about the dangers Rome would face in the interval between the German retreat from the city and the Allies' arrival, in the end there proved to be neither any interval nor anything for the pope to worry about. The last days of May had seen intense fighting south of the city, as dense olive groves gave cover to Wehrmacht snipers, while German machine guns fired from six-foot-deep trenches, and snarls of barbed wire blocked the way of Allied troops. But the Allies now pushed quickly through the last line of German defenses. Allied bazooka teams demolished German tanks as Allied soldiers raked the German-infested hillside forests with their automatic guns. Engineers widened the roads, which were soon clogged with Allied tanks, artillery pieces, trucks, and jeeps. On June 3, as the Allies approached the Eternal City, Hitler himself ordered Marshal Kesselring to prevent Rome from becoming a combat zone. The Germans would do nothing to damage it as they retreated.[33]

That evening at eleven P.M. the German military authorities directed Weizsäcker to have the Vatican Secretariat of State transmit Germany's proposals for an evacuation of Rome to the Allies: They called on the Allies to recognize Rome as an open city, with no military forces permitted. In exchange they pledged to engage in no acts of destruction and do nothing to damage the city's water supply or electricity. The next morning Cardinal Maglione summoned Osborne to transmit the German offer. The British envoy did not hesitate to respond on behalf of his government: the proposal to declare Rome an open city could not be taken seriously.[34]

Beginning the night of June 2, an endless procession of German tanks, trucks, and vehicles of all kinds, heading northward, streamed through the city's streets. The Germans had requisitioned any conveyance that could be used for this purpose, from private cars to ox-driven carts. For many Romans, the sight they now witnessed was deeply gratifying. After nine months of living in fear of the Germans and their Italian Fascist allies, they looked on as the dispirited, weary German soldiers hustled northward in the face of the advancing Allied army. Monsignor Tardini observed, "The spectacle is depressing because one sees dejected, demoralized, exhausted soldiers . . . but it is also comforting because one sees the bullies humiliated, the violent ones crushed." Romans watched in silence, afraid that any sign of celebration would lead the Germans to open fire.[35]

On June 4, as the last of the retreating German soldiers were leaving, Allied troops began entering a city rejoicing at its liberation. There had been no battle in Rome, and what shots were heard were fired in the air in celebration. The next day at seven A.M. the pope appeared at the window of his fourth-floor apartment in the Apostolic Palace to bless the crowd. As he looked out, he was annoyed to see an American tank parked in St. Peter's Square below. Over the course of the morning, he would phone Tardini three times to get it removed.[36]

Cardinal Maglione summoned the chargé d'affaires of Italy's Vatican embassy. The cardinal had not been in good health for many months and in recent weeks had frequently been confined to bed. When Babuscio entered the cardinal's office, he could see he was suffering, a condition he blamed in part on having spent the past winter in Vatican palaces completely lacking in heat. Although unwell, the cardinal thought that now that the Germans had left Rome, the matter he wanted to raise could not be delayed. The pope was worried that, after what had transpired over the past months, the victors might not show the "sentiments of clemency" that they should in dealing with the Germans' Italian collaborators. He asked Babuscio to convey this request to the royal government.[37]

At six P.M. on June 6, a large crowd again gathered in St. Peter's Square in what *L'Osservatore Romano,* hailing the pope as the *Defensor Civitatis,* would describe as an expression of the Romans' gratitude to the pope for saving their city. It was a big day for the Allies as well, D-Day, for that morning the massive amphibious landing of Allied troops on the beaches of Normandy had taken place. Over the next days, they would begin their slow and costly battle to escape from their exposed positions and drive the Germans from France.

Cheered on by the crowd that day, the pontiff stepped out onto the loggia perched over the basilica's massive door and offered thanks to God for having inspired "both of the belligerent parties" to spare the Eternal City. "People credit Pope for saving Rome," explained Osborne in reporting the event to London, "though he had nothing to do with it." Had Hitler ordered the Germans to stand and fight, the Romans would not then be in the streets celebrating. But Osborne, in apparent contradiction, added that perhaps Hitler had spared the city in order to stay on Pius XII's good side, "in the hope of retaining the Pope's services as an advocate to mitigate the harshness of eventual armistice or peace terms." A more plausible case for the pope's role in sparing Rome is that both the Germans and the Allies were eager to cast themselves as defenders of Christianity. In this sense, perhaps the pope, or more precisely, the papacy, had indeed saved Rome.[38]

CHAPTER

3 8

MALEVOLENT REPORTS

EARLY ON THE BRIGHT, SUNLIT JUNE MORNING THE DAY BEFORE
Rome's liberation, General Mark Clark had set out from Anzio in
a convoy composed of two armored cars and six jeeps packed with
journalists. It had been almost eleven months since the first Allied
troops had landed in Sicily and begun their bloodsoaked march north,
months in which early hopes of the liberation of Rome had periodically flared up, only to be extinguished. Along its way through the
hills that morning, the convoy stopped to allow the general to pose for
photos next to a large blue and white street sign indicating the direction to "Roma." The festive atmosphere was brusquely interrupted,
though, as amid the clicking of the cameras came the sound of sniper
bullets. The general and his entourage dropped to the ground and
crawled down the hill, taking shelter in a thick-walled house. Only the
next day would the last of the snipers be cleared and the road to Rome
opened.[1]

In the days that followed, as smiling Allied troops pressed candies
into the hands of the throngs of Rome's children who greeted them
and the city rejoiced in its liberation, Allied dignitaries vied for the
honor of a private audience with the pope. General Clark was the first
of these to make his way to the Apostolic Palace, arriving in his jeep on
June 8, 1944, in St. Peter's Square still wearing his battle dress. In preparation for his meeting with Clark, the pope had notes drafted to guide
their discussion. While Tardini likely wrote down the first three of the

four points the pope wanted to make, thanking the Allies for sparing Rome from further damage, the pope added his own fourth point by hand: "We have been informed that the Communists are entering into many of the offices of government. That is cause of considerable worry. We feel that very little good can come of it. We hope that some restraint can be exercised over them."[2]

The next day brought the prime minister of New Zealand, whose troops had taken part in the drive toward Rome. Osborne, who accompanied him, had never seen the pope in such a good mood. The fact that the transition from German to Allied control had come without damage to the city and without any attacks on the church had been a great relief. Indeed, the Vatican had survived the German occupation of Rome relatively unscathed. While the Allies had mounted a propaganda barrage in the previous months claiming German persecution of the Vatican, it was largely just that, propaganda. In mid-June Robert Murphy, America's chief diplomat with the Allied army in Italy, reported back to Washington that "so far no evidence has been obtained in Rome of oppression and persecution of Roman Catholic Church there." What damage had been done was the result of Allied bombardment of the city.[3]

Among the Allied luminaries seeking an audience with Pius XII was Charles de Gaulle, head of the Free French forces, who met with the pope in late June. "It is the actions of the Soviets," recalled the French resistance leader following their conversation, "that fills the Holy Father with anxiety." The pope "believes that Christianity is destined to suffer very cruel ordeals and that only a close union of the European states inspired by Catholicism—Germany, France, Spain, Belgium, Portugal—will be able to curb the danger. I see that this is Pope Pius XII's big objective." A few days later, when De Gaulle returned to Allied headquarters in Algiers, he shared his impressions of the pope with Duff Cooper, the British emissary to De Gaulle's Free French Committee. "General de Gaulle told me last night," Duff Cooper reported to London, "that he had not been very favourably impressed by his interview with the Pope. It appears that his Holiness is mainly concerned at the present time with the sufferings which he fears may befall the unfortunate people of Germany."[4]

Although the pope had been relieved by the smooth transition to Allied control of Rome, he remained unhappy that the Allies had rejected his pleas that Rome be declared an open city. As the Allies had rebuffed the German proposal that the city be demilitarized, might it not now be Germany's turn to subject the city to bombardment? The American secretary of state referred to this fear in an early July letter: "The papal authorities appear unduly apprehensive of danger to Rome in view of the present over-all military situation, especially as to the Allied air supremacy over Italy and other military means at hand. The Joint Chiefs of Staff consider that there is little likelihood of serious German air or other attacks upon the city of Rome now or in the foreseeable future."[5]

Soon after the Allied occupation of Rome, President Roosevelt asked Myron Taylor, his emissary to the pontiff, to return there. Taylor's first reports back to Roosevelt from the Italian capital, in the form of handwritten letters, told how exhilarated he found the pope, who was now receiving thousands of Allied officers and men at his daily audiences. The pontiff had even held a special audience in the papal throne room for members of the press, shaking hands and speaking personally with each of them.

In the lengthy conversations that Taylor had with Pius XII, the pontiff made clear he thought Germany would ultimately be defeated, but he expressed concern at the loss of life that would be necessary to bring it about. He worried, too, that defeat would lead Germany to turn Communist. The pope asked Taylor if he thought he should make a new plea for peace, to which Roosevelt's envoy responded with a firm no. The pope's most recent statement on the subject, in his remarks a few days before the liberation of Rome, Taylor told him, "was interpreted in America . . . as pro German. . . . Nothing should be done that would raise false hopes in Germany or elsewhere as it would prolong the conflict" and, he warned, "it would be misunderstood and resented."[6]

**Myron Taylor and Cardinal Maglione with visiting Henry Lewis Stimson,
U.S. Secretary of War, Vatican City, July 6, 1944**

In early July 1944 the pope received William "Wild Bill" Donovan, legendary director of the Office of Strategic Services, the American intelligence service, for a private audience.[7] Curiously, when meeting with the American spymaster, with whom he shared his worries about Communism and the future of Germany, the pope was under the misimpression that the U.S. president himself was on his way to Rome.[8] He instructed the lone American prelate in the Secretariat of State, Monsignor Walter Carroll, to draft an English-language memo in preparation for the encounter. Although Roosevelt was not in fact coming, the memo offers insight into what the pope and those in the Secretariat of State were thinking in the aftermath of the Allies' conquest of Rome.

The pope thought it important that the Americans, and not the British, play the major role in Italy in the months to come. "The Americans," wrote Carroll, "seem disposed to return to America and leave Europe to the English. It is a return to American isolationism which is extremely dangerous and might well be disastrous for Europe." Behind the American view that they would soon be able to wash their hands of the Italian situation, he advised, was the idea that Italy should be left to the Italians. This was "based on the fundamental error that Italy is ready for a democratic form of government and that American democracy can be transplanted to Italy." Such a view, thought the monsignor, showed an ignorance of both Italian history and the Italian character. It was crucial that the American government exert "a quiet but very effective control over the destiny of the country for some time to come."

The final point that the pope was advised to raise with the American president was the danger that Germany's defeat would lead to Russian domination of Europe. Preparations had to be made to ensure that this did not happen. Now was the time to press Roosevelt, who would "undoubtedly be a candidate for a fourth term" and was "extremely sensitive to reactions and to the popular opinion in Catholic circles in America. . . . He will be most anxious therefore, to know the desires of the Holy See and will most certainly make every effort to satisfy those desires. Hence, this is a logical moment to strike hard."[9]

FOR MANY ALLIED SOLDIERS, the chance to take part in a papal audience in the frescoed halls of the Vatican was too exciting a prospect to resist, and the pontiff delighted in mingling with them. He was now holding large public audiences every day, for the most part in the Sala Regia outside the Sistine Chapel, where a special platform had been built from which he would offer remarks in English before giving his blessing. As he left these audiences, he often stopped to speak with the men within reach and offer them his ring to kiss. "His gracious manner and smile, and the close individual attention which he bestows on each person to whom he speaks," reported Osborne, "never fail to make a most favourable impression."

Yet curiously, the pope was a bit worried by the reception he encountered in his audiences with American soldiers. He told General

Clark, at one of his subsequent audiences with the American military leader, "You know, I think your American soldiers do not like me." Given the large number of GIs who had been clamoring to attend a papal audience, Clark at first thought he was joking, but he was not. When Italians or Germans had attended his audiences, Pius XII explained, they broke out in cheers when he entered the hall, "but when I appear before your American soldiers, they do not utter a sound." Much to the pope's relief, Clark explained that in the United States, a more reverential attitude was thought appropriate on such occasions. Applause and shouts would have seemed disrespectful.[10]

While the pope was exhilarated by the crowds drawn to his daily audiences, he remained preoccupied by fears of a Communist takeover in Italy. At his weekly meetings with Taylor, that worry and his related desire to have the Allied armies remain in Italy for a long time were the two primary topics of discussion. When Osborne met with the pope in late July, he found the same concern: "In discussing the Italian situation to-day the Pope said that he hoped that we should maintain unobtrusive control, if not actual occupation of the country for some time. Otherwise he feared chaos would supervene." Osborne, no friend of the left himself, agreed, but he told Pius XII that the "uncompromising but uninformed champions of democracy in London and Washington would never agree to anything of the sort." Both the American and the British leaders thought the Italians should decide their own future by holding free elections. "The Pope," Osborne reported, "observed that this was admirable in theory, but in practice and in present conditions in the country a doubtful benefit to the Italian people."[11]

Osborne would soon have the unusual opportunity of briefing the British prime minister directly, as Churchill had decided to pay Rome a visit. Hearing of the plans, Francesco Babuscio, once again secure in his status as the official Italian envoy to the Vatican, met with Pius XII on August 17. Italy's royal government had long pressed the Allies to treat Italy as a co-belligerent rather than as a defeated enemy. Now that Italy's capital had been freed of the Germans, the distinction was becoming a more pressing issue for the Italians. Offering Italy recognition as an ally rather than as a vanquished Axis power would mean reestablishing the country's own government's powers rather than having the Allies continue to exercise that authority. Babuscio asked the pope to impress on Churchill the importance of making this move. He also urged the pope to impress the British prime minister with the urgency of supplying Italy with sufficient food that its people could avoid starvation in the coming winter. Italy, said Babuscio, lacked everything: coal, fuel, medicines. With the collapse of the transportation system, even the crops that were harvested often had no way to get where they were so desperately needed.

The pope agreed to speak to the prime minister about all this, but he had a message of his own that he wanted Babuscio to deliver. Let the Italian government know, he said, that he firmly hoped that whatever measures were to be taken against "those responsible for the Italian tragedy"—that is, Mussolini and the Fascist leadership of the country—"not depart from that spirit of clemency that is so innate among our people."[12]

As it happened, the British prime minister's visit came at a particularly bad time for the pope. On August 22, 1944, the day Churchill arrived in Rome, Cardinal Maglione, who had long suffered from heart disease, died. He was sixty-seven years old. A few weeks earlier he had been admitted to the American section of a Neapolitan hospital, but the doctors could not save him. His funeral would be held in Rome a week later, several days after the British prime minister was scheduled to leave the city. Although Maglione had never enjoyed warm relations with Pius XII, and it seemed in recent times that the pope often preferred to deal with his two deputies, Monsignors Montini and Tardini, the Neapolitan cardinal had been a favorite of the foreign diplomatic corps and an astute observer of the international scene. His death left a void that would not soon be filled.[13]

Accompanied by Osborne, Churchill met with Pius XII the day after Maglione's death. Monsignor Tardini, after discussing the upcoming visit with the pope, had drafted points the pope wanted to raise with the British prime minister, which were then translated into English. The bulk of these concerned Italy's political situation, first among them the question of the monarchy. After Victor Emmanuel's two decades of support for Mussolini and the Fascist regime, the monarchy that had founded the Kingdom of Italy now risked being jettisoned. The pope planned to tell the prime minister that it should be retained, arguing that "the change from the monarchical system to that of a republic could likely add to the present distress, embitter discords, and prepare new upheavals for the future." The pope was also eager to discuss his greatest worry: "Communism is a very grave and imminent danger for the Italian people, impoverished, starving and exasperated as it is." Only if the Allies provided Italy with major economic relief, the pope would warn, could the Communist threat be blunted.

The pope also wanted to bring up disturbing reports he was receiving from southern Italy that the Allies were allowing Catholic religious instruction to be dropped from the public schools. The great majority of the members of the Allied Commission for Education, complained the pope, were non-Catholics. Using the excuse that they needed to select anti-Fascists to advise them, the commission had sought advice "from Italian intellectuals, known for their anti-Catholic spirit, who really constitute a negligible minority in comparison with the great body of educated Catholic Italians." What the pope thought the Allies needed instead was the advice of ecclesiastical authorities, especially in the selection of appropriate textbooks for the public schools.

Next on the pope's list of topics to be raised with Churchill were concerns about the future of the Lateran Accords that the Vatican had signed with Mussolini fifteen years earlier: "Some say that the Lateran Agreements were concluded by Fascism and therefore should fall with it." On the contrary, in a revision of history that would quickly become the standard line in the Vatican, the pope was to argue that the Fascist government had never been favorably disposed toward the church. The agreement had been not between the church and Mussolini, who negotiated it and signed it, the pope would insist, but between the church and the Italian king.

Finally, the pope was eager for the Allied authorities to do something about an alarming new development. At the Vatican's insistence, the Fascist regime had repressed all attempts by Protestants to proselytize in Italy, but now, as the war front moved northward, Protestant missionaries were making their way into the country. The effects of allowing "Protestant propaganda" in Italy would be "a) a sad division and a serious disquietude among the people; b) a strong reaction on the part of the bishops, the clergy and Catholic Action; c) an unavoidable attitude of condemnation and opposition on the part of the Holy See."[14]

How many of the points from this memo Pius XII discussed with Churchill in their forty-five-minute meeting is not clear, although he was not shy in speaking his mind with the British prime minister. After the meeting, Churchill told Myron Taylor the pope was "a very forthright and powerful personality." As Churchill might be thought to be rather knowledgeable on the subject of powerful personalities, the comment is revealing. The war had changed the pope, whom many cardinals had earlier feared would be insufficiently tough for the demands of the position. Pius XII still cultivated an ascetic image, and still in private delighted in having his canaries feed from his hands, but he was now far from bashful in making his views known. No longer sharing Rome with Italy's longtime dictator, who had known how to intimidate him, and with Hitler increasingly in retreat, he could now begin to assert himself.[15]

Nowhere were the pope's more imperious instincts clearer than in the question of appointing a new secretary of state. As always at such a time, rumors of who Maglione's successor might be spread quickly. But Pius XII seemed in no hurry to find a replacement. In fact, the pope felt more comfortable without a secretary of state, and he had never been fully at ease with the one he had, for in the pope's eyes Cardinal Maglione had seemed to view himself too much as an equal. In Monsignors Tardini and Montini, the pope had able men whose subservience to him was never in doubt.[16]

On September 1, 1944, the fifth anniversary of the start of the war, and with fierce fighting continuing farther north in Italy, the pope broadcast his first worldwide radio address since Rome's liberation. A new front in the war was forming at the time in northern Italy. Over the summer, Allied troops had advanced rapidly northward from

Rome through Florence, but by the end of August they had stalled at the Germans' new line of defense, the Gothic Line. It stretched from just south of La Spezia on the northwestern coast across the Apennines to Pesaro on the Adriatic. Not helping the Allied cause was the decision of the military command to transfer large numbers of troops from the Italian front to the new front in France. Over the next months as winter descended, the fighting in the northern Apennines would be fierce, with the Germans and their Fascist allies still in control of the northern third of the peninsula.

While Allied officials were relieved that the pope's September 1 radio speech made no direct call for a compromise peace, it did trigger some angry reaction. Particularly unhappy were the Poles, dismayed that on the anniversary of the German invasion of their country, the pope made no mention of it, focusing instead on how much Rome and Italy had suffered from the war. The pope's speech was also poorly received in Britain, where his remarks were interpreted as asking the people of London to forgive the Germans for attacking them. A letter to *The Times* on September 4 offered a common English view, expressed in a typically ironic way:

> I am sorry, indeed, if I have missed the Papal denunciations of Germany's crimes; but I find that my friends are in the same state of woeful ignorance. In fairness to his Holiness, and for the instruction of your readers, perhaps you would permit your correspondent to give us the texts of the pronouncements condemning the German invasions of Poland, France, Holland, Belgium, Norway, Greece, Russia, &c., the systematic slaughter and torture of Poles and Jews, the mass deportations and vast robberies, the bombardments of Warsaw, Rotterdam, Belgrade, London, &c. I have been searching hopefully for such an utterance in your long report . . . of the Pope's broadcast address on the fifth anniversary of the war. I do not find it. There is nothing here to show the historians that the war was not begun by America or Greece.

What particularly upset the pope was that some of the unfavorable comments about his speech were broadcast on Allied military radio, leading to a letter of protest that Montini handed Osborne. "We cannot but be surprised," wrote Montini, "that Allied Press services collect these malevolent and unjust reports, thereby co-operating in their diffusion among the public."[17]

WHILE THE BATTLE OVER the Eternal City had ended, the battle to rewrite its history had barely begun. Rome was filled with men who had played major roles in the Fascist regime and now desperately sought to keep their privileged positions and to avoid admitting to any responsibility for the disaster that had befallen their country. Francesco Babuscio, the Italian emissary to the Holy See, offers a case in point. Along with others like him, he now faced the threat posed by the High Commission for the Purging of the Public Administration. Established by the Italian government several months earlier as part of an Allied-encouraged effort to remove Fascists from public administration, the commission got new life following Rome's liberation. In late August, Babuscio learned that he was being suspended from his position while under investigation by the commission. The suspension never took effect, thanks to the efforts of the government's aristocratic undersecretary for foreign affairs, Giovanni Visconti Venosta. The undersecretary argued that at such a delicate moment, it was best not to do anything that might upset the government's relations with the Holy See.[18]

While Babuscio was left in his place at the Vatican, the proceedings against him went on. The charges were many, from his having risen above others in the foreign service early in his career thanks to his strong Fascist ties, to his service in administering conquered Albania, which led to another promotion, and his appointment in February 1943 as Mussolini's chief of staff at the Foreign Ministry.[19]

If the men who until months earlier had been loyal servants of the Fascist government now found themselves in a compromising position, the same was, at least in theory, true of the many high prelates who had taken such a public role in supporting the Fascist regime and the Axis war. For the pope, allowing action to be taken against any of them would mean admitting the role the church had played in supporting Fascism and the war, both facts of recent history that Vatican officials and leaders of church organizations throughout Italy would now strenuously deny.

One churchman proved to be too compromised even for Pius XII to protect, much as he tried. For almost two decades, Archbishop Angelo Bartolomasi had headed Italy's military chaplaincy, an appointment requiring papal approval. An enthusiastic supporter of Fascism, he had long played a highly visible role in rallying Catholics to support Mussolini and, until the Duce was overthrown, urging Catholic support for the Axis war. But when the Fascist regime fell, the pope made no move to replace him, and indeed months after Rome's liberation, Bartolomasi remained at his post.

In mid-August 1944, at the urging of Italy's minister of war, Babuscio advised the pope that he should remove the source of much embarrassment. When, a month later, the pope still had taken no action, Visconti Venosta, undersecretary of foreign affairs, sent word to the pope that he could delay no longer.[20]

Early in the fall, as the pope still refused to act, Visconti Venosta went to see Monsignor Montini to give vent to his frustration. In an attempt to placate the undersecretary, Montini assured him that while Bartolomasi remained head of the Italian military chaplaincy, he would no longer play any public role in that capacity. Yet despite those assurances, in early October the archbishop took part in his official capacity at the belated funeral honoring Colonel Giuseppe Cordero di Montezemolo, a martyr of the underground resistance. Captured by the Germans, Montezemolo had been the highest-profile victim of the mass execution carried out only a few months earlier at the Fosse Ardeatine. The outrage of Montezomolo's family and friends at the prelate's presence at the funeral of the anti-Fascist hero could hardly have been greater.

An angry Visconti Venosta directed Babuscio to deliver an ultimatum. Up until then, he had done everything he could to prevent the press from attacking the Vatican for leaving the Fascist archbishop in his place, but no longer. Nor would he advise other members of the government to remain quiet. "If one wants to avoid a painful polemic," the undersecretary told Babuscio, "there is only one thing to do. Put the government in a position to declare that Monsignor Bartolomasi is no longer the Military's Bishop."[21]

Babuscio went to see Monsignor Montini. True, Montini admitted, he had assured them that Bartolomasi would never again take part in any public ceremonies as head of the chaplaincy. His appearance at the resistance hero's funeral was, said the monsignor, "not planned." The matter would soon be put to rest, he promised, and Bartolomasi replaced. Finally bowing to the pressure, Pius XII reluctantly agreed to relieve the archbishop of his post.[22]

ALLIED TROOPS HAD ENTERED Paris in late August and were now marching eastward. Over the next month, as the Allies approached the German border, the Germans would evacuate their troops from Greece and Albania. But in Italy the Allied army found itself bogged down in the rugged Apennines south of Bologna. A German engineering unit, employing Italian forced labor, had begun to build the two-hundred-mile series of fortifications stretching across the peninsula the previous spring. With more than two thousand machine-gun nests, innumerable concrete bunkers, air defenses, artillery positions, antitank ditches, and observation posts, it proved a formidable barrier to the Allied advance. The fighting over the next months would be fierce. The cemetery interring German war dead at Futa Pass would ultimately be the final resting place for over thirty thousand, while the Allies suffered forty thousand casualties of their own. Among the latter was a twenty-one-year-old American platoon leader, hit in his shoulder and his back by German fire, and given little chance of surviving. Lapsing into and out of consciousness over the next three years, losing a kidney and the use of his right arm, he somehow survived. The GI, Bob Dole, would go on to serve over a quarter-century in the U.S. Senate and, in 1996, be the Republican candidate for president.[23]

Rome's Jews could now come out of hiding, but Jews in the north were still being herded onto trains bound for the Nazi death camps. A month after Rome's liberation, Palestine's two chief rabbis—Ashkenazi and Sephardic—had sent Maglione a telegram, urging the pope to grant them an audience:

> We understand Apostolic Delegate [responsible for Jerusalem] Father Hughes will these days convey our request audience with His Holiness reference position European Jewry. Since we contacted news arrived position rapidly worsening. The voice of God and our tormented brethren will give us no rest till we confer with His Holiness who has ever proffered helping hand oppressed Israel. View extreme urgency pray petition His Holiness expedite grant audience. Anticipatory thanks.

Well aware of the kind of help the rabbis would be asking of him, the pope judged it best to turn down their request, albeit taking care not to put anything in writing: A note on the newly available Vatican file reads: "As for the audience requested by Chief Rabbi Herzog of Jerusalem, the decision of the Holy Father is this: 'He believes it well not to respond.'"[24]

A GRUESOME
END

A S 1945 BEGAN, THE NORTH OF ITALY WAS STILL A WAR ZONE.
German troops in the Apennines south of Bologna were holding
off the stalled Allied advance, while both the Germans and the forces
of Mussolini's Italian Social Republic were battling the expanding Italian partisan movement. Partisans captured by the Fascist republic's
"Black Brigades" were regularly tortured before being shot. Italy's
rapidly growing Communist Party was not only providing the largest
contingent of partisan fighters but also organizing work stoppages in
the factories. Farther north in Europe, the Germans, following a brief
initial success in the Battle of the Bulge, were in retreat. January 1945
would also see the Soviets liberate Warsaw. The Red Army would
enter Budapest the following month.

In northern Italy conditions were grim. Allied bombs were still
falling on the cities as British nighttime bombers and American day-
time "precision" bombers took aim at the Germans' positions and their
supply lines. Bologna, lying just across the Germans' winter line, suffered the most. Large portions of the porticoed city were leveled as
bombs fell around Bologna almost daily in December and January.[1]

Italians in the north of the peninsula lived in fear of the Germans
and their Italian Fascist comrades, on the hunt for those suspected of
aiding the partisans. In early October, Cardinal Schuster, Milan's archbishop, described the situation in a report to the pope: "Here the regime of terror is progressively increasing as the end comes ever more

clearly in sight." Many parish priests were in hiding, sought after by the Germans and their Fascist cronies for aiding the partisans. Other priests were already imprisoned. Mussolini no longer seemed in control of his own forces. "Last week Mussolini, following my own complaint, ordered the arrest of [Pietro] Koch, head of the autonomous militia that has tortured its victims with the most refined methods. The police chief of Milan, on the personal order of the Duce, had the head of the band arrested along with his principal associates, and subsequently invited a group of medical doctors to examine the instruments of torture they used on their prisoners." But within days, Guido Buffarini, Mussolini's minister of internal affairs, ordered Koch and his henchmen freed and indeed threatened to have the police chief and the prefect arrested. "And so it goes," concluded the archbishop. Two weeks later Schuster sent the pope an update. An Allied bombing raid on Milan had caused six hundred deaths, including a priest and nearly two hundred children whose school was hit.[2]

Chafing at his loss of authority, and perhaps thinking ahead to the slender possibility that he could escape with his life from the unfolding disaster of the war, Mussolini now periodically tried to distance himself from the Germans. His protests to Rudolf Rahn, Germany's ambassador to his government, and to the German military authorities about some of their more egregious executions of Italian civilians were becoming more energetic. Only a few months earlier he had not protested when the Germans executed 335 Italian civilians at the caves outside Rome.

In mid-December Mussolini roused himself from his depression and self-pity to go from his remote villa headquarters on Lake Garda to Milan. There he made the last crowd-rousing appearance of his career. At Milan's Lirico Theater, he offered a stem-winding speech as of old, regularly interrupted by enthusiastic applause and shouts from his die-hard followers. Recounting the ongoing battle of his Fascist republican government against the "reactionary plutocracies" and denouncing the "traitors of July 25," he called nostalgically for a return to the early comradely spirit of Italian Fascism. Over the next two days, he toured Milan in his open-topped car, stopping at Piazza San Sepolcro where, as a thirty-five-year-old veteran of the Great War, he had launched the Fascist movement a quarter-century earlier. Not surprisingly, his euphoria did not last long. To a comrade who later congratulated him on the adulatory reception he had gotten in Milan, he replied, "What is life? Dust and altars, altars and dust."[3]

While not nearly as dramatic as the situation in the north, life in Rome and other liberated parts of the country was a struggle as well. Food was scarce, homes had been destroyed, and the economy was barely functioning. An American intelligence report of the time captured some of the drama of everyday life. Although based on a report filed from Naples, it was presented as representing the broader picture of conditions in the Allied-occupied regions of the country: "In many cases, there is literally no food to be had, and houses are so cold and damp that in the evenings one goes to bed very early." Telephone lines and public transportation functioned only sporadically. The black market, it seemed, was the only market, and food prices were sky high. "People try to steal—a pair of socks here, some butter there, even chestnuts." In their desperation, many women were selling themselves to Allied soldiers: "The men are bitter about what they call the prostitutionalism of their women, yet a great many parents send their daughters out so that the family may have the wherewithal to carry on."

As the American report described it, the public mood was dark, the Italians wallowing in self-pity: "Time and again they speak of themselves contemptuously, saying they are capable of nothing, their leaders are either idiots or crooks, and their military effort a sham. . . . As a whole they are bewildered and confused, and sometimes they react in a pitiful childlike dependency upon the Allies."[4]

While President Roosevelt was receiving these intelligence reports, he was also receiving a stream of requests from his emissary to the pope, Myron Taylor, calling on the United States to send Italy desperately needed supplies. Taylor, who had taken up residence in an elegant town house near the Spanish Steps, was now spending most of his time not on Vatican business but on coordinating American relief programs. On January 15, 1945, he urged the importance of supplying "a very large quantity of shoes," suggesting that a simple design of serviceable shoes for workmen would be best, while adding that women's need for shoes was less pressing because they were accustomed to wearing homemade wooden footwear. The next day he sent a follow-up telegram detailing the shortage of ambulances in Italy and asking that a large number be sent: "Recently in Florence sick people are carried to hospital by hand litter and in one instance with wheelbarrow." He added that the words "American Relief for Italy" should be stenciled prominently on the side of every vehicle.[5]

The problem of prostitution of Italian women with Allied soldiers, cited in the U.S. intelligence report, had been also very much on the pope's mind ever since the Allies seized Rome the previous June. On January 17 the Vatican Secretariat of State sent the president's envoy its latest complaint. "At Via Babuino, no. 186 . . . there has been opened since the month of June 1944 a clandestine house of prostitution. . . . This house is visited continuously by Allied soldiers, almost exclusively colored. . . . The Secretariat of State would appreciate very much the esteemed cooperation of the Personal Representative of the President of the United States in bringing about the termination of this situation so offensive to public morals." On receiving the request, Myron Taylor passed it on to the Allied military command in Rome. "I beg to advise," the American military chief of staff wrote Taylor a few weeks later, that as a result of the Vatican's plea, "the premises have been ordered 'Off limits' for all Allied personnel."[6]

The pope continued to complain about the breakdown of public morality produced by the Allied occupation of Rome. "I absolutely do not intend having Rome become the amusement center for Allied officers," said the pope in early April. "I did not allow such a thing to happen under Fascism; I did not allow it under the Germans, nor will I allow it to the Allies. Every day I hear complaints about the regrettable scandals taking place." The pope went on to explain that what he had in mind were not only "public and private entertainments, which too often assume the aspect of orgies," but also pervasive corruption, presumably here referring to the flourishing black market.[7]

In these final months of the war, no one outside the pope's immediate court had such easy access to the pontiff as the American president's envoy. Although in February and March the pope was ill with the flu, he was always pleased to meet with Taylor. "Myron Taylor," the new French provisional government's envoy to the Vatican observed in mid-March, "pays the Pope visits with a frequency unheard of by all the other foreign diplomats. With his familiar and direct bonhomie, which has earned him unanimous sympathies, he seems to have established himself as some sort of adviser to the Holy See." Indeed, the pope and Taylor shared a certain chemistry, helped, as the French envoy put it, by Taylor's personal friendship with Roosevelt and his "large personal fortune." Widely seen as the face of American economic aid efforts in Italy, Taylor had become one of the most popular foreigners in the peninsula.[8]

For Pius XII, Taylor's importance derived as well from the pope's fears of what the impending German defeat might bring. Since Mussolini's overthrow, the pope had been hoping for what the French envoy described as a "moderate Allied victory," one that would put an end to Hitlerism and to Hitler's puppet Italian government in northern Italy, yet somehow not inflict on Germany "the rigors of total defeat." That way the plague of Communism would remain sealed off in the Soviet Union, leaving the rest of Europe safe. Now, though, with the Red Army marching rapidly toward Berlin, things were turning out differently. The pope thought American support crucial if Italy, and indeed all the Catholic nations of Europe, were to be saved from Communism's spread.[9]

REPORTING TO ROOSEVELT ON his lengthy mid-December papal audience, Myron Taylor had put the matter starkly: "The principal preoccupation of the Pope is the spread of Communism in Europe and Italy." Later in the month, after waiting an unusually long time outside Pius XII's office before their scheduled meeting, Taylor was taken aback when he saw the German ambassador emerge. On greeting the pope, Taylor remarked on the length of time the pontiff had spent with him. The pope replied, defensively, that Ambassador Weizsäcker had never been a Nazi. The man had seemed so unhappy, said the pope, that he thought he should do what he could to console him.[10]

With Allied armies moving eastward across France and Belgium toward the German border and the massive Red Army pushing westward, Weizsäcker was not the only one in a position of authority in the Third Reich who was eager to find an escape. In the face of the Allies' insistence on Germany's unconditional surrender, Pius XII seemed to some to be the only prominent figure in Europe in a position to change their minds. The pope's long-nourished hope that, by remaining neutral in the war, he would ultimately be in a position to broker a peace deal between the two sides was widely known. Now many, both in Italy and in Germany, were eager to avail themselves of his services.

For the Germans occupying northern Italy, as well as for their Italian Fascist associates, Cardinal Schuster was the closest they could hope to get to the pope. As archbishop of Milan, formerly known for his strong backing of the Fascist regime, he was, from the time Rome was lost, the highest-placed Italian prelate in the lands under German control. Among the first to explore this approach was the German ambassador to Mussolini's government, Rudolf Rahn, who stealthily made his way through a side entrance of the archbishop's quarters on January 22, 1945. "He is looking for a bridge," recalled the archbishop of their conversation, "and was hoping that this might be the Roman Pontiff." Because Milan was cut off from direct communication with Rome, Schuster's channel for contacting the Vatican ran through Monsignor Bernardini, the nuncio in Switzerland.[11]

From his headquarters on Lake Garda, Mussolini, in what must have been particularly galling for him, used the same route to seek the pope's assistance. He had a proposal to make for which he needed the pope's help, and to increase his chances of success, he tried two different routes to get to the pontiff.

In early February, Mussolini made his first approach by calling on Father Giusto Pancino, the priest who had earlier helped him contact his daughter in Switzerland. He hoped the priest could use his link with the nuncio in Bern to get a message to the pope. After meeting with Mussolini, Father Pancino wrote the nuncio, asking for his help to get a visa to come see him. His mission, he explained, was to convey "messages of the greatest urgency and importance." They were, he said, from Mussolini and his "friend," whom the nuncio thought might be Hitler. Not sure how to respond, Bernardini wrote the Vatican asking for instructions.

The pope replied quickly: Bernardini should arrange the visa for Father Pancino, but he should take care that the Allies not find out about it.[12]

In early March, using a separate route for the same purpose, Mussolini sent his son Vittorio to Milan to ask Cardinal Schuster to contact the pope through the Swiss nuncio.[13] Although the cardinal and the nuncio were both Italian, Schuster then wrote the nuncio in Latin as an extra precaution against prying eyes. He recounted Vittorio Mussolini's visit and the three-part message his father wanted to send the pope. The first two parts consisted of threats, the third, an offer. First, the Duce informed the archbishop of Milan that while he knew he could not stop the enemy's advance, he would fight "tooth and nail" to the end. He vowed to take Italy down with him as, he noted, Hitler was doing in Germany. "In short," observed Schuster in offering his own gloss on the Duce's threat, "he has acted as Samson among the Philistines."

Second, Mussolini told the archbishop that only one option remained for his forces if the war continued. They would protect themselves for as long as they could "by sacrificing Milan and Lombardy." Here Schuster added another comment: "Is that really their plan or are these empty threats for our benefit?"

Last came the offer. The Duce, his son informed the archbishop, would "gladly make peace with the enemy." All he required was an assurance that no one be punished simply for being loyal to the Fascist cause, but only if found guilty of committing a crime.

Cardinal Schuster told Vittorio that he could hardly refuse to do what he could to help avoid further bloodshed and destruction. He asked only that Mussolini put what he proposed in writing, "in order that I might be able to convey his desires in his very own words to the

Holy See and to his adversaries." Like the pope, Schuster was worried not only by the German occupation but, with Italy's Fascist regime in its final death throes, by a rapidly growing Italian Communist Party. A big political void was about to open in Italy, and the danger that it would be filled by the Communists loomed large. In February Schuster had sent a pastoral letter to all the parish priests in his archdiocese, calling on them to explain to their flocks the fateful choice they faced: "With Christ or with Satan, with Christ or with materialist communism."[14]

Three days after Mussolini's son visited the archbishop, Father Pancino finally reached Bern, bringing the nuncio Mussolini's proposal. Pancino described the sad situation in which northern Italy now found itself, afflicted on one side by "the ferocity of communist partisans guided," the priest said, rather surprisingly, "by Slavic women," and on the other by the atrocities visited on them by the Germans. "Finally," reported Bernardini, Pancino "spoke to me of the intention of Signor Mussolini and Germany (not of Signor Hitler, who does not like to be compromised, but of Signor Himmler) to negotiate with the Allies."

The message that Mussolini wanted to get to the Holy See was this: "Germany and the neo-fascist government intend to pass, under certain conditions, into the Anglo-American camp to block the spread of communism and prevent the bolshevization of Europe." Germany would renounce any claims to an empire and, said Father Pancino, "turns to the Holy See so that it is possible to reach a compromise with the Allies." Asked what the "certain conditions" were that Mussolini's message had mentioned, Pancino said he had not been told. He added that "an analogous request to negotiate with the Allies, accompanied by the threat to destroy Lombardy, was made by Vittorio Mussolini in his father's name to the Cardinal Archbishop of Milan."[15]

The nuncio replied that he thought Mussolini's last-minute proposal had little chance of success, given the Allies' repeated insistence they would never negotiate with either him or the Nazi government. Pancino acknowledged the difficulty but insisted that Mussolini's proposal be sent on to the pope.[16]

While Pius XII continued to be tempted by the prospect of playing his long-dreamt-of role of peacemaker, Monsignor Tardini was doing all he could to discourage him. Shortly after Mussolini's proposals arrived, Tardini prepared a memo for the pope offering his critique: "That Germany and the neo-fascist government . . . intend to pass into the Anglo-American camp to block communism is truly astonishing. While the Anglo-Americans declare that they will not consider any negotiations with the Nazis . . . the Nazis propose an alliance with them." Tardini saw no reason why the Holy See would want to get involved as a middleman in transmitting such a proposal. The Anglo-Americans would undoubtedly reject it, and it would only incite the Russians to increase their attacks on the Vatican. "For both, the Holy See itself might well appear as favorable to saving, in extremis, Nazism and fascism."

Tardini advised the pope to reply to the nuncio in the following terms: The Holy See had recently received confirmation of the Allies' continued insistence on "unconditional surrender"—here Tardini used the English term. "As a result, while the Holy See is so desirous of a true and just peace, it is not in a position to take other steps." Making only minor changes in the proposed text, on March 14 Pius XII instructed Tardini to send the response to Bern.[17]

At the same time, Mussolini's son returned to Milan to bring the archbishop the written proposal he had requested. Schuster in turn sent it to Bernardini in Switzerland to forward to the pope. In sending the report on to Rome, the nuncio added his own note: "These people either ignore or pretend to ignore the fact that the end is rapidly approaching and with threats of destruction and reprisals, with a language that recalls times now past, they present proposals that have no possibility of being considered."[18]

Mussolini's written proposal repeated his threats: Should the German army retreat from Italy, widespread anti-Fascist hatred left his government no other option than to fight until its last bullet was spent. But to prevent further deaths and destruction, and to show they placed their love for Italy above any political interest, "the government of the Italian Social Republic proposes that preliminary agreements be signed with the Supreme Allied Command, on the basis of which the two contracting parties commit to the following points." Among the conditions listed was the Allies' commitment to collaborate with the Fascist forces to repress the partisan bands and the Communists, while the clergy worked to promote a general pacification. The list ended with what Mussolini described as the one "absolute condition." The arrests of those who had remained loyal to the Fascist cause must be stopped and the persecution of Fascists through the commission that had been set up in Rome ended. The Allies were to try only those guilty of "infamous crimes, not attributable to the war." Mussolini promised that following this transitional phase, the Republican Fascist Party would be dissolved and a government of national unity formed.[19]

Still nurturing some hope that he could bring about a negotiated peace, Pius XII, spurning Tardini's advice, decided he could not ignore Mussolini's plea. Do not put anything in writing, Pius XII instructed Tardini on April 2, 1945, but speak with Osborne, Britain's envoy, and through him relay Mussolini's offer to the Allies on condition that Osborne agree to keep the Vatican's role "absolutely secret." The pope himself, still looking ill and tired from his stubborn bout with the flu, had met with Osborne only a few days earlier. He had shared his concern about recent Russian propaganda efforts to remind the world of the Vatican's two-decade-long support for Italian Fascism. It was all, said the pope, part of an effort to discredit the church and bring the Communists to power in Italy.[20]

This worry was likely much in the pope's mind when, only hours after instructing Tardini to contact the British envoy, he changed his mind. He had learned in the meantime of a violent Moscow Radio attack on Switzerland for serving as a transit point for German peace proposals. "For that reason," Tardini recorded in a note, "His Holiness prefers that we say nothing to Signor Osborne."[21]

Meanwhile another desperate effort to enlist the pope's help to avoid the fate that now threatened the Fascist and Nazi leaders was under way within Vatican City itself. Several weeks earlier, while the pope was confined to bed with the flu, the German ambassador had

gone to see Monsignor Tardini. Weizsäcker arrived with a stack of en-
crypted messages from Berlin. They were proposals, he explained, for
the pope to use his influence with the Americans and British to broker
a truce. The Germans had only one card left to play: Weizsäcker argued that Russia's goal was to turn all of continental Europe Communist. The only way to prevent such a calamity was for the three great
powers—the United States, Britain, and Germany—to join together
to defeat it. Nazism, added the ambassador, had been misunderstood.
It was basically only another form of capitalism. Aware that the Nazis'
ongoing extermination of Europe's Jews was not a great selling point
for his argument, he suggested that some kind of arrangement could
be made to relocate Jews outside of Europe. He made no mention of
the fact that his government had already put over half of all of Europe's
Jews to death. When Tardini greeted the ambassador's proposal with
unconcealed skepticism, Weizsäcker asked whether he thought the Allies might take a different attitude if Hitler were no longer in the picture.

Despite Tardini's lack of enthusiasm for the proposal and his incre-
dulity at the ambassador's characterization of Nazism, the German ambassador returned five days later to renew his plea. The democracies
alone could not stop the Communist tidal wave from washing across
Europe, and should Germany lose the war, there was no doubt that all
of Europe would soon turn red. Without specifying to whom he was
referring, Weizsäcker said that the "people in Berlin" were calling on
the Allies to halt their land and air campaign against Germany. This
would allow the Germans to concentrate their forces on the eastern
front and defeat the Russians. They would then negotiate a peace of
"conciliation" with the Allies.

Tardini was unmoved. Were the Vatican to do what Weizsäcker was
asking and serve as the conduit for such a proposal to the western Allies, he replied, it would immediately expose the Holy See to the
charge it was trying to save Nazism just as it was being defeated on the
battlefield. The pope would be criticized for promoting a compromise
peace in the face of the Allies' repeated exclusion of that possibility.

Such a proposal might also lead the Allies to suspect that the Vatican was enabling the Germans to focus their military efforts on defeating the Russians before then turning their full force against their western enemies. To these objections, Weizsäcker replied weakly that the British and Americans might reach their agreement with "other German leaders and not with Nazism." But, thought Tardini, the ambassador was exceedingly vague about what exactly this might mean.

Tardini brought the pope his notes of the encounter. A few days later, having recovered from his illness, the pontiff decided to meet with Weizsäcker to discuss his proposal. Proceeding cautiously, as he always did, he thought it best to first have a word with Myron Taylor. In an effort to end the war without further bloodshed, he asked the president's envoy, might the Allies be willing to enter discussions with the Germans either directly or through a third party, perhaps—although he did not say this—through the Vatican itself? Taylor could not have been more emphatic: there could be no such talks. Only Germany's unconditional surrender would end the war.[22]

Adolf Hitler, Berlin, March 20, 1945

IN BERLIN, THE END was nearing for Hitler and the men around him. But his propaganda minister, Joseph Goebbels, still clung to the slender hope that the Vatican might play a role to save them. "The Catholic press in England, led by the Catholic Herald," Goebbels wrote in his diary on March 30, "continues to attack bolshevism sharply. Its language could not be bettered by the German press. I assume that this violent attack is being made on instructions from the Vatican." His hopes, such as they were, would soon be extinguished. On April 13 Soviet troops entered Vienna as they closed in on the heart of the Third Reich. A month after voicing his hopes in the Vatican, Goebbels and his wife, holed up in Hitler's Berlin bunker, prepared for the end. After directing a medical staff member to give morphine injections to their six children, aged four to twelve, they had Hitler's doctor crush a vial of poison and put it into each of their children's mouths. Goebbels and his wife, Magda, then swallowed the poison themselves.[23]

It was while Hitler and his associates were hunkering down in their Berlin bunker that the pope learned of the fate that had befallen King Victor Emmanuel's daughter, Princess Mafalda. She had returned to Rome from the funeral of her brother-in-law, King Boris of Bulgaria, in September 1943. Her parents were gone, having abandoned the city two weeks earlier, in the hours after the armistice was announced. After visiting her three youngest children, whom Monsignor Montini was sheltering in his Vatican apartment, she had received word that her husband was planning to reach her by telephone at the German embassy. It was a cruel ruse, as, on Hitler's orders, Mafalda was seized on her arrival at the embassy and forced onto a plane bound for Berlin.

Shortly after Rome was liberated, several months after her disappearance, the Vatican made its first attempt to learn of her fate, perhaps prompted by a request from the newly returned royal family. A cyphered telegram in mid-August 1944, bearing the signature of Cardinal Maglione, went to the Vatican nuncio in Berlin: "I will be grateful if Your Most Reverend Excellency can inform me where and how Her Royal Highness Princess Mafalda is. According to the latest information she is at Kassel." In fact, Mafalda had never been allowed to return to her husband's home in Kassel but had been sent shortly after her arrival in Berlin in September 1943 to the Buchenwald concentration camp three hundred kilometers to the southwest. Monsignor Orsenigo, the nuncio in Berlin, could provide the Vatican no news of her.[24]

In March 1945 Monsignor Montini, who had briefly sheltered Mafalda's children in his Vatican apartment two years earlier, sent a new ciphered telegram to Orsenigo in Berlin: "Fervent prayers have been directed to the Holy Father that he interest himself in the fate of Princess Mafalda of Savoy, married to Prince Philipp von Hessen." Montini asked that the nuncio see what steps could be taken to ensure her safety. The telegram, however, came much too late. Nor, perhaps unsurprisingly given the situation in Berlin in these last weeks of the war, did it ever reach the nuncio.[25]

A month later Mafalda's brother, Umberto, urgently contacted Monsignor Montini. Umberto had been made regent of the realm following Rome's liberation when his father reluctantly transferred most of his powers as king to him. What prompted Umberto's new appeal to the Vatican was a newspaper story out of Paris reporting that Mafalda was dead, having died the previous year at Buchenwald. Monsignor Montini quickly cabled the nuncio in Paris, Angelo Roncalli, to see if he could verify the report. Roncalli was able to locate two priests who had recently arrived in Paris from Buchenwald. The future pope John XXIII then cabled news of what he had learned: the princess had been injured during an Allied bombing of the Buchenwald concentration camp the previous summer and had died a few days later. Roncalli added: "corpse preserved and recognizable." The gruesome details of her death, following a botched operation to amputate her badly burned left arm, would only come later.[26]

THE WAR IN ITALY ended in late April, an event that President Roosevelt did not live to see. Within days of the president's death on April 12, 1945, Allied troops broke through the Germans' last line of defense in Italy in the mountains between Florence and Bologna and rushed northward. With the Allied army advancing rapidly and the Germans retreating, popular revolts broke out in cities throughout the north. At eight A.M. on April 25, an underground radio station broadcast a call from the leadership of the Committee for National Liberation in Northern Italy for armed insurrection in all lands still occupied by the "Nazi-Fascists." In Milan, amid a general strike, partisans began taking over strategic points as German troops began their retreat. Desperate carloads of Fascists sped through the streets shooting wildly at their enemies. That same day, in an attempt to avoid a final bloodbath, Cardinal Schuster hosted a meeting bringing Mussolini and his war minister Rodolfo Graziani together with the Resistance leaders. A pallid, physically shrunken Duce asked for guarantees for the safety of himself and his Fascist compatriots, but it was too late, much too late for that.[27]

Benito Mussolini, 1945

Fleeing northward, the Duce made his way to Como, on the southern edge of the lake of the same name. There Clara insisted on joining him. While in Milan, Mussolini had arranged for a plane to take her parents and sister to safety in Spain, but Franco, fearful of the Allies' reaction, was not willing to take in Mussolini himself. The man who had long basked in the cheers and adulation of millions now felt abandoned. The last humiliation was at the archbishop's, where he had been told that the German military command had already entered into negotiations with the Resistance leadership to arrange for their evacuation from Milan, something they had not bothered to tell him.

Along Lake Como, a retreating German convoy agreed to take the Duce and Clara as it headed north to the border, but before it got far, a small group of lightly armed partisans blocked its way.[28] Eager to move on, the German officer in charge agreed to let the partisans search for any Italians hidden among them in exchange for a promise to allow the convoy to proceed. Despite the German uniform he wore and the sunglasses partially covering his well-known face, the Duce was recognized and seized. Clara insisted on being taken with him.

Shocked to find himself with such an illustrious prisoner, the local partisan chief sent word to Milan, asking the Resistance leaders what he should do. After debating whether the fallen dictator should be brought back to Milan alive or simply executed where he was, they made their decision and dispatched a low-level partisan chief, "Colonel Valerio"—in his pre-partisan life Walter Audisio, an accountant—to carry it out. On arriving at the farmhouse on Lake Como where Mussolini and Clara were being held on April 28, Audisio apparently told them he had come with orders to let them go. The details of what transpired over the next hour have inspired a booming editorial business, including a number of contradictory descriptions later given by Audisio himself. Put into a car with "Colonel Valerio" and a number of his fellow partisans, Mussolini and Clara were driven to a short stone wall circling a small villa. There at four P.M., the car pulled over, and the couple were told to get out. It was raining, and Clara, weeping, was wearing her fur coat. Mussolini, sensing his end was near, had a vacant expression. "Are you happy that I followed you to the last?" Clara whispered to him. Mussolini, his mind far away, seems not to have heard.

"By order of the general command of the Committee of National Liberation," the partisan colonel then announced—or at least this is how he subsequently described the events—"I have the task of rendering justice in the name of the Italian people." As he pointed his weapon at them, Clara rushed at him in an effort to turn it away, but in the end he succeeded in his task. Mussolini and Clara fell, mortally wounded, to the wet ground.

The partisans then piled the two bodies into a truck and headed for Milan. There, in Piazzale Loreto, the cadavers of Mussolini and his lover joined those of other Fascist notables who had been executed in much the same way. The choice of Piazzale Loreto was not casual, for the previous summer, in reprisal for a partisan attack on a German military convoy, the head of the Gestapo in Milan had selected fifteen civilians and had them shot there, leaving their putrefying bodies on display for several days. Now in their delirium following years of war and deprivation, the crowd took its revenge on the bodies of the Fascist leaders, spitting on them, cursing them, kicking them, and shooting bullets into them, before Mussolini and Clara, along with their comrades, were hung by their feet from the scaffolding of a gas station bordering the piazza. A priest had tied a rope around Clara's skirt, binding her legs at her thighs, before she was hoisted up, protecting her modesty as she hung from the scaffolding. Drops of the Duce's brain oozed from his damaged head and dripped down on the ground below. Readers of the Vatican newspaper the next day would learn of the dictator's death only from the article in the lower part of the fourth column of page two. It was titled simply: "Shooting of Fascist Chiefs."[29]

THE DAYS THAT FOLLOWED were a time for celebration but also for revenge. A few days after the Duce was hung by the feet at Piazzale Loreto, Archbishop Schuster wrote the pope to describe the orgy of popular violence enveloping Lombardy. He described it as "a wave of communism, inspiring terror." People's tribunals, he told the pope, were ordering many people shot without any real trials: "it is enough to establish the identity of the accused: 'Are you so-and-so? You are dead.'" Among those executed was Father Tullio Calcagno, director of the pro-Fascist Catholic journal *Crociata Italica*. "He was surprised in a German military barracks," the cardinal informed the pope. "He had neither priest, nor sacraments [that is, the administration of last rites]. However, he twice made the sign of the Cross and was then shot. God's justice!" The crowd then attacked the fallen priest, kicking and spitting on his lifeless body. Fortunately, observed the archbishop, a group of young Catholics intervened, removing the priest's black cassock so that it would not be sullied.[30]

MUSSOLINI'S FORMER ACOLYTE, PARTNER, and protector outlived him by only two days. The Führer, having taken refuge in a bunker deep below Berlin's Chancellery as the Red Army closed in, was oddly busy with marriage plans at the time Mussolini was taken out and shot. Shortly after midnight the next day, bowing to his secret lover's greatest wish, Hitler and Eva Braun were married in the bunker by a local Nazi city councilor. Following the small ceremony, champagne and sandwiches were served. The Führer then dictated his final testament, blaming the war on "international Jewry." The following day, having learned of Mussolini's fate, and amid reports that Soviet troops were nearing, Hitler made his final arrangements. Closing the door to his study, he sat on a small sofa alongside his wife. Eva swallowed a prussic acid pill and slumped down. Hitler held a Walther pistol in his right hand, brought it up to his temple, and pulled the trigger.

On discovering the bodies minutes later, Hitler's valet went to fetch blankets and with the help of three SS guards rolled the two bodies onto them. The four men then carried the newlyweds up the stairs from the bunker and out into the Chancellery's garden. There, amid punishing Red Army artillery fire, the two corpses were laid side by side. Large quantities of gasoline were poured over them, and then

Pope Pius XII

they were set ablaze. When the first Soviet soldiers arrived two days later, all that remained of Hitler and Eva were ashes and teeth.[31]

THE POPE'S NAME DAY, June 2, came less than a month after Germany's surrender. Eager to take advantage of the gathering of the cardinals traditionally held that day to honor him, Pius XII did something he had never previously done. He addressed himself directly to the question of National Socialism. He began, defensively, by justifying his signing of the concordat with Germany a few months after Hitler had come to power, an agreement he had helped craft as secretary of state. It was done, he stressed, with the agreement of the German episcopate, and without intending in any way to signal Vatican approval of Nazi doctrine. "In any case," he said, "one must recognize that the Concordat over the following years procured some advantages, or at least prevented greater harm." He then devoted much of his speech to chronicling what he described as the Nazi regime's campaign against the Catholic Church. He highlighted the many Catholic priests, especially in Poland, who were consigned to concentration camps by the Nazis. He did not fail to get in, as well, mention of his 1942 Christmas address, casting himself as following in the footsteps of his predecessor, Pius XI, and his 1937 encyclical denouncing Nazi doctrine.

The speech highlighted the suffering of Catholics and the Catholic Church during the war and represented the Catholics in Germany as the Nazis' victims. He made not even the briefest mention, indeed no mention at all, of the Nazis' extermination of Europe's Jews. If any Jews had been in those concentration camps alongside the valorous Catholic priests and lay Catholics, one would not know it from the pope's speech. Nor did he make any mention of Italy's part in the Axis cause, much less suggest any Italian responsibility for the disasters that had befallen Europe.[32]

Two days after the pope's name day speech came the first anniversary of the liberation of Rome. To mark the day, the youth wing of Italian Catholic Action organized celebrations to offer thanks to Pius XII, heralding him as the savior of Rome and the great Defender of Christianity. The campaign to proclaim him a saint would have to await his death, still years away.[33]

EPILOGUE

———

THE POSTWAR YEARS WERE A TIME FOR FORGETTING. A NEW HISTORY had to be written for Italy, one in which Italians had not been Fascists, Mussolini had not been a popular hero, Italy was not the partner of Nazi Germany, and the pope had not pursued a modus vivendi with Europe's murderous dictators. Throughout the country, cities large and small sprouted centers for the study of the Resistance as temples to worship a past that was as heroic as it was misleading. Centers aimed at shedding light on the two decades of the Fascist regime were notable only for their absence.[1]

Italy's Jews, too, played a part in recasting their country's history, for the alternative was much too painful. The fact that so many of them had responded to the pressure of persecution by abandoning their religion in the hope of an escape through baptism was not something they were eager to acknowledge. Nor were they eager to draw attention to how little protest the racial laws had prompted among their Catholic fellow citizens, indeed how eager so many of those citizens had been to take their Jewish colleagues' positions and their Jewish neighbors' property. Least palatable of all was recognizing how many of their Catholic neighbors during the German occupation had reported on their hiding places to the police, sending their loved ones to their deaths. Better to blame it all on the Germans.[2]

The history of Italy's anti-Jewish racial laws—in brutal force for five years before Mussolini was deposed—began to be rewritten even before the rubble had been removed from the nation's streets. In June 1945 Italy's ambassador to Belgium reported on a local Jewish newspaper's request for information on the measures taken against Italy's Jews. "Naturally," the ambassador reported to Rome, "I emphasized that our racial law not only found scarce application in individual concrete cases, but all the people and virtually all the administrative bodies that were supposed to apply it, competed instead in efforts to completely sabotage it." Only with the arrival of the Germans in September 1943, the ambassador told the journalist, had Jews begun to be persecuted, and that was "exclusively the work of the Germans," while "the Italian people in all strata and the Italian clergy did all they could to hide and save the Jews, almost always at great risk for their own persons and for their families."[3]

Of greatest concern to Pius XII and his immediate advisers, following the liberation of Rome, was the fate of the concordat that Mussolini had negotiated with the pope's brother. It had ended liberal Italy's separation of church and state and offered the church many privileges. A July 30, 1944, memo in the Secretariat of State office already reflected the recasting of history that would characterize the postwar period: "In 1929 the claims by the Church and by Catholics were recognized not by the Fascist Party, which always harbored an unfavorable attitude toward the Catholic Church but by the Italian government."[4]

Not until ten years after the war's end did the church first face a strong challenge to its new narrative, when the scholar Arturo Jemolo published his history of church-state relations in Italy. He wrote: "Whoever looks with a dispassionate eye at the relations between the Church (not only the Holy See, but the episcopate, and the secular and regular clergy) and the Fascist government for a period that includes the eleven years between the conclusion of the Concordat and the beginning of the 1940s cannot fail to recognize that they were cordial, marked by a spirit of collaboration and reciprocal concessions."[5] When, three years later, a book aimed at a broad audience appeared in Italy with much the same thesis, the Vatican quickly responded, denying that the church in Italy had ever supported the Fascist regime. Indeed, *L'Osservatore Romano* ran an attack on the book even before it appeared in bookstores. "The Church," it proclaimed, "has maintained an attitude that has been correct, clear, and consistent in its centuries-long life . . . vigilant, solicitous, careful to protect the many who depend on it from the anger of despots or from the sinister maneuvers of other malefactors; and always immoveable, steadfast in the eternal principles on which its high mission rests."[6]

In 1963 the appearance of the play *The Deputy* posed a new threat to this narrative. Written by the German playwright Rolf Hochhuth, the play portrayed a Pius XII who willingly turned a blind eye to the Holocaust. It was staged despite church protests in both Europe and North America and was scheduled to come to Italy in February 1964. The Vatican applied pressure on the government to prevent it from being performed in Italy, and as a result, state officials banned it.[7]

A positive review of *The Deputy* in a British publication had resulted in a denunciation that could hardly have come from a higher church source. Giovanni Montini offered a vigorous defense of his former mentor, in the form of a letter to *The Tablet*. Coincidentally, the British Catholic journal received it on June 21, 1963, the day Montini was elected to the papacy. Rejecting the playwright's depiction of Pius XII, Montini wrote that the wartime pope had in fact spared "no effort" and left nothing "untried to prevent the horrors of mass deportation and exile." "History," wrote Montini, "will vindicate the conduct of Pius XII when confronted by the criminal excesses of the Nazi regime: history will show how vigilant, persistent, disinterested and courageous that conduct must be judged to have been." Indeed, he argued, Pius XII was "a noble and virile character capable of taking very firm decisions and of adopting, fearlessly, positions that entailed considerable risk." What those courageous actions during the war were he did not say.[8]

An embarrassing example of this repackaging of history is offered by the Vatican's official 1998 statement on the church and the Holocaust, "We Remember." Released by the Vatican's Commission for Religious Relations with the Jews, headed by Cardinal Edward Cassidy, it set out its subject clearly enough: "The fact that the *Shoah* took place in Europe, that is, in countries of long-standing Christian civilization, raises the question of the relation between the Nazi persecution and the attitudes down the centuries of Christians towards the Jews." While acknowledging a long history of "anti-Judaism, of which, unfortunately, Christians also have been guilty," the Vatican statement argues that this demonization of Jews had nothing to do with what made the Holocaust possible. Rather, it attributed the latter to "anti-Semitism, based on theories contrary to the constant teaching of the Church." The Vatican statement completely ignores the heavy use the Fascists and Nazis made of the popes' long history of warnings about the evil influence of Jews and the repressive measures they took against Jews. It ignores as well the church's vigorous defense of the anti-Jewish laws introduced in much of Europe in the decade preceding the Final Solution, a defense found in Vatican-supervised publications as well. "We Remember" based its thesis on a distinction between anti-Judaism and antisemitism that had no basis in the actual history of the wave of antisemitism that swept much of Europe in the years leading up to and during the war. A more accurate title for the document, to which Pope John Paul II added his own letter of presentation, would have been "We Choose Not to Remember."[9]

At the center of this new, well-scrubbed historical narrative stands Pius XII, presented as the heroic champion of the oppressed. Ambiguous phrases buried amid thousands of words of baroque oratory have come to be heralded as clear denunciations of the Nazi extermination of Europe's Jews.[10] All the efforts the pope made to avoid antagonizing Hitler and Mussolini are wiped from view. His role as primate of the Italian church, presiding over a clergy that was actively supporting the Axis war, is likewise forgotten. Only examples of those brave priests who stood up to the Fascists can be discussed. Erased from memory are the pope's regular assurances to the Duce that he need only inform him of anti-Fascist priests, and he would have them silenced.

The speed with which the Fascist regime's influential lay enablers were able to remake their identities after the war was matched by the speed with which influential churchmen were able to remake theirs. Few were the unfortunates like Archbishop Bartolomasi who had to pay a price for having used their church pulpits to drum up support for the Axis cause. Even in such an extreme case as Bartolomasi's and his years of enthusiastic Fascist boosterism, however, it would take months of mounting pressure and papal foot-dragging before Pius XII finally forced the archbishop out as director of Italy's military chaplaincy. Cesare Orsenigo, the Hitler-friendly nuncio in Germany, remained in his position following the end of the war, indeed died while still nuncio there in 1946. Nor did the pope choose a new ambassador to Italy, leaving Francesco Borgongini in his place until elevating him, in 1953, to the cardinalate.

The church has showered honors on some of Mussolini's most influential boosters. Father Agostino Gemelli, after being subject to brief unpleasantness by the postwar Italian commission aimed at rooting out the main figures of the Fascist regime, returned to his post as rector of the Catholic University of Milan. Today Rome's major Catholic hospital is named in his honor. The campaign to make a saint of the archbishop of Milan, Cardinal Schuster, long viewed by the Fascists as one of their most important church supporters, began only three years after his death in 1954. In 1996 he was beatified.

IN THE SUMMER OF 1945, with the war in Europe over, foreign diplomats at the Vatican assumed the pope would finally go off to enjoy the traditional papal retreat in the fresh mountain air of Castel Gandolfo. After his initial stay there in 1939, he had not returned, insisting that while Romans were suffering, his place as their pastor was to remain at their side. But the pope didn't seem particularly eager to leave the Vatican. In mid-July, D'Arcy Osborne sent Churchill a report explaining the pope's decision:

> The real fact is that his "villeggiatura" in the country profoundly bores him and he has therefore been opposing passive resistance to all the endeavours of his court and well-wishers to persuade him to move and get a much needed change of air. He appears to be one of those unfortunates who are unable to relax and who cannot enjoy leisure or natural surroundings. On his

daily walk in the Vatican Gardens he is generally studying one of his speeches and rarely lifts his eyes from the document held close before them to look at the flowers and trees of his gardens or the view over Rome.[11]

The pope's annual Christmas address that year contained something none of his speeches during the war did, a clear denunciation of totalitarian states: "The force of the totalitarian State! Cruel, heart-rending irony! The whole surface of the globe, reddened with the bloodshed in these terrible years, cries aloud the tyranny of such a State." As Osborne observed, the pope had waited to denounce totalitarian states until the only one left was the Soviet Union.[12]

Not only did the pope help recraft the Italian church's history of collaboration with Mussolini's regime and support for the war; he helped remake Italy's history and Germany's as well. Far from sharing any blame for the war, Italians were now cast as its victims. Receiving Pasquale Diana, Italy's new ambassador to the Holy See, in February 1946, the pope described the Italian people as the "victim of a war in which they were involved against the feelings and wishes of the great majority." He went on to offer effusive praise, as Diana reported, "for the behavior of the German clergy for its opposition to the Nazi regime." Only in 2020 would the bishops of the Roman Catholic Church in Germany finally acknowledge how misleading the pope's representation of that history was. In marking the seventy-fifth anniversary of the end of the war, they issued a statement acknowledging that Germany's bishops failed to oppose the Nazi war or Hitler's attempted extermination of Europe's Jews. Neither Italy's church nor the Vatican itself has yet acknowledged any similar responsibility.[13]

The immediate postwar period was a dramatic one for Italy and for the pope. On June 2, 1946, with women having the right to vote for the first time, Italians went to the polls to decide whether to retain the Savoyard monarchy or to launch a new, republican form of government. A few weeks earlier King Victor Emmanuel, compromised by his longtime support for Mussolini and Fascism, had ceded the throne to his son in hopes this might encourage more enthusiasm for the monarchy. But his belated move proved insufficient. A majority voted for the republic. Umberto, king for a month, boarded a plane for Portugal and a life in exile. Italy no longer had a royal family.

The results of the referendum on the monarchy made the pope nervous, as he worried the change would benefit Italy's fast-growing Communist Party. He worried too that a new, democratic government would renounce the Lateran Accords, which from the Vatican perspective had been Mussolini's crowning achievement. In the end, these fears proved groundless. The Italian Communist Party, aiming to win Catholic votes in the heavily Catholic country, was eager to show that Communism and Catholicism were not incompatible. Party leader Palmiro Togliatti surprised many when he announced that the Communists would vote in favor of incorporating the Lateran Accords into the new Italian constitution. They remain there today. In the first election for parliament under the new republican constitution, held in 1948, the newly formed Christian Democratic Party, benefiting from the strong support of Catholic clergy and Catholic activists throughout the country, defeated a joint Communist-Socialist ticket to win a majority.[14]

The pope finally returned to Castel Gandolfo in August 1946, seven years after his last visit. Seventy years old, never in robust health, and having recently suffered through the cold wartime winters, the pope looked weakened. "The doctors," the French chargé d'affaires to the Vatican reported, "long preoccupied by his condition, have declared that they would no longer take any responsibility if the Sovereign Pontiff remained in Rome all summer." But even when he finally moved into the papal villa in the Alban Hills, the pope insisted on staying up late every night, refusing to go to bed before listening to the BBC radio's midnight news.[15]

The end of the war had no effect on the pope's commitment to his annual New Year's reception for the Roman aristocracy. Indeed, he used the occasion to express one of his worries about Italy's new democratic regime. The Fascist censoring of books, theater, and film that both Pius XII and his predecessor had taken ample advantage of was a thing of the past. The Christian concept of liberty, the pope told the assembled nobles, did not permit the press and motion pictures to remain unsupervised, for this would leave public morality unprotected. The pope would do what he could to see that offending materials were kept from the impressionable Italian public. He picked up on this theme the next month in his meeting with the Italian ambassador to the Holy See. "As was to be expected," the ambassador reported, "the Pontiff in the course of the audience also spoke of the antireligious and anticlerical press, expressing his regret that the means had not been found to stop those publications."[16]

The war's end also brought renewed gossip about the pope's failure to appoint a replacement for Cardinal Maglione as secretary of state. Shortly after the war's end, the American envoy Harold Tittmann sent a long report on the matter to Washington: "There is no doubt that being his own Secretary of State is not distasteful to him and that he welcomes the opportunity personally to supervise even the minutest details of administration." Tittmann passed on the rumor that was then spreading on both sides of the Atlantic: the pope wanted to select his friend Archbishop Francis Spellman for the post but thought it best to wait until the international situation died down before appointing an American. While Pius XII did take advantage of his first batch of appointments of new cardinals the next year to elevate Spellman to that rank, he would leave the position of secretary of state unfilled.[17]

By 1948, four years after Maglione's death, the fact the pope had still not filled the secretary of state position was prompting not a little unhappiness in the Vatican. Revealing were the remarks that Monsignor Carbone, on the Secretariat of State staff, confided to an Italian military intelligence informant:

> The Pope is a blessed man, who wants to do everything by himself and has an excessive estimation of his own personal abilities. He ought to remember how precious his own work was as Secretary of State to limit the personalism of Pius XI and he ought to resolve to place a cardinal at his side who has views of his own . . . with whom he can discuss and examine questions from two different points of view. Instead, he does everything

himself, he decides everything himself, because Monsignor Montini, out of fear of losing his confidence, tells him he is right about everything.[18]

This was not an opinion the monsignor would have dared to have the pope hear. Pius XII was not one to take criticism well. Jacques Maritain, the distinguished Catholic philosopher who at war's end had become France's ambassador to the Holy See, expressed his concerns about what he referred to as "the sensitivity of the Pope's temperament": "When the Pope saw his words maligned, or worse, when he saw them ignored . . . it hurt him more than it should. Although those around him continually encouraged him, really he was most alone and needed the encouragement of outside observers." Whenever Maritain found a press clipping that cast the pope in a good light, he sent it along to the pope to cheer him up.[19]

AFTER SAYING MASS AT the papal villa at Castel Gandolfo on September 3, 1948, Pius XII collapsed. Laid out on a nearby couch, he regained consciousness only a half hour later. Characteristically, the pope refused his doctors' advice that he not work so hard. Reporting the incident, the American envoy to the Vatican observed, "Sustained efforts by his intimate advisers to lighten his task by prevailing upon him to fill position of Secretary of State which has been vacant since 1944 . . . still unavailing."[20]

At the conclusion of his three years as ambassador to the Vatican in 1948, Jacques Maritain offered the French foreign minister his impressions. The Holy See, he explained, is a monarchy ruled by old men. Pius XII, eager to do good and to be seen to be doing good, believed it was his duty as pope to act as the defender of Western civilization. As a result, he had increasingly turned his attention to the political domain, a tendency reinforced by his recent successful involvement in keeping the Communists out of the Italian government. Indeed, thought Maritain, the pope's mystical belief in the bond that united the pontiff with the city of Rome had reinforced the Vatican's penchant for viewing the world through an Italian lens, notwithstanding the Holy See's universal mission.

"Of extreme delicacy and sensitivity, wishing not to hurt anyone, hesitating for a long time to take a decision," as the French ambassador described him, the pope could become unbending once he had made up his mind. But, concluded Maritain, "One should not expect from him the liveliness of reflexes and intuitions, the spontaneity and strength of character which marked his predecessor."[21]

Despite his frail health, Pius XII's papacy would last another decade. He would keep pushing himself as hard as he could to the end.

At his summer palace at Castel Gandolfo on October 3, 1958, the pope received a group of American pilgrims headed by his longtime friend Cardinal Spellman. He addressed them in English. The following day Britain's envoy to the Vatican heard rumors that the pope had taken ill. He asked Monsignor Angelo Dell'Acqua, who had replaced Montini as substitute in the Secretariat of State, whether it was anything serious. The pope, replied the monsignor, simply had a sore throat. Two days later the Vatican put out a bulletin with the news that the pope had suffered a stroke.

Pius XII died on the morning of October 9, aged eighty-two, his papacy having lasted nineteen years. "There can be no doubt," the British envoy reported to London, "that he really killed himself with over-work."[22]

At the time of his death, the Vatican secretary of state post was still unfilled, and Domenico Tardini remained in his position as pro-secretary of state for extraordinary ecclesiastical affairs. His longtime colleague Giovanni Montini was no longer with him. Four years earlier, following Cardinal Schuster's death, the pope had appointed Montini to be the new archbishop of Milan.

Life at the Vatican was about to change, as the mild-mannered Angelo Roncalli was elected by the cardinals to succeed Pope Pacelli. In 1953 Pius XII had summoned Roncalli, then nuncio to France, back to Italy, raising him to the cardinalate and appointing him patriarch of Venice. Taking the name John XXIII, Roncalli would soon convene a Second Vatican Council and, through it, seek to bring the Roman

Catholic Church into greater harmony with modern times. Although he would die while the council was still in session, his successor, Giovanni Montini, Pope Paul VI, would see it through to its end. Not the least among the changes it would usher in, the council would put an end to the church's age-old demonization of Jews.

THE SILENCE OF
THE POPE

———

THE CONTROVERSY OVER THE WARTIME POPE HAS LARGELY FOCUSED on his silence during the Holocaust, his failure ever to clearly denounce the Nazis for their ongoing campaign to exterminate Europe's Jews, or even to allow the word "Jew" to escape from his lips as they were being systematically murdered. The Jesuit scholar Pierre Blet, one of the best-informed and most sophisticated defenders of Pius XII, offered an explanation for that silence in 1997 that many others have embraced. The pope, he argued, "had given thought to the possibility of public statements" but in the end decided not to speak out. His decision was based on two considerations. The first was his belief that "protests gain nothing, and they can harm those whom one hopes to assist." The second was of quite a different nature: "Pius XII had to consider that a public statement on his part would have furnished ammunition to Nazi propaganda, which would in turn have presented the pope as an enemy of Germany. . . . It could unsettle the faithful—not all of whom were unaffected by the successes of the regime—in their confidence in the church and its leader." Father Blet was putting the matter delicately, but in plainer language this latter motivation boiled down to the pope's recognition that nearly half the citizens of the enlarged German Reich were Catholic, and millions of them were avid supporters of Hitler. To denounce Hitler and the Nazis as the German army was marching through Europe and rounding up Jews for extermination would be to risk losing their allegiance to the Roman Catholic Church.[1]

What are we to make of Father Blet's first proposition, the one most commonly heard today from those promoting a heroic image of the pope? Pius XII's silence, we are told, was motivated by his belief that if he were to denounce the Nazis' exterminationist campaign, he would be encouraging Hitler to take more severe actions against Europe's Jews. It is a proposition that assumes a Hitler and a Final Solution that are unrecognizable. It also fails to recognize that a large number of the men murdering the Jews, whether shooting them next to ditches they made their victims dig, or herding them into gas chambers, thought of themselves as good Catholics. Indeed, they might well have justified their action by recalling what they had learned from their parish priests about Jews and the danger Jews posed to good Christians, building on a centuries-long tradition of vilification of Jews by the church's lower clergy.

The focus on the pope's wartime actions in Italy, a country where his influence was huge, offers particularly valuable insight into these fraught questions. Can anyone argue that if Pius XII never spoke out against Italy's racial laws, and never declared it unacceptable for good Catholics to cooperate in the Jews' persecution, it was because he was afraid of making matters worse for the country's Jews? If he refused to denounce Mussolini for taking Italy to war at Hitler's side, could it have been because he worried that Italians would then abandon the Roman Catholic Church?

A question that is missing in so many of the polemics over Pius XII's attitudes toward the war and the decisions he made during it is a simple one: when? As I have shown in these pages, the war appeared differently to the pope over time. We can distinguish two broad phases. In the first, the pope had good reason to believe the Axis would win the war. The German army seized Warsaw within weeks of its invasion of Poland in September 1939 and the next year took Paris in a matter of weeks while at the same time driving the British army in humiliating retreat from the continent. The contrast with the trench warfare that

Germany had fought against France and Britain only a quarter-century earlier seemed astonishing at the time. Early in 1941 the German army quickly occupied the Balkans, then in June began a rapid march deep into the Soviet Union. Meanwhile England was reeling from months of devastating bombardment, while the Axis armies were routing British troops in North Africa and German submarines threatened to make North American aid to Britain impossible. In the east, Japan was going from conquest to conquest.

Pius XII's eagerness to remain on good terms with the Italian Fascist regime and to avoid offending Hitler in these years has to be understood in this light. He felt he needed to plan for a future in which Germany would dominate continental Europe. His first and foremost duty, as he saw it, was to protect the institutional church. Having no confidence in Hitler, indeed angered by the Nazis' systematic campaign to weaken the church, he saw in Mussolini his best bet for exercising a moderating influence on the man on whom, it seemed, Europe's fate and that of the church would depend. In an Axis-dominated Europe, too, the church's collaboration with the Fascist regime would guarantee its continued position of influence in Italy, a position that might otherwise be threatened by the spread of Nazi ideology to the Italian peninsula.

Only in late 1942, more than three years after the war began, as Axis reverses in Russia and the weight of America's entry into the war were finally being felt, did the ultimate defeat of the Axis begin to appear likelier than not. This ushered in the second phase of the war. But surprisingly little changed in the pope's approach, aside from occasional phrases that began to creep into his speeches referring to the sufferings of minorities and small nations. Part of the reason for this is that his main fear in the war's first phase—of the implications of an all-powerful Nazi regime for the fate of the church in Europe—was replaced by a new fear, the fate of the church following a victory by the Soviet Union.

The German army's occupation of Rome in September 1943 provided an additional incentive for the pope not to offend Hitler. Eager to protect Vatican City and other church institutions in the world capital of Catholicism, Pius XII was determined to maintain cordial relations with the Nazi authorities. Only in this context can we understand the pope's decision not to protest as a thousand of Rome's Jews were rounded up in October 1943 and shipped off to Auschwitz. The proposition that he did not protest because he feared what would happen to Italy's Jews if he did must be difficult for all but the most credulous to believe.

In justifying the pope's silence as the Nazis went about their systematic slaughter of Europe's Jews, defenders of the wartime pontiff sometimes point to the danger that any papal criticism would have entailed for the Vatican or, indeed, for the very safety of the pope himself. While here we are getting closer to the pope's motivation, this too has to be set in its proper context. As the evidence presented in these pages should make clear, both Nazi Germany and Fascist Italy were invested in portraying themselves as defenders of Christianity. The enemies of the Axis, Italy's Fascist press kept repeating, were the same enemies that had long been fighting the Roman Catholic Church: Jews, Communists, and Protestants. As for the Germans, they never bombed Rome, much less the Vatican. It was the Allies who did.

But let us for a moment indulge in a bit of conjectural history. What if? What if the pope had loudly denounced Hitler and Mussolini, excommunicated them, and warned that any Catholic who participated in the extermination of Europe's Jews would be condemned to an eternity of hell's fires? It is indeed not hard to imagine that in such a case the Germans occupying Rome would have taken action to muzzle him. But if they were thus forced to do so, it would have come at a considerable cost to their war effort, undermining one of their major propaganda claims.

This brings up another part of the story, for among the reasons for the pope's silence is one that is rarely mentioned. He realized that many of the loyal Nazi citizens in the Reich had been raised in the church and indeed continued to see themselves as Catholics. A 1939 census found that only one percent of Germans identified as "unbelievers," while the rest, other than the one percent who were Jewish, saw themselves as Christians. The leaders of the Third Reich regularly reminded them that the state was funding both Protestant and Catholic churches, as it would continue to do until the very end.[2] If Pius XII's silence was motivated by fears of the actions that the Axis powers might take against the church if he spoke out, it was motivated as well by his fears that denouncing the Nazis would alienate millions of Catholics and risk producing a schism in the church.

It is in this context that the ambiguity of the pope's speeches during the war can best be understood. A mixture of opaque theological language and moralistic bromides, his sermons were remarkable for their length and his ability, amid the torrents of oratory, to scatter nuggets that both sides would be able to point to as supporting their cause.[3] While government elites in London, Rome, and Berlin complained behind closed doors about the papal phrases they deemed pleasing to their enemies, both Axis and Allied governments worked tirelessly to promote the public impression that the pope was on their side.

IN EXAMINING THE CONSTRUCTION of the heroic image of Pius XII during the war, the historian Oliver Logan observed that the frail, bespectacled, ascetic figure of the "Man in White" offered the perfect foil to the hardy, black-shirted, barrel-chested, pugnacious Duce. As Mussolini's own fortunes declined, the man cast as Rome's savior would become the focus of an intense personality cult. The emotional attachment that many would have to this image after the war was made all the stronger by its unstated corollary, the pope as the spiritual force behind a church that firmly opposed Fascism and all it stood for.[4]

As the history told in these pages makes clear, the controversy over the pope's "silence" began almost as soon as the first shot of the war was fired. Criticisms of the pope for his support of Italian Fascism and for his eagerness to reach an understanding with Hitler began even before that. In February 1940 the American secretary of the treasury received a report from Kurt Riezler, member of a prominent German Catholic family, who had been a major figure in the Weimar Republic before being forced out when Hitler came to power in 1933. "The Catholic Church," observed Riezler, "made a very good bargain with Italian Fascism—strengthening its position in Italy a good deal. The Pope likes dealing with governments, not with people and elections and public opinion—a deal with a more moderate Nazi Government for the sake of peace—with some concessions to the Catholic Church for good service in mediating peace—would be in his line."[5]

The first criticisms of Pius XII for his silence during the war came when German troops crossed into Poland and began brutalizing the Poles, including, notably, many Roman Catholic priests. "The Pope does not seem to realize the immense authority that he continues to enjoy in the world," wrote the French ambassador to the Vatican in October 1940. "He does not seem to appreciate how important a word, an affirmation, a condemnation coming from him has. He has his weapons, and he either does not know it, or he does not want to use them." The ambassador went on to attribute the pope's timorousness to a lack of self-confidence due partly to his nervous character and partly to the "Fascist dictatorial atmosphere" in which the Vatican was enveloped. Although the men of the Vatican insisted that the pope was doing all he could behind the scenes, added the ambassador, "His initiatives are timid, their results insignificant."[6]

The postwar controversy over the pope's failure to denounce the Nazis began almost immediately following Germany's defeat. In mid-October 1945, a widely read French Swiss newspaper published an article, "Crime and Punishment," that denounced the papal nuncio in Berlin, Monsignor Orsenigo, and the Vatican: "Was the Apostolic Nuncio ignorant of the massacres of the members of the German, Austrian, and Polish clergy? Was the Vatican able to ignore the methods of those with whom it had signed a concordat?" Invoking the familiar biblical verse, the article concluded, "Woe unto those who have eyes but do not see and ears but do not hear." Alarmed, the nuncio in Switzerland wrote to Monsignor Tardini arguing that a Vatican response was "imperative" and requesting evidence to defend Orsenigo. The following May word that the Poles thought the Vatican had done nothing to come to the aid of Polish priests interned in German concentration camps led to a similar request for documents to defend the Vatican, including the correspondence of the nuncio in Berlin. Monsignor Tardini scribbled a note on the text of the request, dated May 30, 1946, expressing his doubt that sending such documentation would help their cause: "I am very uncertain: 1) Monsignor Orsenigo's reports have a tone that is a bit too . . . optimistic: he appears too credulous and rather . . . timid in regard to the Germans. 2) Our dispatches have a bureaucratic tone—and could not be otherwise. All this together is not likely to satisfy—today—the Poles."[7]

The evidence newly available from the Vatican archives offers further support for the astute assessment of Pius XII's wartime role by the prominent European historian István Deák:

> Fearful of Hitler's wrath, the Pope barely raised his voice against Nazi racism and anticlericalism, and spoke even less against Nazi anti-Semitism. He did not take a stand in defense of the suffering Polish Catholic nation, or of the Christian victims of the Nazi euthanasia program, or of the Jews of his own bishopric in Rome. . . .
>
> Pius XII made it his supreme purpose to assure the survival of the Catholic Church in a time of turmoil. In this, he was successful, although it is still not clear just how, when, and by whom that survival was threatened. Providing help to the victims of Nazi persecution, the pope undertook much less than could have been expected of a person of his exalted position.[8]

As Deák points out, Pius XII saw his primary responsibility to be the protection of the institutional church, its property, its prerogatives, and its ability to fulfill its mission as he saw it. But as multiple sources from the war years make clear, he was painfully aware of the criticism that he was failing to perform another role that many sought in the leader of the church, courageous moral leadership. His defensiveness on this score runs through innumerable reports of those who met with him at the time.

As the pope saw it, there were bad Fascists and good Fascists, the bad men of the Nazi regime and the good men. For every Farinacci there was a Ciano, for every Ribbentrop there was a Weizsäcker. What differentiated the good from the bad was their attitude toward the church. Those who respected the church's prerogatives, showed deference to the Catholic clergy, and offered the resources of the state to strengthen the church were good. Those who threatened the church's influence, undercut its institutional activities, and threatened its property and its reputation were bad.

Pius XII would never stand up to Mussolini or to Hitler. Both men clearly intimidated him, a fact that the two dictators recognized and used to their benefit. Defenders of Pius XII's silence who argue that the pope was not in a position to exert influence over Germany's political path have a point that has to be taken seriously, but such a defense has little to recommend it in the case of Italy. The pope was, after all, Italian, as were virtually all the men of the Curia. The Vatican was in Rome, within a couple of miles of Mussolini's Palazzo Venezia and the king's Quirinal Palace, and the pope himself was a Roman. The country was overwhelmingly Catholic and permeated by a massive capillary church organization that reached into the remotest villages. There is no doubt that the pope and the Catholic clergy had vast influence there.

The speed with which the whole apparatus of Fascism crumbled when the king deposed Mussolini on July 25, 1943, with barely a peep of popular protest, shows how tenuous the Duce's hold was on the Italian people in the end. What would have happened if the pope had denounced Italy's impending entry into the war in 1940, had denounced the constant use the Fascists were making of church authority in justifying their demonization of Jews? How many of the men who murdered Jews or helped round them up to be sent to their deaths saw themselves as good Roman Catholics?

Pope Pius XII was certainly not "Hitler's pope," as John Cornwell's intentionally provocative book title would have it. In many ways, the Nazi regime was anathema to the pope and to virtually all those around him in the Vatican. They were alarmed by the Reich's efforts to weaken the church's influence, diminish its hold on youth, and discredit key aspects of its theology. The pope's relation with the Italian Fascist regime was very different, and indeed there is a good case for viewing the Italian state as what scholars refer to as "clerico-Fascist."[9] The pope's interest in maintaining friendly relations with Mussolini was motivated as well by what he saw as his value as intercessor for the Vatican with the German Führer. It was a role that Mussolini and the men around him did indeed occasionally perform. One of the Duce's favorite boasts in speaking with Hitler and the Nazi leadership was of all the benefits he had enjoyed by keeping the pope happy.

If many Italians would prefer to remember Pius XII as a heroic figure, it is not due simply to their identities as Roman Catholics and to an understandable desire to view the leader of the church in a positive light. It is part of a much broader effort to recast Italy's uncomfortable Fascist past that goes well beyond the church. Jews in Italy, and especially those in Rome, have reason to see this past differently. As two of the major historical researchers in Rome's Jewish community recently noted, the pope remained silent while more than a thousand of the city's Jews were rounded up on October 16, 1943, and spent the next two days near the Apostolic Palace waiting to be taken to their deaths at Auschwitz. He never spoke out against any of the atrocities committed by the Nazis, not the mass execution at the Fosse Ardeatine nor any of the Nazis' other brutalities in Rome. The only time the pope made a public protest about events in Rome, one milked for all it was worth by the Fascists and Nazis, was when he condemned the bombing of the city by the Allies without making any mention of what the targets of that bombing were. As the major historian of the German occupation of Italy noted, despite claims by the pope's defenders that a behind-the-scenes protest on his part led to an end to the roundup of Rome's Jews following October 16, "the action of the capture of the Jews did not suffer any pause. On the contrary, it continued by the Germans in an undisturbed manner."[10]

If Pius XII is to be judged for his action in protecting the institutional interests of the Roman Catholic Church at a time of war, there is a good case to made that his papacy was a success. Vatican City was never violated, and amid the ashes of Italy's Fascist regime the church came out of the war with all the privileges it had won under Fascism intact. However, as a moral leader, Pius XII must be judged a failure. He had no love for Hitler, but he was intimidated by him, as he was by Italy's dictator as well. At a time of great uncertainty, Pius XII clung firmly to his determination to do nothing to antagonize either man. In fulfilling this aim, the pope was remarkably successful.

ACKNOWLEDGMENTS

―――

THIS BOOK IS BASED LARGELY ON DOCUMENTS FOUND IN ARCHIVES scattered across five countries, six if one counts Vatican City. For their help in this archival work, I have many people to thank, but among them Roberto Benedetti falls into a category of his own. Roberto, a historian expert in both church history and modern Italian history, has collaborated with me in the larger research project of which this book is one product, and together we have coauthored a number of studies published in scholarly journals. His expert efforts played a crucial role in this research, all the more so as the Covid-19 pandemic greatly reduced the amount of time I could spend in Rome at a crucial point in the research for this book. I am deeply indebted to him, and this book benefits tremendously from his research skills, his expertise in the archives, and his dedication.

For his guidance as I confronted the task of plumbing the German diplomatic archives in Berlin, I thank my colleague Lutz Klinkhammer, the foremost scholar dealing with the German occupation of Italy during the Second World War. For his work in those archives, I thank historian Pierluigi Pironti. Similarly, I am indebted to Meeraal Shafaat-Bokharee, at the time a doctoral candidate in history at Cambridge University, for her skilled work for this project at Britain's National Archives at Kew.

For their aid at the U.S. National Archives in College Park, Maryland, I thank Richard Peuser, then chief of the reading rooms there, for his expert advice and his friendship, and Sim Smiley, whose expertise in those archives proved so helpful to me.

For the German archival materials, I was additionally dependent on several Brown University students for their help in translation, including then undergraduates Talia Rueschemeyer-Bailey and Fabienne Tarrant. In addition, special mention is due to Gunnar Mokosch, who began to work on this project when still a graduate student at Brown. He provided crucial help in translating German-language documents and in other aspects of my work with German sources. It was a pleasure to be able to coauthor two scholarly journal articles with him comparing the Italian and German anti-Jewish campaigns, articles I could not have written on my own. I also owe thanks to Jonathan Petropoulos, author of an excellent book on the von Hessen brothers, for his help in fleshing out the story of Prince Philipp von Hessen's role as go-between linking Hitler and Pius XII.

Many thanks to the heads of the various Vatican archives, and for the time they took to meet with me in advance of the opening of the files for the papacy of Pius XII: Monsignor Sergio Pagano, prefect of the Vatican Apostolic Archives; Monsignor Alejandro Cifres, director of the archive of the Congregation for the Doctrine of the Faith; and Johan Ickx, director of the Historical Archive of the Section for Relations with States of the Vatican Secretariat of State. Thanks as well to Daniel Ponziani at the archive of the Congregation for the Doctrine of the Faith and to Brian Mac Cuarta, S.J., academic director of the central Jesuit archives in Rome.

Others in Rome deserving of thanks include my colleague Mauro Canali, one of Italy's foremost experts on the Fascist *ventennio* and intimate master of the Italian state archives for this period, and Tommaso Dell'Era, who shares my interest in the fraught history of the Holy See's actions as the Jews of Europe were being persecuted and then massacred. Thanks as well to Silvia Haia Antonucci, director of the historical archives of Rome's Jewish community, and to Gadi Luzzatto Voghera, director of the Fondazione Centro di Documentazione Ebraica Contemporanea in Milan, for their advice, and to the staff of Rome's Archivio Centrale dello Stato for their assistance.

I would also like to thank various colleagues at Brown University who offered help along the way, including Massimo Riva, Michael Putnam, and John Bodel. Michael and John's help in compensating for the deficiencies of my high school Latin was aided by Brown University classics doctoral student Erika Valdivieso. Thanks, too, to Kevin McLaughlin, dean of the faculty at Brown, and Ed Steinfeld, director of Brown's Watson Institute for International and Public Affairs, for their support, as well as to Matilde Andrade of the department of anthropology. My final Brown thanks is due to the Paul Dupee, Jr., University Professorship, which has provided invaluable funding for my research.

Deep appreciation goes to my literary agent, Wendy Strothman, for all her expert efforts on my behalf, and to her associate, Lauren MacLeod. I also thank the talented Laura Hartman Maestro for the excellent maps she drew for this book.

I feel incredibly fortunate to have had David Ebershoff as my editor at Random House for this book. David had previously been my editor for *The Pope and Mussolini*. I know of no more talented editor in the United States, or anywhere else, for that matter. At Random House I would also like to thank Andy Ward and Tom Perry, publisher and deputy publisher at Random House for their support, along with Darryl Oliver, Barbara Fillon, and Michelle Jasmine. Special thanks to Christopher Brand for the book's stunning jacket design.

I am deeply grateful to my colleagues, the historians Jonathan Petropoulos and Kevin Spicer, C.S.C., and to my friends Bob Bahr, Katherine Darrow, and Peter Darrow for taking the time to read an earlier draft of this book and provide their valuable suggestions (and in the case of Jonathan and Kevin, corrections). This marks the first time that my wife, Susan Kertzer, has read and offered her suggestions on a draft of a book of mine. Despite our earlier fears, our marriage survived the ordeal, and I am indebted to her both for her helpful suggestions and for her patience (and for much else!).

I can't conclude these acknowledgments without bringing to mind my father, whose presence lingers over the pages of this book. As the Jewish chaplain with the Allied troops at Anzio beachhead in early

1944, Lieutenant Morris Kertzer, then thirty-three years old, officiated over Jewish services in a wine cellar while under German bombardment, comforted wounded GIs at the field hospital, and presided over the funerals of Jewish soldiers. He accompanied the troops when, after months of bloody stalemate, they broke through the German defenses and, in early June 1944, liberated Rome. A few days later, together with the chief rabbi of Rome, he conducted services at Rome's Tempio Maggiore. It was the first service held in Rome's majestic synagogue since German troops had occupied the city the previous September and begun their roundup of the city's Jews for deportation to Auschwitz.

Strange, sometimes, are the paths our lives take, and so I find myself, surprisingly, almost eight decades after those events, returning to Rome, and to a story in which my own father played a part.

ARCHIVAL SOURCES
AND ABBREVIATIONS

———

THE FOLLOWING ABBREVIATIONS ARE USED IN THE ENDNOTES.

ARCHIVAL SOURCES

British Archives

NAK   National Archives, Kew, London

   CAB   War Cabinet

    FO   Foreign Office

   WO   War Office

French Archives

MAEC   Ministère des Affaires Étrangères, La Courneuve

MAEN   Ministère des Affaires Étrangères, Nantes

   RSS   Rome Saint Siège

German Archives

PAAA   Politisches Archiv des Auswärtigen Amts, Berlin

 GARV   Auslandsvertretung Rom-Vatikan

  GBS   Büro des Staatsekretärs

  GPA   Politische Abteilung

  GRK   Reichskonkordat

Italian Archives

ACS   Archivio Centrale dello Stato, Rome

CR   Segreteria Particolare Duce, Carteggio Riservato

DAGR   Direzione Generale Pubblica Sicurezza, Divisione
Affari Generali e Riservati

DAGRA   Direzione Generale Pubblica Sicurezza, Divisione
Affari Generali e Riservati, Annuali

DGPS   Direzione Generale Pubblica Sicurezza

MAT   Fascicoli per Materia (1926–44)

MCPG   Ministero della Cultura Popolare, Gabinetto

MI   Ministero dell'Interno

MIFP   Ministero dell'Interno, Fascicoli Personali

PCM   Presidenza del Consiglio dei Ministri

SPD   Segreteria Particolare del Duce

ASDMAE   Archivio Storico Diplomatico, Ministero degli
Affari Esteri, Rome

AISS   Ambasciata Italiana presso la Santa Sede

APSS   Affari Politici, 1931–1945, Santa Sede

GAB   Gabinetto

SG   Segreteria Generale

ASR   Archivio di Stato, Roma, Galla Placidia, Rome

CAP   Corte d'Assise Speciale

ATMR   Archivio Tribunale Militare, Roma, Rome

AUSSME   Archivio Ufficio Storico Stato Maggiore
dell'Esercito, Rome

SIM   Servizio Informazioni Militare

ISACEM   Istituto per la Storia dell'Azione Cattolica e del
Movimento Cattolico in Italia, Rome

PG   Presidenza Generale, 1922–69

United States Archives

NARA   U.S. National Archive and Records Administration, College Park, Maryland

CDF   Central decimal file

RG   Record Group

FDR Library   Franklin Delano Roosevelt Presidential Library, Hyde Park, New York

md, mr, psfa, psfb, psfc, are all pdf document files available on the internet

Vatican and Ecclesiastical Archives

AAV   Archivio Apostolico Vaticano, Vatican City

AESI   Segreteria di Stato, Affari Ecclesiastici Straordinari, Italia

Segr. Stato   Segreteria di Stato

ACDF   Archivio della Congregazione per la Dottrina della Fede, Vatican City

ARSI   Archivium Romanum Societatis Iesu, Rome

ASRS   Archivio Storico della Segreteria di Stato— Sezione per i Rapporti con gli Stati, Vatican City

AA.EE.SS.   Fondo Congregazione degli Affari Ecclesiastici Straordinari

OTHER ABBREVIATIONS

ADSS   *Actes et Documents du Saint Siège Relatifs à la Seconde Guerre Mondiale*

AI   *L'Avvenire d'Italia*

AR   *L'Avvenire*, Rome

CC   *La Civiltà Cattolica*

CS   *Corriere della Sera*

DDF   *Documents Diplomatiques Français*

DDI   *Documenti Diplomatici Italiani*

DGFP	*Documents of German Foreign Policy*
FDR	Franklin Delano Roosevelt
FRUS	*Foreign Relations of the United States*
OR	*L'Osservatore Romano*
PI	*Il Popolo d'Italia*
RF	*Il Regime Fascista*
RSI	Repubblica Sociale Italiano
b.	*busta*
fasc.	*fascicolo*
f.	*foglio*
ff.	*fogli*
posiz.	*posizione*
prot.	*protocollo*

NOTES

PROLOGUE: THE TWISTED CROSS

1. John R. Putnam, consul general, Florence, to William Phillips, American ambassador, Rome, May 21, 1938, and Putnam's "Memorandum of Visit of Their Excellencies Adolph Hitler and Benito Mussolini, May 9, 1938," NARA, LM 192, reel 7; Milza 2000, pp. 759–61; Kershaw 2000, pp. 98–99; Corvaja 2008, pp. 60–68; Ciano 1980, p. 134, diary entry for May 9, 1938.
2. Pignatti to Ciano, May 5, 1938, DDI, series 8, vol. 9, n. 53.
3. On Hitler's relations with Pius XI, see Wolf 2008 and Godman 2007.

CHAPTER I: DEATH OF A POPE

1. Monsignor Tardini's diary describes the scene; see Pagano 2020, pp. 101–4.
2. https://it.cathopedia.org/wiki/Camerlengo. On the role of the Camerlengo also see Del Re 1970, pp. 297–99.
3. Charles-Roux to French Foreign Ministry, September 5, 1938, MAEC, Europe-Italie 267, ff. 131–32.
4. Gannon 1962, pp. 111–15; Gallagher 2008, pp. 87–88, 146n41; Baudrillart 1996, p. 536, diary entry for June 22, 1937; O'Shea 2011, pp. 130–32; Rivière, Rome, to French Foreign Ministry, July 21, 1937, MAEN, RSS 576, PO/1, 1040.
5. Orsenigo, Berlin, to Cardinal Pacelli, May 14, 1937, AAV, *Arch. Nunz. Svizzera* (1935–53), b. 82, fasc. 21, f. 49r. Monsignor Orsenigo was referring to his conversation with German state secretary Ernst von Weizsäcker. Pacelli notes, "L'Ambasciatore di Francia," February 1, 1933, ASRS, *AA.EE.SS.*, posiz. 430b, fasc. 359, f. 35; Charles-Roux to foreign minister, Paris, February 10, 1932, and May 20, 1933, MAEC, Europe-Saint Siège 37, ff. 62, 71–77; Blet 1996, p. 199; Wolf 2008, pp. 158–65; Chiron 2006, pp. 351–52; Kent 1982, pp. 154–55.
6. Kershaw 1999, p. 180; Report of Maggiore Renzetti, Berlin, June 19–20, 1934, DDI, series 7, vol. 15, n. 419; Mussolini to De Vecchi, June 22, 1934, DDI, series 7, vol. 15, n. 430.
7. "Colloquio fra il Capo del Governo . . . ," July 2, 1934, DDI, series 7, vol. 15, n. 469.
8. "Da fonte vaticana," December 24, 1934, ACS, MCPG, b. 158.
9. "Chronologie des relations Franco-Italiennes," MAEC, Papiers Chauvel, vol. 121, f. 24; Luza 1977, p. 542; Pacelli to Mussolini, March 16, 1938, DDI, series 8, vol. 8, n. 339. When, two weeks later, Austria's bishops took advantage of Sunday Mass to read a statement praising all the good Hitler had done and calling on Catholics to vote in the up-

coming plebiscite for Austria's incorporation in the Third Reich, Pius XI was furious. He was especially outraged by the behavior of the Austrian cardinal primate, Vienna's archbishop, Theodor Innitzer. "He signed everything they put in front of him," the pope complained to a French cardinal, "and then he added, without any prompting, 'Heil Hitler!'" Charles-Roux to Georges Bonnet, April 20, 1938, DDF, series 2, vol. 9, n. 209.

10. Hitler's remark, to the visiting pro-Nazi Roberto Farinacci, came in late January 1939. Attolico, Berlin, to Ciano, January 25, 1939, DDI, series 8, vol. 11, n. 108.

11. Having added millions of people to the Reich in the previous year, concluded the Italian ambassador, Hitler needed a period of peace to fully absorb them. "Those, therefore, from outside Germany who believed they would find in the January 30, 1939, speech the germs and the signs of new 'adventures' will have to agree that, after all, the Führer's speech is, taking into account, I repeat, the man, a pacific one." Attolico, Berlin, to Ciano, January 31, 1939, DDI, series 8, vol. 11, n. 130.

12. This is a story I tell in *The Pope and Mussolini* (Kertzer 2014).

13. Bergen to Secretary of State Ernst von Weizsäcker, Berlin, July 23, 1937, telegram, PAAA, GRk, R103252, 16–18.

14. Pignatti to Ciano, December 12, 1938, n. 152, ASDMAE, AISS, b. 95.

15. Pignatti to Ciano, January 4, 1939, n. 41, ASDMAE, AISS, b. 95. In his recent weighty two-volume study, Coco (2019) offers a rich analysis of the dynamics of Mussolini's relations with Pius XI and Pacelli throughout the years in which Cardinal Pacelli served as secretary of state.

16. Phillips to FDR, January 5, 1939, FDR Library, psfa 400, p. 102.

17. Phillips 1952, p. 188. Ciano's meteoric rise predictably provoked jealousy among his colleagues in the foreign service. As one sniped, "The presence in that high position of an immature and arrogant boy, with his obscene thirst for power, spoiled by unearned honors, and with unlimited impunity, possessing a monstrous power, dominated by likes and hatreds, slave of a morbid impressionability and a morbid boastfulness, represented the clear obliteration of over a half century of tradition, of responsibility and prestige of Italian diplomacy." Di Rienzo 2018, pp. 161–62.

18. Phillips to FDR, January 5, 1939, FDR Library, psfa 400, pp. 101–3. The text of Phillips's memo to the president is also found in FRUS vol. 2, pp. 57–60. On January 26, President Roosevelt wrote back to Phillips: "I have read with a great deal of interest your letter of January 5 and the accompanying memorandum of your conversation with Mussolini concerning the Jewish refugee situation. Although I was naturally disappointed that the Duce was not receptive to my suggestion concerning the settlement of refugees on the East African plateau, I am gratified that he at least appreciates the desirability of finding a real solution of the refugee problem and that he indicated a willingness to be helpful in this connection. I have taken note of his expressed willingness to give sympathetic consideration to a specific plan." FDR Library, psfa 400, p. 100.

19. Edda Mussolini 1975, pp. 40–50, 103.

20. Bottai 1989, p. 141, diary entry for February 4, 1939; Navarra 2004, p. 46; Bosworth 2017, pp. 96–97; Gagliani 2015.

21. "La situazione religiosa nel Reich," OR, January 22, 1939, p. 2; "Dopo il discorso del Cancelliere del Reich," OR, February 3, 1939, p. 1.

22. Sottosegretario di stato per gli affari esteri to Pignatti, January 22, 1939, ASDMAE, AISS, b. 102; Pignatti to Ciano, January 24, 1939, ASDMAE, AISS, b. 102.

In fact, only a week earlier Pignatti had sent Ciano a long report pointing to the importance of a conclave to elect a new pope, one that, given the parlous condition of the pope's health, seemed not far off. "I fear," confided the ambassador, "that there is not much to hope for as long as the current pontificate lasts." As, he recalled, he had told the Duce himself, "The Holy Father is tenacious in his ideas and this, his stubbornness, has only been aggravated by his age and by the illness that afflicts him." But Pignatti remained hopeful. "I am convinced that the next pontificate will differ markedly from the present one." Pignatti to Ciano, January 14, 1939, ASDMAE, AISS, b. 95. For the details of this story, see Kertzer 2014. Tardini's note is quoted in Coco 2019, p. 1155. The ellipsis is in the original.

23. The fullest examination of the project for the encyclical, *Humani Generis Unitas,* is provided by Passelecq and Suchecky 1997. The Vatican archives opened since that book was published, however, offer new insight on the project. See the documents at ASRS, *AA.EE.SS.,* Pio XII, parte 1, Stati Ecclesiastici, posiz. 664 A, B, C. Two other sets of documents on the "hidden encyclical" have not to date been made available to researchers at the Vatican (posiz. 664 D and E).

24. Baudrillart 1996, p. 947, diary entry for February 5, 1939; Charles-Roux 1947, p. 242. Word of the pope's ill health began to spread through Rome, leading the Vatican to put out stories that the pontiff was suffering simply from a minor indisposition. "The Pontiff has a light cold," read the February 8 headline in *Regime Fascista.* The front-page story in the next day's edition of Milan's Catholic daily offered the reassuring headline "The Pope's health is fully satisfactory." "Il Pontefice leggermente raffreddato," RF, February 8, 1939, p. 2; "Le condizioni di salute del Papa sono pienamente soddisfacenti," *L'Italia,* February 9, 1939, p. 1.

25. Ciano 1980, p. 250, diary entry for February 10, 1939; Cianfarra 1944, p. 20; Bottai 1989, p. 142, diary entry for February 9, 1939.

26. "In morte del Sommo Pontefice Pio XI," OR, February 12, 1939, p. 1; "Il Gran Consiglio saluta la memoria del Pontefice," PI, February 11, 1939, p. 1.

27. G. Sommi Picenardi, "Il Papa della pace," RF, February 11, 1939, p. 1.

28. Such a picture would not be one that Mussolini would like to see in circulation. A note on the back of the original photo in the Vatican archive reads: "This photograph of His Excellency Count Galeazzo Ciano . . . before the Body of His Holiness Pius XI, in the Sistine Chapel, was withdrawn at the request of His Excellency the Ambassador of Italy, Count Pignatti, who was acting by the order of his Government, and any public dissemination of it was forbidden." AAV, *Segr. Stato,* 1939, Stati, posiz. 60, ff. 5rv. Ciano's telegram (n. 1963) is found at ASDMAE, APSS, b. 45; Ciano 2002, pp. 250–51. Mussolini's own newspaper, *Il Popolo d'Italia,* in reporting news of the pope's death, included a large front-page photograph of Ciano standing alongside Cardinal Pacelli in the Sistine Chapel where the pope's body lay, with the headline "Representing the Fascist government, Ciano renders homage to the corpse." "Ciano rende omaggio alla Salma in rappresentanza del governo fascista," PI, February 11, 1939, p. 1.

29. Ciano 1980, pp. 251–52, diary entries for February 11 and 12, 1939.

30. Appunto Tardini, February 15, 1939, AAV, *Segr. St.,* 1939, Stati Ecclesiastici, posiz. 576 PO, fasc. 607, ff. 164rv; Ciano 1980, p. 252; Pacelli to Ciano, February 13, 1939, ASDMAE, AISS, b. 95; ASV, AESS, posiz. 576, fasc. 606, ff. 147r–53r. Tardini (AAV, *Segr. St.,* 1939, Stati Ecclesiastici, posiz. 576 PO, fasc. 607, ff. 147r–153r) documented the text of what Pius XI planned to be his speech to the bishops on Feburary 11; Fattorini (2011, pp. 210–15) provides the English text of the pope's planned remarks. "The speech that the dead Pope was supposed to read to the Italian bishops who had come to Rome for the tenth anniversary of Conciliation," Pignatti reported to Ciano on the 22nd, "was read and discussed in one of the cardinals' first meetings. The cardinals unanimously decided not to have it released. . . . The cardinals took this decision because the contents of Pius XI's speech seemed too polemical and too strong, and also because it would have tied the hands of the future Pope." Pignatti to Ciano, February 22, 1939, n. 23, ASDMAE, AISS, b. 95. Cardinal Baudrillart's diary entry of two days later, shortly after he arrived in Rome for the conclave, provides further evidence that Pacelli discussed the matter with the cardinals. Known for his Fascist sympathies, the French cardinal was

clearly relieved at the decision to bury the pope's speech: "Everywhere, here, one keeps repeating how providential it is that Pius XI was not able to give his speech to the Italian bishops. It would have embarrassed his successor. The speech has been printed, but kept secret." Baudrillart 1996, pp. 968–69, diary entry for February 24, 1939.

CHAPTER 2: THE CONCLAVE

1. On the Vatican's view of Pignatti, see Maglione, Paris, to Segreteria di Stato di Sua Santità, May 9, 1935, ufficio cifra n. 509, AAV, AESI, *Segr. Stato,* b. 985/658, f. 23r.

2. Pleased to hear this, the Italian ambassador suggested that it would help their cause if in the coming days the German government did what it could to foster the atmosphere needed to elect a "moderate" pope. The German press, he advised, should begin showing more respect toward the Vatican. Pignatti's second piece of advice to Bergen focused on the role the sizable group of German cardinals would play at the conclave. If they were to tell their colleagues that reaching an agreement with the German government was impossible, "all will be lost." Bergen replied that he, too, had heard many expressions of sympathy for Germany in the Vatican in recent days, something that had been notably lacking in the last years of Pius XI's papacy. Pignatti to Ciano, February 18, 1939, n. 21, ASDMAE, AISS, b. 95.

    Following their meeting Bergen sent an urgent plea to Berlin: The government should prevent the German press from taking any more "swipes against the person of the late Pope and other individuals in the Curia." "Indeed," he added, "calling Pius XI a 'political adventurer,' as happened in the 'Angriff' [a Nazi newspaper] on the 10th of this month . . . should be strictly avoided." Bergen to Weizsäcker, February 18, 1939, tel. 19, PAAA, GRk, R29814, 90.

    Meanwhile Pignatti sought the help of the influential superior general of the Jesuit Order, Wladimir Ledóchowski. The two men had regularly commiserated in the past, sharing their alarm at Pius XI's increasingly hostile attitude toward the Italian Fascist regime. Pignatti's goal was to interest the Jesuit general in having a helpful word with the German cardinals. He was confident, he later told Ciano, that Ledóchowski would do just that. Pignatti to Ciano, February 21, 1939, nn. 21 and 22, ASDMAE, AISS, b. 95.

3. Pignatti to Ciano, February 26, 1939, ASDMAE, AISS, b. 95. Ciano's copy to the Italian ambassador in Berlin is found at ASDMAE, APSS, b. 63. Among the bits of evidence coming to Mussolini and his entourage giving them confidence about the friendly attitude Pacelli would adopt was a police informant report of March 1. It offered details on a conversation with Cardinal Angelo Dolci, a big booster of Pacelli's candidacy. Were Pacelli not elected, the cardinal concluded, it would be "a serious error, because Pacelli is such a good person, a good Italian, and is sympathetic to the Regime." ACS, MCPG, b. 170.

4. Pignatti to Ciano, February 27, 1939, ASDMAE, AISS, b. 95.

5. Baudrillart 1996, p. 965, diary entry for February 22, 1939; Charles-Roux to Paris, March 1, 1939, MAEN, RSS 576, PO/1, 1031; Charles-Roux 1947, pp. 266, 272.

6. The report that the Italian ambassador in Lisbon sent on February 27, 1939, to Ciano was then forwarded to Pignatti. Tel. 207233, ASDMAE, AISS, b. 105.

7. Baudrillart 1996, pp. 973–74, diary entry for March 1, 1939; Papin 1977, pp. 60–61.

8. Baudrillart 1996, pp. 975–76, diary entry for March 2, 1939; Charles-Roux to Paris, March 2, 1939, MAEN, RSS 576, PO/1, 1031.

9. Rhodes 1974, pp. 222–23; Baudrillart 1996, p. 732, diary entry for January 17, 1938.

10. Ventresca 2013, pp. 50–51; Schad 2008, pp. 9, 24–29.

11. The quote is from the diary of Bella Fromm, a German Jewish journalist. Schad 2008, pp. 42–43. See also Tittmann 2004, pp. 92–93.

12. Lehnert 2014, pp. 25–26; Cornwell 1999, p. 101.

13. Sister Pascalina quickly gained an enemy in Pacelli's younger sister, Elisabetta. When Elisabetta and her brother were young, they had been quite close, and Elisabetta would occasionally accompany Eugenio's violin with her mandolin. In recent years, while Sister Pascalina had seen Pacelli every day, Pacelli's sister had rarely gotten to see him. Married to a Vatican functionary, she had never left Rome, and now that he had finally returned, she was not pleased to see that another woman was closer to him. To those who would listen, she shared her view that the nun her brother was so attached to was, as she put it, "authoritarian and very cunning." Schad 2008, pp. 53, 62–63; Coppa 2013, pp. 21, 40–41.

14. Charles-Roux 1947, pp. 74–75; Tardini 1961, pp. 51, 60, 66; Carnahan 1949, pp. 19, 30. For a rich description of the great care Pacelli took in preparing his speeches, see Coco 2020. The pope, observes the prominent church historian Emma Fattorini (2007, p. 54), saw in Eugenio Pacelli all that he was not, "tall, solemn, noble, expert command of languages and able preacher, truly a man of the Curia, of exquisite manners." She provides an excellent, succinct portrait of Pacelli and the complementarity of his relationship with Pius XI.

15. Pignatti to Ciano, March 2, 1939, n. 32, ASDMAE, AISS, b. 95.

16. Ciano 2002, p. 195, diary entry for March 2, 1939.

17. "Pace unita alla giustizia," CS, March 3, 1939, p. 1. Farinacci wrote: "The election of Cardinal Eugenio Pacelli as Supreme Pontiff has been greeted with unanimous pleasure." The German papers, he claimed, were also singing the new pontiff's praises. "Il Pontefice Pio dodicesimo," RF, March 4, 1939, p. 1. Mussolini's ambassador to the Third Reich happened to be in the office of German state secretary Ernst von Weizsäcker in Berlin when news of the new pope's election came in. Having read the reports his own ambassador had been sending him from Rome, Weizsäcker showed little surprise. "It is observed here," wrote Mussolini's ambassador, "that Cardinal Pacelli is, after all, not only a very fine diplomat, but contrary to what is commonly thought, he is not a man with a particularly large or strong will. Thus, he is not, by nature, prone to taking actions that are too politically extreme." Weizsäcker would soon get further support for his cautious optimism from the head of the Reich's Vatican Affairs Department. Following the many years that the new pope had spent in Germany, the department head reported, he could properly be described as a Germanophile, eager to establish friendly relations with the Reich. He added, "Pacelli has always been in favor of good relations with Mussolini and with Fascist Italy." Attolico to Ciano, March 3, 1939, tel. 207459, ASDMAE, AISS, b. 95; Friedländer 1966, pp. 3–5.

18. Lehnert 1984, p. 87; Schad 2008, pp. 24–29, 63–65.

CHAPTER 3: APPEALING TO THE FÜHRER

1. Hitler's "personal message" to the pope, judged Milan's Catholic daily, contained "expressions that are especially reverent and cordial." "Il nuovo Pontefice e la situazione religiosa in Germania," L'Italia, March 12, 1939, p. 1.

2. Bergen to Foreign Ministry, Berlin, March 5, 1939, PAAA, GPA, Beschränkung der diplomatischen Beziehungen zwischen dem Reich und dem Vatikan auf das Altreich, R261178, 02–20. Also published in DGFP, series D, vol. 4, n. 472.

3. The pope's message to Hitler read:

> To the illustrious, Herr Adolf Hitler, Führer and Chancellor of the German Reich!
>
> Here at the beginning of our pontificate we wish to assure you that we remain devoted to the spiritual welfare of the German people entrusted to your

leadership. We implore God the Almighty to grant them that true felicity which springs from religion.

We recall with great pleasure the many years We spent in Germany as Apostolic Nuncio when We did all in our power to establish harmonious relations between Church and State. Now that the responsibilities of our pastoral function have increased our opportunities, how much more ardently do We pray to reach that goal.

May the prosperity of the German people and their progress in every domain come, with God's help, to fruition!

As the pope pointed out later to Bergen in emphasizing the importance he gave to this message, he broke with protocol by signing not only the formal Latin note to the Führer but also a German version, which he had prepared himself. Bergen to State Secretary Weizsäcker personally, March 18, 1939, n. 35, PAAA, GBS, R261178, 04.

4. Malgeri 2006; Tittmann 2004, p. 87. "Il Cardinal Maglione nuovo Segretario di Stato di S. Santità," *L'Italia,* March 12, 1939, p. 3; Ciano 1980, p. 268, diary entry for March 18, 1939. The unsigned, undated Italian Foreign Ministry profile of Maglione is found at ASDMAE, AISS, b. 143. In its enthusiastic front-page announcement of the appointment, Mussolini's newspaper asserted that it would be "greeted everywhere with sincere pleasure and great sympathy." "Il Card. Maglione nominato Segretario di Stato," PI, March 12, 1939, p. 1.

5. "Il popolo verso la Basilica" and "Il rito al cospetto della moltitudine," PI, March 13, 1939, p. 1.

6. Phillips to FDR, March 12, 1939, FDR Library, psfa 400, p. 128; Phillips 1952, pp. 252–54; Ciano 1980, p. 263; Charles-Roux to Paris, March 12, 1939, MAEN, RSS 576, PO/1, 1031–33; "Promemoria," March 12, 1939, ACS, DAGRA, b. 39a; Baudrillart 1996, pp. 988–89, diary entry for March 12, 1939; Lehnert 1984, pp. 85, 96.

7. Doyle 1950; Chadwick 1986, p. 130; Papin 1977, pp. 66–67; Chenaux 2003, pp. 231–32; Lehnert 1984, pp. 86–87, 104, 119; Cianfarra 1944, pp. 87–93; Tardini 1961, pp. 142–43; Baudrillart 1996, p. 986, diary entry for March 10, 1939.

8. "Of all the 'facts' that took place in these fatal years," Dino Grandi, one of Italy's most prominent Fascist leaders, recalled after the war, "this was the determining one." Grandi 1985, p. 459.

9. Bergen to Foreign Ministry, Berlin, March 22, 1939, DGFP, series D, vol. 6, n. 65.

10. Pollard (2005, p. 125) documents the Vatican's heavy dependence on American Catholics "to keep it afloat" from the time Pius XI became pope in 1922.

11. Charles-Roux to foreign minister, Paris, March 4, 1939, MAEN, RSS 576, PO/1, 1031; "La prima giornata del nuovo Papa," PI, March 4, 1939, p. 1; "Pio XII invoca la pace nella carità, nella giustizia, nell'ordine," RF, March 4, 1939, p. 1; "Un grande evento degradato a speculazione politica," CS, March 4, 1939, p. 2. Italy's Catholic dailies followed suit. Rome's *L'Avvenire* ran a front-page editorial by its director featuring the pope's watchword of "peace with justice" and using the opportunity to give vent to an anti-British screed. Novus, "Auspicio e promessa di una pace con giustizia," AR, March 7, 1939, p. 1.

12. François-Poncet 1961, pp. 14, 113–16; Moseley 1999, pp. 4–32; Bastianini 2005, pp. 253–72; Di Rienzo 2018, pp. 64, 161–62; Innocenti 1992, p. 16.

13. Ciano 1980, p. 268, diary entry for March 18, 1939; "Pio XII riceve S. E. Ciano," *L'Italia,* March 19, 1939, p. 1; "Il Ministro Ciano ricevuto da Pio XII," PI, March 19, 1939, p. 1; Kertzer 2014, pp. 55–56. "Pius XII had no hesitation in leading that organization in an opposite direction," observed the ambassador. Pignatti to Ciano, April 5, 1939, ASDMAE, AISS, b. 116. Pizzardo's official title was President of the Central Office of Catholic Action. Trionfini 2015.

14. Farinacci, "Uomo singolare," RF, December 15, 1939, p. 1.

15. The fact that Father Tacchi Venturi had at least seven meetings with the pope in 1939 alone offers strong evidence of the value that Pius XII saw in making use of the Jesuit's high-level contacts with the leaders of the Fascist regime. AAV, *Prefettura Casa Pontif.,* Udienze, b. 38–41.

16. The official appointment schedule for Pius XII shows that he met with Tacchi Venturi on March 22, 1939. AAV, *Prefettura Casa Pontif.,* Udienze, b. 38.

17. Tacchi Venturi to Maglione, March 28, 1939, ADSS, vol. 6, n. 5. The text of the document the Jesuit envoy left with Mussolini is also found there. Tacchi Venturi's own notes on the meeting, dated March 27, 1939, are found at ARSI, Fondo Tacchi Venturi, Miscellanea, b. 11, fasc. 33, carte non numerate.

18. "Pio XII benedice la Spagna," *L'Italia,* April 2, 1939, p. 1; Fattorini 2007, p. 104; Halls 1995, p. 33. On the exchange of messages between Pius XII and Franco, and on the special Mass held on April 13, 1939, at the Church of the Gesù, see AAV, *Segr. Stato,* 1939, Stati, posiz. 27, ff. 1r–28r. Pignatti sent the text of the pope's April 18 radio broadcast to Ciano, judging it to be "very satisfactory." Pignatti to Ciano, April 18, 1939, n. 1312/378, ASDMAE, AISS, b. 125. A large folder of Vatican documentation on the pope's telegram congratulating Franco on his victory and the organization of the special Mass held celebrating Franco's victory at Rome's Church of Gesù is found at AAV, *Segr. Stato,* 1939, Stati, posiz. 27.

19. Raul Hilberg (1961, p. 5) published a useful chart setting Nazi anti-Jewish measures alongside their Canonical counterparts. See also Kertzer 2001.

20. D. Mondrone, S.I., "Passio Christi: Passio Ecclesiae," CC 90, no. 2, Quaderno 2131 (April 1939), pp. 3–15. For other examples of the pope's emissaries' efforts in these months on behalf of baptized Jews, see ADSS, vol. 6. For more on the Fascist regime's use of church authority to encourage popular support for its antisemitic campaign, see Kertzer and Benedetti 2021 and Kertzer and Mokosch 2019, 2020.

21. Riccardo Di Segni (2015, pp. 27–28), chief rabbi of Rome, documented the sharp rise in baptism among Rome's Jews with the introduction of the new "racial" policies. While in the two years preceding the new policy an average of 32 Roman Jews were baptized each year, in 1938, 412 Roman Jews were baptized. He found, as well, that the Jews who succeeded in getting baptized were much more likely to survive the Shoah (pp. 45–46).

22. "Shoah, lettera ai figli di papà Emilio," *Report* 6, no. 22 (January 27, 2017), https://www .reportpistoia.com/archivio/agora/item/44653-shoah-lettera-ai-figli-di-papa-emilio .html. The rush to the baptismal font in the wake of the racial laws is one of the embarrassing, if perhaps understandable, facts of Italian Jewish history. From the time Mussolini announced the racial campaign in mid-1938 through the first four months of Pius XII's papacy the following year, four thousand Jews—close to a tenth of all the Jews in the country—succeeded in getting baptized. The converts were not simply those on the fringes of the Jewish community but included some of its most prominent members, as the case of Dr. Pio Tagliacozzo, former president of Rome's Jewish community, and his family illustrates. Michaelis 1978, pp. 238–39.

Even if the baptisms were too recent for the state to recognize their effect in purging Jews of their non-Aryan identity, they gave the newly baptized a source of support they were otherwise lacking. Such converts could now appeal for help to the country's most influential institution outside the state itself, the Roman Catholic Church. Indeed, the Vatican's recently opened archives are filled with such appeals. They contain, too, thousands of pages of documents detailing Vatican efforts to convince the Fascist authorities not to treat such converts as Jews. Minerbi 2010, p. 409.

CHAPTER 4 : THE PEACEMAKER

1. Report of March 31, 1939, MAEC, Papiers Chauvel, vol. 121; Phillips to FDR, March 17, 1939, FDR Library, psfa 400, p. 129.

2. François-Poncet 1961, pp. 101–2; MAEC, Papiers Chauvel, vol. 121, 875; Cannistraro 1982, pp. 9–10; Ciano 1980, pp. 284–85, diary entry for April 16, 1939. In Grandi's (1985, pp. 463–64) later account, which must be read with a critical eye, it was Ciano who had pushed for the invasion of Albania, while Mussolini had to be convinced.

3. "Tutti i principali centri dell'Albania, occupati dalle magnifiche truppe italiane" and "L'Albania liberata da una indegna schiavitù," *L'Italia,* April 11, 1939, p. 2; "Omaggio al Duce del Vescovo di Coriza," AR, April 21, 1939, p. 1; Phillips to FDR, April 14, 1939, FDR Library, psfa 400, pp. 134–35.

4. Pignatti to Ciano, April 14, 1939, DDI, series 8, vol. 11, n. 543; Pignatti to Ciano, May 2, 1939, DDI, series 8, vol. 11, n. 623; Phillips to FDR, April 14, 1939, FDR Library, psfa 400, pp. 132–36.

5. Tacchi Venturi's notes on his May 1 and May 2, 1939, meetings with Mussolini are found at ARSI, Fondo Tacchi Venturi, Miscellanea, b. 11, fasc. 33, carte non numerate. Maglione asked the Vatican envoys to bring the pope's proposal to the government ministers and cable back their replies. Maglione to the nuncios in Paris, Berlin, and Warsaw, and to the apostolic delegate in London, May 3, 1939, ADSS, vol. 1, n. 19.

6. Orsenigo, Berlin, to Maglione, May 6, 1939, ADSS, vol. 1, n. 29; Memorandum Foreign Minister's Personal Staff, Munich, May 10, 1939, DGFP, series D, vol. 6, n. 331; Kershaw 2000, p. 25.

7. The records of the French Foreign Ministry discussions, dated May 7, 1939, are found at MAEN, RSS 576, PO/1, 1108.

8. As for the future, Ciano quoted, in French, what Mussolini had told him: The Axis motto should be *"toujours parler de la paix et préparer la guerre,"* always speak of peace and prepare for war. Discussions of Ribbentrop and Ciano in Milan, May 6–7, memorandum dated May 18, 1939, DGFP, series D, vol. 6, n. 341; Hassell 2011, p. xix. Milan's Catholic newspaper heralded the outcome of the meeting of the two foreign ministers with a front-page headline: "The Axis, instrument of peace and not a supporter of war, leaves further strengthened by the discussions at Milan." "L'Asse, strumento di pace e non fautore di guerra, esce ulteriormente rafforzato dai colloqui di Milano," *L'Italia,* May 7, 1939, p. 1.

 Pignatti, charged with letting the pope know of Mussolini's rejection of his peace proposal, had barely begun to raise the subject with Cardinal Maglione when the cardinal told him how pleased the pope had been by what he had heard about Hitler's reaction to his peace proposal from the nuncio in Berlin. "The Cardinal," the ambassador reported, "did not hide from me that His Holiness had received an excellent impression of Signor Hitler's meeting with Mons. Orsenigo." Pignatti to Ciano, May 9, 1939, tel. 85, ASDMAE, Gab., b. 1125.

 Once the pope learned of Mussolini's opposition to his plan, however, he had Maglione inform the nuncios in Berlin, Warsaw, and Paris, and the papal delegate in London that a peace conference under papal sponsorship was not feasible at the moment. But as Maglione explained in his message, the initiative had borne some fruit, for "the Holy See has received assurances of the goodwill and the intention of the various governments of keeping the peace." Maglione notes, May 9, 1939, ADSS, vol. 1, n. 36; Maglione to the nuncios, ADSS, vol. 1, n. 38.

9. Weizsäcker to Ribbentrop, May 12, 1939, DGFP, series D, vol. 6, n. 372. The original is found at PAAA, GRk, R29814, 94–96. Knowledge of the Polish reaction to the pope's proposal comes from France's ambassador in Warsaw, who discussed it with Poland's

foreign minister. Besides rejecting the notion that the Italians should be part of any discussion of Poland's differences with Germany, the Polish foreign minister suspected the pope's motives in making the proposal. Knowing that Italian public opinion was decidedly against war, the minister speculated, the pope no doubt thought that casting himself as a peacemaker would win him great popularity at the start of his papacy and, at the same time, inspire the Fascist government to take more favorable measures in dealing with the church in Italy. Leon Nobel, French ambassador to Poland, Warsaw, to French Foreign Ministry, May 13, 1939, MAEC, Papiers Duparc, 30-31.

10. It might have been worse, the ambassador reported, for they had succeeded in preventing the pope from stopping along the way at the Campidoglio, Rome's ancient hilltop capital. "He wanted to reevoke," observed Pignatti, "a scene from past times, when Rome was under papal rule." Fortunately, the day had gone without mishap, "but I hope," wrote the ambassador, "the pope never repeats the experience of traversing the city in an open car, at walking speed, accompanied only by a handful of motorcycle police." It was the pope himself, he had learned, who had at the last minute decided on using the open car and directed it to go at such slow speed. The ambassador's concern was not simply with the question of security. "I don't think that the Pope can be allowed to travel through the city outside of the precise agreements taken with the Royal authorities, just as I suppose it is not in the intentions of the Fascist government to tolerate demonstrations of this kind on Italian soil." Pignatti to Ciano and to Direzione Generale Culti, Ministero Interno, May 20, 1939, tel. 1650/493, ASDMAE, APSS, b. 49. The initial request made by the nuncio is found in Borgongini Duca to Ufficio Cerimoniale, Ministero degli Affari Esteri, May 13, 1939, AAV, *Arch. Nunz. Italia,* b. 20, fasc. 47, ff. 2r-3r.

11. Heinrich Brüning, former German chancellor and prominent Catholic dissident, commented that Orsenigo "never stops working for Mr. Hitler." Biffi 1997, pp. 74-96. Corbin, ambassadeur de France, to Delbos, ministre des affaires étrangères, Paris, July 21, 1937, DDF, series 2, vol. 6, n. 257. Word soon reached Mussolini that the Nazis might be responding positively to the pope's efforts. Two German newspapers had recently published articles praising Pius XII for his congratulatory message to Franco. With international tensions now so great, thought the Duce's ambassador in Berlin, the Nazis might find themselves in need of Vatican support. Attolico to Ciano, April 18, 1939, tel. 2972/911, DDI, series 8, vol. 11, n. 572; Conway 1968, p. 229.

12. The unsigned memo was clearly written by Bergen, May 16, 1939, DGFP, series D, vol. 6, n. 395. Mussolini and his son-in-law were meanwhile doing what they could to encourage their Nazi partners to find a path to peace with the pope, and Ciano saw some signs they were succeeding. During a visit to Berlin in late May, he spoke at length with Heinrich Himmler, head of the SS, about the German government's relations with the church. Himmler remarked that he and his colleagues found the new pope sympathetic and thought it possible to reach a modus vivendi with him. "I encouraged him in pursuing this path," Ciano confided that day to his diary, "saying that an agreement between the Reich and the Vatican would also be useful in promoting the popularity of the Axis." Ciano 1980, pp. 299-300, diary entry for May 21, 1939.

13. Fritz Menshausen, second-in-command of the German embassy to the Holy See, sent the Foreign Ministry in Berlin a long critique of Bottai's Easter speech and his subsequent audience with the pope, May 25, 1939, PAAA, GARV, R711.

14. Bottai 1989, p. 148, diary entry for May 19, 1939.

15. Among the valuable sources of insight into the pope's character, see Tardini 1961; Baudrillart 1998, pp. 94-96; Cianfarra 1944, pp. 81-85; Charles-Roux 1947, pp. 74-75; Rhodes 1974, p. 222; O'Connell 1958, p. 366; Katz 2003, p. 54. Following a dinner together on January 24, 1940, as he walked outside the Apostolic Palace just before mid-

night with his two companions, Monsignor Montini pointed out the light illuminating the fourth-floor window of the pope's study. It was never switched off, said Montini, before two A.M. (Mazzei 2021, p. 221).

16. Phillips himself was fast souring on Mussolini, offended most recently by his offhanded remark at a dinner that the United States was being run by Jews. But he still viewed the Italian dictator as one of the only people in the world who could dissuade Hitler from embarking on a horrific war. To encourage the Duce to follow such a course, Phillips, at his frequent meetings with Ciano, kept repeating the same mantra: while he had little confidence in the German dictator, he "had confidence in Mussolini" and trusted "that he would apply the brakes on Hitler." "Personally," the ambassador told the president, "I believe that Mussolini is so anxious to avoid war that we may hope for his calming influence on Hitler." Phillips to FDR, May 26, 1939, FDR Library, psfa 401, pp. 4–8. On Mussolini's communicative powers, see Bollone 2007, pp. 43–44.

17. Cardinal Maglione notes, May 29, 1939, ADSS, vol. 1, n. 160.

18. That did not mean, suggested Mussolini, that they needed to wait until then before striking against the enemy. He offered Hitler various ideas as to how they might in the meantime soften the enemy up, suggesting that they foster antisemitic campaigns worldwide, promote separatist movements in Alsace, Brittany, Corsica, and Ireland, and incite revolt among Britain's and France's colonial subjects. Ciano to Ribbentrop, May 31, 1939, with enclosure, Mussolini to Hitler, May 30, DGFP, series D, vol. 6, n. 459.

19. Tacchi Venturi to Tardini, June 7, 1939, ARSI, Fondo Tacchi Venturi, Miscellanea, b. 11, fasc. 33, carte non numerate.

CHAPTER 5: "PLEASE DO NOT TALK TO ME ABOUT JEWS"

1. Chadwick 1986, pp. 13–15, 125, 128; Tittmann 2004, p. 98; Lammers 1971, pp. 69, 77–78; French embassy to the Holy See to French Foreign Ministry, October 1943, MAEN, RSS 576, PO/1, 1183.

2. Tardini notes, July 4, 1939, ADSS, vol. 1, n. 197; Pignatti to Ciano, July 3, 1939, DDI, series 8, vol. 12, n. 442. A few days later, on the pope's orders, Maglione called Pignatti in again to repeat the warning: both England and France were "absolutely decided to declare war on Germany" should it attack Danzig. Maglione notes, July 7, 1939, ADSS, vol. 1, n. 200; Pignatti to Ciano, July 7, 1939, DDI, series 8, vol. 12, n. 500.

3. Biddle, Warsaw, to FDR, June 20, 1939, FDR Library, psfa 449, pp. 88–94; Mons. Valeri, Paris, to Maglione, June 20 and 21, 1939, ADSS, vol. 1, nn. 66, 68.

   What was especially upsetting to Pius XII about these signs of his declining popularity was how little he seemed to be accomplishing in his attempts to reach an understanding with the Nazi authorities. He had remained publicly silent while Germany annexed Austria and then invaded Czechoslovakia, yet the German government continued its efforts to weaken the church. Indeed, things were only getting worse. Catholic schools were being closed, church property seized, and priests harassed if they showed insufficient support for the Nazi regime. The pope sent Cardinal Maglione to issue a warning to Italy's ambassador. If the situation in Germany did not improve soon, he would have to speak out. It would be one of the first of a long line of toothless threats. Mussolini's ambassador himself was sympathetic and shared the pope's dismay at the Germans' failure to follow the Fascist path to conciliation with the church. "The Holy Father," he said, "knew that [Ciano] had repeatedly intervened in Berlin to advise moderation and advise reaching an agreement with the Holy See." Pignatti to Ciano, July 5, 1939, DDI, series 8, vol. 12, n. 478.

4. On July 3, 1933, Von Papen, then vice chancellor of the German Reich who would soon sign the concordat with Pacelli, had sent a telegram to Hitler from Rome: "Mussolini

received me today and asked me in detail about the state of the negotiations for the Concordat. He instructed me to tell the Chancellor that, in his view, making the Vatican conclude a Concordat would be an enormous benefit for Germany in its current isolated situation. Germany would win the favor of global opinion. Mussolini concluded by saying: 'I entreat you not to depart before the Concordat has reached port.'" PAAA, GRk, R72095, 07.

5. Charles-Roux report, July 6, 1939, to Paris on his audience the previous day with the pope, MAEC, Papiers Duparc, ff. 68–72.

6. "Il Sant'Uffizio revoca la proibizione della lettura dell'Action Française," AI, July 16, 1939, p. 2; Pignatti to Ciano, July 17, 1939, tel. 2341/733, ASDMAE, APSS, b. 47. Mussolini was getting other encouraging news about the new pope, learning of the remarks the papal nuncio in Switzerland had made after his recent visit to the Vatican. Following Pius XII's ascension to the papacy, observed the nuncio, the atmosphere there was completely changed. He had talked with the pope, who spoke "with great sympathy for Fascism and with sincere admiration for the Duce." The pope explained that he had completely reorganized Catholic Action to prevent it from creating any further conflict with the government. The pope had also said he was eager to arrive at an agreement with the Führer. Referring to Hitler's visit to Italy in May 1938, the pope told the nuncio that "he had tried in vain to prevent his predecessor from protesting against the exhibition of the swastika in Rome." Attilio Tamaro, Bern, to Ciano, July 21, 1939, tel. 3461/1236, ASDMAE, APSS, b. 43.

7. "Colloquio con Rev.mo Padre Tacchi Venturi, May 11, 1939," ASRS, *AA.EE.SS.,* Pio XII, Asterisco Italia, posiz. 1054*, ff. 248–49. In August, Father Tacchi Venturi successfully urged Pius XII to make two appeals on behalf of baptized Jews, albeit not publicly. The first regarded the government decision, in ejecting all Jewish children from the country's public schools, to apply the ban to children of Jewish parents who had been baptized after October 1938. The second regarded the law prohibiting Catholics who were considered to be "of Jewish race," that is, converts or children of converts, from marrying those of "Aryan race," that is, Catholics not descended from Jews. Montini notes, August 12, 1939, ADSS, vol. 6, n. 49; Maglione to Borgongini Duca, August 23, 1939, n. 51.

8. De Felice 1974, p. 299, 1981, p. 280; D'Aroma 1958, p. 218; Moellhausen 1948, pp. 203–5; Innocenti 1992, p. 169. Attempts by the Vatican to get Ciano to intervene to have Catholics who had converted from Judaism treated as "Aryans" were rebuffed out of hand. "I beg you not to make me get involved with the Jews," Ciano replied to the nuncio's plea in April. Borgongini to Maglione, April 19, 1939, ASRS, *AA.EE.SS.,* Pio XII, Parte Asterisco, Italia, posiz. 1054*, ff. 231r–32r.

9. For documentation on Buffarini profiting financially from the racial laws, in collaboration with Antonio Le Pera, director of the office in charge of administering them, see the materials in the 1944 inquiry found at ACS, Ministero delle Finanze, Profitti di regime, b. 7. See also Canali and Volpini 2019; Giovanni and Palla 2019.

10. Borgongini Duca to Maglione, August 30, 1939, ADSS, vol. 6, nn. 126 and 127. At the same time the German bishops were showing considerable solicitude for the plight of what they referred to as "non-Aryan Catholics," as reflected in their memo: "Grave Situation of Catholics of the Jewish Race in Germany." ASRS, *AA.EE.SS.,* Pio XII, parte Asterisco, Stati Ecclesiastici, posiz. 575*, ff. 184r–96r.

11. There are multiple Italian and German accounts of the Salzburg meetings, which lasted two days, but they coincide remarkably well: Ciano 1980, pp. 326–27, diary entries for August 10, 11, and 12, 1939; Grandi 1985, pp. 505–8; Foreign Ministry Secretariat, Berlin, Record of conversation at Obersalzberg, memorandum, August 12 and 13, 1939, DGFP, series D, vol. 7, nn. 43 and 47. See also Kershaw 1999, pp. 282–83, and Kershaw 2000, pp. 203–4.

CHAPTER 6: THE NAZI PRINCE

1. There have been some hints however that such talks may have been occurring, most notably from a reference in Ciano's diary on January 8, 1940, to comments that Prince von Hessen had made alluding to the likelihood of a deal being reached between the Vatican and the German Reich (Ciano 1980, p. 384). In his book on the von Hessen brothers, Jonathan Petropoulos (2006, pp. 275–76) noted this reference as well as the enigmatic remark that Philipp von Hessen made about the talks in his Nuremburg war crimes trial after the war: "Pope Pius XII placed special trust in me and personally charged me with an important mission. I don't think it right that I give information about the purpose or nature of this mission without special approval." Petropoulos added, "Unfortunately, the Vatican's refusal to open its archives for this period and Philipp's reticence after the war on his dealings with Pius XII leave this history very sketchy."

2. Petropoulos (2006, pp. 67–72) uncovered considerable detail documenting Philipp's affair with Sassoon. Philipp's homosexuality was known to Mussolini's political police by 1934, and so most likely to Mussolini as well (informatore n. 571, July 12, 1934, ACS, MI, Polizia Politica, Materia, b. 40, carte non numerate).

3. Serri 2015.

4. The quote, from Machtan, is cited by Petropoulos 2006, p. 4. On German aristocrats' support for Hitler, see Malinowski 2020. Pius XII knew quite a bit about von Hessen before the secret negotiations began, as his marriage to King Victor Emmanuel's daughter Mafalda had resulted in a series of lengthy reports to the Vatican Secretariat of State in 1936–37. At issue was von Hessen's failure to abide by the negotiated agreement at the time of his marriage, which had bound him to raise his children Catholic. "It seems that the two children, although baptized," Monsignor Pizzardo, Tardini's predecessor as secretary of extraordinary ecclesiastical affairs, observed late in 1936, "have been educated as Protestants." Pizzardo to Borgongini, December 11, 1936, AAV, *Arch. Nunz. Italia,* b. 18, fasc. 1, f. 304r. On Hitler's use of aristocrats in international relations, see Urbach 2015.

5. The police informant folder on Travaglini, on which the above description is based, is found at ACS, MIFP, b. 1371.

6. Travaglini added, "And if National Socialism will give the possibility of finding a road of understanding and agreement . . . there was no person better than Pope Pacelli, sincere friend of Germany, better disposed to finding a solution." Cardinal Lauri forwarded the letter to the pope. Travaglini to Lauri, March 9, 1939, ASRS, *AA.EE.SS.,* Pio XII, parte 1, Germania, posiz. 774, ff. 3r–4r.

7. "Yesterday, Sunday," Travaglini wrote to the cardinal, "His Royal Highness Prince Philipp von Hessen, son-in-law of our Emperor King, called me to Villa Savoia [the royal residence in Rome] to tell me that . . . he was studying with the Führer and with Goering the possibility of directly proposing to the Holy Father an exchange of ideas to bring about a conciliation on new bases between the Holy See and Germany. . . . Prince Philipp von Hessen will probably be called upon to arrange a secret meeting with the Holy Father and then give the Embassies the general outlines for a diplomatic agreement. . . . Perhaps I will have to accept the delicate task of assisting the above-mentioned Prince in his secret steps. To reach the Holy Father I will have to avail myself of the friendly services of Your Eminence." Travaglini to Lauri, April 17, 1939, ASRS, *AA.EE.SS.,* Pio XII, parte 1, Germania, posiz. 774, f. 5r.

    Following Princess Mafalda's marriage to von Hessen, King Victor Emmanuel gave them their own separate home, the Villa Polissena, which was part of the complex of the Villa Savoia. Petropoulos 2006, pp. 76–77.

8. Von Hessen spoke not only Italian but English and French as well. Petropoulos 2006, p. 13.

9. In the same folder is a note from Bishop Alois Hudal addressed, it seems, to Monsignor Montini, containing the same date, March 14, 1938: "I ask that perhaps with a telegram in cypher a notice be given to the Nunciature in Vienna so that in the Bishops' Curias and in the Archives of the Congregations and Orders in Austria all the material regarding cases of immorality of priests is immediately and without exception burned and also the numbers of the protocols cancelled. . . . The matter is extremely delicate but very urgent." The recommendation to the Vatican Secretariat of State apparently came from the Holy Office. ASRS, *AA.EE.SS.*, Fondo Spogli, Scatole bianche, posiz. 1, ff. 25–30. Underlining in original.

10. A report on the initial investigation of the German clergy, presented by Germany's Justice Minister, is described in "'Shocking' sexual abuse of children by German clergy detailed in report," *The Guardian*, September 25, 2018, https://www.theguardian.com /world/2018/sep/25/report-details-sexual-abuse-german-catholic-church. Follow-up investigations on the topic include a 2021 report focusing on the diocese of Cologne in the years 1975–2018, described in "Report finds hundreds of child sex abuse cases in German diocese," *Barron's*, March 17, 2021, https://www.barrons.com/news/german-diocese -faces-moment-of-truth-in-abuse-crisis-01616039706.

11. "Konferenz Seiner Heiligkeit mit dem Prinz von Hessen, 11. Mai 1939," ASRS, *AA.EE.SS.*, Pio XII, parte I, Stati Ecclesiastici, posiz. 802, ff. 555–59.

12. "Relazione sulla conversazione," Travaglini, June 1, 1939, ASRS, *AA.EE.SS.*, Pio XII, parte 1, Germania, posiz. 774, ff. 8r–9r.

13. Travaglini to Lauri, July 3, 1939, ASRS, *AA.EE.SS.*, Pio XII, parte 1, Germania, posiz. 774, ff. 10r–12r.

14. Travaglini to Lauri, August 21, 1939, ASRS, *AA.EE.SS.*, Pio XII, parte 1, Germania, posiz. 774, ff. 14r–16r.

15. Travaglini to Lauri, August 24, 1939, ASRS, *AA.EE.SS.*, Pio XII, parte 1, Germania, posiz. 774, ff. 17rv; Lauri to Pius XII, August 25, 1939, ASRS, *AA.EE.SS.*, Pio XII, parte 1, Germania, posiz. 774, f. 20r.

16. "Geheim-Audienz S.K.H. des Prinzen Philipp von Hessen, Samstag 26 Aug. 1939; Abends 6 Uhr," ASRS, *AA.EE.SS.*, Pio XII, parte 1, Germania, posiz. 774, ff. 22r–24r. Thanks to Gunnar Mokosch for his English translation of this and other German-language documents.

CHAPTER 7: SAVING FACE

1. Phillips to FDR, August 18, 1939, FDR Library, psfa 401, pp. 20–23.

2. Grandi 1985, p. 529, diary entry for August 21, 1939.

3. Petacci 2011, p. 423; Bosworth 2017, p. 106; Monelli 1953, pp. 155–56.

4. Petacci 2011, p. 173, diary entry for August 21, 1939.

5. Bastianini 2005, pp. 69–73. In the account Bastianini gives of this encounter, he too was shocked by Mussolini's reaction and tried to convince the Duce not to join Hitler in the war. This aspect of his account must be treated with considerable skepticism, as with other post hoc accounts by the top Fascists. Attolico, a career diplomat, is a different story and from all accounts was not enthusiastic about Italy joining Hitler's side in the war. On Attolico, see Losito 1994.

6. Tardini notes, August 24, 1939, ADSS, vol. 1, n. 116. First word of the pact was published in *The New York Times* on August 22: "Germany and Russia agree on non-aggression: Ribbentrop going to Moscow to draft pact; Berlin sees quick showdown with Poland," p. 1.

7. See Coco 2019. The two main sections of the Secretariat of State, which followed the 1908 reorganization plan, consisted of the First Section, dealing with "extraordinary

ecclesiastical affairs," headed by the Secretary of the Congregation for Extraordinary Ecclesiastical Affairs, and the Second Section of "ordinary affairs," headed by the *sostituto,* or substitute. However, as Graham (1984, pp. 70–71) noted, Pius XII never took this distinction too seriously and so the division of responsibilities between Tardini (of the first section) and Montini (of the second section) was never hard and fast.

8. D'Ormesson final report, October 28, 1940, MAEC, Guerre Vichy, 550. Cardinal Baudrillart's diary entry on a day he met with both men captures the contrast that struck many others as well: "Montini refined and distinguished, Tardini, a bit common of manners." Baudrillart 1996, p. 969, diary entry for February 25, 1939. "A bluff and breezy Roman, friendly, cheerful and voluble," was the way the British envoy to the Vatican described Tardini. Osborne report, June 6, 1946, NAK, FO 371, 60812, ZM, 1993, 1946. See also Casula 1989, pp. 207–12, and Riccardi 1982. For a good biographical sketch of Tardini, see Sergio Pagano's introduction to Tardini's diary, Pagano 2020, pp. vii–xxxii.

9. Osborne would likewise predict, in his 1946 biographical sketch of Montini for London, that "he may well be the next Pope but one," a prediction that turned out to be exactly on target. Osborne report, June 6, 1946, NAK, FO 371, 60812, ZM, 1993, 1946.

10. Pignatti to Ciano, August 25, 1939, DDI, series 8, vol. 13, n. 270; Friedländer 1966, pp. 28–31; Tardini notes, August 26, 1939, ADSS, vol. 1, n. 127.

11. Grandi 1985, p. 532, diary entry for August 25, 1939.

12. Mackensen to Ribbentrop, August 25, 1939, DGFP, series D, vol. 7, n. 280.

13. Later in the day, Hitler added a second note, renewing his request to have the Italian military compel the French to devote a sizable contingent of their troops to the Italian border. Should the Polish invasion lead to a wider war, added the Führer, he would, after quickly dispatching Poland, attack the West with great force. "I must now ask a great favor of you, Duce. In this difficult struggle you and your people can best help me by sending me Italian workers, both for industrial and agricultural purposes." Mussolini to Hitler (relayed by telephone by Ciano to Attolico in Berlin), August 26, 1939; Hitler to Mussolini, August 26, 1939; Hitler to Mussolini (communicated via Mackensen), August 26, 1939, DGFP, series D, vol. 7, nn. 301, 307, 341.

14. Petacci 2011, pp. 174–75, diary entry for August 27, 1939. Each morning Mussolini's police chief brought him new evidence of his countrymen's lack of enthusiasm for war. In a typical report, sent the same day as the Duce was waving to the crowd outside Palazzo Venezia, a Roman informant observed: "Here people still don't believe that Italy is about to be involved in the war, if there is one, and most are, at heart, against it." Beyond the "Romans' traditional apathy," explained the informant, the people were influenced by the pope's pleas for peace and their recognition that almost no preparations had been made for a war, as no antiaircraft installations had been mounted in Rome nor had any bomb shelters been built. Informativa da Roma (n. 535—Mezzabotta), August 27, 1939, ACS, MI, MAT, b. 220. The identification of police informants in these notes is based on the work of Mauro Canali (2004), who compiled a list attaching a name to each numeric code used in the police files.

Mussolini still harbored some hope that he could play a starring role in Europe's drama by again acting as mediator. As the German ambassador, who had brought Hitler's letter to Mussolini, reported: "The Duce repeated, in forcible terms, the view he had already advanced yesterday, namely that he still believed it possible to attain all our objectives without resort to war." Not wanting to seem weak, Mussolini added that of course in three or four years they might well wage war against the Western powers, and by then they would be in a much stronger position. Mackensen to Ribbentrop, August 27, 1939, DGFP, series D, vol. 7, n. 349.

15. Montini and Tardini notes, August 28, 1939, ADSS, vol. 1, n. 144; Tardini notes, August 28, 1939, ADSS, vol. 1, n. 143. At the same time, the pope also called on his nuncio to the

Italian government to meet with Mussolini's undersecretary, Buffarini, to see what he could learn. At their meeting, Buffarini said Hitler was convinced he could conquer Poland in three weeks' time and that neither France nor Britain would go to war on Poland's behalf. "The Honorable Buffarini," the nuncio added in reporting the conversation, "sung the praises of the Holy Father, telling me, 'He is just the Pope that is needed.'" Borgongini Duca to Maglione, September 1, 1939, ADSS, vol. 1, n. 178.

To complete these frenetic, last-minute efforts, Cardinal Maglione, who had hurried back from his Neapolitan vacation, summoned the Italian ambassador. The cardinal, the ambassador reported to Ciano, "told me that the Holy See was following with admiration the work of the Duce and of Your Excellency to prevent catastrophe. Cardinal Maglione expressed the hope, on behalf of the Pope, that the Duce and Your Excellency leave no stone unturned in achieving the goal of bringing peace among the opposing parties." Pignatti to Ciano, August 29, 1939, tel. 4065R, ASDMAE, Gab., b. 1125.

16. Tardini notes, August 29, 1939, ADSS, vol. 1, n. 148. Tacchi Venturi's note on his audience with Mussolini, dated August 29, 1939, is found at ARSI, Fondo Tacchi Venturi, Miscellanea, b. 11, fasc. 33, carte non numerate.

17. Maglione to Orsenigo, Berlin, August 29, 1939, ADSS, vol. 1, n. 147; Tacchi Venturi to Maglione, August 30, 1939, ADSS, vol. 1, n. 151.

18. The ellipsis, something of a favored rhetorical device of Tardini, is in the original. The revised text of the message to the nuncio in Warsaw did, however, reflect some of Tardini's concerns. Rather than identify the source of the proposal as an unnamed "diplomat," as had the pope's message to Berlin, the message to Warsaw referred more generically to a "responsible source." Longer than the Berlin telegram, it also added language about the pope's "special affection for Poland." Tardini to Maglione, August 30, 1939, and Maglione to Cortesi, nuncio in Warsaw, August 30, 1939, ADSS, vol. 1, nn. 152, 153.

19. Bérard to Darlan, February 22, 1941, referring to a conversation that took place at Castel Gandolfo on August 30, 1939. MAEC, Guerre Vichy, 551. Again, it was the British who seemed to have the most confidence that the pope might be able to do what the leaders of Europe's great powers could not. In a telegram marked "extremely urgent," Attolico advised Ciano that the British ambassador in Berlin had proposed that, all other efforts having failed, the British and Italian dipomats should call on the pope to intervene with a concrete peace proposal that Britain and Italy could then jointly recommend to Warsaw and Berlin. The British and Italian ambassadors in Berlin had discussed how their governments might craft such a plea to the pope and what the proposal might consist of. In urging consideration for the proposed papal intervention, Attolico, eager to prevent Mussolini from throwing Italy into a war at Germany's side, added that it would have the beneficial effect of allowing Italy to play a key role in mediating the dispute. Attolico to ministro degli esteri, August 30, 1939, tel. 4109R, ASDMAE, Gab., b. 1125.

20. Charles-Roux 1947, p. 332. The French text of the pope's message, dated August 31, 1939, is found at MAEN, RSS 576, PO/1, 1108. Maglione's meetings that day are also described in Tardini notes, ADSS, vol. 1, n. 159. For Bergen's cover letter to Berlin, dated August 31, along with the text of the pope's message, see DGFP, series D, vol. 7, n. 473.

On September 2, Cardinal Maglione took the unusual step of going to visit Tacchi Venturi to ask him to bring Mussolini a message from the pope. The pope had followed the Duce's advice and sent the requested message for the nuncio in Warsaw to give to the Polish president. It was not clear, though, whether the cable to Warsaw had gotten through. "One thing is certain from the events following the night of August 31," wrote Tacchi Venturi in his letter to Mussolini drafted the following day, "that is to say that the result, whether because the [cable] arrived too late or because the President did not decide to follow the Pope's advice, was not that which His Holiness and with him all the world's wise ones desired." ARSI, Fondo Tacchi Venturi, Miscellanea, b. 11, fasc. 33, carte non numerate.

21. Petacci 2011, pp. 184–85, diary entry for August 30, 1939.

CHAPTER 8: WAR BEGINS

1. Lewy 1964. Rarkowski was consecrated a bishop the previous year by Nuncio Cesare Orsenigo, alongside two of Germany's most prominent archbishops: Konrad von Preysing and Clemens August von Galen. See "Bishop Franz Justus Rarkowski, S.M.," catholic-hierarchy.org/bishop/brark.html, and Brandt 1983, pp. 594–95. The quote is reproduced in Friedländer 1966, p. 34.

2. Details on the German assault are from Moorhouse 2020 and Rossino 2003.

3. Bérard to Pétain, February 22, 1941, MAEC, Guerre Vichy, 551; Roger Moorhouse, "The Brutal Blitzkrieg: The 1939 Invasion of Poland," *BBC History Magazine* (2019), https://www.historyextra.com/period/second-world-war/brutal-blitzkrieg-1939 -invasion-poland-start-ww2-roger-moorhouse/.

4. Fonogramma della questura di Roma alla DGPS, September 1, 1939, n. 189826, ACS, MI, DAGRA 39, b. 38; Informativa da Roma, September 1, 1939, ACS, MI, MAT, b. 221.

5. Charles-Roux to French Foreign Ministry, September 3, 1939, MAEN, RSS 576, PO/1, 1108.

6. Ciano 1980, p. 340, diary entry for September 1, 1939; Mackensen to German Foreign Ministry, September 1, 1939, DGFP, series D, vol. 7, n. 507. "I thank you most cordially for the diplomatic and political support which you have been giving recently to Germany," the Führer's telegram began. "I do not expect to need Italy's military support in these circumstances." DGFP, series D, vol. 7, n. 500.

7. Bottai 1989, pp. 156–57, diary entry for September 1, 1939; Grandi 1985, pp. 513–15; De Felice 1981, p. 674.

8. Bottai 1989, pp. 159–60, diary entry for September 5, 1939.

9. Pignatti to Ciano, September 2, 1939, n. 152, ASDMAE, AISS, b. 116.

10. One of the founders of the Fascist movement in 1919, with a well-cultivated reputation of being the most Fascist of the Fascists, Farinacci had long demonstrated a violent streak. He had lost a hand during the Ethiopian war, not as a result of enemy action but, characteristically perhaps, while tossing hand grenades into a lake to catch fish. He was also one of the few Fascist leaders who saw himself as the Duce's equal. Early in his career, as the Fascist *ras,* or boss, of the northern city of Cremona, he discovered that having a newspaper would greatly increase his influence. Funded by sympathetic industrialists and major agricultural financial interests, these early efforts evolved into *Il Regime Fascista.* Having come to Fascism from a revolutionary socialist past, as had Mussolini, he never abandoned the anticlericalism of that earlier time. Among the major Fascist figures, no one was a greater admirer of Hitler than Farinacci. Innocenti 1992, pp. 147–50; Bosworth 2002, pp. 204–5.

11. ACS, MIFP, serie B, b. 3, Gonella, September 3, 1939.

12. "He told me," Pignatti reported, "that, as of yesterday, Sunday, *L'Osservatore Romano* received the order to publish only news and no commentary and, in case of any doubts, to contact the Secretariat of State." Pignatti to Ciano, September 4, 1939, tel. 157, ASDMAE, AISS, b. 116.

13. Pignatti to Ciano, September 6, 1939, tel. 159, ASDMAE, AISS, b. 116; Appunto, September 7, 1939, and Pro-Memoria, September 8, 1939, ACS, MIFP, serie B, b. 3, Gonella; Pignatti to Ciano, September 14, 1939, n. 2998, ASDMAE, AISS, b. 116. Unbeknownst

to Maglione or the pope, one of the paper's journalists was a police spy. Three days after the arrest, he reported that it had "produced an enormous impression at *L'Osservatore Romano* and in the Vatican." The other journalists, afraid of being suspected of anti-Fascism, "are all quaking from fear of being arrested themselves." Informativa da Roma (n. 726—Scattolini), September 5, 1939, ACS, MIFP, serie B, b. 3, Gonella.

14. Huener (2021) offers a detailed study of this destruction. It was accompanied, in part, by efforts to transform the Catholic churches in western Poland from Polish to German institutions, including efforts to forbid the use of the Polish language and to insert ethnically German priests in the place of Polish priests. Rossino (2003, p. 134) reports that instructions from Germany's High Army Command in July 1939 had already noted that "this [Polish] Catholic clergy is primarily responsible for nationalistic rabble-rousing."

15. The September 2 request to the pope is described in Tardini's diary, Pagano 2020, pp. 145–46. Charles-Roux to French Foreign Ministry, September 2 and 3, 1939, MAEN, RSS 576, PO/1, 1108; Visita dell'Ambasciatore di Polonia, September 12, 1939, AAV, *Segr. Stato,* 1940, Stati e Corpo Diplomatico, b. 275, f. 3r.

16. Charles-Roux to Tardini, September 11, 1939, ADSS, vol. 1, n. 198; Charles-Roux to French Foreign Ministry, September 13 and 15, 1939, MAEN, RSS 576, PO/1, 1108. In meeting with Monsignor Tardini on September 18, the French ambassador let his anger at the pope's silence show. Tardini recorded the episode in his diary entry that day: "Then the ambassador goes on the offensive to deplore the fact that the Holy See had not said one word on behalf of Poland, which had been so unjustly attacked. He observed that France and England were fighting for morality, justice, Christian civilization, and the Holy See was doing nothing . . . for Christian civilization!" Tardini, whose ellipsis is in the original diary entry, added, "I laugh and I congratulate His Excellency for his oratorical ability." Pagano 2020, p. 163.

17. Tisserant's plea was sent to Monsignor Montini, as quoted in Fouilloux 2011, p. 286.

18. The pope, it seemed to the ambassador, felt powerless, although this should "never, for a spiritual power, be an excuse to keep quiet." Charles-Roux to Foreign Ministry, Paris, September 18 and 29, 1939, MAEN, RSS 576, PO/1, 1108.

19. The Polish ambassador, his French colleague reported, "had hoped that the Holy Father would at least express his disapproval for the fate inflicted on Poland by the Germans and Russians." This the pope chose not to do. Responding to the French ambassador's complaints, Monsignor Montini justified the pope's failure to say anything about the German invasion by suggesting that the pope had not wanted to risk reprisals against millions of Catholics, not only in Poland but in Germany as well. Osborne, annual report for 1939, NAK, AR 1939, p. 2; Charles-Roux to Foreign Ministry, Paris, September 30 and October 3, 1939, MAEN, RSS 576, PO/1, 1108. Typical of the coverage of the pope's remarks in the Italian Catholic press was the editorial by the director of *L'Avvenire d'Italia:* "His Holiness Pius XII gave the Polish people the spiritual vaticum for this dark night of sorrow. Not hatred. Not rebellion . . . but strength in Faith." The editorial made no mention of the fact that it was Germany that had invaded Poland. "Pio XII al popolo polacco," AI, October 1, 1939, p. 1.

20. Quoted in Friedländer 1966, p. 34.

CHAPTER 9: THE PRINCE RETURNS

1. Petacci 2011, p. 188, diary entry for September 10, 1939.

2. Ciano 1980, p. 343, diary entry for September 6, 1939; Petacci 2011, p. 188, diary entry for September 10, 1939; Visani 2007, p. 36; "Discorso del Duce ai Gerarchi Genovesi," September 30, 1939, AAV, *Arch. Nunz. Italia,* b. 24, fasc. 9, ff. 9r–11r. Nor was there

much evidence of enthusiasm for their German ally in the Italian military officer corps. At the Church of St. Louis of the French, Rome's magnificent Baroque church, an Italian officer arrived unannounced with an engineer. He told the priest who greeted them that they had come to take measurements to be prepared for fighting fires that could result from an air raid. But surely there was no need, the priest replied, since neither British nor French planes would ever dare bomb the Eternal City. "It is not against the French or the English that we will be battling," responded the officer, "but rather against those dirty Germans!" Charles-Roux to French Foreign Ministry, September 23, 1939, MAEN, RSS 576, PO/1, 1108.

3.   Petacci 2011, pp. 199–200, diary entry for September 19, 1939.

4.   "Everything the Pope in person and Vatican diplomacy said and did to ward off the approaching war as it grew more imminent," observed the French ambassador, "was done in harmony with, if not in coordination with, what the Italian government was doing at the same time." He added that he had recently spoken with Monsignor Montini, who expressed some confidence that Italy would remain out of the war and assured the Frenchman that the Vatican would do everything it could to press Italy to stay out of it. Charles-Roux to Foreign Ministry, Paris, September 28, 1939, MAEN, RSS 576, PO/1, 1108.

5.   Pignatti to Ciano, September 16, 1939, ASDMAE, AISS, b. 116. Mussolini had reason to be concerned about the Vatican paper, whose circulation continued to grow. "These days," an informant reported in mid-September, "the public has, as never before, thirst for news and, above all, for the truth, and so they look for it in *L'Osservatore Romano*." Notizia fiduciaria [n. 40—Troiani], September 17, 1939, ACS, MI, MAT, b. 241.

6.   "I will tell the pope tomorrow," the ambassador said, advising Ciano of his upcoming papal audience, "that the fact that Jews, masons, and all the antifascists in general make such fervent propaganda for *L'Osservatore Romano* certainly does not redound to the prestige of the Apostolic See." Pignatti to Ciano, September 28, 1939, n. 3147, ASDMAE, AISS, b. 116.

7.   "It is exact to say," Pignatti had reported the previous month, "that Count Dalla Torre, director of *L'Osservatore Romano,* and thorough Francophile, is not viewed well by the [Vatican] Secretariat of State. I hope and I believe that the Pope will in the end throw him out." But the pope could act, he cautioned, only if Italy's press stopped criticizing the paper's director, for the pontiff could not allow himself to be seen doing Mussolini's bidding. According to one of the government's spies in the Vatican—and the Duce was particularly well supplied with spies inside the offices of the Vatican daily—Dalla Torre himself feared he would soon be dismissed. Pignatti to Ciano, March 29, 1939, n. 1079/311, ASDMAE, AISS, b. 113; Informativa da Roma (n. 675—Di Legge), April 4, 1939, ACS, MIFP, b. 379; Informativa da Roma (n. 726—Scattolini), April 27 and May 22, 1939, ACS, MIFP, b. 379. The informant, referring to Dalla Torre, added, "He has the support of Cardinal Maglione, who has been casting about for reasons to have the Pope see him, but the pope does not want to."

The German ambassador, referring to Dalla Torre's stream of attacks on the Third Reich in the Vatican newspaper under Pius XI, advised Berlin that "under the new pontificate [Dalla Torre's] activities in this area are almost completely prohibited." In mid-April Dalla Torre sent a handwritten note to the Vatican secretary of state, politely objecting to the "silence" the pope had imposed on the Vatican paper in reporting German offenses against the church. His request to allow such criticisms was denied. German embassy to the Holy See to Foreign Ministry, Berlin, n.d. (1939), PAAA, GARV, R549; Dalla Torre, April 18, 1939, ASRS, *AA.EE.SS.,* Pio XII, Parte Asterisco, Stati Ecclesiastici, posiz. 378*, ff. 4, 5, 6–8.

Britain's envoy to the Vatican got to know Dalla Torre and his family—who lived in Vatican City—well during the war and was pleased by his faith that the Allies would ultimately win. While Dalla Torre, who had been director of *L'Osservatore Romano* for two decades, had been close to Pius XI, he never developed the same relationship with his successor, and his relations with Montini and Tardini were also somewhat fraught. OSS report, interview with Dalla Torre, February 21, 1945, NARA, RG 226, Microfilm M1642, roll 103, pp. 58–63; Osborne to Foreign Office, London, June 6, 1946, NAK, FO 371, 60812, ZM 1993, 1946; Alessandrini 1982, pp. 150–53.

Pius XII discussed his reservations about Dalla Torre with Monsignor Tardini on September 22, as discussed in Tardini's diary entry that day. Pagano 2020, p. 170. The pope returned to the subject again in speaking with Tardini four days later: "His Holiness again tells me of his unhappiness with *L'Osservatore Romano*. His attitude toward Count Dalla Torre is very severe. He prefers that he not write" (p. 176).

8. Pignatti to Ciano, September 29, 1939, n. 165, ASDMAE, AISS, b. 116.

9. Pignatti to Ciano, September 30, 1939, n. 166, and Pignatti to Ciano, October 1, 1939, n. 168, ASDMAE, AISS, b. 113. Evidence that the Italian ambassador continued to recognize the need to quiet the press campaign against Dalla Torre if they wanted the pope to get rid of him comes from a mid-October letter he sent to Dino Alfieri, then head of the Ministry of Popular Culture, which oversaw the Italian press: "To obtain the substitution of Count Dalla Torre from the direction of the Vatican newspaper," wrote Pignatti, "it would be necessary for the Italian press to stop writing about him for a long period. I realize that this is difficult." Pignatti to Alfieri, October 18, 1939, ACS, MCPG, 20 vers, b. 10.

10. Osborne to Halifax, London, October 13, 1939, NAK, FO 380/188, n. 99/50/30. Warsaw had surrendered on September 27 and the following day the German and Soviet leaders signed a treaty dividing the country between them. All military operations had been concluded by October 6. Herbert 2019, pp. 315–16.

Responding to criticism of the pope's silence, the Vatican newspaper offered a vigorous rebuttal. The pope had clearly shown his "paternal solicitude toward unfortunate Poland." The reference here was to the words the pope addressed at the end of September to Poland's cardinal primate and the Poles who had accompanied him in his visit to the pope's summer palace in the Alban Hills. Speaking in French, the pope told them, "You have come not to make any demands, nor to express noisy complaints, but to ask for a word of consolation and comfort in your suffering from our heart, from our lips." Here the pope quoted the words of Saint Paul to the Corinthians, "Who of you can suffer without my suffering with you?"

Unhappy with the pope's silence, governments in London and Paris decided to mount a behind-the-scenes campaign to turn up the pressure. British and French cardinals, urged one senior British foreign officer, should write directly to the pope "and point out what an unfortunate effect his silence on the subject of Poland was having on Catholic opinion in our two countries." The archbishop of Paris, told by France's ambassador to the Vatican that the pope's refusal to condemn the German aggression threatened to produce a wave of anticlericalism in the country, wrote the pope his own plea. Sargent memo to secretary of state, October 18, 1939, NAK, FO 800/325, 19; Baudrillart 1998, pp. 233–34, 237, diary entries for October 8 and 11, 1939. The alternative approach, considered by the British Foreign Office, of having the government directly approach the pope through his apostolic delegate in London, seemed less promising to the British foreign service officer. It would, he advised Halifax, be "better to have leading Catholics in this country, such as the Duke of Norfolk and Lord Perth to take up the matter. . . . I think the Pope would be more likely to be impressed if this criticism of his inaction emanated from the faithful in this country rather than from H.M. Government." Halifax quickly followed through with letters to the most prominent Catholics of the British nobility. His letter to the Duke of Norfolk began in a typically understated way,

My dear Bernard,

The attitude which the Pope has publicly adopted hitherto towards the present war, and particularly towards the German invasion of Poland, has been causing me some concern. . . . [I]t is probably true that if he were openly and uncompromisingly to denounce Hitler and all his works he would lose the allegiance of a very considerable number of German Catholics. . . . Nevertheless, making every allowance for the difficulty of the decision confronting His Holiness, one is left with an uncomfortable feeling that his attitude towards Germany's wanton attack on Poland is perhaps a little less courageous than his predecessor's would have been (Halifax to Duke of Norfolk, October 25, 1939, NAK, FO 380/188, no. H/XXXVIII/57).

Perth, in responding to Halifax's request, appeared to have little confidence in the initiative: "My dear Edward, Your letter raises a most difficult problem. . . . I doubt . . . whether the Pope will go so far as to specify in his condemnation Hitler himself or his works: I wonder whether we can expect him to do so, his primary charge being, as he often says, the care of souls." Perth added that he would speak of the matter to Monsignor Godfrey, the papal delegate to Britain, but suggested there was no point speaking to Britain's only cardinal, Arthur Hinsley. "The Cardinal does not, I fear, carry much weight in Rome" (Lord Perth to Halifax, October 26, 1939, NAK, FO 800/325, 23).

11. The pope's remarks were directed to the new Lithuanian ambassador to the Holy See on October 18. Pignatti to Ciano, October 19, 1939, DDI, series 9, vol. 1, n. 811.

12. The English text of *Summi Pontificatus* is found at http://www.vatican.va/content/pius -xii/en/encyclicals/documents/hf_p-xii_enc_20101939_summi-pontificatus.html.

13. Pignatti to Ciano, October 30, 1939, ASDMAE, AISS, b. 100; "La prima enciclica di Pio XII," PI, October 27, 1939, p. 2; Direzione Generale Stampa Estera, Appunto per il ministro, October 28, 1939, ASDMAE, Minculpop, b. 189; "Considerazioni tedesche sull'enciclica," OR, November 5, 1939, p. 2; "L'Enciclica di Pio XII," RF, October 28, 1939, p. 2.

14. Questura di Roma alla DGPS, fonogramma, October 23, 1939, n. 222710, ACS, MI, DAGRA 39, b. 38A; Lauri to Pius XII, October 22, 1939, ASRS, *AA.EE.SS.*, Pio XII, parte 1, Germania, posiz. 774, f. 18r.

15. On the Nazis' views of Christianity, see Steigmann-Gall 2003.

16. Sonder-Audienz für Prinz Philipp v. Hessen, Castel Gandolfo, 24.Okt.1939, 16 Uhr., ASRS, *AA.EE.SS.*, Pio XII, parte 1, Germania, posiz. 774, ff. 26r–28r. It would seem that the labeling of the meeting as taking place in Castel Gandolfo is in error, as according to police reports the pope left there two days earlier.

CHAPTER 10: A PAPAL CURSE

1. Phillips to FDR, October 18, 1939, FDR Library, psfa 401, pp. 43–46.

2. Petacci 2011, pp. 221, 223–24, diary entries for October 20 and 22, 1939.

3. Grandi 1985, pp. 554–56; Charles-Roux reports to Foreign Ministry, Paris, November 2 and 3, 1939, MAEN, RSS 576, PO/1, 1108.

4. The Vatican report, from 1940, is quoted in Huener 2021, p. 98.

5. "Notiziario polacco," OR, November 19, 1939, p. 6; "La 'riserva ebraica di Lublino,'" OR, November 29, 1939, p. 1; Osborne to Ivone Kirkpatrick, Foreign Office, London, November 29, 1939, NAK, FO 380/188, no. C19637; Lewy 1964, p. 245. On the closing of German seminaries, especially those suspected of harboring opponents to the regime, see Burkhard and Weiss 2007.

6. Charles-Roux 1947, pp. 354–55.

7. "La presentazione delle credenziali del nuovo ambasciatore d'Italia," and "Il nuovo Am-

basciatore d'Italia," OR, December 8, 1939, pp. 1–2; Roberto Farinacci, "Un discorso ignorato," RF, December 10, 1939, p. 1.

8. "Il Papa impartisce la benedizione 'Urbi et Orbi' dalla Loggia di S. Maria Maggiore," PI, December 9, 1939, p. 1. A Luce newsreel captured the scene: https://patrimonio .archivioluce.com/luce-web/detail/IL5000022947/2/il-papa-impartisce-benedizione -urbi-et-orbi-davanti-ad-immensa-folla-fedeli.html&jsonVal=.

9. Ciano 1980, pp. 375, 376, diary entries for December 18 and 21, 1939; Le pape Pie XII au roi et à la reine d'Italie, December 21, 1939, and Tardini notes, December 21, 1939, ADSS, vol. 1, nn. 230 and 231; Charles-Roux 1947, p. 357. Mussolini's newspaper, along with papers throughout Italy, devoted page after page to the event. Its front-page sub-title summed up the main message: "Long Discussion with Pius XII—Galeazzo Ciano Accompanies the August Guests—The Pope Blesses a Vigilant, Strong Italy, the Royals, the Head of the Government, and His Collaborators." "L'odierna visita dei Sovrani d'Italia al Sommo Pontefice," PI, December 21, 1939, p. 1. The Italian papers gave special attention to the fact that the pope, in addressing Victor Emmanuel, publicly referred to him with his recently acquired title: "King of Albania."

10. Charles-Roux to Foreign Ministry, Paris, December 22, 1939, MAEN, RSS 576, PO/1, 1090.

11. When word of the planned papal visit reached him at the Italian embassy in Cairo, Sera-fino Mazzolini, Mussolini's ambassador to Egypt, was overjoyed. "The exceptional im-portance of the event," he wrote in his diary, "does not escape anyone. Pius XII is a great pope! And he is Roman! And our king adds a new glorious page to his reign. What an example to the world on the part of Fascist and Catholic Rome!" Rossi 2005, p. 251, diary entry for December 23, 1939.

12. Cardinal Baudrillart (1996, pp. 193–94, diary entry for May 5, 1936) used the term "con-vinced fascist" to describe Schuster. "S.E. il Cardinale restituisce la visita al Federale alla sede della Federazione," L'Italia, December 24, 1939, p. 4. Government reports of Schus-ter's sympathies for Fascism began with his appointment as archbishop of Milan in 1929. August 14, 1929, ACS, SPD, CR-RSI, b. 49; Ferrari 1982, p. 587. In featuring news of the pope's planned visit to the Italian king, Milan's Catholic paper told its readers that it was "only right that the Pope's first visit in his capacity as Sovereign was destined to be to the Sovereign of imperial and fascist Italy." "Pio XII restituirà al Quirinale la visita ai Sovrani d'Italia," L'Italia, December 24, 1939, p. 1.

Cementing the close identification of the pope with Italy's Fascist rulers in the mind of the public, the day before the pope's visit to the king he let Ciano know he would be awarding him a papal knighthood, the Order of the Golden Spur, in recognition of all he had done both for the cause of peace and to promote close church-state relations in Italy. The king reciprocated by naming Cardinal Maglione a royal knight, sending him the ornate collar denoting membership in the Supreme Order of the Most Holy An-nunciation. "Lo Speron d'Oro al conte Ciano," AI, December 27, 1939, p. 2; Ciano 1980, p. 378, diary entry for December 27, 1939. The exchange of decorations was discussed in a British Foreign Office memo, which speculated that the exchange of visits between pope and king had been Ciano's idea "and that Signor Mussolini may have been less en-thusiastic." Foreign Office note, December 27, 1939, NAK, FO 371, 24935, 33.

13. "Lo Storico evento al Quirinale: Il popolo dell'Urbe assisterà oggi in festa alla visita del Pontefice ai Sovrani d'Italia," PI, December 28, 1939, p. 1; booklet of papal visit, Casa di Sua Maestà, December 28, 1939, ASDMAE, AISS, b. 116; "La visita di Pio XII ai Sovrani in una cornice di fasto imperiale," PI, December 29, 1939, pp. 1–2; Charles-Roux 1947, pp. 359–60; Loraine to Halifax, December 29, 1939, NAK, FO 371, 24935, 42–43. Phil-lips, the American ambassador, described the Italian king as "a thin little man with too short legs, a screwed-up face and a bristling mustache, but with a certain dignity in spite of his insignificant appearance." Phillips 1952, p. 192.

14. For his part, the king appeared pleased with the exchange of visits, as he told Borgongini at their New Year's audience, and he praised the remarks the pope had made. Borgongini to Maglione, December 30, 1939, AAV, *Arch. Nunz. Italia,* b. 18, fasc. 4, ff. 71r–73r.

CHAPTER II : MAN OF STEEL

1. Examples include "Relazione sulla situazione politica ed economica della Provincia relativa al periodo 1 ottobre–31 dicembre 1939," tel. 67161/441/042846, Questura di Roma, ACS, MI, DAGRA 41, b. 56; Informativa dalla Città del Vaticano (n. 40—Troiani), January 1, 1940, ACS, MI, MAT, b. 221; Informativa da Roma (n. 561—Alicino), January 5, 1940, ACS, MI, MAT, b. 221. Grandi (1985, p. 559) was of the same view.

2. Menshausen to Foreign Ministry, Berlin, dated December 31, 1939, sent January 1, 1940, tel. 158, PAAA, GBS, 261178, 32.

3. Questura di Roma alla DGPS, fonogramma, February 10, 1940, n. 25720, ACS, MI, DAGRA 40, b. 35B; "La Conciliazione," PI, February 10, 1940, p. 1; "All'Ambasciata d'Italia," OR, February 12, 1940, p. 2; "L'anniversario della Conciliazione," PI, February 12, 1940, p. 2; "L'anniversario della Conciliazione fra Stato e Chiesa," RF, February 11, 1940, p. 1; Alfieri 1955, p. 9.

4. Maglione notes, February 17, 1940, ADSS, vol. 1, n. 247. That Ciano's ongoing attempts to portray himself as their champion in steering Mussolini away from war were not altogether successful is evident from Tardini's diary entry of a few months later. In speaking on May 1 with the Italian embassy's chargé d'affaires, Tardini told him he had never believed in the supposed disagreement between Ciano and Mussolini, with Ciano presumably opposed to war and pro-British, and Mussolini a war-loving Anglophobe. "It is all an act," thought Tardini, aimed at keeping all their options open. Pagano 2020, p. 183.

5. Caviglia 2009, pp. 266–67, diary entry for February 19, 1940.

6. Sumner Welles reports, February 26 and March 1, 1940, FDR Library, psfa 71, pp. 3–14, 27–39.

7. Phillips to FDR, February 26, 1940, FDR Library, psfa 401, pp. 57–61; Sumner Welles report, February 26, 1940, FDR Library, psfa 71, pp. 16–25; Welles to FDR, February 26, 1940, FDR Library, psfa 36, pp. 2–14; Phillips to secretary of state, Washington, D.C., February 28, 1940, FDR Library, psfa 36, pp. 19–21; Ciano 1980, p. 399, diary entry for February 26, 1940.

8. Roosevelt's letter to the pope, dated December 23, 1939, is reproduced in FRUS 1939, vol. 2, pp. 871–72. The president's letter informing Taylor of his appointment, with the same date, is at FRUS 1939, vol. 2, pp. 873–74; Hull to Phillips, Rome, December 23, 1939, FRUS 1939, vol. 2, p. 873; Flynn 1972, pp. 183–85; Chadwick 1986, p. 101. The British ambassador to France, on the day after the appointment, sent a note to the Foreign Office in London, observing: "The Roman Catholic vote was necessary to Pres Roosevelt: hence his recent appointment of Mr. Myron Taylor to the Vatican." NAK, FO 800/325, 404. On Roosevelt's relations with the American church hierarchy, see Fogarty 2003.

9. Myron Taylor to FDR, February 28, 1940, FDR Library, psfa 36, pp. 15–18; Tittmann 2004, p. 8; "Il Sommo Pontefice riceve in solenne udienza il rappresentante del Presidente degli Stati Uniti," OR, February 28, 1940, p. 1. Taylor had been asked to raise another subject with the pope, although there is no record it came up in that first conversation. "Anti-Jewish feeling in Brooklyn, Baltimore and Detroit," wrote the president in his instructions to Taylor, "is said to be encouraged by the church. You should point out that this only causes anti-Catholic feeling in return" (Conway 1975, p. 89n).

10. Appunto, Alfieri, February 29, 1940, ASDMAE, AISS, 1947–54, b. 227; also published in DDI, series 9, vol. 3, n. 409.

11. Travaglini to Cardinal Lauri, January 1, 1940, ASRS, *AA.EE.SS.*, Pio XII, parte 1, Germania, posiz. 774, ff. 29r–30r.

12. Lauri to Pius XII, January 2, 1940, ASRS, *AA.EE.SS.*, Pio XII, parte 1, Germania, posiz. 774, f. 31r. The accompanying note is found at f. 32r.

13. The German-language document containing the text of the pope's five points of January 3, 1940, is found at ASRS, *AA.EE.SS.*, Pio XII, parte 1, Germania, posiz. 774, ff. 63r–71r. At the top of a copy of the pope's German-language document is the handwritten explanation, written in Italian: "Note given privately to Prince von Hessen January 3, 1940, at 6–6:15 P.M. and read and received by him without expressing any difficulty or objection." ASRS, *AA.EE.SS.*, Pio XII, parte 1, Germania, posiz. 774, f. 34r.

14. Travaglini to Lauri, January 4, 1940, ASRS, *AA.EE.SS.*, Pio XII, parte 1, Germania, posiz. 774, f. 35r; Montini note, January 4, 1940, part 1 is at f. 36r.

15. The pope's reply to von Hessen, dated January 5, 1940, is found at ASRS, *AA.EE.SS.*, Pio XII, parte 1, Germania, posiz. 774, ff. 37rv. The record of the cardinal's phone call, apparently prepared by Montini, dated January 8, is at f. 38r.

16. Travaglini to Lauri, February 5, 1940, ASRS, *AA.EE.SS.*, Pio XII, parte 1, Germania, posiz. 774, ff. 39r–40r.

17. The typed note bears the title "Aufzeichnung," with handwritten edits, apparently by the pope, ASRS, *AA.EE.SS.*, Pio XII, parte 1, Germania, posiz. 774, f. 45r.

18. Travaglini to Lauri, February 18, 1940, ASRS, *AA.EE.SS.*, Pio XII, parte 1, Germania, posiz. 774, ff. 48r–50r.

19. The one memo published in those volumes containing a passing allusion to these negotiations, a note by Monsignor Tardini, appears in ADSS with the following sentence excised without any indication that anything is being deleted: "In fact, Travaglini had always said that, once the audience with the Pope was arranged, von Ribbentrop would have found a pretext to come to Italy." Tardini notes, ASRS, *AA.EE.SS.*, Pio XII, parte 1, Germania, posiz. 774, f. 248v; the expurgated text is found at ADSS, vol. 1, n. 257.

20. Cardinal Lauri to Pius XII, March 8, 1940, and Travaglini to Lauri, March 8, 1940, ASRS, *AA.EE.SS.*, Pio XII, parte 1, Germania, posiz. 774, ff. 55r, 56r.

21. Tardini notes, March 9, 1940, ASRS, *AA.EE.SS.*, Pio XII, parte 1, Germania, posiz. 774, f. 246r.

CHAPTER 12: A PROBLEMATIC VISITOR

1. The quote is from Kershaw 1999, pp. 556–57. See Kershaw 1999, p. 774, for the attitude of other Nazi leaders to Ribbentrop.

2. Ribbentrop conversation with Pius XII, March 11, 1940, memorandum, DGFP, series D, vol. 8, n. 668; Pirelli 1984, p. 256, diary entry for March 15, 1940; "La visita in Vaticano," PI, March 12, 1940, p. 1; Ribbentrop udienza Pio XII, March 11, 1940, AAV, *Segr. Stato,* 1940, Stati e Corpo Diplomatico, posiz. 45, ff. 4–13.

3. Für den Empfang des deutschen Reichsaußenministers JOACHIM VON RIBBENTROP beim Heiligen Vater am 11.März 1940, ASRS, *AA.EE.SS.*, Pio XII, parte 1, Germania, posiz. 774, ff. 63r–71r. This German-language memo in preparation for the pope's meeting was proceeded by an Italian-language memo covering the same ground prepared by the Secretariat of State office and given to the pope on the day before the meeting. "Appunto preparato dal Minutante per Sua Santità e l'Em. Cardinale Segretario di Stato in occasione della visita del Sig. von Ribbentrop, ministro degli esteri di Germania, dell'11 marzo 1940," ff. 74r–76r.

4. Bastianini 2005, p. 292.

5. Tardini notes, March 11, 1940, ADSS, vol. 1, n. 257.

6. Maglione notes, March 11, 1940, ADSS, vol. 1, nn. 258 and 259; Bastianini 2005, p. 292.

Bastianini had served as undersecretary for foreign affairs until the previous October, and he would again during Mussolini's last months in office.

Curiously, the pope had sent instructions the previous evening to Maglione telling him that, should Ribbentrop in their meeting bring up the idea of having Franz von Papen replace Bergen as German ambassador to the Holy See, "it would be well to make him understand clearly that he does not seem the most appropriate person." AAV, *Segr. Stato,* 1940, Stati e Corpo Diplomatico, posiz. 45, f. 8r. Franz von Papen was the German chancellor in 1932 and then became Hitler's vice chancellor the following year. Even following Ribbentrop's visit the pope worried that the Germans would replace Bergen with von Papen and sought out the opinion of Berlin's Bishop Konrad von Preysing, referring to it in his letter, written in German on April 22, 1940, as "a matter of utmost confidentiality." "Since this request will be made to the Holy See perhaps very soon as we have been told," wrote the pope, "it will be useful if you could send Us a reply as soon as you receive this letter." Indeed, the matter was so delicate that the pope instructed him to reply by a code: "The words 'request for blessing on the occasion of a wedding' will indicate that the agreement can be given," instructed the pontiff, "the words 'request for the blessing of a very sick person' will indicate that it simply has to be denied."

On April 30, the nuncio in Berlin sent a one-line cable to Maglione: "The bishop of Berlin is requesting the blessing of a very sick person." The following day Bishop Preysing wrote directly to the pope to explain that he opposed the choice of von Papen because appointment of "this type of high-profile National Socialist will appear to be sanctioned by the Church." Von Papen, feared the bishop, would create an entourage in Rome that would seek to spread the false opinion of close, harmonious relations between the National Socialist government and the Vatican. These documents are found at AAV, *Segr. Stato,* 1940, Diocesi, posiz. 306, ff. 114r–16r, 117r, 121r–23v.

7. Relazione del colloquio avvenuto fra il Signor Ribbentrop e Monsignor Tiso, fatta da quest'ultimo a Monsignor [Michal] Buzalka, Vescovo Ausiliare di Tirnava il 7 agosto 1940, ASRS, *AA.EE.SS.,* Pio XII, parte 1, Germania, posiz. 774, f. 156r.

8. Grandi 1985, p. 562; Attolico to Ciano, March 9, 1940, DDI, series 9, vol. 3, n. 502. In his memoir the French ambassador to Italy made a similar point about the significance of Ribbentrop's visit in dating Mussolini's final move toward war. François-Poncet 1961, pp. 161–77.

9. Rauscher 2004, pp. 337–38.

10. The official Italian transcript of the March 10 meeting is found at ASDMAE, Gab., b. 1130A, UC-14, fasc. 2.

11. The Italian transcript of the March 11 conversation is found at DDI, series 9, vol. 3, n. 524; the German memo on it is at DGFP, series D, vol. 8, n. 669.

12. Orsenigo to Maglione, March 17, 1940, ASRS, *AA.EE.SS.,* Pio XII, parte 1, Germania, posiz. 774, ff. 180r–82r.

13. Welles's reports on his March 1 meeting with Ribbentrop and his March 2 meeting with Hitler are found in FDR Library, psfa 72, pp. 27–39, 45–55.

14. At his March 16 meeting with the Duce and Ciano, it was Welles who learned the most important news. Germany, Mussolini told him, planned to conquer France within three or four months, and the Germans were confident Britain would soon crumble as well. The Duce also told the American that Hitler had asked him to come in two days' time to the Brenner Pass for an urgent meeting. The German offensive, predicted the Duce, would take place very soon: "The minute hand is pointing to one minute before midnight." The Duce's parting remark gave Welles some grounds for hope that Italy might remain out of the fighting. "You may wish to remember," Mussolini said, "that, while the German-Italian pact exists, I nevertheless retain complete liberty of action." Welles's report on his March 16 meeting with Mussolini is found at FDR Library, psfa 72,

pp. 97–103. Further telegram correspondence reporting on the visit is found at FDR Library, psfa 36, pp. 60–75.

Welles next met with the Italian king. Asked his view of the Duce, whom he had been meeting twice a week for many years, the king called him "a very great man." When Welles pleaded with the king to do all he could to keep Italy out of the war, Victor Emmanuel demurred. In Italy, he said, the monarch has little power. He was equally dismissive of the American's attempt at flattery. When Welles told him how impressed he was with the devotion and admiration Italians felt for their king, Victor Emmanuel shook his head and, with a wry smile, replied, "My English is getting rusty and I don't know how to phrase exactly what I mean, but I am afraid the impression you have obtained is not true." One thing was clear to Welles: the timorous king was not going to be of any help. FDR Library, psfa 72, pp. 80–87.

15. According to Taylor's Italian-speaking assistant, Harold Tittmann, when he met with the pope, Pius XII always began by speaking to him in English, proud of his knowledge of the language, but then soon, with evident relief, fell back on Italian for the rest of the conversation. Tittmann 2004, p. 93.

16. Welles's report on his March 18 meeting with the pope is found at FDR Library, psfa 72, pp. 107–111; d'Ormesson final report, October 28, 1940, MAEC, Guerre Vichy, 550.

17. "L'incontro Mussolini-Hitler al Brennero," *L'Italia,* March 19, 1940, p. 1.

18. "La partenza di Hitler," *L'Italia,* March 19, 1940, p. 1. The official German memo of the conversation is found at DGFP, series D, vol. 9, n. 1. "L'incontro al Brennero del Capo del Governo italiano col Cancelliere Hitler," OR, March 18, 1940, p. 1; Ciano 1980, p. 408, diary entry for March 18, 1940; Grandi 1985, p. 565; Rauscher 2004, p. 340; Navarra 2004, p. 46.

19. Welles report on his March 19, 1940, meeting with Ciano, FDR Library, psfa 72, pp. 118–23; Welles final report to FDR on European trip, March 1940, FDR Library, psfa 72, pp. 125–33.

20. Visani 2007, pp. 77–78; Ciano 1980, pp. 414–15, diary entry for April 2, 1940.

21. Hitler to Mussolini, April 9, 1940, Hitler phone message for Mussolini, April 10, 1940, and Mackensen to German Foreign Ministry, April 11, 1940, DGFP, series D, vol. 9, nn. 68, 82 and 86.

22. Petacci 2011, pp. 312–14, diary entry for April 11, 1940.

23. Ciano 1980, p. 418, diary entry for April 11, 1940.

CHAPTER 13: AN INOPPORTUNE TIME

1. Ribbentrop to Mackensen, May 7, 1940, DGFP, series D, vol. 9, n. 205; Hitler's letter to Mussolini is at n. 212; Mussolini to Hitler, May 10, 1940, is at n. 232; Ciano 1980, p. 427, diary entry for May 10, 1940; Bottai 1989, p. 190, diary entry for May 12, 1940; Di Rienzo 2018, p. 315.

2. The pope's April 12 letter to Mussolini is found at ASDMAE, Gab., b. 189, UC–73, fasc. 1. The pope also arranged for *L'Osservatore Romano* to publish an article clarifying that when the pope invoked the desire for peace, he was referring not to a peace of the weak but rather, as Mussolini himself kept insisting, a peace "based on justice." Alfieri enthusiastically reported on the OR article ("L'invito del papa") to Ciano, sending him the clipping. Alfieri to Ciano, April 21, 1940, ASDMAE, AISS, b. 113.

3. Mussolini letter to Pius XII, April 30, 1940, ASDMAE, AISS, b. 176; also found in ADSS, vol. 1, n. 290; Ciano 1980, p. 422, diary entry for April 28, 1940.

4. Hull to Phillips (transmitting text of FDR messages to Phillips and to Mussolini), April 29, 1940, FRUS 1940, vol. 2, pp. 691–92; Phillips to Hull, May 1, 1940, FRUS 1940, vol. 2, pp. 693–95. As for the coordination with the pope, Taylor reported to FDR: "The Pope, pledging us to secrecy advised me on Friday last [April 26] that he had ful-

filled his duty of parallel action by direct handwritten message to Mussolini aimed at non-belligerency for Italy." Taylor to FDR, April 30, 1940, FRUS 1940, vol. 2, pp. 692–93. Phillips's memo of meeting with Ciano, May 2, 1940, is found at FRUS 1940, vol. 2, p. 699; Phillips to FDR, May 2, 1940, FDR Library, psfa 401, p. 71; Mussolini to FDR, May 2, 1940, FRUS 1940, vol. 2, p. 698. Mussolini informed the German ambassador of Roosevelt's approach and his own response. In the future, Mussolini told Mackensen, he would no longer meet with the American ambassador nor with any ambassador other than him. Mussolini also wrote to Hitler the day he received Roosevelt's message, sending him a copy of it along with a copy of his response—a response Hitler received before the president did. Characterizing Roosevelt's plea as having a "threatening character," Mussolini added that he felt the "rather drastic tone" of his own response had been called for. Along with his presidential correspondence, the Duce also sent Hitler a copy of the pope's recent plea for peace and his response to the pontiff. Hitler got back to him quickly. "I find your replies to the Pope and Roosevelt also marvelous." Mackensen to German Foreign Ministry, May 1, 1940, DGFP, series D, vol. 9, n. 185; Mussolini to Hitler, May 2, 1940, DGFP, series D, vol. 9, n. 190; Hitler to Mussolini, May 3, 1940, DGFP, series D, vol. 9, n. 192.

5. As accounts of such violent encounters began to flood the Vatican, Pius XII told Maglione to send a coded telegram to the nuncios abroad to let them know what had happened. Memo, May 14, 1940, AAV, *Segr. Stato,* 1940, Stato Città Vaticano, posiz. 63, f. 27r; Mons. Micara, Brussels, to Maglione, May 10, 1940, ADSS, vol. 1, n. 297; Tardini 1961, p. 123; "Messaggi del Santo Padre ai Sovrani del Belgio, dell'Olanda e del Lussemburgo," OR, May 12, 1940, p. 1.

"After having burned all the copies of *L'Osservatore Romano,*" reported the director of Bologna's Catholic newspaper, *L'Avvenire d'Italia,* on May 11, "they burned ours as well. Coming to the offices of the newspaper they seized the entire run of the press . . . burning it on the public street." AAV, *Segr. Stato,* 1940, Stato Città Vaticano, posiz. 63, f. 329r. Maglione summoned the chargé d'affaires of the Italian embassy to the Vatican on May 12 to complain about the violence committed against the Vatican paper and threatened a public protest if it continued. Memo, May 13, 1940, AAV, *Segr. Stato,* 1940, Stato Città Vaticano, posiz. 63, ff. 31r–32r. On May 14 he followed this up by sending a note to many of the nuncios and apostolic delegates to inform them of the violence committed against the newsstands selling copies of the May 12 edition of *L'Osservatore Romano* (ADSS, vol. 1, n. 315). The French texts of the pope's three messages are found in ADSS, vol. 1, nn. 301–3. Accounts of the violence against the Vatican paper were coming from much of the country. "I am saddened to have to report that here in L'Aquila," wrote the Aquila archbishop on May 13, "for the past three days the copies of L'Osservatore Romano have been seized, torn up, and burned, by order, it seems of this Federal Secretary [of the Fascist Party]." That the orders came from on high was also the opinion of Monsignor Montini, who replied, "Evidently the difficulties caused for the distribution of *L'Osservatore Romano* are the result of orders coming, inexplicably, from the upper hierarchies." AAV, *Segr. Stato,* 1940, Stato Città Vaticano, posiz. 63, ff. 36r, 35r.

6. D'Aroma 1957, p. 296; Ciano 1980, p. 429, diary entry for May 12, 1940.

7. Tardini notes, May 10, 1940, with annex telegram of the French government to Charles-Roux, May 10, 1940, ADSS, vol. 1, n. 298; Osborne to Secretariat of State, May 10, 1940, ADSS, vol. 1, nn. 298, 299, 300.

8. Tardini notes, May 13, 1940, ADSS, vol. 1, n. 312.

9. Ambassador Bullitt, Paris, to U.S. secretary of state, May 14, 1940, FRUS 1940, vol. 2, pp. 703–4.

10. The Holy Father, insisted Cardinal Maglione, had already done all that was "just and opportune." Maglione notes, May 14, 1940, ADSS, vol. 1, n. 316. "His Holiness is persuaded that Italy will enter the war within a month or shortly thereafter," wrote Tardini

in his diary on May 15. "His Holiness believes that the Germans will win, because they have both air and mechanical superiority." Pagano 2020, p. 187.

11. Alfieri 1955, pp. 13–14.

12. Ciano 1980, pp. 421–22, diary entry for April 26, 1940; Goeschel 2018, p. 179.

13. Before he met with the pope for his final audience as ambassador to the Holy See, Alfieri went to see Cardinal Maglione. Maglione took advantage of the occasion to complain about the violence suffered by the vendors and readers of the Vatican newspaper. Did this, asked the cardinal, reflect a government decision to end "the atmosphere of cordiality and mutual collaboration which had been happily restored" under the new pope? Alfieri insisted that the government had nothing to do with it, blaming the violence on "the impulsivity of a handful of youths in a moment of legitimate tension in public opinion." Eager to see peace restored, the cardinal, as the ambassador reported to Ciano, "repeatedly, together with Mons. Montini, asked me to let Your Excellency know that the Vatican lacked any intention of in any way harming the national government. . . . He repeated to me, with great emotion, his deep attachment to Italy and the deep feeling with which he wished for the best fortunes for the common Fatherland." Alfieri to Ciano, May 12, 1940, n. 1375/575, ASDMAE, AISS, b. 113.

14. Montini notes, May 13, 1940, ADSS, vol. 1, n. 313. Following his meeting with the pontiff, Alfieri hastened to brief Mackensen on what the pope had said. He was especially eager to tell the German ambassador that, in response to the complaint about the pope's three telegrams, Pius XII had replied that he had spent hours crafting his texts in such a way as to scrupulously avoid "any word of political import, such as 'invasion,' that might imply a viewpoint." Whether he explicitly told the German ambassador of the pope's eagerness to get a message to Hitler is less clear. Mackensen to Berlin, telegram, May 13, 1940, quoted in Friedländer 1966, pp. 49–50. As he was departing Rome, Alfieri handwrote a letter to the pope, thanking him for the benevolence the pope had shown him the previous day and vaunting the fact that in performing his duties both "as ambassador and as Catholic" he had helped bring about understanding between the government and the church. Alfieri concluded, "I leave with a more tranquil spirit, satisfied at having concluded my high mission [as ambassador to the Holy See] with one last intervention of mine, that of this morning, which shows again my position toward the Church and my profound, immutable devotion to Your Holiness." Alfieri to Pius XII, May 14, 1940, AAV, *Segr. Stato,* 1940, Stato Città Vaticano, posiz. 63, ff. 69r–70v.

15. Eager to maintain good relations with Italy's new ambassador to Germany, the pope instructed Montini to go to the train station to see him off, but mistakenly thinking that the train was to depart at midnight, the monsignor arrived after it had left. Montini to Alfieri, May 15, 1940, ACS, Archivi di Personalità della Politica e della Pubblica Amministrazione, Alfieri, b. 10, Vaticano.

16. Di Rienzo 2018, p. 310; Alfieri to Ciano, May 23, 1940, DDI, series 9, vol. 4, n. 553. Göring, meeting with Alfieri after the bestowal of the Italian honor, was eager to ply him for news of the pope and to talk about Germany's relations with the Catholic Church. Göring compared Germany's clergy unfavorably to Italy's. In Italy the great majority of the clergy supported the government and supported Fascism, he said, while in Germany there were cases of high prelates who stood decisively against Nazism. Alfieri to Ciano, May 23, 1940, DDI, series 9, vol. 4, n. 553.

17. "I must add," observed the nuncio in Paris, in reporting the meeting to Cardinal Maglione, "that this idea of excommunication had not germinated by itself in Mr. Bullitt's mind." Indeed, only the previous evening a French senator, speaking on behalf of members of France's Senate Committee on Foreign Affairs, had come to see the nuncio to ask whether the moment had not come for the pope to excommunicate Hitler, before then raising the same question about Mussolini.

18. Mons. Valeri to Maglione, May 15, 1940; Maglione to Valeri, May 17, 1940, ADSS,

vol. 1, nn. 317 and 324. Pleas to the pope to speak out more clearly were coming from within the church as well. The same day as the nuncio wrote, the archbishop of Paris sent an anguished letter to the pope, begging him to do more to prevent Mussolini from joining Hitler in the assault on France. Some indication of the sense of urgency felt at the time is evident from the fact that the French ambassador delivered Cardinal Suhard's letter to the Apostolic Palace at eleven-fifteen P.M. the night of May 17. AAV, *Segr. Stato,* 1940, Diocesi, posiz. 123, f. 8r. The pope replied that he had already done all he could to keep Italy out of the conflict. Archbishop Suhard, Paris, to Pius XII, May 15, 1940; Maglione to Suhard, May 25, 1940, ADSS, vol. 1, nn. 319 and 329. Related documentation on Cardinal Suhard's plea and the pope's response can be found at AAV, *Segr. Stato,* 1940, Diocesi, posiz. 123, ff. 1r–13r.

The Duce's success in intimidating the pope by unleashing attacks on the Vatican newspaper was clear to the French ambassador at the Vatican as well. Writing to Paris on May 16, Charles-Roux described Montini as "suffering visibly from the blow inflicted by a campaign of intimidation aimed against the Holy See by the Fascist Party and probably inspired by the numerous German agents who are found in Rome. The people in the Vatican, impressionable and easily intimidated by physical brutality, seem to me to yield in this moment to an exaggerated fear." Charles-Roux to French Foreign Ministry, May 16, 1940, MAEC, Papiers Duparc.

19. Stefano Vitti to Pius XII, May 14, 1940, AAV, *Segr. Stato,* anno 1940, Stato Città Vaticano, b. 63, f. 111r.

20. Una Italiana Civile e Cristiana to Pius XII, n.d., AAV, *Segr. Stato,* 1940, Stato Città Vaticano, posiz. 63, ff. 139r–40r.

21. Le donne Cattoliche d'Italia to Pius XII, n.d., AAV, *Segr. Stato,* 1940, Stato Città Vaticano, posiz. 63, f. 120r.

22. Alfieri to Ciano, May 23, 1940, DDI, series 9, vol. 4, n. 553.

23. Foreign Office, London, to Osborne, May 18, 1940, R5999/55/22, NAK, FO 371, 24935, 92; Dixon handwritten note, June 3, 1942, NAK, FO 371, 33411, 152; Informativa da Roma (n. 535—Mezzabotta), May 20, 1940, ACS, MI, MAT, b. 217.

24. Cardinal Hlond to Montini, May 13, 1940; and Montini to Hlond, May 20, 1940, AAV, *Segr. Stato,* 1940, Stati e Corpo Diplomatico, posiz. 275, ff. 29r, 26r.

CHAPTER 14: AN HONORABLE DEATH

1. Buffarini, undersecretary of internal affairs, meeting with the nuncio, surprised him by remarking that the Holy See, in publishing the pope's three telegrams, had acted "against all of Europe." What, the nuncio asked, did he mean by "all of Europe"? "But don't you know," replied Buffarini, "that we and the Germans have divided up Europe?" Italy, he added, would enter the war within two weeks but would not be at war long, for it would all be over soon. Borgongini to Maglione, May 23, 1940, reporting on meeting the previous day, ADSS, vol. 1, n. 328.

2. Visani (2007, pp. 133, 144) provides the excerpts from the May 22 Ministry of Popular Culture, Gabinetto report and the May 24 report of the informant in Genoa.

3. Hitler to Mussolini, May 25, 1940; Mackensen to Ribbentrop, May 26, 1940, DGFP, series D, vol. 9, nn. 317, 320; Goeschel 2018, p. 182.

4. On the role played by Pirelli and the other major Italian industrialists as the Fascist regime hurtled toward disaster, see Carace 2021.

5. Borgongini to Maglione, May 28, 1940, ADSS, vol. 1, n. 332; Pirelli 1984, pp. 262–63, diary entry for May 28, 1940. Mackensen's report to Berlin the next day similarly described Ciano as eager to see Italy enter the war and complaining that it was the Italian military command that kept delaying it. "If one went by the military men," Ciano told

the German ambassador, "one would never be ready." Mackensen to Foreign Ministry, Berlin, May 29, 1940, DGFP, series D, vol. 9, n. 343.

6. Petersen 1994, pp. 107, 112–13; Ciano 1980, pp. 421–22, diary entry for April 27, 1940. Eleonora, who was as good-looking and glamorous as her husband was plain and reserved, was perceptive and talented in her own right. Although Attolico had spent five years in Berlin, he never learned to speak German, and when Hitler, who knew only that language, stopped to chat with her husband at receptions, Eleonora stood at his side, translating. Tall, slender, and self-confident, she was not however particularly appreciated by the pope. Following protocol at the Vatican for the presentation of a new ambassador's credentials, Attolico had brought Eleonora with him to meet the pope. Later, Pius XII complained that she had kept talking the whole time. Mackensen to Foreign Ministry, Berlin, April 30, 1940, DGFP, series D, vol. 9, n. 181; Informativa da Roma (n. 352—Montuschi), May 2, 1940, ACS, MI, MAT, b. 217; Mackensen to Foreign Ministry, Berlin, April 30, 1940, DGFP, series D, vol. 9, n. 181; d'Ormesson to Vichy, July 21, 1940, MAEC, Guerre Vichy, 559.

7. Attolico to Ciano, May 21, 1940, ASDMAE, AISS, b. 113. The Montini quote is from Babuscio Rizzo's report of his conversation with him on May 21. Appunto per l'Eccellenza l'Ambasciatore, ASDMAE, AISS, b. 113. Montini's May 18 conversation with Attolico is reported in a note dated the next day, at AAV, *Segr. Stato,* 1940, Stato Città Vaticano, posiz. 63, ff. 56rv.

8. The result was soon evident to all, as the British envoy in the Vatican reported to London. While in the past the newspaper had offered the only objective account of world events to be found in Italy, "its columns are now almost entirely devoted to information of a religious nature, and it no longer makes any attempt at enlightenment or comment on world affairs. It has died an honourable death, or has at any rate honourably succumbed to temporary extinction, as an organ of information and interpretation." Osborne to Halifax, May 21, 1940, NAK, FO 371, 24935, 84–85; Attolico to Ciano, May 22, 1940, ASDMAE, AISS, b. 113. The May 25 OR article is quoted in Pighin 2010, pp. 43–44.

9. Indeed, reported the ambassador, Pius XII said that he "would be pleased to be notified of any desire we may have, in such a way to be able—to the extent possible—to satisfy us." Now that the conflict over *L'Osservatore Romano* had been put behind them, Attolico asked the pope at their late May meeting if he had any other matters particularly dear to him. Yes, replied the pontiff, he did, for he was concerned about how the Italian government would treat foreign diplomats to the Holy See in case Italy entered the war. Those representing countries Italy regarded as enemies, said the pope, should be allowed to remain unmolested in Rome.

The Vatican had raised the question before, and Attolico had a response ready. While the Lateran Accords did guarantee the Holy See the right to freely engage in diplomatic relations with other countries, international law did not require a nation at war to allow diplomats from enemy nations to remain on its soil.

Perhaps that was true, replied the pope, but the government should consider the consequences of taking such a stance. "If these diplomats take refuge in the Vatican, something I am unable to prevent, they will be less easily under surveillance by the Royal Authorities." It was an argument that would have little sway with the Duce, who had no lack of spies in the Vatican. Attolico to Ciano, May 30, 1939 (reporting on papal audience of May 29), n. 1565/692, ASDMAE, AISS, b. 152.

10. Mackensen to Foreign Ministry, May 30, 1940, and Mussolini to Hitler, May 30, 1940, DGFP, series D, vol. 9, nn. 350, 356; Ciano 1980, p. 436, diary entry for May 30, 1940; Phillips to FDR, May 31, 1940, FDR Library, pfsa 401, pp. 73–75. As the ambassador put it in a letter to Welles the same day, "Mussolini is evidently bewitched by the accom-

plishments of Germany by brute force and sees an easy and cheap victory ahead for himself and a means to his own aggrandizement." Phillips to Welles, FDR Library, psfa 401, pp. 82–83.

11. Phillips told President Roosevelt that Mussolini "undoubtedly has the Caesar complex of adding to the Empire by hook or crook." The ambassador thought Mussolini's eagerness to go to war was all the more remarkable because Germany had shown no need for Italy's assistance. Phillips to FDR, May 31, 1940, FDR Library, psfa 401, pp. 73–77; Milza 2000, pp. 834–35.

CHAPTER 15: A SHORT WAR

1. Ciano to all foreign diplomats, June 10, 1940, DDI, series 9, vol. 4, n. 842; Grandi 1985, p. 586; François-Poncet 1961, pp. 178–79; Bottai 1989, p. 193, diary entry for June 10, 1940.

2. De Felice 1981, pp. 841–42.

3. Petacci 2011, p. 327, diary entry for June 10, 1940; Grandi 1985, pp. 588–89.

4. Roberts 2018, p. 553. On June 10 the French foreign minister notified the papal nuncio in Paris that the French government was vacating the city that day. The German army would enter the French capital four days later. A few days after that, the nuncio sent a letter to the Vatican: "God be thanked, all is now passed in Paris and I am well. The occupation of the city took place amid the greatest calm and correctly. The authorities have given me as well every assurance. The Cardinal Archbishop [of Paris] has remained here, with the entire Curia and virtually all the clergy." French foreign minister to Valeri, Paris, June 10, 1940, and Valeri to Maglione, June 20, 1940 (sent via the nuncio in Berlin), AAV, Nunz. Parigi, Nunziatura Valeri, b. 574, fasc. 368, ff. 1r, 12r.

5. A few hours before Mussolini's declaration of war, the military attaché at the American embassy in Rome had sent Washington a critique of Mussolini's motives: "Due to the unprepared position of Italy to sustain a long war it would appear that if Italy does enter the war now the Duce is convinced that the war will be over within several months. . . . If his estimate is not correct and the war continues for a long period of time, it is believed that Italy cannot sustain herself and will be ruined." Col. G. H. Paine, Rome, June 10, 1940, NARA, RG 165, 2062-716, 3, color 125.

6. Friedländer 1966, p. 54; Paxton 1972, pp. 13–14. Although the pope never made any move to replace Orsenigo, there is some evidence that he himself was concerned that his nuncio in Berlin was overly worried about doing anything that might offend Hitler. A telegram from Cardinal Maglione to Orsenigo on April 13, 1940, had a clearly admonitory tone: "It is the wish of the Holy Father that Your Most Reverend Excellency transmit all the reports that the Bishops desire to send him, as is their right and duty, and that Your Excellency neither obstruct nor discourage these Bishops, who judge it the duty of their pastoral ministry to present in such a manner complaints and protests against the violations of the rights and the freedoms of the Church. The Holy Father trusts that this Nunciature will carry out this, his order exactly." ASRS, *AA.EE.SS.*, Pio XII, parte Extracta, Germania, posiz. 600, f. 5r. That same file contains a 1956 note by Monsignor Tardini on Orsenigo's attitude toward Nazism, which he termed overly "passive." Tardini claimed that Orsenigo "always remained doubtful and suspicious toward the Most Eminent Cardinal Pacelli" (ff. 89v–90r).

7. Maglione, meeting with the new French ambassador on the morning of June 11, recounted this story prior to asking him to plead with his government to have the Allies spare Rome from bombardment, now that Italy had declared war. D'Ormesson to French Foreign Ministry, June 11, 1940, MAEC, Guerre Vichy, 461.

8. D'Ormesson to Foreign Ministry, Paris, June 2, 1940, MAEC, Papiers Duparc. The fact that the pope's speech "contained no word of warning against Italian entry into the

war," observed the British envoy to the Vatican, "is an evident sign that he regards the decision as irrevocable." Osborne to Halifax, June 4, 1940, NAK, FO 380/48, n. 86.

9. "Pio XII, Padre dei popoli, invoca da Dio 'una pace giusta, onorevole e duratura,'" AR, June 4, 1940, p. 1. The Italian ambassador, who sent Ciano a copy of the speech, noted that the pope had studiously avoided any "polemical" political comments. Indeed, he told Ciano, the pope had indicated sympathy for the Italian position. He pointed in particular to the pope's citation of Saint Augustine's phrase, *bellum geritur, ut pax acquiratur* (war is waged for peace to be obtained), which, he remarked, "seems significant in this regard to me and almost serves as a bridge between the Christian concept of peace, which the Pope as pope can hardly fail to preach and to wish for, and the realistic, current necessities of war." Attolico to Ciano, June 2, 1940, tel. 1602/710, ASDMAE, APSS, b. 48.

10. Guariglia to Ciano, May 30, 1940, tel. 3480, ASDMAE, APSS, b. 49; Charles-Roux conversation with Guariglia, May 1940, MAEC, Papiers Chauvel, vol. 121; "Il nuovo Ambasciatore di Francia," OR, June 10, 1940, p. 2; Chassard 2015, p. 11; Osborne annual report for 1940, Osborne to Eden, November 13, 1941, NAK, R 10496/30/507, pp. 7–8.

11. D'Ormesson report on his June 9 audience with the pope, June 11, 1940, MAEC, Guerre Vichy, 544; Chassard 2015, pp. 36–37.

12. Montini, June 12, 1940, AAV, *Segr. Stato,* 1940, Stato Città Vaticano, posiz. 63, ff. 73r–74r.

13. Montini, June 12, 1940, AAV, *Segr. Stato,* 1940, Stato Città Vaticano, posiz. 63, ff. 78r–79v.

14. The pope's instructions were recorded in a handwritten memo by Montini, June 12, 1940, AAV, *Segr. Stato,* 1940, Stato Città Vaticano, b. 63, ff. 75r–76r.

15. Attolico to Ciano, June 13, 1940, n. 1752, ASDMAE, AISS, b. 113.

16. R. Manzini, "L'ora del *L'Italia,*" and "Dovere," AI, June 11, 1940, p. 1; "Il Card. Arcivescovo di Bologna invita il popolo alla preghiera," AI, June 12, 1940, p. 2.

17. "La dichiarazione di guerra dell'Italia alla Francia e alla Gran Bretagna," OR, June 12, 1940, p. 1; Visani 2007, p. 127; d'Ormesson to French Foreign Ministry, June 13, 1940, MAEN, RSS 576, PO/1, 1183.

18. Later in the war another French ambassador to the Holy See would likewise note that the pope had no patience for Tisserant, adding that there was a deep incompatibility between the pope's Roman, sensitive, diplomatic nature and the "rough son of the Lorraine." More typical of the cardinals of the Vatican was Nicola Canali, the leading figure of the three cardinals responsible for the administration of Vatican City. The British envoy described him as "a feared and disliked autocrat," adding that "he is said to be pious and just, but is hard and obstinate." D'Ormesson went to see the corpulent and querulous Canali shortly after moving in. "Poor Italy!" said the cardinal in response to the ambassador's complaints about Mussolini, but his words were accompanied by no sign of actual indignation. "Moreover," added d'Ormesson, "Cardinal Canali's sympathies for the Fascist regime are notorious." D'Ormesson to French Foreign Ministry, June 11, 1940, MAEN, RSS 576, PO/1, 1183; Fouilloux 2011, pp. 292–93; d'Ormesson to French Foreign Ministry, June 13, 1940, MAEN, RSS 576, PO/1, 1183; Osborne to Foreign Office, London, June 6, 1946, NAK, FO 371, 60812, ZM 1993, 1946; Chadwick 1986, p. 125; Chassard 2015, pp. 62, 168; Attolico to Foreign Ministry, December 9, 1940, ASDMAE, AISS, b. 164; Baudrillart 1998, p. 786, diary entry for January 10, 1941. For descriptions of police efforts to follow Tisserant on his movements through Rome, see ACS, MIFP, serie B, b. 25.

19. Not surprisingly, perhaps, the German police intercepted Tisserant's letter, and it worked its way up to the head of the German police, Reinhard Heydrich. He in turn sent a copy to Rome, where the Italian police chief brought it directly to Mussolini. Chenaux 2003, p. 250; Fouilloux 2011, pp. 293–94; Divisione Polizia Politica, October 6, 1940, n. 500.28246, ACS, MIFP, Serie-B, b. 25.

20. Farinacci to Mussolini, June 12, 1940, ACS, MI, MAT, b. 263. The informant also warned about another French prelate in the Vatican, Mons. René Fontenelle, whom he dubbed "a French spy." He, too, said the informant, regularly left Vatican City undisturbed. It was crucial, the informant concluded, that the Regime establish "extremely rigorous services of vigilance" outside the Vatican walls. "To neglect this," he remarked, "could be very costly!"

21. D'Ormesson to French Foreign Ministry, June 13, 1940, MAEN, RSS 576, PO/1, 1183. Farinacci wrote his letter, addressed to Mussolini (as "Caro Presidente") on his stationery as President of the Legislative Commission of Justice of the Camera dei Fasci e delle Corporazioni, datelined Rome, June 12, 1940, ACS, MI, MAT, b. 263. That Bocchini did not appreciate Farinacci's implication that he was not doing his job is clear from the sarcastic, handwritten note scribbled at the bottom of the typed informant report: "But these world saviors must think that we are sleeping!"

22. Bishop Colli's call was featured in many publications, including "Il patriottico appello dell'ACI," AR, June 14, 1940, p. 1; "Un nobilissimo appello del Direttore Generale dell'ACI," L'Italia, June 14, 1940, p. 2; "Patriottico appello dell'ACI," AI, June 14, 1940, p. 2; "Il clero italiano per la vittoria delle nostre armi," PI, June 14, 1940. The letter by Piero Panighi, national president of Catholic Men, appeared with the same title, "I doveri verso la Patria in armi," in both AR (June 23, p. 2) and AI (June 25, p. 2) and was sent to the Foreign Ministry on June 23 by Attolico's Vatican embassy (ASDMAE, AISS, b. 164). Father Giuseppe Borghino, national vice director of Catholic Action, wrote to Montini to give him the welcome news that Alfieri, then Italian ambassador to Germany, had written directly to Monsignor Colli to congratulate him on his public appeal for support of the war. July 6, 1940, AAV, *Segr. Stato,* 1940, Associazioni Cattoliche, posiz. 96, ff. 2r–4r.

23. "As soon as this [war] was declared," wrote Attolico, "the Italian Episcopate and clergy rushed to be among the first to remind the faithful of their duty to serve the Fatherland generously and to express their wish for Italy's victory and greater fortune. All the bishops sent out instructions for the conduct the parish priests and other priests would have to follow." Among these were those from the bishop of La Spezia. Tailoring his message to his maritime diocese, he wrote, "Italy, guided by the always victorious Emperor King and by the Duce, creator of its present greatness, is fighting for the freedom of its sea." The message that the bishop of Acqui addressed to his clergy and members of his diocese reminded them that the Duce had concluded his declaration of war with the watchword "Victory . . . to finally give a long period of peace and justice to Italy, to Europe, to the world," while the king had urged that once again "the victory of our glorious armies be assured." The bishop concluded, "God grant that these wishes which are the wishes of all Italians be fulfilled." The report of the Italian embassy, containing reports of several calls for support of the war on the part of Italy's episcopate, dated June 15, 1940, is at ASDMAE, AISS, b. 164.

24. Ambassador Attolico sent Ciano newspaper clippings about Gemelli's speech. Attolico to Ciano, June 21, 1940, n. 1838/814, ASDMAE, AISS, b. 164. Among the many Catholic and Fascist papers giving major coverage to Gemelli's speech, see "Patriottico appello di Padre Gemelli," PI, June 19, 1940; "Un nobile appello di Padre Gemelli ai professori e studenti dell'Università Cattolica," AI, June 20, 1940, p. 2; "Un nobile appello di Padre Gemelli," L'Italia, June 19, 1940, p. 3.

CHAPTER 16: SURVEILLANCE

1. Valeri, Bordeaux, to Maglione, June 15, 1940; Tardini notes, June 18, 1940; Maglione to Valeri, June 18, 1940, ADSS, vol. 1, nn. 344, 345, 346. My account of the military opera-

tions is based largely on Gooch 2020, pp. 96–104. The confusion among Italy's top generals in the first days of the war is examined in light of General Rodolfo Graziani's diary entries by Canali 2021.

2. D'Ormesson to French Foreign Ministry, June 23, 1940, n. 484, MAEC, Guerre Vichy, 461.

3. Record of Hitler-Mussolini conversation, Munich, June 18, 1940, DGFP, series D, vol. 9, n. 479; Goeschel 2018, p. 187.

4. Di Rienzo 2018, p. 330; Phillips 1952, pp. 283–84; "Elenco delle vittime dell'incursione aerea su Palermo," PI, June 27, 1940, p. 3.

5. D'Ormesson to French foreign minister, June 11, 1940, MAEC, Guerre Vichy, 461. In relaying this news to the Italian ambassador, Cardinal Maglione told him the pope would renew his plea, but it was important that his request not seem to be made in collaboration with the Italian authorities. Rather, he said, it must "retain the mark of being entirely a Vatican initiative." Attolico to Ciano, June 11 and 18, 1940, tel. 2837, ASDMAE, Gab., b. 1192, UC-76, fasc. 1. The underlining is in the original. Also see Osborne's annual report to London for 1940, NAK, Osborne to Eden, November 13, 1941, NAK, R 10496/30/507, pp. 4–5.

6. "With this most recent, high demonstration by the Sovereign Pontiff," concluded the ambassador in reporting the pope's words, "one can regard the Vatican as having now placed itself—on the patriotic and national plane—perfectly in line." Attolico to Ciano, June 21, 1940, n. 1838/814, ASDMAE, AISS, b. 164.

7. D'Ormesson to French Foreign Ministry, June 23, 1940, MAEC, Guerre Vichy, 461; Chassard 2015, p. 45.

8. Osborne's annual report for 1940, Osborne to Eden, November 13, 1941, NAK, R 10496/30/507, p. 1.

9. A series of Vatican secretary of state documents dealing with the papal plea is found at ADSS, vol. 1, nn. 366–78; Halifax to Osborne, July 3, 1940, NAK, FO 380/61, n. 62, 87/6/40; Conway 1973, p. 167; Mons. William Godfrey to Halifax, n.d., Osborne to Eden, November 13, 1941, NAK, R 10496/30/507, pp. 3–4. For Osborne's account of his long discussion with the pope on July 1 about his call for a peace conference, see NAK, FO 380/46, and Osborne's annual report for 1940, Osborne to Eden, November 13, 1941, NAK, R 10496/30/507, p. 4.

10. Gooch 2020, pp. 104–7.

11. Chadwick (1986, p. 137) makes this point.

12. Italian embassy to Holy See, memo, July 1, 1940, ASDMAE, AISS, b. 164. Gemelli's article was likewise sent by the Italian embassy to the Foreign Ministry on July 1 and is found in the same archival file.

13. Attolico reported the *Civiltà Cattolica* article supporting the war in a July 1, 1940, letter to Ciano, n. 1935/862, ASDMAE, AISS, b. 164. Among the front-page stories devoted to it in the daily Catholic press see: "Una nazione in guerra," AR, July 3, 1940, p. 1; "La nazione in Guerra. Una nota della Civiltà Cattolica," AI, July 3, 1940, p. 1.

14. Nota del Commissario di Borgo al Questore di Roma, July 3, 1940, ACS, DAGRA, A5G, IIGM, b. 29.

15. Attolico to Ciano, July 2, 1940, n. 1943/877, ASDMAE, AISS, b. 194.

16. D'Ormesson to French Foreign Ministry, July 9, 1940, MAEC, Guerre Vichy, 555.

17. D'Ormesson's final report, October 28, 1940, MAEC, Guerre Vichy, 550; Bérard to Pétain, February 2, 1942, MAEC, Guerre Vichy, 551.

18. Osborne to Halifax, July 17, 1940, NAK, FO 371, 24962, 42–44.

19. D'Ormesson to French Foreign Ministry, July 9, 1940, MAEC, Guerre Vichy, 553.

20. Bastianini 2005, p. 286; Ciano 1980, pp. 450–51, diary entries for July 5–10, 1940.

21. Returning to the theme at the beginning of August, d'Ormesson reported that the pope could not understand how the French had caved in so quickly in the face of the German

attack and thought the French troops had simply turned and run. "In effect," wrote the French ambassador, "they consider us as a nation that is infinitely sicker than our worst adversaries suppose." D'Ormesson to Charles-Roux, August 1, 1940, MAEC, Guerre Vichy, 551.

22. D'Ormesson to French Foreign Ministry, July 14, 1940, MAEC, Guerre Vichy, 547; d'Ormesson to French Foreign Ministry, July 18, 1940, MAEC, Guerre Vichy, 553.

23. Informativa da Roma, July 7, 1940, ACS, MCPG, b. 164.

24. Knowing of the suspicion with which the diplomats from the hostile countries now lodged in Vatican City were viewed, the Vatican authorities arranged for a police agent to stand guard outside their residence and, the French ambassador was convinced, immediately reported their movements and visitors to the Italian police. The Vatican had also adopted its own censorship of the diplomats' correspondence. It wanted to do all it could, explained d'Ormesson, to avoid upsetting the Italian authorities. D'Ormesson to French Foreign Ministry, July 21, 1940, MAEC, Guerre Vichy, 550; d'Ormesson to French Foreign Ministry, July 24, 1940, MAEC, Guerre Vichy, 547.

25. It was likewise notable, the ambassador added, that "the Holy See's organ is publicizing Father Gemelli's action and, in a certain way, extolling it." Attolico to Ciano, July 24, 1940, n. 2147/968, ASDMAE, AISS, b. 113. Three days later, no doubt further pleasing the Italian ambassador, the Vatican paper published a story that had been eagerly covered the previous day by Mussolini's newspaper, detailing the visit that the archbishop of Milan had made to rooms set up by the Fascist Party for soldiers in transit at Milan's train station. "The cardinal," reported *L'Osservatore Romano,* was "received by the Federal Secretary [of the Fascist Party] . . . by the representative of the women's Fascist organization . . . by a group of Fascist women and by numerous army officers." He distributed prayer books for the soldiers and handed each a religious medallion. "Il Cardinale Schuster visita il posto di ristoro per i soldati," OR, July 27, 1940, p. 4; "Il Cardinale fra i militari del posto di ristoro alla Stazione Centrale," PI, July 26, 1940, p. 2.

26. Attolico to Bocchini, June 28, 1940, and Bocchini to Attolico, July 3, 1940, ACS, DAGR, A5G, IIGM, b. 72; De Felice 1996a, pp. 464–66. Attolico was also at the time urging Ciano to be sure the police kept a close eye on all the movements of *L'Osservatore Romano* director Giuseppe Dalla Torre, who, he reported, was repeatedly meeting with the British envoy D'Arcy Osborne. Attolico to Ciano, July 30, 1940, tel. 2201/996, ASDMAE, AISS, b. 194.

27. Montini to Dalla Torre, August 19, 1940, AAV, Segr. Stato, 1940, Pubblicazioni, posiz. 730, f. 5r. Dalla Torre's notice to his staff is found at f. 3r.

28. D'Ormesson offered much the same view of the pope's thinking in his August 12 report to the French Foreign Ministry (MAEC, Guerre Vichy, 549). On the bombing of Britain, see Rauscher 2004, pp. 368–69; Roberts 2018, p. 588. It was in August as well that Britain began sending its warplanes to bomb Germany, beginning with an attack on Berlin on August 25. Herbert 2019, p. 340.

29. D'Ormesson to French Foreign Ministry, August 23, 1940, MAEC, Guerre Vichy, 553; d'Ormesson to Baudouin, minister of foreign affairs, MAEC, Guerre Vichy, 545. The ellipses are in the original.

30. L.M., "Il Nuovo ordine europeo," *L'Italia,* August 28, 1940, p. 1.

CHAPTER 17: THE FECKLESS ALLY

1. The text of the pope's speech was published on the front page of Rome's *L'Avvenire.* "L'Apostolica orazione di S.S. Pio XII," AR, September 5, 1940, as well as on the first page of that day's OR: "Luminose e fondamentali direttive del Sommo Pontefice Pio XII ai collaboratori dell'Apostolato Gerarchico per il trionfo del Regno di Cristo." Attolico

enthusiastically reported the pope's remarks to Ciano that same day. The Fascist news-papers added their praise, offering excerpts from the pope's remarks. Even Farinacci praised the speech, albeit faulting the pontiff for neglecting to mention the "anti-Jewish struggle." When the French ambassador came to the Vatican to complain about the way the Fascist press was trumpeting the pope's words, an exasperated Monsignor Tardini replied that all that the pope had done was to restate long-standing church doctrine. That defense, unsurprisingly, found little favor in Britain, then under heavy Axis bom-bardment. The British press did nothing to conceal its hostility, offering such titles to its stories as "Pope's Advice to Catholics: Die for Country." Attolico to Ciano, September 4, 1940, tel. 2206/1134, ASDMAE, APSS, b. 48; d'Ormesson to French Foreign Ministry, September 7, 1940, MAEC, Guerre Vichy, 559; Roberto Farinacci, "Verrà giorno . . . ," RF, September 6, 1940, p. 1; Roberts 2018, p. 592; d'Ormesson to French Foreign Min-istry, September 7, 1940, MAEC, Guerre Vichy, 461. In the London Foreign Office, a typed report on the pope's speech bears a handwritten comment from one of the staff: "The Vatican, au fond, is Italian & not international." NAK, FO 371, 24962[A].

Renato Moro (1988, pp. 79–80), one of Italy's most prominent historians of church-state relations in the twentieth century, stressed the significance of this papal speech in announcing a new "modus vivendi" between the Fascist regime and the nation's Catho-lics.

2. Appunto, DGPS, per il gabinetto, ministro dell'Interno, September 10, 1940, n. 500.25231, ACS, MI, MAT, b. 205; "L'Apostolica orazione di S.S. Pio XII sulla missione religiosa, civile e nazionale dell'Azione Cattolica Italiana," AR, September 5, 1940, p. 1.

3. D'Ormesson to French Foreign Ministry, September 13, 1940, MAEC, Guerre Vichy, 553.

4. Osborne to Foreign Office, London, June 6, 1946, NAK, FO 371, 60812, ZM, 1993, 1946.

5. Fogarty 1996, pp. 558–59; Spellman to FDR, March 21, 1940, FDR Library, psfc 117, pp. 13–14, clippings pp. 16–23. Spellman had long cultivated friendly relations with Mussolini's regime, making Farinacci's attack seem to the Vatican all the more unjusti-fied. Indeed, in 1937 the Italian government had conferred a special honor on Spellman, Grand Official of the Order of the Italian Crown. G. Segre, Italian consul, Boston, to Italian ambassador, Washington, D.C., August 11, 1936, and March 31, 1937, n. 10, ASDMAE, AISS, b. 1993.

6. "Cinematografia," RF, September 24, 1940, p. 1. Spellman had also been the first arch-bishop of New York to preach to Italian immigrants in St. Patrick's Cathedral in their own language. Now, in the wake of Mussolini's decision to marry his cause to Hitler's, Spellman, like much of the American church hierarchy that had earlier shown sympathy for the Fascist regime, was fast losing it. But as Italy's ambassador in Washington noted, there were still some pro-Fascist and even more numerous anti-British currents in the Catholic Church in the United States, for the clergy was dominated by the Irish. Indeed, Spellman himself was the child of Irish immigrants. No friends of Britain, the Irish Americans were, wrote the ambassador, "predominantly isolationists and in large part not dragged down by anti-totalitarian currents." The attacks on Spellman, he advised, were counterproductive, producing "a painful impression on that part of the Catholic clergy who are favorable to us and . . . exploited to our detriment by those elements of the clergy who are hostile to us." The ambassador's original report to the Foreign Min-istry, dated September 8, 1940, as well as its reproduction in a message sent by the For-eign Ministry to the Ministry of Popular Culture, are found at ASDMAE, APSS, b. 49. For an extreme example of pro-Nazi currents in the American Catholic church at the time, see Gallagher 2021.

7. The telegram, dated September 25, 1940, is found at ACS, PCM 1940–43, n. 1783/2.5, b. 2936, F2–5.

8. Attolico to Ciano, September 23, 1940, n. 2686, ASDMAE, AISS, b. 113. Attached was the clipping from the September 21 issue of *Il Popolo di Roma,* titled "Civiltà francese."

9. Attolico to Ciano, September 28, 1940, n. 2805, ASDMAE, AISS, b. 113.

10. A. Brucculeri, "Verso l'ordine nuovo," CC, 91 II, Quaderno 2166 (September 21, 1940), pp. 401–13; Attolico to Ciano, October 7, 1940, n. 2889/1329, ASDMAE, AISS, b. 164.

11. r.m. [Raimondo Manzini], "Giovane Europa," AI, October 11, 1940, p. 1; r.m., "Volti del tempo," AI, October 27, 1940, p. 1. For an analysis of the role of Italy's Catholic daily press in promoting popular support for the war, see Kertzer and Benedetti 2020.

12. Weizsäcker memo, Berlin, September 30, 1940, DGFP, series D, vol. 11, n. 135; De Felice 1996a, pp. 189–90; Ciano 1980, p. 471, diary entries for October 17 and 18. Ciano's push to invade Greece is also known from Mackensen's contemporaneous reports. Mackensen to Foreign Ministry, Berlin, October 18, 1940, DGFP, series D, vol. 11, n. 191, and Bastianini 2005, p. 287.

13. Metaxas was also not regarded at the time as a friend of the Roman Catholic Church. Since Metaxas had established his "totalitarian regime," the father general of the order of the Cappuccini reported from Athens to the Vatican, Metaxas, who had previously been seen as kindly disposed to the Catholic Church, had "changed completely." Now that he had become a dictator, his regime relied on support from the Orthodox Church. The Orthodox Metropolitan of Athens, described by the father general as "our enemy," along with his predecessor, were responsible for "all of the anti-Catholic legislation" that the government had recently imposed. Padre Riccardo, relazione, March 22, 1941, ASRS, *AA.EE.SS.,* Pio XII, parte 1, Grecia, posiz. 45, ff. 12r–25r.

14. Ciano 1980, p. 472, diary entry for October 24, 1940; Pirelli 1984, p. 280, diary entry for October 25, 1940; Bismarck, chargé d'affaires, to German Foreign Ministry, October 27, 1940, DGFP, series D, vol. 11, n. 242; Record of conversation Hitler, Duce, October 28, 1940, DGFP, series D, vol. 11, n. 246; Corvaja 2008, pp. 142–44.

CHAPTER 18: THE GREEK FIASCO

1. Gedeon 1997; Morris 2015.

2. Hitler to Mussolini, November 20, 1940, DGFP, series D, vol. 11, n. 369; Mussolini to Hitler, November 22, 1940, DGFP, series D, vol. 11, n. 383.

3. Cardinal Maglione suggested to the French chargé d'affaires that there was a brighter side to Italy's military debacle. "Not knowing how to make war at times like this," he remarked, "may be a sign of civilization." His comment is recorded in a memo dated November 22, 1940, written by the French chargé d'affaires to the Vatican but intercepted by the Italian censors. ACS, MI, MAT, b. 263.

4. De Felice 1996a, pp. 308–9, 1966b, p. 728; Goeschel 2018, p. 197.

5. D'Ormesson, final report, October 28, 1940, MAEC, Guerre Vichy, 550.

6. Corvaja 2008, pp. 142–45.

7. D'Ormesson to French Foreign Ministry, October 30, 1940, MAEC, Guerre Vichy, 551; Attolico to Ciano, October 30, 1940, n. 3117/1419, ASDMAE, AISS, b. 164. The pope's blessing of the Italian soldiers and his words to them on the day after the Greek invasion triggered protests from both the British and the Australians. Maglione to Apostolic Delegate Panico, Sydney, November 6, 1940; and Maglione to Apostolic Delegate Godfrey, London, November 19, 1940, ADSS, vol. 4, nn. 152, 171.

8. A copy of the memo from Kazimierz Papée to Cardinal Maglione, dated November 8, 1940, was sent to Myron Taylor on November 23. Taylor in turn sent it to FDR on February 4, 1941. FDR Library, psfa 394, pp. 21–29. The pope was similarly being pressured by the British to speak out. "It is beyond doubt," a memo prepared by the British envoy to the Vatican charged, "that the Nazis are leading a deliberate campaign to make Catholics believe, as much in the occupied countries as elsewhere, that a new agreement between the Vatican and the Reich is in the process of being put into force, and that the new order of the Axis will satisfy the conditions the Pope enunciated as essential for the

establishment of a just and durable peace." Osborne went on to complain, "One must unfortunately recognize that few eminent Catholics in the occupied countries have distinguished themselves in the struggle to oppose Nazi doctrine or to support the spirit of independence in the face of a brutal aggression." November 14, 1940, ADSS, vol. 4, n. 165. Osborne, at the urging of London, returned later in November to ask the pope to speak out against the Germans' indiscriminate massacre of civilians in their daily bombings of London and other British cities. "I spoke strongly on the subject," he reported back to the Foreign Office, "but I am not sanguine of results." Osborne to Halifax, November 21, 1940, n. 50, NAK, FO 380/61.

9. As they all reflected on the pope's inspiring words, said the bishop, they should think with pride of Italy's many Catholic Action members who had died in the wars in Ethiopia and Spain, in the conquest of Albania, and in the current war. Each of them had answered the pope's patriotic call with their own enthusiastic (Fascist) shout of *"Presente!"* Attolico to Ministero degli Affari Esteri, PCM, and PNF, November 21, 1940, tel. 14/00670/c, ACS, PCM 1940–43, b. 2936, F2–5. The event received major coverage in both the Fascist and Catholic press: "L'udienza del Papa a circa 5000 Giovani cattolici," PI, November 11, 1940, p. 3; "La parola di Pio XII ai giovani d'Italia" and "S.E. Mons. Colli esalta nella Basilica Vaticana le glorie religiose e nazionali dei Giovani Cattolici d'Italia," AR, November 12, 1940, pp. 1–2.

10. "Le solenni onoranze funebri alla Salma del Capo della Polizia Italiana," AR, November 22, 1940, p. 4.

11. "L'omelia di Sua Santità," OR, November 25, 1940, p. 1.

12. Attolico to Ciano, November 24, 1940, tel. 136, ASDMAE, AISS, b. 194; the copy sent on to Mussolini on November 26, tel. 000671, is found at ASDMAE, APSS, b. 48. "La Messa papale in suffragio dei caduti in guerra," PI, November 25, 1940, p. 3; "Pio XII celebra in San Pietro una Messa per i caduti in guerra," RF, November 26, 1940, p. 2.

13. Osborne to Halifax, November 30, 1940, with English translation of papal address of November 24, NAK, FO 371, 24962.

CHAPTER 19: A NEW WORLD ORDER

1. Sarfatti 2006, pp. 138–41; Impagliazzo 1997. For the impact of the racial laws on Jewish children in Italy, see Maida 2013.

2. "L'allontanamento degli ebrei," OR, March 17, 1939, p. 6; "La cancellazione dagli albi dei professionisti considerati di razza ebraica," OR, March 2, 1940, p. 4.

3. Sarfatti 2006, pp. 141–43; Capogreco 2004.

4. Phillips reported on the confining of foreign Jews to concentration camps in Italy as early as June 21, 1940, in his report to the U.S. State Department. NARA, RG 84, box 74, Phillips Correspondence 1940, 840.1, p. 44. On the mixed marriage case, see Cardinal Lauri to Montini, August 20, 1940, and Mons. Lombardi, handwritten notes, August 23, 1940, AAV, *Segr. Stato,* 1940, Varie, posiz. 1120, ff. 5r–8r. See also Dell'Era 2018.

5. The original documents are found at ASRS, *AA.EE.SS.,* Pio XII, Parte Asterisco, Serie Stati Ecclesiastici, posiz. 575*, ff. 732–50. The underlining is in the original. The reproduction of the (edited) documents is found in ADSS, vol. 6, n. 341. The editors also cut from their presentation of the document Tardini's typed note that referred to the gift as coming from "rich American Jews."

6. Attolico to Alessandro Pavolini, November 26, 1940, ASDMAE, AISS, b. 116.

7. To cite only a couple of such articles appearing in *Il Regime Fascista* in December: "Pio Nono per il razzismo fascista," RF, December 5, 1940, p. 3; "La Chiesa cattolica contro i Giudei," RF, December 8, 1940, p. 3. As Semelein (2018, p. 200) has recently noted, referring to the new French anti-Jewish laws under Pétain, "the Catholic hierarchy broadly accepted the status of Jews as second-class citizens." For more on the use, by

both the Fascist and the Catholic press, of church authority in support of the antisemitic campaign, see Kertzer and Mokosch 2019, 2020, and Kertzer and Benedetti 2021. On *La Croix,* see Cointet 1998, pp. 187–88. On the French Catholic reaction to the new anti-Jewish laws, see also Bernay 2012, pp. 149–50; Duquesne 1966, pp. 265–69; and Paxton 1972, p. 174. On French reaction more generally, see Marrus and Paxton 2019.

8. Goeschel 2018, pp. 197–200; Di Rienzo 2018, p. 345; Ciano 1980, pp. 484–85, 487, diary entries for December 4 and 11, 1940.

9. The U.S. military attaché's December 16 report is found at NARA, RG 165, 2062, 5–6, color 125.

10. "Text of Prime Minister Winston Churchill's speech to the Italian People, December 23rd, 1940," https://www.churchillbookcollector.com/pages/books/000462/winston-s -churchill/text-of-prime-minister-winston-churchills-speech-to-the-italian-people -december-23rd-1940.

11. Informativa Città del Vaticano, December 28, 1940, ACS, SPD, CR, b. 324.

12. A draft of the pope's Christmas speech, showing his revisions of the earlier draft, is found at AAV, *Carte Pio XII,* Discorsi, b. 3, 1940, fasc. 38, ff. 1r–15r.

13. Attolico to Ciano, December 24, 1940, n. 3699/1646, ASDMAE, AISS, b. 194; Informativa, Città del Vaticano, December 28, 1940, ACS, SPD, CR, b. 324 (underlining in the original). For the text and for church coverage of the talk, see ISACEM, *Bolletino* 19, n.1 (1941), pp. 1–9; "Il Sommo Pontefice nell'auspicio e nella visione di una pace giusta e duratura," OR, December 25, 1940, pp. 1–2. For the coverage given by Mussolini's paper: "Discorso di Pio XII al Collegio cardinalizio," PI, November 25, 1940, p. 6.

14. For some biographical background, see Chassard 2015, pp. 11–19, 99–101.

15. Bérard to French Foreign Ministry, December 9, 1940, MAEC, Guerre Vichy, 544; Bérard to French Foreign Ministry, December 24, 1940, MAEC, Guerre Vichy, 551.

16. Attolico to Ciano, December 28, 1940, n. 147, ASDMAE, AISS, b. 164.

17. Borgongini to Maglione, December 31, 1940, AAV, *Arch. Nunz. Italia,* b. 18, fasc. 4, ff. 82r–85r.

CHAPTER 20: HITLER TO THE RESCUE

1. General Rintelen report to Wehrmacht High Command, January 2, 1941, DGFP, series D, vol. 11, n. 597; Bosworth 2002, p. 376; U.S. consul, Palermo, report, February 1941, NARA, RG 165, 2062–72, color 126, 9.

2. Harvey 1985.

3. It would be best, the pope decided, to have an appropriate message delivered through Evasio Colli, the bishop heading Italian Catholic Action, whose patriotic message at the beginning of the war the government had so appreciated. On January 9, 1941, Monsignor Colli issued the new appeal: "If there is a circumstance in which Catholics worthy of this name must honor the Gospel and behave as loyal, perfect citizens, obedient to Authority . . . such is the present." Merging Fascist and church watchwords, Colli declared, "The Catholics, for whom obedience, devotion, and sacrifice are transcendent values, must not remain second to anyone in this cooperation." The Vatican newspaper published the bishop's appeal and Rome's Catholic newspaper featured it as well. Attolico to Ciano, January 8, 1941, tel. 78/25, ASDMAE, APSS, b. 55; Mons. Colli, "Comunicati per la Patria nell'ora presente," January 9, 1940, in ISACEM, *Bollettino* 19, n. 2 (February 1941); "Un indirizzo di Mons. Colli all'Azione Cattolica Italiana," OR, January 13, 1941, p. 2. Rome's Catholic newspaper aptly titled its coverage of Colli's address "Italian Catholic Action for the Fatherland in Arms." In an editorial immediately below the text, the paper's director praised the words of the "great bishop" as offering "clarity of Catholic doctrine and practice." Enveloping the Fascist cause in a papal blanket, he concluded: "Rome is still today the seat of the Successor of Peter, in which Christ per-

petuates his *Romanità*. In the Cross that always dominates Rome's sky we are certain of winning. In the watchword 'pray and work' we remain committed to be worthy of Victory." "L'Azione Cattolica Italiana per la Patria in armi," AR, January 11, 1941, p. 1.

4. As was his custom, the archbishop ended his appeal by identifying the Fascist cause with God's own: "On this road . . . our magnificent Armed Forces march and with the soldiers the Italian people, strong in their resolve, faithful to God, trusting in God. It is the path to Victory!" R.m. [Raimondo Manzini], "L'alta visione," AI, January 15, 1941, p. 1; "Un alto messaggio dell'Ordinario militare ai Cappellani delle Forze Armate," AR, January 15, 1941, p. 1. On January 11, 1941, the Polish ambassador to the Holy See complained about Bishop Colli's statement in the press claiming that the recent Italian church initiatives praying for Axis victory had the pope's blessings. The result was a series of memos back and forth in the Vatican Secretariat of State office leading to the advice to Colli (and Archbishop Bartolomasi) not to cite the pope in these efforts. AAV, *Segr. Stato,* 1941, Associazioni Cattoliche, posiz. 5, ff. 1r–8v.

5. Borgongini to Maglione, January 17, 1941, ADSS, vol. 4, n. 237.

6. Informativa, Città del Vaticano, January 5, 1941, ACS, SPD, CR, b. 324; U.S. military attaché report, Rome, January 18, 1941, NARA, RG 165, 2062-716, color 125, 8–9; Bismarck to German Foreign Ministry, January 29, 1941, DGFP, series D, vol. 11, n. 731.

7. Agostino Gemelli, "Per una grande manifestazione di Fede," AI, January 22, 1941, p. 2; R. Manzini, "Fede di un Popolo," AI, February 2, 1941, p. 1; "Solenni funzioni nelle Chiese d'Italia per la vittoria e per la consacrazione del popolo al S. Cuore," AR, February 4, 1941, p. 2. A week later, the paper returned to herald the great success of the event, quoting from various letters from parish priests stating that the number of parishioners who attended rivaled those who came for Easter mass. One ecstatic priest reported that of his fifteen hundred parishioners, thirteen hundred had taken communion at the ceremony. "I trionfi della Fede nella giornata propiziatoria," AR, February 11, 1941, p. 3.

That the pope would expose himself by offering his formal blessings to a mass glorifying the Axis war in the name of the Sacred Heart of Jesus seems surprising, and in fact, notwithstanding the two different sources for this claim, and the fact that it was widely presented as fact by the Catholic press at the time, the notes published by the Vatican suggest that the pope declined the request. According to Monsignor Montini's late January notes, the pope, asked by Gemelli to give his apostolic blessing for the event, did not. Montini notes, January 28, 1941, ADSS, vol. 4, n. 247.

8. Tranfaglia 2005, pp. 155, 344; Informativa dalla Città del Vaticano, February 14, 1941, ACS, SPD, CR, b. 325.

9. Phillips to FDR, February 24, 1941, FDR Library, psfa 401, pp. 98–99; U.S. military attaché report, Rome, February 25, 1941, NARA, RG 165, 2062-718, color 125, 15; Informativa dalla Città del Vaticano, February 14, 1941, ACS, SPD, CR, b. 325. De Felice (1996b, pp. 732–43) similarly concludes that Italian public opinion began to improve in late February and that most believed the war would end in Axis victory by September.

10. Bérard to French Foreign Ministry, March 4, 1941, MAEC, Guerre Vichy, 551; Attolico to Ciano, February 27, 1941, n. 640/298, ASDMAE, AISS, b. 193.

11. Present was the national president of the organization, Aldo Moro, future Italian prime minister and Christian Democratic martyr, who offered what the police informant described as "a warm and patriotic speech." Informativa da Roma, February 25, 1941, ACS, SPD, CR, b. 325.

12. Attolico had been unhappy to learn in March that government authorities in Cremona had embargoed the diocesan bulletin containing the bishop's Easter message, deemed guilty of having referred to war as a punishment from God. If there had been something regarded as offensive in the bishop's message, argued the ambassador, he should have been advised and he could have lodged a complaint at the Vatican, "but, for Heaven's sake, one doesn't engage in confiscations that can be seen as true violations of the Con-

cordat." Worse, he thought, such actions could lead people to conclude that the church was not being supportive of the war. Attolico to Ciano, March 7, 1941, n. 715/328, ASDMAE, APSS, b. 55; Attolico to Ciano, March 30, 1941, tel. 945/438, ASDMAE, APSS, b. 55.

13. Buffarini to Ministero degli Affari Esteri, Gabinetto, March 16, 1941, ASDMAE, APSS, b. 55; Attolico to Ciano, March 22, 1941, tel. 863, ASDMAE, APSS, b. 55.

14. Attolico sent his praise of the cardinal not only to Ciano but also to the Ministry of Internal Affairs and the Ministry of Popular Culture. March 17, 1941, tel. 811/370, ASDMAE, APSS, b. 55. Even Farinacci, no doubt for his own purposes, was hailing the strong support shown by the high Italian clergy for the war effort. In a front-page piece on the March 23 national celebrations marking the anniversary of the founding of the Fascist movement, he devoted a section to the festivities in Milan. Held at a church bordering the same piazza where that now legendary gathering of Fascist founders had taken place twenty-two years earlier, the ceremony featured the consecration by Cardinal Schuster of the new pennant of the local Fascist party chapter, named in honor of Mussolini's dead brother Arnaldo. "Tutto il popolo italiano stretto intorno al Duce," RF, March 25, 1941, p. 1.

15. "Patriottica pastorale del vescovo di Recanati e Loreto," CS, March 20, 1941, p. 2. On the Corriere della Sera and its involvement in the racial campaign, see Allotti and Liucci 2021, chapter 13.

16. Attolico to Ciano, February 4, 1941, n. 387/160, ASDMAE, APSS, b. 54.

17. The documents on the plans for the seizure of the church bells and Attolico's negotiations with Cardinal Maglione are found at ASDMAE, APSS, b. 54. On March 28, 1941, a police informant from Milan reported that on receiving the circular from the government regarding the census of church bells for their eventual requisition for war purposes, the bishops had written for instructions to the Vatican. They received in return instructions from the Secretariat of State, reported the informant, telling the clergy to express their displeasure but not to issue any public protest. ACS, SPD, CR, b. 325.

Even before the war ended, calls for the return of the bells from the dioceses in liberated Italy began to come in. In December 1944 the royal government signed a legislative decree calling for the bells' return, although the actual return of the surviving bells and the construction of the replacements for those melted down began only in the summer of 1947. De Marchis 2013, pp. 42–44.

18. Del Boca 1996. "Will it prove true," a police informant in Rome asked at midmonth, "that the blacks will not come back to power and there will not be danger of reprisals? Will it prove true that, according to the assurances that the Pontiff made to the Duchess of Aosta, that the Apostolic Nuncio has assumed responsibility for the protection of the whites?" Informativa da Roma, April 11, 1941, ACS, SPD, CR, b. 326.

19. Boiardi et al. 1990, p. 9; Goeschel 2018, pp. 200–10; Rauscher 2004, p. 393.

20. Phillips to FDR, April 14, 1941, FDR Library, psfa 401, pp. 126–27; U.S. military attaché, Rome, April 15, 1941, NARA, RG 165, 2062-716, color 125, 18–20.

21. Prelates in the Vatican were nervous at the time about spies in their midst, spies not only for Mussolini but also for foreign powers. See Alvarez 2002. For an example of extensive discussion about a frequenter of the Vatican Secret Archive suspected of being a German spy during the first months of 1941, see AAV, Segr. Stato, 1941, Varie, posiz. 231, ff. 1r–20r.

22. Colonello Cesare Amé, Capo servizio, SIM-Sezione "Bonsignore," Roma, April 16, 1941, ACS, PCM 19940-43, b. 3168, cat. G9-1, Sez. "Bonsignore"; Informativa dalla Città del Vaticano, April 9, 1941, ACS, SPD, CR, b. 326; Osborne annual report for 1941, Osborne to Eden, October 28, 1942, NAK, R 7915/7915/57, p. 5. At the same time, Osborne again pleaded with Cardinal Maglione to have the pope speak out against Nazi aggression, this time their unprovoked attack on Yugoslavia and Greece. "This attack

and the maneuvers that preceded it," argued the British envoy, "have earned the virtually universal condemnation of the civilized world and there will certainly be an inclination to reproach the Vatican for its silence." Osborne to Maglione, April 7, 1941, ADSS,
vol. 4, n. 313. On Vatican radio, see Perin 2017.

23.   At the top of Cardinal Lauri's April 2 request for rescheduling the meeting for that same
day or the next (when, in fact, it was held), Tardini later penciled in his own note of
explanation: "The Most Eminent Cardinal Lauri was the protector of Signor Travaglini,
whom he arranged to have named a viscount." Cardinal Lauri to Pius XII, March 29,
March 31, and April 2, 1941, ASRS, *AA.EE.SS.,* Pio XII, parte 1, Germania, posiz. 774,
ff. 253r, 254r, 255r.

     Curiously, in his memoirs Harold Tittmann (2004, p. 27) recalls that in early 1941 he
had been "invited several times to lunch or dine with Prince Philip of Hesse and his wife,
the frail Princess Mafalda."

24.   Tittmann 2004, p. 37.

25.   Attolico to Mackensen, May 5, 1941, ASDMAE, AISS, b. 131.

26.   Tardini notes, May 6 and May 8, 1941, ADSS, vol. 4, nn. 338, 340.

27.   "Alto discorso di Pio XII," AI, May 24, 1941, p. 1; "La Crociata della purezza nella sublime allocuzione del Santo Padre alla Gioventù femminile di Azione Cattolica," AR,
May 24, 1941, p. 4; Commissario di Borgo report, May 25, 1941, ACS, DAGRA 1941,
b. 35.

28.   "Relativa alla persona del Papa," August 1, 1941, ACS, SPD, CR, b. 328. Several years
later Pascalina had only strengthened her influence in the Vatican, as J. Graham Parsons,
the American envoy at the Vatican, reported to the American secretary of state in 1947.
He quoted from a recent Italian news story: "The woman in closest association with the
Pope is the famous Sister P, Pius XII's 'housekeeper,' superioress of an order of nuns
formed exclusively of Germans or Swiss from Germanic cantons . . . a good woman, no
longer young . . . very fond of the Pope, whom she has been caring for in a truly laud-
able way for many years. . . . But Sister P is like a too-loving and impressionable mother.
The other Vatican dignitaries and prelates willingly pardon her for her indiscreet and
exaggerated chatter, in view of the fact that her work with the Pope would be irreplace-
able. . . . She is the only person who sees the Pope more than once a day, and it seems
that her advice is always taken." August 13, 1947, NARA, RG 59, CDF 1945–49, 8661.00,
box 6971, p. 9.

29.   Phillips to Roosevelt, January 21, 1941, FDR Library, psfa 394, p. 14.

30.   Ciano 1980, p. 513, diary entry for May 16, 1941.

31.   De Felice 1996b, pp. 1070–74. The finance minister's comment was quoted by Ciano
(1980, p. 559) in his diary entry of November 20, 1941. "Speaking of the recent measures
that forbid the use of gasoline in private cars," one such police informant reported at the
time, "Monsignor Monticone, archivist of [the Vatican congregation of] Propaganda
Fide said: 'now we'll see the Petacci Family's three automobiles alone in driving through
Rome, provoking great scandal among all Romans.'" Informatore n. 390 (Pozzi), July
26, 1941, ACS, MIFP, b. 10. The Petaccis would later claim that their Roman home,
notwithstanding "calumnious and tendentious claims of enemy propaganda," had been
purchased entirely by a combination of funds that Clara's mother had inherited and
money that her father had earned as a doctor. Undated document found in ACS, Archivi
di famiglie e di persone, Clara Petacci, b. 5, fasc. 85.

32.   Ciano 1980, pp. 513, 516, 517, diary entries for May 16, 26, and 28.

33.   Phillips to FDR, May 17, 1941, FDR Library, psfa 401, pp. 143–47; FDR to Phillips, May
24, 1941, FDR Library, psfa 401, p. 130.

     As the summer of 1941 approached, Vatican relations with the Italian government
remained good. Following his late May meeting with Pius XII, the Italian ambassador
told Ciano that the pope "spoke a number of times with great deference of the Duce and

of Your Excellency." The pope had stressed how much he was counting on Italy's leaders to protect the Vatican should, as seemed likely, the Axis win the war. "One can now
say," concluded the Italian ambassador, "that in the face of Germany's hostile attitude
toward the church those in positions of authority in the Vatican are almost unanimous
in seeing in Italy their base of support for the future." Attolico to Ciano, May 30, 1941,
tel. 5029, ASDMAE, APSS, b. 54.

CHAPTER 21: THE CRUSADE

1. Hitler to Mussolini, June 21, 1941, DGFP, series D, vol. 12, n. 660; Bismarck to Ribbentrop, June 22, 1941, DGFP, series D, vol. 12, n. 666; Rauscher 2004, p. 403; Robert Citino,
   "Operation Barbarossa: The Biggest of All Time," National World War II Museum,
   June 18, 2021, https://www.nationalww2museum.org/war/articles/operation-barbarossa.
   That the operation had long been planned is evident from Hitler's December 18, 1940,
   directive that gave the operation its name. DGFP, series D, vol. 11, n. 532. See also Herbert 2019, p. 343.

2. Roberts 2018, p. 659; Attolico to Foreign Ministry, June 23, 1941, tel. 000373, ASDMAE,
   AISS, b. 193; Herbert 2019, p. 344.

3. Ciano 1980, p. 527, diary entry for June 23, 1941; Mussolini to Hitler, June 23, 1941,
   DGFP, series D, vol. 13, n. 7. For an examination of the Italian role in the Soviet campaign, see Scianna 2019.

4. Attolico to Ciano, June 26, 1941, n. 1842/818, ASDMAE, AISS, b. 193; Raimondo Manzini, "Le potenze dell'Asse contro l'Unione delle Repubbliche Sovietiche," AI, June 24,
   1941, p. 1; N., "La situazione," AR, June 27, 1941, p. 1.

5. "The Secretariat of State, in keeping with the promises made to us some time ago,"
   observed Ambassador Attolico, "is not failing to continue that action in the periphery
   aimed at a full and sincere collaboration of the Italian clergy in the national cause." Attolico to Ciano, July 1, 1941, tel. 1900/836, ASDMAE, APSS, b. 55.

6. Attività del Clero, prefetto di Salerno, July 3, 1941, ASDMAE, AISS, b. 130; Attolico to
   Ciano, July 1, 1941, tel. 1900/836, ASDMAE, APSS, b. 55.

7. The archbishop continued, "So today we salute and bless the Italian legions, which go to
   join the allied armies in the common effort to open the immense prison that holds Russia, depriving it of the right to see the light, to freely believe and profess the faith." The
   Roman legions, concluded the archbishop, "will thus have accomplished the dual tasks
   of saving civilization and defending the faith!" "Patriottica pastorale del Principe arcivescovo di Gorizia," PI, July 20, 1941, p. 6.

8. Foreign Ministry to Attolico, June 29, 1941, tel. 24901, ASDMAE, AISS, 1947–1954,
   b. 227. Among the various police informant reports from the Vatican that detail a secret
   agreement of this type, see Informativa (Galantini), July 24, 1941, ACS, SPD, CR,
   b. 327.

9. Babuscio Rizzo, Appunto per gli Atti, August 1, 1941, ASDMAE, AISS, b. 193; Attolico
   to Ciano, August 2, 1941, DDI, series 9, vol. 7, n. 450. In the wake of the German invasion of the Soviet Union, high-ranking members of the Italian clergy offered their outspoken support for the war. In a speech highlighted in the Fascist press, Monsignor
   Celso Costantini, secretary of the Congregation of Propaganda Fide, offered his own
   prayers for Axis victory. "We fervently wish with all our heart," he said, "that this battle
   brings us a conclusive victory and the end of bolshevism." He invoked "the blessing of
   the Almighty on the Italian and German combatants in the struggle for the defence of
   our freedom against the red barbarities." Attolico thought the speech especially notable,
   because, he reported, underlining his words for emphasis: "he would not have spoken
   without the agreement of the Holy See."
      It was also important to note, he added, that the major Catholic press was not alone

in exalting the Axis war now that it had turned against the USSR. "Even more significant," he observed, "are all the articles appearing in the minor organs of the religious associations and of Catholic Action, due to the capillarity of their distribution and the particularity of the public to which they are directed, making them, I would say, even more efficient and expressive." Attolico to Ciano and Ministry of Popular Culture, August 9, 1941, n. 2352/1028, ASDMAE, AISS, b. 193. The monthly reports on church activity in the provinces sent in by the prefects were painting a similar picture. In the past month, read a mid-August report from the prefect of Bologna, "the priests and Catholics in general continued to praise the struggle against Bolshevik Russia and to call ever greater attention to the ideal motives that inspire the peoples of the Axis in the war." Attività del Clero, prefetto di Bologna, August 12, 1941, n. 388, ASDMAE, AISS, b. 130. Likewise, the following month, the prefect reported, "The local clergy, following the directives of the Curia, has continued to give proof of their orientation in favor of the national goals that the Regime proposes to reach, placing themselves in every circumstance at the side of the Party, to ensure confidence in the victory of our arms among the faithful." September 8, 1941, n. 388, ASDMAE, AISS, b. 130.

Monsignor Costantini's blessing for the Axis war attracted the attention of the Germans as well. Fritz Menshausen, Bergen's number two at the German embassy to the Holy See, sent in his own report on the prelate's invocation of God's blessings on the Italian and German armies. Well-informed sources, he told the German state secretary in late August, had told him that by a phrase in a previous radio address, "Pope XII sought to express his hope that the great sacrifices required by the war would not be in vain and that they would lead to victory over Bolshevism in line with the will of Divine Providence." Menshausen to Weizsäcker, August 23, 1941, PAAA, GBS, R29816, 24–28. The following month a speech by one of the most prominent cardinals of the Curia, Cardinal Camillo Caccia Dominioni, offered additional evidence of the impact that the German attack on the Soviet Union had. "I can confirm," wrote Attolico in reporting the speech, "that today the entire Italian Catholic world is squarely on the side of the Regime in the battle against Bolshevism." Attolico to Ciano and Ministry of Popular Culture, September 11, 1941, n. 2655, ASDMAE, AISS, b. 193.

10. Osborne to Eden, July 24, 1941, NAK, FO 380/71, n. 60/1/41. Osborne took the opportunity of meeting with Cardinal Maglione in early August to renew the British government's admonition that the pope not involve himself in any Nazi-sponsored peace effort. The cardinal told him not to worry, reminding the envoy of the "extreme caution" the Vatican had pursued in such matters. Osborne to Eden, August 4, 1941, NAK, FO 380/71, n. 60/3/41. Two months later Osborne reiterated his belief that the pope would not involve himself in a peace initiative that had no chance of success, but he added: "Nevertheless it would be prudent to bear in mind that the Pope's passionate desire to see peace restored, his undoubted ambition personally to contribute thereto and his susceptibility to pressure from the Italian Government and to appeals to his sentiments for the Italian people would all combine to urge him towards support of any initiative that offered a reasonable prospect of success." Osborne to Eden, August 25, 1941, NAK, FO 380/71, n. 60/6/41.

11. Bérard to French Foreign Ministry, July 19, 1941, MAEC, Guerre Vichy, 551. Further documentation on the pope's radio message is found at AAV, Segr. Stato, 1941, Sommo Pontefice, posiz. 69, ff. 1r–30r.

12. Maglione to Mons. Cicognani, Washington, D.C., August 11, 1941, ADSS, vol. 5, n. 41.

13. Spellman to Pius XII, September 4, 1941, ADSS, vol. 5, n. 61. On Hurley, see Gallagher 2008.

14. Ciano, who had been suffering from months of throat pain and was about to have a tonsillectomy, did not make the trip. On learning of Ciano's surgery, Borgongini went to the Foreign Ministry to express the Vatican's well wishes, reporting back to Maglione.

The cardinal told him that the pope was following Ciano's recovery with great interest and wanted the nuncio to convey the pope's blessing on the Italian foreign minister for a speedy recovery. Borgongini to Maglione, August 29, 1941, and Maglione to Borgongini, August 30, 1941, AAV, *Arch. Nunz. Italia,* b. 20, fasc. 49, ff. 2r, 5r. That the pope was following Ciano's illness with great interest is clear from the documentation at AAV, *Segr. Stato,* 1941, Stati, posiz. 203, ff. 10r–14r.

15. The war, said Hitler, was now one of annihilation of the enemy, paving the way for a new European order. Once the Russian campaign was completed, the long-delayed invasion of Britain could begin, and with it the war's final act. After that, he added, he looked forward to spending time in Florence, a city he loved for its remarkable art and beautiful surroundings. Record of Duce's conversation with Hitler, August 25, 1941, DGFP, series D, vol. 13, n. 242; Corvaja 2008, pp. 186–200.

16. This paragraph is based on what Tardini told the French ambassador: Bérard to Darlan, September 4, 1941, MAEN, RSS 576, PO/1, 1183. Tardini would put this in different terms in speaking in early September with Attolico, who was once again pleading to have the pope explicitly bless the Axis war against the Soviet Union. Instead of using the church image of the crusade, as the Italian ambassador suggested, more appropriate, thought Tardini, was another: "un diavolo scaccia l'altro," "one devil drives out the other" (a pithier version of a line from Matthew 9:34). Tardini notes, September 5, 1941, ADSS, vol. 5, n. 62.

17. Capo di gabinetto, Ministero degli Affari Esteri, to Babuscio Rizzo, September 9, 1941, ASDMAE, AISS, 1947–54, b. 227.

18. Phillips to FDR, March 10, 1941, FDR Library, psfa 401, pp. 100–3; Osborne to Howard, September 25, 1942, NAK, FO 371, 33430, 18–21; Tittmann 2004, p. 129.

19. Taylor to the president and to Secretary Hull, memorandum, September 21, 1941, FDR Library, psfa 394, pp. 68–73; Maglione notes, September 10, 1941, ADSS, vol. 5, n. 69. Maglione's September 11 notes on the meeting can be found at ADSS, vol. 5, n. 73.

Taylor also gave the pope a separate letter from Roosevelt, dated September 3, 1941, which sought to quell the pope's worries about the Soviet Union. Roosevelt admitted that the USSR was "governed by a dictatorship as rigid in its manner of being as is the dictatorship in Germany," but argued that it was Germany that was more dangerous to other nations as, while the USSR worked through propaganda, Germany relied on "military aggression." He added his belief that Russia was less dangerous to the survival of religion than was Germany. AAV, *Segr. Stato,* 1941, Stati, posiz. 73, ff. 19rv.

20. Attolico to Ciano, September 11, 1941, ASDMAE, AISS, 1947–54, b. 227. After receiving Attolico's detailed report on his conversation with the cardinal, Ciano gave a copy to Otto von Bismarck at the German embassy. Mackensen to German Foreign Ministry, September 13, 1941, DGFP, series D, vol. 13, n. 315.

21. Tardini notes, September 12, 1941, ADSS, vol. 5, n. 74.

22. Projet de réponse au Président Roosevelt, September 14, 1941, ADSS, vol. 5, n. 75. The remarks the pope planned to make verbally to Taylor on September 16, 1941, in English, are found at AAV, *Segr. Stato,* 1941, Stati, posiz. 73, f. 34r.

23. Attolico to Ciano, September 16, 1941, n. 2702, ASDMAE, AISS, 1947–54, b. 227. Within twenty-four hours of receiving Attolico's report on his meeting with the pope, Ciano again had a copy delivered to Mackensen, with its account of the pope's fears that after his victory Hitler might move against the Vatican itself. The report also dealt with a matter of great interest to both Mussolini and Hitler, the purpose of Myron Taylor's visit to the pope. In his meeting with Attolico, the pontiff had downplayed its significance and expressed his belief that American intervention in the war was not imminent. Again, Mackensen was told that the report was highly confidential and that not even the German ambassador to the Holy See was being informed. There was no doubt about Mackensen's Nazi loyalties. PAAA, GPA, Politische Lage im Vatikan, R261177, 18–24,

September 17, 1941. Ciano likewise gave Mackensen a copy of Attolico's report of the conversation that Taylor had had with Monsignor Tardini, dated September 18, 1939. PAAA, GPA, Politische Lage im Vatikan, R261177, 25–27.

24. Chenaux 2003, p. 282. Given the distinction being made between Christians and Jews as the basis for selecting who were targets for deportation and death in the Axis-controlled lands, large numbers of Jews were clamoring to be baptized. In December 1941, when the nuncio in Bucharest requested guidance on how to respond to "the huge influx of Jews" in Romania who were asking to be baptized, the Holy Office took up the question. ACDF, DV 1942, n. 10, ff. 41r–43r.

25. Quoted in Chenaux 2003, p. 267. In mid-October, Cardinal Maglione replied to the nuncio in France, who had written him about his recent meeting with the archbishop of Lyon. "It was very opportune," the secretary of state told the nuncio, "that you reminded [the archbishop] and then also the Spanish ambassador [to France] what goodness and indulgence His Holiness has always shown to Signor Hitler." Maglione offered as evidence the "benevolent expressions contained in the handwritten letter the Holy Father sent him having barely ascended to Saint Peter's throne." To offer the nuncio further ammunition, Maglione recalled that during Ribbentrop's visit to the pope the previous year, the German foreign minister had been "so impressed by the Holy Father's benevolent and paternal interest in Germany that, immediately after the audience, he told me these very words: 'one sees that His Holiness's heart is always in Germany.'" Maglione to Valeri, October 18, 1941, ADSS, vol. 5, n. 121.

26. Yad Vashem, Zarasai county, U.S. Holocaust Memorial Museum, *Holocaust Encyclopedia,* https://www.yadvashem.org/YV/en/about/institute/killing_sites_catalog_details_full.asp?region=Zarasai&title=Zarasai%20county. On the activities of the *Einsatzgruppen* in Poland, see Matthäus, Böhler, and Mallmann 2014 and Herbert 2019, pp. 318–19.

27. Chenaux 2003, p. 267; Le chargé d'affaires à Presbourg Burzio au cardinal Maglione, October 27, 1941, ADSS, vol. 8, n. 184; fonogramma Questura di Roma alla DGPS e alla prefettura di Roma, October 27, 1941, ACS, MI, DAGRA 41, b. 35, n. 218792; informativa, October 28, 1941, ACS, SPD, CR, b. 328.

A police informant report offered more detail on the pope's audiences with German soldiers. "His Holiness continues to receive and see, always with pleasure, the German soldiers. . . . His Holiness often offers each of them words of comfort and of pleasure, saying that he loves their country. . . . He always gladly agrees to their requests for photographs." The report concludes, "That the Pope takes much pleasure from receiving such soldiers is demonstrated finally by the fact that contrary to the normal practice of the Vatican, he received some groups of them in the afternoon—dedicated by custom instead only to some private and reserved audiences." November 1, 1941, ACS, MI, DAGRA 41, b. 35. In a November 26, 1941, police informant report, titled "This morning's reception at the Vatican," the informant wrote, "His Holiness this morning in the Vatican, in receiving German officials and other soldiers of undetermined nationality, said, 'If you have done your duty to your country, be always proud of it.'" ACS, SPD, CR, b. 329. According to Herbert (2019, p. 381) the *Einsatzgruppen* murdered hundreds of thousands of Soviet Jews in October and November 1941 alone.

28. Father Scavizzi's diary entries and his account of his meetings with the pope are found in Manzo 1997. Quotes are here from pp. 128–31.

CHAPTER 22: A NEW PRINCE

1. https://it.wikisource.org/wiki/Italia_-_11_dicembre_1941,_Annuncio_della_dichiarazione_di_guerra_agli_Stati_Uniti.

2. Informativa, December 8, 1941, ACS, DAGR, A5, G II, GM, b. 72; Phillips to secretary of state, Washington, D.C., December 11, 1941, FDR Library, psfa 401, p. 176; Bottai

1989, p. 292, diary entry for December 11, 1941. The men around the pope were critical of Roosevelt's decision to throw the United States into the war, reported Attolico. America's entry, they thought, would only prolong the bloodshed. Attolico to Ciano, December 12, 1941, n. 3681/1561, ASDMAE, AISS, b. 193.

3. The French ambassador reported the news along with the *Osservatore Romano* story to Vichy. Bérard to Darlan, December 16, 1941, MAEN, RSS 576, PO/1, 1183.

4. Osborne to Foreign Office, December 17, 1941, NAK, FO 371, 33410, 4–6. What the pope's true feelings were about the honor are not clear. A police informant reported the common impression that the pope was extremely moved and pleased by the ennobling of his brother's family and greatly impressed by the Duce's gesture. Notizia fiduciaria, December 20, 1941, ACS, SPD, CR, b. 329.

For the Fascist government, American entry into the war offered new ways for the Vatican to prove useful. Among the early targets was Latin America, given worries that the Latin American countries, most of which continued to trade with Italy, would follow the U.S. example and break off relations. These fears were magnified when, shortly after Pearl Harbor, Colombia announced that it was doing just that, and word arrived that the foreign ministers of all the Americas had decided to meet the next month to discuss if they should do the same.

When Attolico told Cardinal Maglione that Mussolini hoped to get the Vatican's help, he was pleased to find him receptive. Attolico to Ciano, December 17 and 20, 1941, DDI, series 9, vol. 8, nn. 36 and 49. Ciano cabled Italy's ambassadors in the Latin American countries to tell them the news: "I inform you that Cardinal Secretary of State Maglione had, on his own initiative, told the Royal Ambassador to the Holy See that— albeit with the necessary caution—the Vatican had acted and is acting in all of South America in a sense favorable to the maintenance of neutrality." "This is an area," explained Ciano, "where our interests and those of the Holy See coincide perfectly and where, as a result, a mutually agreed upon and parallel action of mutual benefit might be taken, aimed at reaching the same results." At the upcoming foreign ministers' summit in Rio de Janeiro, the importance of having the South American countries resist U.S. pressure was clear. "In this context," he instructed, "act also, insofar as it seems opportune and possible, and where the local circumstances permit, in collaboration or in agreement with the local Catholic circles and in particular with the Vatican representatives." Ciano sent Attolico a copy of his telegram, telling him to let the cardinal know he had sent it. December 29, 1941, tel. 424, ASDMAE, AISS, b. 176. The telegram Ciano sent to the ambassadors in South America can also be found in published form in DDI, series 9, vol. 8, n. 74. While not all the Italian ambassadors in Latin America thought the suggestion worth pursuing, a number did. Italy's ambassador to Brazil assured Ciano that even before receiving his instructions, he had been in contact with the nuncio there, and the two were already working together to discourage the government from bowing to American pressure. Ambasciatore a Rio de Janeiro, Sola, to Ciano, December 29, 1941, DDI, series 9, vol. 8, n. 77.

5. Both the Vatican paper and the major Italian Catholic newspapers published the full text. "Il radiomessaggio natalizio del Sommo Pontefice Pio XII," OR, December 25, 1941, pp. 1–2; "Il Messaggio Natalizio del Papa al Mondo," *L'Italia*, December 25, 1941, p. 1; "I presupposti essenziali dell'ordine internazionale," AR, December 25, 1941, pp. 1–2.

6. Radiomessaggio Pio XII, ISACEM, *Bollettino* 20, n. 2 (febbraio 1942), pp. 25–29; Bérard to Foreign Ministry, Vichy, December 24, 1941, MAEC, Guerre Vichy, 551.

7. "Natale in Vaticano. Il radiomessaggio del Papa," PI, December 25, 1941, p. 2; "La parola del Papa," RF, December 25, 1941, p. 1; Bernardini to Maglione, January 11, 1942, AAV, *Arch. Nunz. Svizzera,* b. 218, fasc. 620, ff. 29r–30r. On the same day the *Regime Fascista* article appeared, Attolico had a copy sent on to Ciano's office, ASDMAE, AISS, b. 194.

Farinacci's true thoughts about the pope come through from the transcript of a wiretapped phone conversation he had with Alessandro Pavolini, minister of popular culture, in early July 1941, which somehow came into possession of the Vatican Secretariat of State. There he complains that Ciano was too soft on the Vatican and its newspaper and asks in addition why the state radio continued to broadcast the pope's radio addresses. "Conversazione svoltasi il giorno 3/7/1941 ore 10,20 fra Pavolini e Farinacci," ASRS, *AA.EE.SS.*, Pio XII, parte I, Italia, posiz. 1336, f. 304r.

8. Osborne to Foreign Office, London, December 24, 25, NAK, FO 371, 33410, 20–23. The Foreign Office reported on the content of the German Foreign Ministry newsletter. Osborne had asked for instruction as to whether at his upcoming New Year's audience he should offer words of encouragement to the pope regarding the papal Christmas address. A series of marginal comments on the document by different members of the Foreign Office expressed their disapproval, ending with the January 25, 1942, note by the deputy undersecretary, Orme Sargent, "I agree. The Pope must be content with the approval which has been expressed by Farinacci and the German Foreign Office!"

9. Osborne to Foreign Office, December 29, 1941, NAK, FO 371, 33410, 7–10; Osborne annual report for 1941, NAK, AR 1941, p. 1. The text of Churchill's speech to Congress is at https://www.nationalchurchillmuseum.org/churchill-address-to-congress.html.

10. This account is based on the Notes de la Secrétairerie d'État, January 6, 1942, ADSS, vol. 5, n. 191. Had the pope seen the actual text of the Duce's remarks, he would have been even more alarmed. "Factions in the Catholic world are opposing the Axis. . . . Moreover they are preaching pacifism. . . . All these tendencies of pacifism . . . must be identified, isolated, and denounced by the Party. The police will take care of the rest." http://bibliotecafascista.blogspot.com/2012/03/discorso-al-direttorio-nazionale-del_4 .html. See Moro 1988, p. 81.

11. Borgongini Duca to Maglione, January 9, 1942, ADSS, vol. 5, n. 195.

12. "We are pastors," the bishop concluded, "and we must unmask the wolf, we must defend the flock even at the cost of our lives." "Allocuzione antibolscevica del Vescovo di Trieste," PI, January 15, 1942, p. 6; Attolico to Ciano and Ministry of Popular Culture, January 23, 1942, tel. 246/88, ASDMAE, AISS, b. 164.

13. Italian embassy to the Holy See to Ciano and Ministry of Popular Culture, January 23, 1942, tel. 246/88, ASDMAE, AISS, b. 164. A couple of weeks earlier, Cardinal Salotti had sent Attolico a letter thanking him for his assistance in having a priest who worked under him freed after the priest had made remarks judged unpatriotic by the police. "It is my duty," wrote Cardinal Salotti, "to warn the above-mentioned priest, so that he is more cautious in the future to avoid in his speeches any phrases or expressions that can be misunderstood. We are at a moment in which everyone must try to keep Italians' morale high, awaiting the longed-for victory." Italian embassy to Holy See to Ciano, January 12, 1942, tel. 155/40, with copy of the January 10 letter by Cardinal Carlo Salotti (prefect, Congregation of Rites) to Attolico, ASDMAE, APSS, b. 58.

14. Osborne sent a long report on the article to London. One of the Foreign Office officials added a note: "This Jesuit paper champions the rights of the 'have nots' to share with the 'haves' & as Mr Osborne remarks comes very near to supporting the Axis claim to vital space." Osborne to Foreign Office, February 5, 1942, NAK, FO 371, 33411, 37–39.

15. Pietro Fedele to Mussolini, January 16, 1942, ACS, Archivi di famiglie e di persone, Clara Petacci, b. 5, fasc. 84.

16. Maestro di Camera di Sua Santità, December 14, 1941, and typed memo, January 10, 1942, ASRS, *AA.EE.SS.*, Pio XII, parte I, Germania, posiz. 826, ff. 2r, 5r.

"They hardly have any illusions here," reported the French ambassador, "about the fate that would be reserved for the church in the case where the success of their arms would give the Germans full freedom of maneuver. That Hitler's regime shows such little regard for the Christian denominations in the Reich is considered in the Vatican as an indication of the radical measures that would be taken in the aftermath of victory." Bérard to Foreign Ministry, Vichy, January 21, 1942, MAEC, Guerre Vichy, 551. Bérard elaborated on this same theme of the pope's fear of what would happen to the church in the case of a Nazi victory in his report to Pétain on February 2, 1942. MAEC, Guerre Vichy, 551.

The pope's fear of what a Nazi victory would mean for the church had become so great that, following many months in which he had allowed no criticism of Germany's anti-church policies to appear in the Vatican paper, it published a front-page article titled "The Religious Situation in Germany." Although its language was diplomatic, its message was clear enough: "Certain newspapers," it began, "have published reassuring news about the situation of the Catholic Church in Germany. We are very sorry to be obliged to state that unfortunately we cannot share or confirm these views." Osborne sent the clipping to London with an approving note. A note from the Foreign Office recommended that it be brought to the attention of the BBC for broadcast to Italy, Spain, and South America. Osborne to Foreign Office, January 22, 1942, NAK, FO 371, 33410, 91. *La Civiltà Cattolica* also quoted extensively from the January 22 OR story. "Cronaca contemporanea," CC, 93 I, Quaderno 2199 (February 1942), pp. 240–41.

The German ambassador to the Holy See sent an unusually long report to Berlin on the state of relations between Germany and the Holy See, highlighting the pope's fears about German postwar plans regarding the church, but also citing the pope as the only member of the church in Italy who was not naturally hostile to Germany, identified by Italy's prelates as the land of the Reformation. Bergen to Foreign Ministry, Berlin, February 21, 1942, PAAA, GPA, Beschränkung der diplomatischen Beziehungen zwischen dem Reich und dem Vatikan auf das Altreich, R261178, 02-20.

17. Notes du père Salza, February 8, 1942, ADSS, vol. 5, n. 243.

18. Ciano 1980, pp. 588–89, diary entry for February 9, 1942; Rossi 2005, p. 359; Bérard to Darlan, Vichy, February 12, 1942, MAEN, RSS 576, PO/1, 1183; Harold Tittmann to U.S. secretary of state, February 13, 1942, NARA, RG 59, CDF 1940–44, 701.6566A, p. 2.

19. Guariglia 1950, pp. 490–92; Babuscio Rizzo to Lanza d'Ajeta, capo gabinetto Ministero degli Affari Esteri, February 13, 1942, ASDMAE, AISS, b. 152; De la Flotte, Foreign Ministry, Vichy, to Bérard, March 18, 1942, MAEC, Guerre Vichy, 546.

20. Guariglia memo, February 26, 1942, n. 644/233, ASDMAE, AISS, b. 152.

21. Guariglia to Ciano, March 23, 1942, n. 907, ASDMAE, APSS, b. 58.

22. The pope's meeting with Father Scavizzi is noted in AAV, *Prefettura Casa Pontif.*, Udienze, b. 50.

23. Scavizzi, "La questione ebraica," in Manzo 1997, pp. 132–36, 215–16.

24. Manzo 1997, pp. 137–39, 229–32.

25. Le chargé d'affaires à Presbourg Burzio au cardinal Maglione, March 9, 1942, ADSS, vol. 8, n. 298. Cardinal Maglione, notified by the nuncio in Budapest of the impending deportation of the Slovakian Jews and the request by the chief rabbi of that city that the pope act to prevent it, summoned the Slovakian ambassador to the Holy See and asked him to contact his government immediately with a Vatican request that the action be nullified. Le nonce à Budapest Rotta au cardinal Maglione, March 20, 1942, and Montini notes, March 24, 1942, nn. 317, 322. It was also in March that the pope received a detailed report prepared by the Swiss representative of the Jewish World Congress, forwarded to Rome by the nuncio in Bern, documenting many cases of mass executions of Jews in Poland, Romania, and other parts of German-controlled Europe. Chenaux 2003, p. 284. On Tiso as priest, politician, and Nazi collaborator, see Ward 2013. It was in March 1942 as well that the mass deportation of French Jews eastward to the death camps began. Herbert 2019, p. 372.

26. Tacchi Venturi to Maglione, March 26, 1942, ADSS, vol. 8, n. 331. Cardinal Maglione himself had met with Buffarini on March 6 to argue that baptized Jews should not be subject to the racial laws, again voicing no objection to the application of the laws to Jews who had not renounced their religion. Colloquio tra l'Emo Card. Maglione e l'on. Buffarini, memo prepared by Tacchi Venturi, March 6, 1942, ASRS, *AA.EE.SS.,* Pio XII, Asterisco Italia, posiz. 1054*, f. 983.

CHAPTER 23: BEST TO SAY NOTHING

1. Rome's Catholic daily had announced the pope's election with a huge picture of Pacelli and the banner headline, "God has given the Church Pius XII and given the world the *Pastore Angelico,*" followed on the first anniversary of his election with the headline "The World Salutes in the PASTOR ANGELICUS the Prince of Peace." Novus (Imolo Marconi), "Dio ha dato alla Chiesa Pio XII e al mondo il Pastore Angelico," AR, March 4, 1939, p. 1; "Il Mondo saluta nel 'PASTOR ANGELICUS' il Principe della Dace," AR, March 5, 1940, pp. 3–4.

2. "Il terzo anno di Pontificato di Sua Santità Pio XII," OR, March 12, 1942, pp. 1, 3–4; Remo Branca, "Vita e arte nel 'Pastor Angelicus,'" and M.M., "Per meglio apprezzare la visione," OR, December 13, 1941, p. 4. On April 27, 1942, the Italian embassy would alert Ciano and the Ministry of Popular Culture to the fact that filming of the movie had begun the previous month and that plans were being made to have it distributed throughout the world. N. 1316/495, ASDMAE, APSS, b. 64.

3. On Mussolini's contribution, see the documentation dated April 1 and 5, 1942, at ACS, PCM 1940–43, b. 2937, ff. 2–5.

4. Father Scavizzi's third report, May 12, 1942, based on his observations aboard the military hospital train in April, is found at Manzo 1997, pp. 233–40.

5. Attolico to Ciano, February 27, 1941, tel. 642/300, ASDMAE, AISS, b. 148; Attolico's report was then forwarded to Italy's ambassador in Berlin (Alfieri), tel. 05264, ASDMAE, APSS, b. 52.

6. The Italian diplomat concluded his report remarking that the nuncio "spoke in a serene and elevated tone without any acrimony, indeed saying he was not afraid of being considered an optimist." Ministero degli Affari Esteri to Italian embassy, Holy See, report of Italian embassy secretary, Berlin, June 20, 1942, tel. 14751, ASDMAE, AISS, b. 148. Not even the bishop of Berlin seems to have been happy with the job Orsenigo was doing, as he had sent a letter of complaint about him directly to the pope the previous April. Konrad von Preysing to Pius XII, April 5, 1940, AAV, *Segr. Stato,* 1940, Diocesi, posiz. 306, f. 93r.

7. Tacchi Venturi to Maglione, June 17, 1942, ADSS, vol. 8, n. 399.

8. "Giudaismo. Roberto Farinacci illustra il problema," PI, July 5, 1942, p. 3; Roberto Farinacci, "Cattolici e cattolici," RF, July 14, 1942, pp. 1–2.

9. "20.000 ebrei rastrellati a Parigi," *L'Italia,* July 18, 1942; Cointet 1998, p. 222. According to Cointet, the number of Jews seized in the July 16–17 roundup in Paris was 12,884, composed primarily of women and children.

10. De Felice 1996b, p. 757; Ciano 1980, pp. 626, 631, diary entries for June 2 and June 21; Roberts 2018, pp. 738–40.

11. Osborne to Howard, London, July 12, 1942, NAK, FO 371, 33426, 2–4. The pope had over the previous few months been engaged in a battle of wills with the British government over their request that the Italian prelate who served as apostolic delegate to Egypt and Palestine be replaced, as the British viewed him as compromised by his Italian allegiances. This had led in March 1942 to a request made by Maglione to the nuncio in Washington to "see if it is not opportune to have a word about this with [the American]

government." Maglione to Cicognani, March 28, 1942, AAV, Segr. Stato, 1941, Stati, posiz. 73, f. 14r. It was yet another example of how the pope found the American government more kindly disposed to the Vatican than the British government.

12. "It is however distressing," wrote Tardini in his notes of the visits, "to see this coalition of diplomats who are guests of the Holy See, who are treated exceedingly well, who can see every day the superiority of the Holy See's action, all in agreement and all stubborn in a belief and an attitude that is as false as it is offensive for those who are so good and so kind to them." Tardini notes, July 20, 21, 24, 1942, ADSS, vol. 5, n. 414.

13. Osborne to Tardini, July 21, 1942, ADSS, vol. 5, n. 416. After delivering the letter, Osborne reported back to its author, Douglas Howard, at the Foreign Office in London, saying it had been his intention to give it personally to the pope, but, as his audience had been delayed, he decided to give it to Tardini to deliver to the pontiff. Tardini had told him he should take the matter up directly with the pope. "This I shall do," Osborne pledged. "Several of my colleagues are also speaking on the same lines at the Vatican," he informed London, "but I cannot say that I look forward with confidence to any results." Osborne to Howard, July 22, 1942, NAK, FO 371, 33412, 60–61.

14. Osborne to Pius XII, July 30, 1942, ASRS, *AA.EE.SS.*, Pio XII, parte 1, Germania, posiz. 847, ff. 48r, 49r–50r. At the same time Orsenigo responded to the Secretariat of State's latest request for information on the fate of the Jews who were being deported from Germany and Austria. Characteristically, Orsenigo's long response repeatedly referred to Jews as "non-Aryans," while explaining that it had become dangerous for people to ask about where they were being taken or what had happened to them. "Unfortunately," he wrote, "one hears reports, difficult to verify, of disastrous trips and even massacres. Even every intervention in favor only of Catholic non-Aryans has so far been rejected with the usual response that baptismal water does not change Judaic blood and that the German Reich is defending itself from the non-Aryan race, not from the religious confession of the baptized Jews." Orsenigo to Maglione, July 28, 1942, ASRS, *AA.EE.SS.*, Pio XII, parte 1, Germania, posiz. 742, ff. 30r–31r.

Around the same time, Monsignor Godfrey, the apostolic delegate in London, sent a message to the Vatican asking if it could confirm reports appearing in the British press that the pope had protested the deportation of Jews under way in France. Maglione replied saying that he had no basis for confirming such a report. Godfrey to Maglione, August 8, 1943, and Maglione to Godfrey, August 11, 1942, AAV, Segr. Stato, 1942, *Commissione Soccorsi*, b. 301, fasc. 19, ff. 2r, 3r.

15. Osborne's diary entry for July 31 is quoted in Chadwick 1984, pp. 452–53.

16. Ciano 1980, p. 380, diary entry for December 30, 1939.

17. Monsignor Tardini's diary describes Maria José's papal audience, accompanied by her husband, on May 6, at which the pope told her that he had it on good authority that the Germans were planning to invade both her own natal land and the Netherlands within the next few days. "This evening at 9," Tardini wrote on May 8, "I see from American radio that the alarm in the Netherlands was caused by a letter that the Princess of Piedmont apparently wrote to a woman in Belgium after her visit to the Vatican." Pagano 2020, pp. 184–85.

18. Montini notes, September 3, 1942, ADSS, vol. 5, n. 454; Di Nolfo and Serra 2010, pp. 18–19; Regolo 2002, 2013. In a June 21, 1943, handwritten note at the British Foreign Office, Denis Laskey observed "The Crown Princess is probably the most forceful member of the Royal Family and there have been many reports that she is working against the regime—though there has so far been nothing to substantiate this." To this, Pierson Dixon added his own comment the same day: "We have heard for so long & so regularly that the Crown Princess is working against the régime that we can safely discount the value of her efforts." NAK, FO 371, 37556.

19. Osborne to Eden, September 8, 1942, NAK, FO 371, 33412, 96–105.

20. Andrea Szeptzyckyj, Metropolita ruteno di Leopoli, to Pius XII, August 29, 1942, ASRS, *AA.EE.SS.*, Pio XII, parte 1, Germania, posiz. 742, f. 11r.

21. P. Lopinot, Ferramonti-Tarsia, to Borgongini Duca, September 10, 1942, ADSS, vol. 8, n. 471; "Life in Ferramonti," Italy and the Holocaust Foundation, 2014, http://www .italyandtheholocaust.org/places-life-in-Life-In-Ferramonti-2.aspx.

22. Montini notes, September 18, 1942, ASRS, *AA.EE.SS.*, Pio XII, parte 1, Germania, posiz. 742, f. 12r.

23. American envoy Harold Tittmann reported the new effort to Washington at the end of July. Like the other Allied diplomats, he had been housed since his country's entry in the war at the Santa Marta guest house in Vatican City. Tittmann recalled that in his previous dispatches, he had repeatedly "called attention to the opinion that the failure of the Holy See to protest publicly against Nazi atrocities is endangering its moral prestige and is undermining faith both in the Church and in the Holy Father Himself." The answer he and his colleagues always got, he reported, was that the pope had already condemned offenses against morality and that "to be specific now would only make matters worse." Tittmann expressed his doubt that the letter campaign that the Brazilian ambassador was sponsoring would get the pope to change his mind, but said he thought it could do no harm. A few days later, the American secretary of state sent word of his support for the coordinated appeal. Tittmann to Hull, Washington, July 30, 1942, NARA, RG 59, Entry 1070, box 29, pp. 125–26; Hull to Tittmann, August 4, 1942, FRUS 1942, vol. 3, p. 773.

24. In a note newly found in the Vatican archives, Tardini's annoyance with their visit shines through: Belgium's ambassador proceeded to read at length from the document they had brought, before then passing the sheets over to his Polish colleague. "He, following the same system (but with a voice even more stentorian and with wearisome slowness), read up to page 21." Tardini note, September 15, 1942, ASRS, *AA.EE.SS.*, Pio XII, parte 1, Germania, posiz. 847, f. 29r.

25. Tittmann to secretary of state, Washington, D.C., September 11, 1942, NARA, RG 59, Entry 1070, box 29, pp. 121–22; L'ambassadeur de Belgique Nieuwenhuys et de Pologne Papée au cardinal Maglione, September 12, 1942, L'ambassadeur du Bresil Accioli au cardinal Maglione, September 14, 1942, Osborne to Maglione, September 14, 1942, ADSS, vol. 5, nn. 465–67; Tittmann to Maglione, September 14, 1942; and Tittmann to Hull, September 14, 1942, FRUS 1942, pp. 3:774–75.

26. Peruvian ambassador to the Holy See, September 17, 1942 (but arriving September 28), ASRS, *AA.EE.SS.*, Pio XII, parte 1, Germania, posiz. 847, f. 47r. The additional note is found at f. 52.

27. Taylor report, September 19, 1942, FDR Library, psfa 494a, pp. 14–24. The pope's copies of Taylor's briefs are found at AAV, Segr. Stato, 1942, Stati, posiz. 204, ff. 59r–71r.

28. Taylor memo given to Pius XII, September 22, 1942, FDR Library, psfa 494a, p. 40. The original is found at ASRS, *AA.EE.SS.*, Pio XII, parte 1, Germania, posiz. 742, ff. 16r–19r.

29. Taylor memo to Maglione, September 26, 1942, FDR Library, psfa 494a, pp. 138–39. The Italian translation of the memo is found at ASRS, *AA.EE.SS.*, Pio XII, Parte Extracta, Germania Extracta, posiz. 742, Ebrei, ff. 21r–23r, along with a note "Il Santo Padre ne ha preso visione" (The Holy Father has seen it), f. 14r.

30. If Roosevelt had harbored any hopes that Italy could be separated from its Axis partner, Taylor's reports from the Vatican doused them. "Over a long period of years," Taylor told the president, "no authoritative voice has made itself heard publicly against the totalitarian regime." Any notion that the king might help rid Italy of Mussolini was likewise to be dismissed, for "no hope is to be placed in the Dynasty, which has always shown the most absolute submission to the regime." Mussolini would be overthrown someday, thought Taylor, but "only when Germany's defeat has been accomplished." Indeed, one of the pope's worries was what would happen in Italy should the Axis be

defeated. "It is the opinion in Vatican circles," Taylor reported, "expressed both by the Pope and the Cardinal, that great disorder will prevail, and both have some doubt as to the ability of the United Nations [i.e., the Allies] or other influences to suppress it." Taylor to FDR, September 24, 1942, FDR Library, psfa 495, pp. 44–45; Memorandum of Conference between the Cardinal Secretary of State Maglione and Myron Taylor, September 25, 1942, FDR Library, psfa 494a, p. 38.

But Taylor had seen some sign of Italians' unhappiness with the regime. Giuseppe Dalla Torre, director of the Vatican newspaper, had smuggled a secret memo to him during his stay, offering his analysis of the various Italian groups that opposed the Duce. In addition to the obvious candidates from the anti-Fascist parties that Mussolini had suppressed many years earlier, he named two prominent generals as well as members of what he referred to as the Catholic aristocracy. He also passed on the rumor that Princess Maria José was herself making efforts to get in contact with the aristocrats eager to have Italy exit the war. But Communists were also trying to promote opposition to the regime, he warned, and they were having some success infiltrating the war factories. Giuseppe Dalla Torre, September 26, 1942, NAK, FO 371, 33430, 39.

Taylor left Rome on September 29 and wrote Roosevelt the next day from Madrid. His mission, he reported, had had two main goals: to convince the pope that he should not attempt to broker any peace with the Axis, and to plant the idea that when the Allies were in a position to offer adequate assistance to Italy, it "should in her future interest abandon Hitler." "This," wrote Taylor, "impressed the Pope and the Vatican authorities greatly." Taylor to FDR, September 29, 1942, FDR Library, psfa 494a, p. 184.

Mussolini followed Taylor's visit with great interest, relying in part on accounts from Guariglia, his ambassador to the Vatican. Guariglia to Ciano, October 2, 1942, DDI, series 9, vol. 9, n. 179. He would hear other accounts of the American's talks with the pope as well. One came from his ambassador in Madrid in the wake of Taylor's brief stopover there. Roosevelt's goal in sending his envoy, reported the ambassador, was to win the pope's help in getting Italy to agree to a separate peace with the Allies. A report from a police informant in the Vatican added another twist: Taylor had brought with him an additional inducement for the pope to avoid doing anything to alienate the Americans. Archbishop Spellman, Taylor informed the pope, had recently deposited $2 million in an American bank in the pope's name, the result of a collection taken among New York's Catholics. L'ambasciatore a Madrid, Lequio, to Ciano, October 2, 1942, DDI, series 9, vol. 9, n. 177; Informativa, Vaticano, October 17, 1942, ACS, DAGR, A5G, IIGM, b. 72. At the same time, the French ambassador in Lisbon was reporting rumors that in an effort to separate the pope from Fascist Italy, Taylor's mission was aimed at convincing the pope to leave Rome and establish a new base for the Holy See in Spain or Portugal. Gentil, Lisbon, to French Foreign Ministry, October 6, 1942, MAEC, Guerre Vichy, 550, 484–85.

31. Memo, Segreteria di Stato di Sua Santità, October 1, 1942, ASRS, *AA.EE.SS.,* Pio XII, parte 1, Germania, posiz. 742, f. 24r.

32. In their "Introduction" to volume 6 of ADSS, the Jesuit editors identified Monsignor Angelo Dell'Acqua as "the first section of the Secretariat of State's specialist on all questions concerning the non-Aryans" (p. 25).

33. The October 2 memo by Dell'Acqua is found at ASRS, *AA.EE.SS.,* Pio XII, Parte Extracta, Germania, posiz. 742, Ebrei, f. 25r. For studies of Dell'Acqua, see Melloni 2004.

34. Report on the stationery of the Polish embassy to the Holy See, datelined Vatican, October 3, 1942, ASRS, *AA.EE.SS.,* Pio XII, parte Extracta, Germania, posiz. 742, f. 35r.

35. Relazione di Scavizzi, October 7, 1942, ASRS, *AA.EE.SS.,* Pio XII, parte Extracta, Germania, posiz. 742, f. 26r.

36. Tittmann to Hull, October 10, 1942, NARA, RG 59, CDF 1940–44, 740.00116, box 2917,

pp. 2, 3; also published in FRUS 1942, vol. 3, pp. 777–78. The Vatican copy is found at ASRS, *AA.EE.SS.,* Pio XII, parte Extracta, Germania, posiz. 742, f. 27r. Over the next many months, Monsignor Bernardini, the nuncio in Bern, would pass along to the Vatican a series of documents from Jewish organizations detailing the extermination of the Jews of Central and Eastern Europe. AAV, *Arch. Nunz. Svizzera,* b. 221, fasc. 626, ff. 93r–120r.

CHAPTER 24: ESCAPING BLAME

1. Gioannini 2012, p. 80.
2. Rauscher 2004, pp. 441–42; Davis 2006, pp. 77–78, 138; "75(nz) squadron," https://75nzsquadron.wordpress.com/october-1942/; "Second Battle of El Alamein," National Army Museum, https://www.nam.ac.uk/explore/battle-alamein.
3. In the end, the ambassador thought he had convinced the Duce it would be best not to accuse the Vatican of complicity in the attacks on Italy's cities. But he was surprised the next day to find Farinacci's editorial on the front page of *Il Regime Fascista* containing word for word all the charges Mussolini had leveled. It seems likely that Mussolini himself asked Farinacci to print the piece. Guariglia 1950, pp. 528–29; Ciano 1980, p. 659, diary entry for October 26, 1942.
4. "Relazione circa la situazione religiosa in Austria e nel Lussemburgo richiesta dal Santo Padre," October 7, 1942, ASRS, *AA.EE.SS.,* Pio XII, parte 1, Germania, posiz. 854, ff. 31r–36r.
5. Bergen to Foreign Ministry, Berlin, October 12, 1942, tel. 264, PAAA, GPA, Beschränkung der diplomatischen Beziehungen zwischen dem Reich und dem Vatikan auf das Altreich, R261178, 100–2. While all this was going on, Italians would see little indication that the church was anything other than supportive of the Axis cause. An early October editorial by Father Busti, director of Milan's Catholic daily, was typical, as he renewed his praise of the Axis war, being fought, he wrote, to bring about "a new order of justice and peace," and to counter "the politics of hatred introduced by England with the Treaty of Versailles." D.m.b. (Don Mario Busti), "Ritorno alla tradizione," *L'Italia,* October 4, 1942, p. 1.

   An editorial later in the month by Father Busti, celebrating the twentieth anniversary of Mussolini's coming to power, recalled an interview the Duce had given a journalist some years earlier, when the subject of religion had come up.

   "Recently," the interviewer said to Mussolini, "you have paid homage to Caesar, but placed Jesus above him, if I am not mistaken."

   "Caesar comes after him—replied the Duce with conviction—Jesus is the greatest!" "1922–28 ottobre–1942 Le Opere del Ventennio," *L'Italia,* October 28, 1942, p. 3.

   The Duce meanwhile kept up his pressure on the pope. On October 8, he had Buffarini, his undersecretary, summon the nuncio to his office. Mussolini, the undersecretary told him, was "beside himself" with fury, having gotten a report—which Buffarini handed to the nuncio—that Cardinal Salotti had expressed anti-Fascist sentiments at a dinner party two months earlier. "Cardinal or no Cardinal," said the Duce, "I will have him arrested, and then we'll see what happens."

   A few days later the nuncio returned and handed Buffarini the cardinal's lengthy letter of defense. The informant report was a pack of lies and distortions, said Salotti. The only charge that had any truth to it was the claim that he had said "Hitler's victory would signal an all-out war on the Catholic religion."

   With the pope newly warned, and the cardinal professing his hope for an Axis victory, Mussolini let the matter rest. The series of documents bearing on this dispute is found at AAV, Segr. Stato, 1942, Cardinali, posiz. 51, ff. 1r–19r.

   The country's Catholic press had taken advantage of the recent twentieth anniversary of the Fascist March on Rome, which had brought Mussolini to power, to renew its praise for all that the Duce had accomplished. In reporting this to Ciano, Ambassador Guariglia particularly called his attention to the article that Rome's Catholic daily had published, written by a prominent *Civiltà Cattolica* author. "Those who look at the picture of the past two decades," wrote the Jesuit, "are stupefied by the multiplicity and historical importance of the events that have occurred under the dynamism of the Fascist Regime." Guariglia to Ministero degli Affari Esteri e Ministero di Cultura Popolare, November 13, 1942, tel. 3436/1339, ASDMAE, APSS, b. 62.

Revealing too was the Vatican's response to an editorial that appeared in a Fascist newspaper of Salerno, which argued that Fascism was incompatible with Catholicism. The reaction was swift. On November 30, Cardinal Maglione summoned the Italian ambassador, showed him the clipping, and asked to have another Fascist newspaper publish a refutation. There was, insisted the cardinal, no incompatibility between Fascism and Catholicism. Guariglia appunto, November 30, 1942, ASDMAE, AISS, b. 164.

6. Bottai 1989, p. 335, diary entry for November 19, 1942.
7. "Bombardamento a Torino," https://www.museotorino.it/view/s/acb7d7d49d6147e188377fb9e9c491ef.
8. Osborne to Eden, November 22, 1942, NAK, FO 371, 33412, 157–60. The archbishop's correspondence with the pope is found at FDR Library, psfc 117, pp. 61–67, and includes materials sent by the Vatican to Archbishop Spellman and from Spellman to FDR.
9. Hassell 2011, p. xxi; Herbert 2019, pp. 411–17; Ian Johnson, "Stalingrad: WWII's Turning Point," *Origins,* https://origins.osu.edu/milestones/august-2017-stalingrad-75-turning-point-world-war-ii-europe. A good, concise examination of the turn in the tide on the eastern front is given by Hartmann 2013.
10. Clara Petacci diary pages, November 30 and December 2, 1942, ACS, Archivi di famiglie e di persone, Clara Petacci, b. 10, fasc. 157.
11. In reporting the conversation to Cardinal Maglione, the nuncio admitted to remaining a bit perplexed by the king's mention of "Lutherans." The king's reference to Jews and Bolsheviks was clear enough, but by Lutherans was he referring to the Germans? Or had he misspoken and meant to say "Anglicans"? With the king, who had a dim view of humanity in general, it was hard to be sure. Borgongini to Maglione, November 27, 1942, ADSS, vol. 7, n. 115.
12. Maglione to Cicognani, Washington, December 3, 1942, and Cicognani to Maglione, December 4, 1942, ADSS, vol. 7, nn. 43–44; Trisco 2003, p. 226.
13. Following their December 4 meeting, Guariglia prepared a memo for Ciano reporting what Maglione had told him. Curiously, he gave a copy to Maglione, who scribbled a comment at the bottom:

> This note of the Ambassador of the Italian Government refers exactly to the conversation he had with me, excepting only the last sentence: "it would be necessary to move at least the principal of these [military] objectives." I had said "it would be necessary to move the military objectives." I pointed this out to the Ambassador. He responded that in reality I had spoken "of the military objectives," of all and not only the principal ones. He added, however, that he had not thought he could cite my phrase as it was, because he did not believe it possible to move all the military objectives and he thought that suggesting moving (all) the military objectives would appear excessive to the Head of the Government (ASRS, *AA.EE.SS.,* Pio XII, parte I, Volumi bianchi I, ff. 256r–57v).

14. Guariglia Appunto, December 4, 1942, n. 3650, ASDMAE, Gab., b. 1192, UC-76, fasc. 3; Maglione to Guariglia, December 4, 1942, ADSS, vol. 7, n. 45. Mussolini, in discussing the Vatican request, told his son-in-law he would not want anyone to say he tried to stay

"under Catholicism's umbrella in order to protect himself from the English bombs." Ciano 1980, p. 674, diary entry for December 5, 1942.

On December 18, Mussolini told his ambassador to the Holy See to inform the Vatican that both the Italian and German military commands would soon leave Rome and that he too would likely join them outside the city. But he made clear his reluctance to appear to be depending on the pope to protect his capital. Adding to his annoyance was the stream of people flooding into Rome, regarding it as the safest place to be as British air attacks threatened the rest of the country. Guariglia to Ciano, December 18, 1942, n. 3797, ASDMAE, Gab., b. 1192, UC-76, fasc. 3.

15. The Vatican documents detailing these intense meetings in mid-December 1942 are found in ASRS, *AA.EE.SS.*, Pio XII, parte I, Volumi bianchi I, ff. 259r–81r. The excerpt from Osborne's diary entry for December 14 is found in Chadwick 1986, p. 216.

16. Ministero della Guerra to Ministero dell'Interno, December 3, 1942, ACS, MI, Gab., RSI, b. 51, n.160860; "Solenni riti religiosi in tutta Italia a propiziazione della Vittoria," AR, December 8, 1942, p. 1; "Patriottico discorso dell'Arcivescovo di Bologna," PI, December 9, 1942, p. 4. The rites were also covered in Bologna's Catholic daily: "Riti propiziatori per la patria in Guerra," AI, December 10, 1942, p. 2. On the pope's authorization of the masses honoring Arnaldo Mussolini, see AAV, Segr. Stato, 1941, posiz. 1950, ff. 11–18r.

17. Segretariato per la Moralità, ACI, "Relazione sugli Spettacoli di Varietà," December 8, 1942, ISACEM, PG XII, b. 22.

18. Cardinal Lavitrano to Mussolini, December 19, 1942, ISACEM, PG XII, b. 22.

CHAPTER 25: PAPAL PREMIERE

1. A mid-December 1942 British intelligence report, describing the German influx, concluded that it was now unlikely the Italians "would be in a position to break away from the Axis." OSS report, "Political Situation in Italy," December 18, 1942, NARA, RG 165, color 278.

2. The anticlerical wing of the National Socialist government was unhappy about the German soldiers' visits to the pope, not thinking their officers and enlisted men's interest in the Vatican was healthy and worried that they would be overly impressed by all the majesty that surrounded the pope. Previous decrees notwithstanding, read a December 8, 1942, report from the Nazi Party Chancellery to the German Foreign Ministry, members of the army continued to make visits to the pope. NSDAP Party Chancellery to FO, Legation Councilor Büttner, PAAA, GPA, Vatikan Kirche 3, R98832, 10–11. Three days later Goebbels (1948, p. 246) wrote in his diary, "Visits of German soldiers and officers to the Pope have by no means grown less in number despite his assurances to the contrary. It would be a good thing to bring about a change of personnel there. I am gathering data to take to the Führer."

3. He was passing this information on, Maglione explained, so that, at opportune moments, the nuncio might cautiously make use of it in conversations with men in the Spanish government and in the "Spanish political-ecclesiastical world." Maglione to nuncio Madrid, Gaetano Cicognani, December 15, 1942, ADSS, vol. 7, n. 61.

4. Underlining is in the original.

5. "I fear," Osborne reported to London, "that the fact is that the Pope is determined not to condemn any specific crime, however monstrous, in order to preserve an appearance of neutrality that will one day enable him to play a part in restoring peace. He does not see that by his silence he is hopelessly prejudicing his prospects of being listened to." Osborne memo, December 18, 1942, NAK, FO 380/75, no. 21/28/42. The memo Osborne handed Tardini to give the pope was titled, "Persecution of the Jews." Chadwick 1986, pp. 216–17.

6. If the pope were to condemn the Nazi crimes, replied Tardini, he would need to condemn the crimes that the Soviets had committed against the Poles as well. Fine, replied the ambassador. What was important was for the pope's condemnation to be public and be unequivocal. Libionka 2008, pp. 286–87.

7. Guariglia to Ciano, December 18 and 19, 1942, nn. 3796 and 3814, ASDMAE, AISS, b. 194. On the pope's Christmas 1942 broadcast, see Coco 2020.

8. Chadwick 1986, p. 218.

9. Ruozzi 2015, pp. 162–64; Osborne annual report for 1942, Osborne to Eden, March 22, 1943, NAK, R 3904/3904/57, p. 2. Among the articles appearing in the Catholic press on the launch of the film, see Enrico Pucci, "La luce del 'Pastor Angelicus' s'irradierà propizia sul mondo," AR, December 18, 1942, p. 3; M.M., "Pio XII: Pastor Angelicus," *L'Italia,* December 18, 1942, p. 2; elledici, "Entusiasmo e commozione di popolo alla visione del 'PASTOR ANGELICUS,'" AR, December 20, 1942, p. 3.

10. Clara Petacci diary, December 20, 1942, ACS, Archivi di famiglie e di persone, Clara Petacci, b. 10, fasc. 157; Bosworth 2017, p. 167.

11. Bosworth 2017, pp. 167–68; Bosworth 2002, pp. 385–89; De Felice 1996b, pp. 1079–85.

12. Ciano 1980, p. 679, diary entry for December 24, 1942.

13. "Il radiomessaggio del Pontefice," PI, December 25, 1942, p. 1; Rossi 2005, p. 394. "The Holy Father's radio Christmas speech," reported Bologna's prefect, offering a perspective of the reception of the address outside Rome, "was met by broad consensus." Loudspeakers had been placed outside parish churches throughout the province so that the faithful could hear the pope's words. "The fundamental principles of the Pontiff's speech," wrote the prefect, were "very cautious, but decisively contrary to the communist ideologies and to the non-Catholic states." "Attività del Clero," prefetto, Bologna, January 7, 1943, n. 301, ASDMAE, AISS, b. 130.

14. Phayer (2008, pp. 53–56) offers a more balanced examination of the pope's speech and the motives behind it. The text of the pope's speech can be found at https://www.vatican.va/content/pius-xii/it/speeches/1942/documents/hf_p-xii_spe_19421224_radiomessage-christmas.html.

15. Osborne to Eden, December 28, 1942, NAK, FO 371, 37537, 6–16; Osborne annual report for 1942, Osborne to Eden, March 22, 1943, NAK, R 3904/3904/57, p. 2; Friedländer 1966, pp. 130–31; Hennesey 1974, p. 36; Tittmann to Hull, December 30, 1942, NARA, RG 59, Entry 1070, box 29, pp. 5–7. Meanwhile the pleas for the pope to speak out against the slaughter of Europe's Jews kept coming in. A batch of them, including a plea from a rabbi heading a London-based Jewish organization and another from the leaders of the orthodox rabbis of North America, are found in the newly opened Vatican archives. They are placed in a folder with a note dated Christmas Day recording the pope's instructions to have the apostolic delegates in Washington and London offer a response orally: "the Holy See is doing what it can." The same Vatican file has copies of the instructions subsequently sent to the apostolic delegates in London and Washington. ASRS, *AA.EE.SS.,* Pio XII, parte 1, Germania, posiz. 742, ff. 52r–59r.

16. Libionka 2008, p. 288. At his end-of-year audience with the pope, Harold Tittmann also noted the pope's defensiveness when he told him his Christmas speech was regarded by many as a disappointment for not explicitly condemning the Nazi atrocities. In addition to offering the reason that he could not condemn the Nazis without condemning the "Bolsheviks" or their atrocities, he led Tittmann to believe that, as the American envoy put it, "he felt there had been some exaggeration for purpose of propaganda" in the accounts of Nazi atrocities. Tittmann 2004, pp. 123–24.

17. Friedländer 1966, pp. 175–76.

18. De Felice 1996b, p. 767.

CHAPTER 26: DISASTER FORETOLD

1. Ciano 1980, pp. 690, 691, diary entries for January 19 and 22, 1943.

2. Relazione Triennale 1940–1942, AAV, *Arch. Nunz. Italia,* b. 13, fasc. 18, ff. 3r–25r. Maglione had requested the report in a letter to Borgongini on June 3, 1942, AAV, *Arch. Nunz. Italia,* b. 13, fasc. 18, ff. 2rv. For background on the Vatican use of the Fascist government to prevent Protestant proselytizing in Italy, see Madigan 2021.

3. "La missione delle classi dirigenti," AI, January 12, 1943, p. 1. The handwritten comment on Osborne's report of the event at the Foreign Office was not sympathetic: "Despite the reference to social reform I should call this a thoroughly reactionary speech as out of date as the ceremony itself." Osborne to Eden, January 12, 1943, NAK, FO 371, 37537.

4. Montini notes, January 12, 1943, ADSS, vol. 7, n. 88, Ciano recorded his own account of the meeting in his diary that day, making clear his belief that Monsignor Montini—and not Cardinal Maglione or Monsignor Tardini—was the pope's closest confidant. "He was prudent, measured, and Italian," observed Ciano, and while Montini did not express any judgments on the war, he had said that the prelates of the Vatican did not believe it would end anytime soon. "He added that anything that it was possible for him to do on behalf of our country, he was entirely at our disposition." Ciano 1980, p. 688, diary entry for January 12, 1943.

5. Davis 2006, p. 93; Rauscher 2004, p. 452; Di Rienzo 2018, p. 425.

6. Libionka 2008, pp. 291–93.

7. Hennesey 1974, p. 40.

8. Ciano 1980, p. 696, diary entry for February 5, 1943; Edda Ciano 1975, p. 169; De Felice 1996b, pp. 1047–48. Edda was convinced that the decision to dismiss her husband was the work of what she referred to as the Petacci clan, Clara's family and their clients. They were, Edda believed, angry that she and her husband had been trying to put an end to the growing public scandal about the riches and favors that the Duce was showering on them. Edda Mussolini 1975, p. 171. For the informant report, see Informativa da Roma (n. 484—Nicosia), February 28, 1943, ACS, MI, MAT, b. 239.

9. Later that morning Mussolini phoned his son-in-law telling him he decided to hold off on appointing him ambassador to the Holy See. "They will say," the Duce told him, "that you've been pensioned off, and you're too young to be pensioned off." It was too late, Ciano replied. The Vatican had already been informed of the decision. Ciano 1980, p. 696, diary entry for February 6, 1943. In his recent biography of Ciano, Di Rienzo (2018, p. 490) disputes Ciano's account that Mussolini had second thoughts about his appointment to the Vatican. However, it is verified by Guariglia's (1950, p. 534) own account. At noon that same day, Guariglia recalled, he had gone to assure Ciano that he had notified Cardinal Maglione. "He was very glad," recalled Guariglia, "because just a half hour earlier Mussolini had telephoned him from Palazzo Venezia to say he had changed his mind and wanted him to go somewhere else. To which Ciano told him that it was no longer possible to make a change, as I had already officially made the request." Ciano's account is further confirmed by Pirelli's (1984, p. 401) February 9, 1943, diary entry.

10. Bergen to Foreign Ministry, Berlin, February 7, 1943, PAAA, GBS, 29818, 12, tel. 46; London, Report n. 54450: "Italy," February 26, 1943, NARA, RG 165, color 279; Pirelli 1984, p. 401, diary entry for February 9, 1943; Tittmann to Hull, Washington, February 9, 1943, NARA, RG 59, CDF 1940–44, 701.6566A, pp. 7–8.

11. Montini notes, February 6, 1943, ADSS, vol. 7, n. 105. The nuncio took the opportunity to send Ciano a letter of appreciation, thanking him for his personal courtesies and attentions, "cooperating effectively with Your high authority to maintain the good rela-

tions between the Holy See and Italy even when difficult questions have come up."
Borgongini to Ciano, February 8, 1943, ASDMAE, AISS, b. 148.

12. Petacci to Mussolini, n.d., ACS, Archivi di famiglie e di persone, Clara Petaccci, b. 4, fasc. 51.

13. "L'Annuale dei Patti Lateranensi. Avvenimento storico," PI, February 12, 1943, p. 1.

14. A few days before the Lateran anniversary, Osborne informed London that Soviet military successes were reviving Vatican anxiety about the "Bolshevisation of Europe." Meeting two days later with Maglione, Osborne found the cardinal preoccupied with the German military's precarious position in Russia. Osborne to Foreign Office, February 5 and 7, 1943, NAK, FO 371, 37538, 17 and 19. Osborne struck a similar note later in the month: "Vatican alarm as a result of continuing Russian victories seems to be growing." February 22, 1943, NAK, FO 371, 37538, 47.

15. D.m.b., "La diga," L'Italia, February 21, 1943, p. 1. Three days later the Italian embassy at the Holy See sent it to the Ministry of Popular Culture and the Foreign Ministry, tel. 599, ASDMAE, APSS, b. 68.

16. Tittmann to Hull, February 13, 1943, NARA, RG 59, CDF 1940–44, 701.6566A, pp. 9–11. It was not only the Americans who were hearing rumors that Mussolini's dramatic cabinet overhaul was linked to a secret peace plan involving the Vatican. Ribbentrop unexpectedly arrived in Rome at the end of the month, triggering a wave of speculation as to why he had come. "He wanted to see for himself," wrote Luca Pietromarchi in his diary, "the significance of the ministerial crisis of three weeks ago. The Germans are always afraid of the possibility that Italy will seek a separate peace. They never know whether the Holy See might lend a hand by becoming a go-between." Quoted in De Felice 1996b, p. 1050; Pietromarchi 2009.

17. Among those unhappy with the apparently indiscriminate bombing campaign was the British envoy to the Vatican, who found himself in an awkward position having been repeatedly instructed to complain to the pope about German attacks on civilian targets. In early 1943, Osborne's unhappiness became the subject of a discussion at the highest levels of the British Foreign Office. "There can be no doubt that a large portion of the weight of our attacks," observed Denis Laskey, one of the foreign secretary's advisers, "is now directed against centres of towns and not against strictly military objectives such as barracks, factories or railways, the object being to disorganize to the maximum the life of the civilians engaged on war production." It was a fact that they could never acknowledge publicly, but Laskey advised, "I think it would be more honest to admit, at least among ourselves, that we do try to kill or maim as many civilians as possible and that our attacks are as indiscriminate as any of those carried out by the Germans and Italians against London in 1940–41." Laskey said all this by way of preface to his argument that the bombing was doing more harm than good. Rather than making Italians more likely to rebel against their leaders and withdraw Italy from the war, which had been its intention, the bombing campaign had simply generated resentment against their tormentors. Much better, he advised, for the British to return to the high ground and limit their raids to military targets.

Responding to these recommendations, the undersecretary of foreign affairs, Orme Sargent, admitted that there was no use in "beating around the bush, for our strategy as regards Italy at present . . . definitely requires indiscriminate bombing by us in order to achieve the object of bringing about a breakdown of Italian morale without having to resort to actual military invasion of the mainland of Italy." Although Sargent added his own doubt that the strategy was sound, he said that as it had been decided upon by the military Chiefs of Staff, there was no point voicing Foreign Office objection. At the bottom of the memo, below these comments, was a handwritten note by Foreign Secretary Anthony Eden: "I agree with Sir O. Sargent."

Two weeks later, Eden elaborated on Britain's strategy in Italy in a letter to President Roosevelt and Secretary of State Hull. "Our aim," Eden wrote, "must be to knock Italy out of the war as quickly as possible and this could be achieved with almost equal effect whether Italy made a separate peace or whether dissatisfaction and disorder within the country attained such serious proportions that the Germans were forced to establish a full scale occupation." The latter would have the advantage of forcing Germany to shift much-needed troops to Italy while depriving the Germans of the Italian troops who were fighting with them in Russia and the Balkans. Having Italy switch sides in the war had little appeal, as Britain's military leaders, the foreign secretary reported, thought little of the value of recruiting the Italian military to fight against the Germans. Rather, the British command thought it was more in the Allies' interest to have the Italians remain part of the Axis coalition and become "an increasing drain on German strength" (Montgomery to Howard, December 31, 1942, with comments by Laskey, January 20, 1943, D. Howard, January 22, 1943, O.G. Garton, January 25, 1943, and (undated, but following January 25), A.E. [Anthony Eden], NAK, FO 371, 37538; Eden to FDR and Hull, January 14, 1943, conveyed by Matthews, U.S. chargé d'affaires in London, January 15, 1943, FRUS 1943, vol. 2, pp. 318–20).

18. Notes de Mgr Arborio Mella di S. Elia, February 24, 1943, ADSS, vol. 7, n. 125. Curiously, an American intelligence report, shown to President Roosevelt, told that a "very dependable source believes that the Pope will intercede to have Mussolini retire of his own volition, and also to have the King abdicate in favor of Prince Humbert. He will be supported by an army under the leadership of Badoglio." OSS report, March 20, 1943, FDR Library, mr 435, p. 199.

19. Pirelli 1984, pp. 418–23, diary entry for March 26, 1943.

20. The Italian embassy at the Holy See highlighted the latest of these in early April, in an article that appeared in the Roman Catholic daily featuring patriotic Easter messages sent by two of Italy's bishops. "While our glorious army is mobilized," said the Sicilian bishop of Trapani, "not every citizen can be a combatant. Everyone however must contribute to the victory. . . . This is exactly what Catholic Action wants so that the Reign of Christ is consolidated in the new Europe." Circolare Gabinetto Ministero dell'Interno al prefetto di Verona, February 4, 1943, ACS, DAGR, A5G, IIGM, b. 27; Ambasciata alla Santa Sede to Ministry of Popular Culture, April 8, 1943, tel. 1124, ASDMAE, APSS, b. 68. The quotes are from the April 2 issue of *L'Avvenire*.

21. De Felice 1996b, p. 941; Davis 2006, p. 89. Among the reports used here are several found in ACS, MI, MAT, b. 239.

22. Maglione notes, April 6, 1943, ADSS, vol. 7, n. 163. Tardini also met with Osborne before his departure for London and criticized the Allies' demand that Italy surrender unconditionally, saying it would be too humiliating for Italy to accept. At the same time, he told Osborne that the Allies should not put any faith in Italy's political exiles, as not only were they out of touch with the reality of life in Italy, but they were animated by a desire for revenge. Tardini recalled that meeting more than a year later in a note dated September 4, 1944, ASRS, *AA.EE.SS.*, Pio XII, parte I, Italia, posiz. 1356, ff. 5r–8r.

CHAPTER 27: A THORNY PROBLEM

1. Roncalli telegram, March 13, 1943, ASRS, *AA.EE.SS.*, Pio XII, parte I, Turchia, posiz. 223 II, f. 143. The ellipsis is found in the original text.

2. Di Meglio held the title of "Addetto" in the first section (relations with states) of the Vatican's Secretariat of State. *Annuario Pontificio,* 1943, p. 618.

3. The ellipsis is in the original document.

4. Di Meglio attributed British support for settling Jews in Palestine to the fact that England "is filo-Semitic and, at least in its roots, anti-Catholic." He added, "The English

government cannot ignore that giving Palestine to the Jews represents a favoritism toward them and an affront to the detriment of Catholicism." Di Meglio's mid-March 1943 report and Tardini's notes dated April 13 are found at ASRS, *AA.EE.SS.,* Pio XII, parte 1, Turchia, posiz. 223 II, ff. 223–233c.

5. Maglione telegram to Roncalli, Istanbul, May 4, 1943, with handwritten note, "approved by the Holy Father," ASRS, *AA.EE.SS.,* Pio XII, parte 1, Turchia, posiz. 223 II, f. 144.

6. Roncalli telegram, Istanbul, May 31, 1943, and Dell'Acqua typed note on it, June 1, 1943, ASRS, *AA.EE.SS.,* Pio XII, parte 1, Serie Turchia, posiz. 223 II, f. 146.

7. Among the recent reports on the ongoing slaughter of Europe's Jews were those coming from the Polish ambassador to the Holy See and from the nuncio in Switzerland. Ambasciata di Polonia, February 2, 1943; Bernardini to Maglione, February 24 and 27, 1943, ASRS, *AA.EE.SS.,* Pio XII, parte 1, Germania, posiz. 742, ff. 72r–76v, 92r–98v.

8. Generoso Pope's telegram to Pius XII is dated March 5, 1943; Maglione's reply was prepared March 7. ASRS, *AA.EE.SS.,* Pio XII, parte 1, Germania, posiz. 742, ff. 177r–80r. Generoso Pope, like much of the leadership of the Italian-American community, had earlier been a strong supporter of Mussolini. On the attitudes of Italian-Americans to Mussolini and Fascism, see Luconi 2000.

9. Cicognani to Maglione, March 26, 1943, ASRS, *AA.EE.SS.,* Pio XII, parte 1, Germania, posiz. 742, f. 100r. In his reply of April 3, Maglione instructed Cicognani to inform the rabbis "that the Holy See continues to concern itself in favor of the Jews," f. 102r.

10. Mussolini had not named a replacement for Ciano as foreign minister in February, but instead retained for himself the Foreign Ministry, naming Bastianini his undersecretary.

11. Tacchi Venturi to Maglione, April 14, 1943, ADSS, vol. 7, n. 152; Pirelli 1984, p. 430, diary entry for April 23, 1943. Italian military commanders rejected the Germans' repeated deportation requests, placing the Jews in these areas instead into Italian-supervised concentration camps. Documents bearing on Vatican negotiations with Bastianini on the matter of the Nazi request can be found at ADSS, vol. 7, nn. 104, 105, 122, 127, 140, and 146. For Bastianini's own account, see Bastianini 2005, p. 98. On the question of how Italian authorities dealt with the German requests to turn over Jews from Italian-controlled territory in France, see Fenoglio 2020.

12. Rauscher 2004, p. 461; Bottai 1989, p. 374, diary entry for April 14, 1943; Pirelli 1984, p. 428, diary entry for April 22, 1943; Bastianini 2005, p. 128.

CHAPTER 28: AN AWKWARD REQUEST

1. "Evolution de l'Italie en 1943," May 5, 1943, MAEC, Papiers Chauvel, vol. 121, 197–98. A note for the Duce from the Italian embassy to the Vatican reported that Scorza's remarks had pleased the prelates in the Secretariat of State, who were nervous about the new party secretary, associating him with earlier attacks on Catholic Action. Appunto per il Duce, May 7, 1943, ASDMAE, AISS, b. 164.

2. Ambasciata italiana, Santa Sede, to Ministry of Popular Culture, May 13, 1943, tel. 1553, ASDMAE, APSS, b. 68. The story appeared in the May 9 issue of *L'Avvenire di Roma.*

On May 1, Rome's major newspaper carried a story titled "May the Burning Heart of the Fatherland Foretell Victory." The article consisted of the text of Cardinal Salotti's recent message to Siena's *podestà.* His words, praising Italy's soldiers as "true authentic heroes, strenuously fighting up to the point of sacrificing their lives," ended with the call for Axis victory that became the story's title. Given the cardinal's position in the Curia, heading the Sacred Congregation of Rites, his bellicose remarks occasioned both a complaint from Harold Tittmann, the American envoy, and an impassioned protest from the Brazilian ambassador to the Holy See. The documentation on this case is found at AAV, *Segr. Stato,* 1942, Cardinali, posiz. 51, ff. 231–341.

3. "Incessante attività del Supremo Pastore per lenire le sofferenze della guerra e Sua invocazione per il ritorno della vera pace nel mondo," OR, June 3, 1943, p. 1.

4. Osborne to Foreign Office, June 3, 1943, NAK, FO 371, 37537, 37–39.

5. Ciano, June 4, 1943, tel. 3751, ASDMAE, APSS, b. 64.

6. Schlemmer 2009.

7. Tittmann 2004, p. 146.

8. Tardini notes, May 10, 1943, ADSS, vol. 7, n. 181, underlining in original.

9. Pius XII to Mussolini, May 12, 1943, ADSS, vol. 7, n. 185.

10. Maglione notes, May 12, 1943, ADSS, vol. 7, n. 186.

11. Mussolini to Pius XII, May 12, 1943, ASDMAE, Gab., b. 1189.

12. Ciano also shared some highly sensitive government secrets with the cardinal, telling him that the head of Italy's military had termed the situation desperate. Another high-ranking general, Ciano added, had informed him that Palermo and Marsala, in western Sicily, had been largely destroyed, while Catania on the eastern coast of the island had suffered incalculable damage from the constant Allied bombardments. Allied planes, said Ciano, were now covering the skies like swarms of flies. Soon they would be covering the rest of Italy's cities and, he pointed out, the country had no remaining air defenses. Maglione notes, May 13, 1943, ADSS, vol. 7, nn. 189 and 190.

13. Hassell 2011, p. xxii; Davis 2006, p. 117.

14. Dalla Torre had recently sent a brief note to Cardinal Maglione. An influential group was planning to meet with the king to discuss how to extricate Italy from the war. It included three top military officers—the two marshals of the Italian army, First World War hero Enrico Caviglia and recently deposed supreme commander Pietro Badoglio, along with Admiral Thaon di Revel, Mussolini's first naval minister—together with two of the country's pre-Fascist prime ministers, including Ivanoe Bonomi. Should Victor Emmanuel decline to meet with them, Bonomi, the most influential non-Fascist political figure in the country, intended to let the king know it would leave them no alternative to exploring a future that would have no place for the monarchy. Dalla Torre to Maglione, May 12, 1943, ADSS, vol. 7, n. 188. A month later Dalla Torre provided a detailed follow-up report on the efforts under way to get the indecisive king to act. Dalla Torre to Maglione, June 11, 1943, ADSS, vol. 7, n. 244.

15. Pirelli 1984, pp. 432–33, diary entry for May 12, 1943. Bonomi would meet with the king on June 2, asking that he remove Mussolini and appoint a provisional military government to end the alliance with Germany, to be followed by a civilian coalition government of anti-Fascists. The king replied that he did not want to empower the anti-Fascists. Boiardi et al. 1990, p. 12.

16. Raccolta di prove documentali, May 12, 1943, ASR, Galla Placidia, CAP, Sezione istruttoria, b. 1669, f. 1010; De Felice 1996b, p. 1181.

17. Cicognani, Washington, to Maglione, February 10, 1943, ADSS, vol. 7, n. 110.

18. At the war's end, in May 1945, Federzoni, one of the pillars of the Fascist regime, would receive a sentence of life in prison. Thanks to the help given him by Monsignor Montini, he was able to escape prison by taking refuge in the Ukrainian Pontifical College in Rome. Then in May 1946, with Vatican help, he succeeded in fleeing to Brazil. Mola 2019, p. xxii; Ciccozzi 2019, pp. lxxiv–lxxv.

19. Maglione to Cicognani, Washington, D.C., May 22, 1943, ADSS, vol. 7, n. 208.

20. Pius XII to President Roosevelt, May 19, 1943, FDR Library, psfa 495, pp. 73–75, reproduced in FRUS 1943, vol. 2, pp. 916–17.

21. Algiers conference planning meeting minutes, May 29–June 3, 1943, FDR Library, mr 844, pp. 9–10.

22. Cicognagni to Maglione, May 29, 1943, ADSS, vol. 7, n. 215.

23. Tardini notes, May 31, 1943, ADSS, vol. 7, n. 219.

24. Maglione to Cicognani, June 1, 1943, ADSS, vol. 7, n. 223.

25. Tardini notes, June 1, 1943, ADSS, vol. 7, n. 221.

26. Cicognani to Maglione, June 12, 1943, ADSS, vol. 7, n. 246.

27. Borgongini to Maglione, June 17, 1943, ADSS, vol. 7, n. 252; Borgongini to Maglione, June 18, 1943, AAV, *Arch. Nunz. Italia,* b. 18, fasc. 4, ff. 124r–25r.

28. Some chaplains, hearing of the plan, expressed their unease, and Cardinal Maglione called on Bartolomasi to come to see him. The result was a referral of the matter to the Vatican's Consistorial Congregation, which called on the archbishop to "suspend" his request to the chaplains, concluding that having the chaplains play this role in the current climate would produce "the aversion of the population to the Clergy." AAV, *Segr. Stato,* 1943, Diocesi, posiz. 179, ff. 1r–6v.

29. Tardini notes, May 30, 1943, ADSS, vol. 7, n. 216.

30. The note was sent to FDR via the nuncio in Washington. Cicognani to Myron Taylor, June 15, 1943, FRUS 1943, vol. 2, pp. 918–19.

31. Combined Chiefs of Staff to Eisenhower, Algiers, June 15, 1943, FDR Library, mr 303, p. 105. That same day, Roosevelt wrote a letter to Pius XII, copying Churchill. Italy had started the war, noted FDR. While Americans greatly valued Italy's religious shrines and monuments, they were determined to win the war. He added, "In the event it should be found militarily necessary for Allied planes to operate over Rome our aviators are thoroughly informed as to the location of the Vatican and have been specifically instructed to prevent bombs from falling within the Vatican City." FDR Library, psfa 495, pp. 69–71.

32. The contrast between the British prime minister's pugnacious stance and the solicitous attitude of the American president had long been clear to the pope, who would repeatedly turn to Roosevelt rather than to Churchill for support. The memo that the British government sent in late June to the Vatican secretary of state made this contrast apparent. "For immediate practical purposes it is not possible to discriminate between Italian Fascist leadership and policy on the one hand and the Italian people on the other, and Italy is inevitably identified with Mussolini and his policy." In England, where people unhappy with the government were free to change it, the Foreign Office explained, "the blind submission of the Italian people to Mussolinian leadership is partly incomprehensible and, in so far as it is appreciated, a matter for mixed pity and contempt." Not only had there been no sign from the Italian king or the Italian people that they disapproved of Mussolini's policies, but there was good reason to suppose that had Mussolini been able to win the war in short order as he thought he would, "he would have been acclaimed by the Italian people as an astute statesman and a brilliant leader and benefactor of his country." It was impossible to have any sympathy for the Italians; nor could any thought be given to allowing the country to bargain its way out of the war that it had so wantonly begun. Fascism had to be destroyed, and Italy had to surrender unconditionally. Légation de Grande Bretagne à la Secrétairerie d'État, Vatican City, June 28, 1943, ADSS, vol. 7, n. 271.

33. Hull to FDR, June 29, 1943, FDR Library, psfa 495, pp. 83–86.

34. Bishop Colli, director of Italian Catholic Action, the diplomat pointed out, had recently issued a similar appeal: "Now that the war is totalitarian, to subtract yourself from certain social duties means to be a deserter; it might also mean, in certain cases, to become a traitor." D'Ajeta to Ministero degli Affari Esteri, June 12, 1943, n. 1882/717, ASDMAE, AISS, b. 164.

35. Osborne to Foreign Office, and Montgomery to Foreign Office, June 13, 1943, NAK, FO 371, 37537, 61–66. The June 15 report from Berlin was sent on by the Italian Foreign Ministry to its embassy to the Holy See on June 18, tel. 19700, ASDMAE, APSS, b. 68.

Mussolini's *Il Popolo d'Italia* also devoted a long, respectful article to the pope's speech. "Il discorso del Papa contro il bolscevismo," June 15, 1943, p. 4. On the strikes in northern Italy, see Gooch 2020, p. 365.

36. Maglione to Babuscio Rizzo, May 3, 1943; Babuscio Rizzo to Maglione, May 5, 1943; Babuscio Rizzo to Generale Cesare A.M.E., Capo del S.I.M., Roma, June 3, 1943, AAV, *Carte Babuscio Rizzo,* b. 1, fasc. 4, sottofasc. 8, ff. 2r–3r, 4r–5r, 6r–7r. "It is with great pleasure," wrote Monsignor Luigi Micara, the nuncio, to Babuscio in an effusive letter of thanks in mid-June, "that I learned the news from my nephew of his new posting in your Ministry." Mons. Luigi Micara to Babuscio Rizzo, June 12, 1943, AAV, *Carte Babuscio Rizzo,* b. 1, fasc. 4, sottofasc. 8, ff. 8r–9v.

37. In mid-June, the French ambassador to the Holy See wrote to Vichy to warn that the men in the Vatican thought that the Allies would likely land not on Italian territory but on the Mediterranean coast of France, intending to make Provence their base for an assault on northern Italy. Bérard to Laval and Rochat, June 14, 1939, MAEC, Guerre Vichy, 544.

CHAPTER 29: THE GOOD NAZI

1. Report to Mussolini, July 5, 1943, ACS, SPD, CR, b. 12; "La presentazione delle credenziali del nuovo Ambasciatore di Germania," OR, July 5, 1943, p. 1.

2. Welles report, March 1, 1940, FDR Library, psfa 71, pp. 41–43; Wheeler-Bennett 1954, p. 416; Hill 1987, p. 477; Hill 1967, pp. 138–41; Namier 1952, p. 63; Lippman 1997, pp. 107–8. As a December 1944 OSS report concluded of von Weizsäcker, "his own nationalist aspirations for Germany and his long experience as a diplomat make him very useful to the Nazis." FDR Library, psf 794, p. 91.

3. Rossi Longhi, Ministero degli Affari Esteri, to Orsenigo, Berlin, April 21, 1943, tel. 13312, ASDMAE, APSS, b. 66. The appointment to the Vatican embassy signaled a dramatic demotion for the German state secretary. Ribbentrop, who had been a salesman before his rapid rise through the Nazi hierarchy, had become increasingly uncomfortable with the polished diplomat who served under him. Compared to Ribbentrop's warmongering, Weizsäcker was a moderate, and the foreign minister finally got rid of him by sending him far from Berlin to a post he had earlier considered abolishing. But for Weizsäcker, the change was not without its attractions. With the war turning against the Axis, the Vatican appeared as the most promising place to explore bringing about a compromise peace that might save him and others like him. Hill 1967, p. 143.

4. On the request regarding a religious studies course, see Di Meglio notes, July 9, 1943, ASRS, *AA.EE.SS.,* Pio XII, parte 1, Germania, posiz. 866, ff. 14rv.

5. Weizsäcker to Foreign Ministry, Berlin, July 5, 1943, tel. 271, PAAA, GBS, 29818, 17–18; Chadwick 1977, pp. 181–82; Miccoli 2000, p. 237.

6. Regia Prefettura di Roma, nota, controllo dell'attività del clero, July 5, 1943, ACS, MI, Gab., RSI, b. 51, n. 10952.

7. De Felice 1996b, pp. 1151, 1184 (based on Puntoni's diary entry, July 5, 1943).

8. FDR to Churchill, July 9, 1943, FDR Library, mr 21, pp. 44–45; Eden and Halifax to Washington and Algiers, July 9, 1943, NAK, CAB, 122/866, 7–8.

9. Atkinson 2007. At the time of the Allied landing, according to Gooch (2020, p. 378) the Germans had 28,000 troops in Sicily, the Italians 175,000.

10. Tardini notes, July 11, 1943, ADSS, vol. 7, n. 287. The original documentation on Roosevelt's message and the pope's response can be found at AAV, *Segr. Stato,* 1943, Stati e Corpo Diplomatico, posiz. 199, ff. 1r–15r.

11. Ciano appunto, July 13, 1943, n. 2252, ASDMAE, Gab., b. 1198, UC-82; Tittmann 2004, p. 159.

12. Maglione to Cicognani, Washington, July 15, 1943, ADSS, vol. 7, n. 297.

13. Pirelli 1984, p. 450, diary entry for July 19, 1943; Tittmann 2004, p. 177. In De Felice's (1996b, pp. 1316–17) examination of the Fummi affair, he writes that before taking his initiative, Bastianini had gotten an indication from Mussolini that he was open to negotiations, and indeed, Bastianini thought the Duce should not be overthrown as only he would be in a position to convince Hitler to allow Italy to withdraw from the war. See also De Felice 1970.

14. Bastianini 2005, p. 131.

15. Edda Mussolini 1975, pp. 174–75; Bosworth 2017, p. 170; Festorazzi 2012, pp. 89–95; General Carboni report, in De Felice 1996b, p. 1536.

16. De Felice 1996b, pp. 1537–40.

17. Bosworth 2017, pp. 169, 171; Gagliani 2015.

CHAPTER 30: DEPOSING THE DUCE

1. Bottai 1989, pp. 392–98, diary entry for July 16, 1943.

2. De Felice 1996b, pp. 1322–38; Kershaw 2000, pp. 592–93.

3. Tittmann 2004, pp. 162–63.

4. Eisenhower report, July 20, 1943, FDR Library, mr 303, pp. 84–86, 88; report from Air Force, Cairo, July 20, 1943, FDR Library, mr 303, pp. 87, 89–90; Davis 2006, p. 130.

5. Roberts 2018, p. 789; Pirelli 1984, p. 457, diary entry for July 23, 1943.

6. Police reports of the pope's July 19, 1943, visit to the site of the bombing, dated July 19 and July 20, nn. 22901 and 149268, are found at ACS, MI, DAGRA 1943, b. 71, and ACS, SPD, CR, b. 127.

7. Bastianini 2005, p. 141; Pirelli 1984, p. 457, diary entry for July 23, 1943.

8. Marco Maffei, "Il Papa si inginocchia sulle macerie della distrutta Basilica di San Lorenzo," and "La promessa del bugiardo," PI, July 20, 1943, p. 1. Two days later the newspaper returned to the theme, titling its front-page story, "The Weeping of the Pope at the Ruins of the Basilica of San Lorenzo." It quoted the rector of the basilica as saying the pope had been so moved by the sight of the destruction that he could barely speak. "He broke out in tears; for the whole time he remained there to pray the tears ran in furrows down his face. The Holy Father's tears," said the rector, "were more eloquent than any speech, they were the most severe condemnation of the authors of the vile attack." "Il pianto del Papa sulle rovine della basilica di S. Lorenzo," PI, July 22, 1943, p. 1. Farinacci's newspaper carried similar stories portraying the heroic pope amid the ruins of the basilica, e.g., "Il Pontefice tra i sinistrati della zona Tiburtina," RF, July 20, 1943, p. 1.

9. Maglione to the nuncios and apostolic delegates, July 20, 1943, ADSS, vol. 7, n. 302. At the same time the pope sent a long message directly to President Roosevelt, expressing his sorrow at the large number of civilians killed by the bombings and adding that given the nature of Rome, it "cannot be attacked without inflicting an incomparable loss on the patrimony of Religion and Civilization." Pius XII to FDR, July 20, 1943, ADSS, vol. 7, n. 303. A copy of the pope's original letter is found at FDR Library, psfa 495, pp. 104–8.

    On receiving the pope's instructions, the nuncio in Spain passed them on to the Spanish primate, the archbishop of Toledo. He in turn promptly sent a message to Roosevelt. Writing on behalf of the Spanish Catholic episcopacy, he called on the president never to bomb Rome again. Secretary of State Cordell Hull was not sympathetic. Instructing the American ambassador in Madrid to give the archbishop no such assurance, he added a further thought: "It is not recalled, incidentally, that the Spanish Episcopacy ever protested against the unchristian acts that have characterized Axis warfare. Our bombing of Rome, made necessary by the Italian Government, was carried out with great care to inflict as little damage as possible on cultural monuments and church property, and it may be remarked that from this as well as from the military standpoint the raid was remarkably successful." U.S. Ambassador Hayes, Madrid, to Hull, July 21, 1943, and Hull to Hayes, July 24, 1943, FRUS 1943, vol. 2, pp. 933–34.

10. Osborne to Eden, July 21, 1943, NAK, FO 371, 37537, pp. 148–51. Here I use the English translation that Osborne provided to London (found at pp. 152–55 of his report). The original text of the pope's letter can be found in "Una Lettera del Sommo Pontefice al Cardinale Vicario in Roma," OR, July 22, 1943, p. 1. Taylor to FDR and Hull, July 24, 1943, FDR Library, psfa 495, p. 116.

11. "Il bombardamento di Roma: La deplorazione del Pontefice bolla di eterna ignominia gli aggressori," RF, July 23, 1943, p. 1.

12. Hennesey 1974, p. 49, McCormick diary entry for July 24, 1943.

13. Bottai 1989, pp. 402–4, diary entry for July 22, 1943.

14. Pirelli 1984, p. 451, diary entry for July 23, 1943.

15. Many first-person accounts by the men at that historic Grand Council meeting exist. Needless to say, they are all self-serving and offer a kaleidoscope of conflicting narratives. Emilio Gentile (2018) has recently devoted an entire book to trying to disentangle them. Among the other accounts relied on here are Bottai's 1989, pp. 404–21, diary entry for July 24, 1943; and Bastianini 2005, p. 291. A good assortment of materials on the meeting collected by the French diplomatic service is found at MAEC, Papiers Chauvel, vol. 121, pp. 901–61. See also Carace 2021.

16. Pighin 2010, pp. 179–80; Montini notes, July 25, 1943, ADSS, vol. 7, n. 313. Apparently, Ciano also rushed a copy of the Grand Council's resolution to Cardinal Maglione that morning. Di Rienzo 2018, p. 515.

17. Ivone 2002, p. 27.

18. Bosworth 2017, p. 171.

19. Clara quotes from her July 25, 1943, letter to Mussolini in a letter she wrote him on its first anniversary, ACS, Archivi di famiglie e di persone, Clara Petacci, b. 4, fasc. 63.

20. De Felice 1996b, pp. 1391–1401. A rich, dramatic account of Mussolini's state of mind over the following two days, while he was confined at a military installation in Rome, was composed by the military doctor who visited him throughout his time there and had several conversations with him. Somehow his account, which ranges from Mussolini's medical history to his musings on the current state of Italy and the war, ended up in the office of the Vatican Secretariat of State, where it can now be found. ASRS, *AA.EE.SS.*, Pio XII, Parte I, Italia, posiz. 1336, ff. 76r–78r.

21. "Il Maresciallo Badoglio Primo Ministro," OR, July 26, 1943, p. 1; "Il nuovo governo italiano," OR, July 28, 1943, p. 1; Pighin 2010, pp. 180–81.

22. "L'esultanza di Milano," CS, July 26, 1943, p. 1; Pighin 2010, pp. 184–85; Tramontin 1982, p. 633.

23. The handwritten note on Tardini's report reads: "His Eminence [Maglione] discussed these arguments with His Holiness in the audience of July 26, 1943. The Holy Father deigned to dwell on the question: in the face of an official request, how could the Pope refuse to take part after having so often recommended peace?" ASRS, *AA.EE.SS.*, Pio XII, Parte I, Italia, posiz. 1336, ff. 123r–28r. The underlines are in the original.

24. Babuscio report, signed Pucci, n.d., AAV, *Carte Babuscio Rizzo*, b. 1, fasc. 2, ff. 110–11.

CHAPTER 31: MUSICAL CHAIRS

1. OSS report, July 28, 1943, FDR Library, mr 436, pp. 111–12.

2. Ivone 2002, p. 27; Grandi 1985, pp. 602–3; Cannistraro 1982, pp. 53–55.

3. FDR to Churchill, July 25, 1943, FDR Library, mr 159, p. 153; Churchill to FDR, July 28, 1943, FDR Library, mr 159, pp. 142–44; Hull 1948, vol. 2, p. 1361; Osborne to Maglione, August 4, 1943, ADSS, vol. 7, n. 328. The ellipsis is in the original.

4. Eisenhower to War Department, July 26, 1943, FDR Library, mr 159, pp. 150–51; FDR

to Churchill, July 27 and 28, 1943, FDR Library, mr 21, pp. 117–19 and 122–23. For the final text of Eisenhower's message to the Italian people, see War Department to Eisenhower, July 28, 1943, FDR Library, mr 159, p. 132.

5. Churchill to FDR, July 29, 1943, FDR Library, mr 159, pp. 125–26. On the British POWs in Italy in August 1943, see Teresa Malice, "Prigionieri militari nella Seconda guerra mondiale tra Italia e Inghilterra," *E-Review: Rivista degli Istituti Storici dell'Emilia Romagna in Rete* (2013), doi: 10.12977/ereview44.

In the wake of Mussolini's overthrow, the German government was eager to extract British POWs to Germany, afraid that if they remained in Italy they might be freed. On August 25, Babuscio gave Cardinal Maglione a typed sheet reporting a conversation he had had the previous day with Otto von Bismarck, from the German embassy in Rome. Bismarck had told him that "Germany is urgently requesting all the prisoners of war that German troops captured in North Africa and Sicily," saying that the "German army has the right to have these prisoners." The Germans were demanding that at least fifty thousand POWs be transported immediately to Germany. ASRS, *AA.EE.SS.,* Pio XII, parte I, Italia, posiz. 1336, ff. 249rv.

6. Goebbels 1948, pp. 407–16, diary entry for July 27, 1943.

7. Maglione notes, July 27, 1943, ADSS, vol. 7, n. 316. The list of Mussolini family members is found with Maglione's handwritten note, dated August 28, 1943, at ASRS, *AA.EE.SS.,* Pio XII, parte I, Italia, posiz. 1336, ff. 250r–51r. On the ties that members of the Mussolini family, including Rachele, had with the Vatican, see also the government informant reports at ACS, MIFP, serie B, b. 8, "Mussolini famiglia."

8. The previous morning the pope had met with another leading member of the Fascist Grand Council, Luigi Federzoni, for an hourlong private audience. See the undated report found at AAV, *Carte Babuscio Rizzo,* b. 1, fasc. 2, f. 113r.

9. Grandi 1985, pp. 651–52. Grandi would be the beneficiary of Vatican support following the fall of Fascism, relying in good part on Monsignor Montini. See the thick file of correspondence at AAV, *Segr. Stato,* 1950–54, Stati e Corpo diplomatico, posiz. 352.

10. Bastianini 2005, pp. 223–27.

11. Guariglia 1950, pp. 739–40.

12. Guariglia to Babuscio Rizzo, July 30, 1943, tel. 23678, ASDMAE, Gab., b. 1198, UC–82; Guariglia 1950, pp. 739–40; Weizsäcker to Foreign Ministry, Berlin, August 4, 1943, tel. 339, PAAA, GBS, 29818, 24–25. More detail on Babuscio's diplomatic career, including his PNF membership booklet, can be found in ASDMAE, Personale Serie VII, Babuscio Rizzo.

13. Tortoreto 1956; Di Capua 2005, pp. 414–15.

14. OSS report, August 1, 1943, FDR Library, mr 436, p. 52; Colli, August 2, 1943, ASDMAE, AISS, b. 130. In its first report on the Catholic press under the new regime, the Italian embassy to the Holy See told how all of the country's major Catholic press had immediately called for good Catholics to support the new government. August 5, 1943, tel. 2502, ACS, MCPG, b. 133. Fear of popular disorder following the regime's collapse and especially fear of a Communist uprising in Italy's northern cities led the government to turn to the Vatican for help. The head of the propaganda ministry sent a note to Guariglia, the new foreign minister. In the wake of the dissolution of the Fascist Party and the installation of the new government, he advised, there was urgent need for a propaganda effort, aimed particularly at the industrial workers and their families, to combat the subversive movements active among them: "The aid of the clergy would seem to be particularly indicated." The memo suggested that Guariglia sound out the Vatican, so that the propaganda ministry could "inform the Prefects of the Kingdom of the resulting agreements for a necessary action of coordination with the religious Authorities."

Guariglia took the proposal to Cardinal Maglione and Monsignor Montini, who voiced their full support. Catholic Action had already issued a call for obedience to the new authorities, and the cardinal said that many of Italy's bishops were spontaneously making pleas of this kind as well. A similar report of the support by Italy's high clergy was sent to Guariglia by Babuscio Rizzo from the Italian embassy to the Vatican on August 10; n. 2572/979, ASDMAE, AISS, b. 164.

At the same time, Maglione made a request of the foreign minister. The Vatican had learned that the new government was planning to replace Luigi Federzoni as head of the prestigious Royal Academy of Italy with the renowned humanist, Benedetto Croce, a man known for his diffidence toward the institutional church. Such an appointment, argued the cardinal, would be offensive to all good Catholics. Responding to his request, Guariglia assured him that there was no plan to appoint a new head of the academy. Indeed, having been established under Fascism and closely bound to it, the academy would be allowed to die. Rocco, Ministry of Popular Culture, Appunto per Guariglia, August 9, 1943, and Guariglia reply, August 10, 1943, nn. 29648, 2602/989, ASDMAE, AISS, b. 130. See also AAV, *Arch. Nunz. Italia,* b. 31, fasc. 7, ff. 2r, 3r, 4r.

15.   The other security issue facing the pope in the wake of the fall of the Fascist government concerned the sporadic cases of German soldiers seeking haven in Vatican City. On August 25, the commander of the Pontifical Gendarmes, a separate unit from the Swiss Guards, responded to the request communicated to him by Cardinal Maglione "to formulate proposals with the aim of avoiding a repetition of the incidents recently provoked by the deserters Henry Hannemann and Augustus Filusch." The cardinal had reached a secret agreement with the Italian police to have it station "a special service of vigilance near the entrances of the [Vatican] State to intervene before the soldiers cross into the territory of Vatican City with the intention of seeking refuge there or when the soldiers themselves, having been turned away at one of the entrances, try to sneak into Vatican City through another entrance." AAV, Segr. Stato, 1943, Stato Città Vaticano, posiz. 108, ff. 1r–33r.

16.   Marras report to Badoglio, July 30, 1943, ASDMAE, Gab., b. 1159A, UC–43 fasc. 1.

17.   July 31 reports found at ASDMAE, Gab., b. 1159A, UC–43, fasc. 3.

18.   Rauscher 2004, p. 480.

19.   Maglione notes, July 31, 1943, ADSS, vol. 7, n. 321.

20.   Weizsäcker to Foreign Ministry, Berlin, August 1, 1943, PAAA, GARV, R235, 09.

21.   Italian embassy to the Secretariat of State, July 31, 1943; Maglione to Cicognani, Washington, August 1, 1943; and Maglione to Godfrey, London, August 2, 1943, ADSS, vol. 7, nn. 322, 323, 324.

22.   Cicognani, Washington, D.C., to Welles, August 2, 1943, FRUS 1943, vol. 2, pp. 938–39; War Department to Eisenhower, August 2, 1943, FDR Library, mr 303, p. 80; Eisenhower to General Marshall, August 3, 1943, FDR Library, mr 303, pp. 76–77; Eisenhower to Marshall, August 3, 1943, FDR Library, mr 303, p. 75.

23.   "Draft conditions for open city," U.S. War Department, August 2, 1943, FDR Library, mr 303, pp. 46–47; FDR to Churchill, August 3, 1943, FDR Library, mr 303, p. 42; Churchill to FDR, August 3, 1943, FDR Library, mr 303, pp. 43–33, 78.

24.   Eisenhower to Marshall, August 4, 1943, FDR Library, mr 303, pp. 72–73.

25.   Churchill to FDR, August 4, 1943, FRUS 1943, vol. 2, pp. 939–40.

26.   US Joint Chiefs to FDR, August 5, 1943, FDR Library, mr 303, pp. 35–37.

CHAPTER 32 : BETRAYAL

1.   Rauscher 2004, pp. 480–81.

2.   Pirelli 1984, pp. 460–61, diary entry for August 3, 1943.

3.   Tardini notes, August 4, 1943, ADSS, vol. 7, n. 327; De Blesson report, October 1943, MAEN, RSS 576, PO/1, 1183. The day earlier Tittmann had sent in a report on the mood

in the Vatican, highlighting fears there of a German takeover. He added his own observation that Romans' apathy "suggests popular uprising against Germans near future is unlikely." The Romans were certainly eager for peace, but, he observed, "people are counting on us rather than own efforts to get them out of war." Tittmann to Hull, August 3, 1943, FRUS 1943, vol. 2, pp. 345–46.

4. Weizsäcker to Foreign Ministry, Berlin, August 4, 1943, PAAA, GBS, 29818, 24–25.

5. Hennesey 1974, pp. 51–52. The quotes from the pope's call to prayer are taken from the English translation that Osborne provided in his August 10, 1943, report to Eden, NAK, FO 371, 37537, 166–69.

6. British Consul General, Tangiers, to Foreign Office, London, FDR Library, mr 159, pp. 74–76. The quotes are from the consul general's report of his conversation with the Italian emissary.

7. Tardini handwritten note, July 30, 1943, ASRS, *AA.EE.SS.*, Pio XII, parte I, Italia, posiz. 1336, ff. 1311–32r.

8. Tacchi Venturi to Maglione, August 10, 1943. ADSS, vol. 9, n. 289.

9. Maglione to Tacchi Venturi, August 18, 1943, ADSS, vol. 9, nn. 289, 296.

10. Tacchi Venturi to Maglione, August 29, 1943, ADSS, vol. 9, n. 317.

11. Davis 2006, 148; De Wyss 1945, p. 83; Questura di Roma alla Prefettura et al., August 13, 1943, ACS, MI, DAGRA 1943, b. 71, n. 161250-066695.

12. Questura di Roma al Capo della polizia e al Prefetto di Roma, August 14, 1943, ACS, DAGR, A5G, IIGM, b. 134, n. 05161; Rossi 2005, pp. 419–20.

13. KKADC Quebec to War Department, August 14, 1943, FDR Library, mr 303, p. 68; Eisenhower, Algiers, to War Department, August 15, 1943, FDR Library, mr 303, p. 63; Combined Chiefs of Staff to Eisenhower, August 15, 1943, FDR Library, mr 303, pp. 62 and 64. The next two weeks saw a constant stream of messages back and forth between Cardinal Maglione and the apostolic delegate in Washington, as they pleaded with the Allies to stop the bombing of Rome. The cardinal's messages made clear a point he had initially avoided: if the Italian government remained publicly committed to the Axis cause, it was only because it was paralyzed by the prospect of German military intervention. Some of this correspondence can be found in ADSS, vol. 7, including nn. 355, 576, but see the account in the August 21, 1943, U.S. Chronicle, FDR Library, psfa 495, p. 138. See also the memo that Cicognani sent to the U.S. State Department on August 18, FRUS 1943, vol. 3, pp. 944–45.

For his part, on August 16, Monsignor Godfrey, the apostolic delegate in London, reported to Maglione on what Britain's minister of information, Brendan Bracken, described as an "intimate friend of Churchill," told him. The British understood that Badoglio was in a difficult position, but as time passed, public opinion was becoming hostile to the new Italian government, "and now it is said openly that the departure of Mussolini has only decapitated Fascism, leaving its body substantially intact." The notion that some kind of deal could be had that would leave Italian soil free from Allied occupation, said the British minister, was a pure "fantasy," as the Allies were intent on occupying any part of the country that would prove useful to prosecuting their war on Germany. Godfrey to Maglione, August 16, 1943, ASRS, Gab., Pio XII, parte I, Italia, posiz. 1336, ff. 181r–82r.

14. De Wyss 1945, p. 94.

15. On the Petaccis, see Montevecchi 2011; Chessa and Raggi 2010; Bosworth 2017, pp. 174, 180–81. Clara Petacci's jail-time diary entries are found in ACS, Archivi di famiglie e di persone, Clara Petacci, b. 10, fasc. 159. Reports of the popular joy greeting word of the Petacci family's fall can be found in "Le sorelle Petacci arrestate per spionaggio?" *L'Italia,* August 30, 1943, p. 1; and "Raccolta delle prove documentali [informative da Città del Vaticano per il periodo dicembre 1942–settembre 1943] per il procedimento penale istruito contro Trojani Virginio di Nerfa," ASR, Galla Placidia, CAP, Sezione Istruttoria,

b. 1669, f. 1010. In the wake of the liberation of Rome, the Italian government was also launching investigations into the corruption of leading figures in the Fascist regime; see Canali and Volpini 2019.

16. Guariglia, Memorandum per Badoglio, August 28, 1943, ASDMAE, Gab., b. 1159, UC–43, fasc. 6.

17. Tittmann 2004, p. 82. On Galeazzi, see Informativa n. 40 (Troiani), January 18, 1940, ACS, MIFP, b. 546, and other police informant files found at b. 546; Comando Supremo S.I.M., Centro C.S. di Roma, October 7, 1944, AUSSME, SIM, Div. 1, faldone n. 67. Osborne would later refer to Galeazzi as "a great personal friend of the Pope" and "certainly the most influential layman" in the Vatican. Osborne to Foreign Office, June 6, 1946, NAK, FO 371, 60812, ZM 1993, 1946.

18. The Galeazzi mission is explained by Tardini in a note written on June 26, 1944, and placed as an annex to the document containing Galeazzi's instructions. Maglione to Cicognani, August 28, 1943, ADSS, vol. 7, n. 374. A note by Tardini records the pope's approval for the text given on August 28.

19. Osborne to Foreign Office, London, September 2, 1943, NAK, FO 371, 37537, 163–64; Bérard to Foreign Ministry, Vichy, September 4, 1943, MAEC, Guerre Vichy, 544; Babuscio Rizzo to Foreign Ministry, Rome, September 5, 1943, tel. 24683, ASDMAE, APSS, b. 64. A Luce video of the pope's radio address is accessible at https://patrimonio .archivioluce.com/luce-web/detail/IL5000018619/2/sommo-pontefice-invia-messaggio -al-mondo-pace-e-giustizia-i-popoli.html.

20. Robert Murphy to FDR, September 8, 1943, FDR Library, mr 855, pp. 228–36.

21. Eisenhower, Algiers, to War Department, and Algiers to War Department, September 1, 1943, FDR Library, mr 160, pp. 50–51, 53–56.

22. FDR and Churchill to Eisenhower, Algiers, September 2, 1943, FDR Library, mr 160, p. 48. At the same time, the two leaders wrote to Stalin to explain their plan: "Our invasion of the mainland begins almost immediately, and the heavy blow called AVALANCHE will be struck in the next week or so. The difficulties of the Italian Government and people in extricating themselves from Hitler's clutches may make a still more daring enterprise necessary, for which General Eisenhower will need as much Italian help as he can get. The Italian acceptance of the terms is largely based on the fact that we shall send an airborne division to Rome to enable them to hold off the Germans, who have gathered Panzer strength in that vicinity and who may replace the Badoglio Government with a Quisling administration probably under Farinacci." FDR and Churchill to Stalin, September 2, 1943, FDR Library, mr 160, pp. 45–46.

23. Eisenhower, Algiers, to USFOR London and War Department, September 3, 1943, FDR Library, mr 160, p. 41; Algiers to War Department, September 6, 1943, FDR Library, mr 160, p. 36.

24. Badoglio to Eisenhower, September 8, 1943, DDI, series 9, vol. 10, n. 769; Eisenhower to War Department, September 8, 1943, FDR Library, mr 160, p. 25.

25. War Department to Eisenhower, September 8, 1943, FDR Library, mr 160, p. 19; Eisenhower, Algiers, to Badoglio, September 8, 1943, DDI, series 9, vol. 10, n. 770.

26. Gabinetto, Questura Roma, al MI-DGPS, September 8, 1943, ACS, DAGR, A5G, IIGM, b. 146, n. 176776/Gab.; MAEC, Papiers Chauvel, vol. 121, pp. 923–34; Klinkhammer 1993, pp. 32–33.

CHAPTER 33: FAKE NEWS

1. On Mafalda's arrest, imprisonment, and death at Buchenwald, see D'Assia 1992 and Barneschi 1982. A number of historians have speculated that the king's escape was facilitated by the German general Kesselring, who thought having the king gone would lead to less resistance by the Italian military to the taking of Rome. Mattesini 2015, pp. 91–92.

2. Eisenhower to War Department, Algiers, telegram, September 18, 1943, FRUS 1943, vol. 2, p. 331.

3. Notes, Secrétairerie d'État, September 9, 1943, and Montini notes, September 9, 1943, ADSS, vol. 7, nn. 389, 391; Guariglia 1950, p. 718.

4. Goebbels 1948, p. 427, diary entry for September 9, 1943; "Evolution de l'Italie en 1943," MAEC, Papiers Chauvel, vol. 121, pp. 216–17; Davis 2006, p. 173.

5. Montini notes, September 9, 1943, ADSS, vol. 7, n. 390; Weizsäcker to Berlin, telegrams, September 9 and 10, 1943, PAAA, GBS, 29818, 31, 32, 33.

6. Montini notes, September 10, 1943, ADSS, vol. 7, nn. 392, 394, 397; Goebbels 1948, pp. 443–44, diary entry for September 11, 1943. Before reaching Kesselring's aide on September 10, Weizsäcker had sent a telegram to Berlin reporting his meeting with Maglione and asking that, as his contact with Kesselring had been broken, the German military commanders in Rome contact him immediately. PAAA, GBS, 29818, 34.

7. Eisenhower to Badoglio, and Churchill and FDR to Badoglio and the Italian people, September 10, 1943, FDR Library, mr 160, pp. 4–5, 6–7.

8. De Felice 1997, pp. 78, 155; Goeschel 2018, p. 260. On Italian soldiers imprisoned in Germany, see Avagliano and Palmieri 2020. On Italians doing forced labor in Germany, see D'Amico, Guerrini, and Mantelli 2020.

9. Pighin 2010, pp. 195–97.

10. Stefani report, September 15, 1943, NAK, FO 371, 37571; unsigned, undated report, NARA, RG 84, box 5, 800 It-Vatican, p. 28; French embassy, Vatican, to French Foreign Ministry, Vichy, October 1943, MAEN, RSS 576, PO/1, 1183. On the agreement with the Germans that led to the posting of German military guards, see Weizsäcker to Berlin, September 15, 1943, PAAA, GPA, Vatikan Kirche 6, R98833, 06.

11. De Felice 1997, pp. 37–43, 52–73; Boiardi et al. 1990, pp. 12–14; A. Rosso diary, September 15, 1943, n. 097835, ASDMAE, RSI, Gab., b. 1; Bosworth 2017, pp. 181–82.

12. Montini notes, September 16, 1943, ADSS, vol. 7, n. 406.

13. Franz von Sonnleithner (assistant to Ribbentrop) to Weizsäcker, September 17, 1943, and Weizsäcker to Berlin, September 18, 1943, PAAA, GBS, 29818, 35–36.

14. Weizsäcker to Berlin, September 18, 1943, PAAA, GPA, Vatikan Kirche 6, R98833, 02–03.

15. Weizsäcker to Berlin, September 21 and 22, 1943, PAAA, GBS, 29818, 37–38 and 40–41. Ribbentrop's continued concern about the Allies' propaganda efforts to portray the pope as endangered by the German occupation of Rome continued in the following month. He sent long instructions to Weizsäcker telling him to ask for a meeting with the pope to urge him to publicly denounce the propaganda, including a statement made by President Roosevelt himself. Ribbentrop to Weizsäcker, October 1943, PAAA, GBS, 29818, 52–53.

16. Weizsäcker to Reich foreign minister and the state secretary, September 23, 1943, PAAA, GBS, 29818, 44.

17. Steengracht to Weizsäcker, September 24, 1943, PAAA, GBS, 29818, 48–51.

18. One indication of how this dilemma presented itself to Pius XII comes from a request sent by Father Gemelli, rector of the Catholic University of Milan, who had been until recently one of Mussolini's greatest boosters in the upper ranks of Italy's clergy. In late September Gemelli sent one of his trusted fellow clerics to Rome with an urgent request for the pope. What should he do, he asked, if, as seemed not unlikely, he was called upon to pledge loyalty to Mussolini's new government? Early the next month, his emissary returned to Rome, where he met with Montini. "Events force me," wrote Gemelli in the note he sent with his envoy, "to again send you a trusted person to ask for further instructions, for which I greatly feel the necessity given the new situation. . . . Milan will not only be a land occupied by the Reich, but public instruction there will depend on the Ministry of National Education of the new republican Fascist Government."

Gemelli's request shows how the Vatican could in these months make use of the ambiguous position of Babuscio, in charge of Italy's embassy to the Holy See. As long as neither Babuscio nor the pope wanted to force the issue, each of the two competing governments could claim that the embassy represented it. "I asked His Excellency Babuscio," wrote Montini, "to confidentially recommend to the Minister of National Education (new Government!) not to place the Catholic University in the necessity of declaring itself for or against." As for Gemelli, he was instructed to keep the university open but do all possible to avoid any events that could have a political connotation. In a confidential note of October 12, Montini let the rector know that they had received "a good assurance that, given the current state of things, this Fascist Republican Government will not require the Catholic University to give it any official recognition, nor impose any compromising actions on it." At this time too the pope sent instructions to all members of the Vatican Secretariat of State: when speaking of the current political situation, the less they said the better. The documentation involving Gemelli's requests and the response from the Vatican Secretariat of State in September and October 1943 are found at AAV, Segr. Stato, 1943, Seminari e Università, posiz. 35, ff. 2r–14r; Maglione notes, September 27, 1943, ADSS, vol. 7, n. 415. The pope's October 4 instructions are found at AAV, Segr. Stato, 1943, Curia Romana, posiz. 95, f. 2r. As a report from the French embassy to the Vatican put it in October: "Vatican Secretary of State hopes to avoid having to recognize the fascist, republican pseudo-government without at the same time having to formally refuse a request from Mussolini." MAEN, RSS 576, PO/1, 1183; Malgeri 1986, p. 314.

19. Macmillan and Murphy to FDR, September 20, 1943, FDR Library, mr 855, pp. 212–15.

20. Press department, Foreign Ministry, Berlin, October 6, 1943, PAAA, GPA Inland ID—Kirchenpolitik "Vatikan," Heft 1, R98841, 09–15. Kurzman (2007) devoted a book to promoting this story, which the prominent European historian István Deák (2008), in his review, poked holes in. It has been denied as well by Moellhausen (1948, pp. 157–58), who was in a good position to know.

21. Chadwick 1986, p. 275. Weizsäcker offered a further report to Berlin on October 12 on the British propaganda effort portraying a German plot to kidnap the pope, then being spread by the Reuters news agency; PAAA, GBS, 29818, 76. Perhaps as a result of Allied efforts, the rumors that the Germans were planning to kidnap the pope made their way as well into Italian police informant reports. "It is said that General Stahel has a plan to have German troops invade Vatican City" read one such report in the fall of 1943. It went on to say that the plan included kidnapping the pope. "Informazione dal Ministro dell'Interno," October–November 1943, AAV, Segr. Stato, *Commissione Soccorsi,* b. 328, fasc. 227, ff. 65r–84r.

22. Weizsäcker to Berlin, October 9, 1943, PAAA, GBS, 29818, 58–59 and 71–74.

23. Maglione notes, October 14, 1943, ADSS, vol. 7, n. 435; Weizsäcker to Berlin, October 14, 1943, PAAA, GBS, 29818, 78; Maglione to Cicognani, Washington, D.C., October 12, 1943, ADSS, vol. 7, n. 433; Cicognani cover letter, October 12, 1943, FDR Library, psfa 495, p. 165.

24. The intercepted telegram, from (Albert) Reissmann, Berlin, to Rome, is found at NAK, HW, 19/238. For background on Prinzing, see Hausmann 2002. Prinzing was also responsible for aligning the German Cultural Institutes in Italy with Nazi policies. On Nazi intelligence services in Italy, see Paehler 2017.

25. Weizsäcker to Foreign Ministry, Berlin, October 9, 1943, tel. 115, PAAA, GBS, 60–62.

CHAPTER 34: THE POPE'S JEWS

1. Picciotto Fargion 2002, p. 878.

2. The German use of mobile gas vans for killing Jews had begun in late 1941, after *Ein-*

satzgruppe members complained of fatigue and discomfort at having to shoot large numbers of women and children. Only in 1942, however, were stationary gas chambers first established in concentration camps located in Poland. See "Gassing Operations," *Holocaust Encyclopedia,* https://encyclopedia.ushmm.org/content/en/article/gassing-operations. For a timeline of events, see also https://www.ushmm.org/learn/timeline-of-events/1942–1945.

3. Klinkhammer 2016, p. 49; Sarfatti 2000, pp. 238–39; Picciotto Fargion 1994, p. 159; Katz 2003, p. 55. The size of the Jewish population in Italy at this date (even aside from the issue of how to count the thousands of Jews who had converted to Catholicism in an effort to escape persecution) is not known precisely. Since the imposition of the racial laws in 1938, many Italian Jews had fled the country, but many Jews escaping persecution in central Europe had come into Italy.

4. Coen 1993, pp. 432–45. Zolli's conversion to Catholicism in January 1945 would create a great scandal in the Jewish world. There is now a rather large literature on him, e.g., Rigano 2006; Weisbord and Sillanpoa 1992.

5. See Kertzer 2001.

6. Moellhausen 1948, pp. 112–17; Breitman and Wolfe 2005, pp. 79–80; Chadwick 1977, p. 187; Rigano 2016, p. 72; Klinkhammer 2016, p. 52. A typed note in the Vatican Secretariat of State files, dated September 27, 1943, reads, "Mons. Arata reports: Doctor Foà, Grand Rabbi of Rome, was summoned by the German police, which commanded him to deliver 50 kilograms of gold by tomorrow at 11 A.M." AAV, Segr. Stato, *Commissione Soccorsi,* b. 326, fasc. 216, f. 108r. An account of these events from the diary of Rosina Sorani, a staff member of Rome's Jewish community, is found in Avagliano and Palmieri 2011, pp. 177–79.

7. The report of this incident to the Vatican Secretariat of State office came from Marchese Serlupi, October 19, 1943, AAV, Segr. Stato, *Commissione Soccorsi,* b. 326, fasc. 216, ff. 110rv.

8. Coen 1993, pp. 64–85; Debenedetti 2001, pp. 40–46; Klinkhammer 2016, pp. 56–61; Osti Guerazzi 2017, pp. 82–83, 209–10; Chadwick 1977, pp. 190–91; Hudal to Stahel, October 16, 1943, ADSS, vol. 9, n. 373.

9. The German Jesuit Father Peter Gumpel has offered this account of the princess's hurried visit to the pope that morning. It might profit from some further confirmation, although it has been widely used by those promoting sainthood for Pius XII. Emanuele D'Onofrio, "Pio XII e la Shoah: ecco cosa raccontano i documenti dell'Archivio segreto," *Aleteria,* January 27, 2014, https://it.aleteia.org/2014/01/27/pio-xii-e-la-shoah-ecco-cosa-raccontano-i-documenti-dellarchivio-segreto/2/; Blet 1999, p. 215.

10. Susan Zuccotti (2000) aptly titled her excellent study of these events *Under His Very Windows,* referring to the imprisonment of the thousand Jews of Rome so close to Vatican City.

11. The pope's decision not to take any action that might stop the deportation of Rome's Jews, or even that might publicly show his displeasure, was no doubt due in part to his eagerness not to upset the harmonious relations he had established with the occupying German military. It is revealing that the one action taken by the papal nuncio to Italy on the day Rome's Jews were being rounded up had nothing to do with protecting the Jews. He wrote Mussolini's minister of war, Rodolfo Graziani, with a request that the Vatican be allowed to augment its Palatine Guard force to protect papal properties and the Vatican City from "disturbing elements." La Nonciature en Italie aux Autorités militaires italiennes, October 16, 1943, ADSS, vol. 9, n. 371. It is perhaps also revealing that the dramatic roundup of Rome's Jews did not distract one of the national leaders of the university branch of Catholic Action from taking time that day in Rome to write Monsignor Montini to warn of a different threat he thought required the Vatican's attention: the appearance of "Catholic communists." The writer, Giulio Andreotti, would later go

on to serve three terms as Italy's Christian Democratic prime minister. AAV, Segr. Stato, 1943, Popolazioni, posiz. 18, ff. 1r–2r.

12. Chadwick 1977, p. 194.

13. Osti Guerrazzi 2017, pp. 209–10; Mme X au cardinal Maglione, October 17, 1943, ADSS, vol. 9, n. 375; Montini notes, October 18, 1943, ADSS, vol. 9, n. 376. These appeals to the pope are also discussed in Kühlwein's (2019) recent book examining Pius XII's reaction to the October 16 roundup of Rome's Jews.

14. The report was by Don Igino Quadraroli, October 17, 1943, AAV, Segr. Stato, *Commissione Soccorsi*, b. 326, fasc. 216, f. 109. It is reproduced in ADSS, vol. 9, n. 374.

15. Ciro Giannelli to Montini, October 16, 1943, AAV, Segr. Stato, *Commissione Soccorsi*, b. 326, fasc. 216, ff. 453r–55r.

16. Montini notes, October 16, 1943, n. 369; Montini notes, October 18, 1943, ADSS, vol. 9, nn. 376 and 377. The correspondence from the Legazione del Sovrano Militare Ordine di Malta is found at AAV, Segr. Stato, *Commissione Soccorsi*, b. 326, fasc. 216, ff. 444r–49r. A list of baptized Jews on whose behalf the Vatican Secretariat of State asked the German embassy to arrange their release, dated October 23, 1943, is found at AAV, Segr. Stato, *Commissione Soccorsi*, b. 326, fasc. 216, ff. 530r–40r.

17. Coen 1993, pp. 89–93.

18. Montini notes, October 18, 1943, ADSS, vol. 9, n. 376; Klinkhammer 1993, p. 404.

19. Secretariat of State notes, October 19 and 21, 1943, AAV, Segr. Stato, *Commissione Soccorsi*, b. 326, fasc. 216, ff. 86r–88v.

20. Osti Guerrazzi 2017, p. 82; Coen 1993, pp. 103–5; Breitman and Wolfe 2005, p. 81; Katz 2003, p. 114; Calimani 2015, p. 613.

21. Osborne to Foreign Office, London, October 18, 1943, NAK, CAB, 122/866, 9. Oddly, Osborne made only indirect reference to the roundup of Rome's Jews in his report. He said he told the pope "it was the opinion of a number of people that he underestimated his own moral authority and the reluctant respect in which it was held by the Nazis because of the Catholic population in Germany; I added that I was inclined to share this opinion." On October 28, Giuseppe Dalla Torre offered the pope further reason to believe that the German command intended to leave Rome intact, sending Cardinal Maglione a report he had gotten from a member of the German embassy in Rome. It stated that an earlier German military plan to blow up Rome's bridges and other structures of military importance when they eventually retreated from the city had been disapproved by Berlin. Dalla Torre ended his report, "Therefore, although it seems incredible, we can conclude that the destruction that the Germans will wreak in Rome in the days of their evacuation will be minimal." Dalla Torre to Maglione, October 28, 1943, ASRS, AA.EE.SS., Pio XII, parte I, Italia, posiz. 1336, ff. 292r–93v.

22. Tittmann to secretary of state, Washington, D.C., October 19, 1943, FDR Library, psfa 495, p. 106.

23. Pighin 2010, pp. 216–17.

24. These documents are found at AAV, Segr. Stato, *Commissione Soccorsi*, b. 326, fasc. 216, ff. 530r–40r.

25. Panzieri to Pius XII, October 27, 1943, ADSS, vol. 9, n. 394; Secrétairerie d'État à Ambassade d'Allemagne, October 29, 1943, ADSS, vol. 9, n. 397; Maglione to Weizsäcker, November 6, 1943, ADSS, vol. 9, n. 416.

26. Oddly, given the continuing roundup of Jews that would take place over the following months in Rome, Weizsäcker added, perhaps in a fit of wishful thinking, "Since no more German measures towards the Jewish question can be expected to be carried out here in Rome, one could expect that this issue, which is rather unpleasant for German-Vatican relations, is gone." Weizsäcker to Berlin, October 28, 1943, PAAA, GPA, Inland ID—Kirchenpolitik "Vatikan," Heft 2, R98842, 02–03.

27. AAV, *Segr. Stato, Commissione Soccorsi,* b. 326, fasc. 216, f. 119, reproduced in ADSS, vol. 9, n. 388.

28. The documentation on this case, beginning with the October 22, 1943, letter from Ugo Di Nola to Pius XII, is found at AAV, *Segr. Stato, Commissione Soccorsi,* b. 326, fasc. 216, ff. 399r–415r. Marina and Claudio, born in Rome in 1937 and 1939 respectively, were both baptized on October 2, 1940. On the deaths of Nella, Marina, and Claudio, see Picciotto Fargion 2002.

CHAPTER 35: BASELESS RUMORS

1. Tardini notes, undated but written after the fact in 1944, ADSS, vol. 7, n. 453; Bérard to Vichy, November 10, 1943, MAEC, Guerre Vichy, 544; Tittmann to Hull, November 6, 1943, FDR Library, mr 303, p. 58; Ministero degli Affari Esteri, Appunto per il Duce, November 7, 1943, n. 096686, ASDMAE, RSI, Gab., b. 23.

2. Eden to Halifax (copy of telegram sent to Algiers), November 6, 1943, NAK, CAB, 122/865, 1; AGWAR Surles to Eisenhower, November 6, 1943, NARA, RG 84, box 5, p. 26.

3. Text Rome radio, November 6, 1943, NAK, FO 371, 37548; McGoldrick 2016, p. 777; "La Città del Vaticano bombardato," RF, November 7, 1943, p. 1. Subsequent articles told of the Catholic world's indignation at the Anglo-American assault on the Vatican. In his editorials, Farinacci suggested that the king and Badoglio might also have been involved in planning the attack, as they were, he claimed, notorious Freemasons and enemies of the Catholic Church. Roberto Farinacci, "Le bombe sul Vaticano," November 9, 1943, p. 1; "Anglicani e Badogliani contro il Vaticano," RF, November 13, 1943, p. 1.

    In replying to the Vatican request for an investigation, Osborne reminded Cardinal Maglione of his oft-repeated warning that the Germans were holding captured Allied planes ready to employ them at an opportune time to bomb the Vatican in an effort to discredit the Allies. "There is also the possibility," he reported back to London, "that some Fascists might have executed the attack without German knowledge or approval and that the Germans are now making the best propaganda use of it." Osborne to Foreign Office, London, November 6 and 7, 1943, tel. 409, 411, NAK, FO 371, 37548.

4. Eisenhower for Arnold and Surles, November 7, 1943. Eisenhower followed this up by sending Washington additional details. On the night in question, nine Allied planes had been flying in the vicinity of Rome, but visibility had been good and none reported bombing anywhere near Vatican City. "The advantage to the Germans of such a bombing," Eisenhower added, "is of course obvious. The same night it should be noted that German aircraft bombed Naples." November 7, 1943, FDR Library, mr 303, pp. 54–55, 57.

5. Conclusions of meeting of War Cabinet, 10 Downing Street, November 8, 1943, NAK, CAB, 65, 1943, p. 145.

6. On November 12 the Foreign Office sent a telegram to Osborne informing him that it had replied to the Apostolic Delegate in London's request by drawing his attention to Eisenhower's November 7 statement affirming that no Allied plane dropped bombs on the Vatican. Resident minister, Algiers, to Foreign Office, November 8, 1943, NAK, FO 371, 37548; U.S. State Department press release, November 9, 1943, n. 469, and Foreign Office to Osborne, November 12, 1943, tel. 275, NAK, FO, 371, 37548.

7. Tardini notes, undated but written after the fact in 1944, ADSS, vol. 7, n. 453. Documentation on the Vatican's own investigation of the bombing is found at ASRS, *AA.EE.SS.,* Pio XII, parte I, Stati Ecclesiastici, posiz. 755, ff. 48r–76r. Further complicating the story, a Rome police intercept recorded a November 8 phone call made by a priest, Father Giuseppe, to Father Tacchi Venturi. He had recently returned from Vit-

erbo, where a witness at the city's airport had told him that the bombing of the Vatican had been carried out by Farinacci himself, on board a plane with a Roman pilot. The transcript is reproduced in Guspini 1973, p. 249. The recent opening of the Vatican archives now introduces yet another twist in the story. The secretary of state files contains the presumed transcript of a November 7, 1943, telephone conversation in which Francesco Barracu, undersecretary to Mussolini, sent word to him that "the Vatican affair is going well, we have succeeded in misdirecting the investigations." Tardini's note on the transcript reads "Bombing of 5-XI-43" and recounts that it was taken directly to the pope. ASRS, *AA.EE.SS.*, Pio XII, Parte I, Italia, posiz. 1336, ff. 298r–303r.

8. Chessa and Raggi 2010, pp. 46–47; Aga-Rossi 2011, p. 13.

9. The radio address Mussolini was to give on October 28, one Roman police informant report asserted, had no aim other than demonstrating that he was still alive. "Raccolta delle prove documentali per il procedimento penale istruito contro Trojani," ASR, Galla Placidia, CAP, Sezione istruttoria, b.1669, fasc. 1010.

10. The Germans had even posted little papal flags around the Vatican-linked properties throughout Rome along with a notice in German and Italian signed by General Stahel proclaiming their extraterritorial status. In late October, Monsignor Costantini, secretary of the Vatican Congregation of Propaganda Fide, recorded in his diary with relief that both the German authorities and Mussolini's new republican government were treating the church deferentially. Pighin 2010, pp. 220–21.

11. Weizsäcker to Berlin, October 9, 1943, tel. 115, PAAA, GBS, 29818, 60–62.

12. Maglione notes, October 29, 1943, ADSS, vol. 7, n. 449; "Cronaca contemporanea," CC, 94 IV, Quaderno 2242 (1943), p. 267. I use, with slight changes, the English translation here that Osborne furnished in reporting the story to London on October 30. NAK, FO 371, 37571.

13. AAV, *Prefettura Casa Pontif.*, Udienze, buste 56–59. From early in the war, reports of the German priest's sympathy for the Axis cause had come into Mussolini's intelligence service. Among the relevant reports was one of July 25, 1941, recounting a conversation in which Father Pfeiffer revealed "his pride and his joy for the triumph of the Axis armies and his faith in their complete victory. He also expressed hope that Hitler will be able in the future to alter his attitude toward religion." Notizia fiduciaria, ACS, SPD, CR, b. 327. On Pfeiffer, see Samerski 2013.

14. A few days later Pius XII received Father Pfeiffer at the Apostolic Palace, where his visitor boasted of the valuable role he was playing on the pope's behalf. Among those attending the dinner, in addition to the top German military officers in Rome and Germany's ambassadors to Italy and to the Holy See, was Rodolfo Graziani, defense minister of Mussolini's new republic. Before the meal, Father Pfeiffer offered to serve as translator for Graziani's conversation with General Stahel, who complimented the priest on all the help he had provided in promoting amicable relations with the Vatican. Pfeiffer notes, November 5, 1943, ADSS, vol. 9, n. 414; original at ASRS, *AA.EE.SS.*, Pio XII, parte I, Italia, posiz. 1336, ff. 294r–95r. That Pfeiffer was regarded as something of a braggart in the Vatican is hinted at by Monsignor Tardini's handwritten comment next to the Father's account of the praise Weizsäcker had offered him: "The German ambassador in the Secretariat of State office often deplored Father Pancrazio's meddling."

Pfeiffer's presence at the dinner with with generals Stahel and Graziani did not go unnoticed by members of the Italian resistance. In the Vatican files a typed sheet can be found, signed "The Committee of National Liberation." It warned that Father Pfeiffer's frequenting of German and Fascist circles was being noted and added, "Among other things the meals consumed at the same table with General Stahel and General Graziani are not being ignored." AAV, Segr. Stato, *Commissione Soccorsi*, b. 326, fasc. 227, f. 135r. The warning was received by the Vatican in the first days of November 1943.

15. As Osborne put it in his annual report for 1943, late in the year Babuscio took up resi-

dence in Vatican City, "where he presumably continued to represent the House of Savoy and the Badoglio Government, although in a tactfully unobtrusive manner." Osborne annual report for 1943, Osborne to Eden, March 24, 1944, NAK, R 6770/ 6770/57, p. 8.

16.   As the Vatican itself had no direct contact with Badoglio, Babuscio had asked the cardinal to send the nuncio in Madrid a note he had written with a request to pass it on to the Italian ambassador there. It read: "Ambassador Babuscio Rizzo asks Ambassador Paulucci to inform Marshal Badoglio that all of the personnel of the Italian Embassy to the Holy See are faithful to His Majesty's Government, remain at their post, and neither the functionaries nor the embassy itself have thus far been molested." n. 3133, ASDMAE, APSS, b. 77, and ADSS, vol. 7, n. 437. The letter he succeeded in sending Paulucci through other channels on December 7, 1943, is found at ASDMAE, APSS, b. 72. Thus far, he explained, he had resisted all pressures to move into Vatican City. "The facts," he added, "have proved me right because . . . no damage has, at least to date, been done to either people or property." This was especially notable because outside the entrance to the embassy, alongside the papal coat of arms, he had placed the "original" royal Italian coat of arms, that is, one lacking the Fascist symbol that Mussolini had inserted at its center. "In this way," wrote Babuscio, "the Embassy, albeit although closed, has continued to exist in Rome." In fairness, he added, it must be said that no one from the Foreign Ministry (now in the hands of Mussolini's government) had exerted pressure on him to move to the new government headquarters in northern Italy or even asked his opinion. "In other words, the Embassy was officially 'ignored.' Such a favorable situation has naturally been able to be sustained thanks to the understanding of our colleagues and because it ties in closely with the decision taken by the occupiers and by those occupied not to raise the question of the Apostolic Nunciature (and, in general, of the Holy See)." Two weeks later Babuscio sent a new message. After further reflection, although he had not gotten any precise pressure to do so, he had decided to move into Vatican City and bring with him part of the embassy's archive and the items of greatest value. Babuscio Rizzo to R. Governo Brindisi, December 21, 1943, tel. 3/3, ASDMAE, APSS, b. 72.

17.   In late September, Spain's ambassador to the Holy See asked Cardinal Maglione what the Vatican would do if Mussolini called on it to publicly recognize his government. "I want to hope that such a request not be made of the Holy See," he replied. While the decision would be for the pope to decide, Maglione said, he thought they should follow their previous policy of not giving formal recognition to governments formed as a result of war, during the war, when a previously recognized legal government still existed. Maglione notes, September 27, 1943, ASRS, *AA.EE.SS.*, Pio XII, parte I, Italia, posiz. 1352b, ff. 18rv.

18.   Renato Prunas to Major General Kenyon Joyce, November 12, 1943, n. 303, ASDMAE, SG, b. 27. On the status of the racial laws at the time, see the October 1943 report at ACS, PCM43-44, Salerno-Gab., b. 11, fasc. 3–16.

19.   Prunas, Appunto per il Capo del Governo, Brindisi, November 15, 1943, ASDMAE, SG, b. 27.

20.   On the plight of Jews in Italy during the German occupation, see Osti Guerrazzi 2020.

21.   Zuccotti (2000, pp. 189–201). Zuccotti's book offers an excellent examination of the experience of Rome's Jews seeking shelter in Catholic institutions in the aftermath of October 16, 1943.

22.   Sacerdote Saverio Quadri to Secretariat of State, n.d., AAV, *Segr. Stato, Commissione Soccorsi*, b. 326, fasc. 216, f. 449r. An internal note on the priest's request in the Secretariat of State file reads, in Latin, "Quid faciendum?" (What to do?). A second handwritten note responds: "One doesn't see how the Secretariat of State can intervene."

23.   Three months after the big roundup of Jews in Rome, the Vatican Secretariat of State received a report that the Gestapo was employing the pretext of conducting a census of

artwork in the city to look for "Jewish and non-Jewish" refugees hidden in Rome's convents. A warning was sent out with the instruction that "The priors must be wary of them and ensure that during their visits they do not encounter any suspicious people." Appunto, January 22, 1944, AAV, *Segr. Stato, Commissione Soccorsi,* b. 332, fasc. 307, ff. 2r–9r.

24. Sister M. Margherita Vaccari to Pope Pius XII, August 8, 1943, AAV, *Segr. Stato, 1943,* Varie, posiz. 1632, ff. 1r–3r. The note on the nuncio's conversation with Chief of Police Carmine Senise was handwritten by Cardinal Maglione on the nun's letter.

25. The original order can be found in ACS, MI, Gabinetto RSI, Carte del Ministro Buffarini (1938–45), fasc. 75. See also Klinkhammer 1993, p. 406. News of the order made the December 1 front page both of Milan's major paper ("L'arresto di tutti gli ebrei," *Corriere della Sera*) and of Farinacci's *Il Regime Fascista* ("Tutti gli Ebrei saranno inviati in appositi campi di concentramento").

    Two weeks earlier, Father Tacchi Venturi had met with Buffarini to follow up on the Vatican's request for him to help convince the German occupation authorities to allow the number of armed Palatine Guards at the Vatican to be increased to two thousand. Buffarini assured the Jesuit emissary that he would do all he could to help. Tacchi Venturi to Maglione, November 12, 1943, AAV, *Segr. Stato, Commissione Soccorsi,* b. 326, fasc. 227, f. 137r.

26. Maglione to Weizsäcker, November 26, 1943, ADSS, vol. 9, n. 441.

27. Cardinal Rossi to Maglione, December 6, 1943, ADSS, vol. 9, n. 455. The letter by German consul Koester to Berlin is published in Friedländer 1966, pp. 209–11. The consul, in his report to Berlin, apparently thought it prudent not to admit to receiving the church dignitary at his consulate and cast the patriarch's visit as having been made not to the consulate but to "a friend of mine," who had reported the conversation in detail to him.

28. "Carità civile," OR, December 3, 1943, p. 1.

29. Southern European Analysis Radio & Press Intelligence no. 12: "The Vatican on Anti-Semitism," December 9, 1943, NARA, RG 165, color 279; Klinkhammer 1993, p. 405.

30. Avagliano and Palmieri 2011, pp. 304–6.

31. Notes de la Secrétairerie d'État, December 17, 1943, ADSS, vol. 9, n. 469.

32. Tacchi Venturi, "Nota verbale sulla situazione ebraica in Italia," December 19, 1943, ASRS, *AA.EE.SS.,* Pio XII, Asterisco Italia, posiz. 1054★, ff. 1097–1103.

33. Dell'Acqua note, November 24, 1943, ASRS, *AA.EE.SS.,* Pio XII, parte I, Jugoslavia, posiz. 160, f. 268r.

34. Dell'Acqua, December 20, 1943, ASRS, *AA.EE.SS.,* Pio XII, Asterisco Italia, posiz. 1054★, ff. 1104–5. See also Maglione notes, December 20, 1943, ADSS, vol. 9, n. 473. The Vatican Secretariat of State continued to rely on private communications with Rodolfo Graziani in calling for better treatment of Jews being rounded up in Italy. A May 11, 1944, folder in the Vatican archives is labeled "notes that should be given to Marshal Graziani." Among these is the plea: "One requests at least a less harsh treatment for the non-Aryans still detained in Italy (for example in the concentration camp of Fossoli di Carpi, [and] in the Verona prison) and the possibility for priests to have access to them." AAV, Segr. Stato, *Commissione Soccorsi,* b. 331, fasc. 285, f. 5r. This approach never had any chance of success.

    An English translation of the memos by Tacchi Venturi and Dell'Acqua is provided in Kertzer 2020.

35. The news came from General Menotti Chieli, the Italian military head of Rome at the time. Cardinal Maglione had asked the general to encourage Graziani to speak with the Duce about Vatican concerns about the new anti-Jewish measures. Chieli was reporting back on what he had learned.

36. Maglione notes, December 20, 1943, ADSS, vol. 9, n. 473. Shortly after sending in his

memo, Dell'Acqua was asked to evaluate a report the Secretariat of State had received claiming that an underground Jewish organization existed in Rome engaged in preparing false Vatican City identity documents for Jews. In his response, the monsignor said he doubted such an organization existed, but he went on to offer further thoughts on how the Vatican should deal with Jews: "Many times, however, I have been able to note that various people employed in the Vatican or close to the Vatican have concerned themselves too much (in a fashion I would dare say was almost exaggerated) with the Jews, favoring them, perhaps even with some elegant fraud. Recently it seems to me that too many non-Aryan people have been frequenting the Secretariat of State and even in the Secretariat of State itself there is too much talk about the Jews and about the related measures adopted by the Germans and by the Italian Republican Government. I have always held it to be a basic norm of wisdom to use the greatest prudence in talking with Jews." Dell'Acqua memo, December 31, 1943, AAV, Segr. Stato, *Commissione Soccorsi,* b. 302, fasc. 11, f. 3r.

According to the best recent estimates, there were 32,294 Italian Jews and another 6,842 foreign Jews trapped in German-occupied Italy. Of these 7,186 are known to have been either killed in Italy itself or deported to their death at Nazi concentration camps. Of the 32,000 Jews who survived, 6,000 did so by escaping to Switzerland, and 500–600 made their way south to safety in the Allied-controlled regions of the country. Picciotto Fargion 2016, p. 25.

CHAPTER 36: TREASON

1. Moseley 1999, p. 178.
2. Di Rienzo 2018, p. 550.
3. Corvaja 2008, p. 265.
4. On learning that Mussolini's government had arrested Ciano and other members of the Grand Council of Fascism, the pope asked Cardinal Maglione to get word to Graziani, minister of war of the Italian Social Republic, to "show mercy" in dealing with those who had voted against the Duce at that fateful July 24 meeting. Maglione note, November 29, 1943, ASRS, *AA.EE.SS.,* Pio XII, parte I, Italia, posiz. 1352b, f. 237r.
5. The OSS, the American intelligence service, would obtain a copy of twelve hundred pages of Ciano's diary in Switzerland in early February 1945. It was, as the OSS report to the U.S. assistant secretary of state explained, procured "by photographing the original pages which remain in Countess Ciano's possession. The photographing had to be done in haste in the sanatorium where Countess Ciano is hospitalized." Charles S. Cheston, acting director, OSS, to James Dunn, February 6, 1945, NARA, RG 226, Microfilm M1642, roll 21, pp. 69–71.
6. The priest's account, found in the newly opened Vatican archives, is in the form of a letter addressed to Edda Mussolini, with the apparent date of February 3, 1944 (AAV, *Arch. Nunz. Svizzera,* b. 224, fasc. 631, ff. 198rv).
7. These events are described in Moseley 1999, pp. 176–236, and Di Rienzo 2018, pp. 537–76. The official sentence by the Tribunale Speciale Straordinario di Verona, along with a note of its execution the next day, is found at ACS, MI, Gabinetto RSI, Carte del Ministro Buffarini (1938–45), fasc. 33. An eyewitness account of Ciano's execution is also found in the newly opened Vatican files at AAV, *Arch. Nunz. Svizzera,* b. 224, fasc. 631, ff. 191r–95r.
8. The founding manifesto of the reconstituted Italian Fascist regime, voted on at a Republican Fascist Party congress held only a few weeks earlier, had specified that Roman Catholicism was to be the official state religion. The gathering of the party having taken place in Verona in mid-November, the eighteen-point program of the Republican Fas-

cist Party came to be known as the Manifesto of Verona. The establishment of Roman Catholicism as Italy's official state religion was specified in point six. Point one declared the end of the monarchy; point seven proclaimed that "members of the Jewish race are foreigners. During this war they belong to an enemy nation." "Manifesto di Verona," *Storiologia,* https://www.storiologia.it/apricrono/storia/a1943u.htm.

9. Ministero degli Affari Esteri (Giurati) to Serafino Mazzolini, segretario generale, Ministero degli Affari Esteri, January 2, 1944, ASDMAE, RSI, Gab., b. 37.

10. Notes de la Secrétairerie d'État, January 11, 1944, and Annexe, Memorandum du Ministère des Affaires Étrangère de la RSI, n.d., January 1944, ADSS, vol. 11, n. 9; Montini notes, January 17, 1944, ADSS, vol. 11, n. 16. The Giurati memo dated January 12, 1944, is also found at ASDMAE, RSI, Gab., b. 37. It was in everyone's interest, Babuscio told the career foreign service officer, Camillo Giurati, not to call attention to the matter. Cardinal Maglione had given assurances that he wanted to do nothing to alter the precarious balance that currently existed in the Vatican's relations with the two competing Italian governments. Accordingly, the cardinal had suggested to Babuscio that he follow the same advice he had given the nuncio, *dormire,* "go to sleep." Giurati, Rome, to Esteri, January 12, 1944, tel. 176, ASDMAE, RSI, Gab., b. 37. Giurati, like many holdovers in the Italian government in Rome, found himself in an uncomfortable position, remaining at his post and serving Mussolini's republican government while not renouncing his allegiance to the king. He judged it best to try to lower the temperature. Monsignor Testa came to see him in mid-January and told him that Cardinal Maglione had felt compelled to let Babuscio move into Vatican City the previous month because he had said he was otherwise in danger of being arrested by the Germans. But he said the cardinal was eager to play down the incident that Babuscio had created and was not inclined to let any of the other staff members of the Italian embassy move in so that "the oil stain does not grow any larger." The Vatican secretary of state, remarked Giurati in reporting this conversation to the government in the north, greatly appreciated the understanding that the government ministry had shown to date. In a separate note, Giurati asked that the "measures of extreme rigor" adopted in dealing with Babuscio be reconsidered. They would only, he argued, allow Babuscio to wrap himself in the mantle of a martyr. Giurati to Gabinetto, January 15, 1944, tel. 205 and 206, ASDMAE, RSI, Gab., b. 37.

    By this time, Babuscio had finally made contact with the Badoglio government. His report on January 18 tells of the struggle he was having with the republican government and his decision to keep the Italian embassy to the Holy See in Rome rather than to try to move it with him into Vatican City. January 18, 1944, n. 5/5, ASDMAE, APSS, b. 72.

11. Bosworth 2017, p. 190.

12. Chessa and Raggi 2010, p. 5.

13. OSS Official Dispatch, via radiophone, Bern, "Italy: Countess Ciano's story," January 29, 1944, FDR Library, mr 438, p. 220.

14. Mussolini to Petacci, February 4, 1944, Montevecchi 2011, p. 32. The pope had received a similar account of Mussolini's state of mind at the time through the report of remarks Mussolini had recently made to Umberto Guglielmotti, newly appointed director of the *Giornale d'Italia* newspaper. Monsignor Enrico Pucci, semiofficial director of Vatican international news services, had sent them directly to the pope, describing Guglielmotti as "my friend." "Unfortunately," Mussolini said, "Italy today is an occupied country and the Germans are the occupiers. . . . An occupied country, albeit occupied for good reason, but occupied. I myself am limited in what I can do. My own movements are controlled. Even if I need to phone someone, I am forced to pass through the German operator." Pucci to Pius XII, January 13, 1944, ASRS, *AA.EE.SS.,* Pio XII, parte I, Italia, posiz. 1352a, ff. 24r–25r.

15. Mussolini to Clara Petacci, February 26, 1944, Chessa and Raggi 2010, p. 79; Montecchi

2011, p. 110; Clara Petacci to Mussolini, February 26, 1944, ACS, Archivi di famiglie e di persone, Clara Petacci, b. 3, fasc. 23.

16. Bernardini note, March 1944, AAV, *Arch. Nunz. Svizzera,* b. 224, fasc. 631, f. 131r.

17. Tardini notes, February 4, 1944, ADSS, vol. 11, n. 27; Tardini note, February 28, 1944, ADSS, vol. 11, n. 57.

18. Commenting on Pancino's visit, the nuncio reported that Edda had cried a great deal at the special mass she attended with her children to pray for the soul of her husband. The telegram sent by Bernardini to the Vatican reporting on the success of Pancino's mission, dated March 24, 1944, along with Pancino's March 25 letter of thanks to Bernardini "for all that you have done," and Bernardini's March 31 report of Pancino's visit to the Swiss government, are found at AAV, *Arch. Nunz. Svizzera,* b. 224, fasc. 631, ff. 136r–40r. The involvement of Cardinal Maglione and Monsignor Tardini in arranging the meeting is documented at ff. 128r–35r. Bernardini's accounts of Pancino's mission are found at ff. 132r and 140r. In the latter account, dated March 31, 1944, he wrote, "I am convinced that from the spiritual point of view the long conversation [of Edda Mussolini with Father Pancino] did a great deal of good for that poor soul who, distant from God, stubbornly seeks comfort amid the ruins of a world that has crumbled around her." In a subsequent sharply worded letter Edda sent her father, dated May 28, 1944, she proclaimed her pride in her husband and referred angrily to her "servants" and his "bosses." Mussolini's reply, dated simply July 1944, can be found now along with Edda's letter at AAV, *Arch. Nunz. Svizzera,* b. 224, fasc. 631, ff. 200r, 201r.

19. Atkinson 2007, pp. 358–92; Nicolas Roland, "Operation Shingle: Landing at Anzio Italy," Naval History and Heritage Command, 2018, https://www.history.navy.mil /browse-by-topic/wars-conflicts-and-operations/world-war-ii/1944/anzio.html.

20. Katz 2003, pp. 146–49.

21. Osborne to Foreign Office, London, January 26, 1944, NAK, CAB, 122/865, 40.

22. Michaelis 1978, p. 390; Presidenza del Consiglio dei Ministri, Sottosegretario di Stato, Salerno, to On. Comitato Parlamentare Ebraico, Camera dei Comuni, Londra, February 25, 1944, n. 1378, ASDMAE, SG, b. 27.

23. Lehnert 1984, p. 129; Montini notes, January 25, 1944, ADSS, vol. 10, n. 20; Osborne to Foreign Office, London, February 4, 1944, tel. 70, NAK, WO 220/274.

24. Air Ministry, Britain, Eaker memo, February 2, 1944, NARA, RG 84, box 47, p. 48; L. Mathewson, Memorandum for the President, February 22, 1944; Chiefs of Staff, War Department, to AFHQ, February 12, 1944; and Wilson, War Department to British Chiefs of Staff, February 2, 1944, all in FDR Library, mr 293, pp. 51, 55, 56; British Chiefs of Staff memo, February 8, 1944, NAK, CAB, 122/865, 41, 45; Osborne to Foreign Office, London, February 2, 1944, tel. 64, NAK, WO, 220/274.

25. On the activities of Caruso and Koch at this time, see Osti Guerrazzi 2020.

26. Tardini notes, February 4, 1944; Secretariat of State notes, February 4, 1944; Tardini notes, February 4, 1944; Montini notes, February 4, 1944, ADSS, vol. 11, nn. 23, 24, 25, 26. Bérard's account of the events in his February 5 report to Vichy is found at MAEC, Guerre Vichy, 461. Babuscio Rizzo's account, dated February 7, 1944, is found at ASDMAE, AISS, b. 186.

The San Paolo raid was not the first joint Italian-German invasion of a major Catholic institution in Rome aimed at capturing refugees hiding there. In late December 1943, a number of such institutions were raided, including the Lombard Seminary, the Oriental Institute, and the Pontifical Institute of Archaeology. Refugees were discovered in each and seized. According to one of the reports found in the Vatican archives, seven people were arrested at the Lombard Seminary, including an army captain-physician, a young man apparently avoiding conscription, a Communist organizer, a man listed as a Roman Jew, and three men each identified as a "baptized Jew" together with the year of baptism. AAV, Segr. Stato, *Commissione Soccorsi,* b. 332, fasc. 307, f. 18r.

Rich documentation on these raids is found in this fascicolo at ff. 11r–37r. In this case, too, Father Pancrazio initially claimed the Germans had taken no part in the raids but was then confronted with evidence by the Secretariat of State that in fact they were (f. 25r).

27. It seems that the cardinal had given a copy of the draft protest to the Brazilian ambassador, who had mentioned it to his German colleague.

28. Maglione notes, February 5, 1944, ADSS, vol. 11, n. 27. Although the cardinal thought it prudent not to accuse the Germans of any responsibility or even knowledge of the assault on San Paolo, he had good reason to believe at the time that this was untrue. Not only had monks at the abbey testified to seeing German police cars outside at the time, but they told of Germans struggling to speak Italian among the men who were interrogating the people caught inside. Tardini notes, February 5, 1944, and February 7, 1944, Secrétairerie d'État aux Missions diplomatiques près le S. Siège, February 7, 1944, ADSS, vol. 11, nn. 23, 28, 31, 32.

29. Notes de la Secrétairerie d'État, February 9–11, 1944, ADSS, vol. 11, n. 35. Caruso would not live to see the end of the year, executed by a firing squad in Rome on September 22, 1944. Osti Guerrazzi 2005, pp. 94–97.

30. The pope had reasons not to want to bring any public attention to what had happened, as the Italian envoy to the Vatican explained in his report of the incident: "It is clear that the Holy See found itself embarrassed by the fact that some of the refugees were wearing religious robes in the Basilica of San Paolo." Indeed, Fascist newspapers had published photographs of the Italian general being removed from the basilica wearing a monk's tunic. The Vatican was calling for the return of those illegally seized in the raid, Babuscio observed, but "rather than having to enter into direct negotiations with the republican government, it would prefer to leave things the way they are." Babuscio Rizzo to R. Ministero degli Affari Esteri, February 11, 1944, n. 1/4, ASDMAE, APSS, b. 72. Two months later the pope directed Cardinal Maglione to summon the Benedictine monk who served as abbot of San Paolo and tell him not to allow any refugees there to dress in clerical garb. Maglione notes, April 6, 1944, ADSS, vol. 11, n. 30.

An April 26, 1944, note by Cardinal Maglione—in the newly opened Vatican archives—refers to a promise that Buffarini made him that he would see that "little by little all those arrested at San Paolo would be released." Maglione met that same day with Ambassador Weizsäcker, reminding him of this promise and noting that so far it had not been kept. AAV, Segr. Stato, *Commissione Soccorsi,* b. 332, fasc. 307, f. 97v.

31. Shortly after the San Paolo raid, Monsignor Montini received a warning from Rome police commissioner Camillo Liccardi that a raid on St. John in Lateran was imminent by the same group that had raided St. Paul. Its aim, he said, would be to capture any "refugees" found there and to discover a hidden room where it was thought arms might be stored. Tardini later added a handwritten note: "This sheet documents one of the many rumors that, from September 1943 to June 1944, were often repeated and left the responsible authorities quite worried." Appunto per Sua Eccellenza, February 21, 1944, ASRS, *AA.EE.SS.,* Pio XII, parte I, Italia, posiz. 1356, f. 18r.

32. Osti Guerrazzi 2004, p. 65.

33. From *Domine salva nos perimus,* "Lord save us, we perish" (Matt. 8:25).

34. Mgr Anichini au pape Pie XII, February 13, 1944, ADSS, vol. 10, n. 53. The pope's fears of having Vatican City be viewed as harboring Jews and others seeking protection from the Germans were fed by his eagerness to retain productive ties with the German military command in Italy. In February, with Father Pfeiffer as the Vatican's intermediary, private meetings had been arranged between Cardinal Canali, head of the commission overseeing Vatican City, and General Stahel, General Mälzer, and Major Böhm. On February 26, 1944, Enrico Galeazzi was dispatched to represent Vatican City, accompanying Pfeiffer on a trip to Marshal Kesselring's headquarters fifty kilometers from

Rome, to express the hope that this cooperation continue. Galeazzi to Maglione, February 28, 1944, and Galeazzi/Pfeiffer report, February 27, 1944, ASRS, *AA.EE.SS.,* Pio XII, parte I, Italia, posiz. 1336, ff. 314r, 315r–20r.

35. Chirieleison, "Appunto per il Maresciallo d'Italia Rodolfo Graziani," February 13, 1944, ATMR, Processi definiti, 34901, Chirieleison, b. 592-C; Comando Supremo, Promemoria Consegnato al Vaticano February 15, 1944, prot. 10, ASDMAE, APSS, b. 71; Chirieleison, "Promemoria consegnato al Vaticano," February 15, 1944, ATMR, Processi definiti, 34901, Chirieleison, b. 592-C; Maglione to Cicognani, Washington, D.C., February 17, 1944, ADSS, vol. 11, n. 41; Cicognani to FDR, February 17, 1944, FDR Library, psfa 496, pp. 20–21; Osborne to Foreign Office, London, February 17, 1944, NAK, CAB 122/865, 51A and 51B; Secretariat of State to Weizsäcker, February 17, 1944, ADSS, vol. 11, n. 42 (see Osborne reply n. 49); Roberts 2018, p. 812.

36. For the story of the bombing of Montecassino, see Atkinson 2007, pp. 432–41.

37. Tittmann to Hull, February 19, 1944, FRUS 1944, vol. 4, pp. 1282–83; OSS memo, March 31, 1944, reporting for February 21 and 28, NARA, RG 84, box 47, 840.1, pp. 60, 61; Osborne to Foreign Office, London, March 7, 1944, tel. 147, NAK, WO 106/4038.

38. Cardinal Schuster was sending copies of both *Il Regime Fascista* and the new Catholic Fascist journal to the Vatican, where the appearance of well-known priests among their authors was causing some alarm. In April 1944 he shared his suspicion with Cardinal Maglione that "the group of priests behind the Crociata Italica is headed by the Duce." Schuster to Maglione, April 25, 1944, ASRS, *AA.EE.SS.,* Pio XII, parte I, Italia, posiz. 1352a, f. 531. He wrote again to the pope about the publication in July, complaining that it "continues its campaign against L'Osservatore Romano, Holy Father, Clergy." Schuster's letter came to the pope via Bernardini's July 14 telegram from Bern. ASRS, *AA.EE.SS.,* Pio XII, parte I, Italia, posiz. 1356, f. 130r. In notes written in October, Tardini observed that "a mosaic of priests is being formed around Farinacci that is worthy of him. . . . But the harm that these priests are doing with their writings should not be undervalued, also because not all that they write can be called '*sciocchezze*' [foolishness] or 'lies': don Calgano, for example, appears to be an intelligent person." Tardini notes, October 21, 1944, ADSS, vol. 11, n. 397.

39. OSS report, Milan, February 24, 1944, FDR Library, mr 438, p. 177. The previous October American intelligence had already noted the switch in Cardinal Schuster's loyalties, as the republican Fascists were arresting priests and others deemed opponents of their German-backed rule: "Cardinal Schuster issues an edict this week which threatens with excommunication those who 'slanderously' denounce persons to the authorities and accuse them of political crimes or of transgressions against the orders of the military authorities. The Schuster edict points to a veritable epidemic of anonymous denunciations, following the reinstatement of the Fascist regime, leading to the imprisonment and internment of many members of the clergy. . . . The edict is doubly significant because it comes from a prelate well-known for his strongly pro-Fascist leanings." *Weekly Review of Foreign Broadcasts,* FCC 15–21, October 1943, NARA, RG 165, color 279.

40. Roberto Farinacci, "Lettera aperta a S.E. il Card. I. Schuster," RF, May 3, 1944, p. 1. On *Crociata Italica,* see Franzinelli 2012, pp. 81–82. Shortly after the German occupation of northern Italy in September 1943, Cardinal Schuster began sending the pope a series of letters recounting the arrest of priests on suspicion of aiding partisans as well as reports of the deportation and murder of Jews. Among the first of these was a handwritten letter he addressed to the pope on October 15, 1943, describing the brutal arrests of two parish priests, the desecration of crucifixes by members of the German SS, and the murder of all seventeen members of Jewish families staying at a hotel: "Men and women massacred, and then thrown into Lake Maggiore, and the three children killed in the forest and then buried." ASRS, *AA.EE.SS.,* Pio XII, parte I, Italia, posiz. 1352b, ff. 550r–51v.

CHAPTER 37: A GRATIFYING SIGHT

1. "Spezzoni anglo-sassoni sulla Città del Vaticano," RF, March 3, 1944, p. 1. "A few min-
    utes before eight P.M. on 1 March," read the report from American intelligence, "the
    same kind of solitary plane which was responsible for the outrage of 5 November,
    dropped six bombs in the immediate vicinity of Vatican City. . . . Everyone agrees that
    it is a repetition of the first attack on the Vatican City, and that it was devised in the same
    Fascist circles. Such methods, although incredibly stupid, are consistent with Farinacci's
    campaign against the Vatican." OSS memo, March 31, 1944, March 7 entry, NARA, RG
    84, box 47, 840.1, pp. 61–62.

2. Wilson, British AFHQ, to Air Ministry, British Chiefs of Staff, copy to D.C., March 25,
    1944, NARA, RG 84, box 47, 840.4, pp. 58–59; Representatives of British Chiefs of
    Staff, April 4, 1944, and Joint Staff Mission to Chiefs of Staff, memo, April 7, 1944,
    NAK, CAB, 122/865, pp. 76, 70A.

3. OSS memo, March 7, 1944, NARA, RG 84, box 47, 840.1, p. 62; NARA, RG59, Entry
    A1, 1068, box 7, fold 711.6. The *Osservatore Romano* article was prepared at the direction
    of the Vatican secretary of state. Tardini notes, March 4, 1944, ADSS, vol. 11, n. 75.
    Maglione also complained of the bombing to Osborne, who responded that "so long as
    the Germans made use of Rome rail communications for bringing up military reinforce-
    ments and supplies, bombing was justified and necessary." Osborne to Foreign Office,
    London, March 7, 1944, tel. 146, NAK, WO 220/274.

4. Comando Forze di Polizia, Roma to Questura et al., March 11, 1944, ACS, MI, DAGRA
    1944–46, b. 214, n. 6058/18; Légation de Grande Bretagne to Secrétairerie d'État, March
    12, 1944, ADSS, vol. 11, n. 93. Babuscio Rizzo also reported the crowd's disappointment
    with the pope's speech in his report to the royal government. March 21, 1944, n. 10/10,
    ASDMAE, APSS, b. 72.

5. Capo Provincia di Roma to Segreteria Particolare del Duce, March 12, 1944, tel. 3687
    and 3688, ACS, SPD, CR-RSI, b. 18; Cesare Bonzani, *I nove mesi di occupazione tedesca di
    Roma,* March 1946, ATMR, Processi definiti, 34901, Chirieleison, b. 592-C; "Pio XII
    rivolge ai romani la sua nobilissima parola di conforto," *L'Italia,* March 13, 1944, p. 1;
    "I voti le opere la invocazione del Supremo Pastore per ottenere al travagliato genere
    umano la pace con Dio e la pace tra le nazioni," OR, March 13–14, 1944, p. 1.

6. Weizsäcker to Berlin, March 14 and March 21, 1944, tel. 166 and 180, PAAA, GPA,
    R98830, 34–37, 28–29; Osborne to Foreign Office, London, March 18, 1944, tel. 174,
    NAK, WO 106/4038. The following month, a report from the Fascist police force in
    Rome addressed to the Duce put the matter this way: "As despised as the Germans are,
    today the English and Americans are even more. The pope hates both the ones and the
    others . . . massacres on all sides and disasters without end. The people yearn for peace,
    the people don't want to hear about foreigners in Italy." "Promemoria per il Duce,"
    April 18, 1944, ACS, MI, Gabinetto R.S.I., b. 5.

7. Chirieleison, "La Città Aperta di Roma, Relazione sintetica," February 28, 1950,
    AUSSME, RSI, b. 76; Comando Supremo report, July 17, 1944, prot. 10, ASDMAE,
    APSS, b. 71; Appunto per il Duce, segretario particolare, February 15, 1944, ACS, SPD,
    CR-RSI, b. 18; Chirieleison, "Promemoria—Bombardamenti aerei di Roma," March 9,
    1944, ATMR, Processi definiti, 34901, Chirieleison, b. 592-C; Ministero degli Affari Es-
    teri to Ministero Educazione Nazionale, Salerno, July 6, 1944, tel. 5554, ACS, PCM
    1943–44, b. 20, cat. 21.

8. Cardinal Maglione to representatives of the Holy See abroad, March 16, 1944, ADSS,
    vol. 11, n. 102; Kiernan to Maglione, March 17, 1944, ADSS, vol. 11, n. 104. The nuncio
    in Washington wrote to Secretary Hull reporting that Cardinal Maglione had told him
    that "the continued bombings of Rome are lowering the prestige of the Allies, embit-
    tering a populace otherwise well disposed, and producing the further effect of foment-

ing Communism which is already rife in the great mass of the people." Cicognani to Hull, March 22, 1944, FDR Library, psfa 496, pp. 42–43.

9. Tittmann to Tardini, March 19, 1944, and Tardini notes, March 20, 1944, ADSS, vol. 11, n. 108 and 108 Annexe.

10. On the massacre, see Moellhausen 1948, pp. 218–24; Zuccotti 1987, pp. 192–93; and Katz 2003, pp. 249–65.

11. Notes de la Secrétairerie d'État, March 24, 1944, ADSS, vol. 10, n. 115; Deák 2008; Osborne to Foreign Office, March 25, 1944, tel. 195, NAK, WO, 106/4038; Miccoli 2000, pp. 257–62. In mid-May the cardinal vicar of Rome called Montini to request instructions. The local Fascist officials were asking him to issue a proclamation calling on all deserters to come out of hiding and present themselves to the authorities. "Limit yourself to recommend calm and obedience to the public Authorities" was the response. Montini notes, May 13, 1944, ADSS, vol. 11, n. 181.

12. Secrétairerie d'État to Weizsäcker, April 22, 1944, ADSS, vol. 10, n. 159. The copy that Weizsäcker sent to Berlin, on the same date, is found at PAAA, GARV, R997, 14–15.

13. Chassard 2015, p. 171.

14. Secrétairerie d'État to Weizsäcker, April 3, 1944, and Tardini notes, April 2, 1944, ADSS, vol. 11, nn. 145, 144. Worse, Tardini added in his note, the prestige of the Vatican itself was being compromised. "When word got around that the Holy See had succeeded in having Rome declared an 'open city,'" he noted, "the Pope got many letters from people who accused him of thinking only of Rome!"

15. Petacci to Mussolini, April 20, 1944, Petacci diary entry, April 21, 1944, ACS, Archivi di famiglie e di persone, Clara Petacci, b. 3, fasc. 25.

16. Corvaja 2008, pp. 280–85; Deakin 1962, pp. 681–89.

17. Petacci to Mussolini, April 21, 1944, ACS, Archivi di famiglie e di persone, Clara Petacci, b. 3, fasc. 25; Bosworth 2017, pp. 17, 194–95.

18. Osti Guerrazzi 2004, p. 103.

19. The police were of the opinion that these, as one police report put it, were "not the work of the people but of antifascist elements" and of certain Fascist elements interested in maintaining a high state of tension. Rapporto anonimo, ACS, MI, Gabinetto della RSI, b. 5, fogli non numerati, n.d. [April 1944].

20. Osti Guerrazzi 2004, p. 158.

21. "Rapporto del Comando Forze di Polizia della città aperta di Roma del 30 aprile 1944," Ufficio di collegamento con le autorità militari germaniche, ACS, MI, DGPS, DAGR, RSI busta unica, 1943–44, fasc. 1, Segnalazioni incidenti 1944.

22. Rapporto anonimo, ACS, ACS, MI, Gabinetto della RSI, b. 5, fogli non numerati, n.d. [April 1944].

23. Bérard to Vichy, April 8, 1944, MAEC, Guerre Vichy, 551; Babuscio Rizzo to Massimo Magistrati (Italian ambassador to Bern), May 13, 1944, n. 45/35, ASDMAE, APSS, b. 72; AMSSO to Britman, Washington, D.C., April 21, 1944, NAK, WO 220/274, 90A.

24. Osborne to Foreign Office, London, April 24, 1944, tel. 281, NAK, WO 220/274.

25. MEDCOS, re COSMED 104, May 1944, NARA, RG 84, box 47, 840.4, pp. 67–68.

26. Levis Sullam 2018; Foa and Scaraffia 2021.

27. Michaelis 1978, pp. 390–92; Zuccotti 1987, pp. 136, 180–81; Avagliano and Palmieri 2011, pp. 316–17. For accounts of those Italian Jews who managed to escape arrest, see Picciotto Fargion 2017.

28. Secretariat of State notes, April 15, 1944, ADSS, vol. 10, n. 145. Throughout these last months of joint German-Fascist rule of Rome, the Vatican continued to enlist the assistance of the local authorities in its ongoing campaign to stamp out immodest dress as well as publications and films that the church deemed morally objectionable, a campaign ultimately supervised by the pope. See, for example, the report on public immorality in Rome sent by Father Gremigni, interim director of the central office of Italian Catholic

Action, to Monsignor Montini on May 24, 1944, and reviewed by the pope on May 29. AAV, *Segr. Stato,* 1944, Associazioni Cattoliche, posiz. 75, ff. 2r–15r.

29. Secretariat of State notes, June 2, 1944, ADSS, vol. 10, n. 219. In short, few Jews were given refuge in Vatican City, and most had sneaked in despite Vatican attempts to keep them out.

 While few Roman Jews found sanctuary in Vatican City, a large number did find refuge in convents and monasteries scattered across Rome. In March 1945 Myron Taylor reported a conversation on the subject that a member of his staff had had with Monsignor Tardini. During the German occupation of the city, said Tardini, Catholic clergy had given asylum to approximately six thousand Jews, spread among roughly 180 religious homes and institutions. Taylor added, "Monsignor Tardini concluded his remarks by saying that the Holy See is naturally most anxious not to give any publicity to this information lest it bring about retaliatory measures against the Catholic Clergy and communities in Nazi-controlled territories." Taylor to secretary of state, Washington, D.C., March 25, 1945, NARA, RG 59, Entry A1, 1068, box 9, fold 800b, pp. 18–19.

30. Atkinson 2007, pp. 543–45.

31. Tardini notes, May 27, 1944, ADSS, vol. 11, n. 196.

32. The documentation is found at AAV, *Segr. Stato, Commissione Soccorsi,* b. 331, fasc. 254, ff. 3r–10r.

33. Weizsäcker telegram to Foreign Ministry, Berlin, June 3, 1944, PAAA, GARV, R997, 02; Atkinson 2007, pp. 550–64.

34. Weizsäcker telegram to Foreign Ministry, Berlin, June 3, 1944, PAAA, GARV, R997, 03–04; Osborne annual report for 1944, Osborne to Eden, April 4, 1945, NAK, ZM 2608/2608/57, p. 6.

35. Tardini notes, June 3, 4, 1944, ADSS, vol. 11, n. 208; Modigliani 1984, p. 97.

36. Tardini notes, June 5, 1944, ADSS, vol. 11, n. 208.

37. Babuscio Rizzo to Ministero degli Affari Esteri, June 6, 1944, tel. 870, ASDMAE, APSS, b. 71.

38. Osborne to Foreign Office, London, June 6, 1944, tel. 404, NAK, WO, 106/4038; Osborne annual report for 1944, Osborne to Eden, April 4, 1945, NAK, ZM 2608/2608/57, p. 1. For a description of the June 6 acclamation of the pope in St. Peter's Square see the account by Babuscio Rizzo, reporting to the Italian royal government in Salerno, June 6, 1944, ASDMAE, AISS, b. 176. The text of the pope's remarks is found at: https://www.vatican.va/content/pius-xii/it/speeches/1944/documents/hf_p-xii_spe_19440606 _popolo-romano.html.

CHAPTER 38: MALEVOLENT REPORTS

1. Atkinson 2007, pp. 569–71.

2. Secretariat of State notes, June 8, 1944, ADSS, vol. 11, n. 218. Clark (1950, pp. 373–75), in his wartime memoir, offered his own description of that and subsequent audiences with the pope. Upon the arrival of Allied troops in Rome, the pope placed Enrico Galeazzi in charge of mediating with them, aided by the American prelates Monsignors Carroll and McCormick. Their meetings with the Allied military command in the days immediately following liberation are chronicled in ASRS, *AA.EE.SS.,* Pio XII, parte I, Italia, posiz. 1336, ff. 342r–45r.

3. Osborne to Eden, June 9, 1944, NAK, CAB, 122/866; Murphy to U.S. secretary of state, June 17, 1944, NARA, RG 84, box 47, 840.4, p. 66.

4. Chenaux 2003, p. 265; Duff Cooper, Algiers, to Foreign Office, London, July 5, 1944, NAK, WO, 106/4038, n. 1251.

5. Hull to Kirk, July 3, 1944, FRUS 1944, vol. 4, pp. 1313–14.

6. In his report to Roosevelt, Taylor added, "The propaganda continues that American Catholics favor a negotiated peace." Taylor to FDR, June 30, 1944, FDR Library, psfa 496, pp. 111–18; Taylor to FDR, n.d., June 1944, FDR Library, psfc 5, p. 54.

7. "He expressed great interest in your reelection," Donovan wrote Roosevelt following the audience, "and at the end he asked me to say to you that he sends 'all my heart's affection.'" Donovan to FDR, July 3, 1944, NARA, RG 226, Microfilm M1642, roll 24, p. 37.

8. "M. Carroll tells me that Roosevelt will arrive in Rome this evening or tomorrow," reads a July 3 note by Tardini. "He wants to be received, together with Signor Taylor, by His Holiness." ASRS, *AA.EE.SS.,* Pio XII, parte I, Italia, posiz. 1356, f. 387.

9. Mgr. Carroll notes, July 3, 1944, ADSS, vol. 11, n. 271.

10. Osborne to Eden, July 7, 1944, NAK, FO 371, 44217, 9–10.

11. Tardini notes, July 4, 1944, Myron Taylor to Pius XII, July 12, 1944, ADSS, vol. 11, nn. 276, 292; Osborne to Foreign Office, July 29, 1944, tel. 565, NAK, WO, 106/4038.

12. Babuscio Rizzo to Ministry of Foreign Affairs, August 20, 1944, n. 365/251, ASDMAE, APSS, b. 71.

13. Pius XII to Maglione, August 5, 1944, Montini aux représentants du Saint Siège, August 22, 1944, ADSS, vol. 11, nn. 314, 330; Babuscio Rizzo to Ministry of Foreign Affairs, August 30, 1944, tel. 421/286, ASDMAE, APSS, b. 71.

14. Secretariat of State notes, August 23, 1944, ADSS, vol. 11, n. 333.

15. Taylor report, August 25, 1944, FDR Library, psfb 216, p. 101.

16. Chenaux 2003, p. 230. Following Maglione's death, Babuscio Rizzo sent a series of reports to the Ministry of Foreign Affairs discussing the question of how and when the cardinal would be replaced. September 7, 1944, tel. 481/326, ASDMAE, APSS, b. 71; September 16, 1944, tel. 559/375, ASDMAE, AISS, b. 160; October 7, 1944, tel. 709/468, ASDMAE, APSS, b. 71.

17. The English text of the pope's September 1 address can be found attached to Osborne's September 1 report to Eden on the speech, NAK, FO 371, 44217, 87–107. The *Times* letter is found at NAK, FO 371, 44217, 79. The English translation of Montini's letter (written in French) to Osborne is found with Osborne's September 26, 1944, report to Foreign Office, London, NAK, FO 371, 44217, 110–12.

18. Visconti Venosta to Alto Commissariato per l'Epurazione dell'Amministrazione, September 1, 1944, n. 61/00831/6, ASDMAE, Personale Serie VII, Babuscio Rizzo. The prime minister, Ivanoe Bonomi, resolved the dispute between the commission and his undersecretary of foreign affairs by deciding in favor of the latter, pending the commission's final determination of Babuscio's guilt. Bonomi to Alto Commissario, October 9, 1944, prot. 2664, ASDMAE, Personale Serie VII, Babuscio Rizzo.

19. The large documentation on these proceedings, covering many months, is found at ASDMAE, Personale Series VII, Babuscio Rizzo. After some efforts to have him dismissed from the foreign service, in the end he, like many others who had served in similar positions in the Fascist regime, would only have his hand slapped and be temporarily reduced a grade.

20. Babuscio Rizzo to Visconti Venosta, September 14, 1944, ASDMAE, Gab., b. 104.

21. Visconti Venosta to Babuscio Rizzo, October 2, 1944, ASDMAE, Gab., b. 104.

22. Babuscio Rizzo to Visconti Venosta, October 6, 1944, ASDMAE, Gab., b. 104; Visconti Venosta to ministro della Casa Reale, Marchese Falcone Lucifero, October 30, 1944, n. 2/661, ASDMAE, Gab., b. 104. While all this was going on in October, the Italian military intelligence service prepared its own report on Monsignor Bartolomasi, not for public consumption, that offered a clear-eyed view of the role the enthusiastic booster of the Fascist regime had played in representing the Vatican during his many years of service. "He always remained in harmony with the policies of the Holy See," wrote the analyst, "and it always considered him a very well-balanced prelate who merited

special consideration." SIM report, October 9, 1944, AUSSME, SIM, Div. 1, b. 139, ff. 56775–76.

23. Dole 2005.

24. Isaac Herzog and Benzion Uziel to Maglione, July 6, 1944, ASRS, *AA.EE.SS.,* Pio XII, parte 1, Germania, posiz. 742, f. 244r. The internal discussion on how to reply, including the pope's July 18 instructions, is found at ff. 246r–47r. During the last week of August, Herzog went to Cairo to meet with Father Arthur Hughes, the apostolic delegate responsible for Palestine, to urge the pope to intercede to prevent the deportation of the Jews from Hungary. He told Hughes that he "deeply regrets not being able to go to the Vatican . . . but," Hughes reported, "he abides by the decision of the Holy See for the reasons of prudence explained to him." Hughes to Tardini, September 12, 1944, ASRS, *AA.EE.SS.,* Pio XII, Parte Asterisco, Stati Ecclesiastici, posiz. 575*, f. 2069r. Tardini was unhappy with the reply drafted by Monsignor Dell'Acqua, writing in the margin: "This language is too cold. The interest shown by the Holy See should be made clearer. The less one is able to accomplish the more necessary it is to extol the Holy See's action" (f. 2073r).

    In late July, Myron Taylor had asked the pope to help broker an agreement with the men who now ruled northern Italy, aimed at saving the thousands of Jews stranded there. It called for the Allies to send ships to a northern Italian Adriatic port and transport all the Jews being held in Italian concentration camps to safety in Allied-controlled areas of Italy or in Africa. On August 7, Tardini passed the proposal on to the German ambassador, now himself confined to Vatican City. Weizsäcker refused to get involved, saying he was not in a position to help. He suggested they interest the papal nuncio in Berlin in the matter. This they did, but to little effect. Orsenigo replied in late August that he had raised the question in the German Foreign Ministry, but they had said the matter was not their responsibility but that of Mussolini's government.

CHAPTER 39: A GRUESOME END

1. "Bologna bombardata 1943–1945," Biblioteca Digitale dell'Archiginnasio, Bologna, http://badigit.comune.bologna.it/bolognabombardata/cronologia.htm.

2. Bernardini sent the text of Cardinal Schuster's October 5 letter to Tardini on October 24, 1944, ASRS, *AA.EE.SS.,* Pio XII, parte I, Italia, posiz. 1356, ff. 106rv. Schuster's October 20 report on the bombing raid, which Bernardini sent on to Tardini on October 26, is found at f. 99r.

3. Milza 2000, pp. 928–31. Mussolini's reference here was presumably to the phrase "passare dall'altare alla polvere," figuratively, from being an object of highest esteem to a nobody.

4. Memorandum for the President, from Charles S. Cheston, Acting Director, OSS, January 10, 1945, FDR Library, psf 794, pp. 23–27.

5. Taylor to U.S. secretary of state, January 15 and 16, 1945, NARA, RG 59, Entry 1070, box 29, pp. 62, 63; Tittmann 2004, p. 212.

6. Segreteria di Stato di Sua Santità to Myron Taylor, January 17, 1945, and Colonel William A. Wedemeyer to Taylor, February 12, 1945, NARA, RG 59, Entry A1, 1068, box 11, fold 811.5.

7. OSS Headquarters detachment 2677th regt. OSS, Italian division, April 6, 1945, Report no. 131, NARA, RG 226, Entry A1–210, box 340. Even during the German occupation, the pope had been concerned about increasing "immorality" in Allied-occupied southern Italy. In late May he called on Italian Catholic Action to prepare to meet the threat that the arrival of Allied troops in Rome would pose. "Relazione sull'immoralità in Roma," May 24, 1944, AAV, Segr. Stato, 1944, Associazioni Cattoliche, posiz. 75, ff. 2r–5r. Notes on the pope's directive are at f. 2r.

8. Taylor's popularity in Italy was such that in September 1944 the grand master of the Order of Malta let the Vatican know his intention to award the American a high honor. The grand master checked first, though, with the Vatican Secretariat of State, which in turn asked Archbishop Francis Spellman what he thought. Spellman replied that he opposed giving the honor to Taylor, not because of anything he had against him personally, but because he was a Protestant and the Order of Malta was a Catholic organization. Spellman complained that in the past the order had honored a number of Protestants, saying that this had made a bad impression in the United States. A handwritten note on the Secretariat of State's September 30, 1944, memo reporting Spellman's opinion reads: "The Order of Malta has suspended the awarding of the honor." AAV, Segr. Stato, 1944, Ordini religiosi maschili, posiz. 76, f. 2r.

9. Hubert Guérin to Georges Bidault, Ministère des Affaires Etrangères, Paris, March 17, 1945, MAEN, RSS 576, PO/1, 1183.

10. Taylor to FDR, December 12, 1944, FDR Library, psfc 5, pp. 74–78; Taylor to FDR and Hull, December 28, 1944, NARA, RG 59, Entry 1070, box 29, p. 65. The pope had been receiving reports of the high regard in which the German ambassador held him. Earlier in the year Monsignor Pucci had written a letter to the pope recounting the "great admiration" Weizsäcker had for the pope, how inspiring the German thought the pope's sermons were, and after his audiences with the pope, how he "remain[ed] above all struck by that sense of paternal and affable goodness with which Your Holiness puts Your interlocutor at ease, allowing him to open up his soul with filial confidence." Pucci to Pius XII, January 13, 1944, ASRS, *AA.EE.SS.*, Pio XII, parte I, Italia, posiz. 1352a, ff. 25r–26r.

   At this time, too, Mussolini's ambassador in Berlin was reporting the latest news of the activities of Monsignor Orsenigo, the papal nuncio in the German capital. The ambassador had learned from his friends in the German Foreign Ministry that "in recent days," Orsenigo was "multiplying his steps to get closer to the German authorities." Joining a lunch that Hitler's Foreign Ministry had arranged with the ambassadors of the Axis-allied countries, Monsignor Orsenigo "expressed himself, in an unusual fashion, in a markedly friendly way toward Germany and openly approved of some of the fervently anti-communist remarks of his fellow diners." Anfuso, Berlin, to RSI Foreign Ministry, December 19, 1944, tel. 10089, ASDMAE, RSI, Affari Commerciali, b. 203.

11. Schuster to Bernardini, January 22, 1945, ADSS, vol. 11, n. 494.

12. Pancino's letter to Bernardini, dated February 5, 1945, is at AAV, *Arch. Nunz. Svizzera*, b. 224, fasc. 631, ff. 162rv; Bernardini to Tardini, February 9, 1945, ADSS, vol. 11, n. 501. Father Pancino met with Mussolini on March 5, reporting to him before going on to see the nuncio in Switzerland. Mussolini to Petacci, March 5, 1945, letter 292, Montevecchi 2011, p. 372.

13. Archbishop Schuster was in communication with Mussolini over the previous months, writing the Duce directly a number of times to plead with him to stop the cruelty inflicted on clergy and laypeople alike by his republican government. Among the most recent examples was Schuster's letter to Mussolini of March 1, 1945, *AA.EE.SS.*, Pio XII, parte I, Italia, posiz. 1356, f. 551r.

14. Schuster to Bernardini, March 5, 1945, Annex II to ADSS, vol. 11, n. 514; Sottosegretariato per la Stampa, presidenza, Consiglio dei Ministri, to Ministero degli Affari Esteri, March 15, 1945, prot. 499, ASDMAE, SG, b. 43.

15. Bernardini to Tardini, March 12, 1945, ADSS, vol. 11, n. 512; Schuster to Bernardini, March 5, 1945, Annex I to ADSS, vol. 11, n. 514.

16. Bernardini to Tardini, March 13, 1945, ADSS, vol. 11, n. 514.

17. Tardini notes, March 13, 1945, ADSS, vol. 11, n. 513. The nuncio's fears that spies in Switzerland might get wind of what was going on turned out to be well founded. On the same day as the pope sent his response, the American intelligence service was brief-

ing the American president: Mussolini was sending letters to the papal nuncio in Switzerland through his friend, a priest. "Himmler wishes the Nuncio to advise the Vatican that Germany desires peace and is disposed to facilitate the entrance of Anglo-American but not Soviet troops." The OSS reports from Berlin to Secretary of State Hull, seen by FDR, were sent on March 14 and 16, 1945, FDR Library, psf 799, pp. 4, 9–10, and NARA, RG 226, Microfilm M1642, roll 21, pp. 66–68.

18. Bernardini to Tardini, March 26, 1945, ADSS, vol. 11, n. 528.

19. Schuster to Bernardini, March 13, 1945, ADSS, vol. 11, n. 515.

20. Osborne to Foreign Office, London, March 28, 1945, tel. 14, NAK, WO, 106/4038.

21. Bernardini to Tardini, March 26, 1945, ADSS, vol. 11, n. 528. Three days after the pope's discussion with Tardini, the pontiff met with Myron Taylor and told him of Mussolini's approach to Cardinal Schuster and the existence of the written peace proposal, assuring him at the same time that the pope had immediately responded that it was not worth passing it on as the Allies had made clear their demand for unconditional surrender. Taylor asked to have a copy of the proposal to send to Roosevelt. At Tardini's urging, the pope had Monsignor Carroll first translate the document into English so that the original text remained secret. Tardini notes, April 5, 1945, ADSS, vol. 11, n. 533.

22. Tardini notes, February 20, 25, March 1, 1945, ADSS, vol. 11, nn. 504, 505, 508. On the pope's illness, see Fonogramma dall'Ufficio speciale di S. Pietro to Segreteria del Capo della Polizia, April 7, 1945, ACS, MI, DAGRA, 1944–46, b. 214, n. 046-1.

23. Weizsäcker [although unsigned] to Foreign Ministry, Berlin, March 28, 1945, PAAA, GARV, R997; Kershaw 2000, pp. 832–33.

24. AAV, Segr. Stato, Commissione Soccorsi, b. 57, fasc. 908, ff. 3r–4r. As the telegram signed by Maglione is dated August 17, 1944, five days before his death, it appears that it was in fact written by Monsignor Montini, as the handwriting on the draft of the telegram dated the previous day seems to suggest.

25. A handwritten note at the bottom of the Secretariat of State copy of the telegram reads: "The present cypher does not seem to have arrived at its addressee." AAV, Segr. Stato, Commissione Soccorsi, b. 57, fasc. 908, f. 6r.

26. The documentation on this exchange, and the pope's subsequent telegram of condolences to Mafalda's brother, Prince Umberto, are found at AAV, Segr. Stato, Commissione Soccorsi, b. 57, fasc. 908, ff. 1r–29r. The story of her death, datelined Paris, was reported in The New York Times, April 24, 1945, p. 13. Mafalda's eldest child, Maurizio, was serving in the German army at the time she was seized.

27. The following day Schuster reported to the pope on the April 25 meeting. Once Mussolini had left, the archbishop reported, the German consul general came to meet with the Resistance heads in his office. ASRS, AA.EE.SS., Pio XII, parte I, Italia, posiz. 1356, f. 624r.

28. Chessa and Raggi 2010, p. 29.

29. Based primarily on the description offered by Milza 2000, pp. 935–47. Taylor himself noted the placement of the Osservatore Romano note on Mussolini's death in his May 1, 1945, report to U.S. secretary of state, NARA, RG 59, Entry 1070, box 29.

30. Schuster to Tardini, May 4, 1945, ASRS, AA.EE.SS., Pio XII, parte I, Italia, posiz. 1356, ff. 626r–27r. Schuster had written a string of complaints about Calcagno and regarded him as a disgrace to the priesthood.

31. Kershaw 2000, pp. 820–31.

32. The text of the pope's address to the Sacred College is found at https://www.vatican.va/content/pius-xii/it/speeches/1945/documents/hf_p-xii_spe_19450602_accogliere.html. D'Arcy Osborne, the British envoy to the Vatican, in sending a copy of the pope's speech to British foreign secretary Anthony Eden, explained, "The main purpose of the Allocution appears to be a justification of—and to some extent perhaps an apologia for—the attitude of the Catholic Church towards the Nazi regime." Osborne to Eden, June 2,

1945, NAK, FO 371, 50062, 3. For the similar view of the speech expressed by the French chargé d'affaires Jean Bourdeillette, see his June 5, 1945, report to French foreign minister Georges Bidault, MAEN, RSS 576, PO/1 1183. See also Miccoli's (2003, pp. 164–65) critique of the pope's June 2 address.

33. The Catholic Action celebration of the anniversary of the liberation of Rome is described in Bourdeillette's June 16 report to Georges Bidault, MAEN, RSS 576, PO/1, 1183.

EPILOGUE

1. There is a considerable literature now on the myth of the good Italian, often contrasting the humane Italian with the evil German during the Second World War and also portraying Italy's colonial enterprise (wrongly) as unusually mild, e.g., Del Boca 2011; Focardi 2013; Allegra 2013.

2. See Osti Guerrazzi 2016 and Levis Sullam 2018.

3. Spataro, Ministero dell'Interno, Gabinetto, Rome, June 26, 1945, AAV, *Segr. Stato, Commissione Soccorsi*, b. 304, fasc. 29, ff. 6rv.

4. ASRS, *AA.EE.SS.,* Pio XII, parte I, Stati Ecclesiastici, posiz. 739, f. 77.

5. Jemolo 1955, p. 270.

6. The book in question was authored by Ernesto Rossi (1958). The *Osservatore Romano* comment is quoted in Mimmo Franzinelli's postscript to the republication of Rossi's book (2000, pp. 337–38).

7. Franzinelli 2000, pp. 339–41.

8. Montini's letter, originally published in the July 6, 1963, issue of *The Tablet,* was republished in *Commonweal,* February 28, 1964, pp. 651–52.

9. The pope's letter of presentation and the text of "We Remember" can be found at https://www.vatican.va/content/john-paul-ii/en/letters/1998/documents/hf_jp-ii_let _19980312_shoah.html. On this topic, see also Caffiero 2009.

10. Most commonly cited in this regard is the pope's 1942 Christmas speech. Strikingly, the Catholic League for Religious and Civil Rights in the United States placed an advertisement in the December 17, 2012, edition of *The New York Times* to call attention to that speech of seventy years earlier. The ad concludes with a statement signed by the organization's president: "We feel confident that when the entire Vatican archives are released, there will be even more reason to salute the heroics of Pope Pius XII."

11. Osborne to Churchill, July 14, 1945, NAK, FO 371, 50062, 115.

12. Osborne to Ernest Bevin, London, December 26, 1945, no. 238. Osborne's report and the official English text of the pope's Christmas speech are found at NAK, FO 371, 60794, ZM77/8/57.

13. Diana to De Gasperi, February 11, 1946, DDI, series 10, vol. 3, n. 179; "Bishops criticize actions of their predecessors in Nazi Germany," *Catholic San Francisco,* April 30, 2020, https://catholic-sf.org/news/bishops-criticize-actions-of-their-predecessors-in-nazi -germany. An English translation of the German bishop's recent statement on the war is available at https://www.dbk.de/fileadmin/redaktion/diverse_downloads/presse_2020 /2020-04-29_DB_107_Englisch.pdf.

14. Diana reported to Prime Minister De Gasperi on July 5, 1946, that the pope had directed Montini to speak with him about the pope's worries regarding the fate of the Lateran Accords and to get assurance that they would be preserved under the new government. DDI, series 10, vol. 3, n. 663. The Lateran Accords consisted of three separate agreements, including the treaty establishing Vatican City as a sovereign state, a concordat governing relations between church and state in Italy, and a financial agreement in which the Italian state made a large payment to the church. In 1984 the Vatican and the

Italian state negotiated a revision of the concordat, partially to reflect changes in the church since the Second Vatican Council. The revised agreement can be found at https://www.vatican.va/roman_curia/secretariat_state/archivio/documents/rc_seg-st_19850603_santa-sede-italia_it.html.

15. Jean Bourgeillette to Georges Bidault, Paris, August 21, 1946, MAEN, RSS 576, PO/1, 1205; Parsons, memorandum of conversation with Tardini, July 30, 1947, NARA, RG 59, Entry A1, 1068, box 15.

16. Franklin Gowen, Vatican City, to U.S. secretary of state, January 8, 1946, NARA, RG 59, CDF 1945–49, 866A.001/1-847, box 6971; Diana to Ministero degli Affari Esteri, February 20, 1947, tel. 407/189, ASDMAE, Gab., b. 104.

17. Tittmann to U.S. secretary of state, July 25, 1945, NARA, RG 59, CDF 1945–49, 8661.00, box 6971, pp. 12–13.

18. Report of January 27, 1948, AUSSME, SIM, Div. 12, b. 364, f. 332588-9.

19. Parsons, Memorandum of conversation with Jacques Maritain, March 18, 1948, NARA, RG 59, Entry A1, 1068, box 19.

20. Gowen to U.S. secretary of state, October 7, 1948, NARA, RG 59, CDF 1945–49, 8661.00, box 6971.

21. The 1948 memo addressed to Georges Bidault in Paris is reproduced in Maritain 1982, pp. 91–96.

22. Marcus Cheke, British Legation to the Holy See, to Selwyn Lloyd, Foreign Office, London, October 9, 1958, NAK, FO 371, 136800.

FINAL THOUGHTS: THE SILENCE OF THE POPE

1. Blet 1999, p. 285. The original French edition of Blet's book appeared in 1997.

2. Munson 2018, p. 4.

3. Chassard 2015, p. 171.

4. Logan 1998, pp. 237–45.

5. Reizler is quoted in Captain William Puleston's report to Secretary of the Treasury Henry Morgenthau, February 25, 1940, FDR Library, md 396, pp. 196–97.

6. Ormesson final report, October 28, 1940, MAEC, Guerre Vichy, 550.

7. The ellipses are in the original. The documentation cited here is found at ASRS, *AA.EE.SS.*, Pio XII, parte I, Germania, posiz. 858, ff. 117r–25r, 186rv. The Swiss article was by Dr. Nerla E. Gun, "Crime et châtiment," *Gazette de Lausanne*, October 17, 1945, clipping at f. 119r. As for the biblical phrase, it appears in the Hebrew Bible in Ezekiel 12:2 and in the New Testament in Mark 8:18.

     Following Germany's defeat, although a request was made by the Allies to have Monsignor Orsenigo immediately removed from his post in Germany, the pope would not replace him. G. Sensi (via Monsignor Bernardini) to Tardini, July 17, 1945, ASRS, *AA.EE.SS.*, Pio XII, parte Extracta, Germania, posiz. 600, f. 56.

8. Deák 2008.

9. On the concept of clerical fascism as applied to Italy, see Pollard 2007 and Valbousquet 2018.

10. Antonucci and Procaccia 2017, p. 21; Klinkhammer 2016, pp. 58–59.

REFERENCES

NOTE: ALL REFERENCES TO ARCHIVAL SOURCES AS WELL AS TO contemporaneous newspapers and magazines are cited in full in the endnotes.

Actes et documents du Saint Siège relatifs à la seconde guerre mondiale, 11 vols. Edited by Pierre Blet, Robert Graham, Angelo Martini, and Burkhart Schneider. Vatican City: Libreria Editrice Vaticana.

Aga-Rossi, Elena. 2011. "L'amore per Clara Petacci." In *Benito Mussolini a Clara. Tutte le lettere a Clara Petacci 1943–1945*. Edited by Luisa Montevecchi, pp. 13–23. Milan: Mondadori.

Alessandrini, Alessandro. 1982. "Giuseppe Dalla Torre." In *Dizionario storico del movimento cattolico in Italia,* vol. 2. Edited by Francesco Tranello and Giorgio Campanini, pp. 150–53. Milan: Marietti.

Alfieri, Dino. 1955. *Dictators Face to Face*. Translated by David Moore. London: Elek.

Allegra, Luciano. 2013. "Italiani, brava gente? Ebrei, fonti inquisitoriali e senso comune." *Quaderni storici* 48 (1): 273–92.

Allotti, Pierluigi, and Raffaele Liucci. 2021. *Il "Corriere della Sera." Biografia di un quotidiano*. Bologna: Il Mulino.

Alvarez, David. 2002. *Spies in the Vatican: Espionage and Intrigue from Napoleon to the Holocaust*. Lawrence: University of Kansas Press.

Antonucci, Silvia Haia, and Claudio Procaccia. 2017. "Introduzione." In *Dopo il 16 ottobre. Gli ebrei a Roma tra occupazione, resistenza, accoglienza e delazioni (1943–44)*. Edited by Antonucci and Procaccia, pp. 1–35. Rome: Viella.

Atkinson, Rick. 2007. *The Day of Battle: The War in Sicily and Italy, 1943–1944*. New York: Henry Holt.

Avagliano, Mario, and Marco Palmieri. 2011. *Gli ebrei sotto la persecuzione in Italia. Diari e lettere 1938–1945*. Turin: Einaudi.

———. 2020. *I militari italiani nei lager nazisti. Una resistenza senz'armi (1943–1945)*. Bologna: Il Mulino.

Barneschi, Renato. 1982. *Frau von Weber: Vita e morte di Mafalda di Savoia a Buchenwald*. Milan: Rusconi.

Bastianini, Giuseppe. 2005. *Volevo fermare Mussolini. Memorie di un diplomatico fascista*. Milan: Rizzoli.

Baudrillart, Alfred. 1996. *Les Carnets du cardinal Baudrillart*. Vol. 2: *20 novembre 1935–11 avril 1939*. Paris: Éditions Cerf.

————. 1998. *Les Carnets du cardinal Baudrillart.* Vol. 3: *11 avril 1939–19 mai 1941.* Paris: Éditions Cerf.

Bernay, Sylvie. 2012. *L'Église de France face à la persécution des Juifs 1940–1944.* Paris: CNRS Éditions.

Biffi, Monica. 1997. *Mons. Cesare Orsenigo nunzio apostolico in Germania (1930–1946).* Milan: NED.

Blet, Pierre, S. J. 1996. "Le Cardinal Pacelli, secrétaire d'état de Pie XI." In *Achille Ratti Pape Pie XI,* pp. 197–213. Rome: Collection de l'École Française de Rome.

————. 1999. *Pius XII and the Second World War According to the Archives of the Vatican.* Translated by Lawrence J. Johnson. New York: Paulist Press.

Boiardi, Franco, et al., eds. 1990. *Il Parlamento italiano. Storia parlamentare e politica dell'Italia 1861–1988.* Vol. 12, tomo 2, *Dal "Consenso" al crollo (1939–1945).* Milan: Nuova CEI.

Bollone, Pierluigi Baima. 2007. *La psicologia di Mussolini.* Milan: Mondadori.

Bosworth, R. J. B. 2002. *Mussolini.* London: Arnold.

————. 2017. *Claretta: Mussolini's Last Lover.* New Haven, Conn.: Yale University Press.

Bottai, Giuseppe. 1989. *Diario, 1935–1944.* Edited by Giordano Bruno Guerri. Milan: Rizzoli.

Brandt, Hans-Jürgen. 1983. "Rarkowski, Franz Justus." In *Die Bischöfe der deutschsprachigen Länder 1785/1803 bis 1945. Ein biographisches Lexikon.* Edited by Erwin Gatz, pp. 594–95. Berlin: Duncker & Humblot.

Breitman, Richard, and Robert Wolfe. 2005. "Case Studies of Genocide." In *U.S. Intelligence and the Nazis.* Edited by Richard Breitman et al., pp. 73–92. New York: Cambridge University Press.

Burkhard, Dominick, and Wolfgang Weiss, eds. 2007. *Katholische Theologie im Nationalsozialismus.* Band I/1, *Institutionen und Strukturen.* Würzburg: Echter.

Caffiero, Marina. 2009. "Introduzione." In *Le radici storiche dell'antisemitismo. Nuove fonti e ricerche.* Edited by Marina Caffiero, pp. 9–18. Rome: Viella.

Calimani, Riccardo. 2015. *Storia degli ebrei italiani.* Vol. 3: *Nel XIX e nel XX secolo.* Milan: Mondadori.

Canali, Mauro. 2004. *Le spie del regime.* Bologna: Il Mulino.

————. 2021. *Rodolfo Graziani. Diari 1940–1941.* Rome: Nuova Argos.

Canali, Mauro, and Clemente Volpini. 2019. *Mussolini e i ladri di regime.* Milan: Mondadori.

Cannistraro, Philip V., ed. 1982. *Historical Dictionary of Fascist Italy.* Westport, Conn.: Greenwood.

Capogreco, Carlo S. 2004. *I campi del Duce. L'internamento civile nell'Italia fascista, 1940–1943.* Turin: Einaudi.

Carace, Paolo. 2021. *Come muore un regime: Il fascismo verso il 25 luglio.* Bologna: Il Mulino.

Carnahan, Ann. 1949. *The Vatican: Behind the Scenes in the Holy City.* New York: Farrar, Straus.

Casula, Carlo Felice. 1989. "Il cardinale Domenico Tardini." *Publications de l'École française de Rome* 113 (1): 207–27.

Caviglia, Enrico. 2009. *I dittatori, le guerre e il piccolo re. Diario 1925–1945.* Edited by Pier Paolo Cervone. Milan: Mursia.

Chadwick, Owen. 1977. "Weizsaecker, the Vatican, and the Jews of Rome." *Journal of Ecclesiastical History* 28 (2): 179–99.

————. 1984. "The Pope and the Jews 1942." In *Persecution and Toleration.* Edited by W. J. Sheils, pp. 435–72. Cambridge, U.K.: Blackwell.

————. 1986. *Britain and the Vatican During the Second World War.* Cambridge, U.K.: Cambridge University Press.

Charles-Roux, François. 1947. *Huit ans au Vatican, 1932–1940.* Paris: Flammarion.

Chassard, Dominique. 2015. *Vichy et le Saint-Siège. Quatre ans de relations diplomatiques: juillet 1940–août 1944.* Paris: Harmattan.

Chenaux, Philippe. 2003. *Pie XII: Diplomate et Pasteur.* Paris: Cerf.

Chessa, Pasquale, and Barbara Raggi. 2010. *L'ultima lettera di Benito. Mussolini e Petacci: amore e politica a Salò, 1943–45*. Milan: Mondadori.

Cianfarra, Camille. 1944. *The Vatican and the War*. New York: Literary Classics.

Ciano, Galeazzo. 1980. *Diario 1937–1943*. Edited by Renzo De Felice. Milan: Rizzoli.

———. 2002. *Diary 1937–1943*. Translated by R. L. Miller and U. Coletti-Perucca. New York: Enigma Books.

Ciccozzi, Erminia, ed. 2019. "Nota biografica." In *Luigi Federzoni. Diario inedito, 1943–1944*, pp. lxix–lxxv. Florence: Pontecorboli.

Clark, Mark. 1950. *Calculated Risk*. New York: Harper.

Coco, Giovanni. 2019. *Il labirinto romano. Il filo delle relazioni Chiesa-Stato tra Pio XI, Pacelli e Mussolini, 1929–1939*, 2 vols. Vatican City: Archivio Segreto Vaticano.

———. 2020. "Gli scritti di Pio XII e il radiomessaggio del Natale 1942." *Rivista di Storia della Chiesa in Italia* 1: 217–41.

Coen, Fausto. 1993. *16 ottobre 1943*. Florence: Giuntina.

Cointet, Michèle. 1998, *L'Église sous Vichy, 1940–1945*. Paris: Perrin.

Conway, John S. 1968. *The Nazi Persecution of the Churches 1933–1945*. New York: Basic Books.

———. 1973. "The Vatican, Great Britain, and Relations with Germany, 1938–1940." *Historical Journal* 16 (1): 147–67.

———. 1975. "Myron C. Taylor's Mission to the Vatican, 1940–1950." *Church History* 44 (1): 85–99.

Coppa, Frank J. 2013. *The Life and Pontificate of Pope Pius XII*. Washington, D.C.: Catholic University of America Press.

Cornwell, John. 1999. *Hitler's Pope*. New York: Viking.

Corvaja, Santi. 2008. *Hitler and Mussolini: The Secret Meetings*. Translated by Robert Miller. New York: Enigma Books.

D'Amico, Giovanna, Irene Guerrini, and Brunello Mantelli, eds. 2020. *Lavorare per il Reich. Fonti archivistiche per lo studio del prelievo di manodopera per la Germania durante la Repubblica Sociale Italiana*. Rome: Novalogos.

D'Aroma, Nino. 1957. *Vent'anni assieme. Vittorio Emanuele e Mussolini*. Rocca San Casciano: Cappelli.

———. 1958. *Mussolini segreto*. Rocca San Casciano: Cappelli.

D'Assia, Enrico. 1992. *Il Lampadario di cristallo*. Milan: Longanesi.

Davis, Richard G. 2006. *Bombing the Axis Powers*. Maxwell Air Force Base, Ala.: Air University Press.

Deák, István. 2008. "Did Hitler Plan to Kidnap the Pope?" *New York Review of Books* 55, no. 10 (June 12, 2008).

Deakin, Frederick W. 1962. *The Brutal Friendship*. New York: Harper & Row.

Debenedetti, Giacomo. 2001. *October 16, 1943: Eight Jews*. Notre Dame, Ind.: Notre Dame University Press.

De Felice, Renzo. 1970. "Bastianini, Giuseppe." *Dizionario biografico degli italiani*, vol. 7, http://www.treccani.it/enciclopedia/giuseppe-bastianini.

———. 1974. *Mussolini il duce. Gli anni del consenso 1929–1936*. Turin: Einaudi.

———. 1981. *Mussolini il duce. Lo Stato totalitario 1936–1940*. Turin: Einaudi.

———. 1996a. *Mussolini l'alleato 1940–1945*. Vol. 1, tomo 1: *L'Italia in guerra 1940–1943. Dalla guerra "breve" alla guerra lunga*. Turin: Einaudi.

———. 1996b. *Mussolini l'alleato 1940–1945*. Vol. 1, tomo 2: *L'Italia in guerra 1940–1943. Crisi e agonia del regime*. Turin: Einaudi.

———. 1997. *Mussolini l'alleato 1940–1945*. Vol. 2: *La guerra civile 1943–1945*. Turin: Einaudi.

Del Boca, Angelo. 1996. *Gli italiani in Africa Orientale*. Vol. 3: *La Caduta dell'Impero*. Milan: Mondadori.

———. 2011. *Italiani, brava gente?* Milan: Neri Pozza Editore.

Dell'Era, Tommaso. 2018. "Leggi razziste, conversione degli ebrei e matrimoni misti a Torino nel 1938: il cardinal Fossati, la S. Sede e il S. Ufficio." *Giornale di Storia Contemporanea* 20 (1): 17–42.

Del Re, Niccolò. 1970. *La Curia romana: lineamenti storico-giuridici,* 3rd edition. Rome: Edizioni di Storia e Letteratura.

De Marchis, Daniele, ed. 2013. *L'archivio della Commissione Centrale per l'Arte Sacra in Italia. Inventario.* Vatican City: Archivio Segreto Vaticano.

De Wyss, Margarita. 1945. *Rome Under the Terror.* London: Hale.

Di Capua, Giovanni. 2005. *Il biennio cruciale (luglio 1943–giugno 1945).* Soveria Mannelli: Rubbettino.

Di Nolfo, Ennio, and Maurizio Serra. 2010. *La gabbia infranta: Gli alleati e l'Italia dal 1943 al 1946.* Rome: Laterza.

Di Rienzo, Eugenio. 2018. *Ciano.* Rome: Salerno Editrice.

Di Segni, Riccardo. 2015. "Battesimi e conversioni all'ebraismo a Roma nella prima metà del Novecento. Indagine preliminare su due registri." *La Rassegna mensile di Israel* 81 (1): 21–49.

Documenti diplomatici italiani 1952–2006. Series 8 (1935–39), vols. 11–13; series 9 (1939–43), vols. 1, 3, 4, 6, 8–10. Rome: Libreria dello Stato.

Documents diplomatiques français. Series 2 (1936–39). 1970. Vol. 6. Paris: Imprimerie Nationale.

Documents of German Foreign Policy 1918–1945. 1953–62. Series D (1937–45), vols. 5–9, 11–13. Washington, D.C.: U.S. Government Printing Office.

Dole, Bob. 2005. *One Soldier's Story.* New York: HarperCollins.

Doyle, Charles H. 1950. *A Day with the Pope.* Garden City, N.Y.: Doubleday.

Duquesne, Jacques. 1966. *Les Catholiques français sous l'occupation.* Paris: Éditions Grasset.

Fattorini, Emma. 2007. *Pio XI, Hitler e Mussolini, la solitudine di un papa.* Turin: Einaudi.

———. 2011. *Hitler, Mussolini and the Vatican: Pope Pius XI and the Speech That Was Never Made.* Translated by Carl Ipsen. Boston: Polity.

Fenoglio, Luca. 2020. "Fascist Policy Toward Jews in South-Eastern France, 1942–1943." In *The "Jewish Question" in the Territories Occupied by Italians 1939–1943.* Edited by Giovanni Orsina and Andrea Ungari, pp. 117–33. Rome: Viella.

Ferrari, Ada. 1982. "Ildefonso Schuster." In *Dizionario storico del movimento cattolico in Italia.* Edited by Francesco Traniello and Giorgio Campanini, pp. 2:586–91. Milan: Marietti.

Festorazzi, Roberto. 2012. *Claretta Petacci.* Argelato: Minerva Edizioni.

Flynn, George. 1972. "Franklin Roosevelt and the Vatican: The Myron Taylor Appointment." *Catholic Historical Review* 58 (2): 171–94.

Foa, Anna, and Lucetta Scaraffia. 2021. *Anime nere. Due donne e due destini nella Roma nazista.* Milan: Marsilio.

Focardi, Filippo. 2013. *Il cattivo tedesco e il bravo italiano.* Rome: Laterza.

Fogarty, Gerald P. 1996. "Pius XI and the Episcopate in the United States." *Publications de l'École Française de Rome* 223 (1): 549–64.

———. 2003. "Roosevelt and the American Catholic Hierarchy." In *Franklin D. Roosevelt, the Vatican, and the Roman Catholic Church in America, 1933–1945.* Edited by David B. Woolner and Richard G. Kurial, pp. 21–43. New York: Palgrave Macmillan.

Foreign Relations of the United States. 1956–65. *1939,* vol. 2; *1940,* vol. 2; *1942,* vol. 3; *1943,* vols. 2–3; *1944,* vol. 4. Washington, D.C.: U.S. Government Printing Office.

Fouilloux, Etienne. 2011. *Eugène, cardinal Tisserant (1884–1972). Une biographie.* Paris: Desclée de Brouwer.

François-Poncet, André. 1961. *Au palais Farnèse. Souvenir d'une ambassade à Rome, 1939–1940.* Paris: Fayard.

Franzinelli, Mimmo. 2000. "Postfazione." In *Il manganello e l'aspersorio,* by Ernesto Rossi, pp. 333–54. Milan: Kaos.

———. 2012. *Il prigioniero di Salò. Mussolini e la tragedia del 1943–1945.* Milan: Mondadori.

Friedländer, Saul. 1966. *Pius XII and the Third Reich: A Documentation.* New York: Knopf.

Gagliani, Dianella. 2015. "Petacci, Clara." *Dizionario biografico degli italiani*, vol. 82, https://www.treccani.it/enciclopedia/ricerca/clara-petacci/.

Gallagher, Charles R. 2008. *Vatican Secret Diplomacy: Joseph P. Hurley and Pope Pius XII*. New Haven, Conn.: Yale University Press.

———. 2021. *Nazis of Copley Square*. Cambridge, Mass.: Harvard University Press.

Gannon, Robert I. 1962. *The Cardinal Spellman Story*. Garden City, N.Y.: Doubleday.

Gedeon, Dimitrios. 1997. *An Abridged History of the Greek-Italian and Greek-German War, 1940–1941*. Athens: Hellenic Army General Staff, Army History Directorate.

Gentile, Emilio. 2018. *25 luglio 1943*. Rome: Laterza.

Gioannini, Marco. 2012. "Bombardare l'Italia. Le strategie alleate e le vittime civili." In *I bombardamenti aerei sull'Italia*. Edited by Nicola Labanca, pp. 79–98. Bologna: Il Mulino.

Giovanni, Paolo, and Marco Palla. 2019. *Il fascismo dalle mani sporche. Dittatura, corruzione, affarismo*. Rome: Laterza.

Godman, Peter. 2007. *Hitler and the Vatican*. New York: Free Press.

Goebbels, Joseph. 1948. *The Goebbels Diaries 1942–1943*. Edited and translated by Louis P. Lochner. Garden City, N.Y.: Doubleday.

Goeschel, Christian. 2018. *Mussolini and Hitler*. New Haven, Conn.: Yale University Press.

Gooch, John. 2020. *Mussolini's War*. New York: Pegasus Books.

Graham, Robert A. 1984. "G. B. Montini Substitut Secretary of State (in tandem with Domenico Tardini)." In *Paul VI et la modernité dans l'Église. Actes du colloque de Rome (2–4 juin 1983)*, pp. 67–84. Rome: École Française de Rome.

Grandi, Dino. 1985. *Il mio paese. Ricordi autobiografici*. Edited by Renzo De Felice. Bologna: Il Mulino.

Guariglia, Raffaele. 1950. *Ricordi, 1922–1946*. Naples: Edizioni Scientifiche Italiane.

Guspini, Ugo. 1973. *L'Orecchio del Regime*. Milan: Mursia.

Halls, W. D. 1995. *Politics, Society, and Christianity in Vichy France*. Oxford: Berg Publishers.

Hartmann, Christian. 2013. *Operation Barbarossa*. Translated by Alexander Starritt. Oxford: Oxford University Press.

Harvey, Stephen. 1985. "The Italian War Effort and the Strategic Bombing of Italy." *History* 20 (228): 32–45.

Hassell, Ulrich von. 2011 (1947). *The von Hassell Diaries, 1938–1944*. London: Frontline.

Hausmann, Frank-Rutger. 2002. *"Auch im Krieg schweigen die Musen nicht." Die Deutschen Wissenschaftlichen Institute im Zweiten Weltkrieg*. 2nd ed. Göttingen: Vandenhoeck & Ruprecht.

Hennesey, James. 1974. "American Jesuit in Wartime Rome: The Diary of Vincent A. McCormick, S.J. (1942–1945)." *Mid-America: An Historical Review* 56: 35–38.

Herbert, Ulrich. 2019. *A History of 20th-Century Germany*. Translated by Ben Fowkes. New York: Oxford University Press.

Hilberg, Raul. 1961. *The Destruction of the European Jews*. Chicago: Quadrangle Books.

Hill, Leonidas E., III. 1967. "The Vatican Embassy of Ernst von Weizsäcker." *Journal of Modern History* 39 (2): 138–59.

———. 1987. "The Genesis and Interpretation of the Memoirs of Ernst von Weizsäcker." *German Studies Review* 10 (3): 443–80.

Huener, Jonathan. 2021. *The Polish Catholic Church Under German Occupation*. Bloomington: Indiana University Press.

Hull, Cordell. 1948. *The Memoirs of Cordell Hull*, 2 vols. New York: Macmillan.

Impagliazzo, Marco. 1997. *La Resistenza silenziosa*. Milan: Guerini.

Innocenti, Marco. 1992. *I gerarchi del fascismo. Storia del ventennio attraverso gli uomini del Duce*. Milan: Mursia.

Ivone, Diomede. 2002. *Raffaele Guariglia e la diplomazia epurata, 1944–1946*. Naples: Editoriale Scientifica.

Jemolo, Arturo C. 1955. *Chiesa e Stato in Italia. Dalla Unificazione ai giorni nostri*. Turin: Einaudi.

Katz, Robert. 2003. *The Battle for Rome*. New York: Simon & Schuster.

Kershaw, Ian. 1999. *Hitler: 1889–1936 Hubris.* New York: Norton.

———. 2000. *Hitler: 1936–1945 Nemesis.* New York: Norton.

Kertzer, David I. 2001. *The Popes Against the Jews.* New York: Knopf.

———. 2014. *The Pope and Mussolini.* New York: Random House.

———. 2020. "The Pope, the Jews, and the Secrets in the Archives." *The Atlantic,* August 24, 2020, https://www.theatlantic.com/ideas/archive/2020/08/the-popes-jews/615736/.

Kertzer, David I., and Roberto Benedetti. 2020. "Italian Catholic Support for the Axis War." *Journal of Modern Italian Studies* 25 (3): 1–39.

———. 2021. "The Italian Catholic Press and the Racial Laws (1938–1943)." *Holocaust and Genocide Studies* 35 (2): 165–84.

Kertzer, David I., and Gunnar Mokosch. 2019. "The Medieval in the Modern: Nazi and Italian Fascist Use of the Ritual Murder Charge." *Holocaust and Genocide Studies* 33 (2): 177–96.

———. 2020. "In the Name of the Cross: Christianity and Anti-Semitic Propaganda in Nazi Germany and Fascist Italy." *Comparative Studies in Society and History* 62 (3): 456–86.

Klinkhammer, Lutz. 1993. *L'occupazione tedesca in Italia, 1943–1945.* Turin: Bollati Borighieri.

———. 2016. "Diplomatici e militari tedeschi a Roma di fronte alla politica di sterminio nazionalsocialista." In *16 ottobre 1943. La deportazione degli ebrei romani tra storia e memoria.* Edited by Martin Baumeister, Amedeo Osti Guerrazzi, and Claudio Procaccia, pp. 41–62. Rome: Viella.

Kühlwein, Klaus. 2019. *Pius XII. und die Deportation der Juden Roms.* Berlin: Peter Lang.

Kurzman, Dan. 2007. *A Special Mission: Hitler's Secret Plot to Seize the Vatican and Kidnap Pope Pius XII.* Cambridge, Mass.: Da Capo Press.

Lammers, Donald. 1971. "Fascism, Communism, and the Foreign Office, 1937–39." *Journal of Contemporary History* 6 (3): 66–86.

Lehnert, Pascalina. 1984. *Pio XII. Il privilegio di servirlo.* Milan: Rusconi.

———. 2014. *His Humble Servant: Sister M. Pascalina Lehnert's Memoirs of Her Years of Service to Eugenio Pacelli, Pope Pius XII.* Translated by Susan Johnson. South Bend, Ind.: St. Augustine's Press.

Levis Sullam, Simon. 2018. *The Italian Executioners: The Genocide of the Jews in Italy.* Translated by Oona Smyth and Claudia Patane. Princeton: Princeton University Press.

Lewy, Guenter. 1964. *The Catholic Church and Nazi Germany.* New York: McGraw-Hill.

Libionka, Dariusz. 2008. "Against a Brick Wall: Interventions of Kazimierz Papée, the Polish Ambassador at the Holy See, with Regard to German Crimes in Poland, November 1942–January 1943." *Holocaust Studies and Materials* 1: 270–93.

Lippman, Matthew. 1997. "The Good Motive Defense: Ernst von Weizsaecker and the Nazi Ministries Case." *Touro International Law Review* 7: 57–175.

Logan, Oliver. 1998. "Pius XII: Romanità, Prophesy and Charisma." *Modern Italy* 3 (2): 237–47.

Losito, Leonardo, ed. 1994. *Bernardo Attolico. Atti e documenti dal convegno internazionale di studi nel primo cinquantenario di morte.* Fasano, Brindisi: Schena Editore.

Luconi, Stefano. 2000. *La "diplomazia parallela." Il regime fascista e la mobilitazione politica degli italo-americani.* Milan: Angeli.

Luza, Radomir. 1977. "Nazi Control of the Austrian Catholic Church, 1939–1941." *Catholic Historical Review* 63 (4): 537–72.

Madigan, Kevin. 2021. *The Popes Against the Protestants.* Cambridge, Mass.: Harvard University Press.

Maida, Bruno. 2013. *La Shoah dei bambini. La persecuzione dell'infanzia ebraica in Italia 1938–1945.* Turin: Einaudi.

Malgeri, Francesco. 1986. "La Chiesa di fronte alla RSI." In *La Repubblica sociale italiana, 1943–1945.* Edited by Pier Paolo Poggio, pp. 313–33. Brescia: Fondazione Luigi Micheletti.

———. 2006. "Maglione, Luigi." *Dizionario biografico degli Italiani* 67: 433–46.

Malinowski, Stephan. 2020. *Nazis and Nobles*. Translated by Jon Andrews. Oxford: Oxford University Press.

Manzo, Michele. 1997. *Don Pirro Scavizzi. Prete romano*. Casale Monferrato: Piemme.

Maritain, Jacques. 1982. "Impressions d'ensemble, Note écrite par Jacques Maritain à l'intention de M. Georges Bidault [1948]." *Cahiers Jacques Maritain* 4 bis, pp. 91–96.

Marrus, Michael R., and Robert O. Paxton. 2019. *Vichy France and the Jews*, 2nd ed. Stanford, Calif.: Stanford University Press.

Mattesini, Francesco. 2015. *Otto settembre: Il dramma della Flotta Italiana*. Rome: Collana Sism.

Matthäus, Jürgen, Jochen Böhler, and Klaus-Michael Mallmann. 2014. *War, Pacification, and Mass Murder, 1939: The Einsatzgruppen in Poland*. Lanham, Md.: Rowman & Littlefield.

Mazzei, Federico. 2021. *Cattolici di opposizione negli anni del fascismo*. Rome: Studium.

McGoldrick, Patricia M. 2016. "Who Bombed the Vatican? The Argentinean Connection." *Catholic Historical Review* 102, no.:4: 771–98.

Melloni, Alberto, ed. 2004. *Angelo dell'Acqua. Prete, diplomatico e cardinale al cuore della politica vaticana (1903–1972)*. Bologna: Il Mulino.

Miccoli, Giovanni. 2000. *I dilemmi e i silenzi di Pio XII*. Milan: Rizzoli.

———. 2003. "L'Italia cattolica e il fascismo." *Rassegna Mensile di Israel* 69 (1): 163–86.

Michaelis, Meir. 1978. *Mussolini and the Jews: German–Italian Relations and the Jewish Question in Italy, 1922–1945*. Oxford: Clarendon.

Milza, Pierre. 2000. *Mussolini*. Translated from French to Italian by Gian Carlo Brioschi and Filippo Scarpelli. Rome: Carocci.

Minerbi, Alessandra. 2010. "Le discriminazioni e il problema dei 'misti.'" In *Storia della Shoah in Italia*. Edited by Marcello Flores, Simon Levis Sullam, Marie-Anne Matard-Bonucci, and Enzo Traverso, pp. 1:403–29. Turin: UTET.

Modigliani, Piero. 1984. *I Nazisti a Roma dal diario di un ebreo*. Rome: Città Nuova.

Moellhausen, Eitel Friedrich. 1948. *La carta perdente. Memorie diplomatiche, 25 luglio 1943–2 maggio 1945*. Edited by Virginio Rusca. Rome: Sestante.

Mola, Aldo A. 2019. "Federzoni, uomo del Re?" In *Luigi Federzoni. Diario inedito (1943–1944)*. Edited by Erminia Ciccozzi, pp. xi–xxvii. Florence: Pontecorboli.

Monelli, Paolo. 1953. *Mussolini: An Intimate Life*. Translated by Brigid Maxwell. London: Thames & Hudson.

Montevecchi, Luisa, ed. 2011. *Benito Mussolini a Clara. Tutte le lettere a Clara Petacci 1943–1945*. Milan: Mondadori.

Moorhouse, Roger. 2020. *First to Fight: The Polish War 1939*. New York: Vintage.

Moro, Renato. 1988. "I cattolici italiani di fronte alla guerra fascista." In *La cultura della pace dalla Resistenza al Patto Atlantico*. Edited by Massimo Pacetti, Massimo Papini, and Marisa Saracinelli, pp. 75–126. Bologna: Il Mulino.

Morris, Roy, Jr. 2015. "Benito Mussolini's Failed Greco-Italian War." *Warfare History Network*, https://warfarehistorynetwork.com/2017/07/20/benito-mussolinis-failed-greco-italian-war/.

Moseley, Ray. 1999. *Mussolini's Shadow: The Double Life of Count Galeazzo Ciano*. New Haven, Conn.: Yale University Press.

Munson, Henry. 2018. "Christianity, Antisemitism, and the Holocaust." *Religions* 9, no. 26, https://www.mdpi.com/2077-1444/9/1/26.

Mussolini, Edda. 1975. *La mia testimonianza*. Milan: Rusconi.

Namier, Lewis B. 1952. *In the Nazi Era*. New York: Macmillan.

Navarra, Quinto. 2004 (1946). *Memorie del cameriere di Mussolini*. Naples: L'Ancora del Mediterraneo.

Noonan, James-Charles, Jr. 1986. *The Church Visible: The Ceremonial Life and Protocol of the Roman Catholic Church*. New York: Viking.

O'Connell, D.J.K. 1958. "Pius XII: Recollections and Impressions." *Irish Quarterly Review* 47 (188): 361–68.

O'Shea, Paul. 2011. *A Cross Too Heavy: Pope Pius XII and the Jews of Europe*. New York: Palgrave Macmillan.

Osti Guerrazzi, Amedeo. 2004. *"La Repubblica necessaria." Il fascismo repubblicano a Roma, 1943–1944*. Milan: Franco Angeli.

———. 2005. *Caino a Roma: I complici romani della Shoah*. Rome: Cooper.

———. 2017. "La persecuzione degli ebrei a Roma. Carnefici e vittime." In *Dopo il 16 ottobre. Gli ebrei a Roma tra occupazione, resistenza, accoglienza e delazioni, 1943–1944*. Edited by Silvia Haia Antonucci and Claudio Procaccia, pp. 81–271. Rome: Viella.

———. 2020. *Gli specialisti dell'odio. Delazioni, arresti, deportazioni di ebrei italiani*. Florence: Giuntina.

Paehler, Katrin. 2017. *The Third Reich's Intelligence Services*. New York: Cambridge University Press.

Pagano, Sergio, ed. 2020. *Diario di un cardinale (1936–1944)*. Milan: San Paolo.

Papin, Chanoine. 1977. *Le dernier étage du Vatican. Témoignage de Pie XI à Paul VI*. Paris: Albatross.

Passelecq, Georges, and Bernard Suchecky. 1997. *The Hidden Encyclical of Pius XI*. Translated by Steven Rendall. New York: Harcourt Brace.

Paxton, Robert. 1972. *Vichy France*. New York: Knopf.

Perin, Raffaella. 2017. *La radio del papa*. Bologna: Il Mulino.

Petacci, Clara. 2011. *Verso il disastro. Mussolini in guerra: diari 1939–1940*. Edited by Mimmo Franzinelli. Milan: Rizzoli.

Petersen, Jens. 1994. "Bernardo Attolico a Berlino (1935–1940)." In *Bernardo Attolico*. Edited by Leonardo A. Losito, pp. 105–15. Fasano, Brindisi: Schena Editore.

Petropoulos, Jonathan. 2006. *Royals and the Reich: The Princes von Hessen in Nazi Germany*. New York: Oxford University Press.

Phayer, Michael. 2008. *Pius XII, the Holocaust, and the Cold War*. Bloomington: Indiana University Press.

Phillips, William. 1952. *Ventures in Diplomacy*. Boston: Beacon.

Picciotto Fargion, Liliana. 1994. *Per ignota destinazione: Gli ebrei sotto il nazismo*. Milan: Mondadori.

———. 2002. *Il libro della memoria. Gli ebrei deportati dall'Italia, 1943–1945*, 3rd ed. Milan: Mursia.

———. 2016. "Italian Jews Who Survived the Shoah: Jewish Self-help and Italian Rescuers, 1943–1945." *Holocaust and Genocide Studies* 30 (1): 20–52.

———. 2017. *Salvarsi. Gli ebrei d'Italia sfuggiti alla Shoah, 1943–1945*. Turin: Einaudi.

Pietromarchi, Luca. 2009. *I diari e le agende di Luca Pietromarchi (1938–1940)*. Edited and with introduction by Ruth Nattermann. Rome: Viella.

Pighin, Bruno F. 2010. *Ai margini della guerra 1938–1947: Diario inedito del Cardinale Celso Costantini*. Venice: Marcianum. [English ed.: *The Secrets of a Vatican Cardinal: Celso Costantini's Wartime Diaries, 1938–1947*. Translated by Laurence Mussio. Montreal: McGill-Queen's University Press, 2014.]

Pirelli, Alberto. 1984. *Taccuini 1922–1943*. Edited by Donato Barbone. Bologna: Il Mulino.

Pollard, John F. 2005. *Money and the Rise of the Modern Papacy*. Cambridge, U.K.: Cambridge University Press.

———. 2007. "'Clerical Fascism': Context, Overview and Conclusion." *Totalitarian Movements and Political Religions* 8 (2): 433–46.

Rauscher, Walter. 2004. *Hitler e Mussolini*. Translated by Loredana Battaglia and Maria Elena Benemerito. Rome: Newton & Compton.

Regolo, Luciano. 2002. *La Regina incompresa*. Milan: Simonelli.

———. 2013. *Così combattevamo il Duce: L'impegno antifascista di Maria José di Savoia*. Rome: Kogoi.

Rhodes, Anthony. 1974. *The Vatican in the Age of the Dictators, 1922–1945*. New York: Holt, Rinehart & Winston.

Riccardi, Andrea. 1982. "Tardini, Domenico." In *Dizionario storico del movimento cattolico in Italia, 1860–1980*. Edited by Francesco Traniello and Giorgio Campanini, pp. 3:832–34. Casale Monferrato: Marietti.

Rigano, Gabriele. 2006. *Il 'Caso Zolli.'* Milan: Guerini.

———. 2016. "Il Vaticano e la razzia del 16 ottobre 1943." In *16 ottobre 1943. La deportazione degli ebrei romani tra storia e memoria*. Edited by Martin Baumeister, Amedeo Osti Guerrazzi, and Claudio Procaccia, pp. 63–85. Rome: Viella.

Roberts, Andrew. 2018. *Churchill: Walking with Destiny*. New York: Viking.

Rossi, Ernesto. 1958. *Il manganello e l'aspersorio: La collusione fra il Vaticano e il regime fascista nel Ventennio*. Firenze: Parenti.

———. 2000. *Il manganello e l'aspersorio. La collusione fra il Vaticano e il regime fascista nel Ventennio*, 2nd ed. Edited by Mimmo Franzinelli. Milan: Kaos.

Rossi, Gianni. 2005. *Mussolini e il diplomatico. La vita e i diari di Serafino Mazzolini, un monarchico a Salò*. Soveria Manneli: Rubbettino.

Rossino, Alexander B. 2003. *Hitler Strikes Poland*. Lawrence: University of Kansas Press.

Ruozzi, Federico. 2015. "Pius XII as Actor and Subject. On the Representation of the Pope in Cinema During the 1940s and 1950s." In *Moralizing Cinema: Film, Catholicism and Power*. Edited by Daniel Biltereyst and Daniela Gennari, pp. 158–72. New York: Routledge.

Samerski, Stefan. 2013. *Pancratius Pfeiffer, der verlängerte Arm von Pius XII. Der Salvatoriangeneral und die deutsche Besetzung Roms 1943/44*. Paderborn: Ferdinand Schöningh.

Sarfatti, Michele. 2000. *Gli ebrei nell'Italia fascista*. Turin: Einaudi.

———. 2006. *The Jews in Mussolini's Italy*. Translated by John and Anne Tedeschi. Madison: University of Wisconsin Press.

Schad, Martha. 2008. *La signora del Sacro Palazzo: Suor Pascalina e Pio XII*. Cinisello Balsamo: San Paolo Edizioni.

Schlemmer, Thomas. 2009. *Invasori non vittime. La campagna italiana di Russia 1941–1943*. Rome: Laterza.

Scianna, Bastian M. 2019. *The Italian War on the Eastern Front, 1941–1943*. New York: Palgrave Macmillan.

Semelin, Jacques. 2018. *The Survival of the Jews in France, 1940–44*. Translated by Cynthia Schoch and Natasha Lehrer. Oxford: Oxford University Press.

Serri, Mirella. 2015. *Gli invisibili. La storia segreta dei prigionieri illustri di Hitler in Italia*. Milan: Longanesi.

Steigmann-Gall, Richard. 2003. *The Holy Reich: Nazi Conceptions of Christianity, 1919–1945*. Cambridge, U.K.: Cambridge University Press.

Tardini, Domenico, ed. 1961. *Memories of Pius XII*. Translated by Rosemary Goldie. Westminster, Md.: Newman Press.

Tittmann, Harold H., Jr. 2004. *Inside the Vatican of Pius XII*. New York: Image Books.

Tortoreto, Emanuele. 1956. "Notizie sul movimento operaio in Milano dal 25 luglio 1943 al marzo 1944." *Movimento di liberazione in Italia* 8 (40): 16–41.

Tramontin, Silvio. 1982. "Pietro Tacchi Venturi." In *Dizionario storico del movimento cattolico in Italia*, vol. 2. Edited by Francesco Tranello and Giorgio Campanini, pp. 631–33. Milan: Marietti.

Tranfaglia, Nicola. 2005. *La stampa del regime 1932–1943. Le veline del Minculpop per orientare l'informazione*. Milan: Bompiani.

Trionfini, Paolo. 2015. "Pizzardo, Giuseppe." *Dizionario biografico degli italiani*, vol. 84. https://www.treccani.it/enciclopedia/giuseppe-pizzardo.

Trisco, Robert. 2003. "The Department of State and the Apostolic Delegation in Washington During World War II." In *Franklin D. Roosevelt, the Vatican, and the Roman Catholic Church in America, 1933–1945.* Edited by David B. Woolner and Richard G. Kurial, pp. 209–51. New York: Palgrave Macmillan.

Urbach, Karina. 2015. *Go-Betweens for Hitler.* Oxford: Oxford University Press.

Valbousquet, Nina. 2018. "Race and Faith: The Catholic Church, Clerical Fascism, and the Shaping of Italian Anti-Semitism and Racism." *Modern Italy* 23 (4): 355–71.

Ventresca, Robert. 2013. *Soldier of Christ: The Life of Pope Pius XII.* Cambridge, Mass.: Harvard University Press.

Visani, Alessandro. 2007. *Verso la guerra. Gli italiani nei mesi della "non belligeranza."* Rome: Edizioni Nuova Cultura.

Ward, James M. 2013. *Priest, Politician, Collaborator: Jozef Tiso and the Making of Fascist Slovakia.* Ithaca, N.Y.: Cornell University Press.

Weisbord, Robert G., and Wallace P. Sillanpoa. 1992. *The Chief Rabbi, the Pope, and the Holocaust.* New Brunswick, N.J.: Transaction.

Wheeler-Bennett, John. 1954. *The Nemesis of Power.* London: Macmillan.

Wolf, Hubert. 2008. *Il Papa e il diavolo. Il Vaticano e il Terzo Reich.* Translated by Paolo Scortini. Rome: Donzelli. [English ed.: *The Pope and the Devil.* Translated by Kenneth Kronenberg. Cambridge, Mass.: Harvard University Press, 2010.]

Zuccotti, Susan. 1987. *The Italians and the Holocaust.* New York: Basic Books.

———. 2000. *Under His Very Windows.* New Haven, Conn.: Yale University Press.

ILLUSTRATION CREDITS

———

FRONTISPIECE: Popperfoto / via Getty Images. Fototeca Gilardi.

1: AAV, *Segr. Stato,* 1939, Stati, posiz. 60, f. 5 @Archivio Apostolico Vaticano 2021. Reproduced by permission of the AAV, all rights reserved.

2: *L'Illustration,* Paris.

3: Biblioteca Statale di Cremona.

4: Sueddeutsche Zeitung Photo / Alamy Stock Photo.

5: Hulton Archive / via Getty Images.

6: AP Images.

7: Keystone / Staff / Hulton Archive/via Getty Images.

8: Keystone-France / Gamma-Keystone / via Getty Images.

9: Istituto Luce Cinecittà.

10: Austrian Archives / Imagno / Alinari Archives.

11: Historic Images.

12: Fototeca Gilardi.

13: Sueddeutsche Zeitung Photo / Alamy Stock Photo.

14: Marka / Universal Images Group / via Getty Images.

15: Sueddeutsche Zeitung Photo / Alamy Stock Photo.

16: Ullstein Picture Dtl. / Contributor / via Getty Images.

17: Ullstein bild Dtl. / Getty Images.

18: Archivio Generale Arcivescovile, Bologna.

19: Popperfoto / via Getty Images.

20: *L'Avvenire* (Rome).

21: Historic Images.

INDEX

Page numbers in *italics* indicate illustrations.

DAVID I. KERTZER is the Paul Dupee, Jr., University Professor of Social Science and professor of anthropology and Italian studies at Brown University, where he previously served as provost. He is the author of twelve previous books, including *The Pope and Mussolini,* winner of the Pulitzer Prize, and *The Kidnapping of Edgardo Mortara,* a National Book Award finalist. He was elected to membership in the American Academy of Arts and Sciences in 2005. Kertzer and his wife, Susan, live in Rhode Island and Maine.

davidkertzer.com

ABOUT THE TYPE

This book was set in Bembo, a typeface based on an old-style Roman face that was used for Cardinal Pietro Bembo's tract *De Aetna* in 1495. Bembo was cut by Francesco Griffo (1450–1518) in the early sixteenth century for Italian Renaissance printer and publisher Aldus Manutius (1449–1515). The Lanston Monotype Company of Philadelphia brought the well-proportioned letterforms of Bembo to the United States in the 1930s.